JAVA

Developer's Guide

Jamie Jaworski

sams.net
201 West 103rd Street
Indianapolis, Indiana 46290

Sams.net Developer's Guide

This book is dedicated to Lisa, Emily, and Jason.

International Standard Book Number: 1-57521-069-X

Library of Congress Catalog Card Number: 95-72939

99 98 97 96 4 3 2 1

Interpretation of the printing code: the rightmost double-digit number is the year of the book's printing; the rightmost single-digit, the number of the book's printing. For example, a printing code of 96-1 shows that the first printing of the book occurred in 1996.

Composed in AGaramond and MCPdigital by Macmillan Computer Publishing

Printed in the United States of America

President, Sams Publishing *Richard K. Swadley*
Publishing Manager *Mark Taber*
Managing Editor *Cindy Morrow*
Marketing Manager *John Pierce*
Assistant Marketing Manager *Kristina Perry*

Acquisitions Editor
Christopher Denny

Development Editor
L. Angelique Brittingham

Software Development Specialist
Merle Newlon

Production Editor
Kitty Wilson

Copy Editor
Kimberly K. Hannel

Technical Reviewer
Christopher M. Stone

Editorial Coordinator
Bill Whitmer

Technical Edit Coordinator
Lynette Quinn

Formatter
Frank Sinclair

Editorial Assistants
Carol Ackerman
Andi Richter
Rhonda Tinch-Mize

Cover Designer
Tim Amrhein

Book Designer
Alyssa Yesh

Copy Writer
Peter Fuller

Production Team Supervisor
Brad Chinn

Production
Mary Ann Abramson, Steve Adams, Georgiana Briggs, Mona Brown, Michael Brumitt, Charlotte Clapp, Jeanne Clark, Bruce Clingaman, Michael Dietsch, Sonja Hart, Jason Hand, Michael Henry, Ayanna Lacey, Clint Lahnen, Paula Lowell, Donna Martin, Steph Mineart, Dana Rhodes, Erich Richter, Craig Small, SA Springer, Mark Walchle

Overview

Contents

IV Window Programming

Acknowledgments

I'd like to thank everyone who helped to see this book to completion. In particular, I'd like to thank George Stones for introducing me to Java, Margo Maley for making the book possible, and everyone at Sams.net for their great support. I'd also like to thank my co-author, Cary Jardin, for helping me finish the book closer to the scheduled deadline.

About the Author

James Jaworski develops advanced systems for the United States Department of Defense. He has used Java in several research and development projects, including a terrain analysis program and a genetic algorithm demonstration.

Introduction

Never before has a new programming language received so much attention and become so popular so quickly. In less than a year, Java evolved from experimental Alpha and Beta versions to its initial 1.0 release. Along the way, it took the Web by storm and became its adopted programming language. The Java phenomenon has captivated the imaginations of Web programmers and content developers and is leading the way toward the next era of Internet application development.

Java's appeal lies in its simplicity, its familiarity, and the careful selection of programming features that it includes and excludes. Java was not designed by a government committee or by a clique of academics. It shares the spirit of its birth with C more than any syntactical similarities. It is a programming language that was designed by programmers for programmers.

This book shows you how to program in Java. It covers all the details of the language, provides you with plenty of programming examples, and most importantly, arms you with the mindset needed to write Java code in a manner that is simple, efficient, and true to the nature of the language.

Who Should Read This Book

If you want someone to teach you how to program in Java, this book is for you. You will learn how to develop standalone Java programs, Java applets, and JavaScript applets. You will learn how to program window GUI controls, work with network sockets, and use stream-based input and output. You will learn to develop object-oriented programs and explore the breadth and depth of the Java application program interface. If you want to become a Java programmer, this book will show you how.

This book is for programmers and those who aspire to become Java programmers. It consists of 40 chapters that are filled with programming examples. If you have written programs in other languages, you will have the necessary background to understand the material presented in this book. If you have programmed in C or C++, then you will be able to quickly get up to speed with Java, since its syntax is based on these languages. If you have never programmed before, then you will have a difficult time using this book, because it assumes familiarity with basic programming concepts such as variables, types, statements, and expressions. I suggest that you pick up an introductory programming book to help you learn this material.

Conventions Used in This Book

This book uses certain conventions that make it easier for you to use.

A `monospaced font` is used to identify program code. An *`italic monospaced font`* is used to identify placeholders used in Java syntax descriptions.

NOTE

Notes like this are used to call your attention to information that is important to understanding and using Java.

TIP

Tips like this are used to identify ways that you can use Java more efficiently or take advantage of undocumented features in the Java Developer's Kit or Java-enabled browsers.

WARNING

Warnings like this are used to help you to avoid common problems encountered when using Java and to keep you clear of potential programming difficulties.

In order to help you understand where you are going and where you have been, each chapter begins with a short description of the information that will be presented and ends with a summary of the material that has been covered.

Getting Started

To use this book with the Java Developer's Kit, you'll need a computer and operating system that are capable of running Java 1.0. There are a wide variety of computers and operating systems that support Java, and Java continues to be ported to new hardware and software platforms.

To effectively use Java with Windows 95, you will need the following:

- A personal computer that is capable of running Windows 95
- At least 8MB of RAM
- At least 10MB of available hard disk space
- A VGA monitor
- A mouse

To effectively use this book, you will need access to a compact disc drive so that you can copy files from the enclosed CD. In addition, an Internet connection will be required to complete some of the networking examples, and a Java-enabled browser, such as Netscape 2.0 or later, will be needed to work with Java applets and JavaScript. A sound card and speakers will be needed to use audio-playing applets.

You can get started if you are able to run Windows 95 and have access to the Web. Chapter 2 shows you how to obtain the Java Developer's Kit from Sun's JavaSoft website. You can add additional hardware, as necessary, to complete the programming examples of each chapter.

The best way to use this book is to start with Chapter 1 and proceed through each chapter, in succession, working through each programming example that is presented. You will learn to program in Java by compiling, running, analyzing, and understanding the sample programs. Additional hands-on learning can be acquired by tinkering with the sample programs, modifying them, and augmenting their capabilities.

I

Introduction to Java

1

The Java Phenomenon

In its brief existence, the World Wide Web has evolved into a truly global information space. Not only does it offer information on any subject, it provides its citizens with the power to globally publish information on any subject and at minimal cost. The massive international participation in the Web has resulted in the creation of many Web pages that are not only informative, but also entertaining. This entertainment value has further fueled the Web's growth and has led to browsing becoming an international pastime.

Browsing involves scanning Web pages for interesting information, following useful links to other pages, and repeating the process until we come across something that makes us temporarily stop and focus. Sometimes we mutter, "Hmm" or "That's interesting!" and create a bookmark. Then, eventually, we move on.

The tendency to move on and continue browsing is natural. We usually don't read the same book over and over. If we have a stack of magazines in front of us, we're likely to flip through them all. Web pages are like magazine pages, except that they are more available, usually free, and have more "next" pages to which to turn.

Computer programs are different. They are active, while books, magazines, and Web pages are static or passive. People do use programs over and over. I still use WordPerfect 5.1. Some people still use CP/M. I have a friend who played DOOM several hours a day for months.

This difference between active computer programs and passive Web pages is what makes Java an attractive addition to the Web. When we click on a Web page containing a Java applet, we don't just read it, listen to it, or watch it—we *interact* with it. Interactivity is the difference between a program and a page, and Java has brought dynamic, interactive content to the Web.

Java's rapidly growing popularity is due to the Web. But Java's inherent power does not come from the fact that it is a Web programming language. The talented software engineers at Sun, in bringing Java to the Web, have elegantly solved a much broader and more significant problem—how to develop network-capable windowing software that will run on almost any 32-bit computer and operating system.

The modern software developer faces enormous headaches and challenges when he tries to develop software that is portable to Microsoft Windows, X Window systems, Motif, MacOS, and OS/2 windowing and networking environments. The usual approach is to pick a target operating system (OS), write software for that OS, and eventually migrate it to the other OS platforms. This usually involves great expense in terms of labor and software development resources.

Java fulfills the software developer's dream of being able to write software in a single language that will support windowing and networking on all major OS platforms, without specialized tailoring *or even recompilation.* But Java's attractiveness does not end here. Sun's engineers were thoughtful enough to develop in Java a language and runtime system that are simple, compact, object-oriented, extendible, and secure. And then they gave it away for free!

The objective of this book is to provide an introduction to using the gift of Java in its broader context—as a platform-independent software development language. Java's capabilities to provide interactive content to Web pages, in the form of applets, are covered within this broader context, but these capabilities do not limit the focus of the book's presentation.

What Is Java?

Forrest Gump might say that Java is as Java does. Java is a programming language, a runtime system, a set of development tools, and an application programming interface (API). The relationships between these elements are depicted in Figure 1.1.

FIGURE 1.1.
Java unveiled.

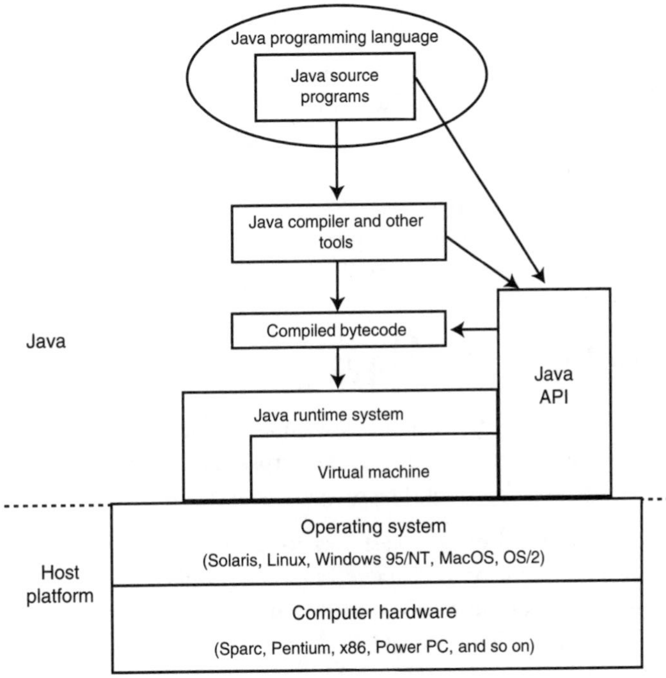

As illustrated in Figure 1.1, a software developer writes programs in the Java language that use predefined software packages of the Java API. The developer compiles his or her programs using the Java compiler. This results in what is known as *compiled bytecode*. Bytecode is in a form that can be executed on the Java virtual machine, the core of the Java runtime system. You can think of the virtual machine as a microprocessor that is implemented in software and runs using the capabilities provided by your operating system and computer hardware. Since the Java virtual machine is not a real microprocessor, the Java bytecode is interpreted, rather than executed directly in the native machine instructions of the host computer. (There are plans to make it possible to translate Java bytecode into machine code on-the-fly.) The Java runtime system consists of the virtual machine plus additional software, such as dynamic link libraries, that are needed to implement the Java API on your operating system and hardware.

The Java API contains predefined software packages with numerous platform-independent "hooks" into the native windowing and networking capabilities of the host operating system. The Java API provides a single common API across all operating systems to which Java is ported.

The keys to Java's portability are its runtime system and its API. The runtime system is very compact, evolving from earlier Sun efforts to build a software platform for consumer electronics. This platform was not designed around any existing microprocessor; it was built from scratch to be simple and efficient. The fact that it was not tied to a given hardware architecture enabled it to be architecture neutral. The simple, efficient, compact, and architecture-neutral nature of the runtime system allows it to be highly portable and still provide effective performance.

The powerful windowing and networking features included in the Java API make it easier for programmers to develop software that is both attractive and platform independent. For example, Ada is a programming language that is highly standardized and supported on most operating systems. Yet Ada applications are not very portable. This is because Ada does not come with a common API that supports windowing and networking on all platforms. Java differs from Ada and all other programming languages in that there is one universal, but powerful, Java API for all operating system platforms. That is why Java is the most portable language.

The Origins of Java

At this point, you may wonder how Sun's engineers were able to develop such a powerful software development environment and surpass all known programming languages. The answer is they didn't—at least not directly. Java evolved from other research projects at Sun.

The development of Java wasn't as accidental or monumental as the discovery of penicillin, but it shares some of its characteristics. The origins of Java trace back to 1991, when Sun was investigating consumer electronics products. At this time, Mosaic and the World Wide Web were just interesting concepts.

James Gosling, the father of Java, was intent on building a low-cost, hardware-independent software platform using C++. For a number of technical reasons, C++ was dropped, and a new language, called Oak, was developed, based on C++, but eliminating its shortcomings. These shortcomings include problems associated with multiple inheritance, automatic type conversion, the use of pointers, and memory management.

Oak was used to develop a small electronics device called *7. This project resulted in the precursors of many of the components of Java: the development environment, runtime system, and API. The technology was explored in a number of consumer applications but was a little ahead of its time.

By 1994 the Web emerged, Oak was renamed Java, and the proverbial light bulb went on in the minds of the Java developers. Java was used as the basis for a Web browser, called WebRunner. WebRunner was successfully demonstrated, and the Java/HotJava project took off.

HotJava, Java, and the Java documentation and source code were made available over the Web, as an alpha version, in early 1995. Initially Java was hosted on SPARC Solaris, and then on Windows NT. In the summer of 1995, Java was ported to Windows 95 and Linux. In the fall of 1995 the Java Beta 1 version was released through Sun's Web site, and Java support was introduced in the Netscape 2.0 browser.

The Java Beta 1 release led scores of vendors to license Java technology, and Java porting efforts were initiated for all major operating systems.

In December 1995 the Java Beta 2 version was released, and JavaScript was announced by Sun and Netscape. Java's success became inevitable when, in early December, both Microsoft and IBM announced their intention to license Java technology.

On January 23, 1996, Java 1.0 was officially released and made available for download over the Internet. JavaScript was also released. Netscape 2.0 now provides support for both Java and JavaScript.

Why Program in Java?

So far we have touched on only two reasons to program in Java—it is platform independent and it supports interactive content on Web pages. Does this mean that Java is for everybody? Certainly not!

If you are developing highly complex, performance-critical number crunching algorithms for a Cray computer, then Java is probably not the language for you. Try FORTRAN. If you are developing patches to legacy code from the 1970s, you might use COBOL. If you are developing software for the U.S. Department of Defense, you should probably use Ada.

So, for what types of software applications is Java well suited? The answer is almost everything else. Figure 1.2 summarizes the types of applications at which Java excels.

Because of its intended use on the Web, where even the smallest security vulnerability could potentially be exploited and cause global mayhem, Java was designed with multiple layers of security countermeasures embedded in the compiler, runtime system, and in browsers that support Java, known as Java-enabled browsers. These countermeasures make Java inherently more secure for developing any type of trusted application software. Chapter 39, "Java Security," is devoted to Java security.

Java is exceptionally well suited to distributed networking applications because of its built-in networking support and the runtime system's capability to dynamically load Java bytecode across the network. Java also provides the capability to dynamically utilize new content and protocol handling software. The HotJava browser, written in Java, is an excellent example of Java's distributed networking capabilities.

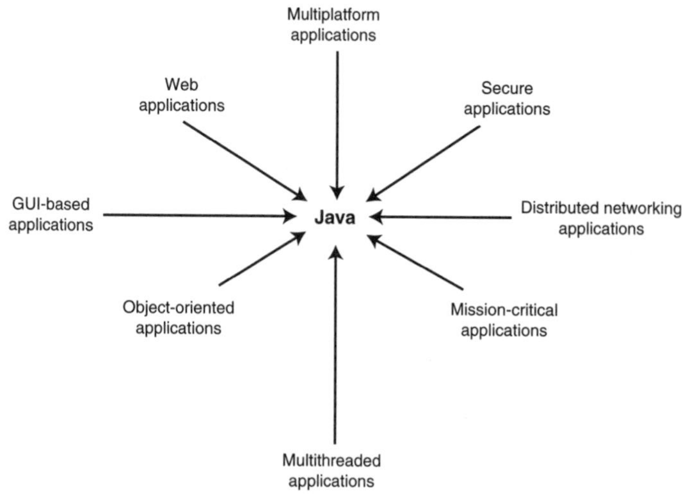

FIGURE 1.2.
Where Java excels.

Java is a sound choice for developing software where reliability is of utmost concern, such as mission-critical applications. Java's object-oriented nature combined with numerous, compile-time and runtime integrity checks eliminate many difficult-to-find programming errors. The Java language has removed many of the dangerous programming capabilities, such as modifiable pointers, unchecked type conversion, and relaxed bounds checking, that are commonly found in other programming languages, such as C and C++.

The Java API provides full support of multithreaded programming. Multithreaded programs can be developed in a single, consistent manner, independent of the vagaries of the host operating system interface.

Java classes and objects directly support the object-oriented concepts of encapsulation, inheritance, messages and methods, and data hiding. Java interfaces provide support for multiple inheritance and polymorphism. The Java language retains all the benefits of object-oriented programming without the performance impacts associated with pure object languages, such as Smalltalk.

The Java API provides extensive support of windowing and graphical user interface development without the complexities associated with maintaining multiple window class libraries. Several visual programming tools have been developed for Java.

Java and HotJava

My first experience with Java was through an early version of HotJava. Java and HotJava are sometimes confused. Java is the language, development and runtime environments, and API. HotJava is a Web browser that is written in Java. HotJava highlights many of the Java features mentioned in the previous section.

HotJava is a Java-enabled browser. This means that HotJava can execute Java applets contained on Web pages. In order to accomplish this, HotJava calls the Java runtime system. The Netscape 2.0 browser, like HotJava, is also Java enabled. It contains a copy of the Java runtime system embedded within it. Figure 1.3 illustrates the operation of HotJava and other Java-enabled browsers.

FIGURE 1.3.
How HotJava and Netscape 2.0 support Java applets.

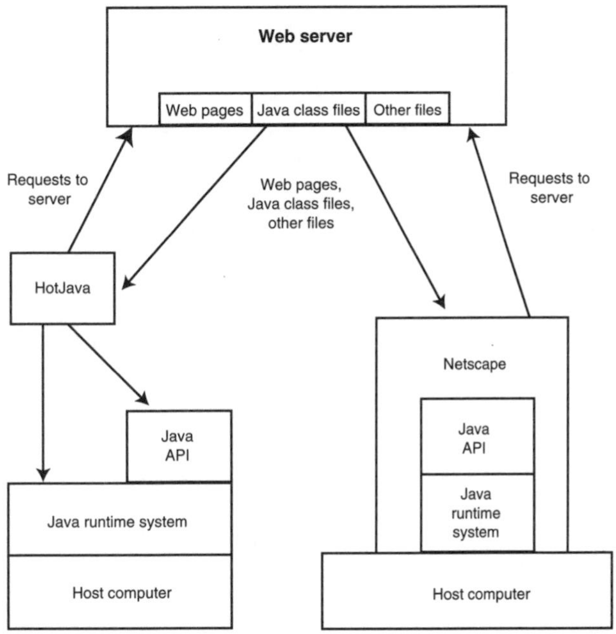

Both HotJava and Netscape request Web pages, written in HTML, from Web servers on the Internet. Since HotJava is written in Java, it uses the Java API and runtime system to display the Web pages to a user. Netscape, on the other hand, is written in C++ and uses C++ functions to display HTML documents.

When either browser encounters an APPLET tag in an HTML file, it requests the Java bytecode file necessary to execute the applet from the Web server. HotJava loads and executes the bytecode file using the Java runtime system. Netscape executes the bytecode file using an embedded version of the Java runtime system.

Summary

This chapter provides a brief description of Java's capabilities. It explains what Java is and why you should be interested in learning to use Java. It also summarizes the history of Java's development. In the next chapter, you will receive a more detailed overview of the Java language, the Java Developer's Kit, and the application programming interface.

2

Java Overview

This chapter lays the foundation for learning Java. It provides an overview of the Java Developer's Kit (JDK), the Java language, and the Java API from the perspective of a software developer.

You will download and install the JDK, and take a quick tour of its contents. You will then learn the features of the Java language that set it apart from its predecessors, C++ and C. You will be introduced to the Java API and learn how Java programs are built from and extend the API. So grab yourself a cup of you-know-what and let's begin.

Getting the JDK

Java is distributed as the JDK. It is available from Sun's Java home page at `http://java.sun.com` or `http://www.javasoft.com`. Figure 2.1 shows the Java home page. From there, you can click on the Products and Services link to download a version of the JDK for your computer and operating system.

FIGURE 2.1.
The Java home page.

Figures 2.2 and 2.3 show some of the pages you are likely to encounter on the way to finding the JDK that is right for you. Sun makes earlier versions of the software available for download. Always download the latest version that is compatible with your hardware and operating system. The examples in this book use JDK 1.0. As long as you are using this version, or later, you will be able to work through these examples. I will be running Java under Windows 95. If you are using another operating system, follow the installation instructions for that operating system.

FIGURE 2.2.
JavaSoft products and services.

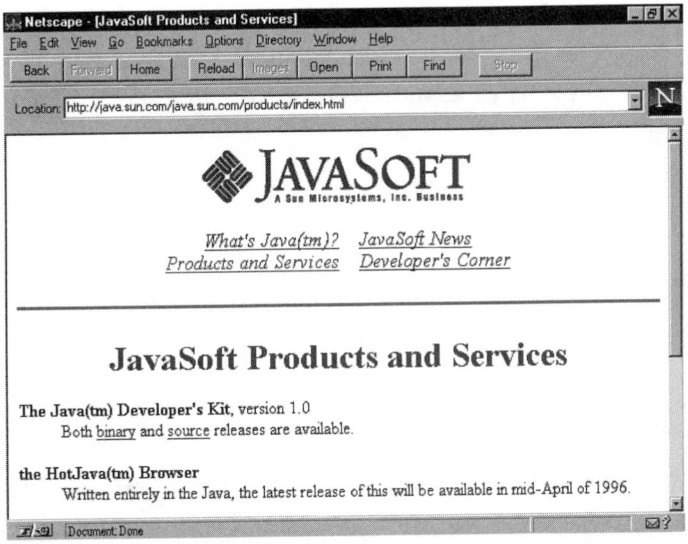

FIGURE 2.3.
The binary code license.

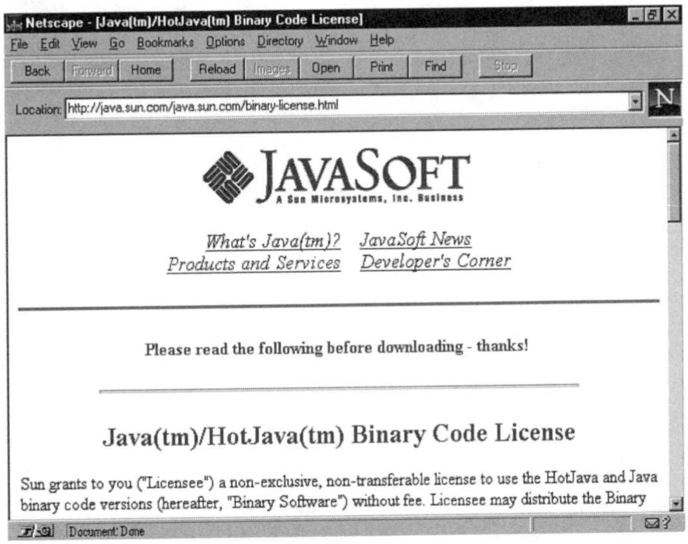

The JDK is distributed as a self-extracting executable file. Move it to a temporary directory and then execute it. It will extract itself and set up its directory structure—a single top-level directory, `java`, with several subdirectories. Move the `java` directory tree from your temporary directory to a permanent home. I suggest `c:\java`. That's where I keep my JDK.

A Quick Tour of the JDK

Now that you have the latest version of the JDK installed on your computer, you're probably wondering what's inside. Let's take a quick look.

Figure 2.4 shows the contents of the `java` directory. It consists of four subdirectories and four files, which are

- The Java copyright and license agreement
- An HTML file that contains information about your JDK and links to online documentation
- A readme file that provides additional information about your JDK release
- A zipped file containing the java source code for the Java API library files

FIGURE 2.4.
The `java` *directory.*

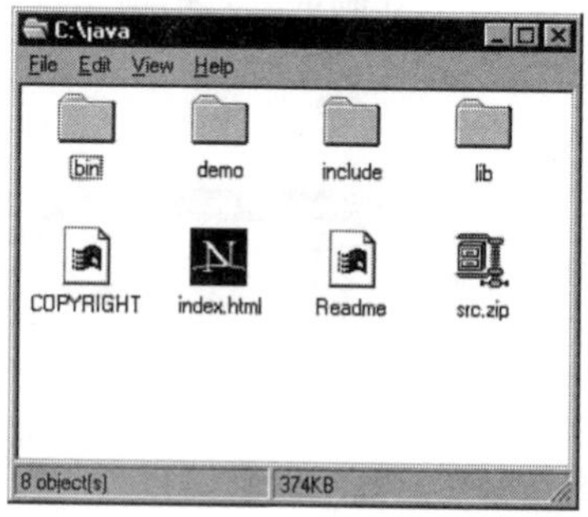

The `java\bin` directory (see Figure 2.5) contains all the executable programs and dynamic link libraries (DLLs) for the JDK toolset. The major software development tools provided with the JDK are the compiler (`javac`), interpreter (`java`), debugger (`jdb`), disassembler (`javap`), documentation generator (`javadoc`), applet viewer (`appletviewer`), and C header file tool (`javah`). We're going to examine each of these tools in Chapter 3, "Using the Java Developer's Kit." If you absolutely can't wait to get your hands on Java, go ahead to Chapter 3, but make sure you come back and browse through the rest of this overview.

The `java\demo` directory, shown in Figure 2.6, contains lots of nifty demos that highlight Java's finer features. I'll show you how to run these demos in Chapter 3. If you can't control the urge to run some of the demos now, click on the HTML files in the demo folders. Be sure to use a Java-enabled browser, such as Netscape 2.0.

The `java\include` directory (see Figure 2.7) contains C header files that are used to write C programs, called *native methods*, that extend the Java API. We won't be getting involved with native methods until Chapter 38, "Creating Native Methods."

FIGURE 2.5.
The Java toolset.

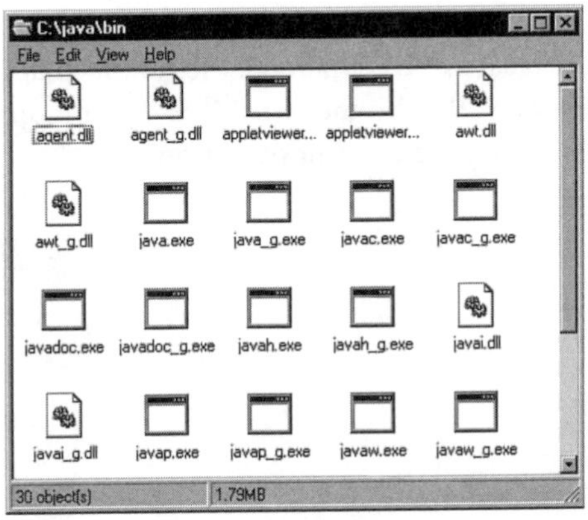

FIGURE 2.6.
Java demos.

FIGURE 2.7.
C header files for writing native methods.

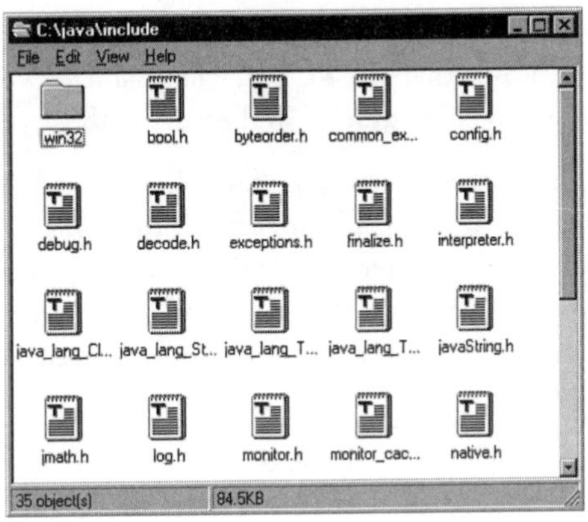

Finally, the `java\lib` directory, shown in Figure 2.8, contains the class library files for the Java API. The file `classes.zip` contains all the compiled library files. The Java compiler and interpreter are able to work with the library files, in compressed form, which saves you some disk space and provides more efficient operation.

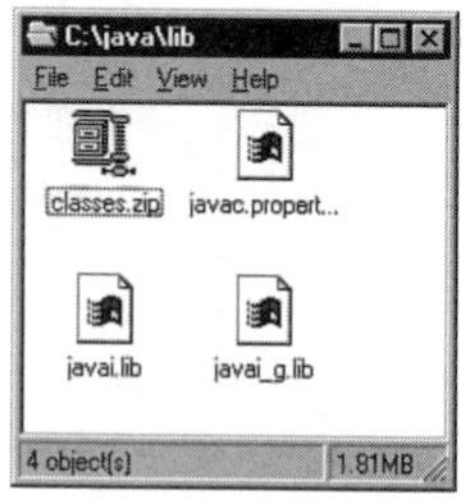

FIGURE 2.8.
Class library files.

Now that you know a little bit about what's inside the JDK, let's quickly cover the Java language and application programming interface so we can get started using the JDK tools.

The Java Language

The Java language is a remarkable example of programming language evolution. Java builds on the familiar and useful features of C++ while removing its complex, dangerous, and superfluous elements. The result is a language that is safer, simpler, and easier to use. The following subsections describe Java in contrast to C++. Appendix B, "Differences Between Java and C++," provides a detailed identification of the differences between the two languages.

Java Is Familiar and Simple

If you have ever programmed in C++, you will find Java's appeal to be instantaneous. Since Java's syntax mirrors that of C++, you will be able to write Java programs within minutes. Your first programs will come quickly and easily, with very little programming overhead.

You will have the feeling that you have eliminated a lot of clutter from your programs—and you will have. All the cryptic header files and preprocessor statements of C and C++ are gone. All the arcane `#define` statements and typedefs have been taken away. You will no longer have to delve through several levels of header files to correctly reference API calls. And no one will have to suffer to figure out how to use your software.

Java programs simply import the software packages they need. These packages may be in another directory, on another drive, or on a machine on the other side of the Internet. The Java compiler and interpreter figure out what objects are referenced and supply the necessary linkage.

Java Is Object-Oriented

If you think C++ is an object-oriented programming language, you are in for a big surprise. After using Java to write a few programs, you'll get a better feeling for what object-oriented software is all about. I know I did.

Java deals with classes and objects, pure and simple. They aren't just more data structures that are available to the programmer—they are the basis for the entire programming language.

In C++, you can declare a class, but you don't have to. You can declare a structure or a union instead. You can declare a whole bunch of loosely associated variables and use them with C-style functions. In Java, classes and objects are at the center of the language. Everything else revolves around them. You can't declare functions and procedures. They don't exist. You can't use structures, unions, or typedefs. They're gone, too. You either use classes and objects or you don't use Java. It's that simple.

Java provides all the luxuries of object-oriented programming: class hierarchy, inheritance, encapsulation, and polymorphism—in a context that is truly useful and efficient. If you are new to object-oriented software, you can find a complete introduction to these topics is provided in Chapter 5, "Classes and Objects." The main reason for developing object-oriented software, beside clarity and simplicity, is the desperate hope that somehow the objects you develop will be reused. Java not only encourages software reuse, it demands it. To write any sort of Java program, no matter how simple, you must build on the classes and methods of the Java API.

Once you have begun developing software in Java, you have two choices:

- Build on the classes you have developed, thereby reusing them.
- Rewrite your software from scratch, copying and tailoring useful parts of existing software.

With Java, the temptation to start from scratch is no longer appealing. Java's object-oriented structure forces you to develop more useful, more tailorable, and much simpler software the first time around.

Java Is Safer and More Reliable

Java is safer to use than C++ because it keeps you from doing the things that you do badly, while making it easier to do the things that you do well.

Java won't automatically convert data types. You have to explicitly convert from one class to another. C++, under the most undesirable conditions, will automatically convert one type to another. It has all the flexibility of assembly code. Java doesn't assume that you know what you are doing. It makes sure that you do.

C++ pointers don't exist in Java. You can no longer access objects indirectly or by chance. You don't need to. You declare objects and reference those objects directly. Complex pointer arithmetic is avoided. If you need an indexed set of objects, you can use an array of objects. The concept of "the address of an object" is eliminated from the programming model, and another assembly language dinosaur is laid to rest. As a result, it becomes much easier to do things correctly in Java.

Java's reliability extends beyond the language level to the compiler and the runtime system. Compile-time checks identify many programming errors that go undetected in other programming languages. These checks go beyond syntactic checking to ensure that statements are semantically correct.

Runtime checks are also more extensive and effective. Remember your teacher or mom telling you to "Check your work twice to make sure it's right"? The Java linker understands class types and performs compiler-level type checking, adding redundancy to reliability. It also performs bounds checking and eliminates indirect object access, even under error conditions.

Java Is Secure

If you gave a skilled hacker a program written in C or C++ and told him to find any security flaws, there are half a dozen things that he would immediately look for: gaining access to the operating system, causing an unexpected return of control, overwriting critical memory areas, acquiring the ability to spoof or modify other programs, browsing for security information, and gaining unauthorized access to the file system.

Why is C or C++ more vulnerable than Java? When a programmer develops software, he or she usually focuses on how to get the software to work correctly and efficiently. C and C++ do not constrain the programmer from meeting these goals and provide a number of flexible features that enable the programmer to meet his end. The hacker is also able to take advantage of these features and use them in ways that weren't originally intended, causing the undesirable consequences identified in the previous paragraph. In short, C and C++ provide a great offense, but no defense. Java, on the other hand, is defensive by nature. Every time a Java-enabled browser downloads a compiled Java class, such as an applet, it runs the risk of running Trojan horse code. Because of this ever-present threat, it subjects the code to a series of checks that ensure that it is correct and secure.

The Java runtime system is designed to enforce a security policy that prevents execution of malicious code. It does this by remembering how objects are stored in memory and enforcing correct and secure access to those objects according to its security rules. It performs bytecode verification by passing compiled classes through a simple theorem prover that either proves that the code is secure or prevents the code from being loaded and executed. The class is Java's basic execution unit and security is implemented at the class level.

The Java runtime system also segregates software according to its origin. Classes from the local system are processed separately from those of other systems. This prevents remote systems from replacing local system software with code that is less trustworthy.

Java-enabled browsers, such as HotJava, allow the user to control the accesses that Java software may make of the local system. When a Java applet needs permission to access local resources, such as files, a security dialog box is presented to the user, requesting explicit user permission. This "Mother may I?" approach ensures that the user always has the final say in the security of his system.

Java security is covered in detail in Chapter 39, "Java Security."

Java Is Multithreaded

Java, like Ada, and unlike other languages, provides built-in language support for multithreading. Multithreading allows more than one thread of execution to take place within a single program. This allows your program to do many things at once: make the Duke dance, play his favorite tune, and interact with the user, seemingly all at the same time. Multithreading is an important asset because it allows the programmer to write programs as independent threads, rather than as a convoluted gaggle of intertwined activities. Multithreading also allows Java to use idle CPU time to perform necessary garbage collection and general system maintenance, enabling these functions to be performed with less impact on program performance.

Writing multithreaded programs is like dating several people concurrently. Everything works fine until the threads start to interact with each other in unexpected ways. Java provides the support necessary to make multithreading work safely and correctly. Java supports multithreading by providing synchronization capabilities that ensure that threads share information and execution time in a way that is *thread safe*. These capabilities are illustrated with several programming examples in Chapter 8, "Multithreading."

Java Is Interpreted and Portable

While it is true that compiled code will almost always run more quickly than interpreted code, it is also true that interpreted code can usually be developed and fielded more inexpensively, more quickly, and in a more flexible manner. It is also usually much more portable.

Java, in order to be a truly platform-independent programming language, must be interpreted. It does not run as fast as compiled native code, but it doesn't run much slower, either. Chapter 36, "The Java Source Code," provides some Java performance benchmarks. For the cases where execution in native machine code is absolutely essential, work is underway to translate Java bytecode into machine code as it is loaded.

The advantages of being interpreted outweigh any performance impacts. Because Java is interpreted, it is much more portable. If an operating system can run the Java interpreter and support the Java API, then it can faithfully run all Java programs.

Interpreted programs are much more easily kept up-to-date. You don't have to recompile them for every change. In Java, recompilation is automatic. The interpreter detects the fact that a program's bytecode file is out-of-date with respect to its source code file and recompiles it as it is loaded.

Because of Java's interpreted nature, linking is also more powerful and flexible. Java's runtime system supports dynamic linking between local class files and those that are downloaded from across the Internet. This feature provides the basis for Web programming.

Java Is the Programming Language of the Web

Java has become the de facto programming language of the Web. It is being licensed by nearly every major software company. It has some offshoots and potential competition, such as JavaScript, VBScript, and Bell Labs's Inferno, but it remains the first Web programming language and the most powerful language for developing platform-independent software.

Java is also evolving beyond the Web and becoming a key component in distributed application development. Sun's release of the NEO and JOE products emphasizes Java's importance to distributed object-based software development. Several other vendors have introduced products that enable Java to be integrated into the Common Object Request Broker Architecture (CORBA), which is the framework for distributed object communication.

The Java API

The Java API is what makes Java attractive and useful. It consists of a set of packages that are distributed with the JDK as class libraries. These packages provide a common interface for developing Java programs on all Java platforms. The Java API furnishes all the capabilities needed to develop console programs, window programs, client and server networking software, applets, and other applications. It is the difference that takes Java from being a really good programming language to making it a very powerful and efficient programming environment.

The Java API consists of eight major development packages and a supporting debug package, as shown in Figure 2.9. *Packages* are collections of related objects. For example, there are separate packages for developing window programs, applets, and networking software.

Java packages contain classes, interfaces, and exceptions, as illustrated in Figure 2.10.

Classes form the basis for object-oriented software development in Java. They contain variables and methods. Variables are data containers. Methods implement operations on the class and its variables. For example, there is a class in the `java.awt` package called `Rectangle`. It consists of variables that specify the position and dimensions of a rectangle, and methods, such as move and resize, that enable operations to be performed on rectangles. Chapter 5 provides an introduction to classes.

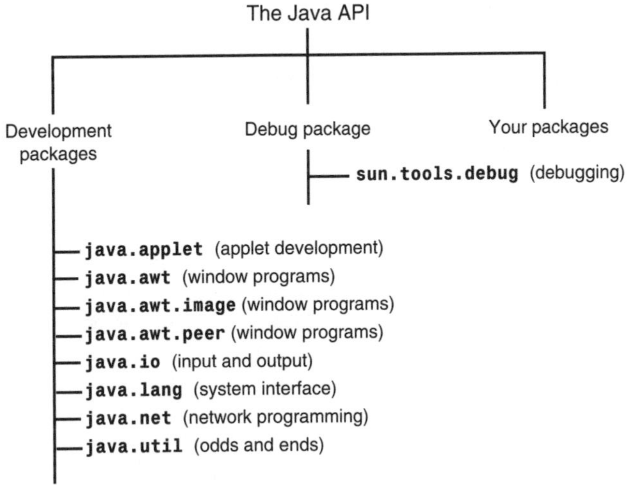

FIGURE 2.9.
The organization of the Java API.

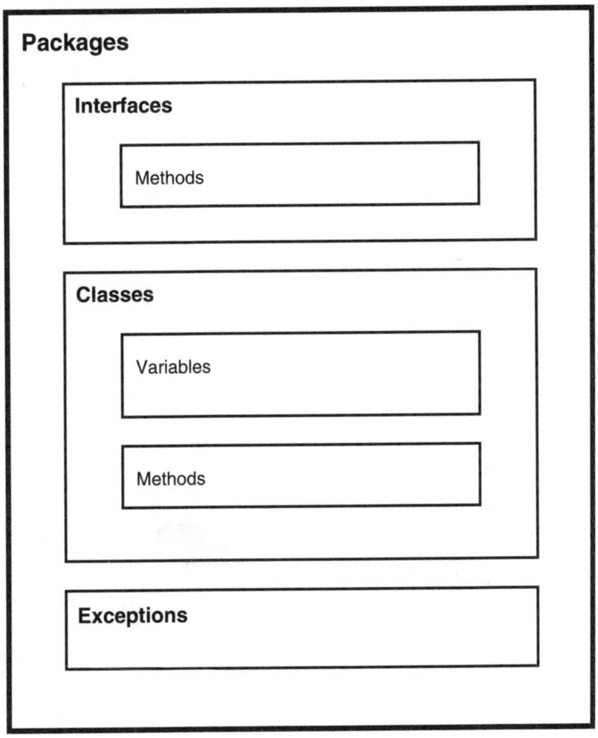

FIGURE 2.10.
How Java packages are organized.

Interfaces are collections of related methods. An example of an interface is the DataInput interface of the `java.io` package. It specifies a collection of methods that must be defined for a class to implement the DataInput interface. Exceptions are events that alter the normal course of program execution. Chapter 6, "Interfaces," introduces interfaces, and Chapter 7, "Exceptions," covers exceptions.

The Java API is used to develop Java programs. Figure 2.11 summarizes this process.

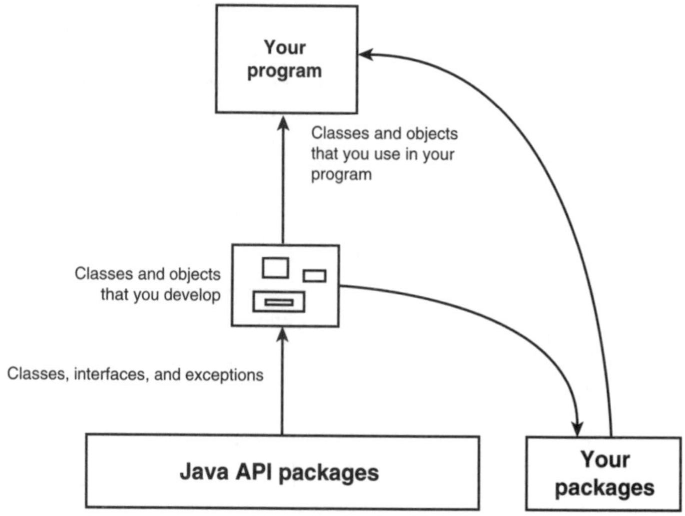

FIGURE 2.11.
Developing software using the Java API.

You write your Java programs using the Java API as a template and building block. You use the API to construct objects that are instances of API classes, implement API interfaces, and respond to API exceptions. These objects are used by your application program, which is itself an instance of a Java API class. Think of your program as a collection of objects that work together to support a common set of operations.

You can also create your own classes, interfaces, and exceptions, building on those that are defined in the API. You can collect them into custom packages that are integrated within and extend the Java API. These API extensions can then be used to develop other programs or even more sophisticated packages and API extensions.

This building-block approach to software development is the essence of object-oriented programming and software reuse. The Java API supports platform-independent software reuse by providing a powerful set of components from which to start.

Summary

In order to learn Java, you have to learn the Java language, learn to use the Java API, and learn how to use the JDK toolset. In this chapter, you have explored the JDK software and learned the tools it contains. In Chapter 3 you will learn how to operate those tools.

This chapter highlights the key features of the Java language. In Part II, "Programming in Java," you will focus on learning Java's syntax and application by developing a series of sample programs. These programs will also familiarize you with using the JDK tools and relevant parts of the Java API.

You have been introduced to the Java API and shown how it is used to construct Java programs. In Part III, "Using the Java API," you will focus on learning the Java API. You will do this by studying the components contained in the API packages and using these components to build Java programs.

By the time you have finished Part III, you will be a competent Java programmer. The rest of the book will show you how to extend your skills by focusing on specific areas of Java software development.

3

Using the Java Developer's Kit

This chapter is an introduction to the software development tools contained in the Java Developer's Kit (JDK). It explains what each tool does and how it is used with the other tools in the toolkit, and shows you how to operate each tool and work with its command-line options. In the last section of this chapter, you'll learn how to run the demo applets included in the JDK.

This chapter has a dual purpose—it serves both as an initial introduction to the JDK and as a JDK reference manual. When reading this chapter for the first time, just try to understand how each of the JDK programs is used. Do not worry about learning all the options that are available to you. These options are illustrated via sample programs during the course of this book. Many of these options are useful only in special circumstances that you might never encounter. When you are working on later chapters, you can refer to this chapter for a full description of the options used in a programming example.

Overview

The purpose of the JDK is to provide a complete set of tools for the development, testing, documentation, and execution of Java programs and applets. The JDK provides tools that support each of these activities, and more. It consists of the following seven programs:

Program Name	*Description*
`javac`	Compiler
`java`	Interpreter
`jdb`	Debugger
`javap`	Disassembler
`appletviewer`	Applet viewer
`javadoc`	Documentation generator
`javah`	C header file generator

Usually, you will write Java programs by using a text editor to develop Java *source files.* These files consist of source code packages that declare Java classes and interfaces. Source files use the `.java` extension.

The Java compiler, `javac`, is used to convert the source files into files that can be executed using the Java interpreter. These files are referred to as *bytecode files* and end with the `.class` extension.

The Java interpreter, `java`, executes classes from the bytecode (`.class`) files. It verifies the integrity, correct operation, and security of each class as it is loaded and executed, and interacts with the host operating system, windowing environment and communication facilities to produce the desired program behavior.

The debugger, `jdb`, is like the interpreter in that it executes Java classes that have been compiled into bytecode files, but it also provides special capabilities to stop program execution at selected breakpoints and to display the values of class variables. These capabilities are very useful in finding programming errors.

The disassembler takes the bytecode files and displays the classes, fields (variables), and methods that have been compiled into the bytecodes. It also identifies the bytecode instructions used to implement each method. The disassembler is a handy tool for recovering the source code design of those compiled Java classes for which no source code is available—for example, those that you would retrieve from the Web.

The applet viewer, `appletviewer`, displays Java applets contained within Web pages, located on your local file system, or at accessible websites. It is used to test applets that you develop.

The automated documentation tool, `javadoc`, is used to convert portions of Java source files into *Hypertext Markup Language* (HTML) files. HTML is the language used to write Web pages. The HTML files generated by `javadoc` document the classes, variables, methods, interfaces, and exceptions contained in Java source files based on special comments inserted into these files.

The C header file tool, `javah`, is used to generate C-language header and source files from a Java bytecode file. The files generated by `javah` are used to develop *native methods*—Java classes that are written in languages other than Java.

Figure 3.1 shows how each of these programs is used and how it interfaces with other programs within the JDK.

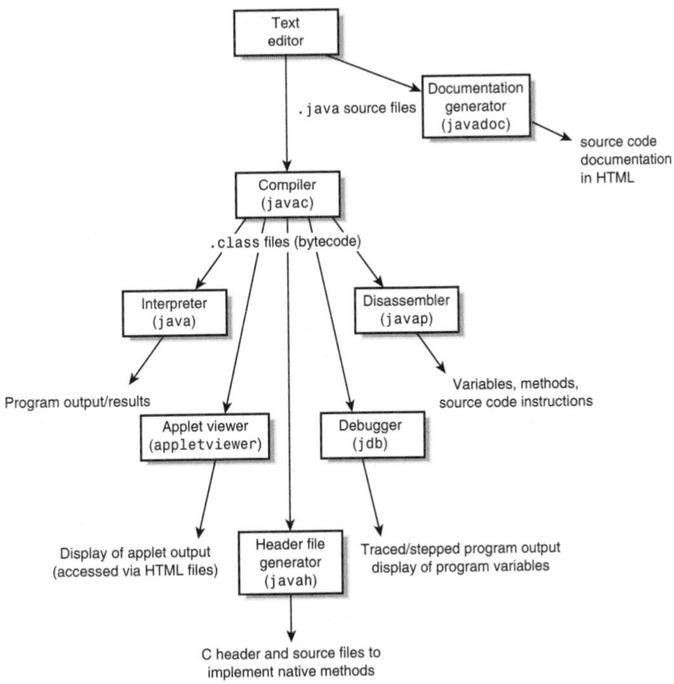

FIGURE 3.1.
How the programs of the JDK interact.

The Compiler

The Java compiler is used to translate Java source code files into bytecode files for execution by the Java interpreter. The source code files must end with the `.java` extension. They are translated into files with the same name, but with the `.class` extension.

For example, suppose the file `test.java` is located in the `c:\myfiles\source` directory. To compile `test.java`, change directories to `c:\myfiles\source` and enter the command `javac test.java`. If your compilation is successful, `javac` will create a file named `test.class` that will contain the compiled bytecodes for `test.java`. If your compile is unsuccessful, you will receive error messages that will help you figure out what went wrong.

> **TIP**
>
> Set your `PATH` variable to the directory containing the JDK executable programs so that your operating system shell can find them. If you installed Java as described in the previous chapter, add `c:\java\bin` to your `PATH`.

In general, the Java compiler is executed as follows:

```
javac options java_source_file
```

Figure 3.2 illustrates the operation of the Java compiler. The compiler options are covered in the following sections. You get hands-on experience using `javac` to compile sample programs in Chapter 4, "First Programs: Hello World! to BlackJack."

FIGURE 3.2.
The operation of the Java compiler.

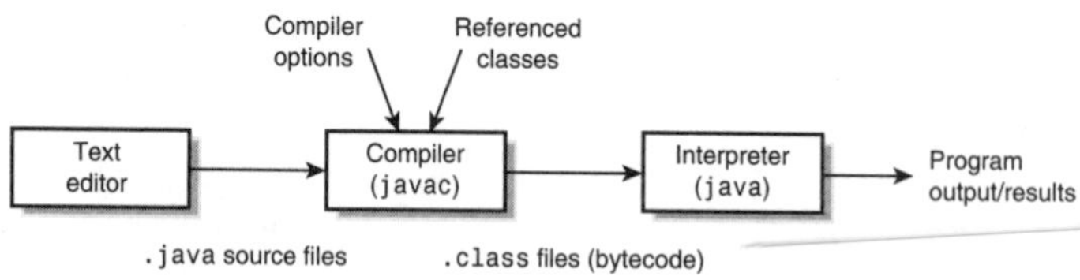

Using Classes from Other Packages

Every Java program uses classes that are defined outside of the program's source code file. Most often these *external classes* are contained in the Java API. However, you will also want to be able to reuse classes that you develop. The Java compiler must be able to locate these external classes in order to determine how to correctly compile code that references them. This section shows how the Java compiler and other programs in the JDK locate compiled classes. Understanding this information is important to using the JDK programs most effectively.

All Java declarations, such as classes, interfaces, and exceptions, are organized into logical units called *packages*. A class or interface must be identified as `public` to be used outside of its package. Only one `public` class or interface is allowed in a given source file. Interfaces are covered in Chapter 6, "Interfaces."

A compiled Java class is identified by its package name followed by a period (`.`) followed by its class name. For example, suppose you've developed and compiled a class called `TestClass` and it is contained in the `TestAPI` package. Your class would be identified by `TestAPI.TestClass`. The identifier, `TestAPI.TestClass`, is referred to as the *fully qualified name* or *full name* of the class `TestClass`. Figure 3.3 shows how package names are combined with class names to produce full class names.

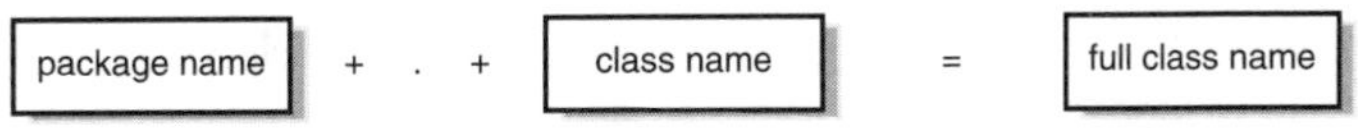

FIGURE 3.3.
How class names are formed.

The full name of a class is used to locate the class with respect to `CLASSPATH`. `CLASSPATH` is a system environment variable containing a list of directories where Java packages can be found. You convert the full name to a path offset by replacing any periods in the name with backslashes (`\`) for Windows 95/NT systems and slashes (`/`) for UNIX systems. This path offset is then combined with directories in `CLASSPATH` to locate the bytecode (`.class`) files containing Java classes.

> **NOTE**
>
> Windows 95 and NT use backslashes (`\`) to indicate and separate directories. UNIX uses slashes (`/`). Because this book is oriented toward Windows 95, it uses the Windows 95 convention. Any other differences for UNIX systems are indicated as appropriate.

The package that contains a particular class is identified using the Java `package` statement. You'll learn how to use this statement in the next chapter. If no package is identified for a class, the class is put in a default package with no name. The full name for the class is then just the class name. Java assumes that the name of the bytecode file containing a class is the name of the class concatenated with the `.class` extension, as illustrated in Figure 3.4.

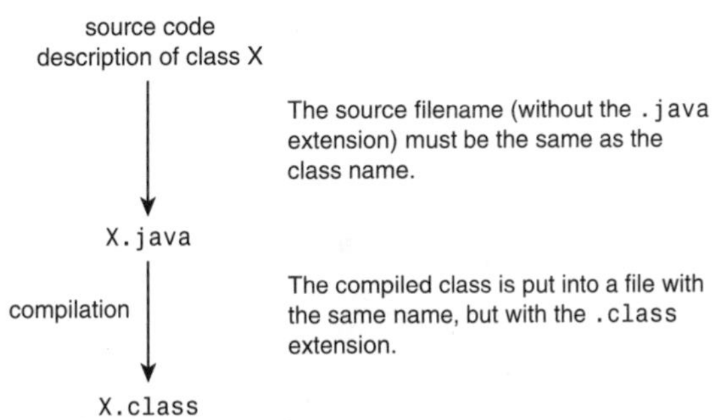

FIGURE 3.4.
The relationship between source code filenames, class names, and bytecode filenames.

Setting CLASSPATH

CLASSPATH tells the JDK programs where to find Java classes. You must set the CLASSPATH to identify the location of your classes. You set CLASSPATH differently depending on your operating system. For Windows 95 and Windows NT, enter the following at the console command line to set your CLASSPATH:

```
set CLASSPATH=path
```

A common CLASSPATH is `.;c:\java;c:\java\lib\classes.zip`. This tells the Java compiler and other JDK tools to use the current directory (`.`), the `c:\java` directory, and the file `c:\java\lib\classes.zip` as a base for finding Java class files. You would enter the following to set this CLASSPATH:

```
set CLASSPATH=.;c:\java;c:\java\lib\classes.zip
```

You can also put this statement in your AUTOEXEC.BAT file so that it will be set automatically each time you start a DOS shell. Windows NT users can use the System option in the Control Panel to set the CLASSPATH variable.

On UNIX systems that use the C shell, you set CLASSPATH using the `setenv` command. Java is typically installed under `/usr/local` on UNIX systems. Suppose that you want to set CLASSPATH to the current directory, your home directory, and the location of the JDK classes. You would enter the following at the shell prompt:

```
setenv CLASSPATH .:~:/usr/local/java/lib/classes.zip
```

For systems that use the Bourne Again shell (`bash`), you would enter the following at the shell prompt:

```
CLASSPATH=.:~:/usr/local/java/lib/classes.zip
export CLASSPATH
```

NOTE

UNIX systems use the colon (`:`) to separate path elements. Windows 95 and NT use the semicolon (`;`).

CLASSPATH can also be set from the `javac` command line using the `-classpath` option. For example, to compile `test.java` with the `.;c:\otherclasses` path, you would use the following command line:

```
javac test.java -classpath .;c:\otherclasses
```

The CLASSPATH set by the `-classpath` option is temporary and only applies to the current file being compiled.

Changing the Root Directory

Normally, `javac` will put the `.class` bytecode file that it generates in the same directory as the `.java` source file that it compiles. You can change this using the `-d` option. For example, to put the `test.class` file generated by compiling `test.java` in the `c:\classes` directory, you would use the following command:

```
javac -d c:\classes test.java
```

The `-d` option does not affect `CLASSPATH`.

Generating Debugging Tables

The Java debugger needs additional information to be placed in `.class` files in order to support enhanced debugging operations. Normally, only information about line numbers is inserted in `.class` files. Additional information about local variables is produced as the result of using the `-g` option. For example, the following produces the `test.class` file with additional debugging information included:

```
javac -g test.java
```

Code Optimization

The bytecode files produced by Java are usually not optimized for execution speed. Optimized files are generally larger, and this is undesirable for some applications, such as Java applets, which may be downloaded over slow Internet connections.

Optimization for execution speed can be turned on using the `-O` option. This results in inline expansion of code, where possible, to reduce delays associated with loading and calling certain methods. Static, final, and private methods are optimized via inline expansion. For example, the following will optimize the `test.class` file for speedier execution:

```
javac -O test.java
```

Suppressing Warnings

Sometimes your `.java` files will contain code that could lead to potential errors. The compiler will warn you about these problem areas. If you do not want to see these warnings, you can turn them off using the `-nowarn` option. For example, the following command will suppress warnings from being generated when compiling `test.java`:

```
javac -nowarn test.java
```

Using Verbose Mode

If you want more detailed information about the compiler's operation, *verbose mode* is for you. When verbose mode is turned on, the compiler identifies the source files that it compiles and the `.class` files that it loads in order to compile these files. Verbose mode is turned on using the `-verbose` option. For example, the following will compile `test.java` and display information on what `.class` files are loaded during the compilation:

```
javac -verbose test.java
```

The Interpreter

The Java interpreter executes the bytecode files produced by the Java compiler. It is invoked using the `java` command, as follows:

```
java options class arguments
```

`class` is the full name of the compiled Java class generated by the Java compiler. In order for the compiler to locate and execute the class, the class must meet the following requirements:

- It must have a valid `main` method. The `main` method is analogous to the `main` function in C and C++ programs. You'll learn how to construct a `main` method in the next chapter.
- It must be contained in a bytecode file with the same name as the class followed by the `.class` extension.
- The location of the class must be determined using `CLASSPATH` and the full name of the class as discussed in the "Using Classes from Other Packages" section earlier in this chapter.

The program arguments are optional parameters that are passed to the `main` method of the class that is executed. They are analogous to command-line arguments that are passed to C and C++ programs. The arguments are processed by the class's `main` method and not by the Java interpreter. For example, suppose that you developed a Java class called `TestClass` with a `main` method that merely displayed the arguments passed to it. Also, assume that `TestClass` is in the `TestAPI` package. The command

```
java TestAPI.TestClass 1 2 3
```

would merely print the numbers 1, 2, and 3.

Interpreter options are used to control different aspects of the interpreter's operation. These options are covered in the following subsections.

Changing CLASSPATH

The Java interpreter has a `-classpath` option that is identical to that of the compiler. It is used to temporarily change `CLASSPATH` for the duration of the class being executed. For example, the following will result in the execution of the `main` method of the compiled `TestClass` located in the file `c:\other\TestAPI.TestClass.class`:

```
java -classpath c:\other TestAPI.TestClass
```

Checking for Source Code Changes

The Java interpreter has a useful option that checks to see if the source code file of the class to be executed has been modified since the last time that it was compiled. This option is the `checksource` option and is identified with `-cs` or `-checksource`. If the date/time of modification of the source code file is more recent than that of the bytecode file, then the source code file is recompiled before the specified class is executed.

For example, suppose you developed and compiled the `TestClass` class, and then later in the day made modifications to the `TestClass.java` file from which `TestClass` was compiled. You have the choice of recompiling `TestClass.java` and executing it using `java` or using the `checksource` option to accomplish compilation and execution with a single command. In the latter case, you could use

```
java -cs TestAPI.TestClass
```

to perform both recompilation and execution.

Verifying Your Code

The Java interpreter has three options to control the bytecode verification of class files that it loads and executes:

`-verify`	Causes the interpreter to verify all code that it loads.
`-noverify`	Causes the interpreter to skip all code verification.
`-verifyremote`	Causes the interpreter to verify all code that is loaded via a classloader. This is the default operation of the interpreter.

Bytecode verification is performed by the Java interpreter to ensure the security, integrity, and correctness of the code it executes. It consists of a series of tests that verify that the code can be safely executed. The advantage of verification is that it promotes security, safety, and reliability. The disadvantage is that it takes time to perform and, therefore, slows down overall program execution.

The default `-verifyremote` option only applies verification to code that is loaded by a classloader. A *classloader* is a Java method that loads classes from remote systems into the local file system. The `-verifyremote` option assumes that local classes are trustworthy and do not need to be verified, but remotely loaded classes are suspect and subject to verification.

Examples of using the verify options are

```
java -verify TestAPI.TestClass
java -noverify TestAPI.TestClass
java -verifyremote TestAPI.TestClass
```

In the first case, all classes are verified as they are loaded. In the second case, no classes are verified. In the last case, only classes that are remotely loaded are verified.

Controlling the Garbage Collector

The Java interpreter automatically allocates and deallocates memory resources as they are needed by Java programs. Memory is allocated as program objects are created and deallocated as the result of the Java *garbage collector*. The Java runtime system keeps track of objects that are created, monitors references to objects, and uses the garbage collector to free the memory associated with objects when no more references to the objects exist.

The garbage collector runs as a separate, low-priority background thread that executes when no other threads are active. It checks object references and frees those objects that are no longer in use. The garbage collector is not explicitly called by executing programs, but operates during periods of low activity. It is said to operate *asynchronously* with respect to program execution.

The `-noasyncgc` option turns off asynchronous garbage collection. This prevents the garbage collector from being run except when a program calls it or the runtime system is out of memory. The `-noasyncgc` option is generally used when a program calls the garbage collector directly. This only occurs in memory-intensive programs that require more direct control over memory resources.

The Java interpreter provides the `-verbosegc` option for monitoring the operation of the garbage collector. This option instructs the garbage collector to display a message to the console window when it frees a previously allocated object. It is used to monitor the operation of the garbage collector and is generally limited to program testing and debugging.

Changing Properties

The Java interpreter allows you to change the values of predefined system parameters, referred to as *system properties*. These properties are used to specify the default values of variables that control the overall behavior of the Java runtime system.

You change or add a property using the -D option. If a property specified by the -D option does not currently exist in the system properties, it will be added to the list of defined properties. For example, the following will change the predefined os.name property from Windows 95 to Windows 96:

```
java -Dos.name="Windows 96" TestAPI.TestClass
```

The following example adds the myProperty property to the list of system properties and gives it the value 1234:

```
java -DmyProperty=1234 TestAPI.TestClass
```

You will learn how to use properties in Chapter 12, "Portable Software and the java.lang Package," when you explore the java.lang.System class.

Setting Memory and Stack Limits

The Java interpreter uses three major memory data structures to execute Java classes. These are the memory allocation pool, the Java code stack, and the C code stack.

The *memory allocation pool* is used to create objects for use in Java programs. It is controlled by the Java runtime system and the garbage collector. It is initially 1MB in size and has a maximum size of 16MB. The -ms and -mx options can be used to change the startup size and maximum size of the memory allocation pool. The memory size may be specified in bytes (default), kilobytes (using the k suffix), or megabytes (using the m suffix). For example, each of the following set the startup size of the memory allocation pool to 2MB and the maximum size to 8MB for the execution of TestClass:

```
java -ms 2097152 -mx 8388608 TestAPI.TestClass
java -ms 2048k -mx 8192k TestAPI.TestClass
java -ms 2m -mx 8m TestAPI.TestClass
```

In general, you should not attempt to change the default memory allocation pool values unless you have a very memory-intensive program or a computer with a less-than-average amount of RAM. The memory allocation pool must be larger than 1,000 bytes, and the default size is 3MB.

A Java code stack is created for every thread of a Java program. It is used to execute the bytecodes that comprise the Java thread. Chapter 37, "The Java Virtual Machine," provides a detailed description of the operation of the Java virtual machine. By increasing the size of the Java code stack, you provide more room for program instructions. By decreasing its size, you lower the memory requirements for your program. The default maximum size of the stack is 400KB. It can be changed using the -oss option. It specifies the stack size in bytes, kilobytes, and megabytes as previously described for the memory allocation pool. For example, the following command will execute TestClass with only 250KB of Java code stack by program thread:

```
java -oss 250k TestAPI.TestClass
```

The Java code stack size should be changed only if you have a program with an unusually large number of Java bytecode instructions or a computer with significantly limited RAM.

The C code stack is similar to the Java code stack. It is used to execute C code for a given thread. Its default size is 128KB and can be changed using the `-ss` option. Its size must be greater than 1,000 bytes. For example, the following command will execute `TestClass` with 256KB of C code stack per program thread:

```
java -ss 256k TestAPI.TestClass
```

The code stack is used to pass parameters to methods and to return the results of a method's calculations. It is similar to the memory functions used in calculators. Unless you plan to use a large amount of C-language native methods in your Java programs, you should never have to change the C code stack size.

Debugging Options

The Java interpreter provides a number of options that support the debugging and testing of Java classes. First and foremost, `java` lets you attach the Java debugger to an executing Java program. The `-debug` option tells the interpreter that you may want to attach the debugger to a Java session. The interpreter responds by displaying an *agent password* to the console window. This password must be entered when you attach the debugger to the active session. Use of the Java debugger is covered in the next section.

The `-verbose` option for the Java interpreter is similar to that used with the compiler. This option causes the interpreter to identify all classes that are loaded during a program's execution. The `-verbose` option can also be identified using `-v`. For example, the command

```
java -verbose TestAPI.TestClass
```

will display all classes that are loaded during the execution of `TestClass`.

There is a special version of the Java interpreter, `java_g`, that is oriented toward debugging. It includes the `-t` option for tracing the instructions executed during the course of a program's execution. Even for very short programs, the amount of data generated by this option can be overwhelming. For example, if you enter

```
java_g -t TestAPI.TestClass
```

you will receive a seemingly endless stream of information concerning the methods and instructions executed.

The Debugger

The Java debugger is used to monitor the execution of Java programs in support of debugging and test activities. It supports debugging of both locally executing and remotely executing Java programs.

The debugger can be started in two ways. In the first way, the debugger is started with a fully qualified class name. The debugger then calls the interpreter with the name of the class to be debugged. For example, the following command line starts the debugger with `TestAPI.TestClass`:

```
jdb TestAPI.TestClass
```

The debugger then invokes the interpreter to load `TestAPI.TestClass`. The interpreter returns control to the debugger before executing any instructions of `TestClass`. Interpreter options can be passed to the interpreter via the debugger command line. For example, the following command passes the `-D` option to the interpreter:

```
jdb -DmyProperty=1234 TestAPI.TestClass
```

The second way of starting the debugger is to attach it to a Java program that has already been started and is still running. The Java program to be debugged must have been started using the `-debug` option, as described in the previous section. The password displayed as the result of starting the program to be debugged is used when attaching the debugger. For example, suppose you initiate execution of `TestClass` using the following command:

```
java -debug TestAPI.TestClass
```

The interpreter will display a password to be used to attach the debugger to this session:

```
Agent password=424ee3
```

You can then attach the debugger to the still-running program using the command

```
jdb -password 424ee3
```

This command will attach the debugger to the execution of `TestClass`, which will result in `TestClass` being suspended and the debugger taking over control of the program's execution.

The debugger may also be used to attach to a program that is executing on a remote computer. Suppose the `TestClass` program is run on a computer named `remote.host.com` and you want to debug it from `my.host.com`. You can do so by entering the following command line:

```
jdb -host remote.host.com -password 424ee3
```

After starting `jdb`, it will announce that it is initializing, identify the class that it is debugging, and print a simple prompt.

Once you are up and running, using the debugger, you can enter a question mark (`?`) at the prompt (`>`) to receive a list of available debugging commands.

Chapter 9, "Using the Debugger," provides a detailed description of how the debugger is used to debug sample programs.

The Disassembler

The Java disassembler, `javap`, is used to reproduce the source code of a compiled Java class. It takes the full name of a class as its input and identifies the variables and methods that have been compiled into the class's bytecodes. It also identifies the source bytecode instructions that implement the class methods.

> **NOTE**
>
> The data components of a class are referred to as either *variables*, *fields*, or *field variables*.

For example, suppose you have the bytecode file of a class that you want to reverse engineer. You can use the disassembler to identify the `public` fields and methods of the class. With this information, you will be able to figure out how to create instances of the class and access their methods.

The debugger is executed as follows:

```
javap options class
```

`class` is the full name of a Java class created by the Java compiler. The options control the type of information displayed by the disassembler.

When no options are used, only the `public` fields and methods of the class are displayed. If the `-p` option is specified, the class's `private` and `protected` fields and methods are also displayed.

The `-c` option is used to display the source bytecode instructions for the class methods.

The `-classpath` option is used in the same way as it is with the compiler and interpreter.

Chapter 37 describes the Java virtual machine, the bytecode instruction set, and the use of the disassembler to analyze compiled classes.

The Applet Viewer

The applet viewer is used to run Java applets and test the applets that you develop. The applet viewer creates a window in which the applet can be viewed. It provides complete support for all applet functions, including networking and multimedia capabilities.

You use the applet viewer as follows:

```
appletviewer options URL
```

`URL` is the universal resource locator of an HTML document containing the applets to be viewed. It can be located on a local machine or on any accessible website. If you just want to

view an applet in a local HTML file, you can use the file's name instead of the entire URL of the file.

The `-debug` option is the only option supported by the applet viewer. It is used to run the applet viewer, using `jdb`, to test and debug the applets contained in the selected HTML document.

The applet viewer is covered in Part VI, "Programming the Web with Applets and Scripts." The last section in this chapter shows how to use it to display the demo applets included with the JDK.

Automating Software Documentation

The Java documentation generator, `javadoc`, is the tool that created the excellent Java API documentation. This documentation can (and should) be obtained from Sun's Java website. Make sure that you get the documentation that is applicable to your Java release. You can find it by pointing your browser at `http://java.sun.com` and then clicking on the documentation icon.

The documentation generator is executed using either the name of a Java source code file, a full class name, or a package name. If it is executed with a class name or package name, it will automatically load the source code associated with the class or with all the classes in the package. If it is executed with a source code file, it will generate documentation for all classes and interfaces defined in the file.

The `javadoc` command line is as follows:

```
javadoc options package
javadoc options class
javadoc options source_file
```

The `javadoc` options are `-classpath`, `-d`, and `-verbose`. The `-classpath` option is the same as with the compiler and interpreter. The `-d` option is used to specify the directory to which the generated HTML files are to be stored. It is similar to the `-d` option used with the compiler. The `-verbose` option results in a comprehensive display of the files that are loaded during the documentation-generation process.

Chapter 10, "Automating Software Documentation," shows how to use `javadoc` to automatically generate Java software documentation.

Header File Generation

The header file generation tool, `javah`, is used to produce the C files required to develop native methods. It produces both header and source files. The header files contain C-language definitions that map to Java class definitions. The source files contain the stubs for C functions that map to class methods.

The command line used to invoke `javah` is

```
javah options class(es)
```

where *`class(es)`* refers to the full class names of the classes for which header files are to be generated. The `javah` options control the way the header files are generated:

- The `-o` option combines all the files generated into a single file.
- The `-d` option identifies the directory where `javah` is to put the header and source files that it generates.
- The `-td` option specifies where `javah` is to store temporary files used in the header file generation process. The default directory is the `\tmp` directory.
- The `-stubs` option causes `javah` to generate C function stubs for class methods.
- The `-verbose` option is used to display status information concerning the files generated.
- The `-classpath` option is used in the same way as it is used with the compiler and interpreter.

See Chapter 38, "Creating Native Methods," for more information on this process.

Running the Demo Programs

The JDK comes with 32 sample applets that demonstrate the capabilities of the Java language and API. These applets are located in the `java\demo` directory of the JDK. If you installed the JDK under your `C:` drive, the applets will be located under `c:\java\demo`. The demo directory has 22 subdirectories, each containing one or more sample applets. To execute any of the applets, open an MS-DOS window and change to the subdirectory of `c:\java\demo` where the applet is located. In the subdirectory are files named `example1.html`, `example2.html`, and so on that are the HTML files containing links to the demo applets. Most of the subdirectories contain only a single example file. To execute the applet, just run `appletviewer` with the name of the HTML file as a command-line argument.

I'll walk you through a few applets so that you can get the hang of it. First, open an MS-DOS window and change directories to `c:\java\demo\Animator`. If you do a directory listing, you will see that it contains the following files:

```
C:\java\demo\Animator>dir

 Volume in drive C is ATHOME
 Volume Serial Number is 1CE3-2551
 Directory of C:\java\demo\Animator

.              <DIR>        01-24-96  6:50p .
..             <DIR>        01-24-96  6:50p ..
IMAGES         <DIR>        01-24-96  6:50p images
ANIMAT~1 JAV        21,410  10-13-95 10:23a Animator.java
```

```
ANIMAT~1 CLA        14,873  10-13-95   1:54a Animator.class
IMAGEN~1 CLA           706  10-13-95   1:54a ImageNotFoundException.class
PARSEE~1 CLA           410  10-13-95   1:54a ParseException.class
INDEX~1  HTM         3,411  10-13-95   1:54a index.html
AUDIO          <DIR>        01-24-96   6:50p audio
EXAMPL~1 HTM           428  10-13-95   1:54a example2.html
EXAMPL~2 HTM           466  10-13-95   1:54a example3.html
EXAMPL~3 HTM           419  10-13-95   1:54a example1.html
         8 file(s)          42,123 bytes
         4 dir(s)      357,564,416 bytes free
```

Entering the command `appletviewer example1.html` results in `appletviewer` being launched with the `example1.html` file. The applet viewer will then load and display any applets pointed to by the HTML file. (See Figure 3.5.)

FIGURE 3.5.
The applet viewer.

This applet displays an animation of the Duke, a kind of mascot of the Java project. As the Duke waves to you, an audio file is played in the background.

My favorite Duke applet is located in the `UnderConstruction` directory. Change to this directory using the command `cd ..\UnderConstruction` and run the applet using the command `appletviewer example1.html`. The applet shows the Duke operating a jackhammer and plays the sound of the jackhammer in the background. (See Figure 3.6.)

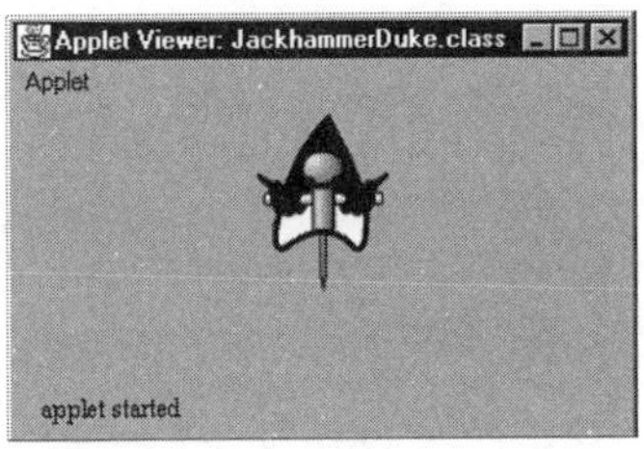

FIGURE 3.6.
Duke operating a jackhammer applet.

Now change to the `BouncingHeads` subdirectory and run the command `appletviewer example1.html`. You'll see images of a person's head bouncing around the screen, complete with background music and occasional grunting sounds. (See Figure 3.7.) This applet shows how Java can combine several multimedia features into a single applet with more than adequate runtime performance.

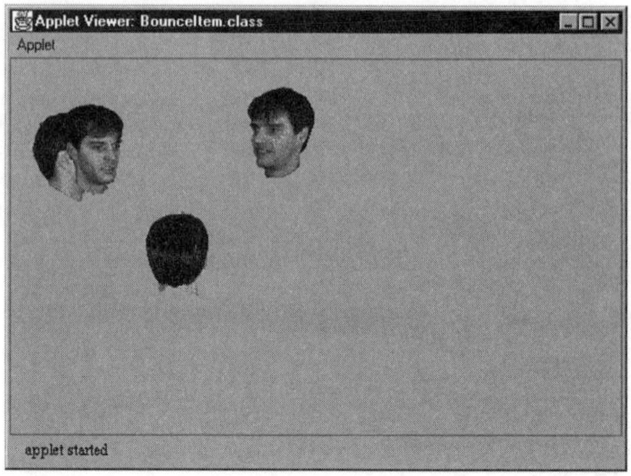

FIGURE 3.7.
The `BouncingHeads` *applet.*

Finally, change to the `TicTacToe` subdirectory and use the applet viewer to run the `example1.html` file. See if you can figure out how to beat the applet—it *can* be done! (See Figure 3.8.)

FIGURE 3.8.
The `TicTacToe` *applet.*

You can experiment with the rest of the demo applets by changing to the subdirectory containing the applet and running `appletviewer` with the appropriate HTML file.

Summary

You have covered a lot of information in this lesson. You have studied the tools of the Java Developer's Kit and learned what each tool does and how it is used with the other tools in the JDK. You have learned how to operate these tools and work with their command-line arguments. Finally, you have had a little fun by running the demo applets that come with the JDK. In Chapter 4 you'll start programming. You'll code, compile, and execute four simple programs that illustrate the basic elements of the Java language.

II

Programming in Java

4

First Programs: Hello World! to BlackJack

This chapter will quickly get you up to speed writing Java programs. If you have previously programmed in C++, this chapter will be a breeze. If you have programmed in some other language, the examples presented here will be familiar; you will just be learning a new syntax. If you have never programmed before, you will face the task of debugging your first programs. It will be easy or difficult depending on the mistakes you make and your ability to find programming errors. You may want to ask for help from someone who has programmed before.

In order to carry out the examples in this chapter and in the rest of the book, you need access to a computer that supports Java 1.0 or later. The type of computer and operating system that you use to write your programs won't matter. After all, that's the beauty of Java. The examples in this book have been developed using Java running under Windows 95. If you use Windows 95, I strongly recommend that you use a text editor other than Notepad or WordPad. These editors do not allow you to save files easily with the `.java` extension and will drive you crazy during program development. I use the shareware program TextPad, from Helios Software Solutions. It works well with both Windows 95 and NT, and is both convenient and affordable. It can be found in most Windows 95 FTP archives. If you are using Solaris, Linux, Windows NT, or any other Java port, you will use a text editor that is native to your system.

Hello World!

Since Brian Kernighan and Dennis Ritchie released the C programming language in 1978, the traditional first program has been to display `Hello World!` on the console display. Who are we to break with tradition?

Fire up your computer and change to the directory where you have Java installed. On my computer, Java is located in the `c:\java` directory. Create a subdirectory called `jdg` under your Java directory (that is, `c:\java\jdg`). If you are using a system such as UNIX or Windows NT, where you may not have write access to the `java` directory, create a `jdg` directory under your home directory.

You will store all the files that you develop under the `jdg` directory. Separate subdirectories will be created for each chapter, as shown in Figure 4.1. Go ahead and create a directory `ch04` for this lesson.

The CD-ROM that accompanies this book has an analogous directory structure to the one that you'll create. It contains the source and bytecode files for each example in the book. If you don't want to type in any of the sample programs, you can simply copy them from the CD-ROM. The CD-ROM also contains images, audio and video files, and other files used in the examples.

I recommend that you type in the first few programs. By doing so you will quickly get a feel for the Java syntax.

FIGURE 4.1.
Files contained on the CD-ROM mirror the ones you'll create.

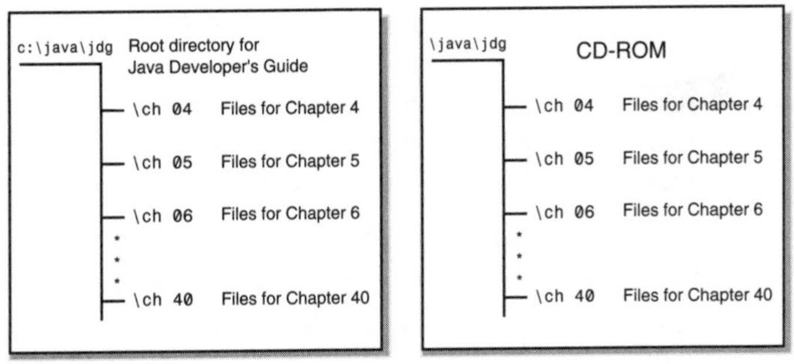

Now start your favorite text editor and key in the Java program in Listing 4.1.

Listing 4.1. The source code of the Hello World! program.

```
package jdg.ch04;

/* HelloWorldApp.java */

import java.lang.System;

class HelloWorldApp {
 /**
 * Traditional "Hello World!" program.
 */
 public static void main (String args[]) {
  // Write to stdout.
  System.out.println("Hello World!");
 }
}
```

Save this program as `HelloWorldApp.java` in the `c:\java\jdg\ch04` directory.

While in the `c:\java\jdg\ch04` directory, enter `javac HelloWorldApp.java`. This invokes the Java compiler and compiles the `HelloWorldApp.java` source file, creating the `HelloWorldApp.class` binary file. A listing of your directory should look similar to the following:

```
C:\java\jdg\ch04>dir

 Volume in drive C is ATHOME
 Volume Serial Number is 1CE3-2551
 Directory of C:\java\jdg\ch04

.              <DIR>        01-24-96 10:42p .
..             <DIR>        01-24-96 10:42p ..
HELLOW~1 JAV           265  01-22-96  3:38p HelloWorldApp.java
HELLOW~1 CLA           487  01-24-96 10:45p HelloWorldApp.class
         2 file(s)            752 bytes
         2 dir(s)     348,585,984 bytes free
```

If you receive any compiler errors, go back to your editor and make sure that you typed the program correctly. Then recompile your program using `javac`. Make sure you set your `PATH` and `CLASSPATH` environment variables as discussed in Chapter 3, "Using the Java Developer's Kit." `PATH` tells your operating system shell where to find your Java Developer's Kit programs. `CLASSPATH` tells the Java runtime system where to find Java classes.

When you're ready to run `HelloWorldApp`, using the Java interpreter, enter `java jdg.ch04.HelloWorldApp` from your shell command prompt. You should get the following output:

```
C:\java\jdg\ch04>java jdg.ch04.HelloWorldApp
Hello World!
```

> **NOTE**
>
> If you get an error message saying that Java can't find the `HelloWorldApp` class, make sure that your `CLASSPATH` is correctly set.

At this point, you are probably not impressed with the power of Java—but you soon will be. Let's walk through the program source code and learn some Java syntax.

Comments

Java allows three kinds of comments. You can use any of these comment styles to document your Java programs. An example of each kind is provided in the `HelloWorldApp.java` source code. The C-style comments begin with `/*` and end with `*/`. Here is an example:

```
/* HelloWorldApp.java */
```

The C++-style comments begin with `//` and continue to the end of a line:

```
// Write to stdout.
```

The Java automated documentation support comments begin with `/**` and end with `*/`. They are found immediately before or after a Java declaration:

```
/**
* Traditional "Hello World!" program.
*/
```

See Chapter 10, "Automating Software Documentation," for more information about this Java feature.

Java Program Structure

Java programs are built from classes and interfaces. A *class* defines a set of data structures, called *variables*, and the operations, referred to as *methods*, that are permitted on the variables. An *interface* defines a collection of methods that are to be implemented by a class. Your

HelloWorldApp program was built from the HelloWorldApp class. It also uses the System class. Figure 4.2 summarizes the Java program structure.

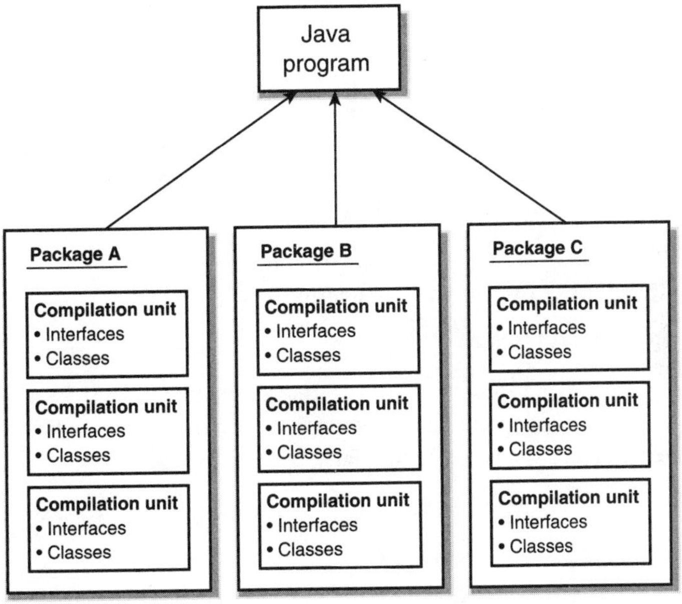

FIGURE 4.2.
The Java program structure.

Classes and interfaces are organized into .java files that are separately compiled. These .java files are called *compilation units*. The HelloWorldApp.java file that you created with your text editor and compiled using javac is an example of a compilation unit.

The classes and interfaces contained in compilation units are organized into *packages*. Packages are used to group related classes and interfaces and to avoid naming conflicts. Your HelloWorldApp class is in the jdg.ch04 package. The System class, referenced by your program, is in the java.lang package.

The package Statement

The *package statement* identifies which package a compilation unit is in. The package statement must be the first statement in a compilation unit. Its syntax is

```
package packageName;
```

For example, the package statement

```
package jdg.ch04;
```

was used to identify the package containing the HelloWorldApp as jdg.ch04.

If a compilation unit does not contain a package statement, the classes and interfaces contained in the compilation unit are put into a default package—the package with no name. This default package is the same for all classes within a particular directory.

The import Statement

The java.lang.System class is used to display Hello World!. The System class is in the java.lang package. In order to tell the compiler to use the System class in the java.lang package (as opposed to the System class in another package), import the System class using the import statement. *Importing* a class tells the compiler to use that class when it compiles your source code file.

The syntax of the import statement is

```
import fullClassName;
```

The class name supplied with the import statement must be a fully qualified class name, as described in Chapter 3. This means that the name of the package containing the class must be prepended to the name of the class.

For example, the following import statement imports the System class from java.lang:

```
import java.lang.System;
```

The * wildcard character can be used instead of the class name in the import statement. It indicates that all classes in the package should be imported. For example, the following import statement imports all classes in the java.lang package:

```
import java.lang.*;
```

An alternative to using the import statement is to prefix the name of a class with its package name. For example, the statement

```
java.lang.System.out.println("Hello World!");
```

could have been used in place of

```
import java.lang.System;
 .
 .
 .
System.out.println("Hello World!");
```

The last statement above would be replaced by the sample prefix statement.

It is generally easier to use the import statement than to spell out package names. In the case where two or more classes of the same name are imported into a compilation unit, you must prepend the package name when referencing one of the ambiguous classes.

Classes and Methods

The `HelloWorldApp` program was built on the `HelloWorldApp` class. This class is declared beginning with

```
class HelloWorldApp {
```

The class declaration ends with the last brace (`}`) of the file. `HelloWorldApp` declares and implements one method—the `main` method:

```
public static void main (String args[]) {
 // Write to stdout.
 System.out.println("Hello World!");
}
```

The `main` method is the method that is executed when a class is run from the command line using the Java interpreter. For example, the statement

```
java jdg.ch04.HelloWorldApp
```

causes the `main` method of the `jdg.ch04.HelloWorldApp` class to be executed.

The `main` method is always defined as `public` (that is, publicly accessible), `static` (applying to the class as a whole), and in the case of `HelloWorldApp`, `void` (no return value). The `args[]` parameter of `main` is defined as an array of class `String`. The `args[]` parameter is used to pass command-line arguments to the `main` method. Don't worry if you don't understand these terms—they will all be defined by the end of Chapter 5, "Classes and Objects."

The implementation of the `main` method consists of the following statement:

```
System.out.println("Hello World!");
```

This statement executes the `println` method of the object referred to by the `out` variable of the `System` class. The `println` method is executed using the `"Hello World!"` parameter. This is what causes `Hello World!` to be displayed on your console window.

The `System` Class

The `System` class provides an interface to a number of useful system resources. Among these are the `System.in` and `System.out` input and output streams. The `System.out` stream was used in the preceding example. The following example illustrates the use of `System.in`.

I Can Read!

This program builds on what you learned from `HelloWorldApp`. `HelloWorldApp` just displayed a message to your console window. The `ICanReadApp` program will read your name from the keyboard characters you type and display it on the console window. It introduces the concepts of identifiers, variable declarations, Java keywords, and object constructors.

Use your text editor to create a file called `ICanReadApp.java` with the Java program in Listing 4.2.

Listing 4.2. The source code of the I Can Read! program.

```
// ICanReadApp.java

import java.lang.System;
import java.io.DataInputStream;
import java.io.IOException;
class ICanReadApp {
 public static void main (String args[]) throws IOException {
  System.out.print("Enter your name: ");
  System.out.flush();
  String name;
  DataInputStream keyboardInput = new DataInputStream(System.in);
  name=keyboardInput.readLine();
  System.out.println("Your name is: "+name);
 }
}
```

Save the file in your `c:\java\jdg\ch04` directory. Compile it with the command line

```
javac ICanReadApp.java
```

This will produce a file named `ICanReadApp.class` that contains the binary compiled code for your program. Run the program with the command line

```
java ICanReadApp
```

Make sure that your `CLASSPATH` is correctly set so that Java can find the `ICanReadApp` class.

The program will prompt you to enter your name. When you enter your name, the program will display it to you. Here is a sample program run:

```
C:\java\jdg\ch04>java ICanReadApp
Enter your name: Jamie
Your name is: Jamie
```

It may seem that you're going nowhere fast, but this little program illustrates some more basic Java syntax. Hang in there—by the time you get to the end of the chapter, you'll be having fun with Java console programming.

Overview of `ICanReadApp`

One of the first things you probably noticed about this program is that it doesn't contain a package statement. That was done deliberately to show you what happens when a package statement is omitted. The package name of the `ICanReadApp` class is set to the no name (blank) package, by default. This means that you don't have to prepend the package name to the class name in order to execute it using the interpreter. Although not using a package name might seem like a benefit, it also limits the extent to which the classes you develop can be accessed by other Java programs. Because the package name is blank and your `CLASSPATH` variable is `.;c:\java`, the `ICanReadApp` class can only be accessed from within the `c:\java\jdg\ch04` directory. However, you can change your `CLASSPATH` to include this directory, as discussed in Chapter 2, "Java Overview."

The first line of the `ICanReadApp` program is a comment that identifies the name of the source file. Three `import` statements are used to import the `java.lang.System`, `java.io.DataInputStream`, and `java.io.IOException` classes into the compilation unit:

```
import java.lang.System;
import java.io.DataInputStream;
import java.io.IOException;
```

The `ICanReadApp` class is then declared. It consists of a single method called `main`. The `main` method contains a `throws` clause that identifies the fact that an `IOException` may be thrown during the course of its execution. When an exception is thrown, program control immediately transfers to an exception handler. This issue is covered in Chapter 7, "Exceptions."

The `main` method consists of the following six statements. These statements are summarized and then explained in the following subsections:

```
System.out.print("Enter your name: ");
System.out.flush();
String name;
DataInputStream keyboardInput = new DataInputStream(System.in);
name=keyboardInput.readLine();
System.out.println("Your name is: "+name);
```

The first statement displays the prompt `Enter your name:` on the console window.

The second statement flushes the output to the console to make sure that the data is displayed, even though a line termination was not sent to the console.

The third statement declares a variable called `name` of class `String`.

The fourth statement declares a variable named `keyboardInput` of class `DataInputStream`. It then creates an object of class `DataInputStream` that is constructed from the `System.in` object. This new object is then assigned to `keyboardInput`.

The fifth statement reads a line of data from the `keyboardInput` object and assigns it to the `name` variable.

The last statement displays the string `Your name is:` followed by the value of the object referred to by the `name` variable.

Declaring Variables and Creating Objects

Statements three and four of the `main` method declare two variables: `name` and `keyboardInput`. Variables are used to refer to data of a predefined Java type, an array of values, an object of a particular Java class, or an object that implements a particular Java interface. Variables are given names, called identifiers. The type of data that the variable refers to is specified in the variable declaration. The `name` variable is declared to refer to an object of class `String`. The `keyboardInput` variable is declared to refer to an object of class `DataInputStream`.

Notice the difference between statements three and four. In statement three, the `name` variable is declared—nothing more. No objects are created and referred to by `name`. It is like a blank street sign. We know it is a street sign, but we don't know on what street it will be posted.

In statement four, after `keyboardInput` is declared, it is assigned a new object of class `DataInputStream` that is created using the `new` operator and the `System.in` parameter. The `new` operator is used to create an object that is an instance of a particular class. You'll learn all about classes in Chapter 5. The `keyboardInput` variable refers to the object that is created.

The `name` variable is assigned an object in line five. When the `readLine` method is applied to the object referred to by `keyboardInput`, an object of class `String` is created. This object is created and initialized with the keyboard data that you type in response to the `Enter your name:` prompt. The assignment statement causes `name` to refer to this newly created `String` object.

Identifiers and Keywords

Identifiers are used to name variables, classes, interfaces, methods, and other Java language elements. An identifier is a sequence of characters that starts with an underscore (_), a dollar sign ($), or a letter (ASCII or Unicode). Subsequent characters may contain these characters plus the digits 0 through 9. Unicode letters come from the Unicode character set and are covered in Chapter 11, "Language Summary." Java reserves certain identifiers as keywords. Their use is restricted by Java and cannot be used in any other way. The reserved Java keywords are also listed in Chapter 11.

The following are valid identifiers:

```
myID
_score
$money
$$99__
```

These are not valid identifiers:

```
2time
dog#
spaced out
```

The problem with `2time` is that it begins with a digit. `dog#` contains a pound (#) character that is not allowed in identifiers. The last example fails because it contains a space character.

Using `System.in`

Console (that is, non-Windows) programs process user keyboard input and display data to the console window. The console window is an MS-DOS window in Windows 95 and NT implementations of Java and a shell, or `xterm` window, in UNIX-based Java implementations. In the `HelloWorldApp` program, you learned how to write to the console window. The `ICanReadApp` program showed how to read from the keyboard.

You might compare `System.in` with `System.out` and wonder why I had to create an object of class `DataInputStream`. The `System.out` variable refers to an object of class `PrintStream`. The `PrintStream` class provides the `println` method for writing to objects of this class. The `System.in` variable refers to an object of the `InputStream` class. The methods provided by the `InputStream` class aren't all that great for reading a line of text entered at the keyboard and returning that data as a string. The `InputStream` methods are fairly primitive. The `DataInputStream` class is a subclass of `FilterInputStream`, which is a subclass of `InputStream`. A subclass is a class that is built on another class as a foundation. The methods of `DataInputStream` build on the methods of `FilterInputStream` and `InputStream`. The `readLine` method is one such method. The example uses the `DataInputStream` class because it provides an easier method of reading keyboard input.

> **NOTE**
>
> Don't worry about learning all the new classes mentioned in this chapter. They are all covered in Part III, "Using the Java API."

In statement four, when the new `DataInputStream` object is created, it uses the object referred to by `System.in` as a foundation.

Type This!

In the `ICanReadApp` program, you were introduced to variable declarations and the construction and assignment of objects to variables. Variables may refer to objects of a particular class, to objects of one of the predefined Java types, to arrays, or to objects that implement a particular interface. You have already encountered the first case. The `TypeThisApp` program introduces the primitive Java types. Arrays are presented in the last example of this chapter. Interfaces are covered in Chapter 6, "Interfaces."

Start up your text editor and enter the program code shown in Listing 4.3. Then save it as `TypeThisApp.java` in your `ch04` directory.

Listing 4.3. The Type This! program.

```
// TypeThisApp.java

import java.lang.System;

class TypeThisApp {
 public static void main (String args[]) {
  // Integer types
  byte oneByte = 57;
  short twoBytes = 1024;
  int fourBytes = 1234567;
  long eightBytes = 0x123456789ABCDEFl;
  // Floating-point types
  float thirtyTwoBits = 1234.56f;
  double sixtyFourBits = 6.282E123;
  // Boolean type
  boolean ownSelf = true;
  // Character type
  char malcolm = 'X';
  System.out.println(oneByte);
  System.out.println(twoBytes);
  System.out.println(fourBytes);
  System.out.println(eightBytes);
  System.out.println(thirtyTwoBits);
  System.out.println(sixtyFourBits);
  System.out.println(ownSelf);
  System.out.println(malcolm);
 }
}
```

Compile the program using the following command line:

```
javac TypeThisApp.java
```

This will produce the `TypeThisApp.class` file that you can execute using

```
java TypeThisApp
```

The following output should be displayed on your console window:

```
C:\java\jdg\ch04>java TypeThisApp
57
1024
1234567
81985529216486895
1234.56
6.282e+123
true
X
```

Overview of `TypeThisApp`

`TypeThisApp`, like `HelloWorldApp` and `ICanReadApp`, declares only one class with a single method—`main`. The `main` method consists of eight variable declarations and assignments followed by eight invocations of the `println` method for the `System.out` object.

The eight variable declarations declare variables of the primitive data types `byte`, `short`, `int`, `long`, `float`, `double`, `boolean`, and `char`. Each of the declarations is combined with an assignment of a literal value to the declared variable.

The Primitive Java Data Types

Java supports four major primitive data types: `integer`, `floating point`, `boolean`, and `character`. The `integer` type has four subtypes: `byte`, `short`, `int`, and `long`. These correspond to 1-byte, 2-byte, 4-byte, and 8-byte integer values. The `floating point` type consists of a 4-byte `float` subtype and an 8-byte `double` subtype. The `floating point` type follows IEEE 754, a recognized standard for floating-point arithmetic developed by the Institute of Electrical and Electronics Engineers.

The `boolean` type consists of the literal values `true` and `false`. `boolean` types are not automatically converted into `integer` types because they are not defined in terms of integers as they are in C and C++. Explicit conversion is required.

The `character` type uses the standard Unicode character set and is a 16-bit unsigned integer. Variables of the `char` type store single characters. The `java.lang.String` class is used to store strings of characters.

Literal Values

`TypeThisApp` illustrates the use of literal values with the primitive types. Integer literals can be expressed as decimal, hexadecimal, or octal values, using the conventions established by C and C++. An integer literal that begins with a `0` is assumed to represent an octal value. An integer literal beginning with `0x` or `0X` is assumed to be a hexadecimal value. An `l` or `L` appended to an integer literal indicates that the literal is of type `long`.

Floating-point literals use the standard exponential notation described in Chapter 11. Floating-point literals are of type `double`, by default. An `f` or `F` appended to a floating-point literal indicates that the literal is of type `float`.

Boolean types simply use the values `true` and `false`.

Character types use standard Unicode, which is a superset of ASCII. Unicode is covered in Chapter 11. The C and C++ conventions for representing character literals are used by Java.

BlackJack

The programs you've written so far in this chapter have been deliberately kept short and simple. Their purpose is to quickly get you started in Java programming and to cover some of the basic elements of the Java language. The next example allows you to spread your wings and have a little fun at the same time. The `BlackJackApp` program that you will develop in this section is a simplified, character-based version of the popular blackjack card game. This example, while entertaining, illustrates the use of Java arrays and provides many examples of Java statements and expressions.

The `BlackJackApp` program is rather long compared to the previous examples. You have the option of copying the source code from the CD-ROM or typing it in yourself. I recommend typing it in. By doing so you will be sure to cover every statement in the program and increase your knowledge of Java syntax. Depending on how accurately you type, you might be called upon to develop some Java debugging skills.

Listing 4.4 is the program source code. Either type it into a file and save it as `c:\java\jdg\ch04\BlackJackApp.java`, or copy the file `\java\jdg\ch04\BlackJackApp.java` from the CD-ROM drive to your `ch04` directory.

Listing 4.4. The source code of the BlackJack program.

```
// BlackJackApp.java

// Import all the Java API classes needed by this program.
import java.lang.System;
import java.lang.Integer;
import java.lang.NumberFormatException;
import java.io.DataInputStream;
import java.io.IOException;
import java.util.Random;

class BlackJackApp {
 public static void main (String args[]) throws IOException {
  // Create a BlackJackGame object ...
  BlackJackGame game = new BlackJackGame();
  // and play it!
  game.play();
 }
}

class BlackJackGame {
 // Variable declarations
 int bet;
 int money;
 Deck deck;
 Hand playersHand;
 Hand dealersHand;
 DataInputStream keyboardInput;

 // Method declarations
```

```
public BlackJackGame() { // Constructor
 bet = 0;
 money = 1000;
 deck = new Deck();
 keyboardInput = new DataInputStream(System.in);
}

void play() throws IOException {
 System.out.println("Welcome to Blackjack!");
 System.out.println("You have $"+Integer.toString(money)+".");
 do {
  placeBet();
  if(bet>0) {
   initialDeal();
   if(playersHand.blackjack()) playerWins();
   else{
    while(playersHand.under(22) && playerTakesAHit()) {
     playersHand.addCard(deck.deal());
     playersHand.show(false,false);
    }
    while(dealersHand.mustHit())
     dealersHand.addCard(deck.deal());
    dealersHand.show(true,false);
    showResults();
   }
  }
 } while (bet>0);
}

void placeBet() throws IOException, NumberFormatException {
 do{
  System.out.print("Enter bet: ");
  System.out.flush();
  bet = Integer.parseInt(keyboardInput.readLine());
 } while(bet<0 || bet>money);
}

void initialDeal() {
 System.out.println("New hand...");
 playersHand = new Hand();
 dealersHand = new Hand();
 for(int i = 0;i<2;++i) {
  playersHand.addCard(deck.deal());
  dealersHand.addCard(deck.deal());
 }
 dealersHand.show(true,true);
 playersHand.show(false,false);
}

void playerWins() {
 money += bet;
 System.out.println("Player wins $"+Integer.toString(bet)+".");
 System.out.println("Player has $"+Integer.toString(money)+".");
}

void dealerWins() {
 money -= bet;
```

continues

Listing 4.4. continued

```
  System.out.println("Player loses $"+Integer.toString(bet)+".");
  System.out.println("Player has $"+Integer.toString(money)+".");
 }

 void tie() {
  System.out.println("Tie.");
  System.out.println("Player has $"+Integer.toString(money)+".");
 }

 boolean playerTakesAHit() throws IOException {
  char ch = ' ';
  do{
   System.out.print("Hit or Stay: ");
   System.out.flush();
   String playersDecision = keyboardInput.readLine();
   try ch = playersDecision.charAt(0);
   catch (StringIndexOutOfBoundsException exception) ;
   if(ch == 'H' || ch == 'h') return true;
   if(ch == 'S' || ch == 's') return false;
  } while(true);
 }

 void showResults() {
  if(playersHand.busted() && dealersHand.busted()) tie();
  else if(playersHand.busted()) dealerWins();
  else if(dealersHand.busted()) playerWins();
  else if(playersHand.bestScore() > dealersHand.bestScore()) playerWins();
  else if(playersHand.bestScore() < dealersHand.bestScore()) dealerWins();
  else tie();
 }
} // End of BlackJackGame class

class Deck {
 // Variable declarations
 int cards[];     // Array of 52 cards
 int topCard;     // 0-51 (index of card in deck)
 Random random;

 // Method declarations
 public Deck() { // Constructor
  cards = new int[52];
  for(int i = 0;i<52;++i) cards[i] = i;
  topCard = 0;
  random = new Random();
  shuffle();
 }

 public void shuffle() {
  // Repeat 52 times
  for(int i = 0;i<52;++i) {
   // Randomly exchange two cards in the deck.
   int j = randomCard();
   int k = randomCard();
   int temp = cards[j];
   cards[j] = cards[k];
   cards[k] = temp;
```

```
  }
 }

 int randomCard() {
  int r = random.nextInt();
  if(r<0) r = 0-r;
  return r%52;
 }

 Card deal() {
  if(topCard>51) {
   shuffle();
   topCard = 0;
  }
  Card card = new Card(cards[topCard]);
  ++topCard;
  return card;
 }
} // End of Deck class

class Hand {
 // Variable declarations
 int numCards;
 Card cards[];
 static int MaxCards = 12;

 //Method declarations
 public Hand() { // Constructor
  numCards = 0;
  cards = new Card[MaxCards];
 }

 void addCard(Card c) {
  cards[numCards] = c;
  ++numCards;
 }

 void show(boolean isDealer,boolean hideFirstCard) {
  if(isDealer) System.out.println("Dealer:");
  else System.out.println("Player:");
  for(int i = 0;i<numCards;++i) {
   if(i == 0 && hideFirstCard) System.out.println("  Hidden");
   else System.out.println("  "+cards[i].value+" of "+cards[i].suit);
  }
 }

boolean blackjack() {
 if(numCards == 2) {
  if(cards[0].iValue == 1 && cards[1].iValue == 10) return true;
  if(cards[1].iValue == 1 && cards[0].iValue == 10) return true;
 }
 return false;
}

boolean under(int n) {
 int points = 0;
 for(int i = 0;i<numCards;++i) points += cards[i].iValue;
```

continues

Listing 4.4. continued

```
 if(points<n) return true;
 else return false;
}

int bestScore() {
 int points = 0;
 boolean haveAce = false;
 for(int i = 0;i<numCards;++i) {
  points += cards[i].iValue;
  if(cards[i].iValue == 1) haveAce = true;
 }
 if(haveAce) {
  if(points+10 < 22) points += 10;
 }
 return points;
}

boolean mustHit() {
 if(bestScore()<17) return true;
 else return false;
}

 boolean busted() {
  if(!under(22)) return true;
  else return false;
 }
} // End of Hand class

class Card {
 // Variable declarations
 int iValue;   // Numeric value corresponding to card.
 String value; // "A" "2" through "9" "T" "J" "Q" "K"
 String suit; // "S" "H" "C" "D"

 // Method declarations
 public Card(int n) { // Constructor
  int iSuit = n/13;
  iValue = n%13+1;
  switch(iSuit) {
   case 0:
    suit = "Spades";
    break;
   case 1:
    suit = "Hearts";
    break;
   case 2:
    suit = "Clubs";
    break;
   default:
    suit = "Diamonds";
  }
  if(iValue == 1) value = "Ace";
  else if(iValue == 10) value = "Ten";
  else if(iValue == 11) value = "Jack";
  else if(iValue == 12) value = "Queen";
  else if(iValue == 13) value = "King";
```

```
  else value = Integer.toString(iValue);
  if(iValue>10) iValue = 10;
 }

 int getValue() {
  return iValue;
 }
} // End of Card class
```

Having produced `BlackJackApp.java`, in one way or another, compile it using the command line

```
javac BlackJackApp.java
```

This will produce the `BlackJackApp.class` file. If your file does not compile, go back and fix any typing errors and try again. Once you have a successful compile, execute the program using

```
java BlackJackApp
```

This will result in the following display:

```
C:\java\jdg\ch04>java BlackJackApp
Welcome to Blackjack!
You have $1000.
Enter bet:
```

The `BlackJackApp` program will provide you with $1000 with which to play blackjack. You use this money to bet. You place a bet between 0 and the amount of money you have, and then the computer, acting as dealer, will deal two cards to you and two to itself. For example, upon entering a bet of `10`, I received the following program output:

```
C:\java\jdg\ch04>java BlackJackApp
Welcome to Blackjack!
You have $1000.
Enter bet: 10
New hand...
Dealer:
  Hidden
  2 of Hearts
Player:
  Queen of Clubs
  3 of Spades
Hit or Stay:
```

I, being the player, was dealt a queen of clubs and a three of spades. This gives me a total of 13 points. Points are calculated as follows:

Card Point	*Value*
Ace	1 or 11 (whichever is better)
2 through 10	face value of card (that is, 2 through 10)
Jack, Queen, King	10

The objective of the game is to get as close to 21 as you can, without going over. Whoever gets the closest wins. If you go over 21, you lose, unless the dealer does also, in which case you tie.

When you are dealt your initial two cards, you are shown one of the dealer's cards. This helps you to determine whether you should take another card, referred to as *hitting*, or *stay* with the cards that you have. You can enter `h` or `s` to inform the dealer of your decision. If you enter `h`, you will be dealt another card. If you enter `s`, the dealer will begin to play its hand.

NOTE

If the point total of your first two cards is 21, you are said to have *blackjack* and immediately win.

The dealer must take a hit until the total points in its hand is 17 or over, at which point it must stay. When both you and the dealer have finished playing your hands, the total number of points acquired by each is used to determine the winner. Play is repeated until you enter a 0 bet.

The following program output shows a game played between myself and the `BlackJackApp` program:

```
C:\java\jdg\ch04>java BlackJackApp
Welcome to Blackjack!
You have $1000.
Enter bet: 10
New hand...
Dealer:
  Hidden
  2 of Hearts
Player:
  Queen of Clubs
  3 of Spades
Hit or Stay: h
Player:
  Queen of Clubs
  3 of Spades
  7 of Spades
Hit or Stay: s
Dealer:
  Queen of Spades
  2 of Hearts
  5 of Spades
Player wins $10.
Player has $1010.
Enter bet: 20
New hand...
Dealer:
  Hidden
  7 of Clubs
```

```
Player:
  King of Clubs
  9 of Spades
Hit or Stay: s
Dealer:
  2 of Clubs
  7 of Clubs
  9 of Clubs
Player wins $20.
Player has $1030.
Enter bet: 0

C:\java\jdg\ch04>
```

On the initial deal, I bet 10 bucks. I was given a queen of clubs and a three of spades, for a total of 13 points. The dealer was given a two of hearts and another (hidden) card. I elected to take a hit and was dealt a seven of spades, bringing the total in my hand up to 20 points—beginner's luck! The dealer turned over the hidden card to reveal a queen of spades. He then drew a five of spades for a total of 17 points. Because the dealer reached 17, he was forced to stay, and I had won $10. Feeling a little lightheaded, I proceeded to double my bet to $20. I was dealt a king of clubs and a nine of spades for a total of 19 points. I decided to stay with that hand. The dealer's hand was revealed to be a two of clubs and a seven of clubs. The dealer drew a nine of clubs for a total of 18 points. I had won again! At that point I elected to take the money and continue writing this book. I entered a 0 bet to end the game.

The point of the example is not to turn you into a blackjack gambler, but to serve as a more interesting example from which to discuss Java arrays, statements, and expressions.

Overview of `BlackJackApp`

The `BlackJackApp.java` file is long, but don't let that daunt you. I'm going to break it down, class by class, and method by method, to explain its operation.

The program begins with a comment identifying the name of the program:

```
// BlackJackApp.java
```

It then imports all the Java API classes it needs to perform its processing:

```
// Import all the Java API classes needed by this program.
import java.lang.System;
import java.lang.Integer;
import java.lang.NumberFormatException;
import java.io.DataInputStream;
import java.io.IOException;
import java.util.Random;
```

Next, it declares the `BlackJackApp` class, the class that implements your blackjack application. This class has a single `main` method, like all the other programs you've developed so far. The `main` method consists of two Java statements. The first declares the `game` variable as having class type BlackJackGame and assigns it a new object of class BlackJackGame. The second statement applies the play() method to the object referenced by game, as shown in the following code:

```
class BlackJackApp {
 public static void main (String args[]) throws IOException {
  // Create a BlackJackGame object ...
  BlackJackGame game = new BlackJackGame();
  // and play it!
  game.play();
 }
}
```

The BlackJackGame Class

The BlackJackGame class is not defined as part of the Java API. I wonder why they left it out? Because it doesn't exist anywhere else, it is a class that must be declared as part of the program. The BlackJackGame class and other classes could have been defined and compiled, separately, but they were combined into a single compilation unit to keep this example somewhat compact.

The BlackJackGame class is rather long. It declares six variables and nine methods. The variables are data structures that represent the state of a blackjack game. The bet variable identifies the amount wagered by the player. The money variable identifies how much money the player has left. The deck variable references an object of class Deck that is used to represent a deck of cards. Two Hand variables are declared, representing the player's hand and the dealer's hand. Finally, our old friend keyboardInput has returned for a repeat performance:

```
class BlackJackGame {
 // Variable declarations
 int bet;
 int money;
 Deck deck;
 Hand playersHand;
 Hand dealersHand;
 DataInputStream keyboardInput;
   .
   .
   .
}
```

The first method declared for BlackJackGame is its *constructor*. A constructor is used to initialize objects that are new instances of a class. In the main method of the BlackJackApp class, the BlackJackGame() constructor is invoked to initialize the newly created BlackJackGame object that is assigned to game:

```
BlackJackGame game = new BlackJackGame();
```

The BlackJackGame() constructor initializes four of the six variables of the BlackJackGame class. The player's bet is set to 0, and the player is given $1000. The playersHand and dealersHand variables are not initialized until the cards are dealt.

A new `Deck` object is created and assigned to the `deck` variable. The new object is initialized using the `Deck()` constructor for the `Deck` class. If you typed in the program, you probably know where to find it in the source code listing.

Finally, the `keyboardInput` variable is assigned a new object of class `DataInputStream`. This object is created using the `DataInputStream()` constructor with the `System.in` variable as an argument:

```
// Method declarations public BlackJackGame() { // Constructor
  bet = 0;
  money = 1000;
  deck = new Deck();
  keyboardInput = new DataInputStream(System.in);
 }
```

NOTE

An *argument* is a value that is provided as an input to a method invocation. It does not denote disagreement.

The second method defined for `BlackJackGame` is the `play()` method. This method is invoked in the `main` method of `BlackJackApp` to cause the `BlackJackGame` object, referenced by `game`, to be played:

```
game.play();
```

The `play()` method begins with the `void` keyword to indicate that it does not return any value. It also identifies the fact that `IOException` may be thrown during its processing. Exceptions are covered in Chapter 7. The general structure of the `play()` method is as follows:

```
void play() throws IOException {
   .
   .
   .
}
```

The `play()` method begins by displaying the `Welcome to Blackjack!` text and the amount of money available to the player. The second `println()` method takes three arguments. First it displays `You have $`, then it displays the contents of the `money` variable, and then it displays a period (.). It converts the integer value of `money` to a `String` value before printing it. `String` is a class defined in the Java API to represent strings of characters. These statements are as follows:

```
System.out.println("Welcome to Blackjack!");
System.out.println("You have $"+Integer.toString(money)+".");
```

The rest of the statements of the `play()` method are surrounded by

```
do {
   .
   .
   .
} while (bet>0);
```

This is a `do` statement, and it causes the statements between the braces to be repeatedly executed while the value of `bet` is greater than 0.

The block of statements within the `do` statement begins with an invocation of the `placeBet()` method. Because no object is identified with the `placeBet()` method, it is invoked using the current object—that which is invoked with the `play()` method:

```
placeBet();
```

The `placeBet()` method, as you'll see shortly, is used to prompt the player to enter his bet. After the `placeBet()` method is invoked, the next statement is an `if` statement that checks whether `bet` is greater than 0. If `bet` is greater than 0, the statements between its braces are executed.

If `bet` is not greater than 0, execution continues after the `if` statement. In this case, the end of the `do` statement is encountered, the `do` statement terminates, the `play()` procedure returns, and the `BlackJackApp main` method finishes its processing. In other words, the game is over.

The following code tests whether `bet` is greater than 0:

```
if(bet>0) {
   .
   .
   .
}
```

If `bet` is greater than 0, the `initialDeal()` method is invoked. This method is used to deal a new hand to the player and to the dealer. It causes the `playersHand` and `dealersHand` variables to each be initialized with an object of class `Hand`. The `initialDeal()` method is invoked using the following code:

```
initialDeal();
```

Another `if` statement is then executed. This `if` statement checks to see if the player was dealt blackjack (21 points). It does this by invoking the `blackjack()` method for the object referenced by the `playersHand` variable. In the case that the `blackjack()` method returns the boolean value `true`, the player wins the bet, and the `playerWins()` method is invoked. If the player was not fortunate enough to be dealt a blackjack, the statements within the `else` part of the `if` statement are executed, as shown in the following code:

```
if(playersHand.blackjack()) playerWins();
else{
   .
   .
   .
}
```

The `else` part begins with a `while` statement. A `while` statement is similar to a `do` statement in that it repeatedly executes the block of statements enclosed by braces. It differs from the `do` statement in that it checks to see if it is finished *before* executing the statement block. The `while` statement checks to see if the player has 21 or fewer points in his hand and whether he wants to take a another card. It does this by invoking the `under()` method for the object referenced by the playersHand variable, passing it the integer 22 as an argument. If the under() method returns the boolean value true, the playerTakesAHit() method is invoked to prompt the player to hit or stay. If the user elects to take a hit, playerTakesAHit() returns a boolean true, and the statements enclosed by the while statement are executed. If either under() or playerTakesAHit() returns false, the next statement after the while statement is executed.

The statements enclosed within the while statement invoke methods for the Hand object referenced by the playersHand variable. The first method causes a card to be added to the player's hand by dealing it from the deck. The second method determines if and how the player's hand should be displayed. The code that performs this processing follows:

```
while(playersHand.under(22) && playerTakesAHit()) {
 playersHand.addCard(deck.deal());
 playersHand.show(false,false);
}
```

The previous while statement is followed by another while statement. This while statement does not enclose a block of statements within braces. It only applies to a single statement:

```
while(dealersHand.mustHit())
 dealersHand.addCard(deck.deal());
```

The while statement is used to play the dealer's hand. It invokes the mustHit() method with the object referenced by the dealersHand variable to determine whether the dealer has fewer than 17 points in his hand and, therefore, must take a hit. If the dealer must take a hit, the addCard() method is invoked to deal a card to the dealer.

After the dealer's hand is played, the show() method is invoked to display it to the console. The showResults() method is then invoked to show the results of the hand. This concludes the description of the play() method. It's a good idea to review the source code of the play() method to make sure that you know how it works before going on. The following statements invoke the show() and showResults() methods:

```
dealersHand.show(true,false);
showResults();
```

The placeBet() method is invoked by the play() method to prompt the player to enter a bet. It declares two potential exceptions in its throw clause.

The placeBet() method uses a do statement to repeatedly prompt the user to enter a bet that is at least 0 and at most is the amount of money that he has left. The statement block enclosed by the do statement displays the prompt, reads the line entered by the user, converts it to an integer, and then assigns it to the bet variable. The source code of the placeBet() method follows:

```
void placeBet() throws IOException, NumberFormatException {
 do{
  System.out.print("Enter bet: ");
  System.out.flush();
  bet = Integer.parseInt(keyboardInput.readLine());
 } while(bet<0 || bet>money);
}
```

The `initialDeal()` method is invoked by the `play()` method to deal a new hand to the player and the dealer. It displays the `New hand...` text to the console window to inform the player that a new hand is being dealt. It then creates two new objects of class `Hand`, initializes them with the `Hand()` constructor, and assigns them to the `playersHand` and `dealersHand` variables. The source code of the `initialDeal()` method follows:

```
void initialDeal() {
 System.out.println("New hand...");
 playersHand = new Hand();
 dealersHand = new Hand();
   .
   .
   .
}
```

After creating the two new hands, the `initialDeal()` method executes a `for` statement. The `for` statement iterates the execution of the block of statements enclosed by braces, based on the conditions identified immediately before the statement block. In this case a variable, `i`, of type `int`, is created for the duration of the `for` statement's execution and assigned a value of 0. The statement block is then executed while `i` is less than 2. Each time the statement block is executed, the value of `i` is incremented by 1. The expression `++i` causes `i` to be incremented by 1.

The `for` statement is used to sequentially deal two cards to the player and two to the dealer by invoking the `addCard()` method. Note that the value returned by the `deal()` method is used as an argument to the `addCard()` method, in both instances. The source code of the `for` statement follows:

```
for(int i = 0;i<2;++i) {
 playersHand.addCard(deck.deal());
 dealersHand.addCard(deck.deal());
}
```

After the player and dealer have been dealt their hands, the mysterious `show()` method is invoked, as shown in the following code, to display the new hands (you'll find out what the boolean values are used for when you study the `show()` method):

```
dealersHand.show(true,true);
playersHand.show(false,false);
```

The next three methods, `playerWins()`, `dealerWins()`, and `tie()`, are used to update the `money` variable based on the `bet` variable and the outcome of the hand:

```
void playerWins() {
 money += bet;
 System.out.println("Player wins $"+Integer.toString(bet)+".");
 System.out.println("Player has $"+Integer.toString(money)+".");
}

void dealerWins() {
 money -= bet;
 System.out.println("Player loses $"+Integer.toString(bet)+".");
 System.out.println("Player has $"+Integer.toString(money)+".");
```

```
}

void tie() {
 System.out.println("Tie.");
 System.out.println("Player has $"+Integer.toString(money)+".");
}
```

These methods also display the results to the player by converting the values of `bet` and `money` to `String` objects. The `+=` operator causes the value of `bet` to be added to the value of `money` and assigned to the `money` variable. Similarly, the `-=` operator causes the value of `bet` to be subtracted from the value of `money` before it is assigned to the `money` variable.

The `playerTakesAHit()` method is an example of a method that returns a result. The `boolean` keyword at the beginning of the method declaration specifies that the method should return a result of type `boolean`. Any valid primitive type, array type, class type, or interface type can be used to specify the return type of a method. For example, the return type could be `long`, `String`, or an array of `double` values.

The method begins by declaring a variable of type `char` and assigning it a space character. It then executes an infinite `do` statement. The statement is infinite because the `while` condition at the end of the `do` statement is literally always `true`. This doesn't mean that the statement will execute forever, though. Return statements within the block of the `do` statement will cause statement execution to return to the method that invoked `playerTakesAHit()`.

The `do` block begins by displaying the `Hit or Stay:` prompt to the player and reads the player's input from the keyboard. A `try` statement is then executed. The `try` statement executes a statement or block of statements and, if an exception is thrown, uses a `catch` clause to process the exception. This `try` statement sets the variable `ch` to the first character of the `playersDecision` variable. The `playersDecision` variable references a `String` object that is created when the player's input is read from the keyboard. The `charAt()` method is defined in the `String` class of the Java API. If the player enters a blank line, the `StringIndexOutOfBoundsException` will be thrown. The `catch` clause is used to prevent the exception from terminating program execution.

If the character assigned to `ch`, via `playersDecision`, is `H` or `h`, the value of `true` is returned as the result of the `playerTakesAHit()` method. If `ch` equals `S` or `s`, `false` is returned. Otherwise, the `do` statement causes the player to be repeatedly prompted until he hits or stays. The `playerTakesAHit()` method follows:

```
boolean playerTakesAHit() throws IOException {
 char ch = ' ';
 do{
  System.out.print("Hit or Stay: ");
  System.out.flush();
  String playersDecision = keyboardInput.readLine();
  try ch = playersDecision.charAt(0);
  catch (StringIndexOutOfBoundsException exception) ;
  if(ch == 'H' || ch == 'h') return true;
  if(ch == 'S' || ch == 's') return false;
 } while(true);
}
```

The showResults() method is the last method declared for the BlackJackGame class. This method illustrates the use of nested if statements. The first if statement checks to see if the player's hand and the dealer's hand are both busted (over 21 points). If so, the tie() method is invoked to display the results to the player. If not, the statement following the else is executed. This turns out to be another if statement.

The second if statement checks to see if the player's hand is busted. Because the else part of the first if statement was executed, it is impossible for both the player and the dealer to be busted. So, if the player is busted, the dealer wins.

The third if statement is executed in the else parts of the first and second if statements. It uses the same logic as the second if statement to determine whether the dealer busted and the player wins.

The fourth if statement is only executed if neither the player nor the dealer busted. It checks the points in both of their hands to see if the player is higher than the dealer and, therefore, is the victor.

The fifth if statement is only executed if neither busts and the player is not higher than the dealer. If the dealer is higher than the player, the dealer wins. If the dealer is not higher than the player, the final else part is executed. At this point, neither has busted, but neither is higher than the other, so both must have the same number of points and a tie is declared. The showResults() method follows:

```
void showResults() {
 if(playersHand.busted() && dealersHand.busted()) tie();
 else if(playersHand.busted()) dealerWins();
 else if(dealersHand.busted()) playerWins();
 else if(playersHand.bestScore() > dealersHand.bestScore()) playerWins();
 else if(playersHand.bestScore() < dealersHand.bestScore()) dealerWins();
 else tie();
}
```

The Deck Class

The third class declared within BlackJackApp.java is the Deck class. It is used to simulate a deck of cards.

The Deck class declares three variables and four methods. The cards[] variable is an example of an *array*. Arrays are objects that contain a number of variables of the same type. The variables contained in an array are referred to as the *component variables* of the array and are referenced using the integer indices 0,…,n–1, where n is the number of components contained within the array. The cards[] array is declared to contain components of type int. The brackets ([]) indicate the declaration of an array.

The topCard variable is an integer that identifies the next card to be dealt from the deck. The random variable is used to generate random numbers. It references objects that are of class java.util.Random, a class defined within the Java API. The variable declarations of the Deck class follow:

```
class Deck {
 // Variable declarations
 int cards[];      // Array of 52 cards
 int topCard;      // 0-51 (index of card in deck)
 Random random;
     .
     .
     .
}
```

The constructor for the `Deck` class allocates an array of 52 integers and assigns it to `cards[]`. The `cards[]` array simulates the 52 cards found in a normal deck of playing cards.

A `for` statement is used to assign 0 to `cards[0]`, 1 to `cards[1]`, 2 to `cards[2]`, and so on, until 51 is assigned to `cards[51]`. This creates a deck of cards in which all the cards are ordered by suit and by value. The integers 0 through 51 are logically mapped to playing cards, as follows:

0 through 12 are mapped to the ace of spades through the king of spades

13 through 25 are mapped to the ace of hearts through the king of hearts

26 through 38 are mapped to the ace of clubs through the king of clubs

39 through 51 are mapped to the ace of diamonds through the king of diamonds

The `topCard` of the deck is set to 0. It is used as an index into the `cards[]` array. The `random` variable is assigned a new object of class `Random`. Finally, the `shuffle()` method is invoked to shuffle the new deck of cards. The constructor of the `Deck` class follows:

```
// Method declarations
public Deck() { // Constructor
 cards = new int[52];
 for(int i = 0;i<52;++i) cards[i] = i;
 topCard = 0;
 random = new Random();
 shuffle();
}
```

The `shuffle()` method shuffles the deck of cards by randomly switching two cards in the deck 52 times. It does this by invoking the `randomCard()` method to generate a random integer between 0 and 51. These random integers are used to randomly select components of cards and exchange their values. The `shuffle()` method follows:

```
public void shuffle() {
 // Repeat 52 times
 for(int i = 0;i<52;++i) {
  // Randomly exchange two cards in the deck.
  int j = randomCard();
  int k = randomCard();
  int temp = cards[j];
  cards[j] = cards[k];
  cards[k] = temp;
 }
}
```

The randomCard() method returns an integer between 0 and 51 inclusive. It identifies the int return value in its method declaration. It begins by declaring a variable r and assigning it a random integer value generated by applying the nextInt() method to the random variable. The nextInt() method is defined in the java.util.Random class. If the value assigned to r is less than 0, it is changed in sign to a positive integer. The randomCard() method then returns an integer between 0 and 51 by returning the random integer modulus 52. The randomCard() method follows:

```
int randomCard() {
 int r = random.nextInt();
 if(r<0) r = 0-r;
 return r%52;
}
```

The deal() method is used to deal a card off the top of the deck. It does this by using the topCard variable as an index into the cards[] array. It starts at 0 and is incremented until it is greater than 51, indicating that all the cards in the deck have been dealt. In this case, the deck is reshuffled, and topCard is set to 0 once again. This creates the effect of another deck being used because the player and dealer are not required to throw back any cards that are currently in their hands before the deck is shuffled.

The Card class is used to translate the integer card values to String values that can be displayed on the console. A card is dealt by constructing a new instance of Card using the value of cards[] indexed by topCard as an argument. topCard is then incremented to move to the next card in the deck. Note that deal() returns the object of class Card that was created using the Card() constructor. The deal() method follows:

```
Card deal() {
 if(topCard>51) {
  shuffle();
  topCard = 0;
 }
 Card card = new Card(cards[topCard]);
 ++topCard;
 return card;
}
```

The Hand Class

The Hand class is used to implement a hand of cards as played by both the player and the dealer. It declares three variables and eight methods.

The numCards variable identifies the number of cards contained in the hand. The cards[] array has the same name as the cards[] array declared in the Deck class, but it is logically and physically distinct. Because it is declared in a separate class, it is contained in objects that are instances of the Hand class and not of the Deck class. The MaxCards variable is declared to be static. This means that it is used with the class, as a whole, and not with individual objects that are instances of the class. You'll learn more about class and instance variables in Chapter 5. MaxCards is used to identify the number of components to be allocated within cards[]. The Hand class is structured as follows:

```
class Hand {
 // Variable declarations
 int numCards;
 Card cards[];
 static int MaxCards = 12;
     .
     .
     .
}
```

The constructor for the `Hand` class sets `numCards` to `0`, to indicate an empty hand, and then creates a `MaxCards` size array of `Card` objects and assigns it to `cards`. The constructor for the `Hand` class follows:

```
//Method declarations
public Hand() { // Constructor
 numCards = 0;
 cards = new Card[MaxCards];
}
```

Cards are added to a hand using the `addCard()` method. This method takes an object of class `Card` as an argument and adds it to the first available position within the `cards[]` array. It then increments `numCards` so that it will index the next available position within `cards[]`. The `addCard()` method follows:

```
void addCard(Card c) {
  cards[numCards] = c;
  ++numCards;
 }
```

The `show()` method displays either the dealer's or the player's hand. It takes two boolean arguments that specify whether the hand belongs to the dealer, and if so, whether the first card should be hidden when the hand is displayed. The `isDealer` parameter is used in the initial `if` statement to determine whether a dealer or a player heading should be displayed. A `for` statement is then used to iterate `numCards` times in order to display each card of the hand. The statement block enclosed by the `for` statement uses the `hideFirstCard` parameter to determine whether the first card should be hidden or displayed. The `show()` method follows:

```
void show(boolean isDealer,boolean hideFirstCard) {
  if(isDealer) System.out.println("Dealer:");
  else System.out.println("Player:");
  for(int i = 0;i<numCards;++i) {
   if(i == 0 && hideFirstCard) System.out.println("  Hidden");
   else System.out.println("  "+cards[i].value+" of "+cards[i].suit);
  }
 }
```

The `blackjack()` method returns a boolean value indicating whether the hand is blackjack. It uses an `if` statement to make sure that there are only two cards in the hand. If there are not two cards, `false` is returned to indicate that the hand is not blackjack. If the number of cards is exactly two, it uses the `iValue` variable of the `Card` objects contained in the `cards[]` array to determine whether the current hand is blackjack. The `iValue` variable is discussed with the `Card` class. It identifies the number of points associated with a card. A card with `iValue = 1` is an ace. Aces can be either 1 or 11 points. The `blackjack()` method follows:

```
boolean blackjack() {
 if(numCards == 2) {
  if(cards[0].iValue == 1 && cards[1].iValue == 10) return true;
  if(cards[1].iValue == 1 && cards[0].iValue == 10) return true;
 }
 return false;
}
```

The `under()` method returns a boolean value indicating whether the number of points in a hand is less than the argument passed via the `n` parameter. It declares a `points` variable of type `int` and uses a `for` statement to sum the points for all cards in the hand. It then checks to see if the number of points in the hand is less than `n` and returns an appropriate value of `true` or `false`. The `under()` method follows:

```
boolean under(int n) {
 int points = 0;
 for(int i = 0;i<numCards;++i) points += cards[i].iValue;
 if(points<n) return true;
 else return false;
}
```

The `bestScore()` method returns an integer value identifying the best possible point score for the hand. It adjusts the value associated with aces to either 1 or 11, depending on whether it causes the hand to go over 21 points. It uses a variable, `haveAce`, of type `boolean`, to identify whether the hand contains an ace. It uses a `for` statement to calculate the minimum number of points in the hand and to determine whether any aces are present. If an ace is found, it determines whether it is better to use the 11- or 1-point value of the ace. The `bestScore()` method follows:

```
int bestScore() {
 int points = 0;
 boolean haveAce = false;
 for(int i = 0;i<numCards;++i) {
  points += cards[i].iValue;
  if(cards[i].iValue == 1) haveAce = true;
 }
 if(haveAce) {
  if(points+10 < 22) points += 10;
 }
 return points;
}
```

The `mustHit()` method is used to play out the dealer's hand. If the `bestScore` of the dealer's hand is lower than 17, the dealer must take a hit. If it is 17 or higher, the dealer must stay. The `mustHit()` method follows:

```
boolean mustHit() {
 if(bestScore()<17) return true;
 else return false;
}
```

The `busted()` method uses an `if` statement to determine whether the number of points in a hand is under 22. If it is not under, the hand is busted, and `true` is returned. Otherwise, `false` is returned. The `busted()` method follows:

```
boolean busted() {
  if(!under(22)) return true;
  else return false;
 }
```

The Card Class

The `Card` class is used to translate the integer value of cards, maintained by objects of the `Deck` class, into objects of type `String`. It declares three variables and two methods.

The `iValue` variable is used to keep track of the number of points associated with a card. It is an abbreviation for "integer value" and is used to differentiate it from the `value` variable. The `value` variable references a text string that is used to describe the face value of a playing card. The `suit` variable is used to identify the suit of a playing card. The variables declared for the `Card` class are shown:

```
class Card {
 // Variable declarations
 int iValue;   // Numeric value corresponding to card.
 String value; // "A" "2" through "9" "T" "J" "Q" "K"
 String suit; // "S" "H" "C" "D"
     .
     .
     .
}
```

The `Card()` constructor is the heart of the `Card` class and is an example of a constructor that takes an argument. It expects a value of 0 through 51 of a card value from the `Deck` class. The `Card` class constructor follows:

```
// Method declarations
 public Card(int n) { // Constructor
     .
     .
     .
 }
```

`Card()` first determines the suit of the card identified by the `n` parameter. It does this by dividing `n` by 13 and assigning the result to an integer variable named `iSuit`. It determines the point value of the card by calculating `n` modulus 13 and adding 1. It adjusts this value later in the method. This is shown in the following code:

```
int iSuit = n/13;
  iValue = n%13+1;
```

`Card()` then uses a `switch` statement to assign the correct text string to the `suit` variable. The `switch` statement takes the `iSuit` variable and compares it to the values identified in each of the `case` labels. If a `case` label matches the value of `iSuit`, control of execution is passed to the statement after the `case` label. These statements consist of assignment statements that set `suit` to the correct text string. The `default` label is used if no other label matches `iSuit`. The `break` statement is used to "jump out" of the execution of the `switch` statement to the statement immediately following the `switch` statement. It is also used with other statements, such as the `for`, `while`, and `do` statements. The `switch` statement follows:

```
switch(iSuit) {
   case 0:
    suit = "Spades";
    break;
   case 1:
    suit = "Hearts";
    break;
   case 2:
    suit = "Clubs";
    break;
   default:
    suit = "Diamonds";
  }
```

The statements following the `switch` statement show how a `switch` statement can be coded using a series of nested `if` statements:

```
if(iValue == 1) value = "Ace";
else if(iValue == 10) value = "Ten";
else if(iValue == 11) value = "Jack";
else if(iValue == 12) value = "Queen";
else if(iValue == 13) value = "King";
else value = Integer.toString(iValue);
if(iValue>10) iValue = 10;
```

These statements are equivalent to the following `switch` statement:

```
value=Integer.toString(iValue);
switch(iValue) {
case 1:
    value = "Ace";
    break;
case 10:
    value = "Ten";
    break;
case 11:
    value = "Jack";
    iValue = 10;
    break;
case 12:
    value = "Queen";
    iValue = 10;
    break;
case 13:
    value = "King";
    iValue = 10;
    break;
}
```

Finally, the `getValue()` method is used to return the value of `iValue`, the point value of the card. It is fairly simple, as far as methods go, but it shows how the values of an object's variables can be made available without having to provide access to the variable itself. The `getValue()` method follows:

```
int getValue() {
  return iValue;
 }
```

Arrays

Arrays are objects that contain a number of variables of the same type. These component variables are referenced using the integer indices $0,\ldots,n-1$, where n is the length of the array. The type of the array is identified by appending `[]` to the type of its components. For example, `int[]` identifies an array of type `int`, `Object[]` identifies an array of type `Object`, and `char[][]` identifies an array of an array of type `char`.

> **NOTE**
>
> Java only supports single-dimensional arrays. Multidimensional-array capabilities can be achieved by using arrays of arrays.

Arrays are declared by declaring a variable to be of an array type. For example, the following declares `nums` to be an array of type `int`:

```
int[] nums;
```

The declaration can also be written as follows:

```
int nums[];
```

You can place the brackets after either the type or the variable name.

Array Allocation

When a variable of an array type is declared, the size of the array is not identified, and the array object is not allocated. To allocate storage for an array, you can use the `new` operator to create an array object of a specific size. For example, the following statement:

```
char ch[] = new char[24];
```

creates a `char` array of length 24, the individual component variables of which can be referenced by `ch[0]`, `ch[2]`, …, `ch[23]`. The following statement creates an array of type `Dice[]` of length 6:

```
Dice[] d = new Dice[6];
```

Arrays can also be allocated by specifying their initial values. For example, the following allocates a `String` array of length 7 that contains abbreviations for the days of the week:

```
String days[] = {"sun", "mon", "tue", "wed", "thu", "fri", "sat"};
```

The length of an array can always be found by appending `.length` to the name of the array. For example, `days.length` returns the integer `7` as the length of `days[]`.

Statements

The `BlackJackApp` example introduces a number of Java statements. These statements implement the bodies of the various methods used in the example. The following subsections describe the types of statements that are used in the `BlackJackApp` example. A complete description of Java statements is provided in Chapter 11. When you read through the following sections and learn about a particular statement, go back through the `BlackJackApp` program and see how many examples of the statement you can find. This will help you to associate the statement's syntax with the different contexts in which it can be used and elevate your understanding from the syntactic to the semantic level.

NOTE

Java statements, like C and C++ statements, are separated by semicolons.

Statement Blocks

Java statements are organized into statement *blocks*. Blocks begin with an opening brace (`{`) and end with a closing brace (`}`). They are used to indicate a group of statements and variable declarations that are to be considered as a single syntactical unit. Blocks are used to define the scope of execution of statements in which they are enclosed. For example, the body of a method can be considered to be a single block. Blocks are used in other statements, such as the `if` and `do` statements, to identify groups of statements that are to be executed as if they were a single statement.

NOTE

Statement blocks can be considered to be syntactically equivalent to a single statement.

An example of a statement block is taken from the `BlackJackGame()` constructor:

```
bet = 0;
money = 1000;
deck = new Deck();
keyboardInput = new DataInputStream(System.in);
}
```

The `if` Statement

The `if` statement is used to decide whether a particular statement should be executed. Its syntax is as follows:

```
if ( BooleanExpression ) Statement1
else Statement2
```

The `else` part of the statement is optional. If the boolean expression, referred to as the *`if` condition*, evaluates to `true`, *`Statement1`* is executed; otherwise, *`Statement2`* is executed. Program execution then continues with the next statement following the `if` statement. If the `else` part is omitted, execution proceeds immediately to the next statement when the `if` condition is false. Either *`Statement1`* or *`Statement2`* can be a statement block.

An example of an `if` statement is taken from the `show()` method of the `Hand` class:

```
if(isDealer) System.out.println("Dealer:");
else System.out.println("Player:");
```

If the value of `isDealer` is `true`, the text `Dealer:` is displayed; otherwise, the text `Player:` is displayed.

The `switch` Statement

The `switch` statement is like a sequence of embedded `if` statements. It is used to transfer control to the first labeled statement within a block of statements that matches the value of the expression in the `switch` expression. The syntax of the `switch` statement is

```
switch ( SwitchExpression ) StatementBlock;
```

where statements within the statement block are labeled by preceding them with prefixes of the form

```
case ConstantExpression :
```

or

```
default :
```

The `switch` expression must evaluate to a value of type `char`, `byte`, `short`, or `int`. The same is true of the constant expressions in the `case` labels. The `switch` statement evaluates the `switch` expression and transfers program execution to the first labeled statement whose constant expression has the same value as the `switch` expression. If no case-labeled expression matches the `switch` expression, control is transferred to the first statement with a `default` label. Otherwise, control is transferred to the next statement following the `switch` statement.

An example of a `switch` statement is taken from the `Card()` constructor:

```
switch(iSuit) {
 case 0:
  suit = "Spades";
  break;
 case 1:
```

```
   suit = "Hearts";
   break;
  case 2:
   suit = "Clubs";
   break;
  default:
   suit = "Diamonds";
}
```

The value of `iSuit` is compared to the values 0, 1, and 2 of the `case` labels. If it matches any of these values, program execution is transferred to the labeled statement. Otherwise, program execution is transferred to the statement labeled as `default`. The `break` statements are used to transfer control to the first statement following the `switch` statement, as you'll learn in the following section.

The `break` Statement

The `break` statement is used to terminate execution of a statement block and transfer control to the first statement following the statement in which the block is enclosed. The syntax of the `break` statement is

```
break;
```

or

```
break label;
```

where *`label`* is an optional label that can be attached to the statement enclosing the statement block. Refer to Chapter 11 for a discussion of the use of labels with the `break` statement.

The `break` statement is used with the `case`, `do`, `while`, and `for` statements to exit the enclosed statement block and transfer control to the first statement following the enclosing statement.

The sample `switch` statement, shown in the previous section, contains several `break` statements that cause program execution to be transferred to the first statement following the `switch` statement.

The `for` Statement

The `for` statement is used to iterate the execution of a statement or statement block. Its syntax is as follows:

```
for (InitializationClause ForExpression; IncrementClause) EnclosedStatement
```

`InitializationClause` consists of a statement that is executed once at the beginning of the `for` statement. The `for` expression is then checked. If it is `false`, the `for` statement ends, and program execution continues with the next statement following the `for` statement. If the `for` expression is `true`, the enclosed statement is executed. The enclosed statement can be a statement block.

When the execution of the enclosed statement is completed, the statement contained in the increment clause is executed. The `for` expression is then reevaluated to determine whether the enclosed statement should be executed again. The enclosed statement, increment statement, and evaluation of the `for` expression repeat their execution until the `for` expression evaluates to `false`, at which point execution of the `for` statement is complete and program execution continues with the statement following the `for` statement.

NOTE

The increment clause does not end with a semicolon (;).

A sample `for` statement is taken from the `under()` method of the `Hand` class:

```
for(int i = 0;i<numCards;++i) points += cards[i].iValue;
```

This statement begins by setting the variable `i` to `0`. It then checks to see if `i` is less than `numCards`. If it is not, the `for` statement terminates. If `i` is less than `numCards`, the statement

```
points += cards[i].iValue;
```

is executed. This statement is used to add the `iValue` variable of the `i`th `card[]` array element to the `points` variable. When execution of this statement is completed, the `++i` statement is executed to increment `i` by 1. The `for` expression, `i<numCards`, is reevaluated, and the `for` statement's execution continues.

NOTE

The operators used by Java are very similar to those of C and C++.

The do Statement

The `do` statement is used to repeatedly execute a statement until a specified condition becomes `false`. The syntax of the `do` statement is

```
do EnclosedStatement while (BooleanExpression) ;
```

The `do` statement repeatedly executes the enclosed statement until the boolean expression becomes `false`. The enclosed statement will be executed at least once because the boolean expression is evaluated after its execution. The enclosed statement can be a statement block.

An example of a `do` statement is taken from the `placeBet()` method of the `BlackJackGame` class:

```
do{
 System.out.print("Enter bet: ");
 System.out.flush();
 bet = Integer.parseInt(keyboardInput.readLine());
} while(bet<0 || bet>money);
```

The `do` statement executes the statement block until a bet between 0 and the value of `money` is entered by the player.

The `while` Statement

The `while` statement is similar to the `do` statement, except that the boolean expression is evaluated before execution of the enclosed statement. If the boolean expression evaluates to `false`, the `while` statement is terminated, and execution continues with the next statement following the `while` statement. The `while` statement syntax is as follows:

```
while (BooleanExpression) EnclosedStatement
```

A sample `while` statement is taken from the `play()` method of the `BlackJackGame` class:

```
while(dealersHand.mustHit())
 dealersHand.addCard(deck.deal());
```

The `while` statement checks to see if the dealer must take a hit and, if so, adds a card to the dealer's hand. The `while` statement repeats this processing until the dealer is no longer required to take a hit.

The `return` Statement

The `return` statement is used to terminate execution of a method and return a value of the type specified in the method's declaration. Its syntax is

```
return Expression;
```

`Expression` must evaluate to a value that is compatible with the result type of the method in which it is used.

A sample `return` statement is taken from the `getValue()` method of the `Card` class:

```
int getValue() {
 return iValue;
}
```

This simple method returns the value `iValue` and completes the execution of the `getValue()` method.

Summary

In this chapter you have toured the elements of the Java language by writing four sample programs. You have learned about the structure of Java programs, how to compile and execute them, and about many Java language elements. You should now be up and running with Java and capable of experimenting with it by writing your own programs. Although this chapter covers many elements of the Java syntax, use Chapter 11 as a complete reference for the Java language. Chapter 5 supplements the information you learned in this chapter with a solid background in Java's support of object-oriented programming.

5

Classes and Objects

In this chapter you'll learn all about Java and object-oriented programming. You'll first cover general object-oriented programming concepts and then learn how to use Java classes to build object-oriented software. You'll use the information you learn to develop a sample Java program that illustrates the benefits of object-oriented programming.

Object-Oriented Programming Concepts

Over the many years since the dawn of computing, people have studied software-development approaches to figure out which approaches are quickest, cheapest, most reliable, and produce the best software. And over the years, many approaches and technologies have reigned as the best. As time goes on, we learn more about software development and are able to modify and adapt our approaches based on what we learn. The type of software we develop also changes over time as a result of improvements in computer hardware, innovations in computer science, and changes in user expectations. These improvements affect our development approaches as well.

Of all the known approaches to developing software, one approach, called the *object-oriented* approach, has repeatedly proven itself to be the best approach for a large class of common software applications. It's likely that the object-oriented approach will undergo further evolution and that a new, improved software-development paradigm will take its place. But for right now, and the foreseeable future, it is recognized as the best approach for the majority of software that we develop today.

Object-oriented programming focuses on the development of self-contained software components, called *objects.* These objects are modeled after things, such as files, forms, buttons, and windows, that appear in the real world. Objects are defined in terms of the information they contain and the operations they provide for using and manipulating this information.

It's an Object-Oriented World

This book is an object. It contains a lot of information. (If you don't believe me, try retyping it.) It also has methods for accessing the information it contains. For example, you can open the book, turn a page, read a paragraph, search the table of contents, and so on. The information contained in the book, together with the methods for accessing it, are what comprise the object known as this book.

In order to read this book, you need some sort of light source. You could be reading it in the open sunshine or by moonlight, but let's assume that you are using a lamp of some kind. A lamp is also an object. It is an example of an object that contains information about its state. The *state* of an object is the particular condition it is in. For example, a lamp can be on or off. The lamp's methods—turn lamp on and turn lamp off—are used to access the state of the lamp.

This book, too, has state information. For example, it can be open or closed. If it is open, it can be opened to a particular page. The pages are objects in their own right. They contain information and can be accessed through the read page method. The book object can be viewed as being composed of page objects. The book's methods provide access to pages, and the page methods provide access to the information contained on a particular page.

The information contained in an object, whether it is state specific or not, is referred to as the object's *data.* The object's methods are said to *access* the data. Some methods return information about the object's data and are said to support *read access.* Other methods cause the data to be modified and are said to provide *write access* to the data. Finally, as you'll learn in later sections, some methods, called *constructors,* are used to create objects.

Composition and Reuse

The fact that one object can be composed of, or built from, other objects is the heart of object-oriented programming. This allows more complex objects to be constructed from simple object components. Just as you would not write a book as one continuous stream of text (unless you are Jack Kerouac), you wouldn't write a program as a single sequence of source code instructions. You design your program as an application object and construct it from other objects that are built or borrowed.

For example, suppose you are developing a drawing program. Your drawing application would consist of objects such as windows, menus, a drawing canvas, a tool palette, a color palette, and so on. Some of these objects would be available in object libraries and others would be built from more primitive components. You would develop your drawing application by gathering and building its component objects and assembling them into an integrated whole.

Object composition not only allows you to simplify the organization of your programs, it also lets you reuse the software you develop. For example, you could develop drawing objects as part of your drawing program and then reuse those objects in a paint program and a desktop-publishing program. You could also package up your drawing objects and give or sell them to others so that they can use them as a foundation for building their own custom objects.

Object reuse provides you with the capability to build or acquire a library of objects from which you can more quickly and easily piece together your programs. Without this capability, you are forced to start from scratch with every program that you develop.

Object reuse is not limited to object composition. It also exploits a powerful capability of object-oriented programming known as *inheritance.* Inheritance not only allows objects to be used as is, but also allows new objects to be created by extending and tailoring existing objects. Before you learn about inheritance, however, the concept of an object's class must be explained.

Classes

At this point, you might be wondering just how you go about developing objects. The answer, of course, depends on the language you are using. Java, C++, Smalltalk, and some other object-oriented languages follow a class-based approach. This approach allows you to declare *classes* that serve as a template from which objects are created.

As you would expect, a *class* defines the type of data that is contained in an object and the methods that are used to access this data. A class also defines one or more methods to be used to create objects that are *instances* of the class. An instance of a class is a concrete manifestation of the class in your computer's memory.

For example, consider a job application form as an object. It contains data—the different form fields that must be filled out. There are also methods for accessing the data—for example, fill in form and read form. Now suppose that you develop an application form for a company that will use it for new job applicants. When a job is advertised, 100 potential applicants show up. In order for these applicants to use your form, they must all be given a unique instance of the form. These form instances are created by using the form you developed as a master copy and then duplicating the master copy as many times as needed to create each instance. The job applicants then fill in their instances of the form, using the fill in form method.

In the preceding example, the master form is analogous to a class. The master form defines the data to be contained in each of its instances and implicitly provides methods by which the data can be accessed. In the same way, a class defines the data that can be contained in an object as well as the methods that can be used to access this data.

Classification and Inheritance

Classification is a common way that we organize knowledge. When we encounter a new object in our daily experience, we try to fit that object in our hierarchical classification scheme. If it fits in an existing category, we know what kind of object it is. If it doesn't fit, we add a new category. Figure 5.1 describes how we use classification to represent knowledge.

FIGURE 5.1.
Hierarchical classification of knowledge.

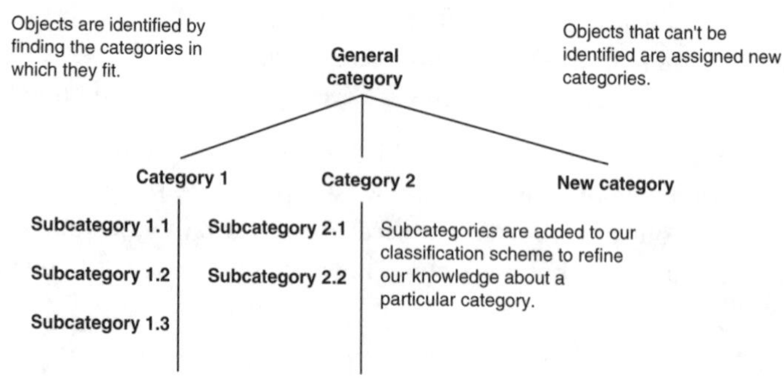

When we classify objects in this hierarchical fashion, the object categories at the top of the classification tree include all the object categories below them. If an object category appears in the classification tree, it satisfies the properties of all object categories above it in the tree. Figure 5.2 presents a classification tree for vehicles. All categories in the tree below the category automobile, for example, share the common characteristics of being four-wheeled, self-powered, and designed for passenger transportation.

FIGURE 5.2.
Vehicle classification tree.

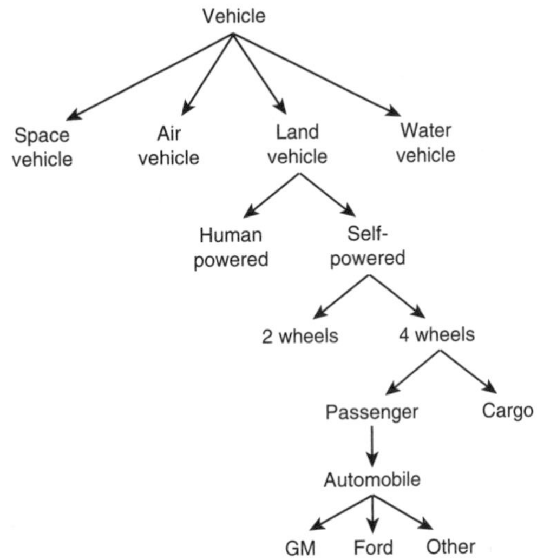

The fact that a lower-level category shares the characteristics of the categories above it on the classification tree is known as *inheritance*. The lower-level categories are said to inherit the characteristics of the categories above them on the tree.

At this point, you're probably wondering what any of this has to do with object-oriented programming in general, and Java software development in particular. We're almost there.

The classes you learned about in the previous section can also be organized in a hierarchical fashion. A class X is said to *extend* another class Y if it contains all the data contained in class Y and implements all the methods implemented by class Y. Class X is said to be a *subclass* of class Y, and class Y is said to be a *superclass*, or *parent class*, of class X.

Classes form a hierarchical classification tree under the subclass relationship. If a class X is a subclass of a class Y, it inherits the properties of Y. This means that all of the data and methods defined for class Y are available to class X.

Most object-oriented programming languages, and Java in particular, allow you to easily define subclasses that automatically inherit the data and methods of the classes they extend. This is a very powerful feature for software reuse. Not only can you reuse classes as they are defined, but you can easily extend and tailor their definitions by adding additional data and access methods to their subclasses.

There are many times that you may have a class definition you can use in your program, but it would be better if it supported additional state information or access methods. Java's support of subclassing enables you to easily extend such classes by supplying only the additional data and methods that are unique to the subclass. This allows you to take advantage of all the features of the superclass without having to implement any of them.

Multiple Inheritance

When a class extends another class, it inherits the data and methods of the class it extends. This is known as *single inheritance.* It is also possible for a class to extend classes on more than one branch of the class hierarchy tree, as shown in Figure 5.3. This is known as *multiple inheritance.*

FIGURE 5.3.
Multiple inheritance.

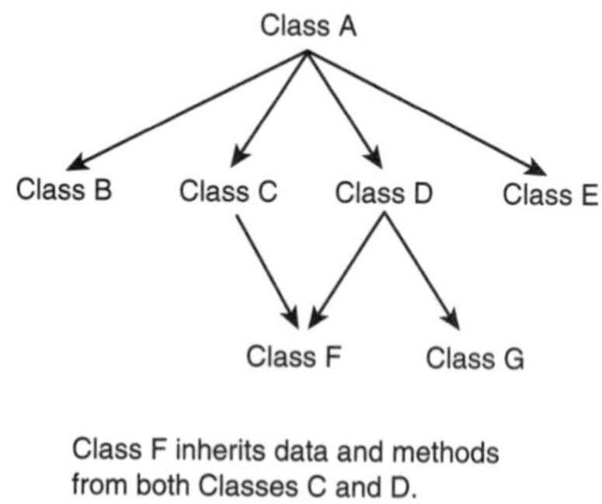

Multiple inheritance poses some difficulties for object-oriented programming. Most of these difficulties stem from the problem of determining which parent of a class to use under certain conditions. Numerous ambiguities arise when a class may have more than one immediate parent. For example, suppose a class X extends both a class Y and a class Z. Both class Y and class Z implement a unique print method. How does the compiler determine what method should be used to print objects of class X? What if the ambiguity arises during runtime for an object that inherits methods over several widely spaced branches of the class hierarchy? What's a poor compiler to do?

It is possible to design compilers and runtime systems that solve the ambiguities resulting from multiple inheritance, but these solutions tend to introduce a significant amount of processing overhead, adversely affecting program size and performance. The developers of Java have opted to support only single inheritance. This greatly simplifies the Java language, compiler, and runtime system. Java uses the interface construct to provide the benefits of multiple inheritance without the drawbacks resulting from parent ambiguity. You'll learn more about this construct in Chapter 6, "Interfaces."

Messages, Methods, and Object Interaction

In a pure object-oriented programming model, such as that used by Smalltalk, objects interact by sending messages to each other. When an object receives a message, the object invokes a method to process the message. The method may change the state of the object, return information contained in the object, or cause objects to be created or deleted.

The object model used by Java is consistent with the concept of message passing, but does not emphasize it. In the Java model, objects interact by invoking each other's methods. *Methods* provide access to the information contained in an object. The type of access varies depending on the method.

Encapsulation

One of the characteristics of object-oriented programming that is often touted in discussions of the subject is *encapsulation.* The term carries the connotation of an object being enclosed in some sort of container—and that is exactly what it means. Encapsulation is the combining of data and the code that manipulates that data into a single component—that is, an object. Encapsulation also refers to the control of access to the details of an object's implementation. Object access is limited to a well-defined, controlled interface. This allows objects to be self-contained and protects them from accidental misuse, both of which are important to reliable software design.

Polymorphism

Polymorphism is the ability to assume different forms. In object-oriented programming, this refers to the ability of objects to have many methods of the same name, but with different forms. The compiler and runtime system support polymorphism by matching each method invocation to the correct method, class, and object. The ability to figure out which method to use, in complex situations, is the essence of polymorphism.

Luckily for us, polymorphism is implemented in the compiler and runtime system—we don't need to do anything to make it happen. We just need to know that it works.

Dynamic Binding

Sometimes a program might need to interface with objects of many different classes. For example, consider a program that has the responsibility of sending out objects over a communication link. The program may not know what class an object belongs to until it is time to send it. The capability to defer until runtime decisions about what class an object belongs to and the methods for accessing the object is known as *dynamic binding.*

Dynamic binding is important to object-oriented programming because it eliminates many potentially constraining assumptions about the classes that an object belongs to and enables objects to be designed in a more general and open manner.

Dynamic binding also provides capabilities that are necessary for the advanced network programming capabilities of Java applets. When a browser executes a Java applet, the applet could require the loading of classes located on other sites across the Internet. Furthermore, these classes could be in a continual state of modification and upgrade. Dynamic binding allows new and modified objects to be used by executing software without requiring recompilation. The compiler and interpreter work together to provide executable code with the capabilities needed to dynamically interface with unknown objects during program execution.

Java Classes

In this section, you will develop a Java program, `CDrawApp`, that illustrates the concepts of encapsulation, composition and reuse, classification and inheritance, polymorphism, and dynamic binding. `CDrawApp` will allow you to draw points, boxes, and text strings on a character-based grid that is displayed using the Java console window.

The program will be introduced as a series of Java classes that cover different aspects of class and object syntax. Each new class will make use of the capabilities provided by previous classes and will provide additional building blocks required for the program's development. It is important that you understand each class that is presented before moving on to subsequent classes.

You should create a `ch05` directory, under `c:\java\jdg`, to store the Java source and bytecode files for this lesson. All classes will be developed in the `jdg.ch05` package.

Class Syntax

The Java language is class and object oriented. Classes are templates for the creation of objects. They define the data contained in an object together with methods for accessing that data.

Classes are declared as follows:

```
ClassModifiers class ClassName ExtendsClause ImplementsClause ClassBody
```

The *`ClassModifiers`*, *`ExtendsClause`*, and *`ImplementsClause`* are optional. Interfaces and the *`ImplementsClause`* are covered in the next chapter. The *`ClassBody`* is enclosed by braces, and contains zero or more field declarations.

An example of a simple class declaration is

```
class SimpleClass {
}
```

It declares a class, named `SimpleClass`, that is a subclass of `Object`, the highest-level class in the Java class hierarchy. `SimpleClass` declares no variables or methods of its own; it has only those that it inherits from `Object`.

The Point Class

The first class that you'll define for the CDrawApp program is the Point class. This class is used to identify a point on a grid by its x- and y-coordinates. The source code for the class declaration follows. (See Listing 5.1.) You should enter the code in a file named Point.java and store it in your c:\java\jdg\ch05 directory. Then compile it using the command javac Point.java.

Listing 5.1. The Point class source code.

```
package jdg.ch05;

// Point.java

public class Point {
 // Variable declarations
 private int x;
 private int y;

 //Method declarations
 public Point() {
  x = 0;
  y = 0;
 }
 public Point(int xValue, int yValue) {
  x = xValue;
  y = yValue;
 }
 public Point(Point p) {
  x = p.x();
  y = p.y();
 }
 public int x() {
  return x;
 }
 public int y() {
  return y;
 }
 public void xSet(int xValue) {
  x = xValue;
 }
 public void ySet(int yValue) {
  y = yValue;
 }
 public Point add(Point p) {
  return new Point(x+p.x(), y+p.y());
 }
 public Point add(int i,int j) {
  return new Point(x+i,y+j);
 }
 public String toString() {
  return new String("("+String.valueOf(x)+","+String.valueOf(y)+")");
 }
}
```

Class Modifiers

The `Point` class is declared using the `public` class modifier. *Class modifiers* are keywords that are used to specify the properties of a class. Three class modifiers are supported: `public`, `final`, and `abstract`. If a class is declared as `public`, it can be accessed outside of its package; otherwise, it cannot. Because `Point` is declared as `public`, it can be accessed outside its package. Only one `public` class or interface is allowed in a compilation unit. `Point` is the only class in `Point.java` and, therefore, follows this rule.

If a class is declared as `final`, it cannot be extended. `Final` classes form the leaves of the class hierarchy tree.

An `abstract` class is used to define the general behavior for an intended set of subclasses. `abstract` classes are used to set the stage for subsequent subclass development. They are, by definition, incomplete and cannot be instantiated in terms of objects. `abstract` classes describe the behavior expected of their subclasses through the declaration of *`abstract` methods*. `abstract` methods must be redefined, or *overridden*, before they can be used. Only `abstract` classes are allowed to declare or inherit `abstract` methods. The `CGObject` class is an example of an `abstract` class. It is presented in the section "The CGObject class," later in this chapter.

Extending Superclasses

When a class declaration does not contain an `extends` clause, the class is automatically made a subclass of the `Object` class. The `Point` class does not contain an `extends` clause and, therefore, is a subclass of `Object`. The `Object` class is at the top of the Java class hierarchy, being the *superclass* of all Java classes.

You can change a class's position in the class hierarchy by identifying its immediate superclass in the class declaration. The *immediate superclass* is the parent class directly above it in the class hierarchy. You identify the immediate superclass of a class using the `extends` clause in the class declaration. For example, you can place `SimpleClass` under `ExampleClass` in the class hierarchy as follows:

```
class SimpleClass extends ExampleClass {
}
```

`SimpleClass` does not have any unique variables or methods of its own, but it inherits those of `ExampleClass` and all superclasses of `ExampleClass`.

Adding Body to Classes

The body of the `Point` class consists of all declarations between the opening and closing braces. If a class is to add any features to its superclass, it does so in its class body. It is here that additional variables and methods are declared. These additional declarations are referred to as *field declarations*.

The field declarations are identified within the opening and closing braces ({ and }) of the class body. You need to supply the braces even if you don't intend to declare any fields, as you saw in the `SimpleClass` example.

Variable Declarations

Variables are the components of an object that store data and state information. They are declared as follows:

```
VariableModifiers Type VariableDeclarators
```

`VariableModifiers` are keywords that identify special properties of the variables being declared. `Type` is the Java type of the declared variables. It may be a primitive type, a class type, an interface type, or an array type. `VariableDeclarators` identify the names of the declared variables and can be used to specify the initial values of these variables.

The `Point` class declares two integer variables: `x` and `y`. They are used to store the location of a point on a two-dimensional grid. These variables are declared with the `private` modifier. This modifier restricts access to the `x` and `y` variables to within the `Point` class. The `Point` class illustrates the principles of encapsulation. Data and methods are combined with a well-defined interface to provide maximum modularity. Access to the internal operation of the class is controlled.

Constructor Declarations

Constructors are special methods that are used to initialize newly created objects. They are used together with the `new` operator to create and initialize objects that are instances of a class.

Constructors are declared in a slightly different manner than other methods. Their syntax is as follows:

```
AccessSpecifier ConstructorDeclarator ThrowsClause ConstructorBody
```

`AccessSpecifier` identifies the type of access allowed to the constructor. `ConstructorDeclarator` identifies a method with the same name as the class and specifies its parameter list. The parameter list is a comma-separated list of parameter declarations where each parameter declaration identifies the type and name of a parameter that is passed to the constructor upon invocation.

`ThrowsClause` is a constructor. Exceptions are covered in Chapter 7, "Exceptions."

`ConstructorBody` contains the code that implements the constructor.

The `Point` class has three constructors:

```
public Point() {
 x = 0;
 y = 0;
}
```

```
public Point(int xValue, int yValue) {
 x = xValue;
 y = yValue;
}
public Point(Point p) {
 x = p.x();
 y = p.y();
}
```

All three constructors are identified as `public`. This allows them to be accessed outside of their package. The first constructor does not have any parameters. It simply initializes the `x` and `y` variables to `0`. The second constructor has two parameters, `xValue` and `yValue`, of integer type. They are used to set the value of `x` and `y`. The third constructor takes an object of class `Point` as its parameter. It sets the values of `x` and `y` based upon the values of the parameter point `p`. It is an example of a *copy constructor* because it creates a new point that is a copy of the point that is passed as its parameter.

The declaration of the three `Point` constructors is an example of *overloading*. Overloading occurs when two or more methods with the same name are declared within a class. The overloaded methods must differ in their parameter lists. The `add()` methods of the `Point` class are also overloaded.

Overloading is an example of polymorphism. When an overloaded method is to be invoked during program execution, the number and type of method arguments used in the invocation determine which method is used.

Access Method Declarations

Methods are executable units of code that provide access to the data stored in variables. Methods that are not constructors are referred to as *nonconstructor* methods, or *access* methods. Access methods are declared within the body of a class as follows:

`MethodModifiers ResultType MethodDeclarator ThrowsClause MethodBody`

`MethodModifiers` identify special properties of a method. All the methods of class `Point` are `public`, allowing them to be accessed outside of their package.

`ResultType` of a method identifies the type of value that is returned by the method. If an access method does not return a value, it must use the `void` return type. Constructors do not have a return type. The access methods of class `Point` have return values of type `int`, `void`, `Point`, and `String`.

`MethodDeclarator` identifies the method, by name, and specifies its parameter list. The parameter list of access methods is specified in the same manner as with constructors.

`MethodBody` contains the code that implements the Java method.

The `Point` class has seven access methods. The `x()` and `y()` methods return the x- and y-coordinates of a point. The `xSet()` and `ySet()` methods set the values of these coordinates based on the values of the `xValue` and `yValue` parameters. The two `add()` methods are used to create a new `Point` object by adding to the coordinates of the point being accessed. The `new` operator creates new instances of a class. It is always followed by a constructor that initializes the newly created instance. The `toString()` method returns an object of class `String` that describes the point as an ordered pair.

The `CGrid` Class

The `CGrid` class is used to define a grid of characters of specified dimensions. It provides a basic set of grid methods and is extended by other classes that add to these methods. Its source code is shown in Listing 5.2. It should be entered into the `CGrid.java` file and compiled using `javac`.

Listing 5.2. The `CGrid` class source code.

```
package jdg.ch05;

// CGrid.java

public class CGrid {
 // Variable declarations
 protected int width;
 protected int depth;
 protected char grid[][];

 // Method declarations
 public CGrid(int widthValue,int depthValue) {
  width = widthValue;
  depth = depthValue;
  grid = new char[depth][width];
  blankGrid();
 }
 public void blankGrid() {
  fillGrid(' ');
 }
 public void fillGrid(char ch) {
  for(int j=0; j<depth; ++j)
   for(int i=0; i<width; ++i)
    grid[j][i]= ch;
 }
 public void putCharAt(char ch,Point p){
  grid[p.y()][p.x()] = ch;
 }
 public char getCharFrom(Point p) {
  return grid[p.y()][p.x()];
 }
}
```

`CGrid` declares three variables: `width`, `depth`, and `grid[][]`. The `width` and `depth` variables are used to specify the horizontal and vertical dimensions of `grid[][]`, an array of character arrays that holds the characters of the grid. The `grid[][]` array is used as a two-dimensional array of characters, even though Java technically does not have multidimensional arrays.

The `CGrid` variables are declared as `protected`. This specifies that they can only be accessed in the package, `jdg.ch05`, in which they are declared, and in any subclasses of `CGrid`.

`CGrid` has a single constructor that sets the values of `width` and `depth`, allocates the `grid[][]` array, and then invokes `blankGrid()` to fill `grid[][]` with spaces.

`CGrid` has four access methods. The `fillGrid()` method sets each element of the `grid[][]` array to the `ch` parameter. The `blankGrid()` method simply calls `fillGrid()` with a space character. The `putCharAt()` and `getCharFrom()` methods are used to set a point in the grid to a particular character and to find out what character is at a given location in the grid.

Note that the `putCharAt()` and `getCharFrom()` methods use the `Point` class to define their parameters. Because `Point` is in the same package as `CGrid`, it does not need to be imported.

The `CGObject` Class

The `CGObject` class is an example of an `abstract` class. `abstract` classes are used to constrain the behavior of their subclasses by defining `abstract` methods. The `abstract` methods must be implemented by any non-`abstract` subclasses. Listing 5.3 shows the source code of the `CGObject` class.

Listing 5.3. The `CGObject` class source code.

```
package jdg.ch05;

// CGObject.java

public abstract class CGObject {
 // Variable declarations
 public Point location;
 public char drawCharacter;

 // Method declarations
 public void addToGrid(PrintCGrid grid) {
  grid.addCGObject(this);
 }
 public abstract void display(PrintCGrid grid);
 public abstract void describe();
}
```

The `CGObject` class is used to define the general behavior of objects that may be displayed on a grid. It declares two variables: `location` and `drawCharacter`. The `location` variable is of type `Point` and is used to specify the point on a grid where an object is located. The `drawCharacter` variable identifies the character that should be used to draw the object.

`CGObject` has three methods and no constructors. `abstract` classes cannot have constructors because they are incompletely defined and, therefore, cannot have object instances.

The first method, addToGrid(), is not abstract. It takes an object of class PrintCGrid as a parameter and invokes the addCGObject() method of PrintCGrid to add this to the grid. The this keyword is used to refer to the current object. Whatever object of a subclass of CGObject that is invoked with the addToGrid() method is added to an object of class PrintCGrid.

CGObject's other two methods are declared with the abstract keyword. This signifies that they must be overridden before they can be used by any non-abstract subclasses of CGObject. The overridden methods must have the same names, parameters, and return values as the abstract methods. The display() method will be used to display an object on a grid of class PrintCGrid. The describe() method will be used to display a description of a grid object.

Don't forget to enter and compile CGObject before going on to the next class. In case you forgot, it should be entered into a file of the same name, with the .java extension—that is, CGObject.java.

The PrintCGrid Class

The PrintCGrid class is a subclass of the CGrid class. It defines additional variables and methods that allow objects to be added to a grid. It also provides methods for displaying the grid. The source code of the PrintCGrid class is shown in Listing 5.4.

Listing 5.4. The PrintCGrid class source code.

```
package jdg.ch05;

import java.lang.System;

// PrintCGrid.java

public class PrintCGrid extends CGrid {
 // Variable declarations
 protected CGObject displayList[];
 protected static final int maxObjects = 100;
 protected int numObjects;

 // Method declarations
 public PrintCGrid(int x,int y) {
  super(x,y);
  numObjects = 0;
  displayList = new CGObject[maxObjects];
 }
 public void addCGObject(CGObject obj) {
  if(numObjects < maxObjects) {
   displayList[numObjects] = obj;
   ++numObjects;
  }
 }
 public void deleteCGObject(int index) {
  if(index < numObjects && numObjects > 0) {
   for(int i = index; i < numObjects -1 ; ++i)
```

continues

Listing 5.4. continued

```
    displayList[i] = displayList[i+1];
   --numObjects;
  }
 }
 public void deleteLastObject() {
   if(numObjects > 0) --numObjects;
 }
 public int getNumObjects() {
  return numObjects;
 }
 public CGObject getObject(int index) {
  return displayList[index];
 }
 public void clearGrid() {
  numObjects = 0;
 }
 public void drawGrid() {
  blankGrid();
  for(int i = 0; i < numObjects ; ++i)
   displayList[i].display(this);
 }
 public void displayGrid() {
  for(int i=0;i<depth;++i)
   System.out.println(String.valueOf(grid[i]));
 }
 public void displayRow(int row) {
  System.out.print(String.valueOf(grid[row]));
 }
 public void show() {
  drawGrid();
  displayGrid();
 }
}
```

`PrintCGrid` is identified as a subclass of `CGrid` by the `extends` clause in the `PrintCGrid` class declaration. This means that all the variables and methods defined in `CGrid` are available to `PrintCGrid`. You should now begin to get a feel for the power of inheritance. `PrintCGrid` uses `CGrid` as a base to which other grid display variables and methods are added.

`PrintCGrid` declares three variables: `displayList[]`, `maxObjects`, and `numObjects`. These variables are declared as `protected`, thereby limiting their access to the `jdg.ch05` package and subclasses of `PrintCGrid`.

The `displayList[]` variable is an array of class `CGObject`. This does not mean that it will contain objects that are instances of this class. That would be impossible, because `CGObject` is `abstract`. Declaring `displayList[]` to be an array of class `CGObject` allows it to hold objects of any class that is a subclass of `CGObject`. In general, if a variable is declared to be of class X, then the variable can be assigned any object of a class that is a subclass of X.

The `maxObjects` variable is declared as both `static` and `final`. Variables that are declared using the `static` modifier are common to all objects that are instances of a class and are not replicated for each instance. Static variables are referred to as class variables. Variables that aren't declared as static are instance variables and are replicated for each object that is an instance of a class.

The final modifier is used to identify a variable as a constant. A variable that is declared with the final modifier must be initialized in its declaration and cannot be assigned a value anywhere else outside its declaration. The maxObjects constant is initialized to 100. It is used to identify the maximum number of objects that can be added to displayList[].

The numObjects variable is used to count the actual number of objects that have been added to the grid's displayList[].

PrintCGrid has a single constructor. This constructor has two parameters, x and y, that represent the horizontal and vertical dimensions of the grid. The constructor invokes the super() method, passing these variables as arguments. The super() method is an example of a *constructor call statement.* It invokes the constructor of PrintCGrid's superclass, that is, CGrid, with the arguments x and y. CGrid's constructor initializes its width and depth variables, allocates the grid[][] array, and fills it with spaces. When CGrid's constructor is finished, PrintCGrid's constructor continues by setting numObjects to 0 and allocating the displayList[] array.

PrintCGrid provides 10 access methods. The addCGObject() method adds an object to the displayList[] array. The deleteCGObject() method deletes the object at the specified index. All subsequent objects in the array are moved to fill the hole left by the deleted object. The deleteLastObject() method deletes the last object by merely decrementing numObjects.

The getNumObjects() method returns the number of objects in displayList[]. The getObject() method returns the object at the specified position within displayList[]. The clearGrid() method clears all objects by setting numObjects to 0.

The drawGrid() method is an interesting example of dynamic binding and the use of abstract classes. It blanks the grid, using the method that it inherits from CGrid, and then invokes the display() method of each object in displayList[]. It does not know what kind of objects are contained in displayList[]. It only knows that they are of some subclass of CGObject, and therefore must implement the display() method. Dynamic binding enables the display() method to be invoked for the correct object class.

The displayGrid() method displays each row of the grid to the console window. It is an example of inheritance. The grid[][] array was defined in the CGrid class and inherited by PrintCGrid. It is updated by drawGrid() and the display() methods of all subclasses of CGObject. It is used by PrintCGrid to print characters to the console window.

The valueOf() method used in displayGrid() is a static method of the String class. It converts an array of characters into a String object. A static method is similar to a static variable in that it applies to the class as a whole rather than to objects that are instances of the class. Because of this class orientation, a static method can access only static variables. All static methods are final. final methods cannot be overridden.

The `displayRow()` method displays a single row of the grid to the console window and the `show()` method combines the `drawGrid()` and `displayGrid()` methods into a single method.

The `BorderedPrintCGrid` Class

The `BorderedPrintCGrid` class further extends the `CGrid` class by subclassing `PrintCGrid`. It adds additional variables and methods for creating a border around objects of class `PrintCGrid`. Listing 5.5 contains the source code of the `BorderedPrintCGrid` class.

Listing 5.5. The `BorderedPrintCGrid` class source code.

```
package jdg.ch05;

// BorderedPrintCGrid.java

public class BorderedPrintCGrid extends PrintCGrid {
 // Variable declarations
 private boolean useBorder;
 private char borderCharacter;
 private String horizEdge;
 private String vertEdge;

 // Method declarations
 public BorderedPrintCGrid() {
  super(75,20);
  setBorderDefaults('*');
 }
 public BorderedPrintCGrid(int x,int y,char ch) {
  super(x,y);
  setBorderDefaults(ch);
 }
 private void setBorderDefaults(char ch) {
  useBorder = true;
  setBorderCharacter(ch);
 }
 public void enableBorder(boolean toggle) {
  useBorder = toggle;
 }
 public void setBorderCharacter(char ch) {
  borderCharacter = ch;
  char border[] = new char[width+2];
  for(int i=0;i<width+2;++i) border[i] = borderCharacter;
  horizEdge = new String(border);
  vertEdge = String.valueOf(borderCharacter);
 }
 public void displayGrid() {
  if(useBorder) {
   System.out.println(horizEdge);
   for(int i=0;i<depth;++i) {
    System.out.print(vertEdge);
    displayRow(i);
    System.out.println(vertEdge);
   }
```

```
   System.out.println(horizEdge);
  }else super.displayGrid();
 }
}
```

BorderedPrintCGrid declares four private variables: useBorder, borderCharacter, horizEdge, and vertEdge. The useBorder variable is of type boolean and determines whether a border should be displayed. The borderCharacter variable contains the character to be used to display the border. The horizEdge and vertEdge variables contain the String objects to be displayed for the horizontal and vertical edges of the border. These objects are computed from the borderEdge character based on the grid[][] dimensions.

BorderedPrintCGrid has two constructors. The first does not take any parameters. It constructs a grid 75 characters wide and 20 rows high by calling the constructor of PrintCGrid. Note that PrintCGrid's constructor passes the call farther up the class hierarchy to CGrid's constructor. This is an example of how classification and inheritance work together to simplify the development of new classes and methods. The setBorderDefaults() method is used to initialize the variables of BorderedPrintCGrid. The second constructor is similar to the first, but provides the capability for the grid's dimensions to be specified directly.

BorderedPrintCGrid provides four access methods. The setBorderDefaults() method initializes the variables of the BorderedPrintCGrid class using the enableBorder() and setBorderCharacter() methods. The enableBorder() method allows the useBorder variable to be set to true or false. The setBorderCharacter() method sets the borderCharacter, horizEdge, and vertEdge variables for use by the displayGrid() method.

The displayGrid() method overrides the displayGrid() method of the PrintCGrid class. By doing so, it redefines the method to suit its own needs. It checks to see if the useBorder variable is true. If it is true, then a bordered grid is displayed using the displayRow() method of PrintCGrid. If it is false, it invokes the displayGrid() method of its superclass, PrintCGrid, to display the grid. The super keyword is used to identify the fact that a superclass method should be used instead of the one defined for the current class. The name of the superclass can also be used to indicate which method should be used. The method invocation could have used PrintCGrid.displayGrid() instead of super.displayGrid().

The CGPoint Class

The CGPoint class shows how a non-abstract class extends an abstract class. The CGPoint class extends CGObject. It does not add any new variables to those that it inherits, and the only methods that it declares are constructors and the abstract methods that it is required to implement. Listing 5.6 shows the source code of the CGPoint class.

Listing 5.6. The `CGPoint` class source code.

```
package jdg.ch05;

// CGPoint.java

public class CGPoint extends CGObject {
 // Method declarations
 public CGPoint(int x, int y,char ch) {
  location = new Point(x,y);
  drawCharacter = ch;
 }
 public CGPoint(int x, int y) {
  this(x,y,'+');
 }
 public CGPoint(Point p) {
  this(p.x(),p.y(),'+');
 }
 public CGPoint(Point p,char ch) {
  this(p.x(),p.y(),ch);
 }
 public void display(PrintCGrid grid) {
  grid.putCharAt(drawCharacter,location);
 }
 public void describe() {
  System.out.print("CGPoint "+String.valueOf(drawCharacter)+" ");
  System.out.println(location.toString());
 }
}
```

`CGPoint` has four constructors. The first takes the x- and y-coordinates of a point and the character to be displayed, and initializes the `location` and `drawCharacter` variables declared in `CGObject`. The remaining constructors invoke the `this()` constructor. The `this()` constructor invokes a constructor for the current class that has a matching argument list. The matching constructor is the first constructor, in all three cases. The second, third, and fourth constructors provide a variety of parameter lists by which objects of `CGPoint` can be constructed. The second and third constructors supply default values for `drawCharacter`.

The `this()` constructor call statement is similar to the `super()` constructor call statement used with the `PrintCGrid` and `BorderedPrintCGrid` classes. Each allows part of the construction details to be handed off to other constructors in the same and parent classes. If no constructor call statement is used, a default `super()` constructor is used. This ensures that when an object is created, constructors from all of its superclasses are called to initialize all variables inherited by the object.

`CGPoint` overrides the `display()` and `describe()` abstract methods defined by `CGObject`. The `display()` method uses the `putCharAt()` method defined for class `CGrid` to draw a character in the `grid[][]` array. The `describe()` method prints a description of the point to the console window. It uses the `toString()` method of the `Point` class.

The CGBox Class

The `CGBox` class also extends `CGObject`. It provides an additional variable to allow a rectangle to be displayed on a grid. Listing 5.7 contains the `CGBox` class source code.

Listing 5.7. The `CGBox` class source code.

```
package jdg.ch05;

// CGBox.java

public class CGBox extends CGObject {
 // Variable declarations
 protected Point lr; // Lower right corner of a box

 // Method declarations
 public CGBox(Point ulCorner, Point lrCorner,char ch) {
  location = ulCorner;
  lr = lrCorner;
  drawCharacter = ch;
 }
 public CGBox(Point ulCorner, Point lrCorner) {
  this(ulCorner,lrCorner,'#');
 }
 public void display(PrintCGrid grid) {
  int width = lr.x() - location.x() + 1;
  int height = lr.y() - location.y() + 1;
  Point topRow = new Point(location);
  Point bottomRow = new Point(location.x(),lr.y());
  for(int i=0; i<width; ++i) {
   grid.putCharAt(drawCharacter,topRow);
   grid.putCharAt(drawCharacter,bottomRow);
   topRow = topRow.add(1,0);
   bottomRow = bottomRow.add(1,0);
  }
  Point leftCol = new Point(location);
  Point rightCol = new Point(lr.x(),location.y());
  for(int i=0;i<height;++i){
   grid.putCharAt(drawCharacter,leftCol);
   grid.putCharAt(drawCharacter,rightCol);
   leftCol = leftCol.add(0,1);
   rightCol = rightCol.add(0,1);
  }
 }
 public void describe() {
  System.out.print("CGBox "+String.valueOf(drawCharacter)+" ");
  System.out.println(location.toString()+" "+lr.toString());
 }
}
```

The `location` variable defined in `CGObject` is used as the upper-left corner of the rectangle. The `lr` variable defined by `CGBox` is the lower-right corner of the rectangle.

CGBox provides two constructors. The first takes arguments for the upper-left and lower-right corners of the rectangle and a character to be used as the drawCharacter. The second constructor provides for a default box drawCharacter and uses a call to the first constructor to accomplish its initialization.

The display() method displays a box on an object of class PrintCGrid. It is a good example of object composition because it uses objects of several different classes to accomplish this purpose. It begins by calculating the box's width and height dimensions from the location and lr variables. The location variable is the upper-left corner of the box, and the lr variable is the lower-right corner. It then creates two points, topRow and bottomRow, that will be used to step through the top and bottom rows of the box's display. The first for statement is used to display the box's top and bottom rows. The putCharAt() method of CGrid is used to display the drawCharacter at the locations specified by topRow and bottomRow. The putCharAt() method is inherited by objects of class PrintCGrid. The x-coordinates of the topRow and bottomRow variables are incremented by 1 to step through the rows' display using the add() method of the Point class.

The display() method creates the leftCol and rightCol points to be used to step through the display of the box's left and right columns. The second for statement displays these columns in a similar manner to the first for statement. The y-coordinates of the leftCol and rightCol variables are incremented by 1 to step through the columns' display.

The describe() method displays a description of a box's parameters to the console window. This description identifies the drawCharacter and upper-left and lower-right corners of the box.

The CGText Class

The CGText class is the third and final subclass of CGObject that is declared in this chapter. (See Listing 5.8.) The CGObject class hierarchy is extended further in Chapter 6.

Listing 5.8. The CGText class source code.

```
package jdg.ch05;

// CGText.java

public class CGText extends CGObject {
 // Variable declarations
 String text;

 // Method declarations
 public CGText(Point p,String s) {
  location = p;
  drawCharacter = ' ';
  text = s;
 }
 public void display(PrintCGrid grid) {
  Point p = new Point(location);
  for(int i=0;i<text.length();++i){
```

```
   grid.putCharAt(text.charAt(i),p);
   p = p.add(1,0);
  }
 }
 public void describe() {
  System.out.println("CGText "+location.toString()+" "+text);
 }
}
```

`CGText` declares one variable, `text`, that is used to store a string of text to be displayed on the grid. It has a single constructor that takes two arguments: a `Point` value that identifies the point on the grid where the text is to be displayed and a `String` value that specifies this text. Because `drawCharacter` is not displayed, it is initialized to a space. `CGText` implements the two abstract methods required of it. The `display()` method displays the text variable at the location specified by the location variable. The `describe()` method displays the location of the point and its text to the console window.

The `KeyboardInput` Class

The `KeyboardInput` class extends the `DataInputStream` class of the Java API to provide a set of common simple methods for getting keyboard input from the user. (See Listing 5.9.)

Listing 5.9. The `KeyboardInput` class source code.

```
package jdg.ch05;

import java.lang.System;
import java.io.DataInputStream;
import java.io.InputStream;
import java.io.IOException;

public class KeyboardInput extends DataInputStream {
 public KeyboardInput(InputStream inStream) {
  super(inStream);
 }
 public char getChar() throws IOException {
  String line = readLine();
  if(line.length()==0) return ' ';
  return line.charAt(0);
 }
 public String getText() throws IOException {
  String line = readLine();
  return line;
 }
 public int getInt() throws IOException {
  String line = readLine();
  Integer i = new Integer(line);
  return i.intValue();
 }
 public Point getPoint() throws IOException {
```

continues

Listing 5.9. continued

```
  System.out.print("  x-coordinate: ");
  System.out.flush();
  int x = getInt();
  System.out.print("  y-coordinate: ");
  System.out.flush();
  int y = getInt();
  return new Point(x,y);
 }
}
```

`KeyboardInput` has a single constructor that takes an object of class `InputStream` as a parameter. This object should be `java.lang.System.in`, but may be mapped to other input streams if necessary. The `KeyboardInput` constructor passes the `InputStream` object to `DataInputStream`'s constructor using the `super()` constructor call.

`KeyboardInput` defines four access methods that get objects of type `char`, `String`, `int`, and `Point` from the user. The `getChar()` method uses the `readLine()` method of `DataInputStream` to read a line of data entered by the user. If the line is blank, it returns the space character; otherwise it returns the first character in the input line. The `getText()` method simply returns the entire line entered by the user, whether it is blank or not. The `getInt()` method works the same way as `getChar()` except that it uses a constructor of the `Integer` class to construct an object of class `Integer` directly from the input line. It then converts the `Integer` object to an object of type `int` before it returns it using the `return` statement. The `Integer` class is an example of a class that wraps the primitive type `int`. Class wrappers are covered in Chapter 12, "Portable Software and the `java.lang` Package."

The `getPoint()` method interacts with the user to get the x- and y-coordinates of a point. It then constructs an object of class `Point` that it uses as its return value. The `getPoint()` method uses the `getInt()` method to get the values of the x- and y-coordinates.

The CDrawApp Program

You're finally ready to use all the classes that you've developed in this chapter to build the `CDrawApp` program. Make sure that you've compiled all the classes that have been introduced. Your `c:\java\jdg\ch05` directory should have compiled classes for `Point.java`, `CGrid.java`, `CGObject.java`, `PrintCGrid.java`, `BorderedPrintCGrid.java`, `CGPoint.java`, `CGBox.java`, `CGText.java`, and `KeyboardInput.java`. The `CDrawApp.java` file is shown in Listing 5.10.

Listing 5.10. The `CDrawApp` and `CDraw` classes.

```
package jdg.ch05;

import java.lang.System;
import java.io.DataInputStream;
import java.io.IOException;
```

```
class CDrawApp {
 public static void main(String args[]) throws IOException {
  CDraw program = new CDraw();
  program.run();
 }
}

class CDraw {
 // Variable declarations
 static KeyboardInput kbd = new KeyboardInput(System.in);
 BorderedPrintCGrid grid;

 // Method declarations
 CDraw() {
  grid = new BorderedPrintCGrid();
 }
 void run() throws IOException {
  boolean finished = false;
  do {
   char command = getCommand();
   switch(command){
    case 'P':
     addPoint();
     System.out.println();
     break;
    case 'B':
     addBox();
     System.out.println();
     break;
    case 'T':
     addText();
     System.out.println();
     break;
    case 'U':
     grid.deleteLastObject();
     System.out.println();
     break;
    case 'C':
     grid.clearGrid();
     System.out.println();
     break;
    case 'S':
     grid.show();
     break;
    case 'X':
     finished = true;
    default:
     System.out.println();
   }
  } while (!finished);
 }
 char getCommand() throws IOException {
  System.out.println("CDrawApp    P - Add a Point   U - Undo Last Add");
  System.out.print("Main Menu   B - Add a Box     C - Clear Grid");
  System.out.println("      X - Exit CDrawApp");
  System.out.print("            T - Add Text      S - Show Grid");
  System.out.print("       Enter command: ");
```

continues

Listing 5.10. continued

```
  System.out.flush();
  return Character.toUpperCase(kbd.getChar());
 }
 void addPoint() throws IOException {
  System.out.println("Add Point Menu");
  System.out.println(" Location:");
  Point p = kbd.getPoint();
  System.out.print(" Character: ");
  System.out.flush();
  char ch = kbd.getChar();
  if(ch==' ') ch = '+';
  CGPoint cgp = new CGPoint(p,ch);
  cgp.addToGrid(grid);
 }
 void addBox() throws IOException {
  System.out.println("Add Box Menu");
  System.out.println(" Upper Left Corner:");
  Point ul = kbd.getPoint();
  System.out.println(" Lower Right Corner:");
  Point lr = kbd.getPoint();
  System.out.print(" Character: ");
  System.out.flush();
  char ch = kbd.getChar();
  if(ch==' ') ch = '#';
  CGBox box = new CGBox(ul,lr,ch);
  box.addToGrid(grid);
 }
 void addText() throws IOException {
  System.out.println("Add Text Menu");
  System.out.println(" Location:");
  Point p = kbd.getPoint();
  System.out.print(" Text: ");
  System.out.flush();
  String text = kbd.getText();
  CGText cgt = new CGText(p,text);
  cgt.addToGrid(grid);
 }
}
```

The declaration of the `CDrawApp` class is very small. It consists of a `main()` method that creates an object of class `CDraw` and then invokes the `run()` method for that object. A separate `CDraw` object is created because the `main()` method is `static`. `static` methods are like `static` variables. They apply to the class as a whole and not to objects that are individual instances of a class. `static` methods can only access variables that they create or that are `static` variables of the class. By creating the `CDraw` class, you are able to avoid any limitations posed by `static`'s `main()` method.

The `CDraw` class declares two variables: `kbd` and `grid`. The `kbd` variable is used to get input from the user. The `grid` variable is used to display objects such as points, boxes, and text. The `kbd` variable is created as a `static` variable of class `KeyboardInput`. It is initialized using the `KeyboardInput()` constructor and the predefined `java.lang.System.in` input stream. A variable initializer is used to create and initialize the value of kbd. Other initializers, called *static initializers*, are also supported by Java. Static initializers allow blocks of statements to be executed during class initialization. They are covered in Chapter 11, "Language Summary."

CDraw has a single constructor that creates an object that is a new instance of BorderedPrintCGrid and assigns it to the grid variable. The BorderedPrintCGrid() constructor creates a default grid 75 characters wide and 20 characters high. The default border character is an asterisk (*).

CDraw has five access methods. The run() method implements the core processing of the CDrawApp program. It uses a do statement that repeatedly processes user keyboard commands. It invokes the getCommand() method to display a menu to the user and retrieve the user's command selection. It then uses a switch statement to process the command. It invokes the addPoint(), addBox(), and addText() methods to add points, boxes, and text to the grid. It invokes the deleteLastObject() and clearGrid() methods of the PrintCGrid class to remove the last object added to the grid or to completely clear the grid of all objects. The show() method of PrintCGrid is used to draw and display the grid. If the user enters a command line beginning with X or x, the boolean variable finished is set to true, the do statement finishes, and the CDrawApp program terminates.

The getCommand() method displays a menu to the user and uses the getChar() method of the KeyboardInput class to get a character command from the user. The static toUpperCase() method of the Character class is used to convert the character returned by getChar() to uppercase.

The addPoint() method queries the user to enter the location of a point and the character to be used to displayed at that location. It uses the getPoint() and getChar() methods of the KeyboardInput class. If a user enters a space for the display character, addPoint() uses the plus (+) character as a default. It uses the data obtained from the user to construct an object of class CGPoint and adds the object to grid using the addToGrid() method of class CGObject that is inherited by class CGPoint.

The addBox() method is similar to the addPoint() method except that it must obtain two points from the user—the upper-left and lower-right corners of a rectangle. It also obtains a box display character from the user, the default value of which is the pound (#) sign. An object of class CGBox is constructed from the user-supplied information and added to the grid using the CGObject addToGrid() method.

The final method of CDraw, addText(), retrieves a location and a text string from the user and uses this information to create an object of class CGText. The new object is then added to the grid in the same manner as the CGPoint and CGBox objects.

Running CDrawApp

Assuming that you have compiled all the classes introduced in this chapter, go ahead and compile CDrawApp. You can then run CDrawApp using the following command line:

```
C:\java\jdg\ch05>java jdg.ch05.CDrawApp
```

`CDrawApp` begins by displaying the following menu:

```
CDrawApp    P - Add a Point   U - Undo Last Add
Main Menu   B - Add a Box     C - Clear Grid      X - Exit CDrawApp
            T - Add Text      S - Show Grid       Enter command:
```

This menu provides you with seven command options: `P`, `B`, `T`, `U`, `C`, `S`, and `X`. Entering `X` will cause `CDrawApp` to terminate. You don't want to do this yet. Entering `S` will cause `CDrawApp` to display the character grid. Go ahead and enter `S`. Your screen should look like this:

```
*****************************************************************************
*                                                                           *
*                                                                           *
*                                                                           *
*                                                                           *
*                                                                           *
*                                                                           *
*                                                                           *
*                                                                           *
*                                                                           *
*                                                                           *
*                                                                           *
*                                                                           *
*                                                                           *
*                                                                           *
*                                                                           *
*                                                                           *
*                                                                           *
*                                                                           *
*                                                                           *
*                                                                           *
*****************************************************************************
CDrawApp    P - Add a Point   U - Undo Last Add
Main Menu   B - Add a Box     C - Clear Grid      X - Exit CDrawApp
            T - Add Text      S - Show Grid       Enter command:
```

`CDrawApp` displays a blank bordered grid using the `show()` method of the `PrintCGrid` class. You should be able to trace program execution up to this point by examining the source code files of the classes used in this chapter. The `CDraw` `run()` and `getCommand()` methods perform most of the user interface processing.

You can add a point to the grid by entering a `P` command. You will get the following display:

```
Add Point Menu
 Location:
  x-coordinate:
```

The Add Point Menu prompt is displayed by the `addPoint()` method of the `CDraw` class. It prompts you to enter the x-coordinate of a grid point. The upper-left corner of the grid is 0,0 and the lower-right corner of the grid is 74,19, where 74 is the maximum x-coordinate and 19 is the maximum y-coordinate. Enter `35` for the x-coordinate. The Add Point Menu then prompts you to enter the y-coordinate:

```
Add Point Menu
 Location:
```

```
  x-coordinate: 35
  y-coordinate:
```

Enter `10` for the y-coordinate. You are prompted to enter the character to be displayed at location 35,10. Enter `x` to finish adding a point:

```
Add Point Menu
 Location:
  x-coordinate: 35
  y-coordinate: 10
 Character: x

CDrawApp    P - Add a Point   U - Undo Last Add
Main Menu   B - Add a Box     C - Clear Grid      X - Exit CDrawApp
            T - Add Text      S - Show Grid       Enter command:
```

The `CDrawApp` main menu is displayed again. To verify that the point you just entered was, in fact, added to the grid, redisplay the grid by entering `S`. You will see the `x` in the middle of the grid:

```
*****************************************************************************
*                                                                           *
*                                                                           *
*                                                                           *
*                                                                           *
*                                                                           *
*                                                                           *
*                                                                           *
*                                                                           *
*                                                                           *
*                                                                           *
*                                   x                                       *
*                                                                           *
*                                                                           *
*                                                                           *
*                                                                           *
*                                                                           *
*                                                                           *
*                                                                           *
*                                                                           *
*                                                                           *
*****************************************************************************
CDrawApp    P - Add a Point   U - Undo Last Add
Main Menu   B - Add a Box     C - Clear Grid      X - Exit CDrawApp
            T - Add Text      S - Show Grid       Enter command:
```

Now use the `B` command to enter a box:

```
CDrawApp    P - Add a Point   U - Undo Last Add
Main Menu   B - Add a Box     C - Clear Grid      X - Exit CDrawApp
            T - Add Text      S - Show Grid       Enter command: b
Add Box Menu
 Upper Left Corner:
  x-coordinate:
```

You will have to enter two points and a character to specify a box. Enter `5` for the x-coordinate of the upper-left corner and `1` for its y-coordinate:

```
Add Box Menu
 Upper Left Corner:
  x-coordinate: 5
  y-coordinate: 1
 Lower Right Corner:
  x-coordinate:
```

Enter `70` for the x-coordinate of the lower-right corner and `18` for its y-coordinate:

```
Add Box Menu
 Upper Left Corner:
  x-coordinate: 5
  y-coordinate: 1
 Lower Right Corner:
  x-coordinate: 70
  y-coordinate: 18
 Character:
```

Finally, set the box character to the equals sign (=):

```
Add Box Menu
 Upper Left Corner:
  x-coordinate: 5
  y-coordinate: 1
 Lower Right Corner:
  x-coordinate: 70
  y-coordinate: 18
 Character: =

CDrawApp     P - Add a Point    U - Undo Last Add
Main Menu    B - Add a Box      C - Clear Grid       X - Exit CDrawApp
             T - Add Text       S - Show Grid        Enter command:
```

Go ahead and redisplay the grid using the `ShowGrid` command:

```
*****************************************************************************
*                                                                           *
*     ==================================================================    *
*     =                                                                =    *
*     =                                                                =    *
*     =                                                                =    *
*     =                                                                =    *
*     =                                                                =    *
*     =                                                                =    *
*     =                                                                =    *
*     =                                                                =    *
*     =                             X                                  =    *
*     =                                                                =    *
*     =                                                                =    *
*     =                                                                =    *
*     =                                                                =    *
*     =                                                                =    *
*     =                                                                =    *
*     =                                                                =    *
*     ==================================================================    *
*                                                                           *
*****************************************************************************
```

```
CDrawApp     P - Add a Point    U - Undo Last Add
Main Menu    B - Add a Box      C - Clear Grid      X - Exit CDrawApp
             T - Add Text       S - Show Grid       Enter command:
```

Notice how the box was added to the grid. Now, let's add text to the grid. Enter `T` to bring up the Add Text Menu prompt:

```
Add Text Menu
 Location:
  x-coordinate:
```

Set the x-coordinate to `36` and the y-coordinate to `11`:

```
Add Text Menu
 Location:
  x-coordinate: 36
  y-coordinate: 11
 Text:
```

Enter `I love Java.` at the `Text:` prompt:

```
Add Text Menu
 Location:
  x-coordinate: 36
  y-coordinate: 11
 Text: I love Java.
```

The `CDrawApp` main menu is displayed. Use the `Show Grid` command to redisplay the grid:

```
******************************************************************************
*                                                                            *
*     ===================================================================    *
*     =                                                                 =    *
*     =                                                                 =    *
*     =                                                                 =    *
*     =                                                                 =    *
*     =                                                                 =    *
*     =                                                                 =    *
*     =                                                                 =    *
*     =                                                                 =    *
*     =                              X                                  =    *
*     =                               I love Java.                      =    *
*     =                                                                 =    *
*     =                                                                 =    *
*     =                                                                 =    *
*     =                                                                 =    *
*     =                                                                 =    *
*     =                                                                 =    *
*     ===================================================================    *
*                                                                            *
******************************************************************************
CDrawApp     P - Add a Point    U - Undo Last Add
Main Menu    B - Add a Box      C - Clear Grid      X - Exit CDrawApp
             T - Add Text       S - Show Grid       Enter command:
```

Enter `U` to invoke the `Undo Last Add` command. This results in the text being deleted from the display. Verify this by redisplaying the grid. Then clear the grid by entering `C`. Once again, use the `Show Grid` command to verify that the command worked correctly.

You have now covered all the commands of `CDrawApp`. Enter `X` to exit the program.

`CDrawApp`'s Implementation of Object-Oriented Concepts

The purpose of `CDrawApp` isn't to bolster your graphics production capabilities. It is used as a comprehensive example of how Java classes, objects, and methods can be used to implement the object-oriented programming concepts studied earlier in the chapter.

In building `CDrawApp`, you created 11 classes, 6 of which extended classes other than `Object`. The class hierarchy for the `CDrawApp` program is shown in Figure 5.4.

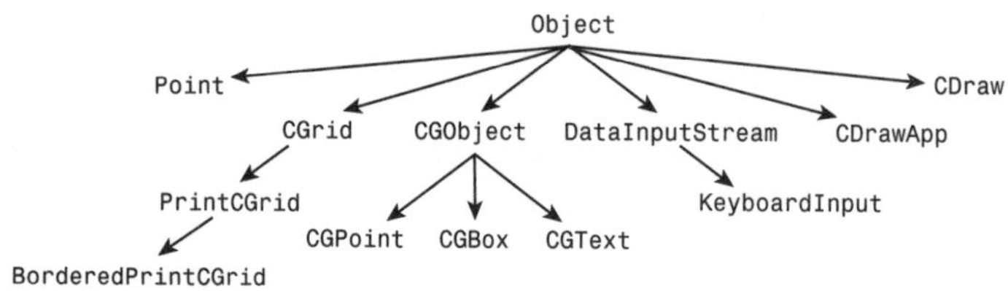

FIGURE 5.4.
The `CDrawApp` *class hierarchy.*

The development of the `CGrid`, `PrintCGrid`, and `BorderedPrintCGrid` classes shows how subclasses extend the data and methods inherited from their parents to successively add more features to their branch of the class hierarchy. `CGrid` provides the basic data and methods to implement character grid objects. `PrintCGrid` adds the capability to add and remove objects from the grid, and to display these objects on the console window. `BorderedPrintCGrid` uses the methods provided by `CGrid` and `PrintCGrid` to develop additional capabilities for displaying a bordered grid.

The `CGObject`, `CGPoint`, `CGBox`, and `CGText` classes are examples of how `abstract` classes are used to specify the behavior of their subclasses. `CGObject` provides the `addToGrid()` method, which is inherited by all of its subclasses. It defines the `display()` and `describe()` methods as `abstract`, requiring all subclasses to implement these methods in a manner that is applicable to the subclass. `CGPoint`, `CGBox`, and `CGText` define specific types of graphical objects that fit within the framework established by `CGObject`.

The `drawGrid()` method of `PrintCGrid` utilizes the `CGObject` class as an abstraction for dealing with objects in the `displayList[]`. The dynamic binding and polymorphic capabilities of the Java compiler and runtime system enable `drawGrid()` to interact with objects of subclasses of `CGObject` without specific knowledge of their class type.

The grid object of class `BorderedPrintCGrid` that is used in the `CDraw` class provides an example of advanced polymorphic behavior. When `grid`'s `show()` method is invoked, the `show()` method of the `PrintCGrid` class is used. The `show()` method invokes the `PrintCGrid` `drawGrid()` method to cause each object in the `displayList[]` to display itself on the grid. It then invokes the `displayGrid()` method to display the grid. `BorderedPrintCGrid` overrides the `displayGrid()`

method of `PrintCGrid`. Which `displayGrid()` method does `show()` invoke—that of `PrintCGrid` or `BorderedPrintCGrid`? The `show()` method is able to discern from runtime information that it is being invoked for an object of class `BorderedPrintCGrid`, so it uses the `BorderedPrintCGrid` `displayGrid()` method. This method checks to see if the `useBorder` variable is `true`, and if so, displays a grid with a border. However, if `useBorder` is `false`, it invokes the `displayGrid()` method of `PrintCGrid`.

The `Point` class is an example of encapsulation. It has a modular, well-defined interface and hides the details of its implementation from other classes. The x- and y-coordinates of a point are inaccessible to methods outside of the `Point` class. Even the methods within `Point` use the `x()` and `y()` methods to access these values. The `Point` class, because of this encapsulation, can be reused in many other applications that use two-dimensional grids.

The `KeyboardInput` class shows how classes from the Java API may be extended by user-defined subclasses. It uses the `readLine()` method from `DataInputStream`, the `charAt()` method from the `String` class, and the `intValue()` method of the `Integer` class to provide convenient methods for accessing user input lines.

The `CDraw` and `CDrawApp` classes illustrate the principle of object composition. They assemble the other classes defined in this chapter into a short, two-page program that uses all of the features provided by these classes.

Summary

In this chapter you have learned some general object-oriented programming concepts and how these concepts apply to Java programs. You have learned how to use classes to develop a sample Java program that illustrates the fundamental elements of Java object-oriented programming.

The classes you developed in this chapter will be reused in Chapters 6 and 7. In Chapter 6 you'll learn how to use interfaces to support features of multiple inheritance. In Chapter 7 you'll learn how to use exceptions to respond to errors and other anomalies during program execution.

6

Interfaces

In this chapter you'll learn how to use Java interfaces to provide a common set of methods by which a group of classes can be accessed and to implement features of multiple inheritance. You'll cover the use of interface constants and learn how to declare objects using interface types. You will also learn how to extend and combine interfaces. When you finish this chapter, you'll be able to use interfaces with your Java classes.

The Purpose of Java Interfaces

The Java interface construct is borrowed from the Objective-C protocol. It is used to identify a common set of methods for the group of classes that implement the interface. It is also used to share constants between classes. Interfaces are used to provide the benefits of multiple inheritance without its implementation difficulties. They allow several classes to share a standard set of methods and constants without requiring these methods and constants to be implemented by a common superclass.

Interfaces provide a standard framework for accessing classes. They are analogous to the interfaces that we encounter in everyday life. Any large class of real-world objects that you regularly manipulate usually has a standard interface. Radios and televisions provide a common set of controls for tuning channels and adjusting audio volume. Cars come with a standard interface for steering, throttling, and braking. Automated bank tellers provide the same general interface for performing bank transactions.

To realize the potential use of Java interfaces, consider the diversity of objects that are manipulated by GUI-building programs. Such programs provide the capability to generate graphical user interfaces by clicking on interface controls and dragging them to appropriate places on the windows and dialog boxes being developed. The objects implementing these controls may support many different sets of methods. For example, one subset of the controls may be required to support cut, copy, and paste operations. These methods might be grouped into an `EditObject` interface. Another subset of the interface controls may be required to support click and double-click operations. These objects might implement a `Clickable` interface. Another subset may support drag-and-drop operations and implement the `Draggable` interface. Other groups of objects may implement multiple interfaces. For example, there might be objects that are both `Clickable` and `Draggable`.

The Benefits of Interfaces

Interfaces provide many advantages to the Java programmer. One is that they allow standard sets of methods to be used across the class hierarchy. For example, you can define the `Editable` interface to support cut, copy, and paste operations. The `Editable` interface can then be implemented by relevant classes and establish a uniform approach to implementing these common operations.

Interface types allow objects to be referenced by the methods they support without considering their location in the class hierarchy. They make maximal use of dynamic binding, allowing objects to be accessed independently of their implementation details. For example, parameters can be defined as interface types and used by methods. These methods can invoke the interface methods of their arguments without having to determine the classes to which the arguments belong.

Interfaces also support *selective* multiple inheritance. They allow various subsets of the features supported by different classes to be shared without mandating that all features of these classes be uniformly imposed as the result of inheritance.

Finally, because interfaces are declared independently of classes, they are unaffected by changes to specific classes or to the class hierarchy as a whole.

Declaring Interfaces

Interfaces, like classes, are not objects, but type definitions that can be used to declare an object. Interfaces are declared as follows:

```
InterfaceModifiers interface InterfaceName ExtendsClause InterfaceBody
```

The allowed interface modifiers are `abstract` and `public`. By default, all interfaces are `abstract`. The `public` access specifier allows interfaces to be accessed outside of the package in which they are declared, in the same manner as with classes. Only one class or interface may be declared `public` in a given compilation unit. The compilation unit must have the same name as its `public` interface or class. The `extends` clause is similar to the class `extends` clause and is covered later in this chapter.

The body of an interface begins with an opening brace (`{`), consists of zero or more variable or method declarations, and ends with a closing brace (`}`).

All variables declared in an interface body are assumed to be both `static` and `final`, must have a constant initializer, and are implemented as constant class variables.

All methods declared in an interface body are assumed to be `abstract` and do not have method bodies. Only access methods can be declared within an interface; constructors are not allowed. The access specifier of a method is that of the interface in which it is declared.

An example of a simple interface declaration is as follows:

```
public interface Clickable {
 void click();
 void doubleClick();
}
```

This `Clickable` interface is declared as `public` so that it can be accessed outside its package. It contains two method declarations, `click()` and `doubleClick()`. These methods must be supported by all classes that implement the `Clickable` interface.

Implementing Interfaces

The interfaces implemented by a class are identified in the `implements` clause of the class declaration. For example, the following class implements the `Scrollable` and `Clickable` interfaces:

```
class ExampleClass implements Scrollable, Clickable {
}
```

A non-`abstract` class must implement all interface methods that are not implemented by its superclasses. `abstract` classes are not required to implement interface methods. They can defer interface implementation to their non-`abstract` subclasses.

The `CDrawApp` Interface Example

To provide a concrete example of the use of interfaces, we'll extend the `CDrawApp` program, introduced in Chapter 5, "Classes and Objects," to include support for editable objects. *Editable objects* are objects that display text on the grid and can be edited using the `CGTextEdit` interface. The `CGText` class will be modified to support this interface. The `CGPoint` and `CGBox` classes will be extended by the subclasses, `CGTextPoint` and `CGTextBox`, both of which provide the capability to display text on the grid. The `CGText`, `CGTextPoint`, and `CGTextBox` classes will implement the `CGTextEdit` interface. Figure 6.1 shows the extensions to the Chapter 5 class hierarchy that were made to support this example.

FIGURE 6.1.
Extensions to the `CDrawApp` *class hierarchy.*

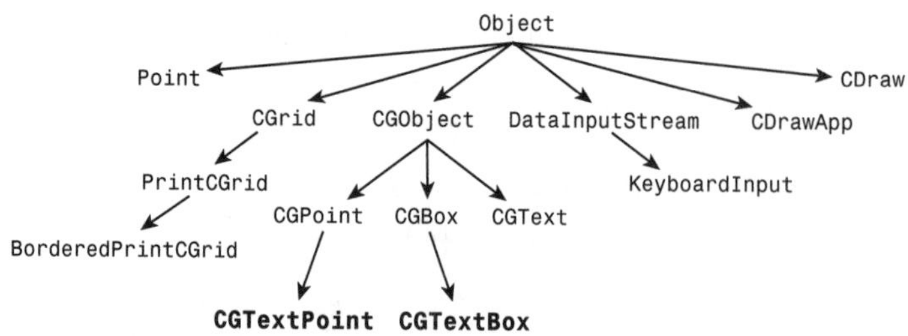

Before going on to edit and compile the source code files for this example, be sure to create a `ch06` subdirectory under `c:\java\jdg`. This subdirectory should be used to store all the source Java files that you develop in this chapter.

The `CGTextEdit` Interface

The `CGTextEdit` interface is quite simple. Its source code is shown in Listing 6.1.

Listing 6.1. The `CGTextEdit` interface source code.

```
package jdg.ch06;

public interface CGTextEdit {
 public void replaceText(String s);
 public void upperCase();
 public void lowerCase();
}
```

The `CGTextEdit` interface source code declares three methods: `replaceText()`, `upperCase()`, and `lowerCase()`. These methods must be provided by all classes that implement the `CGTextEdit` interface. The `replaceString()` method is used to replace the text associated with an object with the text contained in the `String`'s parameter. The `upperCase()` and `lowerCase()` methods are used to convert the text associated with an object to upper- and lowercase, respectively. `CGTextEdit` and all its interfaces are declared as `public`, allowing them to be accessed outside of the `jdg.ch06` package. The `public` modifiers used with the method declarations are redundant. Any method declared in a `public` interface is `public`, by default.

After you have entered the `CGTextEdit` interface into the file, `CGTextEdit.java`, use `javac` to compile `CGTextEdit.java`. Do this from within the `ch06` directory.

Updating the `CGText` Class

The `CGText` class, developed in Chapter 5, will be updated to implement the `CGTextEdit` interface. The easiest way to do this is to copy `CGText.java` from the `c:\java\jdg\ch05` directory to the `c:\java\jdg\ch06` directory and then edit it. Its source code is shown in Listing 6.2.

Listing 6.2. The `CGText` class source code.

```
package jdg.ch06;

import jdg.ch05.CGObject;
import jdg.ch05.Point;
import jdg.ch05.PrintCGrid;
import java.lang.System;

// CGText.java

public class CGText extends CGObject implements CGTextEdit {
 // Variable declarations
 String text;

 // Method declarations
 public CGText(Point p,String s) {
  location = p;
  drawCharacter = ' ';
  text = s;
 }
```

continues

Listing 6.2. continued

```
 public void display(PrintCGrid grid) {
  Point p = new Point(location);
  for(int i=0;i<text.length();++i){
   grid.putCharAt(text.charAt(i),p);
   p = p.add(1,0);
  }
 }
 public void describe() {
  System.out.println("CGText "+location.toString()+" "+text);
 }
 public void replaceText(String s) {
  text=s;
 }
 public void upperCase() {
  text = text.toUpperCase();
 }
 public void lowerCase() {
  text = text.toLowerCase();
 }
}
```

All you need to do is to change the `package` statement, add the `import` statements, edit the class declaration, and add the last three methods that implement the `CGTextEdit` interface.

Because this class is contained in the `jdg.ch06` package, you need to import the `CGObject`, `Point`, and `PrintCGrid` classes from the `jdg.ch05` package.

The class declaration is changed to add the `implements` clause with the `CGTextEdit` interface.

The three new methods are all very simple. The `replaceText()` method assigns `text` to the new value passed by the `s` parameter. The `upperCase()` and `lowerCase()` methods use the `toUpperCase()` and `toLowerCase()` methods of the `String` class to perform their conversions.

You should compile the new `CGText.java` before moving on to the next class.

The `CGTextPoint` Class

The `CGTextPoint` class extends the `CGPoint` class to add the capability to display text along with the character point. (See Listing 6.3.)

Listing 6.3. The `CGTextPoint` class source code.

```
package jdg.ch06;

import jdg.ch05.Point;
import jdg.ch05.CGPoint;
import jdg.ch05.PrintCGrid;
import java.lang.System;

// CGTextPoint.java
```

```
public class CGTextPoint extends CGPoint implements CGTextEdit {
 // Variable declarations
 String text;

 // Method declarations
 public CGTextPoint(Point p,char ch,String s) {
  super(p,ch);
  text = s;
 }
 public CGTextPoint(Point p,String s) {
  super(p);
  text = s;
 }
 public CGTextPoint(Point p,char ch) {
  super(p,ch);
  text = "";
 }
 public CGTextPoint(Point p) {
  super(p);
  text = "";
 }
 public void display(PrintCGrid grid) {
  super.display(grid);
  Point p = location.add(1,0);
  for(int i=0;i<text.length();++i){
   grid.putCharAt(text.charAt(i),p);
   p = p.add(1,0);
  }
 }
 public void describe() {
  System.out.print("CGTextPoint "+String.valueOf(drawCharacter)+" ");
  System.out.println(location.toString()+" "+text);
 }
 public void replaceText(String s) {
  text=s;
 }
 public void upperCase() {
  text = text.toUpperCase();
 }
 public void lowerCase() {
  text = text.toLowerCase();
 }
}
```

`CGTextPoint` declares the variable `text`. This variable is used to store the text associated with the point. It provides four constructors, each of which uses the `super()` constructor call statement to invoke the constructors of the `CGPoint` class. The four constructors allow `CGTextPoint` to be constructed using different combinations of parameters.

The `display()` method invokes the `display()` method of its superclass to display the point at its location on the grid. It then displays the value of the text variable to the immediate right of this point. The `describe()` method displays a description of the text point on the console window. The `replaceText()`, `upperCase()`, and `lowerCase()` methods are the same as those of the new `CGText` class.

The CGTextBox Class

The CGTextBox class extends the CGBox class to add the capability to display text within a box. (See Listing 6.4.) The size of the box is automatically fitted to the size of the text to be displayed.

Listing 6.4. The CGTextBox class source code.

```
package jdg.ch06;

import jdg.ch05.Point;
import jdg.ch05.CGBox;
import jdg.ch05.PrintCGrid;
import java.lang.System;

// CGTextBox.java

public class CGTextBox extends CGBox implements CGTextEdit {
 // Variable declarations
 String text;

 // Method declarations
 public CGTextBox(Point ulCorner, char ch, String s) {
  super(ulCorner,ulCorner.add(s.length()+1,2),ch);
  text = s;
 }
 public CGTextBox(Point ulCorner, String s) {
  super(ulCorner,ulCorner.add(s.length()+1,2));
  text = s;
 }
 public void display(PrintCGrid grid) {
  super.display(grid);
  Point p = location.add(1,1);
  for(int i=0;i<text.length();++i){
   grid.putCharAt(text.charAt(i),p);
   p = p.add(1,0);
  }
 }
 public void describe() {
  System.out.print("CGTextBox "+String.valueOf(drawCharacter)+" ");
  System.out.println(location.toString()+" "+lr.toString()+" "+text);
 }
 public void replaceText(String s) {
  text=s;
  lr=location.add(text.length()+1,2);
 }
 public void upperCase() {
  text = text.toUpperCase();
 }
 public void lowerCase() {
  text = text.toLowerCase();
 }
}
```

The CGTextBox class source code defines the text variable in the same manner as the CGTextPoint class and provides two constructors for initializing objects of its class. Both constructors use calls to the CGBox class to support the initialization. The parameters to these calls calculate the lower-right corner of the box using the upper-left corner as a reference point and adding horizontal and vertical offsets that size the box based on the length of the text it contains.

The display() method displays a box using the display() method of its parent. It then displays text within the box. The describe() method prints a box's parameters on the console window.

The upperCase() and lowerCase() methods are the same as those of the CGTextPoint class, but the replaceText() method is different. It updates the lr variable to correctly resize the box based on changes to the length of the text variable.

Updating the CDraw Class

The CDraw class is updated to support the Edit Text command. This requires changes to all its access methods except the addText() method. The source code of the CDrawApp and CDraw classes is shown in Listing 6.5.

Listing 6.5. The CDrawApp and CDraw classes.

```
package jdg.ch06;

import jdg.ch05.Point;
import jdg.ch05.CGrid;
import jdg.ch05.PrintCGrid;
import jdg.ch05.BorderedPrintCGrid;
import jdg.ch05.CGObject;
import jdg.ch05.CGPoint;
import jdg.ch05.CGBox;
import jdg.ch05.KeyboardInput;
import java.lang.System;
import java.lang.ClassCastException;
import java.io.IOException;

class CDrawApp {
 public static void main(String args[]) throws IOException {
  CDraw program = new CDraw();
  program.run();
 }
}

class CDraw {
 // Variable declarations
 static KeyboardInput kbd = new KeyboardInput(System.in);
 BorderedPrintCGrid grid;

 // Method declarations
 CDraw() {
```

continues

Listing 6.5. continued

```
  grid = new BorderedPrintCGrid();
 }
 void run() throws IOException {
  boolean finished = false;
  do {
   char command = getCommand();
   switch(command){
    case 'P':
     addPoint();
     System.out.println();
     break;
    case 'B':
     addBox();
     System.out.println();
     break;
    case 'T':
     addText();
     System.out.println();
     break;
    case 'U':
     grid.deleteLastObject();
     System.out.println();
     break;
    case 'C':
     grid.clearGrid();
     System.out.println();
     break;
    case 'S':
     grid.show();
     break;
   case 'E':
    editText();
    break;
   case 'X':
    finished = true;
    default:
     System.out.println();
   }
  } while (!finished);
 }
 char getCommand() throws IOException {
  System.out.print("CDrawApp    P - Add a Point   U - Undo Last Add");
  System.out.println("   E - Edit Text");
  System.out.print("Main Menu   B - Add a Box     C - Clear Grid");
  System.out.println("      X - Exit CDrawApp");
  System.out.print("            T - Add Text      S - Show Grid");
  System.out.print("       Enter command: ");
  System.out.flush();
  return Character.toUpperCase(kbd.getChar());
 }
 void addPoint() throws IOException {
  System.out.println("Add Point Menu");
  System.out.println(" Location:");
  Point p = kbd.getPoint();
  System.out.print(" Character: ");
  System.out.flush();
```

```
 char ch = kbd.getChar();
 if(ch==' ') ch = '+';
 System.out.print(" Add text (y/n): ");
 System.out.flush();
 if('Y'==Character.toUpperCase(kbd.getChar())) {
  System.out.print("  Text: ");
  System.out.flush();
  String s = kbd.getText();
  CGTextPoint cgtp = new CGTextPoint(p,ch,s);
  cgtp.addToGrid(grid);
 }else{
  CGPoint cgp = new CGPoint(p,ch);
  cgp.addToGrid(grid);
 }
}
void addBox() throws IOException {
 System.out.println("Add Box Menu");
 System.out.println(" Upper Left Corner:");
 Point ul = kbd.getPoint();
 System.out.print(" Add text (y/n): ");
 System.out.flush();
 if('Y'==Character.toUpperCase(kbd.getChar())) {
  System.out.print("  Text: ");
  System.out.flush();
  String s = kbd.getText();
  System.out.print(" Character: ");
  System.out.flush();
  char ch = kbd.getChar();
  if(ch==' ') ch = '#';
  CGTextBox cgtb = new CGTextBox(ul,ch,s);
  cgtb.addToGrid(grid);
 }else{
  System.out.println(" Lower Right Corner:");
  Point lr = kbd.getPoint();
  System.out.print(" Character: ");
  System.out.flush();
  char ch = kbd.getChar();
  if(ch==' ') ch = '#';
  CGBox box = new CGBox(ul,lr,ch);
  box.addToGrid(grid);
 }
}
void addText() throws IOException {
 System.out.println("Add Text Menu");
 System.out.println(" Location:");
 Point p = kbd.getPoint();
 System.out.print(" Text: ");
 System.out.flush();
 String text = kbd.getText();
 CGText cgt = new CGText(p,text);
 cgt.addToGrid(grid);
}
void editText() throws IOException {
 System.out.println("Current Objects:");
 int numObjects = grid.getNumObjects();
 for(int i=0;i<numObjects;++i){
  System.out.print(" "+String.valueOf(i)+" ");
```

continues

Listing 6.5. continued

```
   grid.getObject(i).describe();
  }
  if(numObjects > 0){
   System.out.print("Select an object to edit: ");
   System.out.flush();
   int objIndex = kbd.getInt();
   CGObject obj = grid.getObject(objIndex);
   try {
    editText((CGTextEdit) obj);
   }catch (ClassCastException ex){
    System.out.println("Object is not editable.");
   }
  }else System.out.println("(none)");
  System.out.println();
 }
 void editText(CGTextEdit obj) throws IOException {
  System.out.println("Text Edit Menu");
  System.out.println(" R - Replace Text");
  System.out.println(" L - Lower Case");
  System.out.println(" U - Upper Case");
  System.out.print("Enter command: ");
  System.out.flush();
  char ch = kbd.getChar();
  ch = Character.toUpperCase(ch);
  switch(ch) {
   case 'R':
    System.out.print("Enter new text: ");
    System.out.flush();
    String s = kbd.getText();
    obj.replaceText(s);
    break;
   case 'L':
    obj.lowerCase();
    break;
   case 'U':
    obj.upperCase();
    break;
  }
 }
}
```

The `run()`, `getCommand()`, `addPoint()`, and `addBox()` methods are updated to support the Edit Text command. The two overloaded `editText()` methods are added to process this command.

The `switch` statement of the `run()` method adds the `'E'` case to its list of command options, calling the `editText()` method to process the Edit Text command. The `getCommand()` method adds the Edit Text command to its menu display.

The `addPoint()` and `addBox()` methods query the user to determine whether text should be added to the point or box. If the user declines to add text, a `CGPoint` or `CGBox` object is created and added to the grid. If the user indicates that he or she wants to add text to the point or box, the user is prompted to enter the text. In this case, `CGTextPoint` and `CGTextBox` objects are created and added to the grid.

The two `editText()` methods share the same name but provide completely different processing. The first `editText()` method is invoked when the user enters the Edit Text command. It displays a list of the objects that are currently added to the grid. It does this by using the `getNumObjects()` method of the `PrintCGrid` class to find out how many objects there are and then retrieving those objects using the `getObject()` method of the `PrintCGrid` class. The following line of code concatenates two method invocations:

```
grid.getObject(i).describe();
```

It retrieves an object of class `CGObject` by invoking the `getObject()` method of the `PrintCGrid` class. It then invokes the object's `describe()` method so that it will display its description on the console window. If there are no objects currently added to the grid, the `editText()` method indicates this fact by displaying `(none)` to the console window. Otherwise, the user is prompted to enter the number of the object to edit. This number is the number listed in the current object display. The number entered by the user is used to retrieve the object to be edited using the `getObject()` method. After the object is retrieved, the `editText()` method tries to edit the text associated with the object by invoking the second `editText()` method. If the object does not implement the `CGTextEdit` interface, a `ClassCastException` is thrown during the invocation of the second `editText()` method. The first `editText()` method catches this exception and reports the selected object as not being editable.

The second `editText()` method displays a Text Edit Menu prompt to the user and invokes the `replaceText()`, `lowerCase()`, and `upperCase()` methods to process the commands entered by the user.

Running the Example

The `CDrawApp` program is compiled and executed in the same manner as its Chapter 5 predecessor. You should notice the additional Edit Text command provided in the `CDrawApp` main menu:

```
C:\java\jdg\ch06>java jdg.ch06.CDrawApp
CDrawApp     P - Add a Point   U - Undo Last Add    E - Edit Text
Main Menu    B - Add a Box     C - Clear Grid       X - Exit CDrawApp
             T - Add Text      S - Show Grid        Enter command:
```

We'll add a few objects to the grid, display them, and then edit their text. After you learn how to use the new program, we'll discuss its features as they relate to interfaces.

Enter `P` to add a point to the grid. Set its x-coordinate to `60`, its y-coordinate to `10`, and its draw character to `@`:

```
Add Point Menu
 Location:
  x-coordinate: 60
  y-coordinate: 10
 Character: @
 Add text (y/n):
```

You are asked whether you want to add text to the point. Press `Y` to add text. You are then prompted to add your text. Enter `at sign` as your text, as shown in the following display output:

```
Add Point Menu
 Location:
  x-coordinate: 60
  y-coordinate: 10
 Character: @
 Add text (y/n): y
  Text:  at sign
```

The `CDrawApp` main menu is then redisplayed. Enter `B` to add a box. Set the box's upper-left corner as follows:

```
Add Box Menu
 Upper Left Corner:
  x-coordinate: 4
  y-coordinate: 4
 Add text (y/n):
```

Enter `Y` to add text to the box. You are prompted to enter your text. Enter the text `Java's interfaces support multiple inheritance.`. Then set the box's draw character to `+`. Your display output should look like the following:

```
Add Box Menu
 Upper Left Corner:
  x-coordinate: 4
  y-coordinate: 4
 Add text (y/n): y
  Text: Java's interfaces support multiple inheritance.
 Character: +
```

Enter `B` to enter another box. This box will not contain any text. Enter the coordinates for the box's corners, as follows:

```
Add Box Menu
 Upper Left Corner:
  x-coordinate: 65
  y-coordinate: 15
 Add text (y/n): n
 Lower Right Corner:
  x-coordinate: 72
  y-coordinate: 18
```

Then set its draw character to a hyphen:

```
Character: -
```

You should have noticed that when a box contains text, its lower-right corner is not specified. That's because the program computes it based on the length of the text to be displayed with the box.

You're almost done adding objects to the grid. Enter `T` to add text to the grid. Set the text's location and value as follows:

```
Add Text Menu
 Location:
  x-coordinate: 1
  y-coordinate: 18
 Text: UPPER CASE Or lower case
```

You now have enough objects to work with. Enter `S` to display the grid. It should look like this:

```
*****************************************************************************
*                                                                           *
*                                                                           *
*                                                                           *
*                                                                           *
*    +++++++++++++++++++++++++++++++++++++++++++++++++                      *
*    +Java's interfaces support multiple inheritance.+                      *
*    +++++++++++++++++++++++++++++++++++++++++++++++++                      *
*                                                                           *
*                                                                           *
*                                                                           *
*                                                            @ at sign      *
*                                                                           *
*                                                                           *
*                                                                           *
*                                                                           *
*                                                                 --------  *
*                                                                 -      -  *
*                                                                 -      -  *
* UPPER CASE Or lower case                                        --------  *
*                                                                           *
*****************************************************************************
```

Let's start editing these objects. Enter `E` to select an object to edit:

```
CDrawApp    P - Add a Point   U - Undo Last Add   E - Edit Text
Main Menu   B - Add a Box     C - Clear Grid      X - Exit CDrawApp
            T - Add Text      S - Show Grid       Enter command: e
Current Objects:
 0 CGTextPoint @ (60,10)  at sign
 1 CGTextBox + (4,4) (52,6) Java's interfaces support multiple inheritance.
 2 CGBox - (65,15) (72,18)
 3 CGText (1,18) UPPER CASE Or lower case
Select an object to edit:
```

A list of the grid's current objects is displayed. Enter `2` to select the object of class `CGBox`. Because this object does not implement the `CGTextEdit` interface, it is identified as not being editable, as shown in the following console output:

```
Object is not editable.
```

See if you can find where this processing was performed within the `CDraw` class. Enter `E` again to edit another object. The list of current objects is again displayed. Enter `1` to select the object of class `CGTextBox`. The Text Edit Menu prompt is displayed as follows:

```
Text Edit Menu
 R - Replace Text
 L - Lower Case
 U - Upper Case
Enter command:
```

This menu allows you to use the methods of the `CGTextEdit` interface to edit the objects that implement the interface. Enter `R` to replace the text associated with the `CGTextBox` object. You are then prompted to enter the new text for this object. Enter `interfaces` to complete the editing. Your display should contain the following output:

```
Enter command: r
Enter new text: interfaces
```

Enter `S` to see how the grid was updated. Notice how the size of the `CGTextBox` was changed to fit the size of the text it contains:

```
++++++++++++
+interfaces+
++++++++++++
```

Enter `E` and then `0` to edit the object of class `CGTextPoint`. Then type `U` to change it to uppercase. Use the `show` command to verify that the text has been changed to uppercase.

Enter `E`, `3`, and `L` in succession to change the case of the text contained in the `CGText` object. Use the Show Grid command to redisplay the grid:

```
******************************************************************************
*                                                                            *
*                                                                            *
*                                                                            *
*                                                                            *
*    ++++++++++++                                                            *
*    +interfaces+                                                            *
*    ++++++++++++                                                            *
*                                                                            *
*                                                                            *
*                                                                            *
*                                                             @ AT SIGN      *
*                                                                            *
*                                                                            *
*                                                                            *
*                                                                            *
*                                                                  --------  *
*                                                                  -      -  *
*                                                                  -      -  *
* upper case or lower case                                         --------  *
*                                                                            *
******************************************************************************
```

Now type `X` to exit the `CDrawApp` program.

Example Summary

The `CDrawApp` program illustrates the use of a simple interface. The `CGTextEdit` interface, used in this example, provides a common set of access methods to three classes on different branches of the `CDrawApp` class hierarchy, as shown in Figure 6.2.

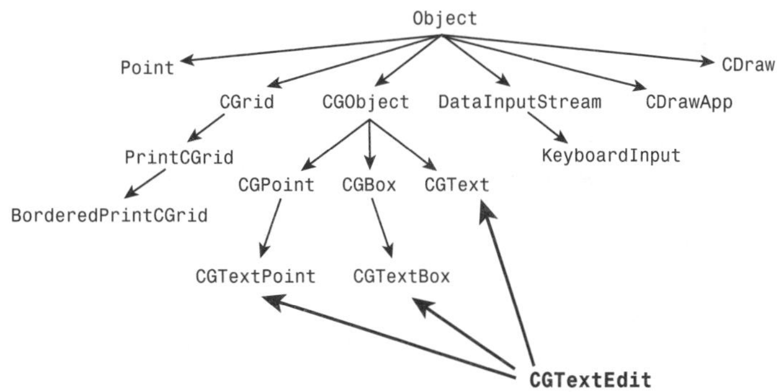

FIGURE 6.2.
The `CGTextEdit` *interface.*

Providing a standard interface to the `CGText`, `CGTextPoint`, and `CGTextBox` classes makes it possible to manipulate objects of these classes as if they belong to a single type. This is illustrated in the second `editText()` method of the `CDraw` class. This method takes an object of the `CGTextEdit` interface type as an argument and edits that object without having to know to which class the object belongs. Although the methods of the `CGTextEdit` interface are very simple, the capability provided by the interface is not. The second `editText()` method is able to manipulate any object that implements the `CGTextEdit` interface, even those that may be defined in the future.

The first `editText()` method of the `CDraw` class also provides an interesting example of the use of interfaces. The first part of the method displays the list of current objects, one of which is selected by the user. The `try` statement tests to see if the selected object implements the `CGTextEdit` interface by trying to cast it to an object of interface type `CGTextEdit`. The casting is performed when the object is used as an argument to the second `editText()` method:

```
try {
 editText((CGTextEdit) obj);
}catch (ClassCastException ex){
 System.out.println("Object is not editable.");
}
```

Casting is the process of changing the type by which an object is accessed. It is covered in Chapter 11, "Language Summary." An object can be cast to an interface type if the object implements the interface; otherwise, a `ClassCastException` is thrown.

The `editText()` method uses casting to determine whether an object implements the `CGTextEdit` interface. If the object implements the `CGTextEdit` interface, the casting is allowed and the second `editText()` method is invoked to edit the object. If the object does not implement the `CGTextEdit` interface, an exception is thrown. This exception is caught by the `catch` part of the `try` statement and the object is identified as not editable.

Using Interfaces as Abstract Types

The preceding example shows how interfaces can be used to declare method parameters. Such declarations require only that the objects passed as arguments during a method invocation implement the identified interface.

In the following example, the `restart()` method of `ExampleClass` declares the `currentSelection` parameter to be of type `ExampleInterface`. The `restart()` method has no idea what class of object is passed to it via `currentSelection`. It only requires it to implement the `ExampleInterface`. The fact that the correct methods are called for the object identified by `currentSelection` is an example of *polymorphism*. The code for `ExampleInterface` follows:

```
interface ExampleInterface {
    void rewind();
    void play();
    void stop();
}
class ExampleClass {
    void restart(ExampleInterface currentSelection) {
         currentSelection.stop();
         currentSelection.rewind();
         currentSelection.play();
    }
}
```

The `restart()` method uses the `ExampleInterface` methods of the `currentSelection` object to perform its processing. Note that `ExampleClass` does not need to implement `ExampleInterface`. The interface only needs to be implemented by the object passed via the `currentSelection` parameter.

Interface Constants

The variables declared in an interface body are available as constants to classes that implement the interface. This enables pools of related constants to be defined and made available to classes that require use of these constants. Common constant pools are color constants, mathematical constants, and formatting constants. Variables declared in an interface are implicitly `static` and `final` and must be initialized in their declaration.

The following example shows how interface variables are used to define a constant pool. Create a file in your `ch06` directory called `ColorConstants.java` and enter the code shown in Listing 6.6.

Listing 6.6. The `ColorConstants` interface defines red, blue, and green constants.

```
package jdg.ch06;

public interface ColorConstants {
 int red = 0xff0000;
 int green = 0xff00;
 int blue = 0xff;
}
```

Compile this code using `javac`. Then create another file called `ColorTestApp.java`, as shown in Listing 6.7.

Listing 6.7. The `ColorTestApp` class source code.

```
package jdg.ch06;

import java.lang.System;

class ColorTestApp implements ColorConstants {
 public static void main(String args[]) {
  System.out.println(red);
  System.out.println(green);
  System.out.println(blue);
 }
}
```

Compile `ColorTestApp.java` and execute it using `java`. Your console window should display the following output:

```
C:\java\jdg\ch06>java jdg.ch06.ColorTestApp
16711680
65280
255
```

The `main()` method of the `ColorTestApp` class is able to access the constants defined in the `ColorConstants` interface as if they were inherited variables. The `main()` function displays these hexadecimal constants as decimal integers.

Extending Interfaces

The interface `extends` clause is similar to the `extends` clause used with classes. An interface is allowed to extend more than one interface, but a class can extend only a single class. The extending interface inherits all the methods and constants defined in the interfaces that it extends. When a class implements an interface X, it must implement all methods of all interfaces that X extends.

The following example declares the `MoreTextEdit` interface as extending the `CGTextEdit` interface. All classes that implement the `MoreTextEdit` interface must implement the methods of both `CGTextEdit` and `MoreTextEdit`:

```
interface MoreTextEdit extends CGTextEdit {
 void insertText(int pos, String s);
 void appendText(String s);
}
```

Combining Interfaces

Two or more interfaces may be combined into a single interface through extension. The following example shows how interfaces are combined:

```
interface TV {
 void changeChannel(int channelNumber);
 void changeVolume(int volumeSetting);
}
interface VCR {
 void play();
 void rewind();
 void record();
}
interface TVCR extends TV, VCR {
}
```

Any non-`abstract` class that implements the `TVCR` interface is required to implement the methods of the `TV` interface and the `VCR` interface.

Summary

In this chapter you have learned how to use Java interfaces to provide a common set of methods by which a group of classes can be accessed. You have added the `CGTextEdit` interface to the `CDrawApp` example from Chapter 5 and learned how to declare objects using interface types. You have also learned how to use interface constants. In Chapter 7, "Exceptions," you'll learn how to use Java exceptions to perform error processing.

7

Exceptions

In this chapter you'll learn how to use exceptions to implement error-handling capabilities in your Java programs. You'll learn how to declare exceptions and identify methods that use them. You'll also learn how to throw exceptions in response to error conditions and how to catch exceptions in support of error processing. When you finish this chapter, you'll be able to use exceptions to handle all sorts of errors in your programs.

Eliminating Software Errors

Programs are reliable, in part, because they are able to cope with errors and exceptions that occur during their execution. The development of reliable, error-tolerant software is a multiphase effort that spans program design, coding, compilation, loading, and execution.

The most serious errors are those that are designed into a program. Many design errors can be eliminated by following a sound development approach, using modern software engineering methods, and making a firm commitment to software quality. The use of an object-oriented approach to software development helps to simplify software design, reduce errors, and promote software reliability.

Programming errors initially occur when a software design is translated into source code. Program verification, validation, analysis, and test activities help to eliminate design and programming errors. The implementation of coding standards and code walkthroughs also reduces the likelihood of undetected programming errors.

The Java language eliminates whole classes of errors that result from the use of dangerous programming constructs such as pointers and automatic type conversions. The simplicity and familiarity of the language also reduce the occurrence of programming errors.

The Java compiler and runtime environment help to keep errors from being introduced into executable Java code. The compiler performs extensive type checking to ensure that objects are correctly referenced and updated and that methods are properly invoked. The runtime system duplicates compile-time checks and implements additional checks to verify that executable code follows established rules for program correctness.

With all the error checking that takes place before a program is executed, you might think that it would be unlikely that errors could still creep into a program. They can and always do, in accordance with Murphy's Law. Runtime error and exception handling is used to identify error conditions and perform processing that minimizes their impact.

Error Processing and Exceptions

Java provides superior support for runtime error and exception handling, allowing programs to check for anomalous conditions and respond to them with minimal impact on the normal flow of program execution. This allows error- and exception-handling code to be added easily to existing methods.

Exceptions are generated by the Java runtime system in response to errors that are detected when classes are loaded and their methods are executed. The runtime system is said to *throw* these *runtime exceptions.* Runtime exceptions are objects of the class `java.lang.RuntimeException` or of its subclasses.

Exceptions may also be thrown directly by Java code using the `throw` statement. These exceptions are thrown when code detects a condition that could potentially lead to a program malfunction. The exceptions thrown by user programs are generally not objects of a subclass of `RuntimeException`. These non-runtime exceptions are referred to as *program* exceptions.

> **NOTE**
>
> It is possible for user programs to throw runtime exceptions, but it is almost always a bad programming practice.

Both program and runtime exceptions must be caught in order for them to be processed by exception-handling code. If a thrown exception is not caught, its thread of execution is terminated and an error message is displayed on the Java console window.

The approach used by Java to catch and handle exceptions is to surround blocks of statements for which exception processing is to be performed with a `try` statement. The `try` statement contains a `catch` clause that identifies what processing is to be performed for different types of exceptions. When an exception occurs, the Java runtime system matches the exception to the appropriate `catch` clause. The `catch` clause then handles the exception in an appropriate manner.

Throwing Exceptions

Exceptions are thrown using the `throw` statement. Its syntax is as follows:

```
throw Expression;
```

`Expression` must evaluate to an object that is an instance of a subclass of the `java.lang.Exception` class. The `Exception` class is defined in the Java API. When an exception is thrown, execution does not continue after the `throw` statement. Instead, it continues with any code that catches the exception. If an exception is not caught, the current thread of execution is terminated and an error is displayed on the console window.

For example, the following statement will throw an exception, using an object of class `ExampleException`:

```
throw new ExampleException();
```

The new operator is invoked with the ExampleException() constructor to allocate and initialize an object of class ExampleException. This object is then thrown by the throw statement.

NOTE

A throw statement can throw an object of any class that is a subclass of java.lang.Throwable; however, it is wise to stick with the standard convention of only throwing objects that are a subclass of class Exception.

Declaring Exceptions

A method's throws clause lists the types of exceptions that can be thrown during a method's execution. The throws clause appears immediately before a method's body in the method declaration. For example, the following method throws the ExampleException:

```
public void exampleMethod() throws ExampleException {
 throw new ExampleException();
}
```

When more than one exception may be thrown during the execution of a method, the exceptions are separated by commas in the throws clause. For example, the following method can throw either the Test1Exception or the Test2Exception:

```
public void testMethod(int i) throws Test1Exception, Test2Exception {
 if(i==1) throw new Test1Exception();
 if(i==2) throw new Test2Exception();
}
```

The types identified in the throws clause must be capable of being legally assigned to the exceptions that may be thrown.

Declare or Catch?

If a program exception can be thrown during the execution of a method, the method must either catch the expression or declare it in the throws clause of its method declaration. If an exception is not caught, it must be declared, even if it is thrown in other methods that are invoked during the method's execution.

For example, suppose that method A of object X invokes method B of object Y, which invokes method C of object Z. If method C throws an exception, it must be caught by method C or declared in method C's throws clause. If it is not caught by method C, it must be caught by method B or declared in method B's throws clause. Similarly, if the exception is not caught by method B, it must be caught by method A or declared in method A's throws clause. The handling of exceptions is a hierarchical process that mirrors the method invocation hierarchy (or *call tree*). Either an exception is caught by a method and removed from the hierarchy or it must be declared and propagated back through the method invocation hierarchy.

NOTE

Because runtime exceptions can occur almost anywhere in a program's execution, the catch-or-declare requirement applies only to program exceptions.

The `CDrawApp` programs of Chapters 5, "Classes and Objects," and 6, "Interfaces," provide an extended example of the declaration of uncaught exceptions. The `jdg.ch05.KeyboardInput` class contains three access methods that use the `readLine()` method: `getChar()`, `getText()`, and `getInt()`. The `readLine()` method is inherited from the `DataInputStream` class. It throws an exception of class `IOException`. Because the `getChar()`, `getText()`, and `getInt()` methods invoke the `readLine()` method, they must either catch the exception or declare it in their `throws` clauses. None of these methods catches `IOException`; therefore, all declare it in their `throws` clauses. The `getCommand()` method of class `CDraw` invokes the `getChar()` method of an object of class `KeyboardMethod`. It does not catch `IOExeption`, so it also must declare it. Because the `run()` method of class `CDraw` invokes the `getCommand()` method, it too is faced with catching or declaring `IOException`. Because `run()` declares `IOException` and the `main()` method of `CDrawApp` invokes the `run()` method for a `CDraw` object, it also must declare `IOException` in its `throws` clause.

At this point you are probably coming to the conclusion that it is a lot easier to catch and handle an exception than to declare it throughout the class hierarchy. If so, you have discovered a key benefit of Java's exception-handling approach. Java makes it easier to develop more-reliable software and harder to develop less-reliable software. If you are a lazy programmer like me, Java will exploit your tendency to do things the easy way to encourage you to do things the right way.

Using the `try` Statement

Statements for which exception processing is to be performed are surrounded by a `try` statement with a valid `catch` or `finally` clause. The syntax of the `try` statement is as follows:

```
try TryBlock CatchClauses FinallyClause;
```

At least one `catch` clause or `finally` clause must be defined. More than one `catch` clause may be used, but no more than one `finally` clause may be identified.

The *`try` block* is a sequence of Java statements that are preceded by an opening brace (`{`) and followed by a closing brace (`}`).

The `catch` clauses are a sequence of clauses of the form:

```
catch (Parameter) {
/*
* Exception handling statements
*/
}
```

Parameter is a variable that is declared to be a class or interface. The statements within the `catch` clause are used to process the exceptions that they "catch," as I'll explain shortly.

The `finally` clause identifies a block of code that is to be executed at the conclusion of the `try` statement and after any `catch` clauses. Its syntax is as follows:

```
finally {
/*
* Statements in finally clause
*/
}
```

The `finally` clause is always executed, no matter whether an exception is thrown.

Catching Exceptions

The `try` statement executes a statement block. If an exception is thrown during the block's execution, it terminates execution of the statement block and checks the `catch` clauses to determine which, if any, of the `catch` clauses can catch the thrown exception. If none of the `catch` clauses can catch the exception, the exception is propagated to the next higher level `try` statement. This process is repeated until the exception is caught or no more `try` statements remain.

A `catch` clause can catch an exception if its argument may be legally assigned the object thrown in the `throw` statement. If the argument of a `catch` clause is a class, the `catch` clause can catch any object whose class is a subclass of this class. If the argument to a `catch` clause is an interface, the `catch` clause can catch any object that implements that interface.

The `try` statement tries each `catch` clause, in order, and selects the first one that can catch the exception that was thrown. It then executes the statements in the `catch` clause. If a `finally` clause occurs in the `try` statement, the statements in the `finally` clause are executed after execution of the `catch` clause has been completed. Execution then continues with the statement following the `try` statement.

The following example shows how `catch` clauses are used to process exceptions that are thrown within the `try` statement. Create a directory `ch07` under `c:\java\jdg` and enter the source code in the file `ExceptionTest.java`. Compile it using the command `javac ExceptionTest.java`. The source code for the `ExceptionTest` program is shown in Listing 7.1.

Listing 7.1. The source code of the `ExceptionTest` program.

```
import jdg.ch05.KeyboardInput;
import java.lang.System;
import java.lang.Exception;
import java.io.IOException;

class VowelException extends Exception {}
class BlankException extends Exception {}
class ExitException extends Exception {}

class ExceptionTest {
 static KeyboardInput kbd = new KeyboardInput(System.in);
 public static void main(String args[]) {
  boolean finished = false;
  do {
   try {
    processUserInput();
   }catch (VowelException x) {
    System.out.println("A vowel exception occurred.");
   }catch (BlankException x) {
    System.out.println("A blank exception occurred.");
   }catch (ExitException x) {
    System.out.println("An exit exception occurred.");
    finished = true;
   }finally {
    System.out.println("This is the finally clause.\n");
   }
  } while(!finished);
 }
 static void processUserInput() throws VowelException, BlankException,
  ExitException {
  System.out.print("Enter a character: ");
  System.out.flush();
  char ch;
  try {
   ch=Character.toUpperCase(kbd.getChar());
  } catch (IOException x) {
   System.out.println("An IOException occurred.");
   return;
  }
  switch(ch) {
   case 'A':
   case 'E':
   case 'I':
   case 'O':
   case 'U':
    throw new VowelException();
   case ' ':
    throw new BlankException();
   case 'X':
    throw new ExitException();
  }
 }
}
```

The ExceptionTest program uses the jdg.ch05.KeyboardInput class to retrieve a character entered by the user. It then throws and catches a VowelException, BlankException, or ExitException based on the user's input.

The ExceptionTest class consists of a single class variable, kbd, that is statically initialized to an object of class KeyboardInput, with System.in as an argument to its constructor.

ExceptionTest provides two static methods, main() and processUserInput(). The main() method consists of a simple do statement that repeatedly tries to invoke processUserInput(). The try statement has three catch clauses and a finally clause. The three catch clauses notify the user of the type of exception they catch. The catch clause with an ExitException parameter causes the do statement and the program to terminate by setting finished to true. The finally clause just displays the fact that it has been executed.

The processUserInput() method prompts the user to enter a character. The actual reading of the character occurs within a try statement. IOException is caught by the try statement, eliminating the need to declare the exception in the processUserInput() throws clause. The IOException is handled by notifying the user that the exception occurred and continuing with program execution.

The processUserInput() method throws one of three exceptions based upon the character entered by the user. If the user enters a vowel, VowelException is thrown. If the user enters a line beginning with a non-printable character, BlankException is thrown. If the user enters x or X, ExitException is thrown.

To run ExceptionTest, type javac ExceptionTest:

```
C:\java\jdg\ch07>java ExceptionTest
Enter a character:
```

The program prompts you to enter a character. Enter a blank line, and the following output is displayed:

```
A blank exception occurred.
This is the finally clause.

Enter a character:
```

The program notifies you that a blank exception has occurred and displays the fact that the finally clause of the main() try statement was executed. The processUserInput() method, upon encountering a space character returned by getChar(), throws the BlankException, which is caught by the main() method. The finally clause always executes no matter whether processUserInput() throws an exception or not.

Enter a at the program prompt, and the following output appears:

```
Enter a character: a
A vowel exception occurred.
This is the finally clause.

Enter a character:
```

Here the program notifies you that a vowel exception has occurred. The processing of the vowel exception is similar to the blank exception. See if you can trace the program flow of control involved in this processing.

Enter `j`, and the following is displayed:

```
Enter a character: j
This is the finally clause.
Enter a character:
```

No exceptions are thrown for the `j` character, but the `finally` clause is executed. The `finally` clause is always executed, no matter what happens during the execution of a `try` statement. Go ahead and type `x` to exit the `ExceptionTest` program. The program displays the following output:

```
Enter a character: x
An exit exception occurred.
This is the finally clause.
```

The exception then returns you to the DOS prompt.

The output acknowledges the fact that the exit exception was thrown by `processUserInput()` and caught by `main()`.

The `ExceptionTest` program provides a simple example of exception throwing and catching. The example in the following section illustrates more complex exception handling.

Nested Exception Handling

`try` statements can be nested to provide multiple levels of exception-handling capabilities. This is accomplished by enclosing a method or block of statements containing a lower-level `try` statement within the try block of a higher-level `try` statement. When an exception is thrown in the `try` block of the lower-level `try` statement that cannot be caught, it continues to be thrown until it reaches the higher-level `try` statement. The higher-level `try` statement can then determine whether the exception can be caught and processed by any of its `catch` clauses. Any number of `try` statements can be nested. Figure 7.1 illustrates this concept.

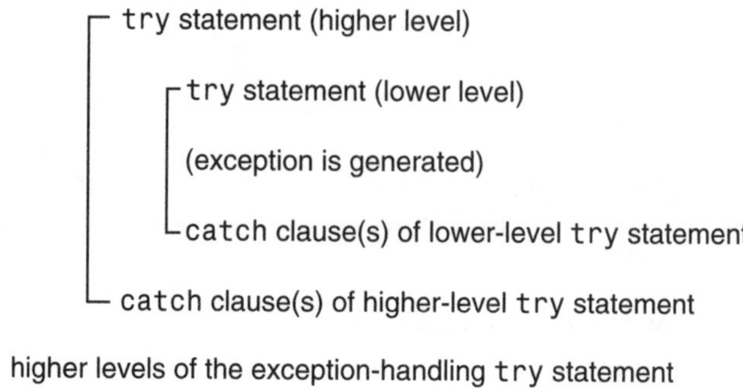

FIGURE 7.1.
Nested exception handling: An exception generated within the lower-level `try` *statement is first passed to its* `catch` *clause(s). If it is not handled, it is propagated to the higher-level* `catch` *clause(s). If it is not handled by the higher-level* `catch` *clause(s), it is propagated further up the exception-handling hierarchy.*

Rethrowing Exceptions

When an exception is caught in the `catch` clause of a `try` statement, that exception may be rethrown. When an exception is rethrown, it can then be caught and processed by the `catch` clause of a higher-level `try` statement. A higher-level `catch` clause can then perform any secondary clean-up processing.

The following example illustrates nested exception handling and the rethrowing of exceptions. Enter the source code shown in Listing 7.2 into `NestedExceptionTest.java` and compile it.

Listing 7.2. The source code of the `NestedExceptionTest` program.

```
import jdg.ch05.KeyboardInput;
import java.lang.System;
import java.lang.Exception;
import java.io.IOException;

class VowelException extends Exception {}
class BlankException extends Exception {}
class ExitException extends Exception {}

class NestedExceptionTest {
 static KeyboardInput kbd = new KeyboardInput(System.in);
 public static void main(String args[]) {
  do{} while(!exitExceptionTest());
 }
 static boolean exitExceptionTest() {
  try {
   vowelExceptionTest();
   System.out.println("Acceptable.\n");
  }catch (ExitException x) {
   try {
    System.out.print("Exit (y/n): ");
    System.out.flush();
    char ch = Character.toUpperCase(kbd.getChar());
```

```
    System.out.println();
    if(ch=='Y') return true;
    else return false;
   }catch (IOException iox) {
    return false;
   }
  }catch (Exception x) {
   System.out.println("Not acceptable. Try again.\n");
  }
  return false;
 }
 static void vowelExceptionTest() throws VowelException, ExitException {
  try {
   blankExceptionTest();
  }catch (BlankException x) {
   System.out.println("Next time type a printable character.\n");
   vowelExceptionTest();
  }catch (VowelException x) {
   System.out.println("You typed a vowel.");
   throw x;
  }
 }
 static void blankExceptionTest() throws VowelException, BlankException,
  ExitException {
  try {
   processUserInput();
  }catch (BlankException x) {
   System.out.println("You entered a blank line. Try again.");
   throw x;
  }
 }
 static void processUserInput() throws VowelException, BlankException,
  ExitException {
  System.out.print("Enter a character: ");
  System.out.flush();
  char ch;
  try {
   ch=Character.toUpperCase(kbd.getChar());
  } catch (IOException x) {
   System.out.println("An IOException occurred.");
   return;
  }
  switch(ch) {
   case 'A':
   case 'E':
   case 'I':
   case 'O':
   case 'U':
    throw new VowelException();
   case ' ':
    throw new BlankException();
   case 'X':
    throw new ExitException();
  }
 }
}
```

This example is based on the previous example, but it is significantly more complex. The exception handling has been removed from the `main()` method and distributed among three nested exception handlers: `exitExceptionTest()`, `vowelExceptionTest()`, and `blankExceptionTest()`.

The `main()` method invokes `exitExceptionTest()` at each iteration of the `do` statement. The `exitExceptionTest()` method returns a `boolean` value indicating whether the `do` statement should terminate. The normal (non-exception) processing performed by `exitExceptionTest()` consists of the following three statements:

```
vowelExceptionTest();
System.out.println("Acceptable.\n");
return false;
```

All other `exitExceptionTest()` processing is error handling. The first two statements are executed within the `try` statement and are subject to error processing. The last statement executes upon completion of the `try` statement, assuming that no transfer of control occurs as the result of exception handling involving the `catch` clauses.

The `try` statement has two `catch` clauses. The first `catch` clause handles `ExitException` processing. It consists of a `try` statement with a `catch` clause that catches the pesky `IOException`. The `try` statement contains a block of statements that asks the user for a confirmation before exiting the program.

The second `catch` clause catches all other objects that are instances of a subclass of `Exception`. It displays a short warning to the user.

The `vowelExceptionTest()` method consists of a `try` statement that invokes `blankExceptionTest()`. The rest of the processing performed by `vowelExceptionTest()` is exception handling. It catches two exceptions: `BlankException` and `VowelException`. It handles `BlankException` by warning the user to type a printable character and reinvoking itself. It handles the vowel exception by notifying the user that he typed a vowel and rethrowing the `VowelException`. By rethrowing the exception, it allows `exitExceptionTest()` to perform additional exception handling. Because `vowelExceptionTest()` rethrows the `VowelException`, it must declare it in its `throws` clause. It also must declare the `ExitException` because the `ExitException` is declared in the `throws` clause of `blankExceptionTest()` and is not caught by `vowelExceptionTest()`.

The `blankExceptionTest()` simply invokes `processUserInput()` as part of its normal processing. It handles one exception thrown by `processUserInput()`: the `BlankException`. It handles the `BlankException` by informing the user that he typed a blank line and that he should try again. It then rethrows the `BlankException` so that it can be rehandled by `vowelExceptionTest()`.

The `processUserInput()` method performs in the same manner as described in the previous example.

Analysis of NestedExceptionTest

If `NestedExceptionTest` seems overly complex, don't worry—it was meant to be. Its purpose is to give you a good understanding of the complex ways that exception handlers can be nested and how exceptions are rethrown. Go ahead and run `NestedExceptionTest` using the command `java NestedExceptionTest`:

```
C:\java\jdg\ch07>java NestedExceptionTest
Enter a character:
```

When you run `NestedExceptionTest`, the `main()` method invokes `exitExceptionTest()`, which invokes `vowelExceptionTest()`, which invokes `blankExceptionTest()`, which invokes `processUserInput()`. The `processUserInput()` method prompts you to enter a character and then does one of four things, depending on the character you enter. If you enter a vowel, it throws a `VowelException`. If you enter a nonprintable character or blank line, it throws a `BlankException`. If you enter `x` or `X`, it throws an `ExitException`. Finally, as a default, if you enter any other printable character, it will simply return control to the `blankExceptionTest()` method.

Let's work through all four scenarios. First, enter `j` to cause normal program processing to occur:

```
Enter a character: j
Acceptable.

Enter a character:
```

The `processUserInput()` method returns control to `blankExceptionTest()`, which returns control to `vowelExceptionTest()`, which returns control to `exitExceptionTest()`. The `exitExceptionTest()` method informs the user that he has entered an acceptable character and returns control to the `main()` method, which starts another character-input cycle.

Now let's go through the case when the user enters a blank line. Just enter a blank line at the prompt:

```
Enter a character:
You entered a blank line. Try again.
Next time type a printable character.

Enter a character:
```

A blank line causes `processUserInput()` to throw the `BlankException`. This exception is caught by `blankExceptionTest()`. The `blankExceptionTest()` method handles the exception by informing the user that he has entered a blank line and that he should try again. It then rethrows the exception, and the rethrown exception is caught by `vowelExceptionTest()`. The `vowelExceptionTest()` method handles the rethrown `BlankException` by telling the user that he should enter a printable character the next time he is prompted. It then invokes itself, starting the character-input cycle all over.

Let's go through the case when the user enters a vowel. Enter `a` at the prompt:

```
Enter a character: a
You typed a vowel.
Not acceptable. Try again.

Enter a character:
```

When a vowel is entered, `processUserInput()` throws the `VowelException`. The `VowelException` is not caught by `blankExceptionTest()` and continues to be thrown until it is caught by `vowelExceptionTest()`. The `vowelExceptionTest()` method handles the exception by informing the user that he has typed a vowel and then rethrows the exception. The rethrown exception is caught by `exitExceptionTest()`, and `exitExceptionTest()` handles it by informing the user that his input is not acceptable. Execution control returns to the `main()` method, which starts another character-input cycle.

This last case examines what happens when the user types `x` at the character prompt. Enter `x` to see what happens:

```
Enter a character: x
Exit (y/n):
```

The `processUserInput()` method throws an `ExitException`, which is not caught by `blankExceptionTest()` nor `vowelExceptionTest()`. The exception continues to be thrown until it is caught by `exitExceptionTest()`. The `exitExceptionTest()` method prompts the user to enter a `y` or `Y` to confirm the fact that he wants to exit the program. If the user enters any other character, control returns to the `main()` method and another character-input cycle is initiated. If the user enters a `y` or `Y`, control is returned to the `main()` method, but the `true` return value is passed, causing the `do` statement and the program to terminate.

Go ahead and type `y` to terminate the `NestedExceptionTest` program.

Summary

In this chapter you have learned how to use Java exceptions to implement error-handling capabilities in your Java programs. You have learned how to throw exceptions in response to error conditions and how to catch exceptions to perform error processing. You have also learned how to implement nested exception handling and how to rethrow exceptions. In Chapter 8, "Multithreading," you will learn how to use Java's multithreading capabilities to write programs that use multiple threads of execution.

8

Multithreading

This chapter introduces you to multithreaded programs and how multithreading is supported in Java. You'll learn how to create, run, and synchronize multiple threads in your programs. You'll also learn about thread scheduling and how a thread's priority determines when it is scheduled. When you finish this chapter you will be able to develop multithreaded programs using Java.

Understanding Multithreading

All the sample programs you developed in the preceding chapters have had only a single thread of execution. Each program proceeded sequentially, one instruction after another, until it completed its processing and terminated.

Multithreaded programs are similar to the single-threaded programs that you have been studying. They differ only in the fact that they support more than one *concurrent* thread of execution—that is, they are able to simultaneously execute multiple sequences of instructions. Each instruction sequence has its own unique flow of control that is independent of all others. These independently executed instruction sequences are known as *threads*.

If your computer has only a single CPU, you might be wondering how it can execute more than one thread at the same time. In single-processor systems, only a single thread of execution occurs at a given instant. The CPU quickly switches back and forth between several threads to create the illusion that the threads are executing at the same time. Single-processor systems support *logical concurrency*, not *physical concurrency*. Logical concurrency is the characteristic exhibited when multiple threads execute with separate, independent flows of control. On multiprocessor systems, several threads do, in fact, execute at the same time, and physical concurrency is achieved. The important feature of multithreaded programs is that they support logical concurrency, not whether physical concurrency is actually achieved.

Many programming languages support *multiprogramming*. Multiprogramming is the logically concurrent execution of multiple programs. For example, a program can request that the operating system execute programs A, B, and C by having it spawn a separate process for each program. These programs can run in parallel, depending upon the multiprogramming features supported by the underlying operating system. Multithreading differs from multiprogramming in that multithreading provides concurrency within the context of a single process and multiprogramming provides concurrency between processes. Threads are not complete processes in and of themselves. They are a separate flow of control that occurs within a process. Figure 8.1 illustrates the difference between multithreading and multiprogramming.

An executing program is generally associated with a single process. The advantage of multithreading is that concurrency can be used within a process to provide multiple simultaneous services to the user. Multithreading also requires less processing overhead than multiprogramming because concurrent threads are able to share common resources more easily. Multiple executing programs tend to duplicate resources and share data as the result of more time-consuming interprocess communication.

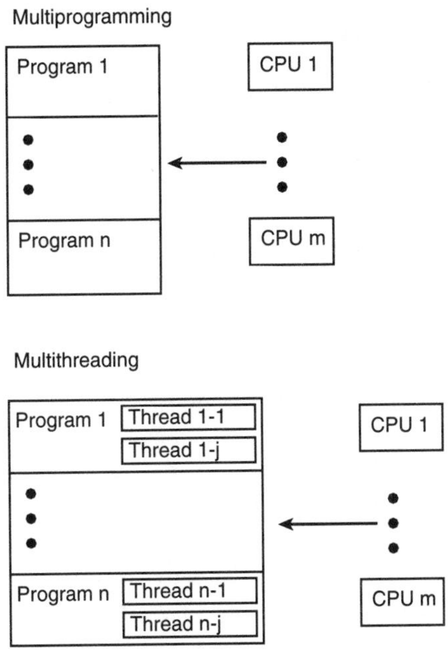

FIGURE 8.1.
Multithreading versus multiprogramming.

How Java Supports Multithreading

Java provides extensive support for both multithreading and multiprogramming. Multithreading is covered in this chapter. Java's support for multiprogramming is covered in Chapter 12, "Portable Software and the `java.lang` Package."

Java's multithreading support is centered around the `java.lang.Thread` class. The `Thread` class provides the capability to create objects of class `Thread`, each with its own separate flow of control. The `Thread` class encapsulates the data and methods associated with separate threads of execution and allows multithreading to be integrated within the object-oriented framework.

Java provides two approaches to creating threads. In the first approach, you create a subclass of class `Thread` and override the `run()` method to provide an entry point into the thread's execution. When you create an instance of your `Thread` subclass, you invoke its `start()` method to cause the thread to execute as an independent sequence of instructions. The `start()` method is inherited from the `Thread` class. It initializes the `Thread` object using your operating system's multithreading capabilities and invokes the `run()` method. You learn how to create threads using this approach in the next section.

NOTE

This chapter makes heavy use of the Java API methods defined for class `Thread` and related classes. If you haven't obtained and installed a copy of the Java API documentation, now is a good time to do so.

The approach to creating threads identified in the previous paragraph is very simple and straightforward. However, it has the drawback of requiring your `Thread` objects to be under the `Thread` class in the class hierarchy. In some cases, as you'll see when you study applets in Part VI, "Programming the Web with Applets and Scripts," this requirement can be somewhat limiting.

Java's other approach to creating threads does not limit the location of your `Thread` objects within the class hierarchy. In this approach, your class implements the `java.lang.Runnable` interface. The `Runnable` interface consists of a single method, the `run()` method, which must be overridden by your class. The `run()` method provides an entry point into your thread's execution. In order to run an object of your class as an independent thread, you pass it as an argument to a constructor of class `Thread`. You learn how to create threads using this approach later in this chapter in the section titled "Implementing `Runnable`."

Creating Subclasses of `Thread`

In this section, you create your first multithreaded program by creating a subclass of `Thread` and then creating, initializing, and starting two `Thread` objects from your class. The threads will execute concurrently and display `Java is hot, aromatic, and invigorating.` to the console window.

Create a `ch08` directory under `c:\java\jdg` and enter the source code from Listing 8.1 into `ThreadTest1.java`. Then compile it using the command `javac ThreadTest1.java`.

Listing 8.1. The source code of the `ThreadTest1` program.

```
import java.lang.Thread;
import java.lang.System;
import java.lang.Math;
import java.lang.InterruptedException;

class ThreadTest1 {
 public static void main(String args[]) {
  MyThread thread1 = new MyThread("thread1: ");
  MyThread thread2 = new MyThread("thread2: ");
  thread1.start();
  thread2.start();
  boolean thread1IsAlive = true;
  boolean thread2IsAlive = true;
  do {
   if(thread1IsAlive && !thread1.isAlive()){
    thread1IsAlive = false;
```

```
    System.out.println("Thread 1 is dead.");
   }
   if(thread2IsAlive && !thread2.isAlive()){
    thread2IsAlive = false;
    System.out.println("Thread 2 is dead.");
   }
  }while(thread1IsAlive || thread2IsAlive);
 }
}
class MyThread extends Thread {
 static String message[] = {"Java","is","hot,","aromatic,","and",
  "invigorating."};
 public MyThread(String id) {
  super(id);
 }
 public void run() {
  String name = getName();
  for(int i=0;i<message.length;++i) {
   randomWait();
   System.out.println(name+message[i]);
  }
 }
 void randomWait(){
  try {
   sleep((long)(3000*Math.random()));
  }catch (InterruptedException x){
   System.out.println("Interrupted!");
  }
 }
}
```

This program creates two threads of execution, `thread1` and `thread2`, from the `MyThread` class. It then starts both threads and executes a `do` statement that waits for the threads to die. The threads display the `Java is hot, aromatic, and invigorating.` message word by word, while waiting a short, random amount of time between each word. Because both threads share the console window, the program's output identifies which threads were able to write to the console at various times during the program's execution.

NOTE

The Java documentation refers to threads that have completed their execution as being *dead*. The term is descriptive, but somewhat morose.

Run `ThreadTest1` to get an idea of the output that it produces. Each time you run the program you might get a different program display. This is because the program uses a random number generator to determine how long each thread should wait before displaying its output. Look at the following output:

```
C:\java\jdg\ch08>java ThreadTest1
thread1: Java
thread2: Java
```

```
thread2: is
thread2: hot,
thread2: aromatic,
thread1: is
thread1: hot,
thread2: and
thread1: aromatic,
thread1: and
thread2: invigorating.
Thread 2 is dead.
thread1: invigorating.
Thread 1 is dead.
```

This output shows that `thread1` executed first and displayed `Java` to the console window. It then waited to execute while `thread2` displayed `Java`, `is`, `hot,`, and `aromatic,`. After that, `thread2` waited while `thread1` continued its execution. `thread1` displayed `is` and then `hot,`. At this point, `thread2` took over again. `thread2` displayed `and` and then went back into waiting. `thread1` then displayed `aromatic,` and `and`. `thread2` finished its execution by displaying `invigorating.`. Having completed its execution, `thread2` died, leaving `thread1` as the only executing task. `thread1` displayed `invigorating.` and then completed its execution.

The `ThreadTest1` class consists of a single `main()` method. This method begins by creating `thread1` and `thread2` as new objects of class `MyThread`. It then starts both threads using the `start()` method. At this point, `main()` enters a `do` loop that continues until both `thread1` and `thread2` are no longer alive. The loop monitors the execution of the two threads and displays a message when it has detected the death of each thread. It uses the `isAlive()` method of the `Thread` class to tell when a thread has died. The `thread1IsAlive` and `thread2IsAlive` variables are used to ensure that a thread's obituary is only displayed once.

The `MyThread` class extends class `Thread`. It declares a statically initialized array, named `message[]`, that contains the message to be displayed by each thread. It has a single constructor that invokes the `Thread` class constructor via `super()`. It contains two access methods: `run()` and `randomWait()`. The `run()` method is required. It uses the `getName()` method of class `Thread` to get the name of the currently executing thread. It then prints each word of the output display message while waiting a random length of time between each print. The `randomWait()` method invokes the `sleep()` method within a `try` statement. The `sleep()` method is another method inherited from class `Thread`. It causes the currently executing task to "go to sleep" or wait until a randomly specified number of milliseconds has transpired. Because the `sleep()` method throws the `InterruptedException` when its sleep is interrupted (how grouchy!), the exception is caught and handled by the `randomWait()` method. The exception is handled by displaying the fact that an interruption has occurred to the console window.

Implementing `Runnable`

In the previous section, you created a multithreaded program by creating the `MyThread` subclass of `Thread`. In this section, you create a program with similar behavior, but you create your threads as objects of the class `MyClass`, which is not a subclass of `Thread`. `MyClass` will implement the `Runnable` interface and objects of `MyClass` will be executed as threads by passing them as arguments to the `Thread` constructor.

The `ThreadTest2` program's source code is shown in Listing 8.2. Enter it into the `ThreadTest2.java` file and compile it.

Listing 8.2. The source code of the `ThreadTest2` program.

```
import java.lang.Thread;
import java.lang.System;
import java.lang.Math;
import java.lang.InterruptedException;
import java.lang.Runnable;

class ThreadTest2 {
 public static void main(String args[]) {
  Thread thread1 = new Thread(new MyClass("thread1: "));
  Thread thread2 = new Thread(new MyClass("thread2: "));
  thread1.start();
  thread2.start();
  boolean thread1IsAlive = true;
  boolean thread2IsAlive = true;
  do {
   if(thread1IsAlive && !thread1.isAlive()){
    thread1IsAlive = false;
    System.out.println("Thread 1 is dead.");
   }
   if(thread2IsAlive && !thread2.isAlive()){
    thread2IsAlive = false;
    System.out.println("Thread 2 is dead.");
   }
  }while(thread1IsAlive || thread2IsAlive);
 }
}
class MyClass implements Runnable {
 static String message[] = {"Java","is","hot,","aromatic,","and",
  "invigorating."};
 String name;
 public MyClass(String id) {
  name = id;
 }
 public void run() {
  for(int i=0;i<message.length;++i) {
   randomWait();
   System.out.println(name+message[i]);
  }
 }
 void randomWait(){
  try {
   Thread.currentThread().sleep((long)(3000*Math.random()));
  }catch (InterruptedException x){
   System.out.println("Interrupted!");
  }
 }
}
```

The ThreadTest2 program is very similar to ThreadTest1. It differs only in the way that the threads are created. You should run ThreadTest2 a few times to examine its output. Here are the results of a sample run I made on my computer:

```
C:\java\jdg\ch08>java ThreadTest2
thread2: Java
thread1: Java
thread2: is
thread2: hot,
thread1: is
thread2: aromatic,
thread1: hot,
thread1: aromatic,
thread1: and
thread2: and
thread1: invigorating.
Thread 1 is dead.
thread2: invigorating.
Thread 2 is dead.
```

These results show thread2 beginning its output before thread1. It does not mean that thread2 began executing before thread1. Thread1 executed first, but went to sleep before generating any output. Thread2 then executed and started its output display before going to sleep. You can follow these results on your own to analyze how thread1 and thread2 switched back and forth during their execution to display their results to the console window.

The main() method of ThreadTest2 differs from that of ThreadTest1 in the way that it creates thread1 and thread2. ThreadTest1 created the threads as new instances of the MyThread class. ThreadTest2 was not able to create the threads directly, because MyClass is not a subclass of Thread. Instead, ThreadTest2 first created instances of MyClass and then passed them to the Thread() constructor, creating instances of class Thread. The Thread() constructor used by ThreadTest2 takes as its argument any class that implements the Runnable interface. This is an example of the flexibility and multiple-inheritance features provided by Java interfaces. The rest of the ThreadTest2 main() method is the same as that of ThreadTest1.

MyClass is declared as implementing the Runnable interface. This is a simple interface to implement; it only requires that you implement the run() method. MyClass declares the name variable to hold the names of MyClass objects that are created. In the first example, the MyThread class did not need to do this because a thread-naming capability was provided by Thread and inherited by MyThread. MyClass contains a simple constructor that initializes the name variable.

The run() methods of ThreadTest2 and ThreadTest1 are nearly identical, differing only with respect to the name issue. This is also true of the randomWait() method. In ThreadTest2, the randomWait() method must use the currentThread() method of class Thread to acquire a reference to an instance of the current thread in order to invoke its sleep() method.

Because these two examples are so similar, you might be wondering why you would pick one approach to creating a class over another. The advantage of using the Runnable interface is that your class does not need to extend the Thread class. This will be very helpful feature when you start using multithreading in applets in Part VI of this book. The only disadvantages to this approach are ones of convenience. You have to do a little more work to create your threads and to access their methods.

Thread States

You have now learned how to declare, create, initialize, start, and run Java threads. The `ThreadTest1` and `ThreadTest2` programs also introduced you to the concept of a thread's death. Threads transition through several states from the time they are created until the time of their death. This section reviews these states.

A thread is created by creating a new object of class `Thread` or of one of its subclasses. When a thread is first created, it does not exist as an independently executing set of instructions. Instead, it is a template from which an executing thread will be created. It first executes as a thread when it is started using the `start()` method and run via the `run()` method. Before a thread is started it is said to be in the *new thread* state. After a thread is started, it is in the *runnable* state. When a class is in the runnable state, it may be executing or temporarily waiting to share processing resources with other threads. A runnable thread enters an extended wait state when one of its methods is invoked that causes it to drop from the runnable state into a not runnable state. In the *not runnable* state, a thread is not just waiting for its share of processing resources, but is blocked waiting for the occurrence of an event that will send it back to the runnable state.

For example, the `sleep()` method was invoked in the `ThreadTest1` and `ThreadTest2` programs to cause a thread to wait for a short period of time so that the other thread could execute. The `sleep()` method causes a thread to enter the not runnable state until the specified time has expired. A thread may also enter the not runnable state while it is waiting for I/O to be completed, or as the result of the invocation of other methods. Chapter 12 provides a detailed description of the methods of the `Thread` class that are inherited by all threads.

NOTE

There is no connection between a thread's runnable state and a class's `Runnable` interface.

A thread leaves the not runnable state and returns to the runnable state when the event that it is waiting for has occurred. For example, a sleeping thread must wait for its specified sleep time to occur. A thread that is waiting on I/O must wait for the I/O operation to be completed.

A thread may transition from the new thread, runnable, or not runnable state to the *dead* state when its `stop()` method is invoked or the thread's execution is completed. When a thread enters the dead state, it's a goner. It can't be revived and returned to any other state.

Thread Priority and Scheduling

From an abstract or a logical perspective, multiple threads execute as concurrent sequences of instructions. This may be physically true for multiprocessor systems, under certain conditions. However, in the general case, multiple threads do not always physically execute at the same time. Instead, the threads share execution time with each other based on the availability of the system's CPU (or CPUs).

The approach used to determining which threads should execute at a given time is referred to as *scheduling*. Scheduling is performed by the Java runtime system. It schedules threads based on their *priority*. The highest-priority thread that is in the runnable state is the thread that is run at any given instant. The highest-priority thread continues to run until it enters the death state, enters the not runnable state, or has its priority lowered, or when a higher-priority thread becomes runnable.

A thread's priority is an integer value between `MIN_PRIORITY` and `MAX_PRIORITY`. These constants are defined in the `Thread` class. In Java 1.0, `MIN_PRIORITY` is 1 and `MAX_PRIORITY` is 10. A thread's priority is set when it is created. It is set to the same priority as the thread that created it. The default priority of a thread is `NORM_PRIORITY` and is equal to 5. The priority of a thread can be changed using the `setPriority()` method.

Java's approach to scheduling is referred to as *preemptive scheduling*. When a thread of higher priority becomes runnable, it preempts threads of lower priority and is immediately executed in their place. If two or more higher-priority threads become runnable, the Java scheduler alternates between them when allocating execution time.

Synchronization

There are many situations in which multiple threads must share access to common objects. For example, all of the programs in this chapter have illustrated the effects of multithreading by having multiple executing threads write to the Java console, a common shared object. These examples have not required any coordination or synchronization in the way the threads access the console window: Whatever thread was currently executing was able to write to the console window. No coordination between concurrent threads was required.

There are times when you might want to coordinate access to shared resources. For example, in a database system, you might not want one thread to be updating a database record while another thread is trying to read it. Java enables you to coordinate the actions of multiple threads using *synchronized methods* and *synchronized statements*.

An object for which access is to be coordinated is accessed through the use of synchronized methods. (Synchronized statements are covered in Chapter 11, "Language Summary.") These methods are declared with the `synchronized` keyword. Only one synchronized method can be invoked for an object at a given point in time. This keeps synchronized methods in multiple threads from conflicting with each other.

All classes and objects are associated with a unique *monitor*. The monitor is used to control the way in which synchronized methods are allowed to access the class or object. When a synchronized method is invoked for a given object, it is said to *acquire* the monitor for that object. No other synchronized method may be invoked for that object until the monitor is released. A monitor is automatically released when the method completes its execution and returns. A monitor may also be released when a synchronized method executes certain methods, such as `wait()`. The thread associated with the currently executing synchronized method becomes not runnable until the wait condition is satisfied and no other method has acquired the object's monitor.

The following example shows how synchronized methods and object monitors are used to coordinate access to a common object by multiple threads. This example adapts the `ThreadTest1` program for use with synchronized methods, as shown in Listing 8.3.

Listing 8.3. The source code of the `ThreadSynchronization` program.

```
import java.lang.Thread;
import java.lang.System;
import java.lang.Math;
import java.lang.InterruptedException;

class ThreadSynchronization {
 public static void main(String args[]) {
  MyThread thread1 = new MyThread("thread1: ");
  MyThread thread2 = new MyThread("thread2: ");
  thread1.start();
  thread2.start();
  boolean thread1IsAlive = true;
  boolean thread2IsAlive = true;
  do {
   if(thread1IsAlive && !thread1.isAlive()){
    thread1IsAlive = false;
    System.out.println("Thread 1 is dead.");
   }
   if(thread2IsAlive && !thread2.isAlive()){
    thread2IsAlive = false;
    System.out.println("Thread 2 is dead.");
   }
  }while(thread1IsAlive || thread2IsAlive);
 }
}
class MyThread extends Thread {
 static String message[] = {"Java","is","hot,","aromatic,",
  "and","invigorating."};
 public MyThread(String id) {
  super(id);
 }
 public void run() {
```

continues

Listing 8.3. continued

```
  SynchronizedOutput.displayList(getName(),message);
 }
 void randomWait(){
  try {
   sleep((long)(3000*Math.random()));
  }catch (InterruptedException x){
   System.out.println("Interrupted!");
  }
 }
}
class SynchronizedOutput {
 public static synchronized void displayList(String name,String list[]) {
  for(int i=0;i<list.length;++i) {
   MyThread t = (MyThread) Thread.currentThread();
   t.randomWait();
   System.out.println(name+list[i]);
  }
 }
}
```

Compile and run the program before going on with its analysis. You might be surprised at the results that you've obtained. Here are the results of an example run on my system:

```
C:\java\jdg\ch08>java ThreadSynchronization
thread1: Java
thread1: is
thread1: hot,
thread1: aromatic,
thread1: and
thread1: invigorating.
Thread 1 is dead.
thread2: Java
thread2: is
thread2: hot,
thread2: aromatic,
thread2: and
thread2: invigorating.
Thread 2 is dead.
```

Now edit `ThreadSynchronization.java` and delete the `synchronized` keyword in the declaration of the `displayList()` method of class `SynchronizedOutput`. It should look like this when you are finished:

```
class SynchronizedOutput {
 public static void displayList(String name,String list[]) {
```

Save `ThreadSynchronization.java`, recompile it, and rerun it with the new change in place. You may now get output similar to this:

```
C:\java\jdg\ch08>java ThreadSynchronization
thread2: Java
thread1: Java
thread1: is
thread2: is
```

```
thread2: hot,
thread2: aromatic,
thread1: hot,
thread2: and
thread2: invigorating.
Thread 2 is dead.
thread1: aromatic,
thread1: and
thread1: invigorating.
Thread 1 is dead.
```

The difference in the program's output should give you a feel for the effects of synchronization upon multithreaded program execution. Let's analyze the program and explain these results.

The `ThreadSynchronization` class is essentially the same as the `ThreadTest1` class. The only difference is the class name.

The `MyThread` class was modified slightly to allow for the use of the `SynchronizedOutput` class. Instead of the output being displayed in the `run()` method, as in `ThreadTest1`, the `run()` method simply invokes the `displayList()` method of the `SynchronizedOutput` class. It is important to understand that the `displayList()` method is `static` and applies to the `SynchronizedOutput` class as a whole, not to any particular instance of the class. The method displays the `Java is hot, aromatic, and invigorating.` message in the same manner as it was displayed in the previous examples of this chapter. It invokes `randomWait()` to wait a random amount of time before displaying each word in the message. The `displayList()` method uses the `currentThread()` method of class `Thread` to reference the current thread in order to invoke `randomWait()`.

What difference, then, does the fact that `displayList()` is synchronized have on the program's execution? When `displayList()` is not synchronized, it may be invoked by one thread, say `thread1`, display some output, and wait while `thread2` executes. When `thread2` executes, it too invokes `displayList()` to display some output. Two separate invocations of `displayList()`, one for `thread1` and the other for `thread2`, execute concurrently. This explains the mixed output display.

When the `synchronized` keyword is used, `thread1` invokes `displayList()`, acquires a monitor for the `SynchronizedOutput` class (because `displayList()` is a `static` method), and `displayList()` proceeds with the output display for `thread1`. Because `thread1` acquired a monitor for the `SynchronizedOutput` class, `thread2` must wait until the monitor is released before it is able to invoke `displayList()` to display its output. This explains why one task's output is completed before the other's.

Daemon Threads

Java borrows the notion of a daemon thread from the UNIX daemon process. A *daemon thread* is a thread that executes in the background and provides services to other threads. It typically executes a continuous loop of instructions that wait for a service request, perform the service, and wait for the next service request. Daemon threads continue to execute until there are no more threads for which services can be provided. At this time, the daemon threads die and the Java interpreter terminates its execution. Any thread can be changed to a daemon thread using the `setDaemon()` method.

Thread Groups

Thread groups are objects that consist of a collection of threads. Every thread is a member of a unique thread group. Thread groups are used to invoke methods that apply to all threads in the group. For example, a thread group can be used to start or stop all threads in a group, to change their priorities, or to change them to daemon threads.

A thread is entered into a thread group when it is created. After the thread enters a thread group, it remains a member of the group throughout its existence. A thread can never become a member of another group.

Threads are entered into a group using `Thread` constructors that take a `ThreadGroup` parameter. These constructors are described in the `Thread` class API documentation. If a thread's group is not specified in its constructor, as is the usual case, the thread is entered into the same group as the thread that created it. The default thread group for a newly executing Java application is the `main` group. All of the threads created in this chapter's examples have been members of the default `main` thread group. The `ThreadGroup` class is covered in Chapter 12.

Summary

In this chapter you have learned how to develop multithreaded programs using Java threads. You have learned how to synchronize multiple threads in order to share common resources. You have also learned how to use thread priorities to control thread scheduling. You have now covered the main features of the Java language. A complete language summary is provided in Chapter 11. In Chapter 9, "Using the Debugger," you'll learn how to use the Java debugger to help debug the programs you develop.

9

Using the Debugger

In this chapter you'll learn to use the Java debugger to trace and debug the Java programs you develop. You'll learn how to invoke the debugger, load class files, and examine classes as they are executed. You'll also explore the commands provided by the debugger and learn to use them through a hands-on tutorial. When you have finished this chapter, you will know how to use the debugger to analyze, test, and debug your Java programs.

Overview of the Debugger

The Java debugger enables Java programmers to debug their programs without having to insert special debugging instructions into their code. The debugger has a number of features, including support for multithreaded programs and remote applications.

The debugger is invoked with the `jdb` command. To get a quick summary of the commands provided by the debugger, enter the debugger command as follows:

```
C:\java\jdg>jdb
Initializing jdb...
>
```

NOTE

The Java debugger has a few bugs of its own. To get the debugger to run properly, you may have to establish an active Internet connection.

The debugger takes a few seconds to initialize and then provides you with the debugger prompt. At the debugger prompt, type `help` to get a description of the commands it supports:

```
C:\java\jdg>jdb
Initializing jdb...
> help
** command list **
threads [threadgroup]     -- list threads
thread <thread id>        -- set default thread
suspend [thread id(s)]    -- suspend threads (default: all)
resume [thread id(s)]     -- resume threads (default: all)
where [thread id] ¦ all   -- dump a thread's stack
threadgroups              -- list threadgroups
threadgroup <name>        -- set current threadgroup

print <id> [id(s)]        -- print object or field
dump <id> [id(s)]         -- print all object information

locals                    -- print all local variables in current stack frame

classes                   -- list currently known classes
methods <class id>        -- list a class's methods

stop in <class id>.<method> -- set a breakpoint in a method
stop at <class id>:<line> -- set a breakpoint at a line
```

```
up [n frames]              -- move up a thread's stack
down [n frames]            -- move down a thread's stack
clear <class id>:<line>    -- clear a breakpoint
step                       -- execute current line
cont                       -- continue execution from breakpoint

catch <class id>           -- break for the specified exception
ignore <class id>          -- ignore the specified exception

list [line number]         -- print source code
use [source file path]     -- display or change the source path

memory                     -- report memory usage
gc                         -- free unused objects

load classname             -- load Java class to be debugged
run <class> [args]         -- start execution of a loaded Java class
!!                         -- repeat last command
help (or ?)                -- list commands
exit (or quit)             -- exit debugger
>
```

Learning the debugger involves learning how to use each of these commands.

An Extended Example

In order to get you quickly up to speed on the operation of the debugger, let's use it to analyze a program that you've already developed. Change directories to the `ch06` directory and recompile the `ch06` source files using the `-g` option. This will result in additional debugging information being inserted into the compiled bytecode files.

```
C:\java\jdg\ch06>javac -g CGTextEdit.java

C:\java\jdg\ch06>javac -g CGText.java

C:\java\jdg\ch06>javac -g CGTextPoint.java

C:\java\jdg\ch06>javac -g CGTextBox.java

C:\java\jdg\ch06>javac -g CDrawApp.java
```

When you have finished compiling the source files, run the debugger by entering the `jdb` command:

```
C:\java\jdg\ch06>jdb
Initializing jdb...
>
```

At the debugger prompt, type `load jdg.ch06.CDrawApp`:

```
> load jdg.ch06.CDrawApp
0x13a41b8:class(jdg.ch06.CDrawApp)
>
```

The debugger responds by loading the `CDrawApp` class. The hexadecimal number preceding the class name is a Java runtime identifier for the `CDrawApp` class. Load the `CDraw` class by typing `load jdg.ch06.CDraw`:

```
> load jdg.ch06.CDraw
0x13a54e8:class(jdg.ch06.CDraw)
>
```

Now that you've loaded these two classes, you want to set a breakpoint in the `main()` method of `CDrawApp`. A *breakpoint* is a place in your program where the debugger stops execution to allow you to enter debugging commands. You set a breakpoint using the `stop in` command:

```
> stop in CDrawApp.main
Breakpoint set in jdg.ch06.CDrawApp.main
>
```

This tells the debugger to stop execution when it encounters the `main()` method of `CDrawApp`. Because the `main()` method is the first method executed in the `CDrawApp` program, the debugger will stop just as it starts to execute `CDrawApp`. Run the debugger for `CDrawApp` to see how the breakpoint works:

```
> run CDrawApp
running ...
main[1]
Breakpoint hit: jdg.ch06.CDrawApp.main (CDrawApp:18)
main[1]
```

The debugger runs `CDrawApp` and stops at the breakpoint. It changes its prompt to `main[1]` to let you know that it is suspended in the number 1 stack frame of the main thread. A stack frame represents the state of the stack of the Java virtual machine as a result of a method invocation. Refer to the section "JVM Stack" in Chapter 37, "The Java Virtual Machine." Now that you've stopped the debugger with your breakpoint, use the `list` command to see where you are in the program's flow of control:

```
main[1] list
14          import java.io.IOException;
15
16          class CDrawApp {
17           public static void main(String args[]) throws IOException {
18       =>   CDraw program = new CDraw();
19            program.run();
20           }
21          }
22
main[1]
```

The arrow indicates that the debugger has stopped at the point where the program instance of `CDrawApp` is about to be created. Now step into the `CDraw()` constructor using the `step` command. This command allows you to control a program's execution one instruction at a time and is used to produce the following debugger output:

```
main[1] step
main[1]
```

```
Breakpoint hit: jdg.ch06.CDraw.<init> (CDraw:29)
main[1]
```

The debugger informs you that it has stopped at a breakpoint in the `CDraw` constructor. The `<init>` identifier is used to indicate a constructor. Enter another `list` command to see where you are:

```
main[1] list
25          static KeyboardInput kbd = new KeyboardInput(System.in);
26          BorderedPrintCGrid grid;
27
28          // Method declarations
29      =>  CDraw() {
30           grid = new BorderedPrintCGrid();
31          }
32          void run() throws IOException {
33           boolean finished = false;
main[1]
```

The debugger indicates that you're about to execute the `CDraw()` constructor. Skip forward in the program's execution until you reach the `run()` method of `CDraw`. Now set a breakpoint at the `run()` method:

```
main[1] stop in CDraw.run
Breakpoint set in jdg.ch06.CDraw.run
main[1]
```

Now continue running the debugger with the `continue` command:

```
main[1] cont
main[1]
Breakpoint hit: jdg.ch06.CDraw.run (CDraw:33)
main[1]
```

The debugger indicates that it stopped at your breakpoint. Use the `list` command to see where the debugger stopped:

```
main[1] list
29          CDraw() {
30           grid = new BorderedPrintCGrid();
31          }
32          void run() throws IOException {
33      =>   boolean finished = false;
34           do {
35            char command = getCommand();
36            switch(command){
37             case 'P':
main[1]
```

You're at the first instruction in the `run()` method. Let's take a little break here and look around a bit. First, use the `methods` command to list the methods that are available to the `CDraw` class:

```
main[1] methods CDraw
void <init>()
void run()
char getCommand()
void addPoint()
```

```
void addBox()
void addText()
void editText()
void editText(CGTextEdit)
void <clinit>()
main[1]
```

The debugger responds by listing all methods declared for `CDraw`, including its constructors, `<init>` and `<clinit>`. These constructors are internal methods generated by the Java virtual machine.

The `classes` command lists all classes that are currently known (loaded) by the debugger. Let's take a look at them:

```
main[1] classes
** classes list **
0x1393008:class(java.lang.Thread)
0x1393018:class(java.lang.Object)
0x1393098:class(java.lang.Class)
0x1393028:class(java.lang.String)
0x1393038:class(java.lang.ThreadDeath)
0x1393048:class(java.lang.Error)
0x1393058:class(java.lang.Throwable)
0x1393068:class(java.lang.Exception)
0x1393078:class(java.lang.RuntimeException)
0x1393088:interface(java.lang.Cloneable)
0x13930b0:class(java.lang.ThreadGroup)
0x13930e0:class(java.lang.System)
0x13930f0:class(java.io.BufferedInputStream)
0x1393100:class(java.io.FilterInputStream)
0x1393110:class(java.io.InputStream)
0x1393128:class(java.io.FileInputStream)
0x1393140:class(java.io.FileDescriptor)
0x1393170:class(java.io.PrintStream)
0x1393180:class(java.io.FilterOutputStream)
0x1393190:class(java.io.OutputStream)
0x13931a8:class(java.io.BufferedOutputStream)
0x13931c0:class(java.io.FileOutputStream)
0x1393208:class(java.lang.StringBuffer)
0x1393240:class(java.lang.Integer)
0x1393250:class(java.lang.Number)
0x13932a8:class(java.lang.NoClassDefFoundError)
0x13932b8:class(java.lang.LinkageError)
0x13932c8:class(java.lang.OutOfMemoryError)
0x13932d8:class(java.lang.VirtualMachineError)
0x13932f0:class(sun.tools.debug.EmptyApp)
0x1393300:class(sun.tools.debug.Agent)
0x1393328:class(java.lang.Runtime)
0x1393370:class(java.util.Properties)
0x1393380:class(java.util.Hashtable)
0x1393390:class(java.util.Dictionary)
0x13933a8:class(java.util.HashtableEntry)
0x1393768:class(java.net.ServerSocket)
0x1393780:class(java.net.PlainSocketImpl)
0x1393790:class(java.net.SocketImpl)
0x13937e0:class(java.net.InetAddress)
0x13938a8:class(java.lang.Math)
```

```
0x13938b8:class(java.util.Random)
0x1393948:class(java.lang.Character)
0x1393a18:class(sun.tools.java.ClassPath)
0x1393a28:class(java.lang.Compiler)
0x1393a58:class(java.io.File)
0x1393aa0:class(sun.tools.java.ClassPathEntry)
0x1393b10:class(sun.tools.zip.ZipFile)
0x1393b40:class(java.io.RandomAccessFile)
0x1393bb0:interface(sun.tools.zip.ZipConstants)
0x1393c00:class(sun.tools.zip.ZipEntry)
0x13a2638:class(sun.tools.debug.BreakpointHandler)
0x13a2670:class(sun.tools.debug.BreakpointQueue)
0x13a26a8:class(java.util.Vector)
0x13a26c8:class(java.net.Socket)
0x13a28f0:class(java.io.DataInputStream)
0x13a2910:class(java.net.SocketInputStream)
0x13a2938:class(sun.tools.debug.ResponseStream)
0x13a2950:class(java.net.SocketOutputStream)
0x13a2978:class(java.io.DataOutputStream)
0x13a29e8:class(sun.tools.debug.AgentOutputStream)
0x13a2ab0:class(java.util.HashtableEnumerator)
0x13a2ad8:class(java.util.VectorEnumerator)
0x13a2f48:interface(java.lang.Runnable)
0x13a37d0:interface(sun.tools.debug.AgentConstants)
0x13a3d18:interface(java.io.DataOutput)
0x13a3d28:interface(java.io.DataInput)
0x13a4130:interface(java.util.Enumeration)
0x13a41b8:class(jdg.ch06.CDrawApp)
0x13a44e0:interface(sun.tools.java.Constants)
0x13a4508:class(sun.tools.java.Identifier)
0x13a54e8:class(jdg.ch06.CDraw)
0x13a54f8:class(jdg.ch05.KeyboardInput)
0x13a5810:interface(sun.tools.java.RuntimeConstants)
0x13a6bf8:class(java.lang.ClassNotFoundException)
0x13a6fc8:class(sun.tools.debug.Field)
0x13a7a38:class(sun.tools.debug.BreakpointSet)
0x13a7dc0:class(sun.tools.debug.MainThread)
0x13a8090:class(sun.tools.debug.StackFrame)
0x13a8168:class(sun.tools.java.Package)
0x13a8230:class(sun.tools.java.ClassFile)
0x13a8318:class(sun.tools.debug.LineNumber)
0x13a9830:class(jdg.ch05.BorderedPrintCGrid)
0x13a9840:class(jdg.ch05.PrintCGrid)
0x13a9850:class(jdg.ch05.CGrid)
0x13a9868:class([[C)
0x13a9878:class([C)
0x13a9930:class(jdg.ch05.CGObject)
main[1]
```

That's quite a number of classes! Look through this list to see if there are any that you recognize. You should be able to identify some classes that are used by the `CDrawApp` program.

The `threadgroups` command lists the threadgroups that are currently defined by the program:

```
main[1] threadgroups
1. (java.lang.ThreadGroup)0x13930b8 system
2. (java.lang.ThreadGroup)0x13939c0 main
3. (java.lang.ThreadGroup)0x13a7d60 jdg.ch06.CDrawApp.main
main[1]
```

The three threadgroups are the `system` threadgroup (used by the Java runtime system), the default `main` threadgroup, and the threadgroup associated with the `CDrawApp` program.

The `threads` command tells you what threads are in a threadgroup:

```
main[1] threads system
Group system:
 1. (java.lang.Thread)0x13931f8                     Finalizer thread
 2. (java.lang.Thread)0x1393918                     Debugger agent
 3. (sun.tools.debug.BreakpointHandler)0x13a2640 Breakpoint handler
Group main:
 4. (java.lang.Thread)0x13930a0 main suspended
Group jdg.ch06.CDrawApp.main:
 5. (sun.tools.debug.MainThread)0x13a7dc8 main at breakpoint
main[1]
```

When you list the threads in the `system` threadgroup, you get a list of all threads maintained by the Java runtime system.

The `memory` command tells you how much memory is available to the Java runtime system:

```
main[1] memory
Free: 2439408, total: 3145720
main[1]
```

The available memory on your computer may differ from mine. For your information, I'm currently running Java on a 486/DX-2 66 computer with 20MB of RAM. Obviously, Java isn't using all of the memory that's available to it.

The `where` command dumps the stack used by the Java virtual machine. It displays the current list of methods that have been invoked to get you to your breakpoint. An example of the `where` command follows:

```
main[1] where
  [1] jdg.ch06.CDraw.run (CDraw:33)
  [2] jdg.ch06.CDrawApp.main (CDrawApp:19)
main[1]
```

The `where` command comes in handy when you are deep in the inner layers of several nested method invocations. It shows you how you got to where you are within the program.

You can use the `up` and `down` commands to move up and down the stack. The `up` command moves you to a higher stack frame within the stack:

```
main[1] up
main[2]
```

Do a `list` command to see the results of the `up` command:

```
main[2] list
15
16          class CDrawApp {
17           public static void main(String args[]) throws IOException {
18            CDraw program = new CDraw();
19       =>   program.run();
20           }
```

```
21          }
22
23          public class CDraw {
main[2]
```

Now use the `down` command to go back down the stack to where you were before:

```
main[2] down
main[1]
```

Do another `list` command to verify that you have returned to where you were before you entered the `up` command:

```
main[1] list
29           CDraw() {
30            grid = new BorderedPrintCGrid();
31           }
32           void run() throws IOException {
33       =>   boolean finished = false;
34            do {
35             char command = getCommand();
36             switch(command){
37              case 'P':
main[1]
```

Now let's look at some variables. Enter the `locals` command to get a list of local variables of the `run()` method:

```
main[1] locals
Local variables and arguments:
  this = jdg.ch06.CDraw@13a7ce8
  finished is not in scope.
  command is not in scope.
main[1]
```

The `finished` and `command` variables are not in the current scope because they have not yet been declared. Step over to the next statement:

```
main[1] step
main[1]
Breakpoint hit: jdg.ch06.CDraw.run (CDraw:35)
main[1]
```

Enter the `list` command to see where you have stepped:

```
main[1] list
31           }
32           void run() throws IOException {
33            boolean finished = false;
34            do {
35       =>    char command = getCommand();
36             switch(command){
37              case 'P':
38                addPoint();
39               System.out.println();
main[1]
```

Do another `locals` command. The `finished` variable should now be in scope:

```
main[1] locals
Local variables and arguments:
  this = jdg.ch06.CDraw@13a7ce8
  finished = false
  command is not in scope.
main[1]
```

You have now covered most of the debugger commands. Now let's go on to debugging multithreaded programs. Type `exit` to exit the debugger.

Debugging Multithreaded Programs

The Java debugger supports the debugging of multithreaded programs. In fact, it provides a great tool for understanding how multithreaded programs work. In this section, you use the debugger to debug the `ThreadTest1` program that you developed in Chapter 8, "Multithreading."

Change directories to the `ch08` directory and enter `javac -g ThreadTest1.java` to add additional debugging information to the `ThreadTest1.class` bytecode file:

```
C:\java\jdg\ch08>javac -g ThreadTest1.java

C:\java\jdg\ch08>
```

Now start `jdb` and load `ThreadTest1` with the command `jdb ThreadTest1`:

```
C:\java\jdg\ch08>jdb ThreadTest1
Initializing jdb...
0x13a41b8:class(ThreadTest1)
>
```

Set a breakpoint at the `main()` method of `ThreadTest1`:

```
> stop in ThreadTest1.main
Breakpoint set in ThreadTest1.main
>
```

Run `ThreadTest1`:

```
> run ThreadTest1
running ...

Breakpoint hit: ThreadTest1.main (ThreadTest1:9)
main[1]
```

The debugger runs `ThreadTest1` and stops at your breakpoint. Do a `list` command to see where the debugger stopped:

```
main[1] list
5          import java.lang.InterruptedException;
6
7          class ThreadTest1 {
8           public static void main(String args[]) {
9       =>   MyThread thread1 = new MyThread("thread1: ");
```

```
10          MyThread thread2 = new MyThread("thread2: ");
11          thread1.start();
12          thread2.start();
13          boolean thread1IsAlive = true;
main[1]
```

The debugger is at the beginning of the `main()` method. It has not created any new threads at this time. Use the `threads` command to verify this:

```
main[1] threads
Group ThreadTest1.main:
 1. (sun.tools.debug.MainThread)0x13a5d88 main at breakpoint
main[1]
```

The only thread is the current main thread of execution. Set a breakpoint to line 11 of `ThreadTest1`, the point where both `thread1` and `thread2` will be declared:

```
main[1] stop at ThreadTest1:11
Breakpoint set at ThreadTest1:11
main[1]
```

Now jump to that point in the program:

```
main[1] cont
main[1]
Breakpoint hit: ThreadTest1.main (ThreadTest1:11)
main[1]
```

Use the `threads` command again to see the effect of the `thread1` and `thread2` declarations:

```
Group ThreadTest1.main:
 1. (sun.tools.debug.MainThread)0x13a5d88 main      at breakpoint
 2. (MyThread)0x13a6b70                   thread1:  zombie
 3. (MyThread)0x13a6b98                   thread2:  zombie
main[1]
```

Both `thread1` and `thread2` are in the New Thread state. The debugger refers to them as *zombies.* That's a curious term considering that the threads have neither started nor died at this point in the program's execution.

Now jump ahead in the program to line 13, where both threads are started. First, set the breakpoint:

```
main[1] stop at ThreadTest1:13
Breakpoint set at ThreadTest1:13
main[1]
```

Now jump ahead to the breakpoint:

```
main[1] cont

Breakpoint hit: ThreadTest1.main (ThreadTest1:13)
main[1]
```

Let's take a quick look around to make sure you are where you want to be:

```
main[1] list
9           MyThread thread1 = new MyThread("thread1: ");
10          MyThread thread2 = new MyThread("thread2: ");
```

```
11          thread1.start();
12          thread2.start();
13     =>   boolean thread1IsAlive = true;
14          boolean thread2IsAlive = true;
15          do {
16           if(thread1IsAlive && !thread1.isAlive()){
17             thread1IsAlive = false;
main[1]
```

You should now get different results when you execute the `threads` command:

```
Group ThreadTest1.main:
 1. (sun.tools.debug.MainThread)0x13a5d88 main      at breakpoint
 2. (MyThread)0x13a6b70                   thread1:  suspended
 3. (MyThread)0x13a6b98                   thread2:  running
main[1]
```

> **NOTE**
>
> Depending on the machine on which you run the `jdb`, you may find that both threads are suspended when you execute the `threads` command.

The debugger tells us that `thread1` is suspended and `thread2` is running. The `suspend` command is used to suspend the execution of a running thread. It takes the number of the thread identified by the `threads` command as its argument. The `suspend` command is used as follows:

```
main[1] suspend 3
main[1]
```

Use the `threads` command to verify that it works:

```
main[1] threads
Group ThreadTest1.main:
 1. (sun.tools.debug.MainThread)0x13a5d88 main      at breakpoint
 2. (MyThread)0x13a6b70                   thread1:  suspended
 3. (MyThread)0x13a6b98                   thread2:  suspended
main[1]
```

Now switch threads to `thread1` using the `thread` command:

```
main[1] thread 2
thread1: [1]
```

Notice how the prompt changed to indicate that you switched to `thread1`. Let's do a `list` command to see where we are in `thread1`. The results of the `list` command follow:

```
thread1: [1] list
36            System.out.println(name+message[i]);
37          }
38         }
39         void randomWait(){
40     =>   try {
41            sleep((long)(3000*Math.random()));
```

```
42            }catch (InterruptedException x){
43             System.out.println("Interrupted!");
44            }
thread1: [1]
```

`Thread1` is in the middle of the `randomWait()` method.

Switch threads to see what `thread2` is up to:

```
thread2: [1] list
36             System.out.println(name+message[i]);
37            }
38           }
39           void randomWait(){
40       =>   try {
41             sleep((long)(3000*Math.random()));
42            }catch (InterruptedException x){
43             System.out.println("Interrupted!");
44            }
thread2: [1]
```

It looks like `thread2` is in the same state as `thread1`.

Set a breakpoint for `thread1` and `thread2`:

```
thread2: [1] stop at MyThread:36
Breakpoint set at MyThread:36
thread2: [1] thread 2
thread1: [1] stop at MyThread:36
Breakpoint set at MyThread:36
thread1: [1]
```

Now continue the execution of `thread1`:

```
thread1: [1] cont
thread1: [1] list
32           public void run() {
33            String name = getName();
34            for(int i=0;i<message.length;++i) {
35             randomWait();
36       =>    System.out.println(name+message[i]);
37            }
38           }
39           void randomWait(){
40            try {
thread1: [1]
```

The thread executes up to the breakpoint. You can verify this by running the `threads` command:

```
thread1: [1] threads
Group ThreadTest1.main:
 1. (sun.tools.debug.MainThread)0x13a5888 main      suspended
 2. (MyThread)0x13a59f0                   thread1:  at breakpoint
 3. (MyThread)0x13a5a18                   thread2:  suspended
thread1: [1]
```

If you use the `step` command, `thread1` becomes suspended and `thread2` reaches the breakpoint:

```
thread1: [1] step
thread1: [1]
Breakpoint hit: MyThread.run (MyThread:36)
thread2: [1] threads
Group ThreadTest1.main:
 1. (sun.tools.debug.MainThread)0x13a5888 main       suspended
 2. (MyThread)0x13a59f0                  thread1:   suspended
 3. (MyThread)0x13a5a18                  thread2:   at breakpoint
thread2: [1]
```

You can use the `print` and `dump` commands to display the values of the message field of `MyThread`:

```
thread2: [1] print MyThread.message
"MyThread" is not a valid field of (MyThread)0x13a5a18
MyThread.message = 0x13a5958 Object[6] = { Java, is, hot,, ... }
thread2: [1] dump MyThread.message
"MyThread" is not a valid field of (MyThread)0x13a5a18
MyThread.message = 0x13a5958 Object[6] = { Java, is, hot,, ... }
thread2: [1]
```

These commands are somewhat buggy. They complain that the fields are not valid, but they display the values of the fields anyway.

At this point, you've covered all the important features of the Java debugger. You can experiment with the debugger to see how the two threads continue their execution. When you are finished, use the `exit` command to terminate the debugger.

Summary

In this chapter you have learned how to use the Java debugger to step through the execution of a Java program. You have learned how to invoke the debugger, load class files, and examine classes as they are executed. In Chapter 10, "Automating Software Documentation," you will learn how to use another program contained in the Java toolkit—the Java documentation tool. You'll see how this tool can help you to quickly and easily develop documentation for your Java programs.

10

Automating Software Documentation

In this chapter you'll learn how to use the Java documentation tool, `javadoc`, to automate the documentation of your software. This is the tool that is used to create the superb Java API documentation. It translates your source code into *Hypertext Markup Language* (HTML) files that can be displayed by a Web browser. When you finish this chapter, you'll be able to quickly and easily document your software using `javadoc`.

How `javadoc` Works

The `javadoc` program examines your source code and generates HTML files that provide a fully integrated set of documentation for your Java software. The HTML files generated by `javadoc` document the classes, interfaces, variables, methods, and exceptions that you declare and use in your programs. These files describe your software at the package and class level. The linking capabilities of HTML are used to provide extensive cross-referencing between related software components. These links allow you to quickly access all of the documentation that is relevant to a particular topic.

`javadoc` differs from other documentation generators in that it goes beyond simple comment-scanning and actually parses your source code in order to generate documentation that describes the structure and behavior of your programs. It makes judicious use of HTML links to generate documentation that allows you to easily traverse the structure of your software.

`javadoc` recognizes special types of comments that you insert in your source code. When it parses your source code, it combines these comments with the structural information it generates. Your comments are then integrated into your software's HTML description. The special comments recognized by `javadoc` consist of doc comments, `javadoc` tags, and HTML tags.

Doc comments are based on the traditional C `/*` and `*/` comment delimiters. They are distinguished from ordinary C comments in that they begin with `/**` instead of `/*`. They are used to identify comments that are to be automatically added to the HTML documentation produced by `javadoc`.

The *`javadoc` tags* are special tags that are embedded in doc comments. These tags allow you to include reference information in your software. For example, you can include a `javadoc` comment that says, `See also: class X`. Some references result in links being automatically inserted into your software's documentation.

`javadoc` also allows you to insert HTML tags directly in your source code. However, `javadoc` recommends that you limit your HTML to small, simple, and correctly formatted HTML elements so as not to conflict with the HTML that it generates. Your HTML tags are combined with those produced by `javadoc` to create an integrated set of HTML pages.

Using javadoc

The best way to understand how `javadoc` works is by using it and then exploring the documentation that it produces. `Javadoc` is so simple to use that it requires only a single command line to generate integrated software documentation for multiple software packages.

To use `javadoc`, create a separate `ch10` directory under your `c:\java\jdg` path. This directory will be used to store the HTML files that `javadoc` produces. You could store these files in the same directory in which you store your Java API documentation, but it's not a good idea to clutter up your API directory with other documentation. Because you will not be storing your documentation in your API directory, you will have to copy the `images` subdirectory from your API directory to `ch10`. The images are needed by your documentation so that Web browsers can display all the fancy icons, images, and bullets that are characteristic of the API documentation. With these images, your documentation looks outstanding. Without the images, your browser will substitute its missing icon images for the Java images, and your documentation will look horrendous.

After you have copied the `images` subdirectory to your `ch10` directory, launch a DOS shell and enter the following DOS command line:

```
C:\java\jdg\ch10>javadoc jdg.ch05 jdg.ch06
Loading source files for jdg.ch05
Loading source files for jdg.ch06
Generating packages.html
generating documentation for class jdg.ch05.BorderedPrintCGrid
generating documentation for class jdg.ch05.CGBox
generating documentation for class jdg.ch05.CGObject
generating documentation for class jdg.ch05.CGPoint
generating documentation for class jdg.ch05.CGText
generating documentation for class jdg.ch05.CGrid
generating documentation for class jdg.ch05.KeyboardInput
generating documentation for class jdg.ch05.Point
generating documentation for class jdg.ch05.PrintCGrid
generating documentation for interface jdg.ch06.CGTextEdit
generating documentation for interface jdg.ch06.ColorConstants
generating documentation for class jdg.ch06.CGText
generating documentation for class jdg.ch06.CGTextBox
generating documentation for class jdg.ch06.CGTextPoint
Generating index
Sorting 90 items . . . done
Generating tree

C:\java\jdg\ch10>
```

As the result of that single command line, `javadoc` generates a complete set of HTML documentation for the software you produced in Chapters 5, "Classes and Objects," and 6, "Interfaces." This documentation will have the same look and feel as the Java API documentation.

When `javadoc` has finished producing the documentation, use your browser to view it. I'll be using Netscape 2.0. It is my favorite browser, and it's Java compatible.

Launch your browser and use its local file open feature to open the file `packages.html`, located in the `ch10` directory. Your browser will display a Sun-style Package Index page, as shown in Figure 10.1.

FIGURE 10.1.
The Package Index page.

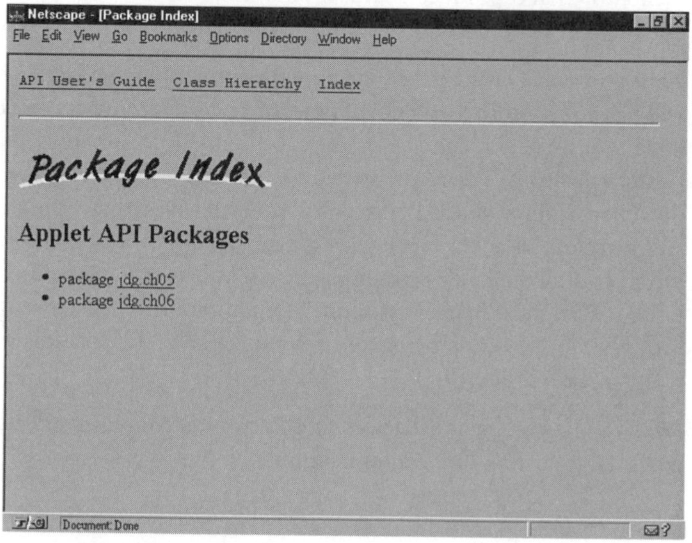

This page looks great, but has two defects owing to the fact that it was not created in the same directory as your Java API. The link to the API User's Guide doesn't work, and your packages are mislabeled as Applet API packages. That's a small price to pay in order to avoid messing up your Java API directory. The rest of the links work fine.

With your browser open to the Package Index, click on the Class Hierarchy link. A Web page showing all the classes in the `jdg.ch05` and `jdg.ch06` packages is presented to you. The page shows how your classes fit within the rest of the Java class hierarchy. It also identifies the interfaces that are implemented by your classes. The information presented in the class hierarchy page is extremely useful in understanding the structure of Java programs. (See Figure 10.2.)

While you have the Class Hierarchy page loaded, click on the Index link. Another great Web page is displayed that contains an alphabetized index of all the fields (variables) and methods declared in the `jdg.ch05` and `jdg.ch06` packages. When I first saw this page, my immediate reaction was, "Where did all this come from?" Go ahead and click around this page to see some of the items that you've used in your programs. When you have finished, click on the All Packages link to go back to the Package Index. (See Figure 10.3.)

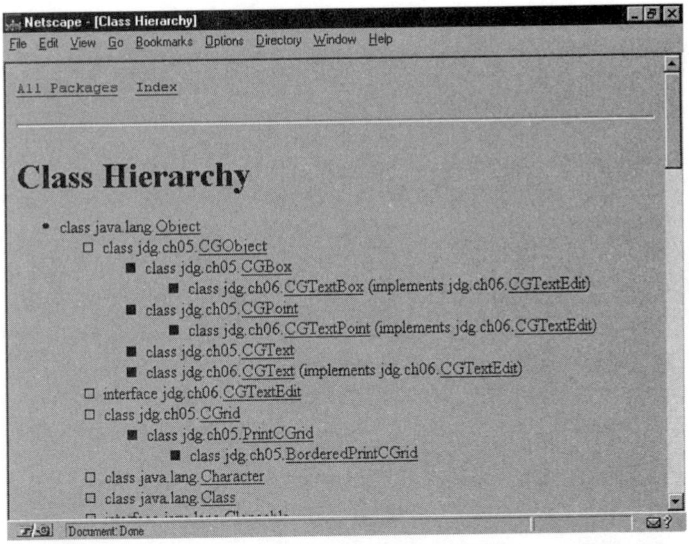

FIGURE 10.2.
The Class Hierarchy description page.

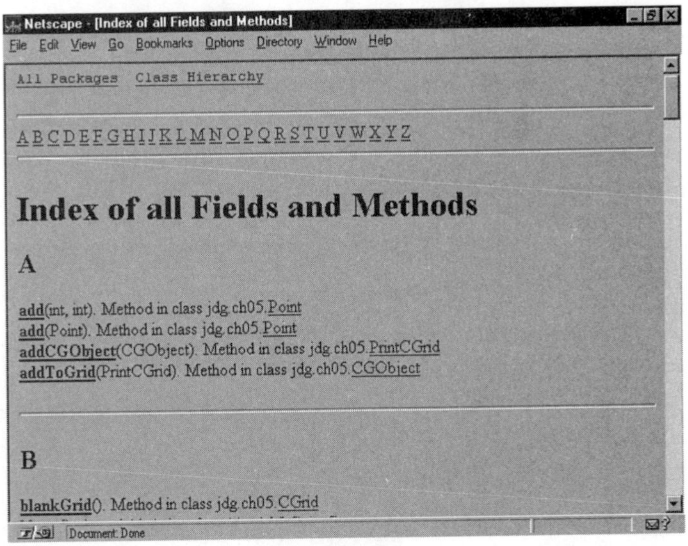

FIGURE 10.3.
The Index of all Fields and Methods page.

From the package index, click on the `jdg.ch05` link. This will bring you into the Class Index for the `jdg.ch05` package. This page documents the classes that are declared in this package. (See Figure 10.4.)

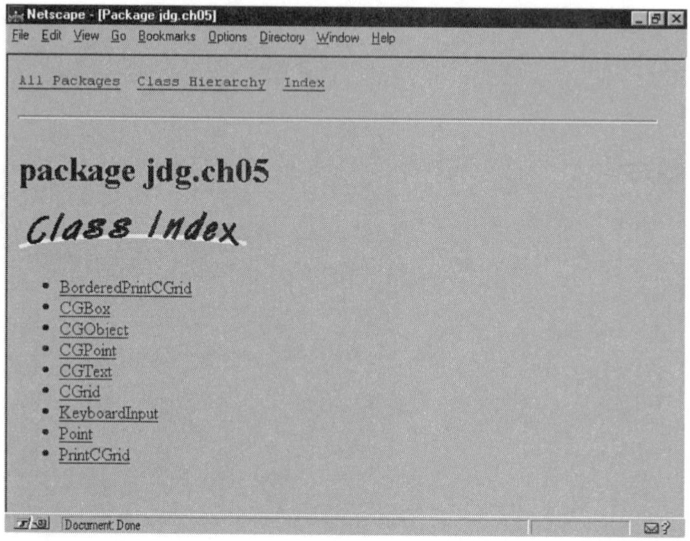

FIGURE 10.4.
The `jdg.ch05` *Class Index page.*

From here, click on the `BorderedPrintCGrid` link. The class's description is displayed. Notice how it identifies the branch of the class hierarchy leading to the `BorderedPrintCGrid` class. You can click on the links in the class hierarchy branch to find out information about the variables and methods that are inherited by a class. A list of constructors appears under the class hierarchy diagram. Click on any of the constructor links to find a more detailed description of the constructors. (See Figure 10.5.)

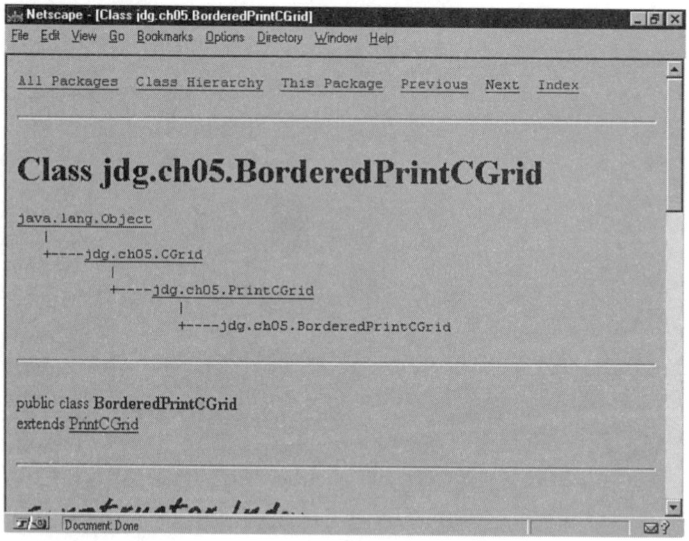

FIGURE 10.5.
The `BorderedPrintCGrid` *class page.*

Under the constructor list is a list of access methods that are declared for the `BorderedPrintCGrid` class. The class-specific Web pages document only the public and protected variables, constructors, and methods of a class. To see a description of class variables, click on the link to the `CGrid` class, at the top of the `BorderedPrintCGrid` Web page. (See Figure 10.6.)

FIGURE 10.6.
The `CGrid` *class page.*

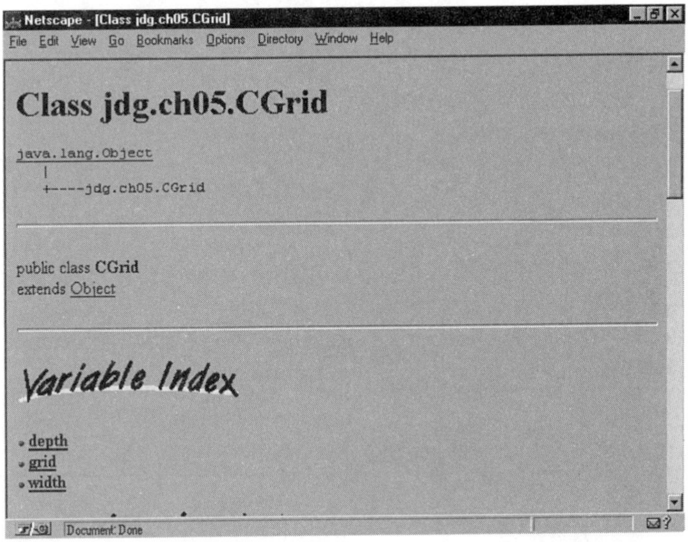

The `CGrid` class defines three protected variables: `depth`, `grid`, and `width`. You can click on the link to the `depth` variable to see how these variables are documented. (See Figure 10.7.)

FIGURE 10.7.
How `javadoc` *describes variables.*

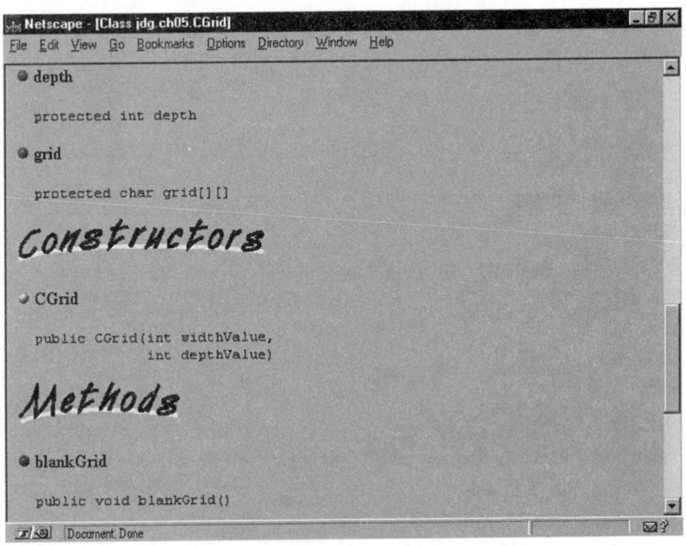

You should now have a pretty good idea of the kind of documentation that can be produced using `javadoc`. The most remarkable fact about the documentation produced in this section is that you did not have to write a single comment in your source code. It was generated automatically and is far more effective than any traditional program comments. However, if this level of documentation is not enough to satisfy your requirements, you can insert additional comments in your source code that will be integrated with the documentation produced by `javadoc`.

Placing Doc Comments

Doc comments, as discussed in the beginning of this chapter, are normal C comments that begin with an extra asterisk. They are easy to insert into your Java programs, and they add implementation-specific information to your documentation. To show how they are used, I've added doc comments to the `CGBox.java` source code. These comments can be easily identified in the new program listing for `CGBox`. (See Listing 10.1.) I haven't included the whole listing, just the part where I've added doc comments.

Listing 10.1. The new `CGBox.java`.

```
package jdg.ch05;

// CGBox.java
/**
 * The CGBox class describes box objects that
 * are displayed on a PrintCGrid.
 */
public class CGBox extends CGObject {
 // Variable declarations

 /**
  * The lr is used to identify the lower right-hand
  * corner of a box.
  */
 protected Point lr; // Lower right corner of a box

 // Method declarations
 /**
  * A CGBox object is constructed using an upper
  * left-hand corner point, a lower right-hand corner
  * point, and a box drawing character.
  */
 public CGBox(Point ulCorner, Point lrCorner,char ch) {
  location = ulCorner;
  lr = lrCorner;
  drawCharacter = ch;
 }
```

You can see how these doc comments were integrated into the appropriate class, variable, and constructor descriptions by looking for them in my browser's display. (See Figure 10.8.)

FIGURE 10.8.
Doc comments as displayed by a browser.

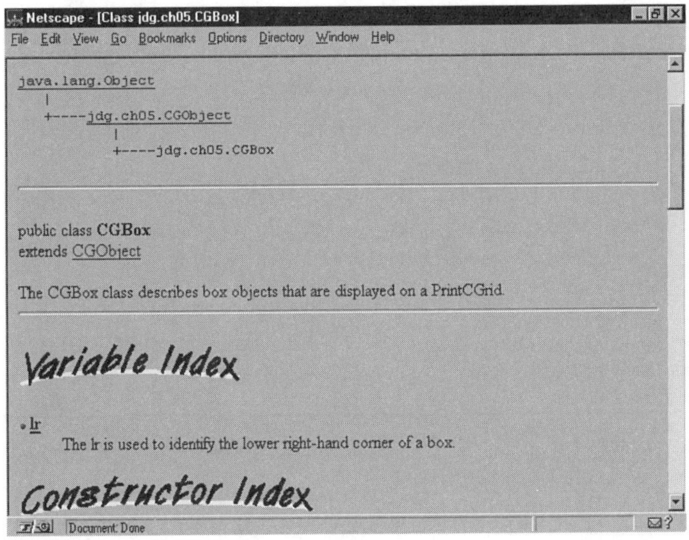

Using javadoc Tags

`javadoc` tags are special tags that are inserted in doc comments. They are used to identify specific references in your code. Special `javadoc` tags are provided for documenting classes, variables, and methods.

`javadoc` tags consist of an at sign (`@`) followed by a tag type and then a specific comment reference. Their syntax is as follows:

```
@tagType commentReference
```

Java classes are allowed to use the `see`, `version`, and `author` tag types. Variables can use only the `see` tag type. Methods are allowed to use the `see`, `param`, `return`, and `exception` tag types.

The `see` tag type has the following syntax:

```
@see className
@see fullClassName
@see fullClassName#methodName
```

The `version` and `author` tag types are used like this:

```
@version versionID
@author authorName
```

The param, return, and exception tags are used as follows:

```
@param parameterName description
@return description
@exception fullClassName description
```

In order to demonstrate the use of these tags, I have modified the `jdg.ch05.CGText.java` file to include param tags. (See Listing 10.2.)

Listing 10.2. The new `CGText`.

```
/**
  * @param p Text location
  * @param s Text string
  */
 public CGText(Point p,String s) {
  location = p;
  drawCharacter = ' ';
  text = s;
 }
```

Figure 10.9 shows how the `javadoc` tags are integrated by `javadoc` and displayed by my browser.

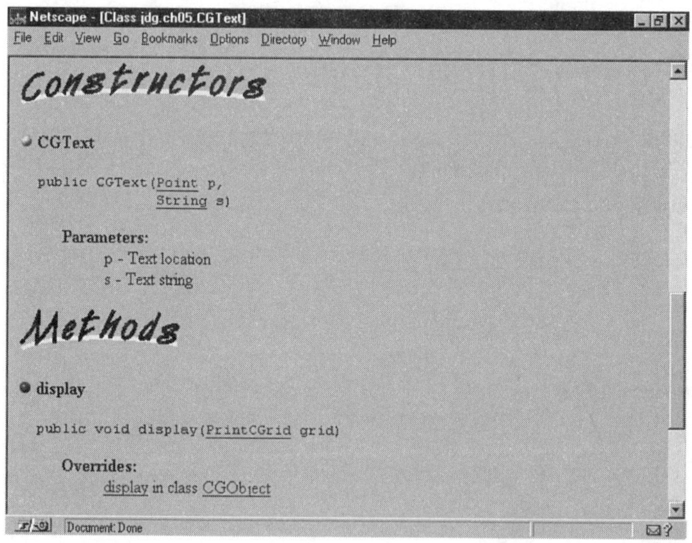

FIGURE 10.9.
The browser's display of the `javadoc` *tags.*

Embedding Standard HTML

If the doc comments and `javadoc` tags still aren't enough to meet your documentation requirements, you can always insert your own HTML markup into a doc comment. However, using HTML is a little bit dangerous because your HTML tags might conflict with the HTML tags inserted by `javadoc`. If you're going to use HTML in your documentation, try to keep it as simple as possible.

I've modified the source code in `CGPoint.java` to include HTML address tags so that I can put my e-mail address in the doc comment. (See Listing 10.3.)

Listing 10.3. The new `CGPoint`.

```
// CGPoint.java
/**
 * Send your bug reports to:
 * <ADDRESS>jamie@jaworski.com</ADDRESS>
 */
public class CGPoint extends CGObject {
 // Method declarations
 public CGPoint(int x, int y,char ch) {
  location = new Point(x,y);
  drawCharacter = ch;
 }
```

Figure 10.10 shows how the HTML tags are integrated by `javadoc` and displayed by my browser.

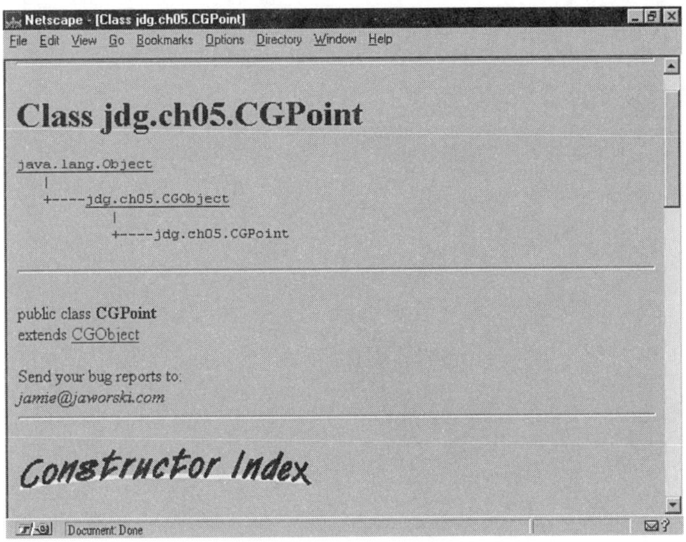

FIGURE 10.10.
How a browser displays `javadoc` *tags.*

Summary

In this chapter you have learned how to use the Java documentation tool `javadoc` to automate the documentation of your software. You have used it to document the software you developed in Chapters 5 and 6. You have also learned how to use doc comments, `javadoc` tags, and

HTML elements with `javadoc`. You have now covered most of the elements of the Java language and have learned how to use the compiler, interpreter, debuggger, and documentation generator. Chapter 11, "Language Summary," provides a complete description of the Java language before you move out of this part of the book and go on to the details of the Java API.

11

Language Summary

In the previous chapters you've covered most of the elements of the Java language and learned how to use those elements through programming examples. This chapter provides a summary of the Java language syntax. You can use it to review what you've learned so far, and also as a quick reference guide when you need to look up a particular aspect of the language.

The `package` Statement

Java programs are organized into *packages*. Packages contain the source code declarations of Java classes and interfaces. Packages are identified by the `package` statement. It is the first statement in a source code file:

```
package packageName;
```

If a `package` statement is omitted, the classes and interfaces declared within the package are put into the default package—the package with no name.

The package name and the `CLASSPATH` are used to find a class. Only one class or interface may be declared as `public` for a given source code file.

The `import` Statement

The `import` statement is used to reference classes and interfaces that are declared in other packages. There are three forms of the `import` statement:

```
import packageName;
```

```
import packageName.className;
```

```
import packageName.*;
```

The first form allows classes and interfaces to be referenced using the last component in the package name. The second form allows the identified classes and interfaces to be referenced without specifying the name of their package. The third form allows all classes and interfaces in the specified package to be referenced without specifying the name of their package.

Comments

Java provides three styles of comments:

```
/* This is a comment. */
```

```
// This is a comment.
```

```
/** This is a javadoc comment */
```

The first comment style supports traditional C-language comments. All text appearing between `/*` and `*/` is treated as a comment. Comments of this style can span multiple lines.

The second comment style supports C++ comments. All text following the `//` until the end of the line is treated as a comment. Comments of this style do not span multiple lines.

The third comment style is used by the `javadoc` documentation-generation tool. All text between the `/**` and `*/` is treated as a `javadoc` comment. `javadoc` comments may span multiple lines.

Comments cannot be nested and cannot appear within string and character literals.

Identifiers

Identifiers are used to name Java language entities. They begin with a letter and consist of letters and digits. Identifiers are case sensitive and cannot be the same as a reserved word.

Reserved Words

The following words are reserved by the Java language; they cannot be used as names or identifiers:

`abstract`	`do`	`implements`	`package`	`throw`
`boolean`	`double`	`import`	`private`	`throws`
`break`	`else`	`inner`	`protected`	`transient`
`byte`	`extends`	`instanceof`	`public`	`try`
`case`	`final`	`int`	`rest`	`var`
`cast`	`finally`	`interface`	`return`	`void`
`catch`	`float`	`long`	`short`	`volatile`
`char`	`for`	`native`	`static`	`while`
`class`	`future`	`new`	`super`	
`const`	`generic`	`null`	`switch`	
`continue`	`goto`	`operator`	`synchronized`	
`default`	`if`	`outer`	`this`	

NOTE

Some of the reserved words have not yet been implemented.

Primitive Data Types and Literal Values

Java defines eight primitive types. Variables that are declared as a *primitive type* are not objects; they are only placeholders to store primitive values. The eight primitive types are `byte`, `short`, `int`, `long`, `float`, `double`, `char`, and `boolean`.

The `byte`, `short`, `int`, and `long` types represent 8-, 16-, 32-, and 64-bit integer values. The literal values of these types are written using positive or negative decimal, hexadecimal, or octal integers. Hexadecimal values are preceded by `0x` or `0X` and use the letters a through f (upper- or lowercase) to represent the digits 10 through 15. Octal numbers are preceded by `0`. Long decimal values have an `l` or `L` appended to the end of the number.

The `float` and `double` types represent 32- and 64-bit IEEE 754 floating-point numbers. `float` numbers have the `f` or `F` suffix. Double numbers have `d` or `D`. If no suffix is provided, the default `double` type is assumed. Floating-point numbers may be written in any of the following four forms:

```
digits . optionalDigits optionalExponentPart suffix

. digits optionalExponentPart suffix

digits exponentPart suffix

NaN
```

`suffix` is optional. It consists of `f`, `F`, `d`, or `D`, as described previously.

`exponentPart` is optional in the first two forms and required in the third form. It consists of an `e` or `E` followed by a signed integer. It is used to identify the exponent of 10 of the number written in scientific notation. For example, 1000000.0 could be represented as 1.0E6.

The special value `NaN` is used to represent the value "not a number" that occurs as the result of undefined mathematical operations such as division by zero.

The `char` type represents 16-bit Unicode characters. *Unicode* is a 16-bit superset of the ASCII character set that provides many foreign-language characters. A single character is specified by putting the character within single quotes (`'`). There are three exceptions: single quote (`'`), double quote (`"`), and backslash (`\`). The backslash character (`\`) is used as an escape code to represent special character values. The character escape codes are shown in Table 11.1.

Table 11.1. Character escape codes.

Escape Code	*Character*
`\b`	backspace
`\t`	tab
`\n`	linefeed

Escape Code	*Character*
`\f`	form feed
`\r`	carriage return
`\"`	double quote
`\'`	single quote
`\\`	backslash

The backslash can also be followed by an 8-bit octal value or by a `u` or `U` followed by a four-digit hexadecimal value. The four-digit value is used to specify the value of Unicode characters.

The `boolean` type represents the logical values `true` and `false`.

String literals are also provided by Java even though strings are not primitive values. Strings consist of characters enclosed by double quotes (`"`). The character escape codes may be used within strings.

The literal value `null` is used to identify the fact that an object is not assigned to a value. It may be used with any variable that is not of a primitive data type.

Class Declarations

Class declarations allow new classes to be defined for use in Java programs. Classes are declared as follows:

```
classModifiers class className extendsClause implementsClause classBody
```

The class modifiers, `extends` clause, and `implements` clause are optional.

The class modifiers are `abstract`, `public`, and `final`. An `abstract` class provides an abstract class declaration that cannot be instantiated. `Abstract` classes are used as building blocks for the declaration of subclasses. A class that is declared as `public` can be referenced outside its package. If a class is not declared as `public`, it can be referenced only within its package. A `final` class cannot be subclassed. A class cannot be declared as both `final` and `abstract`.

The `extends` clause is used to identify the immediate superclass of a class and thereby position the class within the overall class hierarchy. It is written as follows:

```
extends immediateSuperclass
```

The `implements` clause identifies the interfaces that are implemented by a class. It is written as follows:

```
implements interfaceNames
```

`interfaceNames` consists of one or more interface names separated by commas.

The class body declares the variables, constructors, and access methods of a class. It is written as follows:

```
{ fieldDeclarations }
```

`fieldDeclarations` consists of zero or more variable, constructor, or access method declarations or static initializers.

Variable Declarations

Variables are used to refer to objects and primitive data types. They are declared as follows:

```
variableModifiers type extendedVariableName variableInitialization ;
```

`variableModifiers` and `variableInitialization` are optional. A variable's type may be a primitive data type, class type, or interface type. The `extendedVariableName` is a variable name followed by zero or more bracket sets (`[]`) indicating that the variable is an array.

`variableInitialization` consists of an equals sign (=) followed by a variable initialization.

A *variable initialization* is an expression yielding a value of the variable's type. If the variable being declared is an array, it can be assigned to an array initializer. Array initializers are written as follows:

```
{elementInitializers}
```

`elementInitializers` are expressions that yield values that are consistent with the element type of the array.

There are seven variable modifiers: `public`, `protected`, `private`, `static`, `final`, `transient`, and `volatile`.

The `public`, `protected`, and `private` modifiers are used to designate the specific manner in which a variable can be accessed. Variables that are declared as `public` can be accessed anywhere that the class in which they are defined can be accessed. Variables that are declared as `protected` can be accessed within the package in which they are declared and in subclasses of the class in which they are defined. Variables that are declared as `private` are only accessible in the class in which they are defined and not in any of its subclasses. If a variable is declared as neither `public`, `protected`, nor `private`, it can be accessed only within the package in which it is declared.

A variable that is declared as `static` is associated with its class and is shared by objects that are instances of its class. A `static` variable is also known as a *class variable.*

A variable that is declared as `final` is a constant and cannot be modified. `Final` variables must be initialized when they are declared.

A variable that is declared as `transient` refers to objects and primitive values within the Java virtual machine. `Transient` variables have not been implemented within Java 1.0.

A variable that is declared as `volatile` refers to objects and primitive values that can be modified asynchronously. They are treated in a special manner by the compiler to control the manner in which they can be updated.

Constructor Declarations

Constructors are methods that are used to initialize newly created objects of a class. They are declared as follows:

```
constructorModifiers constructorNameAndParameters throwsClause constructorBody
```

The constructor modifiers are `public`, `protected`, and `private`. They control access to the constructor and are used in the same manner as they are for variables.

The constructor name is the same as the class name in which it is declared. It is followed by a parameter list, written as follows:

```
(parameterDeclarations)
```

The parameter list consists of an opening parenthesis followed by zero or more parameter declarations followed by a closing parenthesis. The parameter declarations are separated by commas. Parameter declarations are written as follows:

```
type parameterName
```

Each parameter declaration consists of a type followed by a parameter name. A parameter name may be followed by sets of matched brackets (`[]`) to indicate that it is an array.

The `throws` clause identifies all uncaught exceptions that are thrown within the constructor. It is written as follows:

```
throws uncaughtExceptions
```

The exceptions are separated by whitespace characters.

The body of a constructor specifies the manner in which an object of the constructor's class is to be initialized. It is written as follows:

```
{constructorCallStatement blockBody}
```

The *`constructorCallStatement`* and *`blockBody`* are optional, but the opening and closing braces must be supplied.

The constructor call statement allows another constructor of the class or its superclass to be invoked before the constructor's block body. It is written as follows:

```
this(argumentList);
```

```
super(argumentList);
```

The first form results in a constructor for the current class being invoked with the specified arguments. The second form results in the constructor of the class's superclass being invoked. The argument list consists of expressions that evaluate to the allowed values of a particular constructor.

If no constructor call statement is specified, a default `super()` constructor is invoked before the constructor block body.

Access Method Declarations

Access methods are methods used to perform operations on the data contained in an object or on `static` class variables. They are written as follows:

```
methodModifiers returnType methodNameAndParameters throwsClause methodBody
```

`methodNameAndParameters` is the same as for constructor declarations. Access method names are different from their class names.

The `throws` clause is also the same as for constructor declarations.

The method body differs from the constructor body in that it does not allow a constructor call statement.

The modifiers allowed for a method include the `public`, `protected`, and `private` modifiers defined for constructors as well as the `final`, `static`, `abstract`, `native`, and `synchronized` modifiers.

The `final` modifier identifies a method that cannot be overridden.

The `static` modifier identifies a class method. Class methods are allowed to access `static` class variables only. `Static` methods are `final`.

An `abstract` method is used to identify a method that cannot be invoked and must be overridden by any non-abstract subclasses of the class in which it is declared. An `abstract` method does not have a method body. Instead, it has a semicolon (;).

A `native` method is a method written in a language other than Java. It is like an `abstract` method in that its body is replaced by a semicolon.

A `synchronized` method is a method that must acquire a lock on an object or on a class before it can be executed.

Static Initializers

A *static initializer* is a block of code that is used to initialize the `static` variables of a class. It is written as follows:

```
static block
```

Static initializers can only access `static` class variables. They are executed in the order in which they appear in a class declaration.

Interfaces

An *interface* specifies a collection of abstract methods that must be overridden by classes that implement the interface. Interfaces are declared as follows:

```
interfaceModifiers interface interfaceName extendsClause interfaceBody
```

The interface modifiers are `public` and `abstract`. `public` interfaces can be accessed in other packages. All interfaces are `abstract`. The `abstract` modifier is superfluous.

The optional `extends` clause is used to identify any interfaces that are extended by an interface. It is written as follows:

```
extends interfaceNames
```

The interface names are separated by commas. An interface includes all the methods of all interfaces that it extends.

The interface body consists of zero or more variable and abstract method declarations. They are enclosed within braces (`{` and `}`).

Variables declared within an interface must be `static` and `final`. The `static` and `final` modifiers need not be displayed. Variables declared in a `public` interface are `public`. The `public` keyword need not be specified.

Methods declared within an interface are `abstract`. The `abstract` keyword need not be specified.

Blocks and Block Bodies

Blocks consist of sequences of local variable declarations and statements. They are written as follows:

```
{ blockBody }
```

The `blockBody` is a sequence of local variable declarations or statements.

A block can also consist of a single statement without the enclosing braces.

Local Variable Declarations

Local variables are declared in the same manner as field declarations are, except that local variables do not include modifiers. They are accessible within the block in which they are declared.

The `this` and `super` variables are predefined. They refer to the current object for which a method is invoked and the superclass of the current object being invoked.

Statements

The programming statements provided by Java are described in the following subsections.

Empty Statement

The *empty statement* performs no processing. It consists of a single semicolon (`;`).

Block Statement

A *block statement* consists of a sequence of statements and local variable declarations that are treated as a single statement block. The statements are enclosed within braces (`{` and `}`).

Method Invocation

A *method invocation* invokes a method for an object or a class. Method invocations may be used within an expression or as a separate statement. To be used as a separate statement, the method being invoked must be declared with a void return value. Method invocation statements take the following forms:

```
objectName.methodName(argumentList);
```

```
className.methodName(argumentList);
```

The `argumentList` consists of a comma-separated list of zero or more expressions that are consistent with the method's parameters.

Allocation Statements

When an object is *allocated*, it is typically assigned to a variable. However, it is not required to be assigned when it is allocated. An allocation statement is of the following form:

```
new constructor(argumentList);
```

The `new` operator is used to allocate an object of the class specified by the constructor. The constructor is then invoked to initialize the object using the arguments specified in the argument list.

Assignment Statements

The *assignment statement* assigns an object or value to a variable. Its general form is

```
variableName = expression;
```

where `expression` yields a value that is consistent with the variable's type.

Other assignment operators may be used in addition to the = operator. Refer to the section titled "Operators" later in this chapter.

The `if` Statement

The `if` statement is used to select among alternative paths of execution. It is written in the following two forms:

```
if ( booleanExpression ) statement
```

```
if ( booleanExpression ) statement1 else statement2
```

In the first form, `statement` is executed only if the `boolean` expression is `true`. In the second form, `statement1` is executed if the `boolean` expression is `true`, and `statement2` is executed if the `boolean` expression is `false`.

Statement Labels

A statement can be *labeled* by prefixing an identifier to the statement as follows:

```
label: statement
```

The `label` can be a name or an integer.

The `switch` Statement

The `switch` statement is similar to the `if` statement in that it enables a selection from alternative paths of execution. It is written as follows:

```
switch (expression) caseBlock
```

`expression` must evaluate to a `byte`, `char`, `short`, or `int` value. Control is transferred to the next statement in the block that is labeled with a value that matches the expression.

The `caseBlock` contains a sequence of case-labeled statements. These statements are written as follows:

```
case value: statement
```

An optional default-value statement may also appear in the case block. It is written as follows:

```
default: statement
```

If no value matches the expression and a default-valued statement is provided, control is transferred to this statement. If there is no default-value statement, the next statement following the `switch` statement is executed.

The `break` Statement

The `break` statement is used to transfer control to a labeled statement or out-of-statement block. It takes the following forms:

```
break;
```

```
break label;
```

The first form transfers control to the first statement following the current statement block. The second form transfers control to the statement with the identified label.

The `for` Statement

The `for` statement is used to iteratively execute a statement. It takes the following form:

```
for (initializationStatement booleanExpression ; incrementStatement)
   iteratedStatement
```

The initialization statement is executed at the beginning of the `for` statement, and then the `boolean` expression is tested. If the expression is `true`, the iterated statement is executed. The increment statement is executed after the iterated statement, and then the `boolean` expression is retested. The iterated statement–increment statement loop continues until the `boolean` expression evaluates to `false`.

The `while` Statement

The `while` statement is used to execute a statement while a `boolean` expression is `true`. It is written as follows:

```
while (booleanExpression) iteratedStatement;
```

The `boolean` expression is evaluated; if it is `true` the iterated statement is executed. It continues to execute until the `boolean` expression is `false`.

The do Statement

The do statement, like the while statement, is used to execute a statement until a boolean expression becomes false. The only difference is that the expression is tested after the statement is executed. The do statement is written as follows:

```
do iteratedStatement while (booleanExpression);
```

The continue Statement

The continue statement is used to continue execution of a loop (for, do, or while) without completing execution of the iterated statement. The continue statement may take an optional label. It is written as follows:

```
continue label;
```

If a label is supplied, the loop continues at the labeled loop.

The synchronized Statement

The synchronized statement is used to execute a statement after acquiring a lock on an object. It is written as follows:

```
synchronized ( expression ) statement
```

The expression yields the object for which the lock must be acquired.

The try Statement

The try statement executes a block of statements while setting up exception handlers. If an exception occurs the appropriate handler, if any, is executed to handle the exception. A finally clause may also be specified to perform absolutely required processing.

The try statement is written as follows:

```
try block catchClauses finallyClause
```

At least one catch clause or a finally clause must be provided.

The format of the catch clause is as follows:

```
catch (exceptionDeclaration) block
```

If an exception is thrown within the block executed by the try statement and it can be assigned to the type of exception declared in the catch clause, the block of the catch clause is executed.

The finally clause, if it is provided, is always executed regardless of whether an exception is generated.

The `return` Statement

The `return` statement is used to return an object or a value as the result of a method's invocation. It is written as follows:

```
return expression;
```

The value of the expression must match the return value identified in the method's declaration.

Operators

Java defines arithmetic, relational, logical, bit-manipulation, caste, class, selection, and assignment operators. Table 11.2 summarizes these operators.

Table 11.2. Java operators.

Operator Type	*Operator*	*Description*	*Example*
Arithmetic	`+`	Addition	`a + b`
	`-`	Subtraction	`a - b`
	`*`	Multiplication	`a * b`
	`/`	Division	`a / b`
	`%`	Modulus	`a % b`
Relational	`>`	Greater than	`a > b`
	`<`	Less than	`a < b`
	`>=`	Greater than or equal	`a >= b`
	`<=`	Less than or equal	`a <= b`
	`!=`	Not equal	`a != b`
	`==`	Equal	`a == b`
Logical	`!`	Not	`!a`
	`&&`	AND	`a && b`
	`¦¦`	OR	`a ¦¦ b`
Bit-manipulation	`~`	Complement	`~a`
	`&`	AND	`a & b`
	`¦`	OR	`a ¦ b`
	`^`	Exclusive OR	`a ^ b`
	`<<`	Left shift	`a << b`

Operator Type	*Operator*	*Description*	*Example*
	`>>`	Right shift	`a >> B`
	`>>>`	Zero-filled right shift	`a >>> b`
Assignment	`=`	Assignment	`a = b`
	`++`	Increment and assign	`a++`
	`--`	Decrement and assign	`a--`
	`+=`	Add and assign	`a += b`
	`-=`	Subtract and assign	`a -= b`
	`*=`	Multiply and assign	`a *= b`
	`/=`	Divide and assign	`a /= b`
	`%=`	Take modulus and assign	`a %= b`
	`¦=`	OR and assign	`a ¦= b`
	`&=`	AND and assign	`a &= b`
	`^=`	XOR and assign	`a ^= b`
	`<<=`	Left shift and assign	`a <<= b`
	`>>=`	Right shift and assign	`a >>= b`
	`>>>=`	Zero-filled left shift and assign	`a >>>= b`
Caste	`(type)`	Convert to type	`(char) b`
Instance	`instanceof`	Is instance of class?	`a instanceof b`
Allocation	`new`	Create a new object of a class	`new A()`
Selection	`? :`	If...Then selection	`a ? b : c`

Summary

This chapter provides a summary of the Java language. It reviews the language-specific material covered in Chapters 4 through 10. Part III, "Using the Java API," introduces the Java API.

III

Using the Java API

12

Portable Software and the `java.lang` Package

In this chapter you'll learn how to use the `java.lang` package. This package contains the core API classes of the JDK. It includes the `Object` class, which is the top class in the Java class hierarchy, and the `Class` class, which provides runtime class information for all Java objects. You'll learn about classes that control the operation of the Java runtime system and about the all-important `System` class. You'll also learn how "wrapped" classes are used to convert primitive data types into usable objects. By the time you have completed this chapter, you will have been introduced to all the classes contained in the `java.lang` package.

NOTE

The objective of this part of the book is to familiarize you with each of the packages of the Java API. In order to make the best use of these chapters, you should browse through the pages of the API User's Guide that discuss each of the classes as they are covered here.

The `Object` and `Class` Classes

`Object` and `Class` are two of the most important classes in the Java API. The `Object` class is at the top of the Java class hierarchy. All classes are subclasses of `Object` and therefore inherit its methods. The `Class` class is used to provide class descriptors for all objects created during Java program execution.

`Object`

The `Object` class does not have any variables and has only one constructor. However, it provides 11 methods that are inherited by all Java classes and that support general operations that are used with all objects. For example, the `equals()` and `hashCode()` methods are used to construct hash tables of Java objects. *Hash tables* are like arrays, but they are indexed by key values and dynamically grow in size. They make use of *hash functions* to quickly access the data that they contain. The `hashCode()` method creates a *hash code* for an object. Hash codes are used to quickly determine whether two objects are different. You learn more about hash tables in Chapter 14, "Useful Tools in the `java.util` Package."

The `clone()` method creates an identical copy of an object. The object must implement the `Cloneable` interface. This interface is defined within the `java.lang` package. It contains no methods and is used only to differentiate cloneable from noncloneable classes.

The `getClass()` method identifies the class of an object by returning an object of `Class`. You'll learn how to use this method in the next programming example. (See the "A Touch of Class" section.)

The `toString()` method creates a `String` representation of the value of an object. This method is handy for quickly displaying the contents of an object. When an object is displayed, using `print()` or `println()`, the `toString()` method of its class is automatically called to convert the object into a string before printing. Classes that override the `toString()` method can easily provide a custom display for their objects.

The `finalize()` method of an object is executed when an object is garbage-collected. The method performs no action, by default, and needs to be overridden by any class that requires specialized finalization processing.

The `Object` class provides three `wait()` and two `notify()` methods that support thread control. These methods are implemented by the `Object` class so that they can be made available to threads that are not created from subclasses of class `Thread`. The `wait()` methods cause a thread to wait until it is notified or until a specified amount of time has elapsed. The `notify()` methods are used to notify waiting threads that their wait is over.

Class

The `Class` class provides eight methods that support the runtime processing of an object's class and interface information. This class does not have a constructor. Objects of this class, referred to as *class descriptors*, are automatically created and associated with the objects to which they refer. Despite their name, class descriptors are used for interfaces as well as classes.

The `getName()` and `toString()` methods return the `String` containing the name of a class or interface. The `toString()` method differs in that it prepends the string `class` or `interface`, depending on whether the class descriptor is a class or an interface. The static `forName()` method is used to obtain a class descriptor for the class specified by a `String` object.

The `getSuperclass()` method returns the class descriptor of the superclass of a class. The `isInterface()` method identifies whether a class descriptor applies to a class or an interface. The `getInterface()` method returns an array of `Class` objects that specify the interfaces of a class, if any.

The `newInstance()` method creates an object that is a new instance of the specified class. It can be used in lieu of a class's constructor, although it is generally safer and clearer to use a constructor rather than `newInstance()`.

The `getClassLoader()` method returns the class loader of a class, if one exists. Classes are not usually loaded by a class loader. However, when a class is loaded from outside the `CLASSPATH`, such as over a network, a class loader is used to convert the class byte stream into a class descriptor. The `ClassLoader` class is covered later in this chapter.

A Touch of Class

In order to give you a feel for how the `Object` and `Class` methods can be used, let's create and run a small program called `ClassApp`. If you have not already done so, create a `ch12` directory to be used for this lesson. The program's source code is shown in Listing 12.1.

Listing 12.1. The source code of the `ClassApp` program.

```
import java.lang.System;
import java.lang.Class;
import jdg.ch05.Point;
import jdg.ch06.CGTextPoint;

public class ClassApp {
 public static void main(String args[]) {
  CGTextPoint p = new CGTextPoint(new Point(7,11));
  Object obj = new Object();
  Class cl = p.getClass();
  Class objcl = obj.getClass();
  do {
   describeClass(cl);
   cl = cl.getSuperclass();
  } while(cl!=objcl);
 }
 public static void describeClass(Class classDesc){
  System.out.println("Class: "+classDesc.getName());
  System.out.println("Superclass: "+classDesc.getSuperclass().getName());
  Class interfaces[] = classDesc.getInterfaces();
  for(int i=0;i<interfaces.length;++i)
   System.out.println("has interface: "+interfaces[i].getName());
  System.out.println();
 }
}
```

The program shows how the `Object` and `Class` methods can be used to generate runtime class and interface information about an arbitrary object. It creates an instance of class `CGTextPoint` by importing the classes developed in Chapters 5, "Classes and Objects," and 6, "Interfaces." It also creates a generic instance of class `Object` in order to obtain the class descriptor of that class. The following lines of code use the `Object getClass()` method to obtain the class descriptors of the `CGTextPoint` and `Object` classes:

```
Class cl = p.getClass();
Class objcl = obj.getClass();
```

These class descriptors are instances of `Class`. They are used in a simple `do` loop. The loop invokes the `describeClass()` method for the class identified by `cl` and then assigns `cl` to its superclass. The loop repeats until `cl` becomes the class descriptor for `Object`.

The `describeClass()` method uses the `getName()` method to get the name of the class and its superclass. The `describeClass()` method displays this information to the console. It uses the getInterfaces() method to get all interfaces implemented by a class and the getName() method to get and display the name of each interface.

The program's output is as follows:

```
Class: jdg.ch06.CGTextPoint
Superclass: jdg.ch05.CGPoint
has interface: jdg.ch06.CGTextEdit

Class: jdg.ch05.CGPoint
Superclass: jdg.ch05.CGObject

Class: jdg.ch05.CGObject
Superclass: java.lang.Object
```

It steps up the class hierarchy from CGTextPoint to CGObject to display information about each class. See if you can modify the program to work with objects of other classes. You can do this by assigning the class of these objects to the cl variable in the main() method.

The ClassLoader, SecurityManager, and Runtime Classes

The ClassLoader, SecurityManager, and Runtime classes provide a fine level of control over the operation of the Java runtime system. However, most of the time you will not need or want to exercise this control because Java is set up to perform optimally for a variety of applications. The ClassLoader class allows you to define custom loaders for classes that you load outside of your CLASSPATH—for example, over a network. The SecurityManager class allows you to define a variety of security policies that govern the accesses that classes may make to threads, executable programs, your network, and your file system. The Runtime class provides you with the capability to control and monitor the Java runtime system. It also allows you to execute external programs.

ClassLoader

Classes that are loaded from outside CLASSPATH require a class loader to convert the class byte stream into a class descriptor. ClassLoader is an abstract class that is used to define class loaders. It uses the defineClass() method to convert an array of bytes into a class descriptor. The loadClass() method is used to load a class from its source, usually a network. The resolveClass() method resolves all the classes referenced by a particular class by loading and defining those classes. The findSystemClass() method is used to load classes that are located within CLASSPATH and, therefore, do not require a class loader.

SecurityManager

The `SecurityManager` class is an abstract class that works with class loaders to implement a security policy. It contains several methods that can be overridden to implement customized security policies. This class is covered in Chapter 39, "Java Security," which gets into the details of Java security. For right now, just be aware that it is in `java.lang`.

Runtime

The `Runtime` class provides access to the Java runtime system. It consists of a number of methods that implement system-level services.

The `getRuntime()` method is a static method that is used to obtain access to an object of class `Runtime`. The `exec()` methods are used to execute external programs from the Java runtime system. The `exec()` methods provide a number of alternatives for passing parameters to the executed program. These alternatives are similar to the standard C methods for passing command-line and environment information. The `exec()` methods are subject to security checking to ensure that they are executed by trusted code. See Chapter 39 for more information about runtime security checking.

The `exit()` method is used to exit the Java runtime system with an error code. It is similar to the `exit` function found in standard C libraries.

The `totalMemory()`, `freeMemory()`, and `gc()` methods are used to obtain information about and control the memory used by the runtime system. The `totalMemory()` method identifies the total memory available to the runtime system. The `freeMemory()` method identifies the amount of free (unused) memory. The `gc()` method is used to run the garbage collector to free up memory allocated to objects that are no longer being used. In general, you should not use the `gc()` method, but rather let Java perform its own automated garbage collection.

The `getLocalizedInputStream()` and `getLocalizedOutputStream()` methods are used to convert local (usually ASCII) input and output streams to Unicode-based streams.

The `load()` and `loadLibrary()` methods are used to load dynamic link libraries. This is usually performed in conjunction with native methods, which are described in Chapter 38, "Creating Native Methods."

The `runFinalization()` method causes the `finalize()` method of each object awaiting finalization to be invoked. The `traceInstructions()` and `traceMethodCalls()` methods are used to enable or disable instruction and method tracing. You will most likely never need to use any of these methods in your programs. They are used in programs such as the debugger to trace through the execution of Java methods and instructions.

Using Runtime

Most of the methods provided by Runtime are not typically used in application programs. However, some methods are pretty useful. The program in Listing 12.2 shows how the Runtime methods can be used to display memory status information.

Listing 12.2. The source code of the RuntimeMemApp program.

```
import java.lang.System;
import java.lang.Runtime;
import java.io.IOException;

public class RuntimeMemApp {
 public static void main(String args[]) throws IOException {
  Runtime r = Runtime.getRuntime();
  System.out.println(r.totalMemory());
  System.out.println(r.freeMemory());
 }
}
```

This program uses the static getRuntime() method to get an instance of Runtime that represents the current Java runtime system. The totalMemory() method is used to display the total number of bytes of runtime system memory. The freeMemory() method is used to display the number of bytes of memory that are unallocated and currently available.

When you run the program, you should get results that are similar to the following:

```
3145720
3135888
```

Listing 12.3 demonstrates how to use the Runtime exec() method to execute external programs. This example assumes that you are using Windows 95. It will not work with any other Java implementation. However, it can be easily tailored to launch application programs on other operating-system platforms.

Listing 12.3. The source code of the RuntimeExecApp program.

```
import java.lang.System;
import java.lang.Runtime;
import java.io.IOException;

public class RuntimeExecApp {
 public static void main(String args[]) throws IOException {
  Runtime r = Runtime.getRuntime();
  r.exec("C:\\Windows\\Explorer.exe");
 }
}
```

This program uses `getRuntime()` to get the current instance of the runtime system and then uses `exec()` to execute the Windows Explorer. The double backslashes (`\\`) are Java escape codes for a single backslash (`\`). When you run this program, it should launch a copy of the Windows Explorer. Under Windows 95, the `exec()` function works with true Win32 programs. It cannot be used to execute built-in DOS commands.

The System Class

You are no stranger to the `System` class because you have used it in several previous programming examples. It is one of the most important and useful classes provided by `java.lang`. It provides a standard interface to common system resources and functions. It implements the standard input, output, and error streams, and supplies a set of methods that provide control over the Java runtime system. Some of these methods duplicate those provided by the `Runtime` class.

Property-Related Methods

The `System` class provides three property-related methods. *Properties* are extensions of the `Dictionary` and `Hashtable` classes and are defined in the `java.util` package. A set of system properties is available through the `System` class that describes the general characteristics of the operating system and runtime system that you are using. The `getProperties()` method gets all of the system properties and stores them in an object of class `Properties`. The `getProperty(String)` method gets a single property, as specified by a key. The `setProperties()` method sets the system properties to the values of a `Properties` object. The sample program presented in Listing 12.4 introduces you to these system properties.

Security Manager–Related Methods

The `getSecurityManager()` and `setSecurityManager()` methods provide access to the security manager that is currently in effect. These methods are covered in Chapter 39.

Runtime-Related Methods

Several of the methods defined for the `Runtime` class are made available through the `System` class. These methods are `exit()`, `gc()`, `load()`, `loadLibrary()`, and `runFinalization()`.

Odds and Ends

The `arraycopy()` method is used to copy data from one array to another. This function provides the opportunity for system-specific memory-copy operations to optimize memory-to-memory copies.

The `currentTimeMillis()` method returns the current time in milliseconds since January 1, 1970. If you want more capable date and time methods, check out the `Date` class in `java.util`.

The `getenv()` method is used to obtain the value of an environment variable. However, this method is identified as obsolete in the Java API documentation and can no longer be used.

Time and Properties

The short program in Listing 12.4 illustrates a few of the methods provided by the `System` class. If your heyday was in the 1960s, it will allow you to keep track of the number of milliseconds that have elapsed since the good old days. It also gets and displays the `System` properties. Take a look through these properties to get a feel for the type of information that is provided. Finally, the `exit()` method is used to terminate the program, returning a status code of `13`.

Listing 12.4. The source code of the `SystemApp` program.

```
import java.lang.System;
import java.util.Properties;

public class SystemApp {
 public static void main(String args[]) {
  long time = System.currentTimeMillis();
  System.out.print("Milliseconds elapsed since January 1, 1970: ");
  System.out.println(time);
  Properties p=System.getProperties();
  p.list(System.out);
  System.exit(13);
 }
}
```

The program generated the following output on my computer:

```
Milliseconds elapsed since January 1, 1970: 825298554460
-- listing properties --
java.home=C:\JAVA\BIN\..
awt.toolkit=sun.awt.win32.MToolkit
java.version=1.0
file.separator=\
line.separator=

java.vendor=Sun Microsystems Inc.
user.name=jamie
os.arch=x86
os.name=Windows 95
java.vendor.url=http://www.sun.com/
user.dir=c:\java\jdg\ch12
java.class.path=.;c:\java;c:\java\lib\classes.zip;C:\...
java.class.version=45.3
os.version=4.0
path.separator=;
user.home=\home\jamie
```

Wrapped Classes

Variables that are declared using the primitive Java types are not objects and cannot be created and accessed using methods. Primitive types also cannot be subclassed. To get around the limitations of primitive types, the `java.lang` package defines class *wrappers* for these types. These class wrappers furnish methods that provide basic capabilities such as class conversion, value testing, hash codes, and equality checks. The constructors for the wrapped classes allow objects to be created and converted from primitive values and strings. Be sure to browse the API pages for each of these classes to familiarize yourself with the methods they provide.

The `Boolean` Class

The `Boolean` class is a wrapper for the `boolean` primitive type. It provides the `getBoolean()`, `toString()`, and `booleanValue()` methods to support type and class conversion. The `toString()`, `equals()`, and `hashCode()` methods override those of class `Object`.

The `Character` Class

The `Character` class is a wrapper for the `char` primitive type. It provides several methods that support case, type, and class testing, and conversion. Check out the API pages on these methods. We'll use some of them in the upcoming example.

The `Integer` and `Long` Classes

The `Integer` and `Long` classes wrap the `int` and `long` primitive types. They provide the `MIN_VALUE` and `MAX_VALUE` constants, as well as a number of type and class testing and conversion methods. The `parseInt()` and `parseLong()` methods are used to parse `String` objects and convert them to `Integer` and `Long` objects.

The `Double` and `Float` Classes

The `Double` and `Float` classes wrap the `double` and `float` primitive types. They provide the `MIN_VALUE`, `MAX_VALUE`, `POSITIVE_INFINITY`, and `NEGATIVE_INFINITY` constants, as well as the `NaN` (not-a-number) constant. `NaN` is used as a value that is not equal to any value, including itself. These classes provide a number of type and class testing and conversion methods, including methods that support conversion to and from integer bit representations.

The `Number` Class

The `Number` class is an abstract numeric class that is subclassed by `Integer`, `Long`, `Float`, and `Double`. It provides four methods that support conversion of objects from one class to another.

All Wrapped Up

The program in Listing 12.5 shows some of the methods that can be used with the primitive types when they are wrapped as objects. Look up these methods in the API pages for each class and try to figure out how they work before moving on to their explanations.

Listing 12.5. The source code of the WrappedClassApp program.

```
import java.lang.System;
import java.lang.Boolean;
import java.lang.Character;
import java.lang.Integer;
import java.lang.Long;
import java.lang.Float;
import java.lang.Double;

public class WrappedClassApp {
 public static void main(String args[]) {
  Boolean b1 = new Boolean("TRUE");
  Boolean b2 = new Boolean("FALSE");
  System.out.println(b1.toString()+" or "+b2.toString());
  for(int j=0;j<16;++j)
   System.out.print(Character.forDigit(j,16));
  System.out.println();
  Integer i = new Integer(Integer.parseInt("ef",16));
  Long l = new Long(Long.parseLong("abcd",16));
  long m=l.longValue()*i.longValue();
  System.out.println(Long.toString(m,8));
  System.out.println(Float.MIN_VALUE);
  System.out.println(Double.MAX_VALUE);
 }
}
```

The program examines some of the more useful methods provided by each of the wrapped classes. It creates two objects of class `Boolean` from string arguments passed to their constructors. It assigns these objects to `b1` and `b2` and then converts them back to `String` objects when it displays them. They are displayed in lowercase, as `boolean` values are traditionally represented.

The program then executes a `for` loop that prints out the character corresponding to each of the hexadecimal digits. The static `forDigit()` method of the `Character` class is used to generate the character values of digits in a number system of a different radix.

The static `parseInt()` and `parseLong()` methods are used to parse strings according to different radices. In the example, they are used to convert strings representing hexadecimal numbers into `Integer` and `Long` values. These values are then multiplied together and converted to a string that represents the resulting value in base 8. This is accomplished using an overloaded version of the `toString()` method.

The sample program concludes by displaying the minimum `float` value and the maximum `double` value using the predefined class constants of the `Float` and `Double` classes.

The program's output is as follows:

```
true or false
0123456789abcdef
50062143
1.4013e-045
1.79769e+308
```

The `Math` Class

The `Math` class provides an extensive set of mathematical methods in the form of a static class library. It also defines the mathematical constants `E` and `PI`. The supported methods include arithmetic, trigonometric, exponential, logarithmic, random number, and conversion routines. You should browse the API page of this class to get a feel for the methods it provides. The example in Listing 12.6 only touches on a few of these methods.

Listing 12.6. The source code of the `MathApp` program.

```
import java.lang.System;
import java.lang.Math;

public class MathApp {
 public static void main(String args[]) {
  System.out.println(Math.E);
  System.out.println(Math.PI);
  System.out.println(Math.abs(-1234));
  System.out.println(Math.cos(Math.PI/4));
  System.out.println(Math.sin(Math.PI/2));
  System.out.println(Math.tan(Math.PI/4));
  System.out.println(Math.log(1));
  System.out.println(Math.exp(Math.PI));
  for(int i=0;i<5;++i)
   System.out.print(Math.random()+" ");
  System.out.println();
 }
}
```

This program prints the constants e and π, $|-1234|$, $\cos(\pi/4)$, $\sin(\pi/2)$, $\tan(\pi/4)$, $\ln(1)$, e^{π}, and then five random double numbers between 0.0 and 1.1. Its output is as follows:

```
2.71828
3.14159
1234
0.707107
1
1
0
23.1407
0.831965 0.573099 0.0268818 0.378625 0.164485
```

The random numbers you generate will almost certainly differ from the ones shown here.

The String and StringBuffer Classes

The String and StringBuffer classes are used to support operations on strings of characters. The String class supports constant (unchanging) strings, whereas the StringBuffer class supports growable, modifiable strings. String objects are more compact than StringBuffer objects, but StringBuffer objects are more flexible.

String Literals

String *literals* are strings that are specified using double quotes. "This is a string" and "xyz" are examples of string literals. String literals are different than the literal values used with primitive types. When the javac compiler encounters a String literal, it converts it to a String constructor. For example, the following:

```
String str = "text";
```

is equivalent to this:

```
String str = new String("text");
```

The fact that the compiler automatically supplies String constructors allows you to use String literals everywhere that you could use objects of the String class.

The + Operator and StringBuffer

If String objects are constant, how can they be concatenated with the + operator and be assigned to existing String objects? In the following example, the code will result in the string "ab" being assigned to the s object:

```
String s = "";
s = s + "a" + "b";
```

How can this be possible if Strings are constant? The answer lies in the fact that the Java compiler uses StringBuffer objects to accomplish the string manipulations. This code would be rendered as something similar to the following by the Java compiler:

```
String s = "";
s = new StringBuffer("").append("a").append("b").toString();
```

A new object of class StringBuffer is created with the "" argument. The StringBuffer append() method is used to append the strings "a" and "b" to the new object, and then the object is converted to an object of class String via the toString() method. The toString() method creates a new object of class String before it is assigned to the s variable. In this way, the s variable always refers to a constant (although new) String object.

String Constructors

The String class provides seven constructors for the creation and initialization of String objects. These constructors allow strings to be created from other strings, string literals, arrays of characters, arrays of bytes, and StringBuffer objects. Browse through the API page for the String class to become familiar with these constructors.

String Access Methods

The String class provides a very powerful set of methods for working with String objects. These methods allow you to access individual characters and substrings; test and compare strings; copy, concatenate, and replace parts of strings; convert and create strings; and perform other useful string operations.

The most important String methods are the length() method, which returns an integer value identifying the length of a string; the charAt() method, which allows the individual characters of a string to be accessed; the substring() method, which allows substrings of a string to be accessed; and the valueOf() method, which allows primitive data types to be converted into strings.

In addition to these methods, the Object class provides a toString() method for converting other objects to String objects. This method is often overridden by subclasses to provide a more appropriate object-to-String conversion.

Character and Substring Methods

Several String methods allow you to access individual characters and substrings of a string. These include charAt(), getBytes(), getChars(), indexOf(), lastIndexOf(), and substring(). Whenever you need to perform string manipulations, be sure to check the API documentation to make sure that you don't overlook an easy-to-use, predefined String method.

String Comparison and Test Methods

Several String methods allow you to compare strings, substrings, byte arrays, and other objects with a given string. Some of these methods are compareTo(), endsWith(), equals(), equalsIgnoreCase(), regionMatches(), and startsWith().

Copy, Concatenation, and Replace Methods

The following methods are useful for copying, concatenating, and manipulating strings: concat(), copyValueOf(), replace(), and trim().

String Conversion and Generation

There are a number of string methods that support `String` conversion. These are `intern()`, `toCharArray()`, `toLowerCase()`, `toString()`, `toUpperCase()`, and `valueOf()`. You explore the use of some of these methods in the following example.

Stringing Along

The program in Listing 12.7 provides a glimpse at the operation of some of the methods identified in the previous subsections. Because strings are frequently used in application programs, learning to use the available methods is essential to being able to use the `String` class most effectively.

Listing 12.7. The source code of the `StringApp` program.

```
import java.lang.System;
import java.lang.String;

public class StringApp {
 public static void main(String args[]) {
  String s = "  Java Developer's Guide  ";
  System.out.println(s);
  System.out.println(s.toUpperCase());
  System.out.println(s.toLowerCase());
  System.out.println("["+s+"]");
  s=s.trim();
  System.out.println("["+s+"]");
  s=s.replace('J','X');
  s=s.replace('D','Y');
  s=s.replace('G','Z');
  System.out.println(s);
  int i1 = s.indexOf('X');
  int i2 = s.indexOf('Y');
  int i3 = s.indexOf('Z');
  char ch[] = s.toCharArray();
  ch[i1]='J';
  ch[i2]='D';
  ch[i3]='G';
  s = new String(ch);
  System.out.println(s);
 }
}
```

This program performs several manipulations of a string `s` that is initially set to `"  Java Developer's Guide  "`. It prints the original string and then prints upper- and lowercase versions of it, illustrating the use of the `toUpperCase()` and `toLowerCase()` methods. It prints the string enclosed between two braces to show that it contains leading and trailing spaces. It then trims away these spaces using the `trim()` method and reprints the string to show that these spaces were removed.

The program uses the `replace()` method to replace the letters `'J'`, `'D'`, and `'G'` with `'X'`, `'Y'`, and `'Z'` and prints out the string to show the changes. The `replace()` method is case sensitive. It uses the `indexOf()` method to get the indices of `'X'`, `'Y'`, and `'Z'` within `s`. It uses `toCharArray()` to convert the string to a `char` array. It then uses the indices to put `'J'`, `'D'`, and `'G'` back in their proper locations within the character array. The `String()` constructor is used to construct a new string from the character array. The new string is assigned to `s` and is printed.

The program's output is as follows:

```
  Java Developer's Guide
  JAVA DEVELOPER'S GUIDE
  java developer's guide
[  Java Developer's Guide  ]
[Java Developer's Guide]
Xava Yeveloper's Zuide
Java Developer's Guide
```

The StringBuffer Class

The `StringBuffer` class is the force behind the scene for most complex string manipulations. The compiler automatically declares and manipulates objects of this class to implement common string operations.

The `StringBuffer` class provides three constructors: an empty constructor, an empty constructor with a specified initial buffer length, and a constructor that creates a `StringBuffer` object from a `String` object. In general, you will find yourself constructing `StringBuffer` objects from `String` objects, and the last constructor will be the one you use most often.

The `StringBuffer` class provides several versions of the `append()` method to convert and append other objects and primitive data types to `StringBuffer` objects. It provides a similar set of `insert()` methods for inserting objects and primitive data types into `StringBuffer` objects. It also provides methods to access the character-buffering capacity of `StringBuffer` and methods for accessing the characters contained in a string. It is well worth a visit to the `StringBuffer` API pages to take a look at the methods that it has to offer.

Strung Out

The program in Listing 12.8 shows how `StringBuffer` objects can be manipulated using the `append()`, `insert()`, and `setCharAt()` methods.

Listing 12.8. The source code of the `StringBufferApp` program.

```
import java.lang.System;
import java.lang.String;
import java.lang.StringBuffer;

public class StringBufferApp {
 public static void main(String args[]) {
```

```
    StringBuffer sb = new StringBuffer(" is ");
    sb.append("Hot");
    sb.append('!');
    sb.insert(0,"Java");
    sb.append('\n');
    sb.append("This is ");
    sb.append(true);
    sb.setCharAt(21,'T');
    sb.append('\n');
    sb.append("Java is #");
    sb.append(1);
    String s = sb.toString();
    System.out.println(s);
  }
}
```

The program creates a `StringBuffer` object using the string `" is "`. It appends the string `"Hot"` using the `append()` method and the character `'!'` using an overloaded version of the same method. The `insert()` method is used to insert the string `"Java"` at the beginning of the string buffer.

Three `append`s are used to tack on a newline character (`\n`), the string `"This is "`, and the `boolean` value `true`. The `append()` method is overloaded to support the appending of the primitive data types as well as arbitrary Java objects.

The `setCharAt()` method is used to replace the letter `'t'` at index 21 with the letter `'T'`. The `charAt()` and `setCharAt()` methods allow `StringBuffer` objects to be treated as arrays of characters.

Finally, another newline character is appended to `sb`, followed by the string `"Java is #"` and the `int` value 1. The `StringBuffer` object is then converted to a string and displayed to the console window.

The output of the program is as follows:

```
Java is Hot!
This is True
Java is #1
```

Threads and Processes

Chapter 8, "Multithreading," provides a detailed description of multithreading in Java. This section briefly describes the classes of `java.lang` that support multithreading. It also covers the `Process` class, which is used to manipulate processes that are executed using the `System.exec()` methods.

Runnable

The `Runnable` interface provides a common approach to identifying the code to be executed as part of an active thread. It consists of a single method, `run()`, which is executed when a thread is activated. The `Runnable` interface is implemented by the `Thread` class and by other classes that support threaded execution.

Thread

The `Thread` class is used to construct and access individual threads of execution that are executed as part of a multithreaded program. It defines the priority constants, `MIN_PRIORITY`, `MAX_PRIORITY`, and `NORM_PRIORITY`, that are used to control task scheduling. It provides seven constructors for creating instances of class `Thread`. The four constructors with the `Runnable` parameters are used to construct threads for classes that do not subclass the `Thread` class. The other constructors are used for the construction of `Thread` objects from `Thread` subclasses.

`Thread` supports many methods for accessing `Thread` objects. These methods provide the capabilities to work with a thread's group; obtain detailed information about a thread's activities; set and test a thread's properties; and cause a thread to wait, be interrupted, or be destroyed.

ThreadGroup

The `ThreadGroup` class is used to encapsulate a group of threads as a single object so that they can be accessed as a single unit. A number of access methods are provided for manipulating `ThreadGroup` objects. These methods keep track of the threads and thread groups contained in a thread group and perform global operations on all threads in the group. The global operations are group versions of the operations that are provided by the `Thread` class.

Process

The `Process` class is used to encapsulate processes that are executed with the `System.exec()` methods. An instance of class `Process` is returned by the `Runtime` class `exec()` method when it executes a process that is external to the Java runtime system. This `Process` object can be destroyed using the `destroy()` method and waited on using the `waitFor()` method. The `exitValue()` method returns the system exit value of the process. The `getInputStream()`, `getOutputStream()`, and `getErrorStream()` methods are used to access the standard input, output, and error streams of the process.

Hello Again

The simple program in Listing 12.9 actually performs some pretty complex processing. It is provided as an example of some of the powerful things that can be accomplished using the `Process` class.

Listing 12.9. The source code of the `ProcessApp` program.

```
import java.lang.System;
import java.lang.Runtime;
import java.lang.Process;
import java.io.DataInputStream;
import java.io.IOException;

public class ProcessApp {
 public static void main(String args[]) throws IOException {
  Runtime r = Runtime.getRuntime();
  Process p = r.exec("java jdg.ch04.HelloWorldApp");
  DataInputStream inStream = new DataInputStream(p.getInputStream());
  String line = inStream.readLine();
  System.out.println(line);
 }
}
```

The program uses the static `getRuntime()` method to get the current instance of the Java runtime system. It then uses the `exec()` method to execute another separate copy of the Java interpreter with the `HelloWorldApp` program that was developed in Chapter 4, "First Programs: Hello World! to BlackJack." It creates a `DataInputStream` object, `inStream`, that is connected to the output stream of the `HelloWorldApp` program. It then uses `inStream` to read the output of the `HelloWorldApp` program and display it on the console window as follows:

```
Hello World!
```

The `exec()` methods combined with the `Process` class provide a powerful set of tools by which Java programs can be used to launch and control the execution of other programs.

The Compiler Class

The `Compiler` class consists of five `static` methods that are used to compile Java classes in the rare event that you want to compile classes directly from a program or applet. These methods allow you to build your own customized Java development environment.

Exceptions and Errors

The `java.lang` package establishes the Java exception hierarchy and declares numerous exceptions and errors. Errors are used to indicate the occurrence of abnormal and fatal events that should not be handled within application programs. (See Chapter 7, "Exceptions.")

The `Throwable` Class

The `Throwable` class is at the top of the Java error-and-exception hierarchy. It is extended by the `Error` and `Exception` classes and provides methods that are common to both classes. These methods consist of stack tracing methods, the `getMessage()` method, and the `toString()` method, which is an override of the method inherited from the `Object` class. The `getMessage()` method is used to retrieve any messages that are supplied in the creation of `Throwable` objects.

The `fillInStackTrace()` and `printStackTrace()` methods are used to add information to supply and print information that is used to trace the propagation of exceptions and errors throughout a program's execution.

The `Error` Class

The `Error` class is used to provide a common superclass to define abnormal and fatal events that should not occur. It provides two constructors and no other methods. Four major classes of errors extend the `Error` class: `AWTError`, `LinkageError`, `ThreadDeath`, and `VirtualMachineError`.

The `AWTError` class identifies fatal errors that occur in the Abstract Window Toolkit packages. It is a single identifier for all AWT errors and is not subclassed.

The `LinkageError` class is used to define errors that occur as the result of incompatibilities between dependent classes. These incompatibilities result when a class X that another class Y depends on is changed before class Y can be recompiled. The `LinkageError` class is extensively subclassed to identify specific manifestations of this type of error.

The `ThreadDeath` error class is used to indicate that a thread has been stopped. Instances of this class can be caught and then rethrown to ensure that a thread is gracefully terminated, although this is not recommended. The `ThreadDeath` class is not subclassed.

The `VirtualMachineError` class is used to identify fatal errors occurring in the operation of the Java virtual machine. It has four subclasses: `InternalError`, `OutOfMemoryError`, `StackOverflowError`, and `UnknownError`.

The `Exception` Class

The `Exception` class provides a common superclass for the exceptions that can be defined for Java programs and applets. There are nine subclasses of exceptions that extend the `Exception` class. These exception subclasses are further extended by lower-level subclasses.

Summary

In this chapter you have learned how to use the `java.lang` package. You have taken a tour of its classes and their methods and have written some sample programs that illustrate their use. In the next chapter you'll learn to use the `java.io` package to perform stream-based I/O to files, memory buffers, and the console window.

13

Stream-Based Input/Output and the `java.io` Package

In this chapter you'll learn to use Java streams to perform sophisticated input and output using standard I/O, memory buffers, and files. You'll be introduced to all classes of the `java.io` package. You'll explore the input and output stream class hierarchy and learn to use stream filters to simplify I/O processing. You'll also learn how to perform random-access I/O and how to use the `StreamTokenizer` class to construct input parsers. When you finish this chapter, you'll be able to add sophisticated I/O processing to your Java programs.

Streams

Java input and output is based on the use of streams. *Streams* are sequences of bytes that travel from a source to a destination over a communication path. If your program is writing to a stream, it is the stream's *source*. If it is reading from a stream, it is the stream's *destination*. The communication path is dependent on the type of I/O being performed. It can consist of memory-to-memory transfers, file system, network, and other forms of I/O.

Streams are not complicated. They are powerful because they abstract away the details of the communication path from input and output operations. This allows all I/O to be performed using a common set of methods. These methods can be tailored and extended to provide higher-level custom I/O capabilities.

Java defines two major classes of streams: `InputStream` and `OutputStream`. These streams are subclassed to provide a variety of I/O capabilities.

The `java.io` Class Hierarchy

Figure 13.1 identifies the `java.io` class hierarchy. As described in the previous section, the `InputStream` and `OutputStream` classes are the major components of this hierarchy. Other high-level classes include the `File`, `FileDescriptor`, `RandomAccessFile`, and `StreamTokenizer` classes.

The `InputStream` and `OutputStream` classes have complementary subclasses. For example, both have subclasses for performing I/O via memory buffers, files, and pipes. The `InputStream` subclasses perform the input and the `OutputStream` classes perform the output.

The `InputStream` class has six subclasses. The `ByteArrayInputStream` class is used to convert an array into an input stream. The `StreamBufferInputStream` class uses a `StreamBuffer` as an input stream. The `FileInputStream` allows files to be used as input streams. The `PipedInputStream` class allows a pipe to be constructed between two threads and supports input through the pipe. The `SequenceInputStream` class allows two or more streams to be concatenated into a single stream. The `FilterInputStream` class is an abstract class from which other input-filtering classes are constructed.

FIGURE 13.1.
The classes of the `java.io` *hierarchy.*

```
java.io
 ├─InputStream
 │  ├─FilterInputStream
 │  │  ├─BufferedInputStream
 │  │  ├─DataInputStream
 │  │  ├─LineNumberInputStream
 │  │  └─PushbackInputStream
 │  ├─ByteArrayInputStream
 │  ├─FileInputStream
 │  ├─PipedInputStream
 │  ├─SequenceInputStream
 │  └─StringBufferInputStream
 ├─OutputStream
 │  ├─FilterOutputStream
 │  │  ├─BufferedOutputStream
 │  │  ├─DataOutputStream
 │  │  └─PrintStream
 │  ├─ByteArrayOutputStream
 │  ├─FileOutputStream
 │  └─PipedOutputStream
 ├─File
 ├─RandomAccessFile
 ├─FileDescriptor
 ├─StreamTokenizer
 │
```

Filters are objects that read from one stream and write to another, usually altering the data in some way as they pass it from one stream to another. Filters can be used to buffer data, read and write objects, keep track of line numbers, and perform other operations on the data they move. Filters can be combined, with one filter using the output of another as its input. You can create custom filters by combining existing filters.

`FilterInputStream` has four filtering subclasses. The `BufferedInputStream` class maintains a buffer of the input data that it receives. This eliminates the need to read from the stream's source every time an input byte is needed. The `DataInputStream` class implements the `DataInput` interface, a set of methods that allow objects and primitive data types to be read from a stream. The `LineNumberInputStream` class is used to keep track of input line numbers. The `PushbackInputStream` class provides the capability to push data back onto the stream that it is read from so that it can be read again.

The `OutputStream` class hierarchy consists of four major subclasses. The `ByteArrayOutputStream`, `FileOutputStream`, and `PipedOutputStream` classes are the output complements to the `ByteArrayInputStream`, `FileInputStream`, and `PipedInputStream` classes. The `FilterOutputStream` class provides subclasses that complement the `FilterInputStream` classes.

The BufferedOutputStream class is the output analog to the BufferedInputStream class. It buffers output so that output bytes can be written to devices in larger groups. The DataOutputStream class implements the DataOutput interface. This interface complements the DataInput interface. It provides methods that write objects and primitive data types to streams so that they can be read by the DataInput interface methods. The PrintStream class provides the familiar print() and println() methods used in most of the sample programs that you've developed so far in this book. It provides a number of overloaded methods that simplify data output.

The File class is used to access the files and directories of the local file system. The FileDescriptor class is an encapsulation of the information used by the host system to track files that are being accessed. The RandomAccessFile class provides the capabilities needed to directly access data contained in a file. The StreamTokenizer class is used to create parsers that operate on stream data.

The InputStream Class

The InputStream class is an abstract class that lays the foundation for the Java Input class hierarchy. As such, it provides methods that are inherited by all InputStream classes.

The read() Method

The read() method is the most important method of the InputStream class hierarchy. It reads a byte of data from an input stream and blocks if no data is available. When a method *blocks*, it causes the thread in which it is executing to wait until data becomes available. This is not a problem in multithreaded programs. The read() method takes on several overloaded forms. It can read a single byte or an array of bytes, depending upon what form is used. It returns the number of bytes read or -1 if an end of file is encountered with no bytes read.

The read() method is overridden and overloaded by subclasses to provide custom read capabilities.

The available() Method

The available() method returns the number of bytes that are available to be read without blocking. It is used to peek into the input stream to see how much data is available. However, depending on the input stream, it might not be accurate or useful. Some input streams on some operating systems may always report 0 available bytes. In general, it is not a good idea to blindly rely on this method to perform input processing.

The close() Method

The close() method closes an input stream and releases resources associated with the stream. It is always a good idea to close a stream to ensure that the stream processing is correctly terminated.

Markable Streams

Java supports *markable streams.* These are streams that provide the capability to mark a position in the stream and then later reset the stream so that it can be reread from the marked position. If a stream can be marked, it must contain some memory associated with it to keep track of the data between the mark and the current position of the stream. When this buffering capability is exceeded, the mark becomes invalid.

The `markSupported()` method returns a `boolean` value that identifies whether a stream supports mark and reset capabilities. The `mark()` method marks a position in the stream. It takes an integer parameter that identifies the number of bytes that can be read before the mark becomes invalid. This is used to set the buffering capacity of the stream. The `reset()` method simply repositions the stream to its last marked position.

The `skip()` Method

The `skip()` method skips over a specified number of input bytes. It takes a `long` value as a parameter.

The `OutputStream` Class

The `OutputStream` class is an abstract class that lays the foundation for the output stream hierarchy. It provides a set of methods that are the output analog to the `InputStream` methods.

The `write()` Method

The `write()` method allows bytes to be written to the output stream. It provides three overloaded forms to write a single byte, an array of bytes, or a segment of an array. The `write()` method, like the `read()` method, may block when it tries to write to a stream. The blocking causes the thread executing the `write()` method to wait until the write operation has been completed.

> **NOTE**
>
> The `OutputStream` class defines three overloaded forms for the `write()` method. These forms allow you to write an integer, an array of bytes, or a subarray of bytes to an `OutputStream` object. You will often see several overloaded forms for methods that perform the same operation using different types of data.

The flush() Method

The flush() method causes any buffered data to be immediately written to the output stream. Some subclasses of OutputStream support buffering and override this method to "clean out" their buffers and write all buffered data to the output stream. They must override the OutputStream flush() method because, by default, it does not perform any operations and is used as a placeholder.

The close() Method

It is generally more important to close output streams than input streams, so that any data written to the stream is stored before the stream is deallocated and lost. The close() method of OutputStream is used in the same manner as that of InputStream.

Byte Array I/O

Java supports byte array input and output via the ByteArrayInputStream and ByteArrayOutputStream classes. These classes use memory buffers as the source and destination of the input and output streams. These streams do not have to be used together. They are covered in the same section here because they provide similar and complementary methods. The StringBufferInputStream class is similar to the ByteArrayInput class and is also covered in this section.

The ByteArrayInputStream Class

The ByteArrayInputStream class creates an input stream from a memory buffer. The buffer is an array of bytes. It provides two constructors that use a byte array argument to create the input stream. The class does not support any new methods, but overrides the read(), skip(), available(), and reset() methods of InputStream.

The read() and skip() methods are implemented as specified for InputStream. The method available() is reliable and can be used to check on the number of available bytes in the buffer. The reset() method does not work with a mark() method; it simply resets to the beginning of the buffer.

The ByteArrayOutputStream Class

The ByteArrayOutputStream class is a little more sophisticated than its input complement. It creates an output stream on a byte array, but provides additional capabilities to allow the output array to grow to accommodate new data that is written to it. It also provides the toByteArray() and toString() methods for converting the stream to a byte array or String object.

ByteArrayOutputStream provides two constructors. One takes an integer argument that is used to set the output byte array to an initial size. The other constructor does not take an argument and sets the output buffer to a default size.

ByteArrayOutputStream provides some additional methods not declared for OutputStream. The reset() method resets the output buffer to allow writing to restart at the beginning of the buffer. The size() method returns the current number of bytes that have been written to the buffer. The writeTo() method is new. It takes an object of class OutputStream as an argument and writes the contents of the output buffer to the specified output stream. The write() methods override those of OutputStream to support array output.

The ByteArrayIOApp Program

Having learned about both sides of the byte array I/O classes, you now have a base from which to create a sample program. Remember to create a ch13 directory under \java\jdg in which to store the files created in this chapter. The source code of the ByteArrayIOApp program is provided in Listing 13.1.

Listing 13.1. The source code of the ByteArrayIOApp program.

```
import java.lang.System;
import java.io.ByteArrayInputStream;
import java.io.ByteArrayOutputStream;
import java.io.IOException;

public class ByteArrayIOApp {
 public static void main(String args[]) throws IOException {
  ByteArrayOutputStream outStream = new ByteArrayOutputStream();
  String s = "This is a test.";
  for(int i=0;i<s.length();++i)
   outStream.write(s.charAt(i));
  System.out.println("outstream: "+outStream);
  System.out.println("size: "+outStream.size());
  ByteArrayInputStream inStream;
  inStream = new ByteArrayInputStream(outStream.toByteArray());
  int inBytes = inStream.available();
  System.out.println("inStream has "+inBytes+" available bytes");
  byte inBuf[] = new byte[inBytes];
  int bytesRead = inStream.read(inBuf,0,inBytes);
  System.out.println(bytesRead+" bytes were read");
  System.out.println("They are: "+new String(inBuf,0));
 }
}
```

The program creates a ByteArrayOutputStream object, outStream, and an array, s, that contains the text "This is a test." to be written to the stream. Each character of s is written, one at a time, to outStream. The contents of outstream are then printed, along with the number of bytes written.

A ByteArrayInputStream object, inStream, is created by invoking the toByteArray() method of outStream to create a byte array that is used as an argument to the ByteArrayInputStream constructor. The available() method is used to determine the number of available input bytes stored in the buffer. This number is stored as inBytes and is used to allocate a byte array to store the data that is read. The read() method is invoked for inStream to read inBytes worth of data. The actual number of bytes read is stored in bytesRead. This number is displayed, followed on the next line by the bytes that were read from inStream, as follows:

```
outstream: This is a test.
size: 15
inStream has 15 available bytes
15 bytes were read
They are: This is a test.
```

The StringBufferInputStream Class

StringBufferInputStream is similar to ByteArrayInputStream except that it uses a StringBuffer to store input data. The input stream is constructed using a String argument. Its methods are identical to those provided by ByteArrayInputStream.

File I/O

Java supports stream-based file input and output through the File, FileDescriptor, FileInputStream, and FileOutputStream classes. It supports direct- or random-access I/O using the File, FileDescriptor, and RandomAccessFile classes. Random-access I/O is covered later in this chapter.

The File class provides access to file and directory objects and supports a number of operations on files and directories. The FileDescriptor class encapsulates the information used by the host system to track files that are being accessed. The FileInputStream and FileOutputStream classes provide the capability to read and write to file streams.

The File Class

The File class is used to access file and directory objects. It uses the file-naming conventions of the host operating system. The File class encapsulates these conventions using the File class constants.

File provides constructors for creating files and directories. These constructors take absolute and relative file paths and file and directory names.

The File class provides numerous access methods that can be used to perform all common file and directory operations. It is important for you to review the API page for this class because file I/O and file and directory operations are common to most programs.

File methods allow files to be created, deleted, and renamed. They provide access to a file's path and name and determine whether a File object is a file or directory. These methods also check read and write access permissions.

Directory methods allow directories to be created, deleted, renamed, and listed. Directory methods also allow directory trees to be traversed by providing access to the parent and sibling directories.

The FileDescriptor Class

The FileDescriptor class provides access to the file descriptors maintained by operating systems when files and directories are being accessed. This class is *opaque* in that it does not provide visibility into the specific information maintained by the operating system. It provides only one method, the valid() method, which is used to determine whether a file descriptor object is currently valid.

The FileInputStream Class

The FileInputStream class allows input to be read from a file in the form of a stream. Objects of class FileInputStream are created using a filename string or a File or FileDescriptor object as an argument. FileInputStream overrides the methods of the InputStream class and provides two new methods, finalize() and getFD(). The finalize() method is used to close a stream when it is processed by the Java garbage collector. The getFD() method is used to obtain access to the FileDescriptor associated with the input stream.

The FileOutputStream Class

The FileOutputStream class allows output to be written to a file stream. Objects of class FileOutputStream are created in the same way as those of class FileInputStream, using a filename string, File object, or FileDescriptor object as an argument. FileOutputStream overrides the methods of the OutputStream class and supports the finalize() and getFD() methods described for the FileInputStream class.

The FileIOApp Program

The program in Listing 13.2 illustrates the use of the FileInputStream, FileOutputStream, and File classes. It writes a string to an output file and then reads the file to verify that the output was written correctly. The file used for the I/O is then deleted.

Listing 13.2. The source code of the FileIOApp program.

```
import java.lang.System;
import java.io.FileInputStream;
import java.io.FileOutputStream;
import java.io.File;
import java.io.IOException;

public class FileIOApp {
 public static void main(String args[]) throws IOException {
  FileOutputStream outStream = new FileOutputStream("test.txt");
  String s = "This is a test.";
  for(int i=0;i<s.length();++i)
   outStream.write(s.charAt(i));
  outStream.close();
  FileInputStream inStream = new FileInputStream("test.txt");
  int inBytes = inStream.available();
  System.out.println("inStream has "+inBytes+" available bytes");
  byte inBuf[] = new byte[inBytes];
  int bytesRead = inStream.read(inBuf,0,inBytes);
  System.out.println(bytesRead+" bytes were read");
  System.out.println("They are: "+new String(inBuf,0));
  inStream.close();
  File f = new File("test.txt");
  f.delete();
 }
}
```

The `FileOutputStream` constructor creates an output stream on the file `test.txt`. The file is automatically created in the current working directory. It then writes the string `"This is a test."` to the output file stream. Note the similarity between this program and the previous one. The power of streams is that the same methods can be used no matter what type of stream is being used.

The output stream is closed to make sure that all the data is written to the file. The file is then reopened as an input file by creating an object of class `FileInputStream`. The same methods used in the `ByteArrayIOApp` program are used to determine the number of available bytes in the file and read these bytes into a byte array. The number of bytes read is displayed along with the characters corresponding to those bytes.

The input stream is closed and then a `File` object is created to provide access to the file. The `File` object is used to delete the file using the `delete()` method. The program's output follows:

```
inStream has 15 available bytes
15 bytes were read
They are: This is a test.
```

The SequenceInputStream Class

The SequenceInputStream class is used to combine two or more input streams into a single input stream. The input streams are concatenated, which allows the individual streams to be treated as a single, logical stream. The SequenceInputStream class does not introduce any new access methods. Its power is derived from the two constructors that it provides. One constructor takes two InputStream objects as arguments. The other takes an Enumeration of InputStream objects. The Enumeration interface is described in Chapter 14, "Useful Tools in the java.util Package." It provides methods for dealing with a sequence of related objects.

The SequenceIOApp Program

The program in Listing 13.3 reads the two Java source files, ByteArrayIOApp.java and FileIOApp.java, as a single file courtesy of the SequenceInputStream class.

Listing 13.3. The source code of the SequenceIOApp program.

```
import java.lang.System;
import java.io.FileInputStream;
import java.io.SequenceInputStream;
import java.io.IOException;

public class SequenceIOApp {
 public static void main(String args[]) throws IOException {
  SequenceInputStream inStream;
  FileInputStream f1 = new FileInputStream("ByteArrayIOApp.java");
  FileInputStream f2 = new FileInputStream("FileIOApp.java");
  inStream = new SequenceInputStream(f1,f2);
  boolean eof = false;
  int byteCount = 0;
  while (!eof) {
   int c = inStream.read();
   if(c == -1) eof = true;
   else{
    System.out.print((char) c);
    ++byteCount;
   }
  }
  System.out.println(byteCount+" bytes were read");
  inStream.close();
  f1.close();
  f2.close();
 }
}
```

The program creates two objects of class FileInputStream for the files ByteArrayIOApp.java and FileIOApp.java. The SequenceInputClass constructor is used to construct a single input stream from the two `FileInputStream` objects. The program then uses a `while` loop to read all bytes in the combined file and display them to the console window. The loop stops when the end of the combined file is encountered. This is signaled when the `read()` method returns `-1`. The streams are closed after the combined files have been read. The program's output is as follows:

```
import java.lang.System;
import java.io.ByteArrayInputStream;
import java.io.ByteArrayOutputStream;
import java.io.IOException;

public class ByteArrayIOApp {
 public static void main(String args[]) throws IOException {
  ByteArrayOutputStream outStream = new ByteArrayOutputStream();
  String s = "This is a test.";
  for(int i=0;i<s.length();++i)
   outStream.write(s.charAt(i));
  System.out.println("outstream: "+outStream);
  System.out.println("size: "+outStream.size());
  ByteArrayInputStream inStream;
  inStream = new ByteArrayInputStream(outStream.toByteArray());
  int inBytes = inStream.available();
  System.out.println("inStream has "+inBytes+" available bytes");
  byte inBuf[] = new byte[inBytes];
  int bytesRead = inStream.read(inBuf,0,inBytes);
  System.out.println(bytesRead+" bytes were read");
  System.out.println("They are: "+new String(inBuf,0));
 }
}

import java.lang.System;
import java.io.FileInputStream;
import java.io.FileOutputStream;
import java.io.File;
import java.io.IOException;

public class FileIOApp {
 public static void main(String args[]) throws IOException {
  FileOutputStream outStream = new FileOutputStream("test.txt");
  String s = "This is a test.";
  for(int i=0;i<s.length();++i)
   outStream.write(s.charAt(i));
  outStream.close();
  FileInputStream inStream = new FileInputStream("test.txt");
  int inBytes = inStream.available();
  System.out.println("inStream has "+inBytes+" available bytes");
  byte inBuf[] = new byte[inBytes];
  int bytesRead = inStream.read(inBuf,0,inBytes);
  System.out.println(bytesRead+" bytes were read");
  System.out.println("They are: "+new String(inBuf,0));
  inStream.close();
  File f = new File("test.txt");
  f.delete();
 }
}
1771 bytes were read
```

The SequenceIOApp program displays the combined contents of the two source files followed by a line identifying the number of bytes that were read.

Filtered I/O

The filtered input and output stream classes provide the capability to filter I/O in a number of useful ways. I/O filters are used to adapt streams to specific program needs. These filters sit between an input stream and an output stream and perform special processing on the bytes they transfer from input to output. You can combine filters to perform a sequence of filtering operations where one filter acts on the output of another, as shown in Figure 13.2.

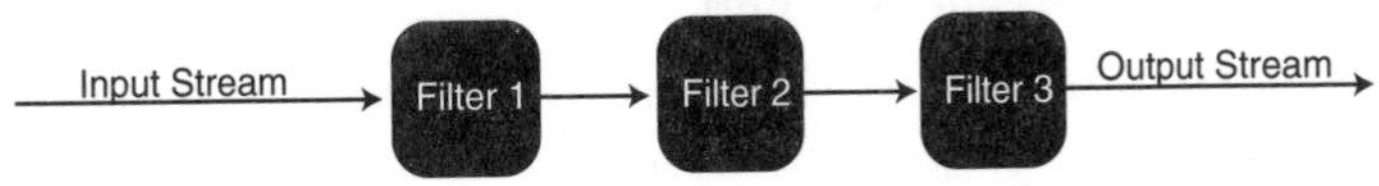

FIGURE 13.2.
Combining filters.

The FilterInputStream Class

The FilterInputStream class is an abstract class that is the parent of all filtered input stream classes. The FilterInputStream class provides the basic capability to create one stream from another. It allows one stream to be read and provided as output as another stream. This is accomplished through the use of the in variable, which is used to maintain a separate object of class InputStream. The design of the FilterInputStream class allows multiple chained filters to be created using several layers of nesting. Each subsequent class accesses the output of the previous class through the in variable. Because the in variable is an object of class InputStream, arbitrary InputStream objects can be filtered.

The FilterOutputStream Class

The FilterOutputStream class is the complement of the FilterInputStream class. It is an abstract class that is the parent of all filtered output stream classes. It is similar to the FilterInputStream class in that it maintains an object of class OutputStream as an out variable. Data written to an object of FilterOutputStream can be modified as needed to perform filtering operations and then forwarded to the out OutputStream object. Because out is declared to be of class OutputStream, arbitrary output streams can be filtered. Multiple FilterOutputStream objects can be combined in a manner that is analogous to FilterInputStream objects. The input of subsequent FilterOutputStream objects is linked to the output of preceding objects.

Buffered I/O

Buffered input and output is used to temporarily cache data that is read from or written to a stream. This allows programs to read and write small amounts of data without adversely affecting system performance. When buffered input is performed, a large number of bytes are read at a single time and stored in an input buffer. When a program reads from the input stream, the input bytes are read from the input buffer. Several reads may be performed before the buffer needs to refilled. Input buffering is used to speed up overall stream input processing.

Output buffering is performed in a manner similar to input buffering. When a program writes to a stream, the output data is stored in an output buffer until the buffer becomes full or the output stream is flushed. Only then is the buffered output actually forwarded to the output stream's destination.

Java implements buffered I/O as filters. The filters maintain and operate the buffer that sits between the program and the source or destination of a buffered stream.

The `BufferedInputStream` Class

The `BufferedInputStream` class supports input buffering by automatically creating and maintaining a buffer for a designated input stream. This allows programs to read data from the stream one byte at a time without degrading system performance. Because the `BufferedInputStream` class is a filter, it can be applied to arbitrary objects of class `InputStream` and combined with other input filters.

The `BufferedInputStream` class uses several variables to implement input buffering. These variables are described in the Java API page for this class. However, because these variables are declared as `protected`, they cannot be directly accessed by your program.

`BufferedInputStream` defines two constructors. One allows the size of an input buffer to be specified and the other does not. Both constructors take an object of class `InputStream` as an argument. It is usually better to let `BufferedInputStream` select the best size for the input buffer than to specify one yourself unless you have specific knowledge that one buffer size is better than another.

`BufferedInputStream` overrides the access methods provided by `InputStream` and does not introduce any new methods of its own.

The `BufferedOutputStream` Class

The `BufferedOutputStream` class performs output buffering in a manner that is analogous to `BufferedInputStream`. It allows the size of the output buffer to be specified in a constructor as well as providing for a default buffer size. It overrides the methods of the `OutputStream` class and does not introduce any new methods of its own.

The `BufferedIOApp` Program

The `BufferedIOApp` program (see Listing 13.4) builds on the `SequenceIOApp` example that was presented previously. It performs buffering on the `SequenceInputStream` object used to combine the input from two separate files. It also performs buffering on program output so that characters do not need to be displayed to the console window a single character at a time.

Listing 13.4. The source code of the BufferedIOApp program.

```
import java.lang.System;
import java.io.BufferedInputStream;
import java.io.BufferedOutputStream;
import java.io.PrintStream;
import java.io.FileInputStream;
import java.io.SequenceInputStream;
import java.io.IOException;

public class BufferedIOApp {
 public static void main(String args[]) throws IOException {
  SequenceInputStream f3;
  FileInputStream f1 = new FileInputStream("ByteArrayIOApp.java");
  FileInputStream f2 = new FileInputStream("FileIOApp.java");
  f3 = new SequenceInputStream(f1,f2);
  BufferedInputStream inStream = new BufferedInputStream(f3);
  BufferedOutputStream bufStream = new BufferedOutputStream(System.out);
  PrintStream outStream = new PrintStream(bufStream);
  inStream.skip(500);
  boolean eof = false;
  int byteCount = 0;
  while (!eof) {
   int c = inStream.read();
   if(c == -1) eof = true;
   else{
    outStream.print((char) c);
    ++byteCount;
   }
  }
  outStream.println(byteCount+" bytes were read");
  inStream.close();
  outStream.close();
  f1.close();
  f2.close();
 }
}
```

The program begins by creating two objects of `FileInputStream` and combining them into a single input stream using the `SequenceInputStream` constructor. It then uses this stream to create an object of `BufferedInputStream` using the default buffer size.

A `BufferedOutputStream` object is created using the `System.out` output stream and a default buffer size. Another filter is applied using the `PrintStream` class. `PrintStream` is an output-filtering subclass of `FilterOutputStream`. It provides several overloaded versions of the `print()` and `println()` methods for facilitating program output.

The `skip()` method is used to skip over 500 bytes of the input stream. This is done for two reasons: to illustrate the use of the `skip()` method and to cut down on the size of the program output. The rest of the input is read and printed as in the previous example.

The program output is similar to that of the preceding example. The `skip()` method was used to skip over 500 bytes of input. These bytes are also absent from the program's output. The program's output is as follows:

```
rrayInputStream inStream;
  inStream = new ByteArrayInputStream(outStream.toByteArray());
  int inBytes = inStream.available();
  System.out.println("inStream has "+inBytes+" available bytes");
  byte inBuf[] = new byte[inBytes];
  int bytesRead = inStream.read(inBuf,0,inBytes);
  System.out.println(bytesRead+" bytes were read");
  System.out.println("They are: "+new String(inBuf,0));
 }
}

import java.lang.System;
import java.io.FileInputStream;
import java.io.FileOutputStream;
import java.io.File;
import java.io.IOException;

public class FileIOApp {
 public static void main(String args[]) throws IOException {
  FileOutputStream outStream = new FileOutputStream("test.txt");
  String s = "This is a test.";
  for(int i=0;i<s.length();++i)
   outStream.write(s.charAt(i));
  outStream.close();
  FileInputStream inStream = new FileInputStream("test.txt");
  int inBytes = inStream.available();
  System.out.println("inStream has "+inBytes+" available bytes");
  byte inBuf[] = new byte[inBytes];
  int bytesRead = inStream.read(inBuf,0,inBytes);
  System.out.println(bytesRead+" bytes were read");
  System.out.println("They are: "+new String(inBuf,0));
  inStream.close();
  File f = new File("test.txt");
  f.delete();
 }
}
1271 bytes were read
```

PushbackInputStream

`PushbackInputStream` is a filter that lets you push a byte that was previously read back onto the input stream so that it can be reread. This type of filter is commonly used with parsers. When a character indicating a new input token is read, it is pushed back onto the input stream until the current input token is processed. It is then reread when processing of the next input token is initiated. `PushbackInputStream` allows only a single byte to be pushed back. This is generally enough for most applications.

The pushback character is stored in a variable named `pushBack`.

The `unread()` method is the only new method introduced by this class. It is used to push a specified character back onto the input stream.

The PushbackIOApp Program

The `PushbackIOApp` program illustrates the use of the `PushbackInputStream` class. (See Listing 13.5.) It adds a pushback filter to the `ByteArrayIOApp` program studied earlier in this chapter.

Listing 13.5. The source code of the PushbackIOApp program.

```
import java.lang.System;
import java.io.PushbackInputStream;
import java.io.ByteArrayInputStream;
import java.io.ByteArrayOutputStream;
import java.io.IOException;

public class PushbackIOApp {
 public static void main(String args[]) throws IOException {
  ByteArrayOutputStream outStream = new ByteArrayOutputStream();
  String s = "This is a test.";
  for(int i=0;i<s.length();++i)
   outStream.write(s.charAt(i));
  System.out.println("outstream: "+outStream);
  System.out.println("size: "+outStream.size());
  ByteArrayInputStream inByteArray;
  inByteArray = new ByteArrayInputStream(outStream.toByteArray());
  PushbackInputStream inStream;
  inStream = new PushbackInputStream(inByteArray);
  char ch = (char) inStream.read();
  System.out.println("First character of inStream is "+ch);
  inStream.unread((int) 't');
  int inBytes = inStream.available();
  System.out.println("inStream has "+inBytes+" available bytes");
  byte inBuf[] = new byte[inBytes];
  for(int i=0;i<inBytes;++i) inBuf[i]=(byte) inStream.read();
  System.out.println("They are: "+new String(inBuf,0));
 }
}
```

`PushbackIOApp` creates a stream to be used for byte array input using the code of the `ByteArrayIOApp` program. It applies a pushback filter to this stream by using the `PushbackInputStream` filter to create an object of class `PushbackInputStream`. It reads the first character of the input stream and displays it. It then pushes back a `t` onto the input stream. Note that any character could have been pushed back upon the input stream. The new input stream is then read and displayed.

The program output shows how the pushback filter was used to change the first character of the input stream from an uppercase `T` to a lowercase `t`. The program output consists of the following:

```
outstream: This is a test.
size: 15
First character of inStream is T
inStream has 15 available bytes
They are: this is a test.
```

The `LineNumberInputStream` Class

The `LineNumberInputStream` class provides a handy capability for keeping track of input line numbers. It is also a subclass of `FilterInputStream`. This class provides two new methods to support line-number processing. The `setLineNumber()` method is used to set the current line number to a particular value. The `getLineNumber()` method is used to obtain the value of the current line number.

The `LineNumIOApp` Program

The `LineNumIOApp` program illustrates the use of this filter class. (See Listing 13.6.)

Listing 13.6. The source code of the `LineNumIOApp` program.

```
import java.lang.System;
import java.io.LineNumberInputStream;
import java.io.FileInputStream;
import java.io.DataInputStream;
import java.io.IOException;

public class LineNumIOApp {
 public static void main(String args[]) throws IOException {
  FileInputStream inFile = new FileInputStream("LineNumIOApp.java");
  LineNumberInputStream inLines = new LineNumberInputStream(inFile);
  DataInputStream inStream = new DataInputStream(inLines);
  String inputLine;
  while ((inputLine=inStream.readLine()) != null) {
   System.out.println(inLines.getLineNumber()+". "+inputLine);
  }
 }
}
```

`LineNumIOApp` reads the `LineNumIOApp.java` source file and displays it using line numbers. It uses three nested input stream objects. First it creates a `FileInputStream` object and assigns it to the `inFile` variable. It then uses this object to create a `LineNumberInputStream` object, which it assigns to `inLines`. Finally, it creates a `DataInputStream` object using `inLines` and assigns it to `inStream`. The `DataInputStream` class is described in the "Data I/O" section of this chapter.

A while loop is used to read every line of the program's source file and display it along with its line number. The readline() method indicates an end-of-file condition by returning a null value. Otherwise, it returns a string with the value of the last line that was read. Notice that the getLineNumber() method was applied to inLines and not to inStream. This is because inStream is an object of DataInputStream and does not support this method.

The program's output provides a nice example of the capabilities of the LineNumberInputStream:

```
1.
2. import java.lang.System;
3. import java.io.LineNumberInputStream;
4. import java.io.FileInputStream;
5. import java.io.DataInputStream;
6. import java.io.IOException;
7.
8. public class LineNumIOApp {
9.  public static void main(String args[]) throws IOException {
10.   FileInputStream inFile = new FileInputStream("LineNumIOApp.java");
11.   LineNumberInputStream inLines = new LineNumberInputStream(inFile);
12.   DataInputStream inStream = new DataInputStream(inLines);
13.   String inputLine;
14.   while ((inputLine=inStream.readLine()) != null) {
15.    System.out.println(inLines.getLineNumber()+". "+inputLine);
16.   }
17.  }
18. }
```

Data I/O

The DataInputStream and DataOutputStream classes implement the DataInput and DataOutput interfaces. These interfaces identify methods that provide the capability to allow arbitrary objects and primitive data types to be read and written from a stream. By implementing these interfaces, the DataInputStream and DataOutputStream classes provide the basis for the implementation of portable input and output streams.

The DataInputStream Class

The DataInputStream class provides the capability to read arbitrary objects and primitive types from an input stream. As you saw in the previous programming example, the filter provided by this class can be nested with other input filters.

This class implements the methods of the DataInput interface. These methods provide a full range of input capabilities. You should check out the Java API pages for the DataInputStream class to familiarize yourself with these methods.

Note that most, but not all, of these methods raise the EOFException when an end of file is encountered. The readLine() method returns a null value to signify a read past the end of a file.

The DataOutputStream Class

The DataOutputStream class provides an output complement to DataInputStream. It allows arbitrary objects and primitive data types to be written to an output stream. It also keeps track of the number of bytes written to the output stream. It is an output filter and can be combined with any output-filtering streams.

The DataIOApp Program

The program in Listing 13.7 shows how DataInputStream and DataOutputStream can be used to easily read and write a variety of values using streams.

Listing 13.7. The source code of the DataIOApp program.

```
import java.lang.System;
import java.io.DataInputStream;
import java.io.DataOutputStream;
import java.io.FileInputStream;
import java.io.FileOutputStream;
import java.io.File;
import java.io.IOException;

public class DataIOApp {
 public static void main(String args[]) throws IOException {
  File file = new File("test.txt");
  FileOutputStream outFile = new FileOutputStream(file);
  DataOutputStream outStream = new DataOutputStream(outFile);
  outStream.writeBoolean(true);
  outStream.writeInt(123456);
  outStream.writeChar('j');
  outStream.writeDouble(1234.56);
  System.out.println(outStream.size()+" bytes were written");
  outStream.close();
  outFile.close();
  FileInputStream inFile = new FileInputStream(file);
  DataInputStream inStream = new DataInputStream(inFile);
  System.out.println(inStream.readBoolean());
  System.out.println(inStream.readInt());
  System.out.println(inStream.readChar());
  System.out.println(inStream.readDouble());
  inStream.close();
  inFile.close();
  file.delete();
 }
}
```

The program creates an object of class File that is used to access the test.txt file. This object is used to create an instance of class FileOutputStream that is assigned to the outFile variable. An object of class DataOutputStream is then constructed as a filter for the FileOutputStream object.

The writeBoolean(), writeChar(), writeInt(), and writeDouble() methods of DataOutputStream are used to write examples of primitive data types to the filtered output stream. The number of bytes written to the output stream is determined from the size() method and displayed to the console window. The output streams are then closed.

The File object, created at the beginning of the program, is then used to create an object of class FileInputStream. The output stream is then filtered by creating an object of DataInputStream.

The primitive data types that were written to the output file in the beginning of the program are now read from the filtered input stream and displayed to the console window.

The program's output shows that the data values were successfully written and read using the data I/O filters:

```
15 bytes were written
true
123456
j
1234.56
```

The PrintStream Class

The PrintStream class should be no stranger to you. The System.out object that you have been using for most of the example programs is an instance of the PrintStream class. It is used to write output to the Java console window.

PrintStream's power lies in the fact that it provides two methods, print() and println(), that are overloaded to print any primitive data type or object. Objects are printed by first converting them to strings using their toString() method inherited from the Object class. To provide custom printing for any class, all you have to do is override the toString() method for that class.

PrintStream provides the capability to automatically flush all output bytes in the stream when a newline character is written to the stream. This feature can be enabled or disabled when the stream is created.

Because PrintStream is a filter, it takes an instance of OutputStream as an argument to its constructor. A second constructor adds the capability to use the autoflushing feature.

PrintStream introduces only one new method besides the extensively overloaded print() and println() methods. The checkError() method is used to flush stream output and determine whether an error occurred on the output stream. This capability is useful for printing output to devices, such as printers, where error status is needed to notify the user of any changes to the device state.

Piped I/O

Piped I/O provides the capability for threads to communicate via streams. A thread sends data to another thread by creating an object of `PipedOutputStream` that it connects to an object of `PipedInputStream`. The output data written by one thread is read by another thread using the `PipedInputStream` object.

The process of connecting piped input and output threads is symmetric. An object of class `PipedInputThread` can also be connected to an existing object of class `PipedOutputThread`.

Java automatically performs synchronization with respect to piped input and output streams. The thread that reads from an input pipe does not have to worry about any conflicts with tasks that are writing to the corresponding output stream thread.

Both `PipedInputStream` and `PipedOutputStream` override the standard I/O methods of `InputStream` and `OutputStream`. The only new method provided by these classes is the `connect()` method. Both classes provide the capability to connect a piped stream when it is constructed by passing the argument of the piped stream to which it is to be connected as an argument to the constructor.

The `PipedIOApp` Program

The `PipedIOApp` program creates two threads of execution, named `Producer` and `Consumer`, that communicate using connected objects of classes `PipedOutputStream` and `PipedInputStream`. `Producer` sends the message `This is a test.` to `Consumer` one character at a time, and `Consumer` reads the message in the same manner. `Producer` displays its name and any characters that it writes to the console window. `Consumer` reads the message and displays its name and the characters it reads to the console window. The source code for the `PipedIOApp` program is shown in Listing 13.8.

Listing 13.8. The source code of the `PipedIOApp` program.

```
import java.lang.Thread;
import java.lang.System;
import java.lang.InterruptedException;
import java.lang.Runnable;
import java.io.PipedInputStream;
import java.io.PipedOutputStream;
import java.io.IOException;

class PipedIOApp {
 public static void main(String args[]) {
  Thread thread1 = new Thread(new PipeOutput("Producer"));
  Thread thread2 = new Thread(new PipeInput("Consumer"));
  thread1.start();
  thread2.start();
  boolean thread1IsAlive = true;
  boolean thread2IsAlive = true;
  do {
```

```
    if(thread1IsAlive && !thread1.isAlive()){
     thread1IsAlive = false;
     System.out.println("Thread 1 is dead.");
    }
    if(thread2IsAlive && !thread2.isAlive()){
     thread2IsAlive = false;
     System.out.println("Thread 2 is dead.");
    }
   }while(thread1IsAlive || thread2IsAlive);
  }
 }
class PipeIO {
 static PipedOutputStream outputPipe = new PipedOutputStream();
 static PipedInputStream inputPipe = new PipedInputStream();
 static {
  try {
   outputPipe.connect(inputPipe);
  }catch (IOException ex) {
   System.out.println("IOException in static initializer");
  }
 }
 String name;
 public PipeIO(String id) {
  name = id;
 }
}
class PipeOutput extends PipeIO implements Runnable {
 public PipeOutput(String id) {
  super(id);
 }
 public void run() {
  String s = "This is a test.";
  try {
   for(int i=0;i<s.length();++i){
    outputPipe.write(s.charAt(i));
    System.out.println(name+" wrote "+s.charAt(i));
   }
   outputPipe.write('!');
  } catch(IOException ex) {
   System.out.println("IOException in PipeOutput");
  }
 }
}
class PipeInput extends PipeIO implements Runnable {
 public PipeInput(String id) {
  super(id);
 }
 public void run() {
  boolean eof = false;
  try {
   while (!eof) {
    int inChar = inputPipe.read();
    if(inChar != -1) {
     char ch = (char) inChar;
     if(ch=='!'){
      eof=true;
      break;
```

continues

Listing 13.8. continued

```
      }else System.out.println(name+" read "+ch);
    }
   }
  } catch(IOException ex) {
   System.out.println("IOException in PipeOutput");
  }
 }
}
```

This program is somewhat longer than the other examples in this chapter due to the overhead needed to set up the threading. The `main()` method creates the two `Producer` and `Consumer` threads as objects of classes `PipeOutput` and `PipeInput`. These classes are subclasses of `PipeIO` that implement the `Runnable` interface. The `main()` method starts both threads and then loops, checking for their death.

The `PipeIO` class is the superclass of the `PipeOutput` and `PipeInput` classes. It contains the `static` variables, `outputPipe` and `inputPipe`, that are used for interthread communication. These variables are assigned objects of classes `PipedOutputStream` and `PipeInputStream`. The `static` initializer is used to connect `outputPipe` with `inputPipe` using the `connect()` method. The `PipeIO` constructor provides the capability to maintain the name of its instances. This is used by the `PipeInput` and `PipeOutput` classes to store thread names.

The `PipeOutput` class extends `PipeIO` and implements the `Runnable` interface, making it eligible to be executed as a separate thread. The required `run()` method performs all thread processing. It loops to write the test message one character at a time to the `outputPipe`. It also displays its name and the characters that it writes to the console window. The `!` character is used to signal the end of the message transmission. Notice that `IOException` is handled within the thread rather than being identified in the `throws` clause of the `run()` method. In order for `run()` to properly implement the `Runnable` interface, it cannot throw any exceptions.

The `PipeInput` class also extends `PipeIO` and implements the `Runnable` interface. It simply loops and reads one character at a time from `inputPipe`, displaying its name and the characters that it reads to the console window. It also handles `IOException` in order to avoid having to identify the exception in its `throws` clause.

The output of `PipeIOApp` shows the time sequencing of the thread input and output taking place using the connected pipe I/O streams. The output generated by running the program on your computer will probably differ because of differences in your computer's execution speed and I/O performance. The output generated when I ran the program is as follows:

```
Producer wrote T
Producer wrote h
Producer wrote i
Producer wrote s
Producer wrote
```

```
Consumer read T
Consumer read h
Consumer read i
Producer wrote i
Producer wrote s
Producer wrote
Consumer read s
Consumer read
Producer wrote a
Producer wrote
Producer wrote t
Consumer read i
Consumer read s
Consumer read
Producer wrote e
Producer wrote s
Consumer read a
Consumer read
Consumer read t
Producer wrote t
Producer wrote .
Thread 1 is dead.
Consumer read e
Consumer read s
Consumer read t
Consumer read .
Thread 2 is dead.
```

The `RandomAccessFile` Class

The `RandomAccessFile` class provides the capability to perform I/O directly to specific locations within a file. The name "random access" comes from the fact that data can be read from or written to random locations within a file rather than as a continuous stream of information. Random access is supported through the `seek()` method, which allows the pointer corresponding to the current file position to be set to arbitrary locations within the file.

`RandomAccessFile` implements both the `DataInput` and `DataOutput` interfaces. This provides the capability to perform I/O using all objects and primitive data types.

`RandomAccessFile` also supports basic file read/write permissions, allowing files to be accessed in read-only or read–write mode. A mode stream argument is passed to the `RandomAccessFile` constructor as `r` or `rw`, indicating read-only and read–write file access. The read-only access attribute may be used to prevent a file from being inadvertently modified.

`RandomAccessFile` introduces several new methods besides those inherited from `Object` and implemented from `DataInput` and `DataOutput`. These methods include `seek()`, `getFilePointer()`, and `length()`. The `seek()` method sets the file pointer to a particular location within the file. The `getFilePointer()` method returns the current location of the file pointer. The `length()` method returns the length of the file in bytes.

The RandomIOApp Program

The RandomIOApp program provides a simple demonstration of the capabilities of random-access I/O. It writes a boolean, int, char, and double value to a file and then uses the seek() method to seek to offset location 1 within the file. This is the position after the first byte in the file. It then reads the int, char, and double values from the file and displays them to the console window. Next, it moves the file pointer to the beginning of the file and reads the boolean value that was first written to the file. This value is also written to the console window. The source code of the RandomIOApp program is shown in Listing 13.9.

Listing 13.9. The source code of the RandomIOApp program.

```
import java.lang.System;
import java.io.RandomAccessFile;
import java.io.IOException;

public class RandomIOApp {
 public static void main(String args[]) throws IOException {
  RandomAccessFile file = new RandomAccessFile("test.txt","rw");
  file.writeBoolean(true);
  file.writeInt(123456);
  file.writeChar('j');
  file.writeDouble(1234.56);
  file.seek(1);
  System.out.println(file.readInt());
  System.out.println(file.readChar());
  System.out.println(file.readDouble());
  file.seek(0);
  System.out.println(file.readBoolean());
  file.close();
 }
}
```

Although the processing performed by RandomIOApp is quite simple, it illustrates how random I/O allows you to move the file pointer to various locations within a file to directly access values and objects contained within the file.

The program's output is as follows:

```
123456
j
1234.56
true
```

The StreamTokenizer Class

The StreamTokenizer class is used by parsers to convert an input stream into a stream of lexical tokens. It uses special methods to identify parser parameters such as ordinary, whitespace, quote, and comment characters. These methods also enable and disable number and end-of-line parsing.

Seven variables are defined for the StreamTokenizer class, four of which are constant class variables. The TT_EOF, TT_EOL, TT_NUMBER, and TT_WORD constants are used to identify the type of input token encountered when parsing the input stream. The ttype variable is set either to one of these constants or to a single character based on the kind of token that is read from the input stream. The TT_ constants are used to indicate a number, word, end of line, or end of file. When a word token is read, the actual word is stored in the sval variable and ttype is set to TT_WORD. When a number token is read, its value is stored in the nval variable and ttype is set to TT_NUMBER. When other special characters, such as @ or *, are read from the input stream, they are assigned directly to the ttype variable.

The StreamTokenizer constructor takes an InputStream object as an argument and generates a StreamTokenizer object. The StreamTokenizer access methods can be divided into two groups: parser parameter–definition methods and stream-processing methods.

The parser parameter–definition methods are used to control the operation of the parser. The commentChar(), slashSlashComments(), and slashStarComments() methods are used to define comments. Comments are ignored by the parser. The whitespaceChars(), wordChars(), quoteChar(), ordinaryChar(), and ordinaryChars() methods are used to set the parser's token-generation parameters. The parseNumbers() and eolIsSignificant() methods toggle number and end-of-line parsing. The lowerCaseMode() method controls whether input words are converted to lowercase, and the resetSyntax() method is used to reset the syntax table, causing all characters to be treated as special characters.

The stream-processing methods are used to read tokens from the input stream, push tokens back out onto the input stream, and return the current line number associated with the input stream. The nextToken() method is used to get the next token from the input stream. The pushBack() method pushes the current token back out onto the input stream. The lineno() method returns the current line number associated with the input stream.

The toString() method of class Object is overwritten to allow printing of the current token.

The StreamTokenApp Program

The StreamTokenApp program demonstrates the ease with which StreamTokenizer can be used to create a parser. This program reads input from the standard input stream, parses input tokens, and displays the token type and value to the console window. (See Listing 13.10.)

Listing 13.10. The source code of the StreamTokenApp program.

```
import java.lang.System;
import java.io.StreamTokenizer;
import java.io.DataInputStream;
```

continues

Listing 13.10. continued

```
import java.io.IOException;

public class StreamTokenApp {
 public static void main(String args[]) throws IOException {
  DataInputStream inData = new DataInputStream(System.in);
  StreamTokenizer inStream = new StreamTokenizer(inData);
  inStream.commentChar('#');
  inStream.eolIsSignificant(true);
  inStream.whitespaceChars(0,32);
  boolean eof = false;
  do {
   int token=inStream.nextToken();
   switch(token){
   case inStream.TT_EOF:
    System.out.println("EOF encountered.");
    eof = true;
    break;
   case inStream.TT_EOL:
    System.out.println("EOL encountered.");
    break;
   case inStream.TT_WORD:
    System.out.println("Word: "+inStream.sval);
    break;
   case inStream.TT_NUMBER:
    System.out.println("Number: "+inStream.nval);
    break;
   default:
    System.out.println((char) token+" encountered.");
    if(token=='!') eof=true;
   }
  } while(!eof);
 }
}
```

The program creates a new object of class `DataInputStream` using `System.in` as an argument. It then converts the `DataInputStream` object into a `StreamTokenizer` object and assigns it to the `inStream` variable. It sets the comment-line character to `#`, makes the end-of-line character a significant token, and identifies all ASCII characters with values between 0 and 32 as whitespace characters.

Having set up the parser, `StreamTokenApp` reads tokens from `inStream` until the end of file is encountered. It uses a `switch` statement to identify the type and value of each token read.

The following is an example of the output produced by `StreamTokenizer`. Try running it with different input lines:

```
This is a test.
Word: This
Word: is
Word: a
Word: test.
```

```
EOL encountered.
123 456
Number: 123
Number: 456
EOL encountered.
12.34 56.78
Number: 12.34
Number: 56.78
EOL encountered.
@ $ % ^
@ encountered.
$ encountered.
% encountered.
^ encountered.
EOL encountered.
#This is a comment.
EOL encountered.
This is #a comment.
Word: This
Word: is
EOL encountered.
!
! encountered.
```

Summary

In this chapter you have learned to work with Java input and output streams to perform input and output using standard I/O, memory buffers, and files. You have explored the input and output stream class hierarchy and learned to use stream filters to simplify I/O processing. You have also learned how to perform random-access I/O and how to use the `StreamTokenizer` class to construct an input parser. In Chapter 14 you will learn how to use the utility classes provided in the `java.util` package.

14

Useful Tools in the `java.util` Package

In this chapter you'll learn how to work with all the useful utility classes contained in the `java.util` package. You'll learn to use the `Date` class to manipulate `Date` objects, to generate random numbers using the `Random` class, and to work with data structures such as dictionaries, stacks, hash tables, vectors, and bit sets. When you finish this chapter you'll be able to make productive use of these utility classes in your own programs.

The Date Class

The `Date` class encapsulates date and time information and allows `Date` objects to be accessed in a system-independent manner. `Date` provides methods for accessing specific date and time measurements, such as year, month, day, date, hours, minutes, and seconds, and for displaying dates in a variety of standard formats.

The `Date` class provides six constructors for creating `Date` objects. The default constructor creates a `Date` object with the current system date and time. Other constructors allow `Date` objects to be set to other dates and times. The access methods defined by the `Date` class support comparisons between dates and provide access to specific date information, including the time zone offset.

If you intend to process date-related information in a program, you should consult the API page for the `Date` class to obtain a full list of the available `Date` methods.

DateApp

The `DateApp` program illustrates the use of the `Date` class. It shows how `Date` objects are created and manipulated using the methods provided by the class. (See Listing 14.1.)

Listing 14.1. The source code of the `DateApp` program.

```
import java.lang.System;
import java.util.Date;

public class DateApp {
 public static void main(String args[]){
  Date today = new Date();
  String days[] = {"Sun","Mon","Tue","Wed","Thu","Fri","Sat"};
  System.out.println("Today's date (locale conventions): "+
   today.toLocaleString());
  System.out.println("Today's date (Unix conventions): "+today.toString());
  System.out.println("Today's date (GMT conventions): "+today.toGMTString());
  System.out.println("Year: "+today.getYear());
  System.out.println("Month: "+today.getMonth());
  System.out.println("Date: "+today.getDate());
  System.out.println("Day: "+days[today.getDay()]);
  System.out.println("Hour: "+today.getHours());
  System.out.println("Minute: "+today.getMinutes());
  System.out.println("Second: "+today.getSeconds());
  Date newYears2000 = new Date(100,0,1);
```

```
  System.out.println("New Years Day 2000: "+newYears2000.toString());
  System.out.println("New Years Day 2000 is "+days[newYears2000.getDay()]);
 }
}
```

The program creates a `Date` object using the default constructor and assigns it to the `today` variable. It then declares an array named `days` and initializes it to the three-letter abbreviations of the days of the week. The `toLocaleString()`, `toString()`, and `toGMTString()` methods are used to convert and print the date using the local operating system and standard UNIX and GMT conventions.

The various `get` methods supported by the `Date` class are used to print out the year, month, date, day, hours, minutes, and seconds corresponding to the current date.

A new `Date` object is constructed and assigned to the `newYears2000` variable. The `Date` constructor takes the arguments `100`, `0`, and `1`. They specify the 100th year after the year 1900, the 0th month (that is, January), and the first day of the month. The date specified is New Year's Day in the year 2000, as you probably guessed from the name of the variable in which it is stored.

The `newYears2000` date is printed followed by the actual day of the week corresponding to the date.

The output of the `DateApp` program is as follows. When you run the program, you will obviously get a different date for the first part of the program's processing. The following are the results that were displayed when I ran the program:

```
Today's date (locale conventions): 03/01/96 09:53:46
Today's date (Unix conventions): Fri Mar 01 09:53:46  1996
Today's date (GMT conventions): 1 Mar 1996 17:53:46 GMT
Year: 96
Month: 2
Date: 1
Day: Fri
Hour: 9
Minute: 53
Second: 46
New Years Day 2000: Sat Jan 01 00:00:00  2000
New Years Day 2000 is Sat
```

The Random Class

The `Random` class provides a template for the creation of random number generators. It differs from the `random()` method of the `java.lang.Math` class in that it allows any number of random number generators to be created as separate objects. The `Math.random()` method provides a `static` function for the generation of random `double` values. This `static` method is shared by all program code.

Objects of the `Random` class generate random numbers using a linear congruential formula. Two constructors are provided for creating `Random` objects. The default constructor initializes the seed of the random number generator using the current system time. The other constructor allows the seed to be set to an initial `long` value.

The Java API page says the random number generator uses a 48-bit seed, but the constructor allows only a 32-bit value to be passed as a seed. In any case, the random number generators that are created as objects of this class should be sufficient for most random number generation needs.

The `Random` class provides six access methods, five of which are used to generate random values. The `nextInt()`, `nextLong()`, `nextFloat()`, and `nextDouble()` methods generate values for the numeric data types. The values generated by `nextFloat()` and `nextDouble()` are between 0.0 and 1.0. The `nextGaussian()` method generates a Gaussian distribution of `double` values with mean 0.0 and standard deviation 1.0.

The `setSeed()` method is used to reset the seed of the random number generator.

RandomApp

The `RandomApp` program demonstrates the use of the `Random` class. (See Listing 14.2.) It creates an object of class `Random` using the default constructor and assigns it to `r`. This causes the random number generator to be seeded using the current system time. Three `for` loops are used to print random `int`, `double`, and Gaussian distributed `double` values. Each loop prints four values.

Listing 14.2. The source code of the `RandomApp` program.

```
import java.lang.System;
import java.util.Random;

public class RandomApp {
 public static void main(String args[]){
  Random r = new Random();
  for(int i=0;i<4;++i) System.out.print(r.nextInt()+" ");
  System.out.println();
  r = new Random(123456789);
  for(int i=0;i<4;++i) System.out.print(r.nextDouble()+" ");
  System.out.println();
  r.setSeed(234567890);
  for(int i=0;i<4;++i) System.out.print(r.nextGaussian()+" ");
  System.out.println();
 }
}
```

The output generated by the program when it was run on my computer produced the following results:

```
1799702397 -2014911382 618703884 -1181330064
0.664038 0.456952 0.390506 0.893341
0.113781 0.412296 -1.57262 0.0756829
```

It will produce different results when it is run on your computer because the first line that is printed uses the `Random()` constructor to generate the output data.

The `Enumeration` Interface

The `Enumeration` interface specifies two methods to be used to index through a set of objects or values: `hasMoreElements()` and `nextElement()`. The `hasMoreElements()` method enables you to determine whether more elements are contained in an `Enumeration` object. The `nextElement()` method returns the next element contained by an object.

Enumeration-implementing objects are said to be *consumed* by their use. This means that the `Enumeration` objects cannot be restarted to reindex through the elements they contain. Their elements may be accessed only once.

The `Enumeration` interface is implemented by the `StringTokenizer` class as discussed later in this chapter in the section "The `StringTokenizer` Class." It is also used to obtain a list of elements contained in a vector, as shown in the programming example in the next section.

The `Vector` Class

The `Vector` class provides the capability to implement a growable array. The array grows larger as more elements are added to it. The array may also be reduced in size, after some of its elements have been deleted. This is accomplished using the `trimToSize()` method.

`Vector` operates by creating an initial storage capacity and then adding to this capacity as needed. It grows by an increment defined by the `capacityIncrement` variable. The initial storage capacity and `capacityIncrement` can be specified in `Vector`'s constructor. A second constructor is used when you want to specify only the initial storage capacity. A third, default constructor specifies neither the initial capacity nor the `capacityIncrement`. This constructor lets Java figure out the best parameters to use for `Vector` objects.

The access methods provided by the `Vector` class support array-like operations and operations related to the size of `Vector` objects. The array-like operations allow elements to be added, deleted, and inserted into vectors. They also allow tests to be performed on the contents of vectors and specific elements to be retrieved. The size-related operations allow the byte size and number of elements of the vector to be determined and the vector size to be increased to a certain capacity or trimmed to the minimum capacity needed. Consult the `Vector` API page for a complete description of these methods.

VectorApp

The VectorApp program illustrates the use of vectors and the Enumeration interface. (See Listing 14.3.)

Listing 14.3. The source code of the VectorApp program.

```
import java.lang.System;
import java.util.Vector;
import java.util.Enumeration;

public class VectorApp {
 public static void main(String args[]){
  Vector v = new Vector();
  v.addElement("one");
  v.addElement("two");
  v.addElement("three");
  v.insertElementAt("zero",0);
  v.insertElementAt("oops",3);
  v.insertElementAt("four",5);
  System.out.println("Size: "+v.size());
  Enumeration enum = v.elements();
  while (enum.hasMoreElements())
   System.out.print(enum.nextElement()+" ");
  System.out.println();
  v.removeElement("oops");
  System.out.println("Size: "+v.size());
  for(int i=0;i<v.size();++i)
   System.out.print(v.elementAt(i)+" ");
  System.out.println();
 }
}
```

The program creates a Vector object using the default constructor and uses the addElement() method to add the strings, "one", "two", and "three" to the vector. It then uses the insertElementAt() method to insert the strings "zero", "oops", and "four" at locations 0, 3, and 5 within the vector. The size() method is used to retrieve the vector size for display to the console window.

The elements() method of the Vector class is used to retrieve an enumeration of the elements that were added to the vector. A while loop is then used to cycle through and print the elements contained in the enumeration. The hasMoreElements() method is used to determine whether the enumeration contains more elements. If it does, the nextElement() method is used to retrieve the object for printing.

The removeElement() of the Vector class is used to remove the vector element containing the string "oops". The new size of the vector is displayed and the elements of the vector are redisplayed. The for loop indexes each element in the vector using the elementAt() method.

The output of the VectorApp program is as follows:

```
Size: 6
zero one two oops three four
Size: 5
zero one two three four
```

The Stack Class

The Stack class provides the capability to create and use stacks within your Java programs. *Stacks* are storage objects that store information by pushing it onto a stack and remove and retrieve information by popping it off the stack. Stacks implement a last-in-first-out storage capability: The last object pushed on a stack is the first object that can be retrieved from the stack. The Stack class extends the Vector class.

The Stack class provides a single default constructor, Stack(), that is used to create an empty stack.

Objects are placed on the stack using the push() method and retrieved from the stack using the pop() method. The search() method allows you to search through a stack to see if a particular object is contained on the stack. The peek() method returns the top element of the stack without popping it off. The empty() method is used to determine whether a stack is empty. The pop() and peek() methods both throw the EmptyStackException if the stack is empty. Use of the empty() method can help to avoid the generation of this exception.

StackApp

The StackApp program demonstrates the operation of a stack. (See Listing 14.4.) It creates a Stack object and then uses the push() method to push the strings "one", "two", and "three" onto the stack. Because the stack operates in last-in-first-out fashion, the top of the stack is the string "three". This is verified by using the peek() method. The contents of the stack are then popped off and printed using a while loop. The empty() method is used to determine when the loop should terminate. The pop() method is used to pop objects off the top of the stack.

Listing 14.4. The source code of the StackApp program.

```
import java.lang.System;
import java.util.Stack;

public class StackApp {
 public static void main(String args[]){
  Stack s = new Stack();
  s.push("one");
  s.push("two");
  s.push("three");
  System.out.println("Top of stack: "+s.peek());
  while (!s.empty())
   System.out.println(s.pop());
 }
}
```

The output of the StackApp program is as follows:

```
Size: 6
zero one two oops three four
Size: 5
zero one two three four
```

The BitSet Class

The BitSet class is used to create objects that maintain a set of bits. The bits are maintained as a growable set. The capacity of the bit set is increased as needed. Bit sets are used to maintain a list of *flags* that indicate the state of each element of a set of conditions. Flags are boolean values that are used to represent the state of an object.

Two BitSet constructors are provided. One allows the initial capacity of a BitSet object to be specified. The other is a default constructor that initializes a BitSet to a default size.

The BitSet access methods provide and, or, and exclusive or logical operations on bit sets; enable specific bits to be set and cleared; and override general methods declared for the Object class.

BitSetApp

The BitSetApp program demonstrates the operation of bit sets. (See Listing 14.5.)

Listing 14.5. The source code of the BitSetApp program.

```
import java.lang.System;
import java.util.BitSet;

public class BitSetApp {
 public static void main(String args[]){
  int size = 8;
  BitSet b1 = new BitSet(size);
  for(int i=0;i<size;++i) b1.set(i);
  BitSet b2 = (BitSet) b1.clone();
  for(int i=0;i<size;i=i+2) b2.clear(i);
  System.out.print("b1: ");
  for(int i=0;i<size;++i) System.out.print(b1.get(i)+" ");
  System.out.print("\nb2: ");
  for(int i=0;i<size;++i) System.out.print(b2.get(i)+" ");
  System.out.println();
  System.out.println("b1: "+b1);
  System.out.println("b2: "+b2);
  b1.xor(b2);
  System.out.println("b1 xor b2 = "+b1);
  b1.and(b2);
  System.out.println("b1 and b2 = "+b1);
  b1.or(b2);
  System.out.println("b1 or b2 = "+b1);
 }
}
```

The program begins by creating a `BitSet` object, `b1`, of size 8. It executes a `for` statement to index through `b1` and set each bit in the bit set. It then uses the `clone()` method to create an identical copy of `b1` and assign it to `b2`. Another `for` statement is executed to clear every even-numbered bit in `b2`. The values of the `b1` and `b2` bit sets are then printed. This results in the display of two lists of `boolean` values. The bit sets are printed as objects, resulting in a set-oriented display. Only the bits with `true boolean` values are identified as members of the displayed bit sets.

The `xor()` method is used to compute the exclusive or of `b1` and `b2`, updating `b1` with the result. The new value of `b1` is then displayed.

The `and()` method is used to calculate the logical and of `b1` and `b2`, again, updating `b1` with the result and displaying `b1`'s new value.

Finally, the logical or of `b1` and `b2` is computed, using the `or()` method. The result is used to update `b1`, and `b1`'s value is displayed.

The output of `BitSetApp` is as follows:

```
b1: true true true true true true true true
b2: false true false true false true false true
b1: {0, 1, 2, 3, 4, 5, 6, 7}
b2: {1, 3, 5, 7}
b1 xor b2 = {0, 2, 4, 6}
b1 and b2 = {}
b1 or b2 = {1, 3, 5, 7}
```

The Dictionary, Hashtable, and Properties Classes

The `Dictionary`, `Hashtable`, and `Properties` classes are three generations of classes that implement the capability to provide key-based data storage and retrieval. The `Dictionary` class is the abstract superclass of `Hashtable`, which is, in turn, the superclass of `Properties`.

Dictionary

`Dictionary` provides the abstract functions used to store and retrieve objects by key–value associations. The class allows any object to be used as a key or value. This provides great flexibility in the design of key-based storage and retrieval classes. `Hashtable` and `Properties` are two examples of these classes.

The `Dictionary` class can be understood using its namesake abstraction. A real-world hardcopy dictionary maps words to their definition. The words can be considered the keys of the dictionary and the definitions as the values of the keys. Java dictionaries operate in the same fashion. One object is used as the key to access another object. This abstraction will become clearer as you investigate the `Hashtable` and `Properties` classes.

The `Dictionary` class defines several methods that are inherited by its subclasses. The `elements()` method is used to return an `Enumeration` object containing the values of the key–value pairs stored within the dictionary. The `keys()` method returns an enumeration of the dictionary keys. The `get()` method is used to retrieve an object from the dictionary based on its key. The `put()` method puts a `Value` object in the dictionary and indexes it using a `Key` object. The `isEmpty()` method determines whether a dictionary contains any elements, and the `size()` method identifies the dictionary's size in terms of the number of elements it contains. The `remove()` method deletes a key–value pair from the dictionary based on the object's key.

Hashtable

The `Hashtable` class implements a hash table data structure. A *hash table* indexes and stores objects in a dictionary using hash codes as the objects' keys. *Hash codes* are integer values that identify objects. They are computed in such a manner that different objects are very likely to have different hash values and therefore different dictionary keys.

The `Object` class implements the `hashCode()` method. This method allows the hash code of an arbitrary Java object to be calculated. All Java classes and objects inherit this method from `Object`. The `hashCode()` method is used to compute the hash code key for storing objects within a hash table. `Object` also implements the `equals()` method. This method is used to determine whether two objects with the same hash code are, in fact, equal.

The Java `Hashtable` class is very similar to the `Dictionary` class from which it is derived. Objects are added to a hash table as key–value pairs. The object used as the key is hashed, using its `hashCode()` method, and the hash code is used as the actual key for the value object. When an object is to be retrieved from a hash table, using a key, the key's hash code is computed and used to find the object.

The `Hashtable` class provides three constructors. The first constructor allows a hash table to be created with a specific initial capacity and load factor. The *load factor* is a float value between 0.0 and 1.0 that identifies the percentage of hash table usage that causes the hash table to be rehashed into a larger table. For example, suppose a hash table is created with a capacity of 100 entries and a 0.70 load factor. When the hash table is 70 percent full, a new, larger hash table will be created, and the current hash table entries will have their hash values recalculated for the larger table.

The second `Hashtable` constructor just specifies the table's initial capacity and ignores the load factor. The default hash table constructor does not specify either hash table parameter.

The access methods defined for the `Hashtable` class allow key–value pairs to be added to and removed from a hash table, search the hash table for a particular key or object value, create an enumeration of the table's keys and values, determine the size of the hash table, and recalculate the hash table, as needed. Many of these methods are inherited or overridden from the `Dictionary` class.

HashApp

The `HashApp` program illustrates the operation and use of hash tables. (See Listing 14.6.)

Listing 14.6. The source code of the `HashApp` program.

```
import java.lang.System;
import java.util.Hashtable;
import java.util.Enumeration;

public class HashApp {
 public static void main(String args[]){
  Hashtable h = new Hashtable();
  h.put("height","6 feet");
  h.put("weight","200 pounds");
  h.put("eye color","blue");
  h.put("hair color","brown");
  System.out.println("h: "+h);
  Enumeration enum = h.keys();
  System.out.print("keys: ");
  while (enum.hasMoreElements()) System.out.print(enum.nextElement()+", ");
  System.out.print("\nelements: ");
  enum = h.elements();
  while (enum.hasMoreElements()) System.out.print(enum.nextElement()+", ");
  System.out.println();
  System.out.println("height: "+h.get("height"));
  System.out.println("weight: "+h.get("weight"));
  System.out.println("eyes: "+h.get("eye color"));
  System.out.println("hair: "+h.get("hair color"));
  h.remove("weight");
  System.out.println("h: "+h);
 }
}
```

The program begins by creating a `Hashtable` object using the default constructor. It then adds four key–value pairs to the hash table using the `put()` method. The hash table is then printed using the default print method for objects of class `Hashtable`.

The `keys()` method is used to create an enumeration of the hash table's keys. These keys are then printed one at a time by indexing through the enumeration object.

The `elements()` method is used to create an enumeration of the hash table's values. This enumeration is printed in the same way as the key enumeration.

The values of the hash table are again displayed by using the `get()` method to get the values corresponding to specific key values.

Finally, the `remove()` method is used to remove the key–value pair associated with the `weight` key and the hash table is reprinted using the default print convention.

The program output is as follows:

```
h: {height=6 feet, weight=200 pounds, eye color=blue, hair color=brown}
keys: height, weight, eye color, hair color,
elements: 6 feet, 200 pounds, blue, brown,
height: 6 feet
weight: 200 pounds
eyes: blue
hair: brown
h: {height=6 feet, eye color=blue, hair color=brown}
```

The Properties Class

The `Properties` class is a subclass of `Hashtable` that can be read from or written to a stream. It also provides the capability to specify a set of default values to be used if a specified key is not found in the table. The default values themselves are specified as an object of class `Properties`. This allows an object of class `Properties` to have a default `Properties` object, which in turn has its own default properties, and so on.

`Properties` supports two constructors: a default constructor with no parameters and a constructor that accepts the default properties to be associated with the `Properties` object being constructed.

The `Properties` class declares several new access methods. The `getProperty()` method allows a property to be retrieved using a `String` object as a key. A second overloaded `getProperty()` method allows a value string to be used as the default in case the key is not contained in the `Properties` object.

The `load()` and `save()` methods are used to load a `Properties` object from an input stream and save it to an output stream. The `save()` method allows an optional header comment to be saved at the beginning of the saved object's position in the output stream.

The `propertyNames()` method provides an enumeration of all the property keys, and the `list()` method provides a convenient way to print a `Properties` object on a `PrintStream` object.

PropApp

The `PropApp` program illustrates the use of the `Properties` class by saving a subset of the system properties to a byte array stream and then loading the properties back in from the byte array stream. (See Listing 14.7.)

Listing 14.7. The source code of the `PropApp` program.

```
import java.lang.System;
import java.util.Properties;
import java.io.ByteArrayOutputStream;
import java.io.ByteArrayInputStream;
import java.io.IOException;

public class PropApp {
 public static void main(String args[]) throws IOException {
```

```
  Properties sysProp = System.getProperties();
  sysProp.list(System.out);
  sysProp.remove("java.home");
  sysProp.remove("file.separator");
  sysProp.remove("line.separator");
  sysProp.remove("java.vendor");
  sysProp.remove("user.name");
  sysProp.remove("java.vendor.url");
  sysProp.remove("user.dir");
  sysProp.remove("java.class.path");
  sysProp.remove("java.class.version");
  sysProp.remove("path.separator");
  sysProp.remove("user.home");
  ByteArrayOutputStream outStream = new ByteArrayOutputStream();
  sysProp.save(outStream,"sysProp");
  System.out.println("\noutputStream:\n"+outStream);
  ByteArrayInputStream inStream;
  inStream = new ByteArrayInputStream(outStream.toByteArray());
  sysProp.load(inStream);
  sysProp.list(System.out);
 }
}
```

The program begins by using the `getProperties()` method of the `System` class to retrieve the system properties and assign them to the `sysProp` variable. The system properties are then listed on the console window using the `list()` method.

Eleven of the properties contained by `sysProp` are removed using the `remove()` method. They were removed to cut down on the amount of program output and to illustrate the use of the `remove()` method.

An object of class `ByteArrayOutputStream` is created and assigned to the `outStream` variable. The `sysProp` `Properties` object is then saved to the output stream using the `save()` method.

The `outStream` is converted to a byte array using the `toByteArray()` method of the `ByteArrayOutputStream` class. The byte array is provided as an argument to a `ByteArrayInputStream` constructor, which uses it to create an object of its class and assign it to the `inStream` variable. The saved properties are reloaded from `inStream` and reassigned to the `sysProp` variable. The contents of the `sysProp` variable are then relisted to show that they were correctly loaded.

The program output is as follows:

```
-- listing properties --
java.home=C:\JAVA\BIN\..
awt.toolkit=sun.awt.win32.MToolkit
java.version=1.0
file.separator=\
line.separator=

java.vendor=Sun Microsystems Inc.
user.name=jaworskij
```

```
os.arch=x86
os.name=Windows 95
java.vendor.url=http://www.sun.com/
user.dir=c:\java\jdg\ch14
java.class.path=.;c:\java;c:\java\lib;;C:\JAVA\BIN\.....
java.class.version=45.3
os.version=4.0
path.separator=;
user.home=\home\jamie

outputStream:
#sysProp
#Fri Mar 01 09:59:00  1996
awt.toolkit=sun.awt.win32.MToolkit
java.version=1.0
os.arch=x86
os.name=Windows 95
os.version=4.0

-- listing properties --
awt.toolkit=sun.awt.win32.MToolkit
java.version=1.0
os.arch=x86
os.name=Windows 95
os.version=4.0
```

The `StringTokenizer` Class

The `StringTokenizer` class is used to create a parser for `String` objects. It parses strings according to a set of delimiter characters. It implements the `Enumeration` interface in order to provide access to the tokens contained within a string. The `StringTokenizer` class is similar to the `StreamTokenizer` class covered in Chapter 13, "Stream-Based Input/Output and the `java.io` Package."

`StringTokenizer` provides three constructors. All three have the input string as a parameter. The first constructor includes two other parameters: a set of delimiters to be using in the string parsing and a `boolean` value used to specify whether the delimiter characters should be returned as tokens. The second constructor accepts the delimiter string but not the return token's toggle. The last constructor uses the default delimiter set consisting of the space, tab, newline, and carriage-return characters.

The access methods provided by `StringTokenizer` include the `Enumeration` methods, `hasMoreElements()` and `nextElement()`, `hasMoreTokens()` and `nextToken()`, and `countTokens()`. The `countTokens()` method returns the number of tokens in the string being parsed.

TokenApp

The `TokenApp` program prompts the user to enter a line of keyboard input and then parses the line, identifying the number and value of the tokens that it found. (See Listing 14.8.)

Listing 14.8. The source code of the TokenApp program.

```
import java.lang.System;
import java.util.StringTokenizer;
import java.io.DataInputStream;
import java.io.IOException;

public class TokenApp {
 public static void main(String args[]) throws IOException {
  DataInputStream keyboardInput = new DataInputStream(System.in);
  int numTokens;
  do {
   System.out.print("=> ");
   System.out.flush();
   StringTokenizer st = new StringTokenizer(keyboardInput.readLine());
   numTokens = st.countTokens();
   System.out.println(numTokens+" tokens");
   while (st.hasMoreTokens())
    System.out.println(" "+st.nextToken());
  } while(numTokens!=0);
 }
}
```

The program begins by creating a `DataInputStream` object using the `System.in` stream as an argument to its constructor. A `do` loop is used to read a line of input from the user, construct a `StringTokenizer` object on the input line, display the number of tokens in the line, and display each token as parsed using the standard delimiter set. The loop continues until a line with no tokens is entered.

The program's output is as follows:

```
=> this is a test
4 tokens
 this
 is
 a
 test
=> 1 2 3 4.5 6
5 tokens
 1
 2
 3
 4.5
 6
=> @ # $ % ^
5 tokens
 @
 #
 $
 %
 ^
=>
0 tokens
```

Observer and Observable

The Observer interface and Observable class are used to implement an abstract system by which observable objects can be observed by objects that implement the Observer interface. *Observable* objects are objects that subclass the abstract Observable class. These objects maintain a list of observers. When an observable object is updated, it invokes the update() method of its observers to notify the observers that it has changed state.

The update() method is the only method that is specified in the Observer interface. The update() method is used to notify an observer that an observable has changed. The method takes the observable object and a second notification message Object as its parameters.

Observable

The Observable class is an abstract class that must be subclassed by observable objects. It provides several methods for adding, deleting, and notifying observers and for manipulating change status. These methods are described in the class's API page.

Summary

In this chapter you have learned how to work with all the useful utility classes contained in the java.util package. You have learned to use the Date class to manipulate Date objects and the Random number class to generate random numbers, and how to work with a range of data structures, including dictionaries, stacks, hash tables, vectors, and bit sets. In Chapter 15, "Window Programming with the java.awt Package," you'll preview the Java Abstract Windows Toolkit (AWT) and learn what window components are available to develop window-based programs using Java.

15

Window Programming with the `java.awt` Package

This chapter introduces the classes of the `java.awt` package. These classes provide the foundation for Java window programming. You'll learn how the `java.awt` package is organized and cover each of the classes that it contains. You'll also cover the `java.awt.image` and `java.awt.peer` packages. This chapter, unlike others in this part, does not provide programming examples. Part IV, "Window Programming," provides a detailed tutorial of Java window programming, including numerous programming examples.

Window Programming Classes

The Java *Abstract Windowing Toolkit* (AWT) provides numerous classes that support window program development. These classes are used to create and organize windows, implement GUI components, handle events, draw text and graphics, perform image processing, and obtain access to the native Windows implementation.

This chapter covers these classes in sections consisting of logically related classes. The "Components and Containers" section introduces the GUI components supported by the AWT and the Windows classes that contain these components. The "Constructing Menus" section describes the classes that are used to implement menu bars and pull-down menus. The "Organizing Windows" section describes the classes that are used to organize windows and lay out the components they contain. The "Handling Events" section introduces the `Event` class and describes the process of Java event handling. The "Working with Images" section introduces the `Image` class and the image-processing classes of the `java.awt.image` class. The "Geometrical Objects" section covers the Java classes that are used to represent points, rectangles, polygons, and dimensions. The "Using Fonts" section introduces the `Font` and `FontMetrics` classes and shows how to use these classes to control the display of text. The "Using the Toolkit" section describes the interface between the platform-independent AWT classes and their native platform-dependent implementations.

Components and Containers

The `Component` class is the superclass of the set of AWT classes that implement graphical user interface controls. These components include windows, dialog boxes, buttons, labels, text fields, and other common GUI components. The `Component` class provides a common set of methods that are used by all these subclasses. These methods include methods for handling events and working with images, fonts, and colors. More than 70 methods are implemented by this class. It is a good idea to browse the API pages of the `Component` class to get a feel for the kinds of methods that are available. You don't have to worry about learning them now. The important methods are covered in Part IV.

Although `Component` contains many GUI-related subclasses, its `Container` subclass is the class used to define Windows objects that contain other objects. As such, it is used to define classes for working with application windows, dialog boxes, panels, and applets. The `Container` class and subclasses are covered in the next section. The classes for GUI controls are covered in later portions of that section.

The `Container` Class

The `Container` class is a subclass of the `Component` class that is used to define components that have the capability to contain other components. It provides methods for adding, retrieving, displaying, counting, and removing the components that it contains. It provides the `deliverEvent()` method for forwarding events to its components. The `Container` class also provides methods for working with layouts. The layout classes control the layout of components within a container.

The `Container` class has two major subclasses: `Window` and `Panel`. `Window` provides a common superclass for application main windows (`Frame` objects) and `Dialog` windows. The `Panel` class is a generic container that can be displayed within a window. It is subclassed by the `java.applet.Applet` class as the base class for all Java applets.

The `Window` Class

The `Window` class provides an encapsulation of a generic `Window` object. It is subclassed by `Frame` and `Dialog` to provide the capabilities needed to support application main windows and dialog boxes.

The `Window` class contains a single constructor that creates a window that has a frame window as its parent. The parent frame window is necessary because only objects of the `Frame` class or its subclasses contain the functionality needed to support the implementation of an independent application window.

The `Window` class implements important methods that are used by its `Frame` and `Dialog` subclasses. The `pack()` method is used to arrange the components contained in the window according to the window layout style. Layout classes are covered later in this chapter. The `show()` method is used to display a window. Windows are hidden (invisible), by default, and are displayed only as a result of invoking their `show()` method. The `toFront()` and `toBack()` methods are used to position windows relative to their frame windows. The `dispose()` method is used to release the resources associated with a window and delete the `Window` object. The `getWarningString()` method is used to retrieve the warning message associated with untrusted windows. Warning messages are associated with windows that are created by applets. The other `Window` methods are used to support peer operations. AWT peers are discussed later in this chapter in the "Using the Toolkit" section.

A `Window` object does not have a border or a menu bar when it is created. In this state it may be used to implement a pop-up window. The default layout for a `Window` object is `BorderLayout`.

Frame

The Frame class is used to provide the main window of an application. It is a subclass of Window that supports the capabilities to specify the icon, cursor, menu bar, and title. Because it implements the MenuContainer interface, it is capable of working with MenuBar objects.

The Frame class defines 14 constants that are used to specify different types of cursors to be used within the frame. Consult the Frame class API page for a description of these constants.

Frame provides two constructors: a default parameterless constructor that creates an untitled frame window and a constructor that accepts a string argument to be used as the frame window's title. The second constructor is typically used.

Frame extends the set of access methods that it inherits from Window by adding methods to get and set the window title, icon image, cursor, and menu bar. Methods for removing the menu bar and specifying whether the window is resizable are also provided.

Dialog

The Dialog class is a subclass of the Window class that is used to implement dialog box windows. A dialog box is a window that takes input from the user. The Dialog class allows dialog boxes that are modal to be constructed. *Modal* dialog boxes must be closed before control returns to the window that launched them. The Dialog class also provides the capability to construct non-modal dialog boxes. *Non-modal* dialog boxes do not need to be closed before other program windows can be accessed.

The Dialog class provides two constructors. Both constructors require the Window object containing the dialog box, as well as the modal flag, to be specified. The second constructor allows the title of the dialog box to be specified.

The Dialog class provides only a handful of access methods. These methods are used to get and set its title, determine whether it is modal, and get and set the dialog box's resizable properties.

FileDialog

The FileDialog class is used to construct dialog boxes that support the selection of files for input and output operations. It is a subset of the Dialog class and provides two constructors. The first constructor identifies the Frame window that contains the dialog box and the title to be used at the top of the dialog box. The second constructor adds a mode parameter that can be set to the LOAD or SAVE constants defined by FileDialog.

FileDialog provides methods that are used to access the directory and filename of the user-selected file and to specify an object that implements the FileNameFilter interface.

The Panel Class

The Panel class is a subclass of the Container class that is used to organize GUI components within other container objects. It provides a single constructor that takes no parameters. The methods used with Panel objects are usually inherited from the Component and Container classes. The Applet class of the java.applet package is a subclass of the Panel class. The default layout for a Panel object is FlowLayout.

The Label Class

The Label class is used to display read-only text labels within a window or other GUI container. It has three constructors. The first constructor takes no parameters and is used to construct a blank label. The second constructor takes a String object as its parameter that is used to specify the label's text. The third constructor has an alignment parameter in addition to the text string. This parameter specifies how the label should be aligned within its container. The Label class defines the LEFT, CENTER, and RIGHT constants for use as alignment values.

The Label class provides methods to get and set the displayed label and its alignment value.

The Button Class

The Button class implements a clickable button GUI control. The button is capable of displaying a text label. Two Button constructors are provided. The first constructor takes no parameters and creates a button with a blank label. The second constructor accepts a String object that is displayed as the button's label. The Button class provides methods for getting and setting its label.

The Checkbox Class

The Checkbox class is used to implement checkbox and radio button GUI controls. The checkbox or radio button is associated with a label. If a Checkbox object is not associated with a CheckboxGroup object, it is implemented as a traditional checkbox. If a Checkbox object is associated with a CheckboxGroup object, it is implemented as a radio button.

The Checkbox class provides three constructors. The first constructor takes no parameters and implements a blank checkbox. The second constructor takes a String parameter that is used as the title of the checkbox. The third constructor allows a CheckboxGroup object and the initial state of the radio button to be specified in addition to its label.

The Checkbox class provides methods for getting and setting the label and state of the checkbox and its CheckboxGroup object, if any. The state of the checkbox is boolean.

CheckboxGroup

The `CheckboxGroup` class is used with the `Checkbox` class to implement radio buttons. All `Checkbox` objects that are associated with a `CheckboxGroup` object are treated as a single set of radio buttons. Only one button in the group may be set or on at a given point in time. The `CheckboxGroup` provides a single, parameterless constructor. It also provides methods for getting and setting the `Checkbox` object.

The `Choice` Class

The `Choice` class is used to implement pull-down lists that can be placed in the main area of a window. These lists are known as *option menus* or a *pop-up menus of choices* and allow the user to select a single menu value. The `Choice` class provides a single, parameterless constructor. It also provides access methods that are used to add items to the list, count the number of items contained in the list, select a list item, and determine which list item is selected.

The `List` Class

The `List` class implements single- and multiple-selection list GUI controls. The lists provided by the `List` class are more sophisticated than those provided by the `Choice` class: The `List` class provides the capability to specify the size of the scrollable window in which the list items are displayed and to select multiple items from the list. The `List` class has two constructors. The first one takes no parameters and constructs a generic `List` object. The second one allows the number of rows of the visible window to be specified and whether or not multiple selections are allowed.

The `List` class provides several access methods that are used to add, delete, and replace list items, count the number of items in the list, determine which items are selected, and select items within the list.

The `TextComponent` Class

The `TextComponent` class is the superclass of all text-based classes. It provides a common set of methods used by its `TextField` and `TextArea` subclasses. It does not provide any constructors and cannot be instantiated. It provides methods for getting and setting the text that is displayed in a text object, setting the text object to an editable or read-only state, or selecting text that is contained within the object.

TextField

The `TextField` class implements a one-line text entry field. It provides four constructors that are used to specify the width of the text field in character columns and the default text to be displayed within the field. It provides several methods for accessing the field's size and for specifying whether the characters typed by the user should be displayed. The `setEchoCharacter()` method is used to specify a character that is to be displayed in lieu of text typed by the user. This method is used to implement password-like fields.

TextArea

The `TextArea` class implements scrollable text entry objects that span multiple lines and columns. It provides four constructors that allow the number of rows and columns and the default text display to be specified. It provides several methods that return the dimensions of the text area and insert, append, and replace the text that is contained in the text area. It also provides the capability to set the text to read-only or edit mode.

The Canvas Class

The `Canvas` class implements a GUI object that supports drawing. Drawing is not implemented on the canvas itself, but on the `Graphics` object provided by the canvas. The `Canvas` class is usually subclassed to implement a custom graphics object. It provides a single, parameterless constructor and one useful method—the `paint()` method, which specifies how its `Graphics` object is to be updated.

Graphics

The `Graphics` class supports the drawing of graphical objects and text within a window. It is used with all graphical applications. The `Graphics` class is an abstract class that is created through methods of other classes. A `Graphics` object is typically provided as an argument to the `paint()` method of a `Canvas` object.

The `Graphics` class provides numerous methods for drawing lines, ovals, rectangles, polygons, text, images, and other objects that can be displayed within a window. It also provides methods for setting the foreground and background colors and the current text font. You should browse through the API description of this class to get a feel for all the methods it provides.

The Scrollbar Class

The `Scrollbar` class is used to implement vertical and horizontal scrollbars. It provides three constructors that allow the orientation of the scrollbar to be specified, as well as parameters that control the scrollbar's operation. It provides several methods that allow the scrollbar's parameters and current value to be read and set. See Chapter 24, "Scrollbars," for more information.

Constructing Menus

Java provides several classes that allow menu bars to be constructed and attached to a `Frame` window. These classes are directly descended from the `Object` class and are not subclasses of the component class.

The `MenuComponent` class is the superclass of the menu-related classes and provides a common set of methods that are used by its subclasses. The `MenuComponent` class provides a default parameterless constructor, although objects of this class should not be directly created. The `getFont()` and `setFont()` methods are used to specify the font to be used with a `MenuComponent` object. The `getParent()` method is used to retrieve an object that implements the `MenuContainer` interface and contains a specified `MenuComponent` object.

The `MenuBar` Class

The `MenuBar` class implements a menu bar that is attached to a `Frame` window. It provides a default parameterless constructor and several access methods for adding and removing `Menu` objects from the menu bar. It also provides methods that are used to return the current number of menus and to get and set a special help menu.

The `MenuItem` Class

The `MenuItem` class is used to implement items that may be selected from a pull-down menu. It is extended by the `Menu` and `CheckboxMenuItem` classes. The `MenuItem` class implements items that can be selected from a pull-down menu. Because it is subclassed by the `Menu` and `CheckboxMenuItem` classes, it provides the capability for objects of these classes to be selected from a pull-down menu. This allows multiple levels of menus to be implemented.

The `MenuItem` class provides a single constructor that takes a `String` object as a parameter. The `String` object is used as the label of the menu item. The `MenuItem` class provides methods for enabling and disabling a menu item and for getting and setting its label.

The `Menu` Class

The `Menu` class implements a single pull-down menu that is attached to a menu bar or other menu. It provides two constructors that allow the menu's label to be specified and determine whether it is to be implemented as a tear-off menu. It also provides methods that are used to add or remove menu items, add menu separators, count the number of items in the menu, and determine what menu item is currently selected.

The CheckboxMenuItem Class

The CheckboxMenuItem class is used to implement menu items that may be checked on or off. It provides a single constructor that contains the label to be used with the checkbox menu item. The setState() and getState() methods are used to determine the checked state of the menu item.

The MenuContainer Class

The MenuContainer interface provides a set of methods that are implemented by classes that contain menus. These methods are getFont(), postEvent(), and remove(). The getFont() method returns the current font associated with a menu object. The postEvent() method is used to generate a menu-related event. The remove() method is used to remove a MenuComponent object.

Organizing Windows

The method by which the components of a Container object are organized is determined by an object that implements the LayoutManager interface. The layout of a Container is specified using the setLayout() method of the Container class. It passes an object that implements the LayoutManager interface as a parameter.

The LayoutManager Class

The LayoutManager interface provides a set of methods that are implemented by classes that control the layout of a container. These methods include those that add or remove components from a layout, specify the size of the container, and lay out the components of the container.

The BorderLayout Class

The BorderLayout class is used to lay out the GUI components contained in a Container object. It lays out components along the north, south, east, and west borders of the container and in the center of the container. The center component gets any space left over from the north, south, east, and west border components. It is the default layout for the Window, Frame, and Dialog classes. It provides the capability to specify the horizontal and vertical gap between the laid out components and the container.

The `CardLayout` Class

The `CardLayout` class is used to lay out the components of a `Container` object in the form of a deck of cards where only one card is visible at a time. The class provides methods that are used to specify the first, last, next, and previous components in the container.

The `FlowLayout` Class

The `FlowLayout` class is used to lay out the components of a `Container` object in a left-to-right, top-to-bottom fashion. It is the default layout used with the `Panel` class. It allows the alignment of the components it lays out to be specified by the `LEFT`, `CENTER`, and `RIGHT` constants.

The `GridLayout` Class

The `GridLayout` class is used to lay out the components of a `Container` object in a grid where all components are the same size. The `GridLayout` constructor is used to specify the number of rows and columns of the grid.

The `GridBagLayout` Class

The `GridBagLayout` class lays out the components of a `Container` object in a grid-like fashion, where some components may occupy more than one row or column. The `GridBagConstraints` class is used to identify the positioning parameters of a component that is contained within an object that is laid out using `GridBagLayout`. The `Insets` class is used to specify the margins associated with an object that is laid out using a `GridBagLayout` object. Refer to the API description of the `GridBagLayout` class for more information on how to use this layout.

Handling Events

The user communicates with window programs by performing actions such as clicking a mouse button or pressing a key on the keyboard. These actions result in the generation of `Event` objects. The process of responding to the occurrence of an event is known as *event handling*. Window programs are said to be *event driven* because they operate by performing actions in response to events.

The `Event` class encapsulates all Windows event processing and is, therefore, a very important class. Because the Windows user interface is event driven, all nontrivial window programs must handle user events.

The `Event` class defines the entire list of events handled by window programs using *class constants*. These constants are used to identify the events that are passed to event-handling methods. You should review the Java API description of the `Event` class to familiarize yourself with these constants.

The Event class provides four constructors for constructing events, but you probably won't need to use these constructors because events are internally generated by the Java runtime system in response to user interface actions. The Event class also provides methods for determining whether the Control, Shift, or Meta (Alt) keys were pressed during the generation of an event.

Working with Images

The Image class is an abstract class that provides a content-independent mechanism for implementing graphical images. Images are created by invoking methods of other classes that create images. The createImage() methods of the Component and Applet classes and the getImage() methods of the Toolkit and Applet classes allow images to be created. Image objects are usually displayed on a Graphics object using the drawImage() method of the Graphics class. The Image class provides several methods for accessing the properties of an image.

The Color Class

The Color class provides a system-independent color implementation and defines several color constants. It provides three constructors that allow a color to be constructed from its red, green, and blue (RGB) color components. Its access methods provide access to the RGB values of a color; brighten and darken a color; and convert colors to a hue, saturation, and brightness (HSB) representation.

The java.awt.image Package

The java.awt.image package defines interfaces and classes that support image generation, storage, and processing. These classes are based on the concept of an image producer and an image consumer. The *image producer* provides the data associated with an image and the *image consumer* uses the data produced by the image producer to process or display an image.

The ImageProducer interface provides a set of methods for classes that produce images. These methods are used to reconstruct or modify an image being produced. The ImageConsumer interface provides a set of constants and methods for accessing image data provided by classes that implement the ImageConsumer interface. The ImageObserver interface provides a set of constants and methods by which objects are notified about an image that is being constructed.

ColorModel

The ColorModel class is an abstract class that provides a general framework for representing colors and maps this framework to the RGB color model. It is extended by the DirectColorModel and IndexColorModel classes.

The DirectColorModel class is used to directly access the color values of a pixel. It specifies a method for directly translating pixel values to their RGB values. The IndexColorModel class translates fixed colormap pixel values to their RGB component colors using pixel values as an index into a color map.

FilteredImageSource

The `FilteredImageSource` class provides the capability to filter an image using an object of class `ImageFilter`. `FilterImageSource` implements the `ImageProducer` interface. Its objects are used as intermediate image producers by filtering the image data produced by an image's original image producer using an object of the `ImageFilter` class. The `FilterImageSource` constructor takes the original image's `ImageProducer` and an `ImageFilter` object as its parameters. Its access methods provide the capability to add and remove image consumers and control the generation of image data.

ImageFilter

The `ImageFilter` class provides a common set of methods for implementing image filters. It does not implement any filtering of its own and must be subclassed to provide a specific filtering mechanism. It is extended by the `CropImageFilter` and `RGBImageFilter` classes.

CropImageFilter

The `CropImageFilter` class is an image filter that is used to crop images to a specific area. Its constructor takes the upper-left coordinate of the location of the cropping rectangle and the rectangle's height and width. Its access methods provide the capability to work with subsets of the pixels of the cropped area.

RGBImageFilter

The `RGBImageFilter` class is an abstract class that is used to create image filters that modify the pixels of the default RGB color model. In order to create a color filter based on this class, you subclass it and override the `filterRGB()` method. This method provides the x- and y-coordinates and RGB value of the pixel at the specified coordinates and returns the filtered color value. Setting the `canFilterIndexColorModel` flag to `true` enables filtering to be performed on the color model instead of the image. This greatly speeds up the filtering process and should be used when the filter is position independent.

PixelGrabber

The `PixelGrabber` class is used to capture the pixels of an image and store them in an array. It provides two constructors that specify the area to be captured and the array where the captured pixels are to be stored. The access methods provided by `PixelGrabber` are used to control the image capture process.

`MemoryImageSource`

The `MemoryImageSource` class is used to create an image using an array of pixel values. It implements the `ImageProducer` interface and provides six constructors for the creation of `ImageProducer` objects based on in-memory descriptions of the image's pixel values.

The `MediaTracker` Class

The `MediaTracker` class provides a set of methods for managing images used to implement multimedia objects. It provides the capability to load a specified set of images, wait on the loading of the images in the set, and maintain the load status of the images. It defines the `COMPLETE`, `ABORTED`, `LOADING`, and `ERRORED` constants to indicate the load status of an image. It provides a single constructor that identifies the `Component` object for which the images are to be loaded. Its access methods are used to manage the image-loading process.

Geometrical Objects

Java provides several classes for working with standard geometrical objects: `Point`, `Rectangle`, `Polygon`, and `Dimension`. These classes are described in the following subsections.

The `Point` Class

The `Point` class is used to represent general two-dimensional x,y-coordinates. It contains a single constructor that takes the x- and y-coordinates as its parameters. The x and y field variables are declared as `public`, providing access to individual coordinates. Methods to perform movement and translation of points are provided.

The `Rectangle` Class

The `Rectangle` class represents a rectangle using the x,y-coordinates of its upper-left corner, its width, and its height. Five constructors are provided to allow rectangles to be created using a variety of approaches. Methods are provided that allow a rectangle's parameters to be accessed, to support movement and translation operations, and to perform other geometrical operations.

The `Polygon` Class

The `Polygon` class represents a polygon as a list of x,y-coordinates that identify the polygon's vertices. It provides a default parameterless constructor and a constructor that identifies the polygon's vertices. The `Polygon` class provides several access methods that are used to access the polygon's vertices, add vertices, test whether a point is contained in a polygon, and get the minimum bounding box containing a polygon.

The `Dimension` Class

The `Dimension` class is used to represent the width and height of a two-dimensional object. It provides three constructors: a default parameterless constructor, a constructor that creates a `Dimension` object using another `Dimension` object, and a constructor that takes width and height parameters. The access methods provided by the `Dimension` class allow the height and width of a dimension to be accessed.

Using Fonts

The `Font` class implements a system-independent set of fonts that control text display. Java font names are mapped to system-supported fonts. The Courier, Dialog, DialogInput, Helvetica, TimesRoman, and ZapfDingbats fonts are the system-independent font names provided by Java. A default font is also supported that may consist of one of the above fonts or may be unique to a given operating-system platform.

Fonts can be specified in terms of font name, style, and point size. The supported styles are defined by the `PLAIN`, `BOLD`, and `ITALIC` constants of the `Font` class. Font styles can be combined by adding these constants. Font sizes can be any integer size supported by the system. The `Font` class provides a single constructor that takes the font name, style constants, and point size as its parameters.

The `Font` class provides several methods for querying the parameters of a font. The `getName()` method returns the Java name for the font. The `getFamily()` method returns the system-dependent font name. The `getStyle()` and `getSize()` methods return the font's style and size parameters. The `isBold()`, `isItalic()`, and `isPlain()` methods provides the capability to test the style parameter.

The `FontMetrics` Class

The `FontMetrics` class is used to access the specific display parameters of a `Font` object. A `FontMetrics` object is usually constructed using the `getFontMetrics()` method of the `Component` class. It provides several methods for determining a font's display parameters, as described in Chapter 22, "Text and Fonts."

The `getHeight()`, `getLeading()`, `getAscent()`, and `getDescent()` methods are used to determine the vertical size properties of a font. The `stringWidth()`, `getWidths()`, `charWidth()`, `charsWidth()`, and `bytesWidth()` methods are used to determine a font's horizontal size properties.

Using the Toolkit

The `Toolkit` class provides the linkage between the platform-independent classes of the AWT and their platform-dependent implementation. It provides the capability to access the platform-dependent peer classes of the subclasses of the `Component` class. These classes can be used to obtain direct access to a component's local implementation. The use of peer classes is discouraged because it limits the portability of any software that utilizes these methods. The `java.awt.peer` package contains the interfaces that are implemented by the platform-dependent AWT software.

The `Toolkit` class also provides several methods that provide access to implementation-dependent characteristics that can be safely used in Java programs. The `getFontList()` method provides a list of the fonts that are supported by the windowing environment. The `getImage()` method allows an image to be retrieved from an URL or the local file system. The `getScreenSize()` and `getScreenResolution()` methods return useful characteristics of the screen display. You should read the API description of this class to familiarize yourself with the methods that it provides.

Summary

This chapter introduces you to the classes of the `java.awt` package, which provide the foundation for Java window programming. You have learned how the `java.awt` package is organized and have covered the classes that it contains. You have also covered the `java.awt.image` and `java.awt.peer` packages. Part IV provides a detailed tutorial of Java window programming with numerous programming examples that will further help you understand the concepts.

16

Web Programming with the java.applet Package

This chapter introduces the classes of the `java.applet` package and explains how applets are integrated within Web documents. It includes a short introduction to HTML. It describes how applets use window components and handle events and identifies the major phases in an applet's life cycle. Applet audio and animation capabilities are also covered. When you finish this chapter, you will have a good understanding of how applets work.

Applets and the World Wide Web

Applets are Java programs that are integrated in Web pages. When a Web page containing an applet is displayed by a Web browser, the applet is loaded and executed. The applet's output is displayed within a subset of the browser's display area. Figure 16.1 illustrates this concept.

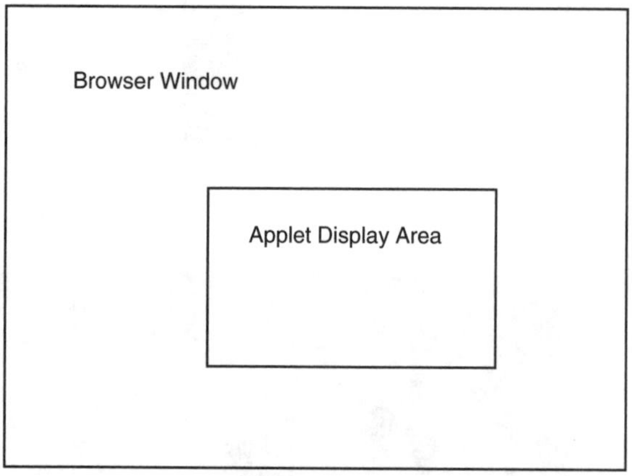

FIGURE 16.1.
How an applet is displayed by a Web browser.

The `Applet` class is a subclass of the `Panel` class, and applets are implemented as a panel within a Web document. You'll learn more about the `Panel` class when you study window programming in Part IV, "Window Programming." Because the `Applet` class is a subclass of the `Panel` class, it inherits all the methods of the `Panel` class and is capable of using most window GUI components. In addition, applet events are handled in the same manner as in standalone Java window programs.

The `Applet` Class

The `java.applet` package is the smallest package in the Java API. It consists of a single class—the `Applet` class—and three interfaces: `AppletContext`, `AppletStub`, and `AudioClip`.

The `Applet` class contains a single default parameterless constructor, which is generally not used. Applets are constructed by the runtime environment when they are loaded and do not have to be explicitly constructed.

The `Applet` class contains 21 access methods that are used to display images, play audio files, respond to events, and obtain information about an applet's execution environment, referred to as the applet's *context.*

The `getImage()` and `getAudioClip()` methods are used to retrieve an `Image` or `AudioClip` object that is identified by an URL. The play methods are used to play an `AudioClip` object.

The `init()`, `start()`, `stop()`, and `destroy()` methods are used to implement each of the four life cycle stages of an applet. The `init()` method is invoked by the runtime environment when an applet is initially loaded. It is invoked to perform any required initialization processing. The `start()` method is invoked by the runtime system when an applet is initially started or restarted as a result of a user switching between Web pages. The `stop()` method is invoked by the runtime system when the user switches from the Web page containing the applet to another Web page or another program. The `destroy()` method is invoked when an applet's execution is terminated, usually as the result of the user exiting the browser. The `isActive()` method is used to determine whether an applet is currently active.

The `getAppletContext()` method is used to obtain the `AppletContext` object associated with an applet. The `AppletContext` interface defines methods by which an applet can access its execution environment. The `getAppletInfo()` method returns a `String` object that provides information about an applet. This information can include version, copyright, and authorship data as well as applet-specific data. The `getAppletInfo()` method is overridden by `Applet` subclasses to provide this information. The `getCodeBase()` method returns the base URL specifying the applet's location. The `getDocumentBase()` method returns the URL of the document in which the applet is contained. The `getParameter()` method is used to obtain parameter data that is passed to an applet in an HTML file. The `getParameterInfo()` method returns an array that describes all the parameters used by an object. It is overriden by `Applet` subclasses in the same manner as the `getAppletInfo()` method.

The `resize()` methods are used to resize an applet. The `setStub()` method is used to set the `AppletStub` associated with the applet. It should not be used unless you are constructing your own custom applet viewer. The `showStatus()` method is used to display a status message using the applet's context.

The `AppletContext` interface defines methods that allow an applet to access the context in which it is being run. This is typically a Web browser, such as Netscape, but could also be the applet viewer. The `AppletContext` interface of an applet is accessed using the `getAppletContext()` method of the `Applet` class. `AppletContext` provides seven methods that allow an applet to obtain information about and manipulate its environment. The `getApplets()` method returns an `Enumeration` object that contains all applets which are accessible in the applet's context. The `getApplet()` method returns an `Applet` object whose name matches a `String` parameter. The `getAudioClip()` method returns an `AudioClip` object that is referenced using an URL. The `getImage()` object returns an `Image` object that is identified by an URL. The two `showDocument()`

methods are used to instruct a Web browser to display the Web document located at a particular URL. The `showStatus()` method is used to display a status message via the Web browser executing the applet.

The `AppletStub` interface is used to implement an applet viewer. It is not generally used by applets. It provides six methods that are used to retrieve applet parameters that can be used to support applet viewing.

The `AudioClip` interface defines three methods: `play()`, `stop()`, and `loop()`. The `play()` method is used to play an audio clip. The `stop()` method is used to terminate the playing of an audio clip. The `loop()` method is used to start and play an audio clip in a continuous loop.

Applets and HTML

Web documents are written in Hypertext Markup Language (HTML). HTML uses *tags* to describe the structure of Web documents. Tags are used to identify headings, paragraphs, and lists, as well as other elements of Web pages such as links, images, forms, and applets. In order to use applets in your Web documents, you need to learn about a few basic HTML tags. While a complete introduction to HTML is beyond the scope of this book, this section provides a quick summary of the basic HTML tags that you will need to work the examples in this book.

NOTE

For more information on HTML, point your Web browser at the URL `http://www.jaworski.com/htmlbook/`. Here you'll find links to introductory tutorials on HTML as well as links to more advanced HTML topics.

Using HTML Tags

HTML tags begin with a < and end with a >. The name of the tag is placed between the opening < and closing >. The tag name may be written using any combination of upper- or lowercase characters. I use the convention of writing tags in uppercase to set them apart from the text to which they apply. For example, the title tag is written `<TITLE>`, the head tag is written `<HEAD>`, and the body tag is written `<BODY>`.

HTML supports two types of tags—separating tags and surrounding tags. Separating tags are placed between the text elements to which they apply. For example, the break tag, written `<BR>`, is used to insert a line break within a line of text. It is placed at the point in the line where the break is desired, as shown in the following HTML:

```
This line ends at the break tag.<BR>This text is displayed on the next line.
```

Surrounding tags consist of pairs of tags that surround the text to which they apply. The first tag in the pair is referred to as the *opening tag* and the second tag is referred to as the *closing tag.* The closing tag contains a / between the opening < and the tag's name. Examples of surrounding tags are <HTML> and </HTML>, <HEAD> and </HEAD>, and <BODY> and </BODY>. You'll learn about these tags in subsequent sections.

Some HTML tags are allowed to specify *attributes.* Attributes are used to identify properties of the tag and are included in the tag between the tag name and the closing >. When attributes are used with surrounding tags, they are included in the opening tag, but not in the closing tag. For example, the applet tag uses attributes to identify the name of the class to be loaded, the dimensions of the applet display region within the browser window, and other properties of the applet. The following HTML is an example of an applet tag that uses attributes:

```
<APPLET CODE="TestApplet" WIDTH=300 HEIGHT=300>
[alternate text to be displayed]
</APPLET>
```

The opening applet tag has three attributes: `CODE`, `WIDTH`, and `HEIGHT`. The `CODE` attribute has the value of `"TestApplet"` and identifies the name of the applet's bytecode file. The `WIDTH` and `HEIGHT` attributes both have the value `300` and specify a 300×300 pixel applet display region within the browser window. The text `[alternate text to be displayed]` appearing between the opening and closing applet tags identifies text that a browser should display if it does not support Java applets.

The HTML, Head, and Body Tags

HTML documents are written in ASCII text. The <HTML> and </HTML> tags mark the beginning and end of an HTML document. HTML documents consist of a single head and a single body. The head is used to identify information about an HTML document, such as its title, while the body contains the information displayed by the HTML document. The head and body are identified using the <HEAD> and </HEAD> and <BODY> and </BODY> tags. The following HTML illustrates the use of these tags:

```
<HTML>
<HEAD>
The document title appears here.
</HEAD>
<BODY>
The information displayed by the HTML document appears here.
</BODY>
</HTML>
```

The Title Tag

The title of an HTML document is typically displayed at the top of the browser window, as shown in Figure 16.2. The title is placed in the head of a Web document and is surrounded by the <TITLE> and </TITLE> tags.

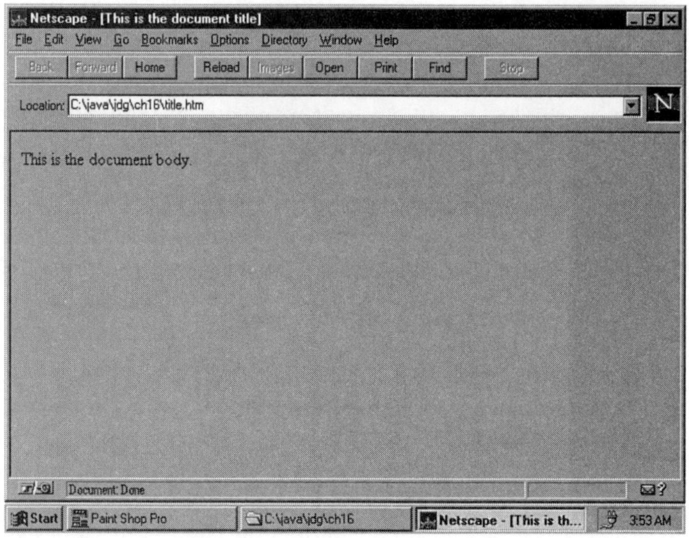

FIGURE 16.2.
The title of a Web document.

The HTML used to create the Web page is shown in Listing 16.1.

Listing 16.1. Using the title tag.

```
<HTML>
<HEAD>
<TITLE>This is the document title</TITLE>
</HEAD>
<BODY>
This is the document body.
</BODY>
</HTML>
```

The Heading and Paragraph Tags

The heading and paragraph tags are the most common tags found within the body of a Web document. The heading tags are used to specify document headings. These headings are used to organize Web documents into sections and subsections in the same manner in which the chapters of this book are organized into sections and subsections. HTML supports six heading levels. First-level headings are identified by the `<H1>` and `</H1>` tags, second-level headings are identified by the `<H2>` and `</H2>` tags, and so on. Sixth-level headings are identified by the `<H6>` and `</H6>` tags. The HTML in Listing 16.2 shows how all six heading levels are displayed.

Listing 16.2 Using heading tags.

```
<HTML>
<HEAD>
```

```
<TITLE>HTML Headings</TITLE>
</HEAD>
<BODY>
<H1>Heading Level 1</H1>
<H2>Heading Level 2</H2>
<H3>Heading Level 3</H3>
<H4>Heading Level 4</H4>
<H5>Heading Level 5</H5>
<H6>Heading Level 6</H6>
</BODY>
</HTML>
```

Figure 16.3 shows how this HTML file is displayed by my Web browser.

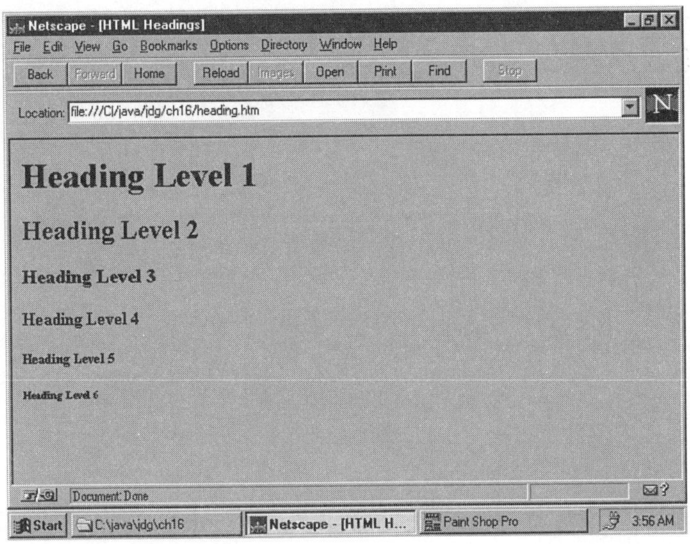

FIGURE 16.3.
HTML heading levels.

Paragraph tags are used to mark paragraphs within HTML documents. In HTML, spaces, tabs, carriage returns, and line feeds are referred to as *whitespace* characters. One or more whitespace characters are normally displayed as a single space by Web browsers. In order to mark the beginning and end of a paragraph, the HTML paragraph tags, `<P>` and `</P>`, must be used. For example, the HTML shown in Listing 16.3 illustrates the use of paragraph tags. Figure 16.4 shows how this HTML is displayed by a Web browser.

Listing 16.3. Using paragraph tags.

```
<HTML>
<HEAD>
<TITLE>HTML Paragraphs</TITLE>
</HEAD>
```

continues

Listing 16.3. continued

```
<BODY>
<H1>How paragraphs are marked in HTML</H1>
<P>This is paragraph 1.</P><P>This is paragraph 2.</P>
<P>This is paragraph 3.
This text also belongs to paragraph 3.
Notice that carriage returns and      multiple spaces     do
not affect the way paragraphs are formatted.</P>
</BODY>
</HTML>
```

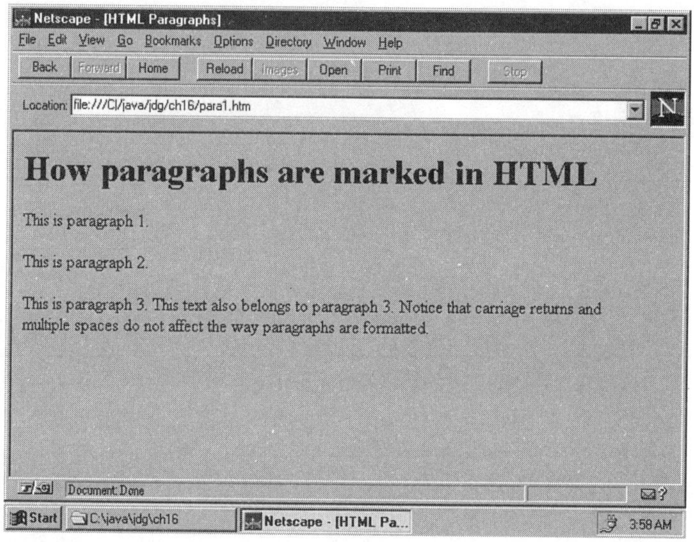

FIGURE 16.4.
HTML paragraphs.

The paragraph tag can also be written as a single separating tag, `<P>`, although this is considered bad practice. The previous example could also have been written as shown in Listing 16.4 using separating paragraph tags rather than surrounding paragraph tags. Figure 16.5 shows how it is displayed by my Web browser.

Listing 16.4. Using paragraph tags as separating tags.

```
<HTML>
<HEAD>
<TITLE>HTML Paragraphs using separating tags</TITLE>
</HEAD>
<BODY>
<H1>How paragraphs are marked in HTML</H1>
This is paragraph 1.<P>This is paragraph 2.
<P>This is paragraph 3.
This text also belongs to paragraph 3.
Notice that carriage returns and      multiple spaces     do
not affect the way paragraphs are formatted.
</BODY>
</HTML>
```

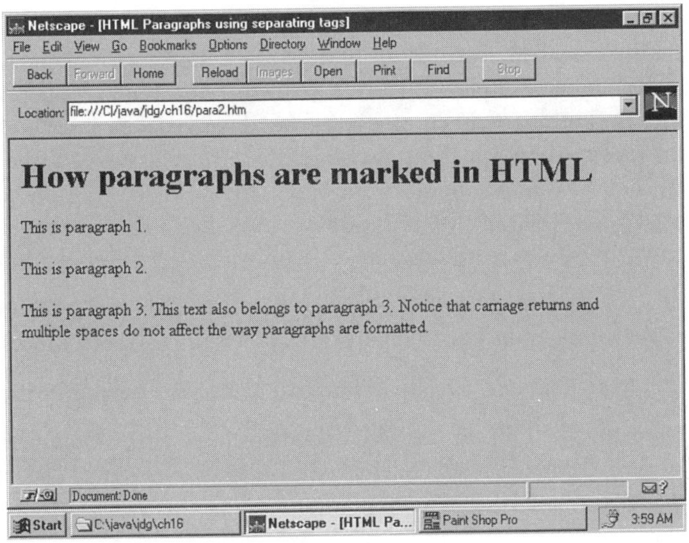

FIGURE 16.5
Marking HTML paragraphs with separating tags.

The Applet and Parameter Tags

While there are a number of different HTML tags that you can learn, the applet and parameter tags are the primary tags of interest for Web programmers.

The applet tag is a surrounding tag. It may surround zero or more parameter tags. It may also surround *alternative text.* Alternative text is text that appears between the `<APPLET>` and `</APPLET>` tags that is not included in a parameter tag. It is displayed by browsers that are not Java enabled as an alternative to the applet's display.

The parameter tag is used to pass named parameters to a Java applet. It is a separating tag that has two attributes: `NAME` and `VALUE`. The `NAME` attribute identifies the name of a parameter and the `VALUE` attribute identifies its value. The following are examples of the use of parameter tags:

```
<PARAM NAME="speed" VALUE="slow">
<PARAM NAME="duration" VALUE="long">
<PARAM NAME="delay" VALUE="short">
```

An applet uses the `getParameter()` method of the `Applet` class to retrieve the value of a parameter. The parameter tag may only appear between the `<APPLET>` and `</APPLET>` tags.

The applet tag supports nine attributes: `ALIGN`, `ALT`, `CODE`, `CODEBASE`, `HEIGHT`, `HSPACE`, `NAME`, `VSPACE`, and `WIDTH`.

The `ALIGN` attribute specifies the alignment of an applet's display region with respect to the rest of the line being displayed by a browser. This line may consist of text, images, or other HTML elements. Values for this attribute are `TOP`, `TEXTTOP`, `BOTTOM`, `ABSBOTTOM`, `BASELINE`, `MIDDLE`, `ABSMIDDLE`, `LEFT`, and `RIGHT`. The `TOP` attribute value causes the top of an applet to be aligned with the top of the line being displayed by a browser. The `TEXTTOP` attribute causes the top of an applet to be aligned with the top of the text being displayed in the current line. The BASELINE and BOTTOM attributes cause the bottom of the applet to be aligned with the baseline of the text in the line being displayed. The ABSBOTTOM attribute causes the bottom of an applet to be aligned with the bottom of the current line being displayed. The MIDDLE attribute causes the middle of the applet to be aligned with the middle of the text displayed in the current line. The ABSMIDDLE attribute causes the middle of the applet to be aligned with the middle of the line being displayed. The LEFT and RIGHT attributes causes the applet to be aligned at the left and right margins of the browser window.

The ALT attribute identifies text that should be displayed by a browser if it understands the applet tags, but does not support Java applets or has applet processing disabled.

The CODE attribute is a relative URL that identifies the name of the bytecode file of the applet.

Normally, the URL of the Web document displaying the applet is used as the base URL for locating the bytecode file referenced by the CODE attribute. The CODEBASE attribute is used to change the base URL to another location.

The HEIGHT attribute identifies the height of the display area required by the applet.

The HSPACE attribute specifies the number of pixels to be used as the left and right margins surrounding an applet.

The NAME attribute is used to assign a name to an applet. This name is used to support inter-applet communication.

The VSPACE attribute specifies the number of pixels to be used as the top and bottom margins surrounding an applet.

The WIDTH attribute identifies the width of the display area required by the applet.

Of the nine applet attributes, only the CODE, HEIGHT, and WIDTH attributes are required.

The HTML file sample.htm, which is shown in Listing 16.5, shows how an applet may be specified in a Web document.

Listing 16.5. The sample.htm file.

```
<HTML>
<HEAD>
<TITLE>Using the Applet Tag</TITLE>
</HEAD>
<BODY>
<H1>An Applet that Displays Text at a Designated Location</H1>
<APPLET CODE="SampleApplet.class" HEIGHT=300 WIDTH=300>
<PARAM NAME="text" VALUE="Applets are fun!">
<PARAM NAME="x" VALUE="50">
<PARAM NAME="y" VALUE="50">
Text displayed by browsers that are not Java-enabled.
```

```
</APPLET>
</BODY>
</HTML>
```

The applet specified in the applet tag displays the text `Applets are fun!` at the coordinate 50,50 within the 300×300 pixel applet display area, as shown in Figure 16.6.

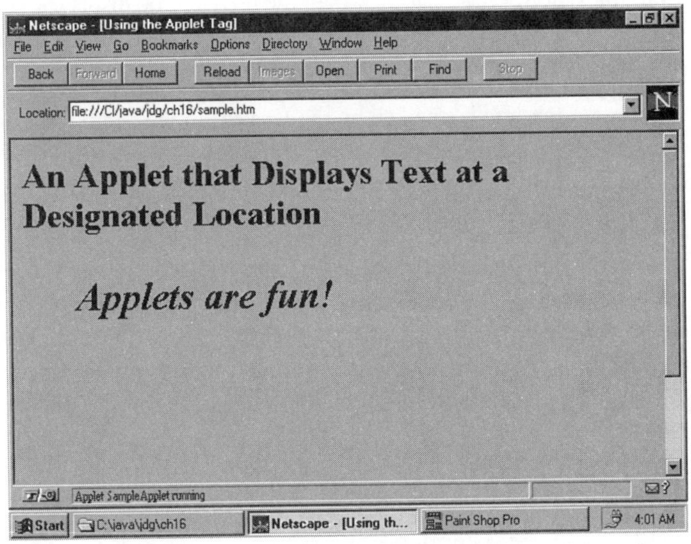

FIGURE 16.6.
The display of `SampleApplet`.

The source code of the `SampleApplet` applet is provided in Listing 16.6.

Listing 16.6. The `SampleApplet.java` source code file.

```
import java.applet.*;
import java.awt.*;

public class SampleApplet extends Applet {
 String text = "error";
 int x = 0;
 int y = 20;
 public void init() {
  text = getParameter("text");
  try {
   x = Integer.parseInt(getParameter("x"));
   y = Integer.parseInt(getParameter("y"));
  }catch(NumberFormatException ex){
  }
 }
 public void paint(Graphics g) {
  g.setFont(new Font("TimesRoman",Font.BOLD+Font.ITALIC,36));
  g.drawString(text,x,y);
 }
}
```

You can compile `SampleApp.java` using the command `javac SampleApplet.java`. Create the `sample.htm` file shown in Listing 16.5 and store it in your `\java\jdg\ch16` directory. Then open the `sample.htm` file using your Web browser. This should result in a display similar to that shown in Figure 16.6.

The `SampleApplet` class extends the `Applet` class. It declares three field variables: `text`, `x`, and `y`. The `text` variable is used to hold the text that is displayed in the `Applet` display area. The `x` and `y` variables specify the location where the text is to be displayed. The default value of the `text` variable is set to `"error"`. The default value of the `x` variable is set to `0`. The default value of the `y` variable is set to `20`.

The `init()` method is invoked by the Java runtime system to perform any required initialization. The `init()` method uses the `getParameter()` method of the `Applet` class to get the value of the `text`, `x`, and `y` parameters. The `parseInt()` method of the `Integer` class is used to convert the `String` value returned by the `getParameter()` method to an `int` value.

The `paint()` method is invoked by the Java runtime system to update the Java display area. It is automatically passed a `Graphics` object as a parameter. This object is used to draw on the applet's display area. The `paint()` method uses the `setFont()` method of the `Graphics` class to set the current font to a 36-point bold italic TimesRoman font. The `drawString()` method of the `Graphics` class is used to display the value of the `text` variable at the `x,y` coordinate.

Other HTML Tags

The HTML tags covered in the preceding sections are the minimum needed to get you started using applets with HTML documents. There are many more HTML tags that you can use with your Web pages. The URL `http://www.jaworski.com/jdg` contains links to Web documents that describe these other HTML tags.

The Life Cycle of an Applet

An applet has a well-defined life cycle, as shown in Figure 16.7. Applets do not need to be explicitly constructed. They are automatically constructed by the runtime environment associated with their applet context—a Web browser or the applet viewer. The `init()` method provides the capability to load applet parameters and perform any necessary initialization processing. The `start()` method serves as the execution entry point for an applet when it is initially executed and restarted as the result of a user returning to the Web page that contains the applet. The `stop()` method provides the capability to `stop()` an applet's execution when the Web page containing the applet is no longer active. The `destroy()` method is used at the end of an applet's life cycle to perform any termination processing.

FIGURE 16.7.
The stages of an applet's life cycle.

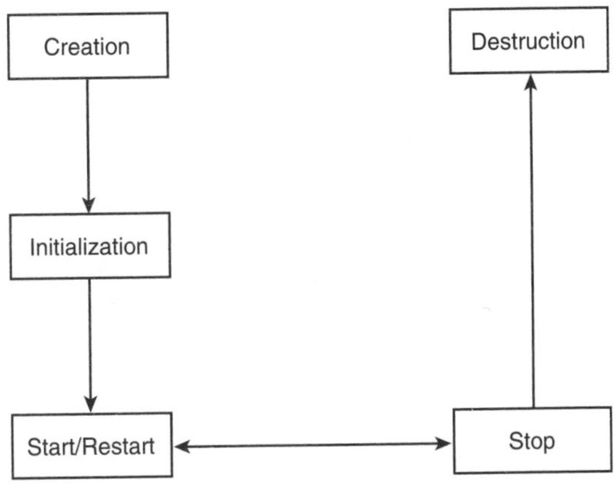

Responding to Events

Because the `Applet` class is a subclass of the `Panel` class and therefore part of the window class hierarchy, applets handle events in the same manner as other window components. All the window event handling approaches that you will learn in Part IV will also apply to `Applet` event handling. The `init()`, `start()`, `stop()`, and `destroy()` methods that you covered in the previous section are used to handle events that are generated by the Java runtime system. These methods are specific to applets and do not apply to other window components.

Using Window Components

Since the `Applet` class is a subclass of the `Panel` class, it can use most of the GUI components that are used by standalone window programs. This includes labels, buttons, checkboxes, radio buttons, lists, text components, canvases, and scrollbars. You will learn to use these components in Part IV. The only major GUI components that cannot be used within an applet are menu components. Menu components are attached to `Frame` objects, which are associated with an application window. It is possible for an applet to create and open a separate application window in the form of a `Frame` object, however such an application window would be labeled as untrusted in accordance with the applet security policy. This prevents the window from masquerading as other programs running on the user's system.

Adding Audio and Animation

The `Applet` class provides the capability to play audio files. These files must be in the Sun audio format and usually end with the `.au` extension. The `play()` method of the `Applet` class can be used to play an audio file that is identified by an URL. A more flexible approach is to load an object that implements the `AudioClip` interface and then invoke the object's `play()`, `loop()`, and `stop()` methods. The `getAudioClip()` method can be used to load an audio file by identifying its URL.

Java also supports the capability to include animation in standalone window programs and applets. Chapter 25, "Using Animation," covers this topic.

Summary

This chapter introduces the classes of the `java.applet` package and explains how applets are integrated within Web documents. It describes how applets use window components and handle events. The major phases in an applet's life cycle are introduced. Applet audio and animation capabilities are also covered. Part VI, "Programming the Web with Applets and Scripts," provides a detailed tutorial on applet programming.

17

Network Programming with the `java.net` Package

In this chapter you'll learn about Java's support of network programming. You'll learn the basics of client/server computing and TCP/IP socket programming. You'll then examine the classes of the `java.net` package and learn how to use them to develop client/server applications. This chapter provides an introduction to the `java.net` package. Part V, "Network Programming," explores the information presented here in greater detail.

The Internet Protocol Suite

The `java.net` package provides a set of classes that support network programming using the communication protocols employed by the Internet. These protocols are known as the *Internet protocol suite* and include the *Internet Protocol* (IP), the *Transport Control Protocol* (TCP), and the *User Datagram Protocol* (UDP) as well as other, less-prominent supporting protocols. Although this section cannot provide a full description of the Internet protocols, it gives you the basic information that you need to get started with Java network programming. In order to take full advantage of this chapter, you need an Internet connection.

What Is the Internet and How Does It Work?

Asking the question What is the Internet? may bring about a heated discussion in some circles. In this book, the *Internet* is defined as the collection of all computers that are able to communicate, using the Internet protocol suite, with the computers and networks registered with the *Internet Network Information Center* (InterNIC). This definition includes all computers to which you can directly (or indirectly through a firewall) send Internet Protocol packets.

Computers on the Internet communicate by exchanging packets of data, known as Internet Protocol, or IP, packets. IP is the network protocol used to send information from one computer to another over the Internet. All computers on the Internet (by our definition in this book) communicate using IP. IP moves information contained in IP packets. The IP packets are routed via special routing algorithms from a source computer that sends the packets to a destination computer that receives them. The routing algorithms figure out the best way to send the packets from source to destination.

In order for IP to send packets from a source computer to a destination computer, it must have some way of identifying these computers. All computers on the Internet are identified using one or more IP addresses. A computer may have more than one IP address if it has more than one interface to computers that are connected to the Internet.

IP addresses are 32-bit numbers. They may be written in decimal, hexadecimal, or other formats, but the most common format is dotted decimal notation. This format breaks the 32-bit address up into four bytes and writes each byte of the address as unsigned decimal integers separated by dots. For example, one of my IP addresses is `0xCCD499C1`. Because `0xCC` = 204, `0xD4` = 212, `0x99` = 153, and `0xC1` = 193, my address in dotted decimal form is `204.212.153.193`.

IP addresses are not easy to remember, even using dotted decimal notation. The Internet has adopted a mechanism, referred to as the *Domain Name System* (DNS), whereby computer names can be associated with IP addresses. These computer names are referred to as *domain names.* The DNS has several rules that determine how domain names are constructed and how they relate to one another. For the purposes of this chapter, it is sufficient to know that domain names are computer names and that they are mapped to IP addresses.

The mapping of domain names to IP addresses is maintained by a system of *domain name servers.* These servers are able to look up the IP address corresponding to a domain name. They also provide the capability to look up the domain name associated with a particular IP address, if one exists.

As I mentioned, IP enables communication between computers on the Internet by routing data from a source computer to a destination computer. However, computer-to-computer communication only solves half of the network communication problem. In order for an application program, such as a mail program, to communicate with another application, such as a mail server, there needs to be a way to send data to specific programs within a computer.

Ports are used to enable communication between programs. A *port* is an address within a computer. Port addresses are 16-bit addresses that are usually associated with a particular application protocol. An application server, such as a Web server or an FTP server, listens on a particular port for service requests, performs whatever service is requested of it, and returns information to the port used by the application program requesting the service.

Popular Internet application protocols are associated with *well-known ports.* The server programs implementing these protocols listen on these ports for service requests. The well-known ports for some common Internet application protocols are

Port	Protocol
21	File Transfer Protocol
23	Telnet Protocol
25	Simple Mail Transfer Protocol
80	Hypertext Transfer Protocol

The well-known ports are used to standardize the location of Internet services.

Connection-Oriented Versus Connectionless Communication

Transport protocols are used to deliver information from one port to another and thereby enable communication between application programs. They use either a connection-oriented or connectionless method of communication. TCP is a connection-oriented protocol and UDP is a connectionless transport protocol.

The TCP connection-oriented protocol establishes a communication link between a source port/IP address and a destination port/IP address. The ports are bound together via this link until the connection is terminated and the link is broken. An example of a connection-oriented protocol is a telephone conversation. A telephone connection is established, communication takes place, and then the connection is terminated.

The reliability of the communication between the source and destination programs is ensured through error-detection and error-correction mechanisms that are implemented within TCP. TCP implements the connection as a stream of bytes from source to destination. This feature allows the use of the stream I/O classes provided by `java.io`.

The UDP connectionless protocol differs from the TCP connection-oriented protocol in that it does not establish a link for the duration of the connection. An example of a connectionless protocol is postal mail. To mail something, you just write down a destination address (and an optional return address) on the envelope of the item you're sending and drop it in a mailbox. When using UDP, an application program writes the destination port and IP address on a datagram and then sends the datagram to its destination. UDP is less reliable than TCP because there are no delivery-assurance or error-detection and -correction mechanisms built into the protocol.

Application protocols such as FTP, SMTP, and HTTP use TCP to provide reliable, stream-based communication between client and server programs. Other protocols, such as the Time Protocol, use UDP because speed of delivery is more important than end-to-end reliability.

Client/Server Computing and the Internet

The Internet provides a variety of services that contribute to its appeal. These services include e-mail, newsgroups, file transfer, remote login, and the Web. Internet services are organized according to a client/server architecture. Client programs, such as Web browsers and file transfer programs, create connections to servers, such as Web and FTP servers. The clients make requests of the server, and the server responds to the requests by providing the service requested by the client.

The Web provides a good example of client/server computing. Web browsers are the clients and Web servers are the servers. Browsers request HTML files from Web servers on your behalf by establishing a connection with a Web server and submitting file requests to the server. The server receives the file requests, retrieves the files, and sends them to the browser over the established connection. The browser receives the files and displays them to your browser window.

Sockets and Client/Server Communication

Clients and servers establish connections and communicate via *sockets.* Connections are communication links that are created over the Internet using TCP. Some client/server applications are also built around the connectionless UDP. These applications also use sockets to communicate.

Sockets are the endpoints of Internet communication. Clients create client sockets and connect them to server sockets. Sockets are associated with a host address and a port address. The host address is the IP address of the host where the client or server program is located. The port address is the communication port used by the client or server program. Server programs use the well-known port number associated with their application protocol.

A client communicates with a server by establishing a connection to the socket of the server. The client and server then exchange data over the connection. Connection-oriented communication is more reliable than connectionless communication because the underlying TCP provides message-acknowledgment, error-detection, and error-recovery services.

When a connectionless protocol is used, the client and server communicate by sending datagrams to each other's socket. The UDP is used for connectionless protocols. It does not support reliable communication like TCP.

Overview of `java.net`

The `java.net` package provides several classes that support socket-based client/server communication.

The `InetAddress` class encapsulates Internet IP addresses and supports conversion between dotted decimal addresses and hostnames.

The `Socket`, `ServerSocket`, and `DatagramSocket` classes implement client and server sockets for connection-oriented and connectionless communication. The `SocketImpl` class and the `SocketImplFactory` interface provide hooks for implementing custom sockets.

The `URL`, `URLConnection`, and `URLEncoder` classes implement high-level browser–server Web connections. The `ContentHandler` and `URLStreamHandler` classes are `abstract` classes that provide the basis for the implementation of Web content and stream handlers. They are supported by the `ContentHandlerFactory` and `URLStreamHandlerFactory` interfaces.

The `InetAddress` Class

The `InetAddress` class encapsulates Internet addresses. It supports both numeric IP addresses and hostnames.

The `InetAddress` class has no `public` variables or constructors. It provides eight access methods that support common operations on Internet addresses. Three of these methods are `static`.

The `getLocalHost()` method is a `static` method that returns an `InetAddress` object representing the Internet address of the local host computer. The `static getByName()` method returns an `InetAddress` object for a specified host. The `static getAllByName()` method returns an array of all Internet addresses associated with a particular host.

The `getAddress()` method gets the numeric IP address of the host identified by the `InetAddress` object, and the `getHostName()` method gets its domain name.

The `equals()`, `hashCode()`, and `toString()` methods override those of the `Object` class.

The `NSLookupApp` program illustrates the use of the `InetAddress` class. It takes a hostname as a parameter and identifies the primary IP address associated with that host. (See Listing 17.1.)

Listing 17.1. The source code of the `NSLookupApp` program.

```
import java.net.InetAddress;
import java.net.UnknownHostException;
import java.lang.System;

public class NSLookupApp {
 public static void main(String args[]) {
  try {
   if(args.length!=1){
    System.out.println("Usage: java NSLookupApp hostName");
    return;
   }
   InetAddress host = InetAddress.getByName(args[0]);
   String hostName = host.getHostName();
   byte ipAddress[] = host.getAddress();
   System.out.println("Host name: "+hostName);
   System.out.print("IP address: ");
   for(int i=0;i<ipAddress.length;++i)
    System.out.print((ipAddress[i]+256)%256+".");
   System.out.println();
  }catch(UnknownHostException ex) {
   System.out.println("Unknown host");
   return;
  }
 }
}
```

Compile `NSLookupApp` and run it as follows:

```
C:\java\jdg\ch17>java NSLookupApp sun.com
Host name: sun.com
IP address: 192.9.9.1.
```

This code example uses `NSLookupApp` to look up the primary IP address associated with the `sun.com` host. Try it with other Internet hostnames to look up their IP addresses.

`NSLookupApp` consists of a single `main()` method. A `try` statement surrounds most of the program's statements. It is used to catch the `UnknownHostException`, which is generated when an invalid hostname is entered by the user or when a hostname cannot be looked up from a DNS server.

`NSLookupApp` first checks the number of arguments supplied in the program invocation to make sure that a hostname argument is provided by the user. It then uses the hostname string of the first user argument with the `static getByName()` method of the `InetAddress` class to create an `InetAddress` object based on the user-supplied hostname. This `InetAddress` object is assigned to the `host` variable. The `getHostName()` method gets the host's name from the host variable and assigns it to the `hostName` variable. The `getAddress()` method returns the four bytes of the host's IP address. The byte array is assigned to the `ipAddress[]` array. The hostname and IP address are then printed to the console window. The bytes of the `ipAddress[]` array are converted to positive 8-bit integers before they are printed.

The Socket Class

The `Socket` class implements client connection-based sockets. These sockets are used to develop applications that utilize services provided by connection-oriented server applications.

The `Socket` class provides four constructors that create sockets and connect them to a destination host and port. The access methods are used to access the I/O streams and connection parameters associated with a connected socket.

The `getInetAddress()` and `getPort()` methods get the IP address of the destination host and the destination host port number to which the socket is connected. The `getLocalPort()` method returns the source host local port number associated with the socket. The `getInputStream()` and `getOutputStream()` methods are used to access the input and output streams associated with a socket. The `close()` method is used to close a socket.

The `setSocketImplFactory()` class method is used to switch from the default Java socket implementation to a custom socket implementation.

The `PortTalkApp` program is used to talk to a particular port on a given host on a line-by-line basis. It provides the option of sending a line to the specified port, receiving a line from the other host, or terminating the connection. Its source code is shown in Listing 17.2.

Listing 17.2. The source code of the `PortTalkApp` program.

```
import java.lang.System;
import java.net.Socket;
import java.net.InetAddress;
import java.net.UnknownHostException;
import java.io.DataInputStream;
import java.io.DataOutputStream;
import java.io.IOException;

public class PortTalkApp {
 public static void main(String args[]){
  PortTalk portTalk = new PortTalk(args);
  portTalk.displayDestinationParameters();
```

continues

Listing 17.2. continued

```
  portTalk.displayLocalParameters();
  portTalk.chat();
  portTalk.shutdown();
 }
}

class PortTalk {
 Socket connection;
 DataOutputStream outStream;
 DataInputStream inStream;
 public PortTalk(String args[]){
  if(args.length!=2) error("Usage: java PortTalkApp host port");
  String destination = args[0];
  int port = 0;
  try {
   port = Integer.valueOf(args[1]).intValue();
  }catch (NumberFormatException ex) error("Invalid port number");
  try{
   connection = new Socket(destination,port);
  }catch (UnknownHostException ex) error("Unknown host");
  catch (IOException ex) error("IO error creating socket");
  try{
   inStream = new DataInputStream(connection.getInputStream());
   outStream = new DataOutputStream(connection.getOutputStream());
  }catch (IOException ex) error("IO error getting streams");
  System.out.println("Connected to "+destination+" at port "+port+".");
 }
 public void displayDestinationParameters(){
  InetAddress destAddress = connection.getInetAddress();
  String name = destAddress.getHostName();
  byte ipAddress[] = destAddress.getAddress();
  int port = connection.getPort();
  displayParameters("Destination ",name,ipAddress,port);
 }
 public void displayLocalParameters(){
  InetAddress localAddress = null;
  try{
   localAddress = InetAddress.getLocalHost();
  }catch (UnknownHostException ex) error("Error getting local host information");
  String name = localAddress.getHostName();
  byte ipAddress[] = localAddress.getAddress();
  int port = connection.getLocalPort();
  displayParameters("Local ",name,ipAddress,port);
 }
 public void displayParameters(String s,String name,byte ipAddress[],int port){
  System.out.println(s+"host is "+name+".");
  System.out.print(s+"IP address is ");
  for(int i=0;i<ipAddress.length;++i)
   System.out.print((ipAddress[i]+256)%256+".");
  System.out.println();
  System.out.println(s+"port number is "+port+".");
 }
 public void chat(){
  DataInputStream keyboardInput = new DataInputStream(System.in);
  boolean finished = false;
  do {
```

```
    try{
     System.out.print("Send, receive, or quit (S/R/Q): ");
     System.out.flush();
     String line = keyboardInput.readLine();
     if(line.length()>0){
      line=line.toUpperCase();
      switch (line.charAt(0)){
      case 'S':
       String sendLine = keyboardInput.readLine();
       outStream.writeBytes(sendLine);
       outStream.write(13);
       outStream.write(10);
       outStream.flush();
       break;
      case 'R':
       int inByte;
       System.out.print("***");
       while ((inByte = inStream.read()) != '\n')
       System.out.write(inByte);
       System.out.println();
       break;
      case 'Q':
       finished=true;
       break;
      default:
       break;
      }
     }
    }catch (IOException ex) error("Error reading from keyboard or socket");
   } while(!finished);
  }
  public void shutdown(){
   try{
    connection.close();
   }catch (IOException ex) error("IO error closing socket");
  }
  public void error(String s){
   System.out.println(s);
   System.exit(1);
  }
 }
```

To see how `PortTalkApp` works, run it using the following command line:

```
C:\java\jdg\ch17>java PortTalkApp jaworski.com 7
Connected to jaworski.com at port 7.
Destination host is jaworski.com.
Destination IP address is 204.212.153.193.
Destination port number is 7.
Local host is athome.jaworski.com.
Local IP address is 204.212.153.194.
Local port number is 1298.
Send, receive, or quit (S/R/Q):
```

PortTalkApp connects to my server at port 7. This is the port number for the echo server application. It is used to test Internet communication between hosts. It identifies my host's name, IP address, and destination port number. In this example, I am connecting from another computer on my local area network. Its name is athome.jaworski.com and has the 204.212.153.194 IP address. When you run the program, your hostname and IP address will be displayed. The local port number that I am connecting from is port 1298.

PortTalkApp asks you whether you want to send a line, receive a line, or quit the program. Whether you elect to send or receive is important. If you decide to receive a line and the host is not sending any data, your program will block while it waits to receive information from a socket-based stream.

Enter an S to send a line and then enter This is a test! on the following line, like this:

```
Send, receive, or quit (S/R/Q): s
This is a test!
Send, receive, or quit (S/R/Q):
```

PortTalkApp will send your line to port 7 on my host and then prompt you for your next command. Enter R to receive a line of text from my server:

```
Send, receive, or quit (S/R/Q): r
***This is a test!
Send, receive, or quit (S/R/Q):
```

PortTalkApp reads a line of text from the socket stream and displays it prefixed with three asterisks. Now enter Q to close the connection and terminate the program. You can also use PortTalkApp to talk to other ports. For example, you can use it to talk to port 25 of hosts that support the Simple Mail Transport Protocol to send e-mail to someone who is served by that host.

PortTalkApp consists of a simple main() function that creates an object of class PortTalk, passing it the user-supplied host and port arguments. It invokes the displayDestinationParameters() and displayLocalParameters() methods of the PortTalk class to provide the initial connection-status information. The chat() method is used to send and receive lines of text over an established connection. The shutdown() method terminates the connection.

The PortTalk class implements the bulk of the processing performed by the program. It declares three field variables. The connection variable keeps track of the socket used with the connection. The inStream and outStream variables maintain the input and output streams derived from the socket.

The PortTalk constructor checks the arguments supplied by the user to make sure that a host and port number were supplied and converts the user-supplied port number to an integer. The error() method is used to display any errors to the console window. A new Socket object is created using the specified destination hostname and port number and is assigned to the connection variable. The getInputStream() and getOutputStream() methods of the Socket class are used to attach input and output streams to the socket identified by the connection variable.

These streams are then filtered as `DataInputStream` and `DataOutputStream` objects and assigned to the `inStream` and `outStream` variables. The constructor ends by displaying a connection status message to the console window.

The `displayDestinationParameters()` method uses the `getInetAdress()` method of the `Socket` class to get the `InetAddress` object associated with the destination host of the connection. It uses the `getHostName()` and `getAddress()` methods of the `InetAddress` class to obtain the name and IP address of the destination host. The `getPort()` method of the `Socket` class is used to get the destination port number. These parameters are displayed using the `displayParameters()` method.

The `displayLocalParameters()` method uses the `getLocalHost()`, `getHostName()`, and `getAddress()` methods of the `InetAddress` class to obtain the `InetAddress` object, name, and IP address of the local host. The `getLocalPort()` method of the `Socket` class is used to get the local port number. These parameters are displayed using the `displayParameters()` method.

The `displayParameters()` method displays the hostname, IP address, and port number of an end of a socket connection. The `s` string parameter is used to differentiate between a local and destination host.

The `chat()` method implements the heart of the `PortTalkApp` program. It displays the `Send, receive, or quit (S/R/Q):` prompt to the user and then reads an input line from the user's keyboard.

If the user enters `S` for send, another line is read from the user's keyboard. This line is then written to the output stream associated with the socket connection. A carriage return and a line-feed character are then written to the output stream to signal an end of line. The carriage return–linefeed combination is the standard end-of-line identifier used with Internet application protocols.

If the user enters `R` for receive, three asterisks (`***`) are written to the console window to indicate input from the destination host. One byte at a time is then read from the input stream associated with the socket and displayed to the console window until a newline (`\n`) character is encountered.

If the user enters `Q` for quit, the `do` loop of the `chat()` method is terminated.

The `shutdown()` method closes the `Socket` object referenced by the connection variable.

The `error()` method prints an error message to the console window and then terminates the program using the `exit()` method of the `System` class.

The `ServerSocket` Class

The `ServerSocket` class implements a TCP server socket. It provides two constructors that specify the port to which the server socket is to listen for incoming connection requests. An optional count parameter may be supplied to specify the amount of time that the socket should listen for an incoming connection.

The accept() method is used to cause the server socket to listen and wait until an incoming connection is established. It returns an object of class Socket once a connection is made. This Socket object is then used to carry out a service for a single client. The getInetAddress() method returns the address of the host to which the socket is connected. The getLocalPort() method returns the port on which the server socket listens for an incoming connection. The toString() method returns the socket's address and port number as a string in preparation for printing.

The close() method closes the server socket.

The static setSocketFactory() method is used to change the default ServerSocket implementation to a custom implementation.

The ReverServerApp program is a simple server that listens on port 1234 for incoming connections from client programs. When ReverServerApp connects to a client, it reads one line of text at a time from the client, reverses the characters in the text line, and sends them back to the client. The source code of ReverServerApp is shown in Listing 17.3.

Listing 17.3. The source code of the ReverServerApp program.

```
import java.lang.System;
import java.net.ServerSocket;
import java.net.Socket;
import java.io.IOException;
import java.io.DataInputStream;
import java.io.DataOutputStream;

public class ReverServerApp {
 public static void main(String args[]){
  try{
   ServerSocket server = new ServerSocket(1234);
   int localPort = server.getLocalPort();
   System.out.println("Reverse Server is listening on port "+localPort+".");
   Socket client = server.accept();
   String destName = client.getInetAddress().getHostName();
   int destPort = client.getPort();
   System.out.println("Accepted connection to "+destName+" on port "+
    destPort+".");
   DataInputStream inStream = new DataInputStream(client.getInputStream());
   DataOutputStream outStream = new DataOutputStream(client.getOutputStream());
   boolean finished = false;
   do {
    String inLine = inStream.readLine();
    System.out.println("Received: "+inLine);
    if(inLine.equalsIgnoreCase("quit")) finished=true;
    String outLine=new ReverseString(inLine.trim()).getString();
    for(int i=0;i<outLine.length();++i)
     outStream.write((byte)outLine.charAt(i));
    outStream.write(13);
```

```
    outStream.write(10);
    outStream.flush();
    System.out.println("Sent: "+outLine);
   } while(!finished);
   inStream.close();
   outStream.close();
   client.close();
   server.close();
  }catch (IOException ex){
   System.out.println("IOException occurred.");
  }
 }
}
class ReverseString {
 String s;
 public ReverseString(String in){
  int len = in.length();
  char outChars[] = new char[len];
  for(int i=0;i<len;++i)
   outChars[len-1-i]=in.charAt(i);
  s = String.valueOf(outChars);
 }
 public String getString(){
  return s;
 }
}
```

To see how `ReverServerApp` works, you need to run it in a separate window and then use `PortTalkApp` to feed it lines of text. First, run `ReverServerApp` using the following command line:

```
C:\java\jdg\ch17>java ReverServerApp
Reverse Server is listening on port 1234.
```

`ReverServerApp` notifies you that it is up and running. Now, in a separate window run `PortTalkApp` as follows, supplying your hostname instead of `athome.jaworski.com`:

```
C:\java\jdg\ch17>java PortTalkApp athome.jaworski.com 1234
Connected to athome.jaworski.com at port 1234.
Destination host is athome.jaworski.com.
Destination IP address is 204.212.153.194.
Destination port number is 1234.
Local host is athome.jaworski.com.
Local IP address is 204.212.153.194.
Local port number is 1302.
Send, receive, or quit (S/R/Q):
```

`PortTalkApp` displays all of the parameters of both endpoints of the connection. If you look in the window where `ReverServerApp` is running, you will see a message similar to the following:

```
Accepted connection to athome.jaworski.com on port 1302.
```

The port number reported by ReverServer is consistent with that reported by PortTalkApp. Now switch back to the PortTalkApp window and enter S to send a line of text, followed by the line of text This is a test!, as shown in the following output:

```
Send, receive, or quit (S/R/Q): s
This is a test!
```

The ReverServerApp window reports the following:

```
Received: This is a test!
Sent: !tset a si sihT
```

Enter an R in the PortTalkApp window, as shown in the following output:

```
Send, receive, or quit (S/R/Q): r
***!tset a si sihT
Send, receive, or quit (S/R/Q):
```

PortTalkApp displays the text that it received from ReverServerApp. Enter the S command followed by a quit text line:

```
Send, receive, or quit (S/R/Q): s
quit
```

The quit line is read by ReverServerApp, causing it to terminate the connection and exit. It displays the following:

```
Received: quit
Sent: tiuq

C:\java\jdg\ch17>
```

In the PortTalkApp window, type Q to terminate PortTalkApp, as shown in the following output:

```
Send, receive, or quit (S/R/Q): q

C:\java\jdg\ch17>
```

The ReverServerApp program is smaller in size than PortTalkApp. It consists of a single main() method. The ReverseString class is also declared.

The main() method begins by creating a ServerSocket object on port 1234. It then uses the getLocalPort() method to get the local port number associated with the socket. This is to verify that it is indeed using port 1234. It then displays the fact that it is up and running and the number of the port on which it is listening for connections.

The accept() method is used to accept an incoming client connection and return the Socket object associated with the connection. The getHostName() and getPort() methods are used to get the hostname and port number associated with the client program. These parameters are displayed to the console window. Input and output streams are then associated with the socket.

The main() method enters a loop where it reads a line of text from the input stream and then checks to see if it is the quit termination signal. The ReverseString() constructor and `getString()` method are used to reverse the line read from the input stream. The reversed line is then written to the output stream. If the `quit` line is received from the client, the loop is terminated and the input stream, output stream, client socket, and server socket are closed.

The `ReverseString` class provides a constructor that reverses a string and a `getString()` method for retrieving the reversed string.

The `DatagramSocket` Class

The `DatagramSocket` class is used to implement client and server sockets using the UDP protocol. UDP is a connectionless protocol that allows application programs (both clients and servers) to exchange information using chunks of data known as *datagrams.*

`DatagramSocket` provides two constructors. The default constructor creates a datagram socket for use by client applications. No port number is specified. The second constructor allows a datagram socket to be created using a specified port. This constructor is typically used with server applications.

The `send()` and `receive()` methods are used to send and receive datagrams using the socket. The datagrams are objects of class `DatagramPacket`. The `getLocalPort()` method returns the local port used in the socket. The `close()` method closes this socket, and the `finalize()` method performs additional socket-termination processing when the socket is deallocated during garbage collection.

The `DatagramPacket` Class

The `DatagramPacket` class encapsulates the actual datagrams that are sent and received using objects of class `DatagramSocket`. Two different constructors are provided: one for datagrams that are received from a datagram socket and one for creating datagrams that are sent over a datagram socket. The arguments to the received datagram constructor are a byte array used as a buffer for the received data and an integer that identifies the number of bytes received and stored in the buffer. The sending datagram constructor adds two additional parameters: the IP address and port where the datagram is to be sent.

Four access methods are provided. The `getAddress()` and `getPort()` methods are used to read the destination IP address and port of the datagram. The `getLength()` and `getData()` methods are used to get the number of bytes of data contained in the datagram and to read the data into a byte array buffer.

The `TimeServerApp` and `GetTimeApp` programs illustrate the use of client/server computing using datagrams. `TimeServerApp` listens on a UDP socket on port 2345 for incoming datagrams. When a datagram is received, it displays the data contained in the datagram to the console window and returns a datagram with the current date and time to the sending client program. It terminates its operation when it receives a datagram with the text `quit` as its data.

The `GetTimeApp` program sends five datagrams with the text `time` in each datagram to local port 2345. After sending each datagram, it waits for a return datagram from `TimeServerApp`. It displays the datagrams that it sends and receives to the console window. It then sends a `quit` datagram to `TimeServerApp` and terminates its operation.

The `TimeServerApp` program listing is shown in Listing 17.4. The code for `GetTimeApp` is in Listing 17.5.

Listing 17.4. The source code of the `TimeServerApp` program.

```
import java.lang.System;
import java.net.DatagramSocket;
import java.net.DatagramPacket;
import java.net.InetAddress;
import java.io.IOException;
import java.util.Date;

public class TimeServerApp {
 public static void main(String args[]){
  try{
   DatagramSocket socket = new DatagramSocket(2345);
   String localAddress = InetAddress.getLocalHost().getHostName().trim();
   int localPort = socket.getLocalPort();
   System.out.print(localAddress+": ");
   System.out.println("Time Server is listening on port "+localPort+".");
   int bufferLength = 256;
   byte packetBuffer[] = new byte[bufferLength];
   DatagramPacket datagram = new DatagramPacket(packetBuffer,bufferLength);
   boolean finished = false;
   do {
    socket.receive(datagram);
    InetAddress destAddress = datagram.getAddress();
    String destHost = destAddress.getHostName().trim();
    int destPort = datagram.getPort();
    System.out.println("\nReceived a datagram from "+destHost+" at port "+
     destPort+".");
    String data = new String(datagram.getData(),0).trim();
    System.out.println("It contained the data: "+data);
    if(data.equalsIgnoreCase("quit")) finished=true;
    String time = new Date().toString();
    time.getBytes(0,time.length(),packetBuffer,0);
    datagram = new DatagramPacket(packetBuffer,bufferLength,destAddress,
     destPort);
    socket.send(datagram);
    System.out.println("Sent "+time+" to "+destHost+" at port "+destPort+".");
   } while(!finished);
  }catch (IOException ex){
   System.out.println("IOException occurred.");
  }
 }
}
```

Listing 17.5. The source code of the GetTimeApp program.

```
import java.lang.System;
import java.net.DatagramSocket;
import java.net.DatagramPacket;
import java.net.InetAddress;
import java.io.IOException;

public class GetTimeApp {
 public static void main(String args[]){
  try{
   DatagramSocket socket = new DatagramSocket();
   InetAddress localAddress = InetAddress.getLocalHost();
   String localHost = localAddress.getHostName();
   int bufferLength = 256;
   byte packetBuffer[];
   DatagramPacket datagram;
   for(int i=0;i<5;++i){
    packetBuffer = new byte[bufferLength];
    "time".getBytes(0,4,packetBuffer,0);
    datagram = new DatagramPacket(packetBuffer,256,localAddress,2345);
    socket.send(datagram);
    System.out.println("\nSent time request to "+localHost+" at port 2345.");
    socket.receive(datagram);
    InetAddress destAddress = datagram.getAddress();
    String destHost = destAddress.getHostName().trim();
    int destPort = datagram.getPort();
    System.out.println("Received a datagram from "+destHost+" at port "+
     destPort+".");
    String data = new String(datagram.getData(),0).trim();
    System.out.println("It contained the following data: "+data);
   }
   packetBuffer = new byte[bufferLength];
   "quit".getBytes(0,4,packetBuffer,0);
   datagram = new DatagramPacket(packetBuffer,256,localAddress,2345);
   socket.send(datagram);
  }catch (IOException ex){
   System.out.println("IOException occurred.");
  }
 }
}
```

TimeServerApp and GetTimeApp should be run in separate windows. First, start TimeServerApp using the following command line:

```
C:\java\jdg\ch17>java TimeServerApp
athome.jaworski.com: Time Server is listening on port 2345.
```

TimeServerApp will respond by letting you know that it is up and running and listening on port 2345.

Next start `GetTimeApp` in a different window, as follows:

```
C:\java\jdg\ch17>java GetTimeApp

Sent time request to athome.jaworski.com at port 2345.
Received a datagram from athome.jaworski.com at port 2345.
It contained the following data: Tue Mar 19 15:12:23  1996

Sent time request to athome.jaworski.com at port 2345.
Received a datagram from athome.jaworski.com at port 2345.
It contained the following data: Tue Mar 19 15:12:23  1996

Sent time request to athome.jaworski.com at port 2345.
Received a datagram from athome.jaworski.com at port 2345.
It contained the following data: Tue Mar 19 15:12:23  1996

Sent time request to athome.jaworski.com at port 2345.
Received a datagram from athome.jaworski.com at port 2345.
It contained the following data: Tue Mar 19 15:12:24  1996

Sent time request to athome.jaworski.com at port 2345.
Received a datagram from athome.jaworski.com at port 2345.
It contained the following data: Tue Mar 19 15:12:24  1996

C:\java\jdg\ch17>
```

`GetTimeApp` reports the packets it sends to and receives from `TimeServerApp` and then terminates. `TimeServerApp` provides a similar display in its window, as shown in the following:

```
Received a datagram from athome.jaworski.com at port 1306.
It contained the data: time
Sent Tue Mar 19 15:12:23  1996 to athome.jaworski.com at port 1306.

Received a datagram from athome.jaworski.com at port 1306.
It contained the data: time
Sent Tue Mar 19 15:12:23  1996 to athome.jaworski.com at port 1306.

Received a datagram from athome.jaworski.com at port 1306.
It contained the data: time
Sent Tue Mar 19 15:12:23  1996 to athome.jaworski.com at port 1306.

Received a datagram from athome.jaworski.com at port 1306.
It contained the data: time
Sent Tue Mar 19 15:12:24  1996 to athome.jaworski.com at port 1306.

Received a datagram from athome.jaworski.com at port 1306.
It contained the data: time
Sent Tue Mar 19 15:12:24  1996 to athome.jaworski.com at port 1306.

Received a datagram from athome.jaworski.com at port 1306.
It contained the data: quit
Sent Tue Mar 19 15:12:24  1996 to athome.jaworski.com at port 1306.

C:\java\jdg\ch17>
```

These two simple programs illustrate the basic mechanisms of datagram-based client/server applications. A UDP client sends a datagram to a UDP server at the server's port address. The UDP server listens on its port for a datagram, processes the datagram, and sends back information to the UDP client.

TimeServerApp

`TimeServerApp` begins by creating a `DatagramSocket` object on port 2345 and assigning it to the socket variable. It then obtains the hostname and local port number using the `getHostName()` and `getLocalPort()` methods and displays this information to the console window.

`TimeServerApp` creates a 256-byte buffer and assigns it to the `packetBuffer[]` array. It then creates a `DatagramPacket` object using the `packetBuffer[]` array and assigns it to the `datagram` variable.

`TimeServerApp` executes a loop where it receives and processes datagrams received from client programs. It receives datagrams using the `receive()` method of the `DatagramSocket` class. It uses the `getAddress()` and `getPort()` methods of the `DatagramPacket` class to get the host address and port of the client program that sent the socket. It displays this information to the console window. It uses the `getData()` method of the `DatagramPacket` class to retrieve the data sent by the client program. It converts this data to a string and displays it on the console window. If the received data contains the `quit` string, it sets the finished flag to `true`. `TimeServerApp` processes the client time request by using the `Date()` constructor of the `java.util` package to construct a new `Date` object, converting the `Date` object to a byte array, and storing the data in `packetBuffer[]`. It then creates a new `DatagramPacket` object, using `packetBuffer[]`, with the destination address and port number of the sending client program. It then sends the datagram to the client using the `send()` method of the `DatagramSocket` class. The console display is then updated with the data that was sent to the client program.

GetTimeApp

The `GetTimeApp` client program creates a `DatagramSocket` object and assigns it to the `socket` variable. It then creates a `DatagramPacket` object in the same manner as the `TimeServerApp` program. `GetTimeApp` uses a `for` statement to loop five times, sending five datagrams to port 2345 of the local host. After each datagram is sent, it waits to receive a return datagram from `TimeServerApp`. It uses the `getAddress()`, `getPort()`, and `getData()` methods of the `DatagramPacket` class to report this information to the console window.

After sending and receiving five datagrams, `GetTimeApp` sends a datagram with the `quit` text to tell `TimeServerApp` that it should terminate its processing.

The `SocketImpl` Class and the `SocketImplFactory` Interface

The `SocketImpl` class is an `abstract` class that is used to define custom socket implementations. It is used with the `SocketImplFactory` interface that must be implemented by new socket implementations.

> **NOTE**
>
> The `setSocketImplFactory()` method of the `Socket` class can be used to set the system `SocketImplFactory`. Once it is set, it cannot be changed.

The `SocketImpl` class provides four variables that are used to define a socket: the destination IP address and port, the local port, and a file descriptor used to create streams. The local IP address of the host is assumed.

Some of the access methods defined by `SocketImpl` are used to perform lower-level socket operations. These include listening for connections, accepting connections, binding a socket to a port, and implementing the actual connection. Datagram sockets are also supported. Other access methods are used to support stream-based I/O and to provide access to the IP address and port parameters of a socket.

Web-Related Classes

In addition to providing the basic TCP- and UDP-based sockets used by almost all Internet client/server applications, the `java.net` package provides a very useful set of classes that support higher-level, Web-specific applications. These classes are centered around the `URL` class, which encapsulates an object on the Web, typically a Web page, by its URL address.

URL stands for *uniform resource locator* and, as its name states, provides a uniform way to locate resources on the Web. Different types of URLs are used with different application protocols, the most common of which are the *Hypertext Transfer Protocol* (HTTP) and the *File Transfer Protocol* (FTP). URLs for these types of protocols are mainly used to identify the location of files, such as Web pages, supporting images, multimedia files, text files, and downloadable programs. HTTP URLs also refer to executable programs, such as CGI scripts, which perform Web-related services. *CGI scripts* are programs, usually written in a scripting language, that receive input and generate output in accordance with the *common gateway interface* (CGI) specification.

URL

The URL class encapsulates Web objects by their URL address. It provides a set of constructors that allow URL objects to be easily constructed and a set of access methods that allow high-level read and write operations to be performed using URLs.

Most, but not all, URLs typically consist of a protocol, hostname, and the path and name of a file on the host. For example, the URL `http://www.jaworski.com/jdg/index.htm` refers to a Web page on my Web server. It specifies the HTTP protocol as the protocol used to access the Web page. It identifies my hostname as `www.jaworski.com`, and it names the file as `/jdg/index.htm` where `/jdg/` is the directory path to the file (relative to my Web server's directory root) and `index.htm` is the file's name. In HTTP URLs, the pathname/filename is optional. For example, the URL `http://www.jaworski.com/jdg/` is equivalent to the previous URL. My Web server uses the filename `index.htm` as the default name for a file. The pathname can also be omitted. The URL `http://www.jaworski.com` would use the `index.htm` file in the Web server's root directory.

The four URL constructors allow URL objects to be created using a variety of URL parameters such as protocol type, hostname, port, and file path. These parameters may be supplied separately or in text form as part of an URL string. The URL class treats a file's path and name as a single entity to provide a more convenient way of working with URL components.

You can construct an URL using its absolute address or using an address that is relative to another URL. Up to now we have been working with the full, complete, or *absolute* address of an URL. A *relative address* is a path/filename or file offset that is specified relative to an absolute URL. For example, the absolute URL `http://www.jaworski.com` can be combined with the relative URL `/jdg/index.htm` to produce the URL to `http://www.jaworski.com/jdg/index.htm`.

The URL access methods provide a full set of URL processing capabilities. The `getProtocol()`, `getHost()`, `getPort()`, `getFile()`, and `getRef()` methods allow the individual address components of the URL to be determined. The `getContent()` and `openStream()` methods allow reading of the Web object pointed to by the URL. The `toExternalForm()` and `toString()` methods enable URLs to be converted into strings to support display and printing. The `equals()` method compares URLs, and the `sameFile()` method compares the Web objects pointed to by the URLs. The `openConnection()` method creates an object of class `URLConnection` to the Web object pointed to by the URL. This class is discussed after the "`URLConnection`" section of this chapter.

The `GetURLApp` program illustrates the power provided by the URL class. This small program implements a primitive Web browser. Just run the program with the name of an URL and it makes a connection to the destination Web server and downloads the referenced document. The program's source code is shown in Listing 17.6.

Listing 17.6. The source code of the `GetURLApp` program.

```
import java.lang.System;
import java.net.URL;
import java.net.MalformedURLException;
import java.io.DataInputStream;
import java.io.IOException;

public class GetURLApp {
 public static void main(String args[]){
  try{
   if(args.length!=1) error("Usage: java GetURLApp URL");
   System.out.println("Fetching URL: "+args[0]);
   URL url = new URL(args[0]);
   DataInputStream inStream = new DataInputStream(url.openStream());
   String line;
   while ((line = inStream.readLine())!= null){
    System.out.println(line);
   }
   inStream.close();
  }catch (MalformedURLException ex){
   error("Bad URL");
  }catch (IOException ex){
   error("IOException occurred.");
  }
 }
 public static void error(String s){
  System.out.println(s);
  System.exit(1);
 }
}
```

After compiling the program, try running it with the URL `http://www.jaworski.com/java/GetURLApp.htm` as follows. Make sure that you use the correct upper- and lowercase characters:

```
C:\java\jdg\ch17>java GetURLApp http://www.jaworski.com/java/GetURLApp.htm
```

The program will respond by displaying the following Web document from my Web server:

```
C:\java\jdg\ch17>java GetURLApp http://www.jaworski.com/java/GetURLApp.htm
Fetching URL: http://www.jaworski.com/java/GetURLApp.htm
<!DOCTYPE HTML PUBLIC "-//SQ//DTD HTML 2.0 HoTMetaL + extensions//EN">
<HTML><HEAD><TITLE>GetURLApp Test Results</TITLE></HEAD>
<BODY><H1>GetURLApp Test Results</H1>
<P>Congratulations! You were able to successfully compile and run GetURLApp.
</P>
</BODY></HTML>

C:\java\jdg\ch17>
```

Try running the program with other URLs to see how they are displayed.

`GetURLApp` consists of a short `main()` method and the `error()` method, used to display error messages to the console window.

The main() method checks the arguments supplied by the user to make sure that the correct number of arguments are present. It then displays a message to the console window identifying the URL that it is trying to fetch. It creates an URL object using the URL name supplied by the user and assigns it to the url variable. It then uses the openStream() method of the URL class to create an input stream from the URL. The input stream is filtered as a DataInputStream object and is assigned to the inStream variable. The inStream variable is used to read and display the input stream one line at a time.

URLConnection

The URLConnnection class is an abstract class that encapsulates an active HTTP connection to a Web object represented by an URL. It provides a number of methods for getting information about the Web object, about the connection to the Web object, and for interacting with the Web object.

URLConnection defines several class variables that specify the connection state and associated parameters. It also supplies numerous methods that provide access to the HTTP-specific fields of the connection. This class is studied, in detail, in Part V of this book. The next programming example covers a few aspects of its use.

URLEncoder

The URLEncoder class is a very simple class that provides a single static method, encode(), for converting text strings to a form that is suitable for use as part of an URL. This format is known as x-www-form-urlencoded and is typically used to encode form data that is sent to a CGI script.

The encode() method converts spaces to plus signs (+) and uses the percent character (%) as an escape code to encode special characters. The two characters that immediately follow a percent sign are interpreted as hexadecimal digits that are combined to produce an eight-bit value.

Listing 17.7 illustrates the use of the encode() method and the URLConnection class. It accesses the echo-query CGI program on my Web server, passing it the "/this/is/extra/path/information" query string and the "Query string with some special characters: @#$%?&+" query string. The query string is encoded using the encode() method of the URLEncoder class. The echo-query CGI program creates an HTML file that describes the parameters passed to it by my Web server and returns this file to the QueryURLApp program. This file shows how the query string was encoded by the encode() method.

Listing 17.7. The source code of the QueryURLApp program.

```
import java.lang.System;
import java.net.URL;
import java.net.URLConnection;
import java.net.URLEncoder;
import java.net.MalformedURLException;
```

continues

Listing 17.7. continued

```
import java.net.UnknownServiceException;
import java.io.DataInputStream;
import java.io.IOException;

public class QueryURLApp {
 public static void main(String args[]){
  try{
   String urlString = "http://www.jaworski.com/cgi-bin/echo-query";
   String extraPathInfo = "/this/is/extra/path/information";
   String queryString =
    URLEncoder.encode("Query string with some special characters: @#$%?&+");
   URL url = new URL(urlString+extraPathInfo+"?"+queryString);
   URLConnection connection = url.openConnection();
   DataInputStream fromURL = new DataInputStream(url.openStream());
   String line;
   while ((line = fromURL.readLine())!= null){
    System.out.println(line);
   }
   fromURL.close();
  }catch (MalformedURLException ex){
   error("Bad URL");
  }catch (UnknownServiceException ex){
   error("UnknownServiceException occurred.");
  }catch (IOException ex){
   error("IOException occurred.");
  }
 }
 public static void error(String s){
  System.out.println(s);
  System.exit(1);
 }
}
```

To run `QueryURLApp`, just type the following command line:

```
C:\java\jdg\ch17>java QueryURLApp
```

`QueryURLApp` queries the echo-query program on my Web server and displays the HTML file generated by the echo-query program. Notice how the query string was encoded:

```
<HTML>
<HEAD>
<TITLE>Echo CGI Request</TITLE>
</HEAD>
<BODY>
<H1>CGI Request</H1>
<H2>Command Line Arguments</H2>
<P>Number of command line arguments: 7</P>
<P>Command line arguments: Query string with some special characters:
➥ @#\$%\?\&+
</P>
<H2>Environment Variables</H2>
<PRE>
AUTH_TYPE =
CONTENT_LENGTH =
```

```
CONTENT_TYPE =
GATEWAY_INTERFACE = CGI/1.1
HTTP_ACCEPT = text/html, image/gif, image/jpeg, *; q=.2, */*; q=.2
HTTP_USER_AGENT = Javainternal_build
PATH_INFO = /this/is/extra/path/information
PATH_TRANSLATED = /usr/local/etc/httpd/htdocs/this/is/extra/path/information
QUERY_STRING =
➥ Query+string+with+some+special+characters%3a+%40%23%24%25%3f%26%2b
REMOTE_ADDR = 204.212.153.194
REMOTE_HOST = athome.jaworski.com
REMOTE_IDENT =
REMOTE_USER =
REQUEST_METHOD = GET
SCRIPT_NAME = /cgi-bin/echo-query
SERVER_NAME = www.jaworski.com
SERVER_PORT = 80
SERVER_PROTOCOL = HTTP/1.0
SERVER_SOFTWARE = NCSA/1.4.2
</PRE>
<H2>Standard Input</H2>
</BODY>
</HTML>

C:\java\jdg\ch17>
```

QueryURLApp creates an URL by concatenating the URL for the echo-query program, the extra path information, and the encoded query string. It then uses the openConnection() method of the URL class to create an URLConnection object, which it assigns to the connection variable. The connection is then read and displayed in the same manner as the GetURLApp program.

The ContentHandler and ContentHandlerFactory Classes

The ContentHandler class is an abstract class that is used to develop specialized objects that are able to extract and process data associated with new MIME types.

MIME, or *multipurpose Internet mail extension,* is a general method by which the content of different types of Internet objects can be identified. MIME was originally developed to include different types of objects, such as sounds, images, and videos, in Internet e-mail messages. It was also adopted and popularized by the Web and is used to identify multimedia and other types of Web objects so that appropriate external viewers or plug-in modules can be used to process and display these objects.

The ContentHandler class provides the basis for developing new viewers for processing MIME types that are not currently supported by Java. It consists of a single method, getContent(), that extracts an object of a particular MIME type from an URL connection. The ContentHandlerFactory interface provides a standard method of associating a content handler with a MIME type.

Chapter 28, "Content Handlers," provides a detailed description of how content handlers are developed.

The `URLStreamHandler` Class and the `URLStreamHandlerFactory` Interface

The `URLStreamHandler` class is an `abstract` class that is used to develop specialized objects that are able to communicate with Web resources using protocols that are currently not supported by Java. For example, suppose you develop a new protocol for a custom client/server application and you want that protocol to be accessible to Web browsers. You would develop an `URLStreamHandler` for that protocol. The `URLStreamHandlerFactory` interface is used to associate a stream handler with a particular protocol. Chapter 28 provides a detailed description of how protocol stream handlers are developed.

Summary

In this chapter you have learned about Java's support of network programming and covered the basics of client/server computing and TCP/IP socket programming. You have toured the classes of the `java.net` package and learned how to use them to develop client/server applications. You have also covered the URL-centric classes that support Web-based applications. You have now completed your introduction to the Java API. The next three parts of this book will show you how to use the Java API to develop Java application programs and applets.

IV

Window Programming

18

Opening Windows

This chapter is the first of eight chapters that cover window programming. It introduces you to Java windows by way of several examples that illustrate different aspects of the classes and methods used to implement simple window applications. Its purpose is to quickly get you up to speed developing window-based programs. Subsequent chapters will fill in the details of the classes and methods that are introduced here. You should approach this chapter by trying to get a good general understanding of what is going on in the sample programs without dwelling on the details. You will learn the details when you study them in later chapters.

Hello Windows!

The first program you wrote in Chapter 4, "First Programs: Hello World! to BlackJack," is the `HelloWorldApp` program. It displays the traditional `Hello World!` text to the console window. The main purpose of the program was to show you how to develop a simple Java program that actually produced some noticeable effect. The same rationale applies to the `HelloWindowsApp` program that you'll develop shortly. The program shows you how to open an application window and write the text `Hello Windows!` to the window. The code for the `HelloWindowsApp` program is shown in Listing 18.1.

Listing 18.1. The source code of the `HelloWindowsApp` program.

```
import java.awt.Frame;
import java.awt.Event;
import java.awt.Graphics;

public class HelloWindowsApp extends Frame {
 public static void main(String args[]){
  HelloWindowsApp app = new HelloWindowsApp();
 }
 public HelloWindowsApp() {
  super("Hello Windows!");
  pack();
  resize(200,200);
  show();
 }
 public void paint(Graphics g) {
  g.drawString("Hello Windows!",50,90);
 }
 public boolean handleEvent(Event event) {
  if(event.id==Event.WINDOW_DESTROY){
   System.exit(0);
   return true;
  }else return false;
 }
}
```

When you compile and run the program it opens a small window in the upper-left corner of your desktop and displays the text `Hello Windows!` in the middle of the window. This program is no giant feat for mankind, but it's a large step for you. It marks your transition from console to window-based programs. Up to this point in the book, console programs served admirably in helping cover the different aspects of the Java language and many of the classes of the API. However, window-based programs and applets (which you learn about in Part VI, "Programming the Web with Applets and Scripts") are the primary areas of interest for most Java programmers. Figure 18.1 shows the window displayed by the `HelloWindowsApp` program.

FIGURE 18.1.
The `HelloWindowsApp` *program display.*

Let's take a look at `HelloWindowsApp` and find out what makes it work. You probably noticed right off the bat that we are now importing classes from the `java.awt` package. The `Frame`, `Event`, and `Graphics` classes shown in the `import` statements are classes that are fundamental to developing window programs. The `Frame` class is used to create `Frame` objects that implement application main windows. The `Event` class is used to process user-generated interface events, such as mouse clicks and keyboard input, and the `Graphics` class is used to update the screen display.

The `HelloWindowsApp` class extends the `Frame` class. This is a typical approach to developing window programs. By subclassing `Frame`, your application class implements a main application window. You still use the same old `main()` method for implementing the entry point to your program. In `HelloWindowsApp`, the `main()` method simply creates a default object of class `HelloWindowsApp`.

The `HelloWindowsApp` constructor uses the `super()` constructor call statement to invoke the `Frame` constructor with the string `"Hello Windows!"`. The `Frame` constructor creates a new application window frame with the specified text as its title. The `pack()` method is used to pack the components of the window and set the window's size based upon the size of these components. It is inherited from the `Window` class, which is the superclass of `Frame`. The `resize()` method then resizes the window to a 200×200 pixel dimension. The `resize()` method is inherited from the `Component` class by way of the `Container`, `Window`, and `Frame` classes. Finally, the `show()` method is used to cause the window to be displayed. It is inherited from the `Window` class.

You might be wondering how the `"Hello Windows!"` text is actually displayed because there is no call from `main()` or `HelloWindowsApp()` to the `paint()` method. When a window or any other object that is in a subclass of `Component` is initially displayed or redisplayed as the result of the window being uncovered or brought to the foreground, the `paint()` method is invoked. It then paints the window according to the current application state.

The `paint()` method used by `HelloWindowsApp` overrides the `paint()` method inherited from the `Component` class. It takes a `Graphics` object as a parameter. The `Graphics` class provides numerous easy-to-use methods for drawing on `Graphics` objects. The `paint()` method uses the `drawString()` method to display the text `"Hello Windows!"` at the screen coordinate 50,90 within the application window.

Window coordinates are organized with the upper-left corner of the window being 0,0. The coordinates of the upper-right corner of the window are *width*,0, where *width* is the horizontal width of the window in pixels. The coordinates of the lower-left corner of the window are 0,*height*, where *height* is the vertical height of the window in pixels. Finally, the coordinates of the lower-right corner of the window are *width,height*. Figure 18.2 illustrates the window coordinate system.

FIGURE 18.2.
Window coordinates.

(0,0)	(1,0)	(2,0)	(3,0)	(4,0)	(5,0)
(0,1)	(1,1)	(2,1)	(3,1)	(4,1)	(5,1)
(0,2)	(1,2)	(2,2)	(3,2)	(4,2)	(5,2)

You probably have been wondering what the `handleEvent()` method is doing in the `HelloWindowsApp` class. The `handleEvent()` method provides a standard approach to event handling in Java applications. *Events* represent actions that occur during the course of program execution. Most events are generated as the result of user actions such as mouse clicks and keyboard actions. The `handleEvent()` method overrides the method inherited from the `Component` class. It takes an object of the `Event` class as a parameter and uses the methods and constants of the `Event` class to determine what event was passed to it and how it should be handled. The `handleEvent()` method returns a `boolean` value indicating whether or not the event has been handled. If a `false` value is returned, the event is propagated to the `handleEvent()` method of the parent of the class that is currently handling the event. If a `true` value is returned, no further event propagation takes place.

The `handleEvent()` method of `HelloWindowsApp` checks the `id` variable of the event to see if it equals the constant `Event.WINDOWS_DESTROY`. The `id` variable and the `WINDOWS_DESTROY` constant both are defined in the API of the `Event` class. The `id` variable is used to identify what type of event occurred, and the `Event` class constants specify the event types. In this example, the event handler only handles the `WINDOW_DESTROY` event. This event occurs when the user closes the main application window by clicking the Close Window icon, as shown in Figure 18.3.

FIGURE 18.3.
Terminating the `HelloWindowsApp` *program.*

The `WINDOW_DESTROY` event is handled by invoking the `exit()` method of the `System` class to terminate the program. The `true` value is returned to indicate that the event was handled.

You might be wondering what would happen if the event handler did not handle the `WINDOW_DESTROY` event. Try deleting the `handleEvent()` method and recompiling and rerunning `HelloWindowsApp` to see what happens when you try to terminate the application.

Going Round in Ovals: A Graphics Program

The `HelloWindowsApp` program provided a simple introduction to window programming. It illustrated many of the basics of writing a window program, but it didn't actually *do* all that much. The `OvalApp` program is also an introductory window program. It introduces more window programming classes and methods such as panels, buttons, layouts, additional event handling, and, of course, oval drawing. The source code of `OvalApp` is shown in Listing 18.2.

Listing 18.2. The source code of the `OvalApp` program.

```
import java.awt.*;
import java.util.Random;

public class OvalApp extends Frame {
 int screenWidth = 400;
 int screenHeight = 400;
 Oval oval;
 public static void main(String args[]){
  OvalApp app = new OvalApp();
 }
 public OvalApp() {
  super("Let's Draw Ovals!");
  Panel buttons = new Panel();
  buttons.add(new Button("Next"));
  buttons.add(new Button("Quit"));
  add("South",buttons);
  oval = new Oval(screenWidth,screenHeight);
  pack();
  resize(screenWidth,screenHeight);
  show();
 }
 public void paint(Graphics g) {
```

continues

Listing 18.2. continued

```
  oval.paint(g);
 }
 public boolean handleEvent(Event event) {
  if(event.id==Event.WINDOW_DESTROY){
   System.exit(0);
   return true;
  }else if(event.id==Event.ACTION_EVENT){
   if(event.target instanceof Button){
    if("Next".equals(event.arg)){
     oval.update();
     repaint();
     return true;
    }else if("Quit".equals(event.arg)){
     System.exit(0);
     return true;
    }
   }
  }
  return false;
 }
}

class Oval {
 int x, y, width, height, maxWidth, maxHeight;
 Color color;
 static Random r = new Random();
 public Oval(int w,int h) {
  super();
  maxWidth = w;
  maxHeight = h;
  update();
 }
 public void update() {
  x = Math.abs(r.nextInt() % (maxWidth-100));
  y = Math.abs(r.nextInt() % (maxHeight-100));
  width = (maxWidth - x)/3;
  height = (maxHeight - y)/3;
  int rgb[] = new int[3];
  for(int i=0;i<3;++i) rgb[i]=Math.abs(r.nextInt()%256);
  color = new Color(rgb[0],rgb[1],rgb[2]);
 }
 public void paint(Graphics g) {
  g.setColor(color);
  g.fillOval(x,y,width,height);
 }
}
```

When you run the `OvalApp` program it displays a window with the title Let's Draw Ovals!. A colored oval is displayed somewhere in the application window, as shown in Figure 18.4.

The window has two buttons, labeled Next and Quit. When you click on the Next button, as shown in Figure 18.5, a different oval is displayed.

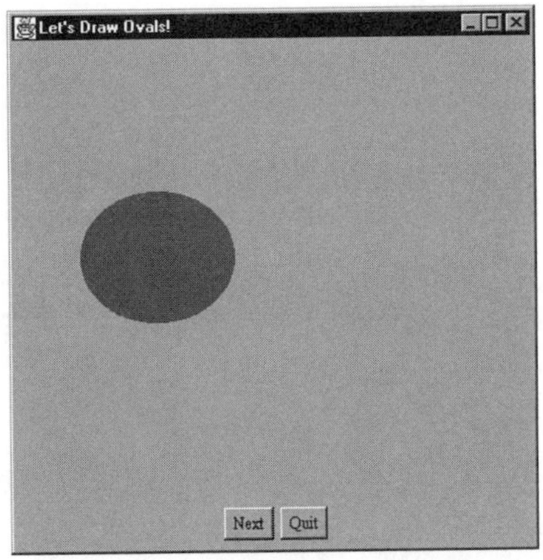

FIGURE 18.4.
The `OvalApp` *startup display.*

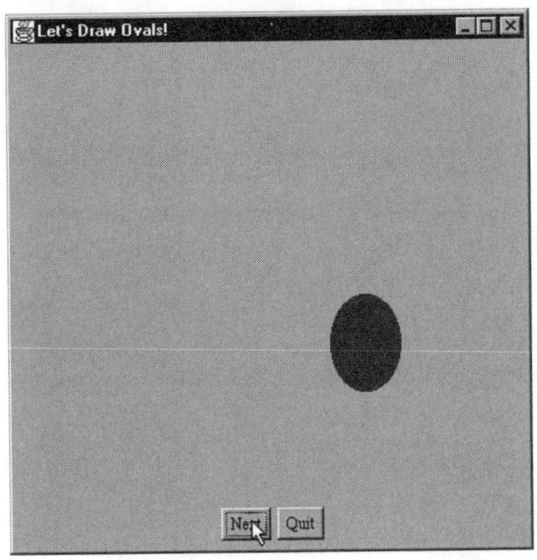

FIGURE 18.5.
The Next button.

You can continue to click on the Next button to cause different colored ovals to be displayed in different parts of the window, as shown in Figure 18.6.

When you have thoroughly amused yourself by drawing ovals, you can click on the Quit button, as shown in Figure 18.7, and terminate the program's execution.

The `OvalApp` program is cute and entertaining, but doesn't perform any useful processing. However, it does provide a good example of some new window programming constructs.

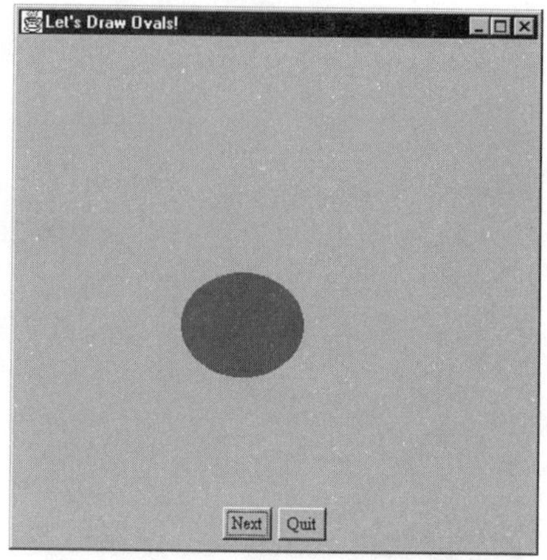

FIGURE 18.6.
A new oval is displayed.

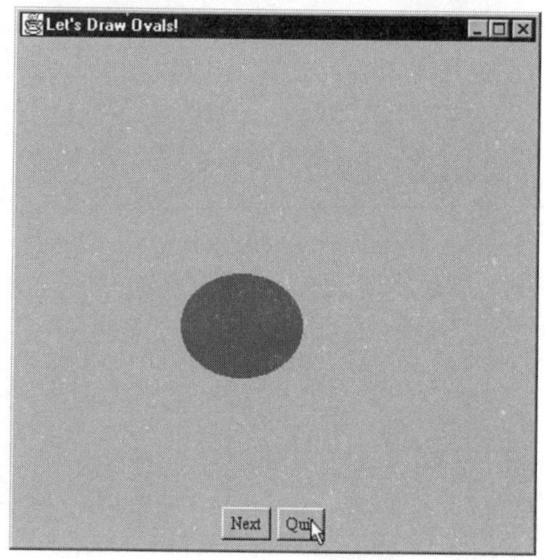

FIGURE 18.7.
The Quit button.

The program begins by doing an import of the relevant classes of the `java.awt` package. The program uses a large number of `java.awt` classes and, rather than listing each one individually, uses the more general package `import` statement to eliminate the trouble of typing each one in individually. The only other class that is included is the `Random` class of the `java.util` package. This class provides the capability to generate random numbers to be used in the oval drawing.

The `OvalApp` class extends `Frame` in the same manner as the `HelloWindowsApp`. Three variables are defined for the `OvalApp` class. The `screenWidth` and `screenHeight` variables define the dimensions of the main window. The `oval` variable is used to refer to the current `Oval` object being displayed. The `main()` method simply creates a new object of class `OvalApp`.

The `OvalApp` constructor sets the window title using the superclass constructor call statement, `super()`. It then creates a `Panel` object called `buttons`. `Panels` are window objects that are used as containers for other objects. They help to organize the way GUI controls are placed in windows. The buttons panel will be used to organize the Next and Quit buttons. The add() method is used with buttons to add two new objects of class Button to the panel. The Button constructor takes a string argument that is the label for the buttons. The add() method is then invoked for the OvalApp object being constructed to add the panel to the OvalApp application window. The OvalApp add() method is inherited from the Container class. The "South" string identifies where the panel should be added in the application window.

The organization of objects within a window container is governed by the *layout* of the container. (Layouts are described in detail in Chapter 19, "Organizing Window Programs.") The default layout for Frame objects and their subclasses is BorderLayout. This type of layout organizes objects within a container by their North, South, East, and West borders. Objects can also be placed in the Center of a container. The add("South",buttons); method invocation adds the buttons panel to the southern (bottom) border of the OvalApp window.

The buttons panel is also associated with a layout. Panels use a FlowLayout object, by default. The FlowLayout class organizes objects in a container in a left-to-right fashion, fitting as many objects as possible in a row before moving on to fill the next row.

The oval variable is assigned a new object of class Oval that is parameterized by the screenWidth and screenHeight dimensions. These arguments are passed to the Oval constructor to make sure that an Oval object is created that is appropriate for the screen size of the OvalApp window. The Oval class is discussed after the OvalApp class's description is completed.

After adding the buttons panel to the window and creating an Oval object, the pack() method is invoked to organize the components of the window and to determine the minimum preferred size of the window. The resize() method then adjusts the screen to the specified width and height dimensions. Finally, the show() method causes the window to be displayed.

The paint() method for the OvalApp class simply passes the task of drawing the window to the Oval class. Notice that it passes on the Graphics object that it receives to the Oval paint() method. Without the Graphics object, Oval's paint() method would have nothing to draw on.

The handleEvent() method for OvalApp doesn't fare as well as the paint() method. Instead of handing off its processing to other classes, it provides a central point for all program event handling. It processes the WINDOWS_DESTROY event in the same manner as the HelloWindowsApp program. It also checks for events of type ACTION_EVENT. Events of this type are typically generated by performing actions on GUI controls—for example, clicking on a button, selecting a menu item, or checking a checkbox. In this case, the method is checking whether the Next or Quit button was clicked. It does this by checking the target variable of the event to see if it is an instance of class Button. The target variable identifies the object that is the target of the event being processed.

The event.arg variable is event specific. It typically provides a value that is used to identify the specific object from its class for which the event was generated. In the case of Button objects, it represents the label of the button. The arg variable is used to determine whether the button being clicked on is the Next button or the Quit button.

When the Next button is clicked, the button-clicked event is handled by invoking the `update()` method of the `oval` variable and repainting the screen. The `update()` method causes the oval's color, position, and size parameters to be changed. The `repaint()` method results in the `paint()` method being reinvoked to redraw an object—in this case, the `OvalApp` window. You should never invoke `paint()` directly—it is under the control of the native windows implementation. Always access it by invoking `repaint()`.

When the Quit button is clicked, the `OvalApp` program terminates in the same manner as when the `WINDOW_DESTROY` event occurs.

The `Oval` class is used to randomly generate ovals of different colors, sizes, and positions and display them in the `OvalApp` window. It defines a number of variables that specify these parameters. The `maxWidth` and `maxHeight` variables store the dimensions of the application window. The `width` and `height` parameters store the actual width and height of an `Oval` object. The `x` and `y` parameters identify its position within the application window. The `color` parameter identifies the color in which the oval is to be drawn. The static `r` variable is an object of class `Random` that is used to generate random numbers that determine the oval's characteristics.

The `Oval` constructor explicitly calls the default constructor call statement, sets the `maxWidth` and `maxHeight` variables, and invokes its `update()` method to randomly generate the values of the rest of the variables defined by the `Oval` class.

The `update()` method sets the upper-left corner of the oval to a random value between (0,0) and (`maxWidth=100`,`maxHeight=100`). This keeps the oval from scrunching up against the window's borders. The width and height of the rectangle are set to one-third of the distance between the upper-left corner of the rectangle and the lower-right corner of the application window.

The red, blue, and green color intensities of the rectangle are randomly generated as values between 0 and 255. In order for the full range of color values to be displayed, your screen must support 24-bit color in its current screen resolution; otherwise, the randomly generated color will be approximated by the next closest color supported by your video card. I rarely set my screen to 24-bit color and usually use 8-bit color to cut down on my video-display memory requirements.

The `paint()` method of the `Oval` class uses the `Graphics` object passed to it by the `OvalApp paint()` method to display the oval. It sets the current color of the `Graphics` object based on the randomly generated color stored in the `color` variable. It then invokes the `fillOval()` method of the `Graphics` class to draw an oval that is filled with the current color. The `fillOval()` method takes the upper-left corner of the `Oval` and its width and height dimensions as parameters.

A Text Editor

Now let's extend your exploration of window applications by developing a primitive text editor. The `TextEditApp` program illustrates more window programming constructs. It introduces menus, dialog boxes, fonts, text processing, and window-based file I/O. It also builds on the event-handling skills that you've developed so far. The source code of the `TextEditApp` program is shown in Listing 18.3.

Listing 18.3. The source code of the `TextEditApp` program.

```
import java.awt.*;
import java.io.*;

public class TextEditApp extends Frame {
 TextArea text;
 MenuBar menuBar;
 FileDialog openFile;
 FileDialog saveFile;
 public static void main(String args[]){
  TextEditApp app = new TextEditApp();
 }
 public TextEditApp() {
  super("Text Editor");
  setup();
  resize(text.minimumSize());
  pack();
  show();
 }
 void setup() {
  setFont(new Font("System",Font.PLAIN,12));
  setBackground(Color.white);
  text = new TextArea(25,80);
  add("Center",text);
  setupMenuBar();
  openFile = new FileDialog(this,"Open File",FileDialog.LOAD);
  saveFile = new FileDialog(this,"Save File As",FileDialog.SAVE);
 }
 void setupMenuBar(){
  menuBar = new MenuBar();
  Menu fileMenu = new Menu("File");
  fileMenu.add(new MenuItem("New"));
  fileMenu.add(new MenuItem("Open"));
  fileMenu.addSeparator();
  fileMenu.add(new MenuItem("Save As"));
  fileMenu.addSeparator();
  fileMenu.add(new MenuItem("Exit"));
  menuBar.add(fileMenu);
  setMenuBar(menuBar);
 }
 public boolean handleEvent(Event event) {
  if(event.id==Event.WINDOW_DESTROY){
   System.exit(0);
   return true;
  }else if(event.id==Event.ACTION_EVENT){
   if(event.target instanceof MenuItem){
    if("New".equals(event.arg)){
     text.setText("");
     return true;
    }else if("Open".equals(event.arg)){
```

continues

Listing 18.3. continued

```
     openFile.show();
     String inFile = openFile.getFile();
     readFile(inFile);
     return true;
    }else if("Save As".equals(event.arg)){
     saveFile.show();
     String outFile = saveFile.getFile();
     writeFile(outFile);
     return true;
    }else if("Exit".equals(event.arg)){
     System.exit(0);
     return true;
    }
   }
  }
  return false;
 }
 public void readFile(String file) {
  DataInputStream inStream;
  try{
   inStream = new DataInputStream(new FileInputStream(file));
  }catch (IOException ex){
   notifyDialog("Error opening file");
   return;
  }
  try{
   String newText="";
   String line;
   while((line=inStream.readLine())!=null)
    newText=newText+line+"\n";
   text.setText(newText);
   inStream.close();
  }catch (IOException ex){
   notifyDialog("Error reading file");
  }
 }
 public void writeFile(String file) {
  DataOutputStream outStream;
  try{
   outStream = new DataOutputStream(new FileOutputStream(file));
  }catch (IOException ex){
   notifyDialog("Error opening file");
   return;
  }
  try{
   outStream.writeBytes(text.getText());
   outStream.close();
  }catch (IOException ex){
   notifyDialog("Error writing file");
  }
 }
 public void notifyDialog(String msg) {
  Notification notification = new Notification(this,msg);
  notification.show();
 }
}
```

```
class Notification extends Dialog {
 String msg;
 public Notification(Frame f,String s) {
  super(f,"Notification",true);
  msg = s;
 }
 public void show() {
  add("North",new Label(msg,Label.CENTER));
  Panel p = new Panel();
  p.add(new Button("OK"));
  add("South",p);
  setBackground(Color.gray);
  resize(160,100);
  super.show();
 }
 public boolean handleEvent(Event event) {
  if(event.id==Event.WINDOW_DESTROY){
   dispose();
   return true;
  }else if(event.id==Event.ACTION_EVENT){
   if(event.target instanceof Button){
    if("OK".equals(event.arg)){
     dispose();
     return true;
    }
   }
  }
  return false;
 }
}
```

The `TextEditApp` program provides quite a bit more functionality than the other window programs that you've written so far. After you've compiled it, run the program. It will begin by launching a blank text-editing window with the Text Editor title, as shown in Figure 18.8.

FIGURE 18.8.
The `TextEditApp` *opening window.*

Click in the editor window and begin experimenting with editing text. Type in whatever text comes to your mind. Experiment with tabs to see how they work. Try typing past the right margin to see how the horizontal scrollbars work. Select text with your cursor and use the keyboard copy, cut, and paste commands. Double-click on a word to select it, and then type another word over it. Try typing a few lines to cause the vertical scrollbars to come into play. Your screen should look somewhat similar to Figure 18.9.

FIGURE 18.9.
Editing text.

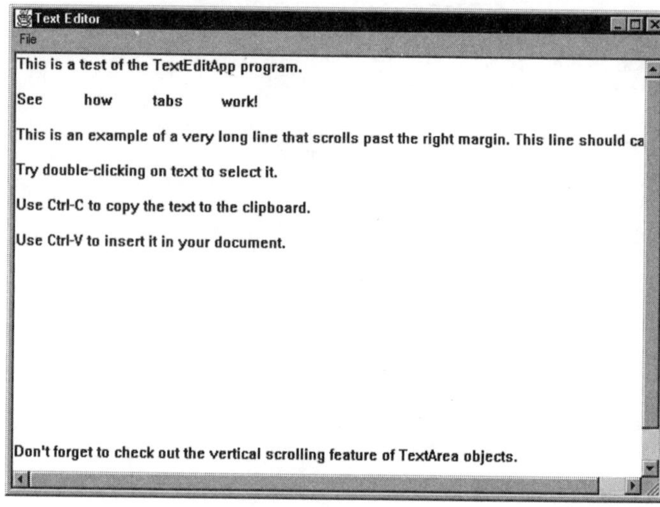

When you have finished editing the text, check out the File pull-down menu shown in Figure 18.10. You'll notice that the File menu supports four commands and contains two separator lines that help organize these commands.

FIGURE 18.10.
The File pull-down menu.

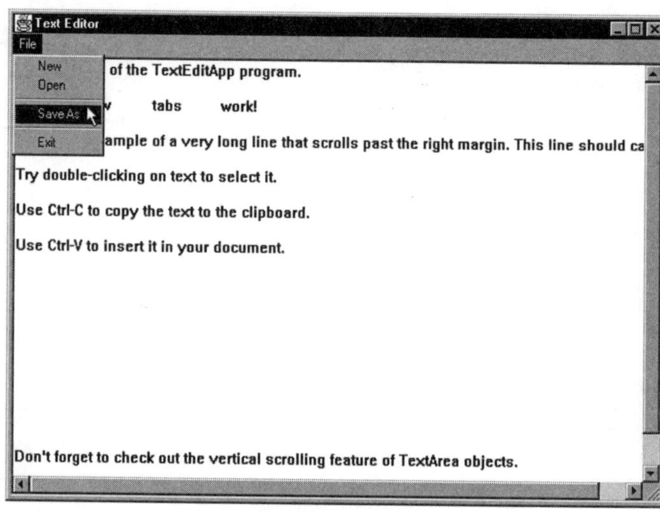

Save your text in the file `test.txt`. A File Save As dialog box appears to help you save your file. The Windows 95 implementation of Java displays a dialog box, as shown in Figure 18.11. If you are using Java on another operating system, the dialog box will look different.

FIGURE 18.11.
Saving text to a file.

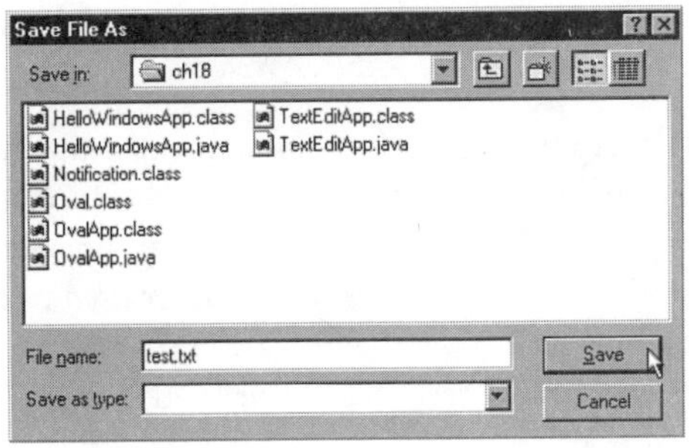

After you have saved your file, select New from the File menu. A new text-editing buffer is displayed. Having cleared the buffer, select Open from the File menu and open the `test.txt` file that you just saved. (See Figure 18.12.) This file will be read in and loaded into the text-editing buffer.

FIGURE 18.12.
Opening a file.

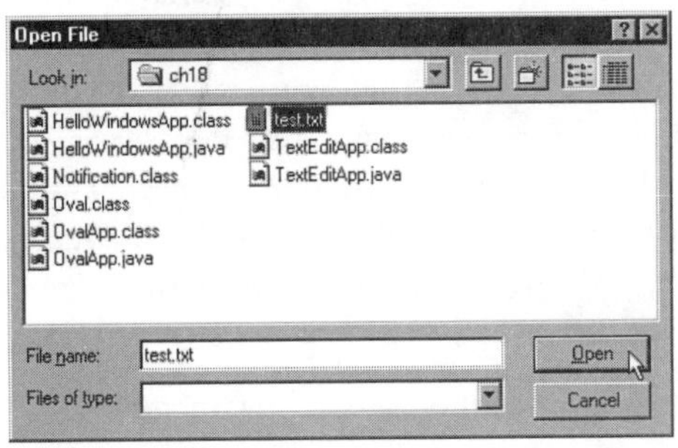

If this seems like a lot of functionality for two pages of code, you're right. Java does most of the work for you. You just need to invoke the correct methods for the `java.awt` API classes.

Let's explore the `TextEditApp` program to see how it works. You'll first notice that it imports the classes of the `java.awt` and `java.io` classes. The `java.awt` package provides the required window classes, and the `java.io` package provides needed file I/O classes.

`TextEditApp` follows the lead of the other window programs developed earlier in this chapter and subclasses the `Frame` class. It declares four field variables: `text`, `menuBar`, `openFile`, and `saveFile`. The text variable is of class `TextArea`. It holds the object that implements the functionality of the text-editing buffer. The `menuBar` variable sets up the File menu. The `openFile` and `saveFile` variables support the file dialog boxes shown in Figures 18.11 and 18.12.

The main() method simply creates an object of TextEditApp. The TextEditApp constructor sets the window title using the constructor of the Frame class and then invokes its setup() method to set up all the objects in the TextEditApp window. The resize() method is called to size the application window based on the minimum size required to implement the TextArea object assigned to text. The pack() and show() methods complete the TextEditApp window setup and display.

The setup() method sets the font to be used in the TextArea object, changes the window's background color, and then sets up the TextArea object, the menu bar, and the file dialog boxes. The setFont() method sets the current font to a newly constructed font. It is inherited from the Component class. The Font class constructor used to create the new font uses the font name (System), text type (PLAIN), and point size (12) of the font as parameters. The Font class defines a number of font parameters that can be used in constructing new font variations.

The setBackground() method sets the background color to white. It is inherited from the Component class. The Color class provides a number of predefined color constants. The text variable is assigned an object of class TextArea that is at least 25 rows by 80 columns. This object implements most of the text-editing capabilities of TextEditApp. It is then added to the center of the TextEditApp window. The setupMenuBar() method is called to set up the File menu.

The openFile and saveFile FileDialog variables are assigned newly created FileDialog objects. The FileDialog constructor takes three arguments. The first is the window that "owns" the dialog box. This is the window to which the file dialog box is attached. The window is attached to the TextEditApp object created by the main() method, so the this argument is supplied to identify the current TextEditApp object. The second parameter is the text string to be displayed at the top of the dialog box. Refer to Figures 18.11 and 18.12 to see how the text string is displayed. The third parameter is either the FileDialog.LOAD or the FileDialog.SAVE constant, indicating whether a file is to be loaded from disk or saved to disk.

The setupMenuBar() method shows how menu bars are created and added to a window. The menuBar variable is assigned an object of class MenuBar. A Menu object is created with the File label and assigned to the fileMenu variable. Menu items and separators are then added to the menu. A Menu object represents a single pull-down menu. A MenuItem object is a pull-down menu selection. A MenuBar object is a collection of Menu objects that is attached to a window.

The MenuItem objects are assigned a label when they are created. They are added to the fileMenu in a top-down fashion. The addSeparator() method is used to add a separator line to a menu. Refer to Figure 18.10 to see how the resulting File menu is displayed. The fileMenu is added to the menuBar object using the add() method of the MenuBar class. The resulting menu bar is added to the TextEditApp window using the setMenuBar() method inherited from the Frame class.

At this point you might have noticed that the TextEditApp class has no paint() method. The TextArea object takes care of drawing itself and does not require an external paint() method. TextArea is a remarkably self-contained and easy-to-use class. Without TextArea, implementing TextEditApp would be considerably more difficult.

The handleEvent() method handles more events than in previous examples. It handles the WINDOW_DESTROY event in the usual manner. This editor is just a prototype—a complete text editor would prompt the user to save any changes before terminating the application. All other events processed are of type ACTION_EVENT and have as their target objects of class MenuItem. In other words, these events process selections from the File menu. MenuItem objects are distinguished by their labels as supplied to the arg variable of an event.

The handling of the New menu item invokes the setText() method of the TextArea class to delete all text in the text variable. The handling of the Open menu item invokes the show() method for the openFile FileDialog, causing the dialog box to be displayed. The getFile() method is invoked to get the name of the file selected for opening by the user. The returned string is then passed to the readFile() method of TextEditApp. The handling of the Save As menu item is similar to that of the Open menu item. The saveFile FileDialog is displayed. A filename is returned and then passed to the writeFile() method of the TextEditApp class. The Exit menu item is handled in the same way as the WINDOW_DESTROY event. Again, a complete editor would prompt the user to save changes before exiting.

The readFile() method reads the file whose name was retrieved via the openFile FileDialog. It first opens the file by creating a new FileInputStream object using the filename and then filtering this stream as a DataInputStream object. The resulting input stream is then assigned to the inStream variable. The try statement has a catch clause that checks for the occurrence of an IOException. If an exception occurs, the notifyDialog is used to warn the user. It displays a dialog box as shown in Figure 18.13. You can cause this dialog box to be generated by trying to open a non-existent file. Try it!

FIGURE 18.13.
The Notification dialog box.

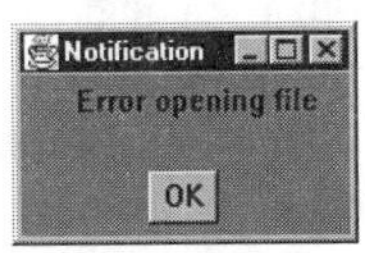

After the file has been opened, its text is read in a line at a time and appended to the newText variable. This results in the input being placed in one long string. The setText() method of the TextArea class is used to move the text into the TextArea object assigned to the text variable. Any I/O errors occurring while the file is being read result in the display of a notification dialog box with the Error reading file message.

The writeFile() method operates in a similar but reverse manner than the readFile() method. It uses the filename retrieved via the saveFile FileDialog to create a FileOutputStream object. It then filters this stream as a DataOutputStream and assigns it to the outStream variable. If any errors occur in the creation of these streams, a dialog box is displayed with the message Error opening file.

After opening the file, the writeBytes() method of the DataOutputStream class is invoked to write the data stored in the TextArea object assigned to the text variable to the output stream.

The `close()` method is then invoked to close the output stream. Any write errors result in the display of an error-notification dialog box.

The `notifyDialog()` method supports the generation and display of dialog boxes by creating new instances of the `Notification` class and passing them the error message. It then invokes their `show()` method to display them.

The `Notification` class actually implements the dialog boxes that are displayed when an error occurs by extending the `Dialog` class. The `Dialog` class, like the `Frame` class, extends the `Window` class. It provides a different set of methods to display dialog boxes as opposed to main application windows. It has one variable, `msg`, that stores the message to be displayed in the dialog box. Its constructor takes two arguments: the application window object to which it is attached and the message to be displayed. It invokes the `Dialog` class constructor using the superclass constructor call statement and passes it the `Frame` object, the string `"Notification"` to be used as the title of the dialog box, and the `true` `boolean` value, which determines whether the dialog box will be modal. A *modal* dialog box is one that must be closed before the user can return to the main application window. (Java currently does not implement this blocking feature of modal dialog boxes.) The constructor then saves the error message argument in the `msg` variable.

The `show()` method of the `Notification` class causes the dialog box to be displayed. It first creates an object of class `Label` with the contents of the `msg` variable being the text assigned to the `Label` object. The `Label.CENTER` constant is used to center the text in the `Label` object. The new label is then added to the North end of the dialog box. `Dialog` objects, like `Frame` objects, use a `BorderLayout` object by default. A `Panel` object is then created, and the OK button is created and added to the panel. The panel is added to the South end of the dialog box. The single button was placed in the panel to cause the button into be displayed in its default dimensions. Instead of the button being stretched to fit the dialog box, the panel in which the button resides is stretched. To see this, try directly inserting the button to the dialog box without using a panel. The background color of the dialog box is set to gray using the `setBackground()` method inherited from the `Component` class and the `Color` class constants. The window is resized to 160×100 pixels and then displayed using the `show()` method of the `Dialog` class. The `super` keyword is used to indicate that the `show()` method of the superclass (`Dialog`) should be used instead of the `show()` method of the current class (`Notification`).

The `Notification` class handles its own events by overriding the `handleEvent()` method. The `WINDOW_DESTROY` event is generated for a dialog box when the user tries to directly close the dialog box without using any of the dialog box buttons. This event is different from the event generated for the main application window. The `Notification` event handler handles the `WINDOW_DESTROY` event by invoking the `dispose()` method inherited from the `Window` class. The `dispose()` method causes the dialog window to be closed and its resources to be returned to the system. The `handleEvent()` method handles the OK button click by looking for an event with an `id` set to `ACTION_EVENT`, checking its target to make sure that it is an instance of the `Button` class and checking its `arg` variable to make sure that it is the OK button. It then invokes the `dispose()` method to close the dialog box.

Summary

This chapter introduces you to window programming by way of several sample programs that illustrate the classes and methods used to implement simple window applications. You should now be comfortable with analyzing window-based programs. Subsequent chapters fill in the details of the classes and methods introduced here. They will help you to become proficient in developing your own window programs. Chapter 19 lays the framework for developing window programs by expanding on the basics introduced here.

19

Organizing Window Programs

This chapter covers the basics of writing window programs. It shows you how window programs are structured and organized and identifies the basic approach to designing most window programs. It covers the details of the `Frame` class and explains how windows are opened and closed. The five basic window layouts are introduced and illustrated through a sample program. The finer points of window event handling are then described. Finally, a window program is created that introduces the most common window GUI controls. When you finish this chapter, you will have had a broad introduction to window programming and will be familiar with most of the common window GUI controls.

Designing Window Programs

The design of most window programs usually involves two basic steps: laying out the program's graphical user interface and providing the functionality that implements the interface.

The first step addresses one of the most important features of window programs—its look and feel. Window programs are preferred to console programs when their look and feel are interesting, innovative, and help the user to accomplish a particular purpose.

A program's look is determined by how it presents itself to users. It consists of all those characteristics that determine its appearance, such as window size, layout, background and foreground colors, menus, and GUI controls. A program's feel is determined by the availability of easy-to-use GUI controls and the contribution of these controls to the program's ultimate intended use. It is the result of the designer's ability to select and implement those GUI controls that enhance a program's capability to satisfy user expectations.

The window's GUI design begins by creating an application window, using the `Frame` class, and determining the basic characteristics of the window such as its size, title, background and foreground colors, and general layout. Next a menu bar is added to the window, and the program's menus and menu items are added to the menu bar. The GUI controls that are to be used in the window are determined, designed, and attached to the window's panels and frame.

At this point, you know what your program will look like and you can concentrate on what it will do. The first step in bringing your program's user interface to life is to add the event-handling software required to respond to events generated as the result of user interaction. The event-handling software will not immediately implement all user actions, but it should respond to them and provide hooks for eventual implementation of all user interface actions. The event-handling software is then fleshed out to provide all the functionality required of the application program. The program's design and implementation reaches an *Alpha stage* when all required user-interface functions have been implemented.

The next stage of program development is to refine and test the program to make it more responsive to its intended purpose. A series of Beta versions of the program are developed that implement user feedback and fix any identified errors or deficiencies. Finally, the program is refined to handle unusual user inputs and to process errors and exceptions.

Figure 19.1 provides an overview of the process of designing and implementing window programs. This chapter covers the basics of creating and organizing window programs and shows how to connect event-handling code to general window components. A window sampler program is provided that illustrates the basic use of common window GUI controls. Subsequent chapters explore the use of these GUI controls in more detail.

FIGURE 19.1.
The process for window design and implementation.

Lay out the program's graphical user interface.

- Create a frame and specify its characteristics.
- Determine the frame's layout.
- Add a menu bar.
- Add panels and GUI components.

Add the functionality that implements the interface.

- Add event-handling software.
- Provide hooks for handling all user interface actions.
- Flesh out event-handling software.
- Refine and test software functions.
- Handle errors and exceptions.
- Respond to user feedback.

Opening and Closing Windows

Opening and closing windows mark the beginning and end of any window program. The `Frame` class provides the basis by which these fundamental window operations are accomplished. A `Frame` object implements an application main window, inheriting many methods that enable it to do so from the `Window`, `Container`, and `Component` classes.

To open an application window, a `Frame` object is created and its `show()` method is invoked. The `show()` method is inherited from the `Window` class. To close an application window, the `WINDOW_DESTROY` event must be handled. The window is disposed of using the `dispose()` method of the `Window` class, or more commonly by invoking the `System.exit()` method after performing any necessary program-termination processing.

The `Frame` class and its ancestors provide a number of methods that control the way in which a window is displayed. The `setBackground()` and `setForeground()` methods inherited from the `Component` class are used to specify a window's background and foreground colors. The `setFont()` method, also inherited from `Component`, is used to specify the default font to be used with a window. The `Frame` class, itself, provides a number of methods that control a window's appearance. The `setTitle()` method allows a window's title to be changed. The `setCursor()` method allows the cursor to be changed while it is in the window's focus. The `setMenuBar()` method enables a menu bar to be attached to a window, and the `setResizable()` method toggles whether a window can or cannot be resized. The `setIconImage()` method allows the window's minimized icon to be changed. This method is not supported by all Java implementations and therefore should be avoided if compatibility is a concern.

The `FrameApp` program shown in Listing 19.1 illustrates the window concepts covered so far and shows the effect of using the basic window controls identified in the previous paragraph.

Listing 19.1. The source code of the `FrameApp` program.

```
import java.awt.*;

public class FrameApp extends Frame {
 String defaultTitle;
 MenuBar defaultMenuBar;
 MenuBar alternativeMenuBar;
 int cursors[] = {CROSSHAIR_CURSOR,DEFAULT_CURSOR,E_RESIZE_CURSOR,HAND_CURSOR,
  MOVE_CURSOR,NE_RESIZE_CURSOR,NW_RESIZE_CURSOR,N_RESIZE_CURSOR,
  SE_RESIZE_CURSOR,SW_RESIZE_CURSOR,S_RESIZE_CURSOR,TEXT_CURSOR,
  WAIT_CURSOR,W_RESIZE_CURSOR};
 Color colors[] = {Color.black,Color.blue,Color.cyan,Color.darkGray,Color.gray,
  Color.green,Color.lightGray,Color.magenta,Color.orange,Color.pink,Color.red,
  Color.white,Color.yellow};
 String fontNames[] = {"Helvetica","TimesRoman","Courier","Dialog",
  "DialogInput","ZapfDingbats"};
 int cursorIndex = 1;
 int backgroundColorIndex = 0;
 int foregroundColorIndex = 0;
 int fontIndex = 0;
 public static void main(String args[]){
  FrameApp app = new FrameApp();
 }
 public FrameApp() {
  super("Exploring Frames");
  defaultTitle = getTitle();
  setup();
  pack();
  resize(400,400);
  show();
 }
 void setup() {
  setupPanels();
```

```
 setupMenuBars();
 setFont(new Font(fontNames[fontIndex],Font.PLAIN,14));
}
void setupPanels() {
 Panel mainPanel = new Panel();
 mainPanel.setLayout(new GridLayout(4,1));
 Label label1 =
  new Label("Change these windows characteristics:",Label.CENTER);
 mainPanel.add(label1);
 Panel panel1 = new Panel();
 panel1.add(new Button("Title"));
 panel1.add(new Button("Menu Bar"));
 panel1.add(new Button("Resizable"));
 mainPanel.add(panel1);
 Label label2 = new Label("Check out these windows options:",Label.CENTER);
 mainPanel.add(label2);
 Panel panel2 = new Panel();
 panel2.add(new Button("Cursor"));
 panel2.add(new Button("Background"));
 panel2.add(new Button("Foreground"));
 panel2.add(new Button("Font"));
 mainPanel.add(panel2);
 add("South",mainPanel);
}
void setupMenuBars() {
 defaultMenuBar = new MenuBar();
 Menu fileMenu = new Menu("File");
 fileMenu.add(new MenuItem("Exit"));
 defaultMenuBar.add(fileMenu);
 setMenuBar(defaultMenuBar);
 alternativeMenuBar = new MenuBar();
 Menu otherMenu = new Menu("Program");
 otherMenu.add(new MenuItem("Quit"));
 alternativeMenuBar.add(otherMenu);
}
public void paint(Graphics g) {
 g.drawString("Sample Text",160,100);
}
public boolean handleEvent(Event event) {
 if(event.id==Event.WINDOW_DESTROY){
  System.exit(0);
  return true;
 }else if(event.id==Event.ACTION_EVENT){
  if(event.target instanceof Button){
   if("Title".equals(event.arg)){
    if(defaultTitle.equals(getTitle()))
     setTitle("Here's an alternative title.");
    else setTitle(defaultTitle);
    return true;
   }else if("Menu Bar".equals(event.arg)){
    if(defaultMenuBar.equals(getMenuBar()))
     setMenuBar(alternativeMenuBar);
    else setMenuBar(defaultMenuBar);
    return true;
   }else if("Resizable".equals(event.arg)){
    setResizable(!isResizable());
    return true;
```

continues

Listing 19.1. continued

```
    }else if("Cursor".equals(event.arg)){
     ++cursorIndex;
     cursorIndex %= cursors.length;
     setCursor(cursors[cursorIndex]);
     return true;
    }else if("Background".equals(event.arg)){
     ++backgroundColorIndex;
     backgroundColorIndex %= colors.length;
     setBackground(colors[backgroundColorIndex]);
     repaint();
     return true;
    }else if("Foreground".equals(event.arg)){
     ++foregroundColorIndex;
     foregroundColorIndex %= colors.length;
     setForeground(colors[foregroundColorIndex]);
     repaint();
     return true;
    }else if("Font".equals(event.arg)){
     ++fontIndex;
     fontIndex %= fontNames.length;
     setFont(new Font(fontNames[fontIndex],Font.PLAIN,14));
     repaint();
     return true;
    }
   }else if(event.target instanceof MenuItem){
    if("Exit".equals(event.arg) || "Quit".equals(event.arg)){
     System.exit(0);
     return true;
    }
   }
  }
  return false;
 }
}
```

After you have compiled `FrameApp`, run it and check out the buttons and menus it provides. When you first launch `FrameApp`, it displays the text `Sample Text` followed by two rows of buttons, as shown in Figure 19.2. The buttons in the first row provide the capability to change the window's title, menu bar, and resizable properties. These buttons are *toggles*—the second time you click a button, the window's characteristic being changed is reverted to its initial default value. The buttons in the second row allow you to step through a sequence of values for the window's cursor, background and foreground colors, and text font. If you are using Windows 95, you will find that it does not support all cursors defined by Java. You will find out which cursors are not supported when you analyze this program's code.

Let's investigate each of the program's features. Click on the Title button and you will notice that the window's title text is changed from `Exploring Frames` to `Here's an alternative title.`, as shown in Figure 19.3. Click on the button a second time and the title changes back to `Exploring Frames`.

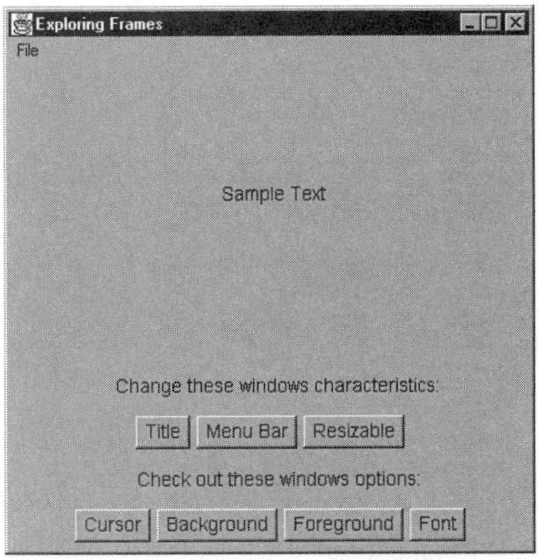

FIGURE 19.2.
The `FrameApp` *initial display.*

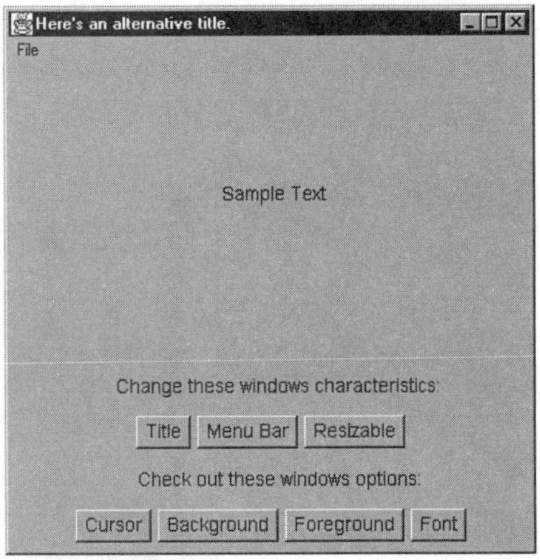

FIGURE 19.3.
Here's an alternative title.

Click on the File menu, but don't select the Exit option. The File menu is replaced by the Program menu, shown in Figure 19.4, when you click on the Menu Bar button. Adding, deleting, and modifying menus are common operations for many window programs.

You will notice that your program window is initially resizable. This means that you can use the cursor at the window's edge to make the window larger or smaller. The cursor changes from a pointer to a resizable icon to let you know that the window can be resized. If you click on the Resizable button, the window is no longer capable of being resized. You can check this by placing your cursor at the window's boundary.

Click on the Cursor button to change the cursor associated with your program's window. Step through the list of available cursors until you reach the crosshair cursor. Then click the cursor button one more time to return to the default cursor.

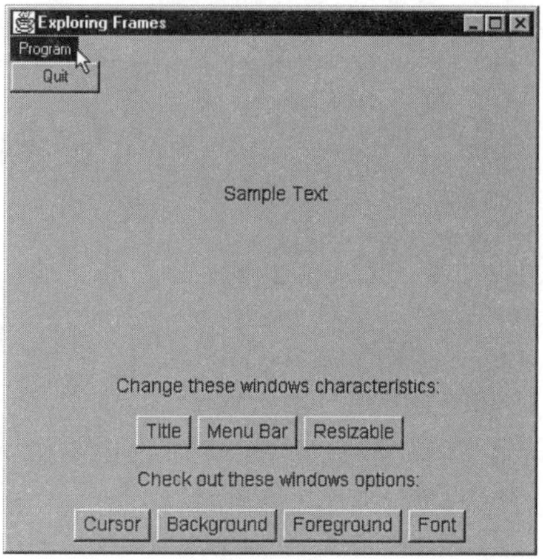

FIGURE 19.4.
The Program menu.

Click the Background button and the program's background color is changed to blue, as shown in Figure 19.5. You can continue to click the Background button to look at other background colors. Notice that the color does not change in the panel used by the program's buttons. Now try clicking on the Foreground button a few times to change the window's foreground color.

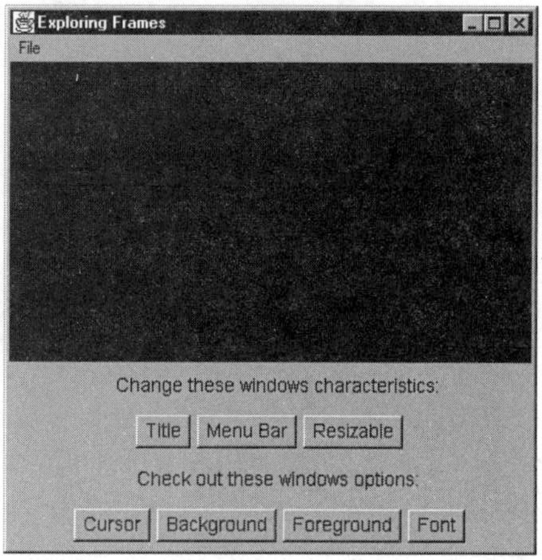

FIGURE 19.5.
Changing the window background.

The Font button allows you to change the font used with the sample text display as shown in Figure 19.6. Cycle through the list of fonts. The last font in the list is the ZapfDingbats font. It is used to display special characters and symbols, as shown in Figure 19.6.

You have covered the program's features. Now let's look at its code to see how it works.

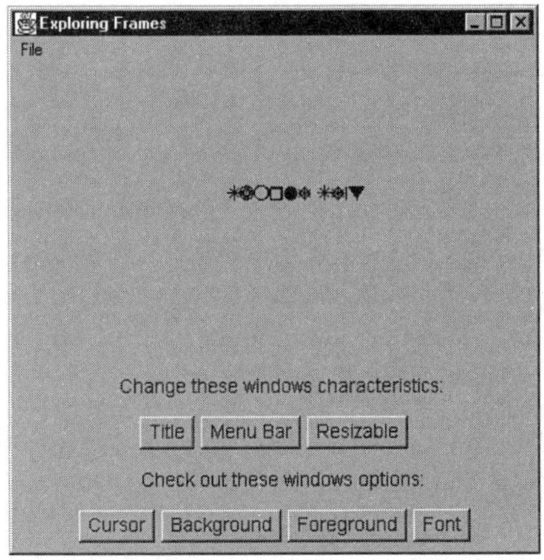

FIGURE 19.6.
ZapfDingbats characters.

The `FrameApp` class defines a number of variables. The `defaultTitle` variable is used to store the default window title so that it can be restored after it has been changed. The `defaultMenuBar` and `alternativeMenuBar` variables are used to store the File and Program menu bars. The `cursors[]` array stores the cursor constants that are defined for the `Frame` class. These constants are stored in an array to make it easier to cycle through them. The `cursorIndex` variable maintains an index to the current cursor being displayed.

The `colors[]` array stores a subset of the colors defined by the `Color` class. These colors are used when the background and foreground colors are changed. The `backgroundColorIndex` and `foregroundColorIndex` variables are used to keep track of the current background and foreground colors.

The `fontNames[]` array stores the names of the fonts known to Java. The `fontIndex` variable is used to point to the current window font.

`FrameApp` has a simple standard `main()` method that creates a new `FrameApp` object. The `FrameApp` constructor invokes the superclass constructor call statement to set the window's title and then uses the `getTitle()` method inherited from `Frame` to store the title in the `defaultTitle` variable. It then invokes the `setup()` method to set up panels, buttons, menu bars, and the default window font. The `pack()` method and the `resize()` methods are used to organize the components of the window and adjust it to the desired size. The `show()` method then causes the window to be opened and displayed.

The `setup()` method invokes the `setupPanels()` and `setupMenuBars()` methods to set up the program's panels, buttons, and menu bars. It invokes the `setFont()` method inherited from the `Component` class to set the default font to be used with the window. The `setFont()` method takes three arguments: the name of the font, the font style, and the size of the font in points. The font names are stored in the `fontNames[]` array. The font style constants are defined in the `Font` class.

The `setupPanels()` method constructs a `Panel` object named `mainPanel` that is to hold the subpanels corresponding to the rows of buttons. The layout of the `mainPanel` is set to a `GridLayout` object of four rows and one column. Layouts are used to specify how objects are to be placed in a container. They are covered in the "Using Layouts" section in this chapter.

A new `Label` object is created with the text `Change these windows characteristics:` and added to the `mainPanel`. The `Label.CENTER` constant specifies how the label should be aligned within its available space. A `Panel` object named `panel1` is created to hold the Title, Menu Bar, and Resizable buttons that are subsequently created and added to the panel. The `panel1` object is then added to the `mainPanel`.

A second `Label` object named `label2` is created to hold the text `Check out these windows options:`. The label is then added to the `mainPanel`. A second `Panel` object named `panel2` is created. The Cursor, Background, Foreground, and Font buttons are then added to `panel2`. The `panel2` object is then added to the `mainPanel`. The `mainPanel` is then added to the southern (bottom) region of the `FrameApp` object being constructed. The "Using Layouts" section in this chapter describes why the `FrameApp` object was organized with a `mainPanel` and two subpanels.

The `setupMenuBars()` method creates a new `MenuBar` object and assigns it to the `defaultMenuBar` variable. It declares the `fileMenu` variable and assigns it a new `Menu` object with the File label. It creates a `MenuItem` object with the Exit label and adds it to the `fileMenu`. The `defaultMenuBar` is then set as the menu bar of the `FrameApp` object being constructed via the `setMenuBar()` method of the `Frame` class. Menus are covered in Chapter 20, "Menus, Buttons, and Dialog Boxes." For now, just remember that a `Frame` has a `MenuBar` that consists of one or more `Menus` that each have one or more `MenuItems`.

The `alternativeMenuBar` is constructed in the same manner as the `defaultMenuBar` except that it contains an `otherMenu` with the File and Exit labels replaced by Program and Quit labels.

The `alternativeMenuBar` is not set to the `FrameApp` using the `setMenuBar()` method. A `Frame` object can have only one menu bar.

The `paint()` method is used to initially draw the window display and then to update it as the result of window operations. It simply displays the text `Sample Text` at pixel location (160,100) within the window `Graphics` object.

The `handleEvent()` method is the last method to be covered. It is responsible for handling all of the user-generated events and provides most of the program's functionality. The `handleEvent()` method handles the `WINDOWS_DESTROY` event by invoking the `System.exit()` method to terminate the program's execution. It also handles the `Button` and `MenuItem` action events. The Exit and Quit menu items also result in the program's execution being terminated.

When the Title button is clicked, `handleEvent()` uses the `getTitle()` method to determine whether the current window title equals the title stored in `defaultTitle`. If they are equal, the window's title is set to Here's an alternative title. If the current title differs from the value stored in `defaultTitle`, the window's title is set using `defaultTitle`.

When the Menu Bar button is clicked, `handleEvent()` uses the `getMenuBar()` method to check whether the window's current menu bar is the same as the value of `defaultMenuBar`. If they are the same, the window's menu bar is set to the value of `alternativeMenuBar`. If they are different, the window's menu bar is set to the value of `defaultMenuBar`.

When the Resizable button is clicked, `handleEvent()` uses the `isResizable()` method to determine whether the window is currently resizable and then sets it to the opposite value.

When the Cursor button is clicked, `handleEvent()` cycles the `cursorIndex` to the next cursor value within the `cursors[]` array and sets the cursor to this value using the `setCursor()` method.

When the Background button is clicked, `handleEvent()` cycles the `backgroundIndex` variable to the next color value within the `color[]` array and sets the background to this value using the `setBackground()` method. It then invokes the `repaint()` method of the `Component` class to cause the screen to be repainted. The Foreground button is handled in a similar manner.

When the Font button is clicked, `handleEvent()` cycles the `fontIndex` to the next font name and creates a new 14-point plain font of that type. It then invokes the `setFont()` method of the `Component` class to change the current font. The `repaint()` method is used to cause the screen to be repainted.

Using Layouts

The `FrameApp` program uses a number of panels and layouts to organize the way that labels and buttons are presented in the application window. The organization of any object that is a subclass of the `Container` class is governed by a layout. The layout determines how objects of class `Component` are positioned when they are added via the `add()` method to the `Container` object. Five types of layouts are provided by Java: `BorderLayout`, `CardLayout`, `FlowLayout`, `GridLayout`, and `GridBagLayout`. Other, custom layouts can also be defined.

The `BorderLayout` class is the default layout used by `Frame` objects. An object of the `Component` class is added to either the North, South, East, West, or Center of the component, as shown in Figure 19.7.

In the `FrameApp` program, the `mainPanel` was added to the South region of the window. The remainder of the program window was used by the program's default `Graphics` object, which was placed in the North region of the window. No `Component` objects were added to the East, West, or Center regions.

The `FlowLayout` class is the default layout used for `Panel` objects. If a container uses a `FlowLayout`, the container is filled left to right from top to bottom. An example of this layout is the two rows of buttons that were added to `panel1` and `panel2`. The `FlowLayout` class causes each component to be centered in its container, by default.

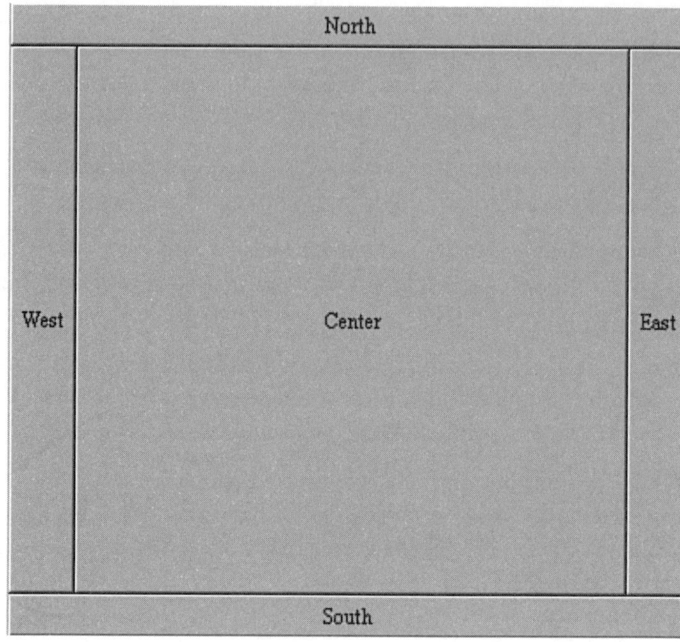

FIGURE 19.7.
A `BorderLayout` *example.*

The `GridLayout` class organizes a container as a grid of *n* rows and *m* columns. Each grid cell is the same size, as shown in Figure 19.8.

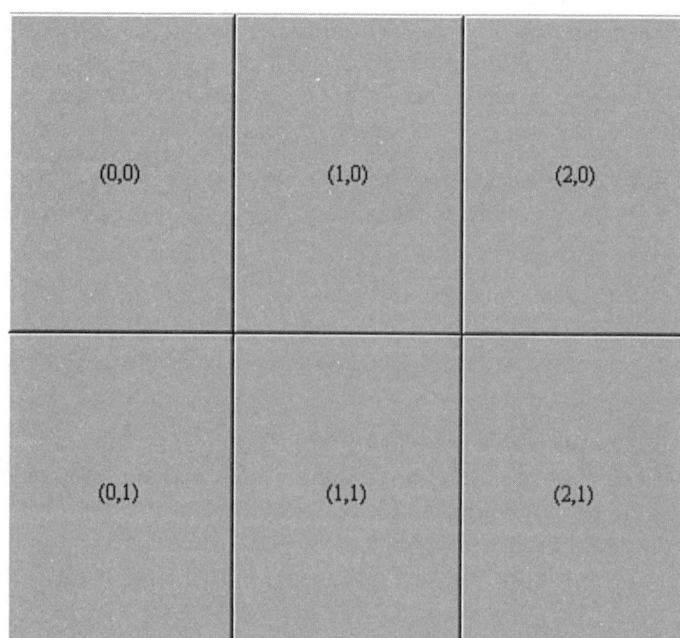

FIGURE 19.8.
A `GridLayout` *example.*

The `GridLayout` class is used with the `mainPanel` in the `FrameApp` program. A grid of four rows and one column is used to stack `panel1` and `panel2` with the two labels to produce the display shown in Figure 19.2.

The `CardLayout` class organizes a container like a deck of cards. The first component in the container is initially displayed. Other components are then displayed using the `next()`, `previous()`, `first()`, `last()`, and `show()` methods of the `CardLayout` class. The `CardLayout` class is illustrated in Listing 19.2.

The `GridBagLayout` class is the most complex and flexible of the layout classes. It is similar to the `GridLayout` class in that it organizes its components in a grid, but it is more flexible because it allows the rows and columns to have different sizes. In addition, components are allowed to span multiple rows and columns. The positioning of each component is controlled by the use of objects of class `GridBagConstraints`. The `GridBagConstraints` objects identify the preferred size of each component and specify constraints on how they should be laid out. You should refer to the API documentation for the `GridBagLayout` and `GridBagConstraints` classes to read the detailed description of the variables and methods of these classes. The `GridBagLayout` class is also demonstrated in the `LayoutApp` program in Listing 19.2.

The `LayoutApp` program illustrates the use of each of the five predefined Java layouts. These layouts position buttons within panels to show how the various layouts are organized and displayed. A `Panel` pull-down menu is used to switch to each of the layout classes.

Listing 19.2. The source code of the `LayoutApp` program.

```
import java.awt.*;

public class LayoutApp extends Frame {
 MenuBar menuBar;
 Panel panels[];
 Panel currentPanel;
 static int border=0;
 static int card=1;
 static int flow=2;
 static int grid=3;
 static int gridBag=4;
 Menu cardMenu;
 public static void main(String args[]){
  LayoutApp app = new LayoutApp();
 }
 public LayoutApp() {
  super("BorderLayout");
  setup();
  pack();
  resize(400,400);
  show();
 }
 void setup() {
  setupMenuBar();
```

continues

Listing 19.2. continued

```
  setupPanels();
 }
 void setupMenuBar() {
  menuBar = new MenuBar();
  Menu fileMenu = new Menu("File");
  fileMenu.add(new MenuItem("Exit"));
  menuBar.add(fileMenu);
  Menu panelMenu = new Menu("Panel");
  panelMenu.add(new MenuItem("BorderLayout"));
  panelMenu.add(new MenuItem("CardLayout"));
  panelMenu.add(new MenuItem("FlowLayout"));
  panelMenu.add(new MenuItem("GridLayout"));
  panelMenu.add(new MenuItem("GridBagLayout"));
  menuBar.add(panelMenu);
  cardMenu = new Menu("Card");
  cardMenu.add(new MenuItem("First"));
  cardMenu.add(new MenuItem("Last"));
  cardMenu.add(new MenuItem("Next"));
  cardMenu.add(new MenuItem("Previous"));
  setMenuBar(menuBar);
 }
 void setupPanels() {
  panels = new Panel[5];
  for(int i=0;i<5;++i) panels[i]=new Panel();
  panels[border].setLayout(new BorderLayout());
  panels[card].setLayout(new CardLayout());
  panels[flow].setLayout(new FlowLayout());
  panels[grid].setLayout(new GridLayout(2,3));
  GridBagLayout gridBagLayout = new GridBagLayout();
  panels[gridBag].setLayout(gridBagLayout);
  panels[border].add("North",new Button("North"));
  panels[border].add("South",new Button("South"));
  panels[border].add("East",new Button("East"));
  panels[border].add("West",new Button("West"));
  panels[border].add("Center",new Button("Center"));
  String cardButtons[] = {"First","Second","Third","Fourth","Last"};
  String flowButtons[] = {"One","Two","Three","Four","Five"};
  String gridButtons[] = {"(0,0)","(1,0)","(2,0)","(0,1)","(1,1)","(2,1)"};
  for(int i=0;i<cardButtons.length;++i)
   panels[card].add(new Button(cardButtons[i]));
  for(int i=0;i<flowButtons.length;++i)
   panels[flow].add(new Button(flowButtons[i]));
  for(int i=0;i<gridButtons.length;++i)
   panels[grid].add(new Button(gridButtons[i]));
  Button gridBagButtons[] = new Button[9];
  for(int i=0;i<9;++i) gridBagButtons[i] = new Button("Button"+i);
  int gridx[] = {0,1,2,0,2,0,1,1,0};
  int gridy[] = {0,0,0,1,1,2,2,3,4};
  int gridwidth[] = {1,1,1,2,1,1,1,2,3};
  int gridheight[] = {1,1,1,1,2,2,1,1,1};
  GridBagConstraints gridBagConstraints[] = new GridBagConstraints[9];
  for(int i=0;i<9;++i) {
   gridBagConstraints[i] = new GridBagConstraints();
   gridBagConstraints[i].fill=GridBagConstraints.BOTH;
   gridBagConstraints[i].gridx=gridx[i];
   gridBagConstraints[i].gridy=gridy[i];
```

```
   gridBagConstraints[i].gridwidth=gridwidth[i];
   gridBagConstraints[i].gridheight=gridheight[i];
   gridBagLayout.setConstraints(gridBagButtons[i],gridBagConstraints[i]);
   panels[gridBag].add(gridBagButtons[i]);
  }
  add("Center",panels[border]);
  currentPanel=panels[border];
 }
 public boolean handleEvent(Event event) {
  if(event.id==Event.WINDOW_DESTROY){
   System.exit(0);
   return true;
  }else if(event.id==Event.ACTION_EVENT){
   if(event.target instanceof MenuItem){
    if("Exit".equals(event.arg)){
     System.exit(0);
     return true;
    }else if("BorderLayout".equals(event.arg)){
     switchPanels(panels[border],"BorderLayout",false);
     return true;
    }else if("CardLayout".equals(event.arg)){
     switchPanels(panels[card],"CardLayout",true);
     return true;
    }else if("FlowLayout".equals(event.arg)){
     switchPanels(panels[flow],"FlowLayout",false);
     return true;
    }else if("GridLayout".equals(event.arg)){
     switchPanels(panels[grid],"GridLayout",false);
     return true;
    }else if("GridBagLayout".equals(event.arg)){
     switchPanels(panels[gridBag],"GridBagLayout",false);
     return true;
    }else if("First".equals(event.arg)){
     CardLayout currentLayout=(CardLayout)currentPanel.getLayout();
     currentLayout.first(currentPanel);
     return true;
    }else if("Last".equals(event.arg)){
     CardLayout currentLayout=(CardLayout)currentPanel.getLayout();
     currentLayout.last(currentPanel);
     return true;
    }else if("Next".equals(event.arg)){
     CardLayout currentLayout=(CardLayout)currentPanel.getLayout();
     currentLayout.next(currentPanel);
     return true;
    }else if("Previous".equals(event.arg)){
     CardLayout currentLayout=(CardLayout)currentPanel.getLayout();
     currentLayout.previous(currentPanel);
     return true;
    }
   }
  }
  return false;
 }
 void switchPanels(Panel newPanel,String newTitle,boolean setCardMenu) {
  remove(currentPanel);
  currentPanel=newPanel;
```

continues

Listing 19.2. continued

```
  add("Center",currentPanel);
  setTitle(newTitle);
  if(setCardMenu) menuBar.add(cardMenu);
  else menuBar.remove(cardMenu);
  show();
 }
}
```

When you compile and run `LayoutApp`, the opening window should look like the one shown in Figure 19.9.

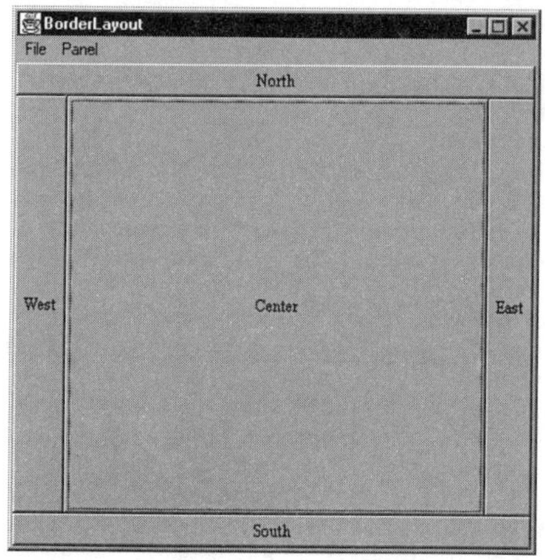

FIGURE 19.9.
The opening window of the `LayoutApp` *program.*

The opening window illustrates the use of the `BorderLayout` class by displaying a panel that uses the `BorderLayout`. Notice that the window's title is BorderLayout. The title is updated when a new layout class is displayed. To switch layouts, use the Panel pull-down menu as shown in Figure 19.10.

Select the CardLayout menu item from the Panel menu. The window displays a panel that uses a `CardLayout` object, and the window's title is updated to identify the new layout. An additional Card pull-down menu is added to the menu bar so that the different button components in the `CardLayout` object can be displayed. (See Figure 19.11.) There are five buttons, labeled First, Second, Third, Fourth, and Last. Use the Next menu item of the Card menu to step through these buttons. After you have reached the button labeled Last, use the Previous menu item to step back through the list of buttons. Next, try using the First and Last menu items to go to the first and last buttons in the panel governed by the `CardLayout` object.

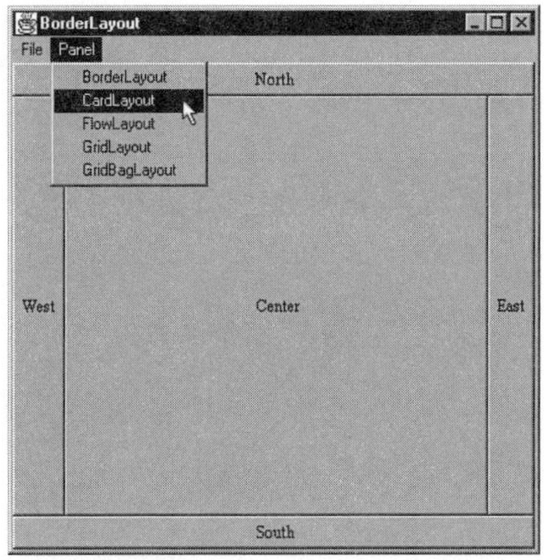

FIGURE 19.10.
The Panel menu.

FIGURE 19.11.
A `CardLayout` *example.*

Select the FlowLayout menu item from the Panel menu. The window displays five buttons, labeled One through Five, across the top of the window as shown in Figure 19.12. The Card pull-down menu is removed and the window's title is changed to FlowLayout.

Select the GridLayout menu item from the Panel menu. The window displays six buttons in a rectangular grid that is two rows by three columns, with each button labeled with its x,y-coordinate, as shown in Figure 19.13. The window's title is changed to GridLayout.

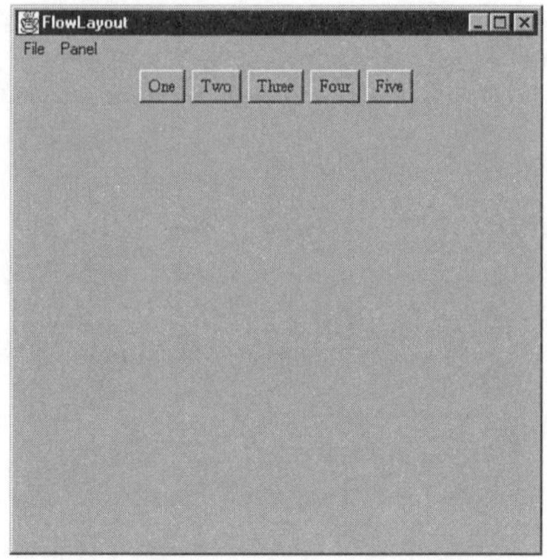

FIGURE 19.12.
A `FlowLayout` *example.*

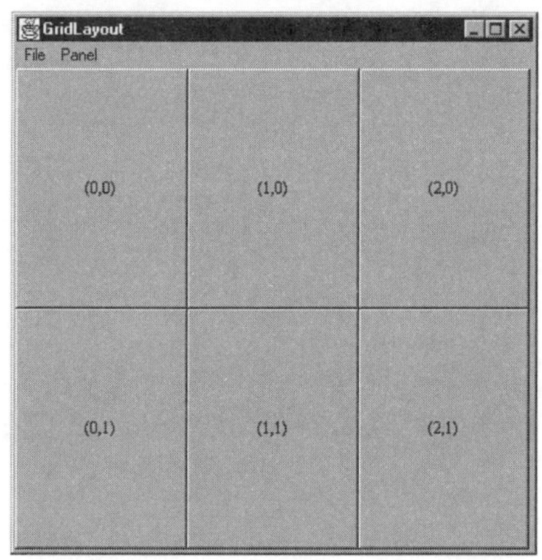

FIGURE 19.13.
A `GridLayout` *example.*

Select the GridBagLayout menu item from the Panel menu. The window displays nine buttons arranged in a free-form manner in a rectangular grid, five rows by three columns, as shown in Figure 19.14. The window's title is changed to GridBagLayout.

Now that you have an idea of what the `LayoutApp` program does, let's see how it works.

The `LayoutApp` class declares several variables and constants. The `menuBar` variable provides the program's menu bar. It is updated by different class methods when it is initially set up and displayed and when the Card menu is added and removed. The `cardMenu` variable is also declared. The `panels[]` array consists of five panels that illustrate the five predefined Java layouts. It is indexed by the `border`, `card`, `flow`, `grid`, and `gridBag` constants. The `currentPanel` variable is used to keep track of the current panel being displayed.

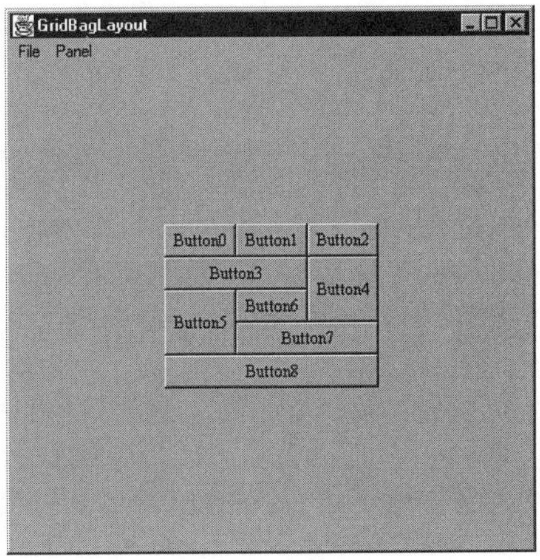

FIGURE 19.14.
A `GridBagLayout` *example.*

The `main()` function should seem to be pretty standard to you by now. It is typical of the `main()` function found in most window programs.

The `LayoutApp` class invokes the superclass constructor with the BorderLayout title. `BorderLayout` is the layout of the first panel to be displayed and is the default layout for `Frame` objects. The `setup()` method is invoked to set up the menu bar and panels used in the program. The rest of the `LayoutApp` constructor is fairly standard. The `pack()`, `resize()`, and `show()` methods are used to organize, resize, open, and display the `LayoutApp` main window.

The `setupMenuBar()` method creates a new menu bar and assigns it to the `menuBar` variable. A File menu is created with an Exit menu item and is then added to the object referenced by `menuBar`. A Panel menu is created and added to the `menuBar` in a similar fashion. The Panel menu is given buttons that identify each of the five layouts. A third Card menu is also created, but is not added to the `menuBar`. It is given the First, Last, Next, and Previous menu items. Finally, the object referenced by `menuBar` is set as the menu bar by invoking the `setMenuBar()` method of the `Frame` class.

The `setupPanels()` method is the most complicated method in this program. It is where all of the five different panels are created and laid out. First, the `panels[]` array is allocated and then five new `Panel` objects are assigned to the array's elements. Then each of the panels is laid out.

The `panels[border]` array element has its layout set to a `BorderLayout` object using the `setLayout()` method of the `Container` class. The `panels[card]` array element has its layout set to a `CardLayout` object. The `panels[flow]` array element has its layout set to a `FlowLayout` object. The `panels[grid]` array element has its layout set to a `GridLayout` object, two rows by three columns. The layout of the `panels[gridBag]` array element is separately created and assigned to the `gridBagLayout` variable. It is used later on when the panel is laid out with objects of class `GridBagConstraints`.

After each of the panels has had its layout set, buttons are added to illustrate how the individual layouts are displayed. The panels[border] panel is given five buttons, labeled North, South, East, West, and Center. These buttons are added to the positions identified by their labels. The buttons for the panels[card], panels[flow], and panels[grid] panels are added by first creating an array of labels for each panel and then using a for statement to step through the arrays, creating buttons and adding them to their respective panels. This approach greatly simplifies the process of creating buttons and adding them to panels.

The buttons for the panels[gridBag] panel are created a little differently by iterating from 0 through 8 and appending each number to the end of the "Button" string. The gridx[], gridy[], gridwidth[], and gridheight[] arrays are used to produce the objects of class GridBagConstraints that are used to lay out the buttons in the panels[gridBag] panel. The gridx[] array identifies the x-coordinate of each button within the 5-by-3 grid. The gridy[] array identifies the y-coordinate. The gridwidth[] array identifies button widths in terms of number of grid cells. The gridheight[] array identifies the height of each button in grid cells.

An array of GridBagConstraint objects is created and assigned to the gridBagConstraints variable. Each of the array's elements is then created and initialized using the gridx[], gridy[], gridwidth[], and gridheight[] arrays. The fill variable of each array element is set to the GridBagConstraints.BOTH constant, indicating that the buttons may grow both vertically and horizontally to fill the space assigned to them as the result of the way they are laid out. The setConstraints() method is used to associate each button with its gridBagConstraints[] element within the GridBagLayout object referenced by gridBagLayout. The last line in the for statement adds each button to the panels[gridBag] panel.

Finally, the panels[border] panel is assigned as the initial panel to be displayed when the program starts up. The currentPanel variable is also initialized to panels[border].

The handleEvent() method handles the processing of user menu selections. The WINDOWS_DESTROY event and the Exit menu option result in immediate program termination. The menu items associated with each layout result in the appropriate panel being selected and displayed. This is accomplished using the switchPanels() method.

The First, Last, Next, and Previous menu items are processed by getting the layout associated with the current panel and then invoking the first(), last(), next(), or previous() methods of the CardLayout class to select the appropriate button to be displayed within the panels[card] panel.

The switchPanels() method is used to provide a common method of switching from one panel to another. It begins by using the remove() method of the Container class to remove the current panel from the LayoutApp main window. The current panel is set based on the Panel object passed to the method via the newPanel parameter. The new current panel is then added to the center of the main window, and the window's title is set based on the newTitle string parameter. The `cardMenu` is added or removed from the menu bar based on the `boolean` `setCardMenu` parameter. Finally, the new panel is displayed by invoking the `show()` method of the `Window` class.

Connecting Code to Events

Although the various graphical user interface subclasses of the `Component` class are what is seen by the user when he interacts with a window program, the event-handling software is what actually connects these components to the code that implements the program's behavior.

Events are generated as the result of the user's interaction with the program's GUI components. These events are defined in the `Event` class and cover a large variety of user actions using the mouse and keyboard.

Until now you've been handling events using monolithic `handleEvent()` methods. Although this approach works, it can sometimes become difficult to manage. An alternative approach is to handle events locally by each GUI component, which allows event handling to be more closely aligned with the components generating the event. Local component event handling is performed using the `handleEvent()`, `action()`, and other methods, such as `mouseUp()` and `mouseDown()`, that are inherited from the `Component` class. Consult the `Component` class API for a detailed list of these methods. In order to perform local event handling you must subclass these components (for example, `Button`, `Checkbox`, `Scrollbar`) and override their event-handling methods.

The `handleEvent()` and `action()` methods are the most common methods used for event handling. You've already used the `handleEvent()` method quite extensively. The `action()` method is used to handle events that have the `ACTION_EVENT` type. These events are typical of GUI components such as menu items, buttons, lists, and checkboxes.

The `action()` method is passed the event along with an object containing the value of the event's `arg` variable. This object describes the `Component` being acted upon. For example, clicking a button results in the button's label being assigned to the `arg` variable. The window sampler program presented in the next section shows how the `action()` method is used.

The Window Sampler Program

The `SamplerApp` program serves a dual purpose. It shows how each of the most common GUI components are displayed and accessed and also demonstrates local event-handling approaches for each of these components. The program displays `Label`, `TextField`, `TextArea`, `Button`, `Canvas`, `Checkbox`, `Choice`, `List`, and `Scrollbar` objects and shows how to handle events associated with these objects. The program's source code is shown in Listing 19.3.

Listing 19.3. The source code of the `SamplerApp` program.

```
import java.awt.*;
import java.lang.System;

public class SamplerApp extends Frame {
 TextArea textArea;
 public static void main(String args[]){
  SamplerApp app = new SamplerApp();
 }
 public SamplerApp() {
  super("Windows Sampler");
  setup();
  pack();
  resize(400,400);
  show();
 }
 void setup() {
  setupMenuBars();
  setupPanels();
 }
 void setupMenuBars() {
  MenuBar menuBar = new MenuBar();
  Menu fileMenu = new Menu("File");
  fileMenu.add(new MenuItem("Exit"));
  menuBar.add(fileMenu);
  setMenuBar(menuBar);
 }
 void setupPanels() {
  Panel mainPanel = new Panel();
  mainPanel.setLayout(new GridLayout(3,3));
  Panel panels[][] = new Panel[3][3];
  for(int i=0;i<3;++i){
   for(int j=0;j<3;++j){
    panels[j][i] = new Panel();
    panels[j][i].setLayout(new FlowLayout(FlowLayout.LEFT));
   }
  }
  panels[0][0].add(new Label("Text Field:"));
  panels[0][0].add(new MyTextField("A text field.",15));
  panels[1][0].add(new Label("Text Area:"));
  textArea = new TextArea("A text area.",5,15);
  panels[1][0].add(textArea);
  panels[2][0].add(new Label("Button:"));
  panels[2][0].add(new MyButton("Blank Text Area",textArea));
  panels[0][1].add(new Label("Canvas:"));
  panels[0][1].add(new MyCanvas());
  String checkboxStrings[] = {"Checkboxes:","Java","Developer's","Guide"};
  panels[1][1].add(new MyCheckboxGroup(checkboxStrings));
  panels[2][1].add(new Label("Choices:"));
  String choiceStrings[] = {"Yes","No","Maybe"};
  panels[2][1].add(new MyChoice(choiceStrings,textArea));
  panels[0][2].add(new Label("List:"));
  String listStrings[] = {"Sleepy","Sneezy","Grumpy","Dopey","Doc",
   "Happy","Bashful"};
  panels[0][2].add(new MyList(listStrings,textArea));
  panels[1][2].setLayout(new BorderLayout());
  panels[1][2].add("Center",new Label("Horizontal Scrollbar:"));
```

```
  panels[1][2].add("South",new MyScrollbar(Scrollbar.HORIZONTAL,50,10,0,
   100,textArea));
  panels[2][2].setLayout(new BorderLayout());
  panels[2][2].add("North",new Label("Vertical Scrollbar:"));
  panels[2][2].add("East",new MyScrollbar(Scrollbar.VERTICAL,50,10,0,
   1000,textArea));
  for(int i=0;i<3;++i)
   for(int j=0;j<3;++j)
    mainPanel.add(panels[j][i]);
  add("Center",mainPanel);
 }
 public boolean handleEvent(Event event) {
  if(event.id==Event.WINDOW_DESTROY){
   System.exit(0);
   return true;
  }else if(event.id==Event.ACTION_EVENT){
   if(event.target instanceof MenuItem){
    if("Exit".equals(event.arg)){
     System.exit(0);
     return true;
    }
   }
  }
  return false;
 }
}
class MyTextField extends TextField {
 public MyTextField(String text,int columns) {
  super(text,columns);
 }
 public boolean action(Event event,Object arg) {
  String text = getText();
  setText(text.toUpperCase());
  return true;
 }
}
class MyButton extends Button {
 TextArea textArea;
 public MyButton(String text,TextArea newTextArea) {
  super(text);
  textArea = newTextArea;
 }
 public boolean action(Event event,Object arg) {
  textArea.setText("");
  return true;
 }
}
class MyCanvas extends Canvas {
 int x = -1;
 int y = -1;
 int boxSize = 10;
 public MyCanvas() {
  super();
  resize(75,75);
  setBackground(Color.white);
  setForeground(Color.red);
  show();
```

continues

Listing 19.3. continued

```
 }
 public boolean mouseDown(Event event,int xClick,int yClick) {
  x = xClick;
  y = yClick;
  repaint();
  return true;
 }
 public void paint(Graphics g) {
  setBackground(Color.white);
  setForeground(Color.red);
  if(x>=0 && y>=0) g.fillRect(x,y,boxSize,boxSize);
 }
}
class MyCheckboxGroup extends Panel {
 String labelString;
 String checkboxLabels[];
 Checkbox checkboxes[];
 int numBoxes;
 TextField results;
 public MyCheckboxGroup(String strings[]) {
  super();
  labelString = strings[0];
  numBoxes = strings.length-1;
  checkboxLabels = new String[numBoxes];
  for(int i=0;i<numBoxes;++i)
   checkboxLabels[i] = strings[i+1];
  results = new TextField("",15);
  setupPanel();
  show();
 }
 void setupPanel() {
  setLayout(new GridLayout(numBoxes+2,1));
  add(new Label(labelString));
  checkboxes = new Checkbox[numBoxes];
  for(int i=0;i<numBoxes;++i){
   checkboxes[i] = new Checkbox(checkboxLabels[i]);
   add(checkboxes[i]);
  }
  add(results);
 }
 public boolean handleEvent(Event event) {
  if(event.id==Event.ACTION_EVENT){
   if(event.target instanceof Checkbox){
    String newResults = "";
    for(int i=0;i<numBoxes;++i)
     if(checkboxes[i].getState())
      newResults = newResults + " " +checkboxes[i].getLabel();
    results.setText(newResults);
   }
  }
  return false;
 }
}
class MyChoice extends Choice {
 TextArea text;
 public MyChoice(String strings[],TextArea textArea) {
```

```
  super();
  try {
   for(int i=0;i<strings.length;++i)
    addItem(strings[i]);
   text = textArea;
  }catch(NullPointerException ex){
   System.exit(0);
  }
 }
 public boolean action(Event event,Object arg) {
  text.setText((String)arg);
  return true;
 }
}
class MyList extends List {
 TextArea text;
 public MyList(String strings[],TextArea textArea) {
  super(3,false);
  for(int i=0;i<strings.length;++i)
   addItem(strings[i]);
  text = textArea;
 }
 public boolean handleEvent(Event event) {
  if(event.id==Event.ACTION_EVENT){
   text.setText("Double-clicked:\n "+event.arg.toString());
   return true;
  }else if(event.id==Event.LIST_SELECT){
   text.setText("Selected:\n "+
    getItem((new Integer(event.arg.toString())).intValue()));
   return true;
  }else if(event.id==Event.LIST_DESELECT){
   text.setText("Deselected:\n "+
    getItem((new Integer(event.arg.toString())).intValue()));
   return true;
  }
  return false;
 }
}
class MyScrollbar extends Scrollbar {
 TextArea text;
 public MyScrollbar(int orientation,int value,int visible,int min,int max,
  TextArea textArea) {
  super(orientation,value,visible,min,max);
  text=textArea;
 }
 public boolean handleEvent(Event event) {
  if(event.id==Event.SCROLL_LINE_UP){
   text.setText("Position: "+getValue());
   return true;
  }else if(event.id==Event.SCROLL_LINE_DOWN){
   text.setText("Position: "+getValue());
   return true;
  }else if(event.id==Event.SCROLL_PAGE_UP){
   text.setText("Position: "+getValue());
   return true;
  }else if(event.id==Event.SCROLL_PAGE_DOWN){
```

continues

Listing 19.3. continued

```
    text.setText("Position: "+getValue());
    return true;
   }else if(event.id==Event.SCROLL_ABSOLUTE){
    text.setText("Position: "+getValue());
    return true;
   }
   return false;
  }
 }
```

After compiling and running the program, the main application window should be displayed, as shown in Figure 19.15. The program presents a number of GUI components at various locations within the window. Labels are used to identify these components.

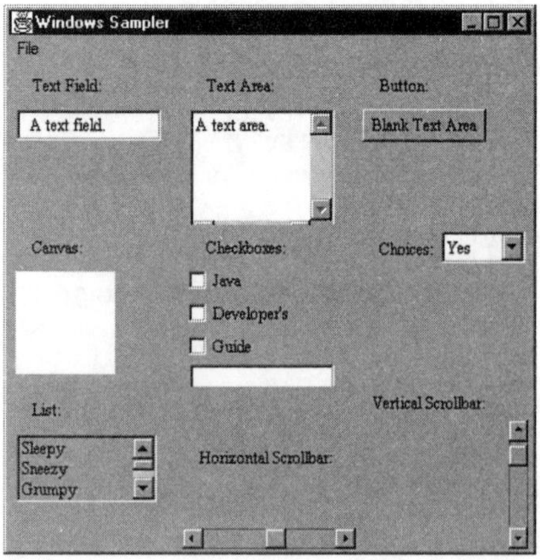

FIGURE 19.15.
The SamplerApp *program display.*

The TextField object presented in the upper left corner of the window allows a user to type some text. When the user presses the Enter key from within the text field, an ACTION_EVENT is generated and the text is automatically converted to uppercase.

The TextArea object allows the user to type in and edit text in a multiline text field. This object is used in the SamplerApp program to display the results of operations on other objects such as the Blank Text Area button, the choices list, the scrollable list, and the horizontal and vertical scrollbars.

The Blank Text Area button causes all text displayed in the TextArea object to be erased. The Canvas object displays a red square at the point where the user clicks within the canvas. When the Checkbox objects are selected, they display the text of their labels in the underlying text field. The value selected from the Choice and List objects is displayed in the TextArea object. The horizontal and vertical scrollbars also display their scrollbar positions in the TextArea object.

Play around with each of the GUI components to familiarize yourself with their operation before moving on to analyze the SamplerApp source code.

The SamplerApp class has one field variable—the textArea variable that is used to hold the TextArea object written to by several GUI components. The main() method and SamplerApp constructor are defined in the standard manner. The setupMenuBars(), setupPanels(), and handleEvent() methods provide the primary processing for this class, with the bulk of the processing being performed in setupPanels().

The setupMenuBars() method creates a File menu with an Exit menu item. The handleEvent() method handles the WINDOW_DESTROY event and the Exit menu item. All other event handling is performed locally by the window components.

The setupPanels() method creates a Panel with a 3-by-3 GridLayout and assigns it to mainPanel. It then declares and initializes a 3-by-3 panels[][] array to hold the nine subpanels of the mainPanel. The layout of elements of the panels[][] array is set to a left-justified FlowLayout. Subsequent code adds GUI components to each of the panels[][] elements.

A TextField: label and an object of MyTextField are added to panels[0][0]. The MyTextField object is assigned a default value of "A text field." and is set to 15 columns. A TextArea: label and a 5-row by 15-column TextArea object with the default text of "A text area." are added to panels[1][0]. A Button: label and a MyButton object are added to panels[2][0]. The MyButton object is given the Blank Text Area label and is passed the name of a TextArea to be updated.

A Canvas: label and a MyCanvas object are added to panels[0][1]. An array of strings is created and passed to the MyCheckBoxGroup() constructor. The resulting MyCheckBoxGroup object is added to panels[1][1]. A Choices: label is added to panels[2][1]. A MyChoice object is created using the choiceStrings[] array and the textArea variable. The object is also added to panels[2][1].

A List: label is added to panels[0][2]. A MyList object is created using the names of the Seven Dwarfs and the textArea variable and is added to panels[1][2]. The layouts for panels[1][2] and panels[2][2] are changed to a BorderLayout object. A Horizontal Scrollbar: label is added to the center of panels[1][2], and a MyScrollBar object is created and added to the South region of panels[1][2]. A Vertical Scrollbar: label is added to the North region of panels[2][2], and a MyScrollBar object is created and added to the East region of panels[2][2].

After the components of all the panels have been created and added to their respective panels, each of the elements of the panels[][] array is added to the mainPanel object. The mainPanel is then added to the center of the SamplerApp window.

After the SamplerApp class is declared, seven new classes are declared that subclass the standard GUI components and provide custom display and event handling.

MyTextField

The TextField class provides the capability for the user to enter and edit a single line of text. The MyTextField class extends the TextField class and handles the event generated when the user presses the Enter key while editing within the text field. The MyTextField() constructor passes the text and columns parameters to the TextField constructor via the superclass constructor call statement. The text parameter identifies a string of text that is to be initially displayed within the text field. The columns parameter specifies the displayed width of the text field in character columns. The action() method handles the event occurring when the user presses the Enter key while editing the text field. It uses the getText() method inherited from the TextComponent class to retrieve the current text displayed within the text field, converts it to uppercase, and then sets the converted text in the text field using the setText() method inherited from TextComponent. The TextComponent class is the parent of both TextField and TextArea.

MyButton

The MyButton class extends the Button class. Its constructor takes two parameters: the string label to be displayed on the button and a reference to the TextArea object that is to be cleared when the button is clicked. The action() method handles the button click and uses the setText() method of TextComponent to set the text of the TextArea object to an empty string.

MyCanvas

The Canvas class provides the capability to add individual drawing components to a container. It is covered extensively in Chapter 23, "The Canvas." The MyCanvas class extends Canvas and provides a minimal drawing capability. It declares the x and y variables to record the last position in which the mouse is clicked within the canvas. Their default values are set to -1 to indicate that the mouse has not yet been clicked on the canvas. The boxSize variable specifies the size of the box to be displayed at the position of the last mouse click.

The MyCanvas constructor sets the canvas size to an area of 75×75 pixels with a white background and a red foreground drawing color. The show() method is used to cause the canvas to be initially displayed.

The mouseDown() method overrides the method defined in the Component class. It provides the capability to handle the MOUSE_DOWN event generated when the user clicks a mouse button. Java assumes a one-button mouse to provide the widest compatibility. The mouseDown() method stores the position of the user's click and then invokes the repaint() method to repaint the canvas.

The paint() method declared for MyCanvas checks to make sure that a click has occurred and fills a rectangle with the upper left corner at the point of the last click and with boxSize dimensions.

MyCheckBoxGroup

The MyCheckBoxGroup class extends the Panel class. It implements a custom panel consisting of a label, an array of Checkbox objects, and a TextField object. The results of clicking on any of the checkboxes are displayed in the results TextField. The MyCheckBoxGroup constructor takes an array of strings as its parameter. It sets the label string to the first string in the array and sets the labels of the checkboxes to the rest of the strings. The `numBoxes` variable specifies the number of `Checkbox` objects to be created. The `results TextField` is created as an empty 15-character `TextField` object.

The `setupPanel()` method sets the layout of the panel to a `GridLayout` that is one column wide and has enough rows to accommodate the label, checkboxes, and text field. The label is created and added to the panel, followed by each of the checkboxes. The `results TextField` is then added to the end of the panel.

The `MyCheckBoxGroup handleEvent()` method is used to handle any actions occurring within the panel and is capable of handling all events for all checkboxes. It handles checkbox events by using the `getState()` and `getLabel()` methods of the `Checkbox` class to query the checked status of each checkbox and to retrieve the labels associated with the checkboxes that are checked. It then displays these labels in the `results TextField` using the `setText()` method.

MyChoice

The `Choice` class is used to implement Motif option menus, which are free-standing pull-down menus that can be used to select a single value from a list. The `MyChoice` class extends the `Choice` class and provides the capability to display selected choices in a `TextArea` object.

The `MyChoice` constructor takes an array of strings to be used as the choices and a `TextArea` object as its parameters. The `addItem()` method of the `Choice` class is used to add the choice strings to the list of choices. The constructor checks for a `NullPointerException` when the strings are added to the `Choice` list because the `addItem()` method throws this exception.

The `action()` method handles the event generated when a user makes a selection from the list. The `arg` parameter contains the label of the selected choice. It is displayed in the `TextArea` object using the `setText()` method.

MyList

The `List` class implements scrollable lists from which a user can select one or more list items. The `MyList` class extends the `List` class and provides support for displaying the selected list items in a `TextArea` field.

The `MyList` constructor takes an array of strings and the `TextArea` object as its parameters. The strings are used as the items of the list. The `super(3,false)` superclass constructor call statement invokes the `List` class constructor and specifies a three-row list with multiple list selections being disabled. Lists are covered in more detail in Chapter 21, "Checkboxes, Choices, and Lists." The `addItem()` method of the `List` class is used to add the strings as items of the list.

The `handleEvent()` method handles the `ACTION_EVENT` occurring when a list item is double-clicked, the `LIST_SELECT` event that is generated when an unselected list item is clicked, and the `LIST_DESELECT` event that occurs when a selected list item is clicked and deselected. The Windows 95 implementation of Java does not correctly handle the `LIST_DESELECT` event. The `handleEvent()` method handles these events by writing the results of the action in the specified `TextArea` object.

MyScrollbar

The `Scrollbar` class encapsulates vertical and horizontal scrollbars. The `MyScrollbar` class extends `Scrollbar` and provides the capability to display the results of scrollbar operations using a `TextArea` object. (See Chapter 24, "Scrollbars," for more information on using scrollbars.)

The `MyScrollbar` constructor takes a number of parameters that determine the characteristics of a scrollbar. These parameters are forwarded to the superclass constructor. A `TextArea` object is also passed as a parameter. The orientation parameter is set to the `HORIZONTAL` and `VERTICAL` constants of the `Scrollbar` class. These constants specify whether the scrollbar should be displayed horizontally or vertically. The `min` and `max` parameters specify a range of integer values that are associated with the scrollbar. The `value` parameter sets the initial position of the scrollbar between the `min` and `max` values. The `visible` parameter identifies the size of the visible portion of the scrollable area. This determines how the current scrollbar position is updated as the result of a page-up or page-down scrollbar operation.

The `handleEvent()` method of the `MyScrollbar` class handles the `SCROLL_LINE_UP`, `SCROLL_LINE_DOWN`, `SCROLL_PAGE_UP`, `SCROLL_PAGE_DOWN`, and `SCROLL_ABSOLUTE` events. The `SCROLL_LINE_UP` and `SCROLL_LINE_DOWN` events are generated when the user clicks on the end arrows of the scrollbar. The `SCROLL_PAGE_UP` and `SCROLL_PAGE_DOWN` events are generated when the user clicks between the end arrows and the scrollbar position marker. The `SCROLL_ABSOLUTE` event is generated when the user moves the scrollbar position marker. The `handleEvent()` method handles these events by displaying the current scrollbar position in the designated `TextArea` object. The `getValue()` method of the `Scrollbar` class is used to obtain the current scrollbar position.

Summary

This chapter covers the basics of writing window programs. It shows how window programs are structured and organized and identifies the basic approach used to design most window programs. It covers the details of the `Frame` class and the five basic window layouts. The process of window event handling is described and illustrated through the `SamplerApp` program. `SamplerApp` also introduces the most common window GUI controls. Subsequent chapters investigate these components in more detail.

20

Menus, Buttons, and Dialog Boxes

This chapter covers the details of using the `Menu`, `Button`, and `Dialog` classes. It describes the available menu and button options and shows you how to quickly and easily construct menus and buttons for your window programs. The use of dialog boxes is explained, and a generic `MessageDialog` component is constructed and explained as part of an example. When you finish this chapter, you will be able to effectively use menus, buttons, and dialog boxes in your Java window programs.

Adding Menus to Windows

Java provides a rich set of menu-related classes to create and interact with pull-down menus. The `MenuComponent` class is the superclass of all menu-related classes. It extends the `Object` class. The `getFont()` and `setFont()` methods are the most useful methods provided by `MenuComponent`. Its two direct superclasses, `MenuBar` and `MenuItem`, provide most of the methods for creating and using menus. The `CheckboxMenuItem` class extends the `MenuItem` class and supports menu items that can be checked on or off. The `Menu` class extends the `MenuItem` class and implements a collection of `MenuItem` objects that can be assigned to a `MenuBar` object.

You are probably somewhat familiar with menus from Chapters 18, "Opening Windows," and 19, "Organizing Window Programs." A program's application window is implemented by a `Frame` object. It can have one and only one `MenuBar` object, which is set using the `setMenuBar()` method. A *menu bar* is a collection of menus. Each menu is represented as a separate pull-down menu on the menu bar. Common examples are the File, Edit, and Help pull-down menus found in many window applications. The `MenuBar` class allows a special menu to be designated as a Help menu, but this feature is not implemented in Windows 95 or NT.

A `Menu` object contains one or more `MenuItem` objects, which can be a normal user-selectable `MenuItem` object, a `CheckboxMenuItem` object, or another `Menu` object. Java supports *tear-off menus,* which are menus that can be removed from a menu bar. A tear-off menu is constructed in the same manner as a regular menu—you only need to set the `boolean` tear-off value in the `Menu()` constructor. Tear-off menus, however, are not implemented within Windows 95 or NT.

The `MenuItem` class is the superclass of the `Menu` class. It allows a menu to be a menu item and is used in constructing cascading, multilevel menus. `MenuItem` is also the superclass of the `CheckboxMenuItem` class and provides the capability to implement menu items that can be checked or unchecked. If a `MenuItem` object is constructed directly with the `MenuItem` constructor, it becomes a normal menu item that is selected from a pull-down menu.

The `MyMenu` Class

The creation and organization of menu bars, menus, and menu items into a program's menu is a straightforward, but tedious, process. You have to create a menu bar, create and add menus to the menu bar, add menu items to the menus, and then add the menu bar to the program's application window. This usually involves the use of a large number of constructors and access methods. To illustrate the use of the menu-related classes and to simplify the menu-creation process, you'll create two classes, `MyMenu` and `MyMenuBar`, that can be used to quickly construct menus for Java programs. These classes implement multiple levels of menus, checkbox menu items, and menu-disabling options. The special Help menu and tear-off menus are not implemented, however, because they are transparent to Windows 95 and NT.

The `MyMenu` class is used to construct menus using an array of objects consisting of `String` objects that represent menu labels, or arrays of objects that represent submenus. Menu labels can be either checkbox menu items or normal menu items and can be either initially enabled or disabled (grayed out). Checkbox menu items can be initially checked or unchecked. The first character of the label's text string is used to indicate what type of label it is. The character conventions are as follows:

+	A checkbox menu item that is initially checked and enabled.
#	A checkbox menu item that is initially checked and disabled.
-	A checkbox menu item that is initially unchecked and enabled. If the label consists of just -, it indicates a separator.
=	A checkbox menu item that is initially unchecked and disabled.
~	A normal menu item that is initially disabled.
	Any other character indicates a normal, enabled menu item. If the first character is !, it is ignored. This allows any menu item to begin with any character.

These conventions apply to menu options. Only the ~ and ! options are used with the menu's main label. Using these options greatly simplifies the process of a menu creation. The source code for the `MyMenu` class is shown in Listing 20.1.

Listing 20.1. The source code of the `MyMenu` class.

```
package jdg.ch20;

import java.awt.*;

public class MyMenu extends Menu {
 public MyMenu(Object labels[]) {
  super((String)labels[0]);
  String menuName = (String) labels[0];
  char firstMenuChar = menuName.charAt(0);
  if(firstMenuChar == '~' || firstMenuChar =='!'){
   setLabel(menuName.substring(1));
   if(firstMenuChar == '~') disable();
  }
  for(int i=1;i<labels.length;++i) {
   if(labels[i] instanceof String){
    if("-".equals(labels[i])) addSeparator();
    else{
```

continues

Listing 20.1. continued

```
     String label = (String)labels[i];
     char firstChar = label.charAt(0);
     switch(firstChar){
     case '+':
      CheckboxMenuItem checkboxItem = new CheckboxMenuItem(label.substring(1));
      checkboxItem.setState(true);
      add(checkboxItem);
      break;
     case '#':
      checkboxItem = new CheckboxMenuItem(label.substring(1));
      checkboxItem.setState(true);
      checkboxItem.disable();
      add(checkboxItem);
      break;
     case '-':
      checkboxItem = new CheckboxMenuItem(label.substring(1));
      checkboxItem.setState(false);
      add(checkboxItem);
      break;
     case '=':
      checkboxItem = new CheckboxMenuItem(label.substring(1));
      checkboxItem.setState(false);
      checkboxItem.disable();
      add(checkboxItem);
      break;
     case '~':
      MenuItem menuItem = new MenuItem(label.substring(1));
      menuItem.disable();
      add(menuItem);
      break;
     case '!':
      add(label.substring(1));
      break;
     default:
      add(label);
     }
    }
   }else{
    add(new MyMenu((Object[])labels[i]));
   }
  }
 }
 public MenuItem getItem(String menuItem) {
  int numItems = countItems();
  for(int i=0;i<numItems;++i)
   if(menuItem.equals(getItem(i).getLabel())) return getItem(i);
  return null;
 }
}
```

The `MyMenu` class specifies that it is in the package `jdg.ch20`. Make sure that you place it in the `jdg/ch20` directory and compile it. You'll be using it quite a bit in subsequent chapters.

`MyMenu` contains no field variables. It consists of a single constructor and the `getItem()` access method. The `getItem()` method retrieves a menu item contained in the menu and based on the menu item's label. It uses the `countItems()` and `getItem()` methods of the `Menu` class to retrieve the menu items contained in a menu and the `getLabel()` method of the `MenuItem` class to match a menu item with the search string.

The `MyMenu` constructor constructs a menu from an array of menu labels and nested menu arrays (representing submenus). For example, to construct a typical File menu, labeled File, with the New and Open menu items followed by a separator and an Exit menu item, you would use the following `MyMenu` constructor:

```
String fileMenuLabels[] = {"File","New","Open","-","Exit"};
MyMenu fileMenu = new MyMenu(fileLabelMenus);
```

The first object in the array must be a `String` object that is the main label associated with the menu. The following objects are either `String` objects identifying the labels of the menu items contained in the menu, separators, or second-level arrays representing submenus. For example, the following creates a multilevel menu:

```
String goMenuLabels[] = {"Go","Beginning","End","Previous","Next"};
String editMenuLabels[] = {"Edit","Copy","Cut","-","Paste","-",goMenuLabels};
MyMenu editLabel = new MyMenu(editMenuLabels);
```

Using the `MyMenu` class is much easier than constructing each of the individual menu items and adding them to a menu.

Let's step through the `MyMenu` constructor to see how it works. It uses the `super()` class constructor call statement to construct a `Menu` object using the first label in the `labels[]` array. This label may contain the `~` or `!` character as the first character. `MyMenu()` checks for these characters and readjusts the menu's label accordingly. If the first character of the menu's label is `~`, `MyMenu()` will disable the entire menu using the `disable()` method of the `MenuItem` class.

After setting up the menu's main label, `MyMenu()` iterates through the list of objects contained in `labels[]`. If the object is an instance of the `String` class, and is therefore a label, `MyMenu()` checks the first letter of the label and processes it accordingly. If the object is not an instance of the `String` class, `MyMenu()` calls itself again, passing the object to itself as another array of objects. It then adds the resulting `MyMenu` object to itself using the `add()` method of the `Menu` class. This allows submenus to be processed in a recursive fashion.

`MyMenu()` processes the menu item labels by using a `switch` statement to check the first character of the label to see if it matches the `+`, `#`, `-`, `=`, `~`, or `!` character. If it does not match any of these characters, the label is added as a normal menu item. If the label equals `-`, a separator is added.

If the first character is `+`, an enabled and checked `CheckboxMenuItem` object is added to the menu. The `setState()` method of the `CheckboxMenuItem` class is used to set the state of the menu item to checked. If the first character is `#`, a checked, but disabled, `CheckboxMenuItem` object is added. The `disable()` method of the `MenuItem` class is used to disable the menu item. The cases in which the first character of the label is - or = are processed in a similar manner, except that the CheckboxMenuItem object is initially unchecked.

When the first character of the label is ~, a normal MenuItem object is added to the menu. The menu item is disabled.

The ! character is an escape character that is used to create a normal menu item beginning with any of the special characters previously mentioned. When the first character of a label is !, the actual label generated begins with the subsequent character.

The MyMenuBar Class

The MyMenuBar class uses the MyMenu class presented in the previous section to quickly create an entire menu bar. Whereas the MyMenu class uses an array of labels and submenus to create a menu, the MyMenuBar class uses an array of these arrays to create the entire menu bar. For example, the following statements will construct a menu bar with File, Edit, and Help menus, each consisting of individual menu items:

```
String menuBarLabels[] = {
 {"File","New","Open","-","~Save As","-","Exit"};
 {"Edit","Copy","Cut","-","~Paste"};
 {"Help","Index"};
};
MyMenuBar menuBar = new MyMenuBar(menuBarLabels);
```

Note that the Save As and Paste menu items are initially disabled.

The source code of the MyMenuBar class is shown in Listing 20.2.

Listing 20.2. The source code of the MyMenuBar class.

```
package jdg.ch20;

import java.awt.*;

public class MyMenuBar extends MenuBar {
 public MyMenuBar(Object labels[][]) {
  super();
  for(int i=0;i<labels.length;++i)
   add(new MyMenu(labels[i]));
 }
 public MyMenu getMenu(String menuName) {
  int numMenus = countMenus();
  for(int i=0;i<numMenus;++i)
   if(menuName.equals(getMenu(i).getLabel())) return((MyMenu)getMenu(i));
  return null;
 }
}
```

The `MyMenuBar` constructor simply iterates through the outer array and passes the first-level elements (which are themselves `Object` arrays) to the `MyMenu` constructor to construct `MyMenu` objects. These objects are then added to the `MyMenuBar` object being constructed using the `add()` method inherited from the `MenuBar` class.

The `getMenu()` method retrieves a `MyMenu` object from a `MyMenuBar` object based on the label associated with the `MyMenu` object. It uses the `countMenus()` and `getMenu()` methods of the `MenuBar` class to retrieve each `MyMenu` object contained in the menu bar. The `getLabel()` method of the `MenuItem` class is used to check the labels of the `MyMenu` objects against the search string.

The MenuApp Program

The `MenuApp` program illustrates the use of the `MyMenuBar` and `MyMenu` classes. Its source code is shown in Listing 20.3.

Listing 20.3. The source code of the MenuApp program.

```
import java.awt.*;
import jdg.ch20.MyMenu;
import jdg.ch20.MyMenuBar;

public class MenuApp extends Frame {
 MyMenuBar menuBar;
 public static void main(String args[]){
  MenuApp app = new MenuApp();
 }
 public MenuApp() {
  super("Menu Madness");
  setup();
  pack();
  resize(400,400);
  show();
 }
 void setup() {
  setBackground(Color.white);
  setupMenuBar();
 }
 void setupMenuBar(){
  String gotoMenu[] = {"Go To","Beginning","End","-","Line Number"};
  Object menuItems[][] = {
   {"File","New","Open","-","~Save","~Save As","-","Exit"},
   {"Edit","Copy","Cut","-","~Paste"},
   {"Search","Find","~Find Next","~Find Previous","-", gotoMenu},
   {"View","-Hex","+Line Number","+Column Number"},
   {"Help","About Menu Madness"},
  };
  menuBar = new MyMenuBar(menuItems);
  setMenuBar(menuBar);
 }
```

continues

Listing 20.3. continued

```
 public boolean handleEvent(Event event) {
  if(event.id==Event.WINDOW_DESTROY){
   System.exit(0);
   return true;
  }else if(event.id==Event.ACTION_EVENT){
   if(event.target instanceof MenuItem){
    if("Exit".equals(event.arg)){
     System.exit(0);
     return true;
    }else if("New".equals(event.arg) || "Open".equals(event.arg)){
     menuBar.getMenu("File").getItem("Save").enable();
     menuBar.getMenu("File").getItem("Save As").enable();
     return true;
    }else if("Copy".equals(event.arg) || "Cut".equals(event.arg)){
     menuBar.getMenu("Edit").getItem("Paste").enable();
     return true;
    }else if("Find".equals(event.arg)){
     menuBar.getMenu("Search").getItem("Find Next").enable();
     menuBar.getMenu("Search").getItem("Find Previous").enable();
     return true;
    }else if("Hex".equals(event.arg)){
     CheckboxMenuItem hexMenuItem =
      (CheckboxMenuItem) menuBar.getMenu("View").getItem("Hex");
     CheckboxMenuItem lineMenuItem =
      (CheckboxMenuItem) menuBar.getMenu("View").getItem("Line Number");
     CheckboxMenuItem colMenuItem =
      (CheckboxMenuItem) menuBar.getMenu("View").getItem("Column Number");
     boolean hexState = hexMenuItem.getState();
     lineMenuItem.setState(!hexState);
     colMenuItem.setState(!hexState);
     return true;
    }else if("Line Number".equals(event.arg) ||
     "Column Number".equals(event.arg)){
     CheckboxMenuItem hexMenuItem =
      (CheckboxMenuItem) menuBar.getMenu("View").getItem("Hex");
     CheckboxMenuItem lineMenuItem =
      (CheckboxMenuItem) menuBar.getMenu("View").getItem("Line Number");
     CheckboxMenuItem colMenuItem =
      (CheckboxMenuItem) menuBar.getMenu("View").getItem("Column Number");
     boolean lineState = lineMenuItem.getState();
     boolean columnState = colMenuItem.getState();
     hexMenuItem.setState(!(lineState | columnState));
     return true;
    }else if("About Menu Madness".equals(event.arg)){
     menuBar.getMenu("Help").disable();
     return true;
    }
   }
  }
  return false;
 }
}
```

`MenuApp` shows how the `MyMenuBar` and `MyMenu` classes are used to easily create a menu bar and to support the processing of menu-related events. When the program is executed, it displays a blank opening screen and a menu bar with five pull-down menus, as shown in Figure 20.1.

FIGURE 20.1.
The `MenuApp` *opening window.*

Click on the File menu and select the New menu item as shown in Figure 20.2. This will cause the Save and Save As menu items to become enabled. You can verify this by clicking on the File menu once again.

FIGURE 20.2.
The File menu.

Click on the Edit menu and select the Copy menu item as shown in Figure 20.3. This results in the Paste menu item becoming enabled.

FIGURE 20.3.
The Edit menu.

Click on the Search menu and then on the Go To menu item as shown in Figure 20.4. The Go To menu item is a second-level menu that is attached to the Search menu.

FIGURE 20.4.
The Search menu.

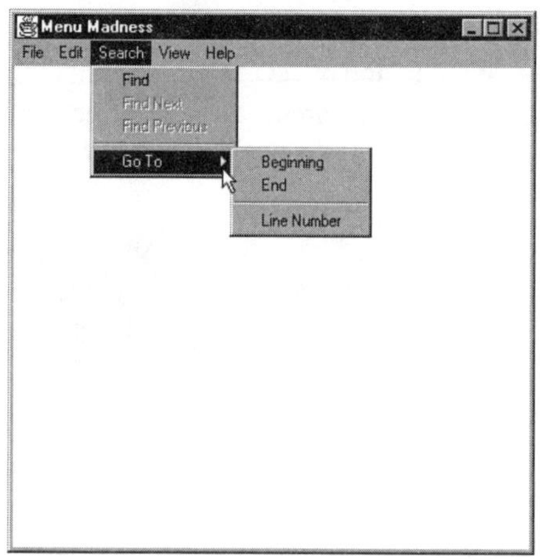

Click on the View menu and select the Hex checkbox menu item as shown in Figure 20.5. Notice that the Line Number and Column Number menu items that are initially checked become unchecked, as shown in Figure 20.6.

FIGURE 20.5.
The View menu.

FIGURE 20.6.
The View menu after checking Hex.

Click on the Help menu and select About Menu Madness, as shown in Figure 20.7. This Help menu isn't much help at all because it is programmed to disable itself, as shown in Figure 20.8.

You've completed the tour of the `MenuApp` program. Select Exit from the File menu to terminate the program's operation.

FIGURE 20.7.
The Help menu.

FIGURE 20.8.
The Help menu disabled.

Inside MenuApp

The `MenuApp` class consists of a single field variable, `menuBar`, that is an object of class `MyMenuBar`. The `MenuApp` constructor creates a 400×400 frame window with the title Menu Madness and invokes the `setup()` method to set up the background color and the menu bar. The `setup()` method invokes `setupMenuBar()` to actually perform the menu bar setup.

The `setupMenuBar()` method creates a `gotoMenu[]` array as the labels of a submenu that will be attached to the Search menu. The `menuItems[][]` array is used to define the labels associated with the menu bar and its first-level menus. The `gotoMenu[]` array is included as an object in this array. Notice the use of the first-character conventions for disabling menu items and specifying menu items that are checkboxes. The menu bar is created, assigned to the `menuBar` variable, and set as the menu bar for the `MenuApp` frame.

Creating the menu bar was a snap using the `MyMenuBar` class. However, creating the menu bar is only half the work. You also need to write event-handling code that acts on the menu items selected by the user. The event-handling code of `MenuApp` is used to illustrate the use of the various methods provided with menus and menu items.

The `WINDOWS_DESTROY` event and the Exit menu item are handled by terminating the program's execution. The New and Open menu items cause the Save and Save As menu items to be enabled. The `getMenu()` method of `MyMenuBar` and the `getItem()` method of `MyMenu` are used to retrieve the Save and Save As `MenuItem` objects. The `enable()` method of the `MenuItem` class is used to enable these menu items. Note that the Save and Save As menu items, as well as some other menu items, are not handled. Selecting these menu items results in no action being performed by `MenuApp`.

The Copy and Cut menu items are processed in a similar manner as the New and Open menu items. Selecting Copy or Cut menu items results in the Paste menu item being enabled.

The Find menu item causes the Find Next and Find Previous menu items to be enabled.

The Hex checkbox menu item is handled by using the `getState()` method to determine the state of its associated checkbox and then setting the checkbox state of the Line Number and Column Number checkbox menu items to the opposite state.

The Line Number and Column Number menu items are set and reset independent of each other, but they are combined to determine the state of the Hex menu item. If both the Line Number and Column Number menu items are unchecked, the state of the Hex menu item is set to checked. Otherwise, the Hex menu item is set to unchecked.

The handling of the About Menu Madness menu item shows how an entire menu can be disabled.

Working with Buttons

Buttons are one of the easiest GUI components to use in a Java window program. You create them using the `Button` constructor and add them to your program using the `add()` method of their container. After that, you just handle the events associated with them and, optionally, change their labels.

The `ButtonBar` Class

To do something a little bit creative with labels, you can design a `ButtonBar` class. This class creates a dialog box with a specified label and adds a list of buttons to the dialog box, in the form of a button bar. It also allows the buttons in the button bar to be arranged in a vertical or horizontal fashion. The source code for the `ButtonBar` class is shown in Listing 20.4.

Listing 20.4. The source code of the `ButtonBar` class.

```
package jdg.ch20;

import java.awt.*;

public class ButtonBar extends Dialog {
 public static int HORIZONTAL = 0;
 public static int VERTICAL = 1;
 public ButtonBar(Frame parent,String title,String labels[],int orientation) {
  super(parent,title,false);
  int length = labels.length;
  if(orientation == HORIZONTAL) setLayout(new GridLayout(1,length));
  else setLayout(new GridLayout(length,1));
  for(int i=0;i<length;++i) add(new Button(labels[i]));
  pack();
  resize(minimumSize());
 }
 public boolean handleEvent(Event event) {
  if(event.id==Event.WINDOW_DESTROY) show(false);
  return false;
 }
}
```

The `HORIZONTAL` and `VERTICAL` constants are used to specify the orientation of the button bar. The constructor uses the `parent`, `title`, `labels[]`, and `orientation` parameters. The `parent` and `title` parameters are passed to the `Dialog` class constructor via the `super()` constructor call statement. The `false` value indicates that the button bar is not modal. The orientation parameter is used to determine the type of `GridLayout` associated with the button bar. After the orientation is specified, the `Button` objects, whose labels are specified by the `labels[]` array, are added to the button bar. The button bar dialog box is then packed and resized to the minimum size needed to contain the buttons.

A single event is handled by the `ButtonBar` class. The `WINDOWS_DESTROY` event is generated when a user tries to close the button bar dialog box. When this happens, the `show()` method inherited from the `Window` class is used to hide the dialog box. The `handleEvent()` method returns the `false` value, allowing the event to be processed by the window containing the dialog box.

The `ButtonApp` Program

The `ButtonApp` program illustrates the operation of the `ButtonBar` class. Its source code is shown in Listing 20.5.

Listing 20.5. The source code of the `ButtonApp` program.

```
import java.awt.*;
import jdg.ch20.MyMenu;
import jdg.ch20.MyMenuBar;
```

```
import jdg.ch20.ButtonBar;

public class ButtonApp extends Frame {
 MyMenuBar menuBar;
 ButtonBar buttonBar;
 public static void main(String args[]){
  ButtonApp app = new ButtonApp();
 }
 public ButtonApp() {
  super("ButtonApp");
  setup();
  pack();
  resize(400,400);
  show();
 }
 void setup() {
  setBackground(Color.white);
  setupMenuBar();
  String buttons[] = {"this","is","a","test"};
  buttonBar = new ButtonBar(this,"Button Bar",buttons,ButtonBar.HORIZONTAL);
 }
 void setupMenuBar(){
  Object menuItems[][] = {
   {"File","Exit"},
   {"View","-Button Bar"},
  };
  menuBar = new MyMenuBar(menuItems);
  setMenuBar(menuBar);
 }
 public boolean handleEvent(Event event) {
  if(event.id==Event.WINDOW_DESTROY){
   if(event.target instanceof ButtonBar){
     CheckboxMenuItem buttonItem =
      (CheckboxMenuItem)menuBar.getMenu("View").getItem("Button Bar");
     buttonItem.setState(false);
     return true;
   }
   System.exit(0);
   return true;
  }else if(event.id==Event.ACTION_EVENT){
   if(event.target instanceof MenuItem){
    if("Exit".equals(event.arg)){
     System.exit(0);
     return true;
    }else if("Button Bar".equals(event.arg)){
     CheckboxMenuItem buttonItem =
      (CheckboxMenuItem)menuBar.getMenu("View").getItem("Button Bar");
     boolean viewButtonBar = buttonItem.getState();
     buttonBar.show(viewButtonBar);
     return true;
    }
   }
  }
  return false;
 }
}
```

When you execute `ButtonApp`, it displays the opening window shown in Figure 20.9.

FIGURE 20.9.
The `ButtonApp` *opening window.*

Select Button Bar from the View menu, as shown in Figure 20.10.

FIGURE 20.10.
Selecting Button Bar from the View menu.

The button bar shown in Figure 20.11 is displayed on top of the main `ButtonApp` window. If you select the View menu once more, you will notice that the Button Bar menu item is implemented as a pull-down menu. It is checked or unchecked depending on whether the button bar is displayed.

FIGURE 20.11.
The button bar.

The ButtonApp program consists mostly of setup and event-handling software. It declares two field variables, menuBar and buttonBar, that are used to reference the program's menu bar and the button bar. The constructor follows the typical approach to constructing a frame window and creates a 400×400 window with the ButtonApp title.

The setup() method sets the background to white, creates a menu bar using the MyMenuBar class, and constructs a horizontal button bar using the ButtonBar class constructor introduced in the previous section. The rest of the program consists of event handling.

The WINDOW_DESTROY event is handled a little differently than the typical approach. Remember that this event can be generated for the main application window or for the button bar dialog box. The event.target variable is checked to see if the event was generated for an instance of the ButtonBar class. If so, the checkbox associated with the Button Bar menu is unchecked.

If the WINDOW_DESTROY event was generated for the main application window or the Exit menu item is selected, the program is terminated.

If the Button Bar menu item is selected, the state of the checkbox associated with that menu item is used to determine whether the button bar should be displayed. The show() method inherited from the Component class is used to turn the button bar display on and off.

Using Dialog Boxes

The ButtonBar class illustrates some of the typical methods used with dialog boxes. Most of these methods are not specific to the Dialog class, which provides few methods of its own. Rather, they are inherited from the Window and Component classes, which are superclasses of the Dialog class.

The Dialog class is used to construct a window that is displayed separately from the application menu. The window associated with a Dialog object is not allowed to contain a menu bar. It may be specified as being *modal*, meaning that it is displayed on top of the main application window until it is hidden or disposed of using the show() and dispose() methods. Most dialog boxes are not as elaborate as that made with the ButtonBar class. They are mainly used to display information to the user and get the user's response via a button click.

The MessageDialog Class

The `MessageDialog` class provides a custom component that implements the most common types of dialog boxes. It provides a convenient constructor for creating dialog boxes and partially handles the `WINDOW_DESTROY` event by hiding a dialog box from view. The source code is shown in Listing 20.6.

Listing 20.6. The source code of the `MessageDialog` class.

```
package jdg.ch20;

import java.awt.*;

public class MessageDialog extends Dialog {
 public MessageDialog(Frame parent,String title,boolean modal,String text[],
  String buttons[]) {
  super(parent,title,modal);
  int textLines = text.length;
  int numButtons = buttons.length;
  Panel textPanel = new Panel();
  Panel buttonPanel = new Panel();
  textPanel.setLayout(new GridLayout(textLines,1));
  for(int i=0;i<textLines;++i) textPanel.add(new Label(text[i]));
  for(int i=0;i<numButtons;++i) buttonPanel.add(new Button(buttons[i]));
  add("North",textPanel);
  add("South",buttonPanel);
  setBackground(Color.lightGray);
  setForeground(Color.white);
  pack();
  resize(minimumSize());
 }
 public boolean handleEvent(Event event) {
  if(event.id==Event.WINDOW_DESTROY) show(false);
  else if(event.id==Event.ACTION_EVENT && event.target instanceof Button)
   show(false);
  return false;
 }
}
```

The `MessageDialog` constructor uses the `parent`, `title`, `modal`, `text[]`, and `buttons[]` parameters. The `parent`, `title`, and `modal` parameters are passed to the `Dialog` constructor of its parent class. Two `Panel` objects are created and assigned to `textPanel` and `buttonPanel`. The `textPanel` layout is specified as a `GridLayout` object and the `buttonPanel` layout is the default `FlowLayout` object. The `text[]` lines are arranged in a vertical grid in the `textPanel`. The `buttons[]` are laid out in a centered horizontal fashion within the `buttonPanel`. The layout for the `MessageDialog` object is `BorderLayout`, by default. The `textPanel` is added to the top of the dialog box and the `buttonPanel` is added to the bottom. The foreground and background colors are set to light gray and white. The dialog box is packed and resized to the minimum size needed to contain the two panels.

The MessageApp Program

The MessageApp program shows how the MessageDialog class can be used to implement traditional dialog box functions found in typical window programs. Its source code is shown in Listing 20.7.

Listing 20.7. The source code of the MessageApp program.

```
import java.awt.*;
import jdg.ch20.MyMenu;
import jdg.ch20.MyMenuBar;
import jdg.ch20.MessageDialog;

public class MessageApp extends Frame {
 MyMenuBar menuBar;
 MessageDialog dialog;
 public static void main(String args[]){
  MessageApp app = new MessageApp();
 }
 public MessageApp() {
  super("MessageApp");
  setup();
  pack();
  resize(400,400);
  show();
 }
 void setup() {
  setBackground(Color.white);
  setupMenuBar();
 }
 void setupMenuBar(){
  Object menuItems[][] = {
   {"File","Exit"},
   {"View","Information","Confirmation","Selection"},
  };
  menuBar = new MyMenuBar(menuItems);
  setMenuBar(menuBar);
 }
 public boolean handleEvent(Event event) {
  if(event.id==Event.WINDOW_DESTROY){
   if(event.target instanceof MessageDialog) return true;
   System.exit(0);
   return true;
  }else if(event.id==Event.ACTION_EVENT){
   if(event.target instanceof MenuItem){
    if("Exit".equals(event.arg)){
     System.exit(0);
     return true;
```

continues

Listing 20.7. continued

```
    }else if("Information".equals(event.arg)){
     String text[] = {"Don't look now, but your shoelace is untied."};
     String buttons[] = {"OK"};
     dialog = new MessageDialog(this,"Information",true,text,buttons);
     dialog.show();
     return true;
    }else if("Confirmation".equals(event.arg)){
     String text[] = {"Do you really want to do this?"};
     String buttons[] = {"Yes","No","Cancel"};
     dialog = new MessageDialog(this,"Confirmation",true,text,buttons);
     dialog.show();
     return true;
    }else if("Selection".equals(event.arg)){
     String text[] = {"What direction do you want to go?",
       "North: cold", "South: warm", "East: humid", "West: arid"};
     String buttons[] = {"North","South","East","West"};
     dialog = new MessageDialog(this,"Selection",true,text,buttons);
     dialog.show();
     return true;
    }
   }
  }
  return false;
 }
}
```

The `MessageApp` opening window is shown in Figure 20.12. It supports the File and View pull-down menus.

FIGURE 20.12.
The `MessageApp` *opening window.*

Select the Information menu item from the View pull-down menu, as shown in Figure 20.13.

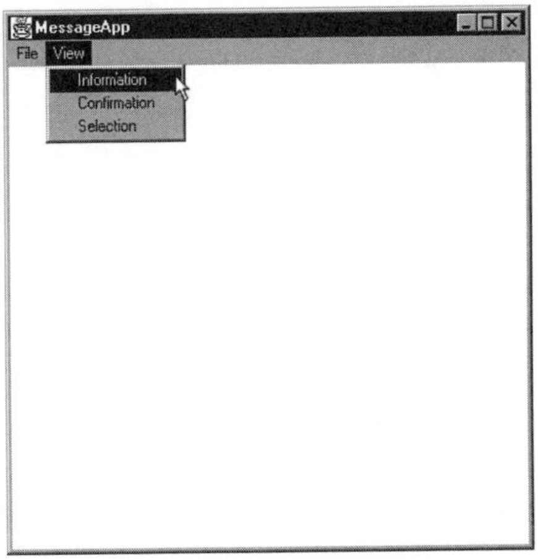

FIGURE 20.13.
Selecting Information from the View menu.

A helpful Information dialog box is displayed, as shown in Figure 20.14. This type of dialog box is typically used to provide information to the user. When the dialog box is displayed, the user acknowledges the information by clicking on the OK button.

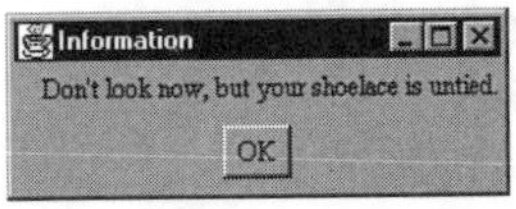

FIGURE 20.14.
The Information dialog box.

Selecting Confirmation from the View menu results in a Confirmation dialog box being displayed to the user, as shown in Figure 20.15. This type of dialog box requests confirmation from the user before attempting to perform an operation that may require the user's approval. If the user clicks the Yes button, the action is performed. If the user clicks No, the operation is not performed. If the user clicks Cancel, an entire series of actions leading up to the confirmation dialog box is aborted.

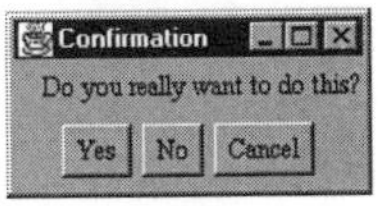

FIGURE 20.15.
The Confirmation dialog box.

Choosing the Selection menu item from the View menu results in a multiple-choice Selection dialog box displayed to the user. The user is allowed to pick one from several alternative paths of program execution. (See Figure 20.16.)

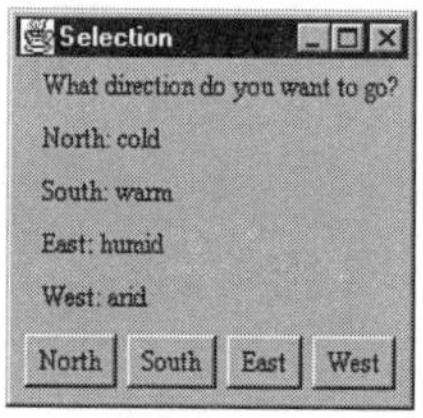

FIGURE 20.16.
The Selection dialog box.

The `MessageApp` constructor creates a 400×400 window, titled MessageApp. It uses the `MyMenuBar` class to construct the program's menu bar. No special processing of note is performed in the application window's construction. The dialog boxes, previously shown, are created by the program's event-handling software.

The `handleEvent()` method takes the message dialog boxes into account when processing the `WINDOW_DESTROY` message. It checks to see if the target of the event is a dialog box and, if so, continues with program execution. If the Information menu item is selected, a new `MessageDialog` object is created with the information shown in Figure 20.14 and the dialog box is displayed to the user using the `show()` method. The dialog box is modal. The Confirmation and Selection menu items are handled in a similar manner. They create the dialog boxes shown in Figures 20.15 and 20.16 using the `MessageDialog()` constructor.

The `FileDialog` Class

The `FileDialog` class is a custom subclass of the `Dialog` class. The `FileDialog` class uses the operating system's native dialog boxes to query the user for the name of a file to be loaded or saved. The `getDirectory()` and `getFile()` methods return the file's directory and filename. The `setDirectory()` and `setFile()` methods are used to set the state of the dialog box to a particular directory and file when it is initially opened. The `getMode()` method returns the `LOAD` or `SAVE` mode of the dialog box. The `setFileNameFilter()` and `getFileNameFilter()` methods are used to associate an object of the `FileNameFilter` interface with the dialog box. No classes that implement this interface are currently provided by the Java API. The `TextEdit` example in Chapter 18 illustrates the use of the `FileDialog` class in performing file load and save operations.

Summary

This chapter shows you how to use the `Menu`, `Button`, and `Dialog` classes. It describes the available menu and button options and shows you how to quickly and easily construct menus and buttons for your window programs using the `MyMenu`, `MyMenuBar`, and `ButtonBar` classes. The use of dialog boxes is also covered. You have created the `MessageDialog` class, which you can reuse in other programs. Chapter 21, "Checkboxes, Choices, and Lists," shows you how to work with those elements.

21

Checkboxes, Choices, and Lists

This chapter covers the details of using the `Checkbox`, `Choice`, and `List` classes. It shows you how to create and use objects of these classes and how to create custom components that simplify the use of these GUI controls. When you finish this chapter, you will be able to effectively use checkboxes, radio buttons, choices, and lists in your Java window programs.

Using Checkboxes

Checkboxes are a common type of GUI control. They are typically used in form-like windows to simplify yes/no or true/false selections. The user checks a checkbox to indicate yes or true, and leaves it unchecked to indicate no or false.

The name of the `Checkbox` class is somewhat misleading in that `Checkbox` objects are used to implement traditional checkboxes as well as radio buttons.

Radio buttons are similar to traditional checkboxes in that they are in either an on or off state. They are different from traditional checkboxes in that only one radio button in a group may be on at a given time. They are aptly named after the buttons on a car radio, which can only be used to select a single radio channel at a given time.

When `Checkbox` objects are used as radio buttons, they are associated with a `CheckboxGroup` object that enforces mutual exclusion among the `Checkbox` objects in its group.

The `CheckboxPanel` Class

Checkboxes, like menus, are easy to use but tedious to construct and organize. The `CheckboxPanel` class provides a more convenient approach to creating and organizing checkboxes. (See Listing 21.1.) Typically, checkboxes are created in groups and organized in a panel that is given a title. The `CheckboxPanel` class provides a constructor for quickly creating objects of this type. It also provides access methods for getting and setting the value of an individual checkbox within the panel, based on the checkbox's label.

Listing 21.1. The `CheckboxPanel` class source code.

```
package jdg.ch21;

import java.awt.*;

public class CheckboxPanel extends Panel {
 public static int HORIZONTAL = 0;
 public static int VERTICAL = 1;
 public CheckboxPanel(String title,String labels[],int orientation) {
  super();
  int length = labels.length;
  if(orientation == HORIZONTAL) setLayout(new GridLayout(1,length+1));
  else setLayout(new GridLayout(length+1,1));
  add(new Label(title));
  for(int i=0;i<length;++i) add(new Checkbox(labels[i]));
```

```
 }
 public CheckboxPanel(String title,String labels[],boolean state[],
  int orientation) {
  super();
  int length = labels.length;
  if(orientation == HORIZONTAL) setLayout(new GridLayout(1,length+1));
  else setLayout(new GridLayout(length+1,1));
  add(new Label(title));
  for(int i=0;i<length;++i){
   Checkbox checkBox = new Checkbox(labels[i]);
   checkBox.setState(state[i]);
   add(checkBox);
  }
 }
 public boolean getState(String label) {
  Checkbox boxes[] = (Checkbox[])getComponents();
  for(int i=0;i<boxes.length;++i)
   if(label.equals(boxes[i].getLabel())) return boxes[i].getState();
  return false;
 }
 public void setState(String label,boolean state) {
  Checkbox boxes[] = (Checkbox[])getComponents();
  for(int i=0;i<boxes.length;++i)
   if(label.equals(boxes[i].getLabel())) boxes[i].setState(state);
 }
}
```

Two `CheckboxPanel` constructors are provided. The first constructor uses a `title` string for the panel, an array of `labels[]` to be associated with checkboxes, and an `orientation` parameter that specifies whether the panel is to be organized in a vertical or horizontal fashion.

A `GridLayout` object is used to organize the `Label` and `Checkbox` objects placed within the panel. The title `Label` is added at the top of vertical panels and on the left side of horizontal panels. Then the checkboxes are created, one at a time, and fill in the rest of the panel.

The second constructor is similar to the first constructor, except that it uses an additional `state[]` array to set the initial state of the checkboxes that are added to the panel. The state of each checkbox is set using the `setState()` method of the `Checkbox` class.

The `getState()` method takes the label of a checkbox as its parameter and searches the checkboxes contained in the panel for one whose label matches the specified label. It then returns the state of this checkbox. If no matching checkbox is found, it returns `false`.

The `setState()` method is similar to the `getState()` method. It is used to update a checkbox with a given label.

Working with Radio Buttons

Radio buttons are created using the `Checkbox` class and are transformed from checkboxes into radio buttons when they are associated with a `CheckboxGroup` object. A `CheckboxGroup` can be assigned with the `Checkbox` constructor or using the `setCheckboxGroup()` method. Only one object in the checkbox group is allowed to be set at any given time.

The `CheckboxGroupPanel` Class

The `CheckboxGroupPanel` class extends the `CheckboxPanel` class to work with radio buttons. Its source code is shown in Listing 21.2.

Listing 21.2. The source code for the `CheckboxGroupPanel` class.

```
package jdg.ch21;

import java.awt.*;

public class CheckboxGroupPanel extends CheckboxPanel {
 public CheckboxGroupPanel(String title,String labels[],int orientation) {
  super(title,labels,orientation);
  putInGroup();
 }
 public CheckboxGroupPanel(String title,String labels[],boolean state[],
  int orientation) {
  super(title,labels,state,orientation);
  putInGroup();
 }
 void putInGroup() {
  Component components[] = getComponents();
  int length = components.length;
  CheckboxGroup group = new CheckboxGroup();
  for(int i=1;i<length;++i){
   Checkbox checkBox = (Checkbox) components[i];
   checkBox.setCheckboxGroup(group);
  }
 }
}
```

The `Checkbox` panel constructors are overridden to place the checkboxes in the panel in a single group. If the second constructor is used, only one checkbox should be specified as being in the on state.

The `putInGroup()` method uses the `getComponents()` method inherited from the `Container` class to create an array of the components contained in the panel. It creates a `CheckboxGroup` object and then indexes through the array, putting all checkboxes into this group using the `setCheckboxGroup()` method. The first component is skipped because it is the title of the panel.

The `CheckboxApp` Program

The `CheckboxApp` program illustrates the use of the `CheckboxPanel` and `CheckboxGroupPanel` classes. Its source code is shown in Listing 21.3.

Listing 21.3. The source code for the CheckboxApp program.

```
import java.awt.*;
import jdg.ch20.MyMenu;
import jdg.ch20.MyMenuBar;
import jdg.ch20.MessageDialog;
import jdg.ch21.CheckboxPanel;
import jdg.ch21.CheckboxGroupPanel;

public class CheckboxApp extends Frame {
 MyMenuBar menuBar;
 MessageDialog dialog;
 CheckboxPanel checkboxPanel;
 CheckboxGroupPanel checkboxGroupPanel;
 public static void main(String args[]){
  CheckboxApp app = new CheckboxApp();
 }
 public CheckboxApp() {
  super("CheckboxApp");
  setup();
  pack();
  resize(minimumSize());
  show();
 }
 void setup() {
  setBackground(Color.white);
  setupMenuBar();
  setupCheckboxes();
 }
 void setupMenuBar(){
  Object menuItems[][] = {
   {"File","Exit"},
  };
  menuBar = new MyMenuBar(menuItems);
  setMenuBar(menuBar);
 }
 void setupCheckboxes(){
  setLayout(new GridLayout(1,2));
  String sports[] = {"Baseball","Basketball","Football","Hockey","Soccer"};
  checkboxPanel = new CheckboxPanel("What team sports do you like?  ",
   sports,CheckboxPanel.VERTICAL);
  add(checkboxPanel);
  String ages[] = {"under 20","20 - 39","40 - 59","60 - 79","80 and over"};
  checkboxGroupPanel = new CheckboxGroupPanel("What is your age?  ",
   ages,CheckboxPanel.VERTICAL);
  add(checkboxGroupPanel);
 }
 public boolean handleEvent(Event event) {
  if(event.id==Event.WINDOW_DESTROY){
   if(event.target instanceof MessageDialog) return true;
   System.exit(0);
   return true;
  }else if(event.id==Event.ACTION_EVENT){
   if(event.target instanceof MenuItem){
    if("Exit".equals(event.arg)){
     System.exit(0);
     return true;
```

continues

Listing 21.3. continued

```
    }
   }else if(event.target instanceof Checkbox){
    String status;
    Checkbox checkbox = (Checkbox)event.target;
    if(checkbox.getState()) status = "You checked: ";
    else status = "You unchecked: ";
    String text[] = {status+checkbox.getLabel()+"    "};
    String buttons[] = {"OK"};
    dialog = new MessageDialog(this,"Guess what?",true,text,buttons);
    dialog.show();
    return true;
   }
  }
  return false;
 }
}
```

When you execute the program, it displays the window shown in Figure 21.1. The left side of the window displays a `CheckboxPanel` object, and the right side displays a `CheckboxPanelGroup` object. Notice that traditional checkboxes are displayed on the left, and radio buttons are displayed on the right.

FIGURE 21.1.
The `CheckboxApp` *opening window.*

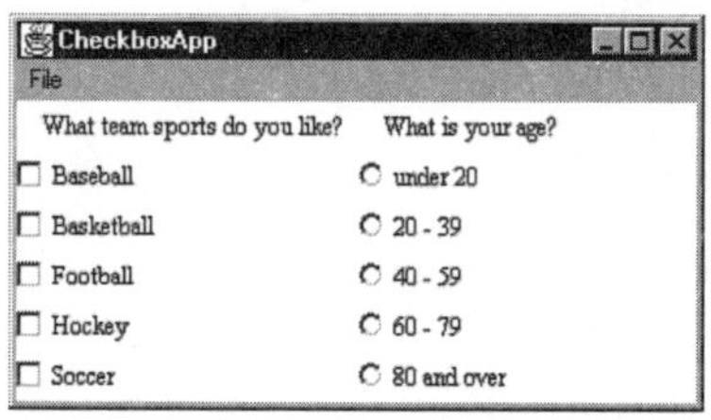

Click on the Basketball checkbox, as shown in Figure 21.2. The checkbox is checked and the dialog box shown in Figure 21.3 is displayed as the result of handling this event. Click on the Basketball checkbox again, and the dialog box shown in Figure 21.4 is displayed. The purpose of this type of dialog box is to illustrate checkbox event handling. It is not normally part of any application that uses checkboxes because the checkbox display indicates the state of a checkbox.

FIGURE 21.2.
Checking Basketball.

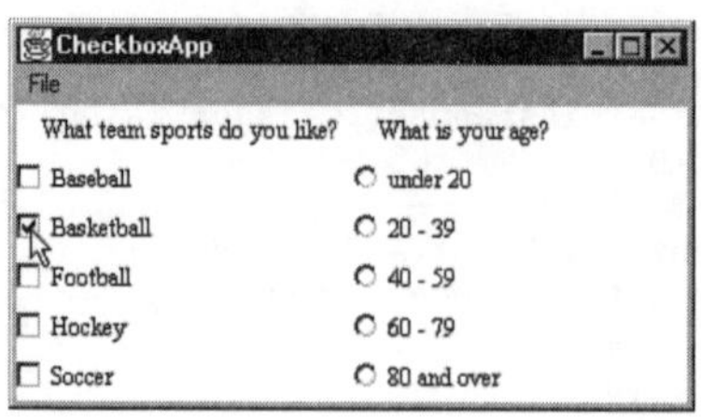

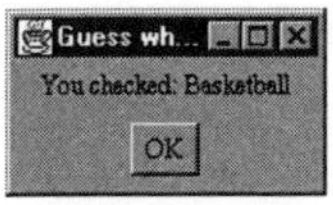

FIGURE 21.3.
You checked Basketball.

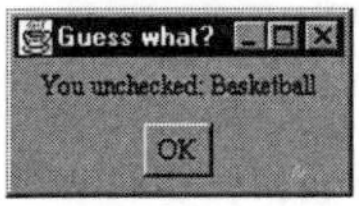

FIGURE 21.4.
You unchecked Basketball.

Go ahead and check your favorite sports, and then turn your attention to the radio buttons. Select your age group, as shown in Figure 21.5. The program notifies you of your selection. Go ahead and select another age group, as shown in Figure 21.6. Notice that you can't select more than one age group at a given time. That's the idea behind radio buttons.

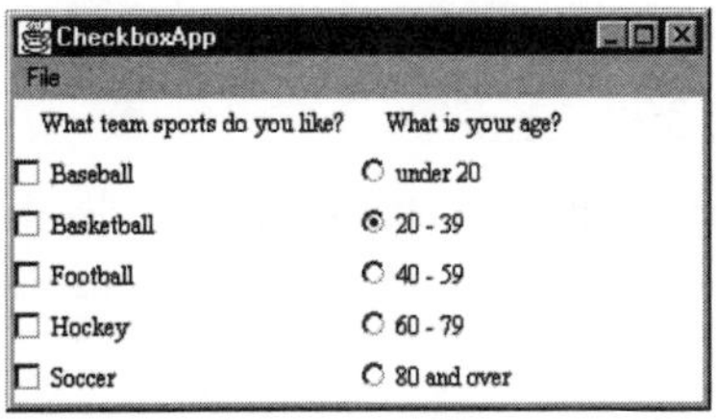

FIGURE 21.5.
Select your age group.

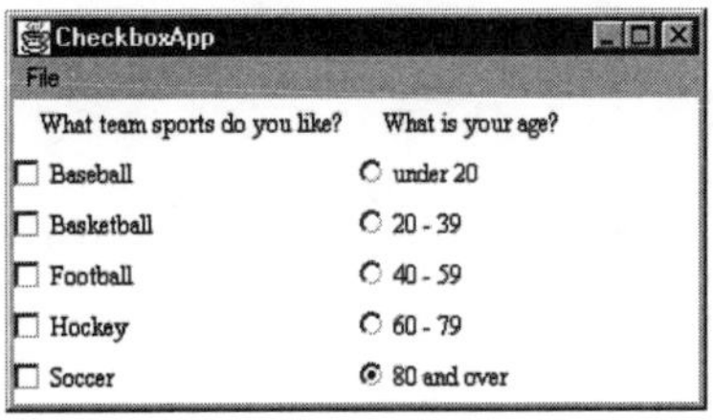

FIGURE 21.6.
Now select a different age group.

The `CheckboxApp` program makes use of several custom components that you've built so far, including the `MyMenu`, `MyMenuBar`, `MessageDialog`, `CheckboxPanel`, and `CheckboxGroupPanel` classes. Try rewriting this program without using these classes and you'll find out how time-consuming and tedious it can be to write programs without custom classes. You should now be getting used to using this class-building approach to simplify your Java programming.

The `setupCheckboxes()` method sets up the checkbox and radio button panels displayed in the previous figures. A `GridLayout` object is used to organize the main application window. The `checkboxPanel` variable is assigned the `CheckboxPanel` object that is created using the `sports[]` array, and the `checkboxGroupPanel` variable is assigned the `CheckboxGroupPanel` object that is created using the `ages[]` array. Both panels are then added to the `Frame` object being constructed. That's all the code required to create the GUI controls shown in Figure 21.1.

The `handleEvent()` method looks to see if the target of an `ACTION_EVENT` is an instance of the `Checkbox` class. This will be true for both checkboxes and radio buttons. It then retrieves the checkbox from the `event.target` variable and uses the `getState()` method to obtain the state of the `Checkbox` object. Then it retrieves the label of the `Checkbox` object using the `getLabel()` method and passes this information to the user via a `MessageDialog` object.

Making Choices

The `Choice` class allows Motif-style choice lists to be used in Java window programs. These GUI controls are also supported in Windows 95 and NT programs. A *choice list* is a pull-down menu that allows a user to select a single item from a list. When a choice selection is made, an `ACTION_EVENT` is generated, and the program is then able to respond to that selection. Choices are like menus that are placed in the middle of a window.

The `MyChoice` Class

`MyChoice` is a short and sweet class that simplifies the construction of a `Choice` object. Its source code is shown in Listing 21.4.

Listing 21.4. The source code for the `MyChoice` class.

```
package jdg.ch21;

import java.awt.*;

public class MyChoice extends Choice {
 public MyChoice(String labels[]) {
  super();
  int length = labels.length;
  for(int i=0;i<length;++i) {
   try {
    addItem(labels[i]);
   }catch (NullPointerException ex) {
    addItem("");
   }
  }
 }
}
```

Rather than constructing a `Choice` object and adding all of the items in the choice list, the `MyChoice` constructor takes an array of labels and adds them to the `Choice` object as it is constructed. The `addItem()` method of the `Choice` class throws the `NullPointerException` and is handled by adding a blank item to the choice list when a `null` pointer is encountered.

Selecting from Lists

The `List` class is a tad more sophisticated that the `Choice` class. It is similar in that it allows a user to select from a list of items that are displayed in a window component. It is different because it provides the capability to support multiple menu selections, to specify the size of the list window, and to dynamically update the list during program execution.

The `List` class provides two constructors. The default constructor takes no parameters. The second constructor specifies the number of visible rows to be identified and whether multiple selections are allowed.

The access methods supported by the `List` class are also more extensive than the `Choice` class. In particular, the `delItem()`, `clear()`, and `replaceItem()` methods allow `List` objects to be dynamically updated.

The `MyList` Class

The `MyList` class is very similar to the `MyChoice` class in that it enables a list to be constructed using an array of list items. (See Listing 21.5.) The `MyList` constructor also allows the number of rows displayed in the list and the multiple-selection parameter to be specified. The `MyList` constructor sets the foreground and background colors of the list box that is displayed. This is used to override any colors that might be set for the foreground and background of the list's container.

Listing 21.5. The source code for the `MyList` class.

```
package jdg.ch21;

import java.awt.*;

public class MyList extends List {
 public MyList(int rows,boolean multiple,String labels[]) {
  super(rows,multiple);
  int length = labels.length;
  for(int i=0;i<length;++i) {
   try {
    addItem(labels[i]);
   }catch (NullPointerException ex) {
    addItem("");
   }
  }
  setBackground(Color.white);
  setForeground(Color.black);
 }
}
```

The ChoiceListApp Program

The `ChoiceListApp` program illustrates the use of the `MyChoice` and `MyList` classes. (See Listing 21.6.) It provides the capability to decide what you want to eat for your next meal and can be very handy when a moment of indecision arrives. The following source code lists only a basic set of menu items, but additional menu items can be added easily.

Listing 21.6. The source code for the `ChoiceListApp` program.

```
import java.awt.*;
import jdg.ch20.MyMenu;
import jdg.ch20.MyMenuBar;
import jdg.ch21.MyChoice;
import jdg.ch21.MyList;

public class ChoiceListApp extends Frame {
 MyMenuBar menuBar;
 MyChoice mealChoice;
 MyList currentList;
 MyList mealList[];
 String meals[] = {"Breakfast","Lunch","Dinner"};
 String mealChoices[][] = {
  {"pancakes","eggs","bacon","ham","sausage","cereal",
   "toast","coffee","juice"},
  {"pizza","hamburger","hot dog","burrito","salad","fries",
   "chips","soda","milk"},
  {"spaghetti","carne asada","barbequed chicken","soup","salad",
   "bread","wine","beer","soda","milk"}
 };
 TextField text;
 public static void main(String args[]){
  ChoiceListApp app = new ChoiceListApp();
 }
 public ChoiceListApp() {
  super("ChoiceListApp");
  setup();
  pack();
  resize(275,175);
  show();
 }
 void setup() {
  setBackground(Color.white);
  setupMenuBar();
  setupChoice();
  setupLists();
  text = new TextField(40);
  add("North",new Label("Place your order:"));
  add("South",text);
  add("West",mealChoice);
  currentList = mealList[0];
  add("East",currentList);
 }
 void setupMenuBar(){
```

```
 Object menuItems[][] = {
  {"File","Exit"},
 };
 menuBar = new MyMenuBar(menuItems);
 setMenuBar(menuBar);
}
void setupChoice(){
 mealChoice = new MyChoice(meals);
}
void setupLists(){
 mealList = new MyList[meals.length];
 for(int i=0;i<meals.length;++i)
  mealList[i] = new MyList(5,true,mealChoices[i]);
}
public boolean handleEvent(Event event) {
 if(event.id==Event.WINDOW_DESTROY){
  System.exit(0);
  return true;
 }else if(event.id==Event.ACTION_EVENT){
  if(event.target instanceof MenuItem){
   if("Exit".equals(event.arg)){
    System.exit(0);
    return true;
   }
  }else if(event.target instanceof Choice){
   for(int i=0;i<meals.length;++i)
    if(meals[i].equals(event.arg)){
     remove(currentList);
     currentList = mealList[i];
     add("East",currentList);
     text.setText(meals[i]);
    }
   show();
   return true;
  }else if(event.target instanceof List){
   updateTextField();
   return true;
  }
 }else if(event.id==Event.LIST_SELECT || event.id==Event.LIST_DESELECT){
  updateTextField();
  return true;
 }
 return false;
}
void updateTextField() {
 String order = mealChoice.getSelectedItem()+": ";
 String items[] = currentList.getSelectedItems();
 for(int i=0;i<items.length;++i) order += items[i]+" ";
 text.setText(order);
}
}
```

Make sure that you have food on hand when you run the `ChoiceListApp` program. Its opening window is shown in Figure 21.7.

FIGURE 21.7.
The `ChoiceListApp` *opening window.*

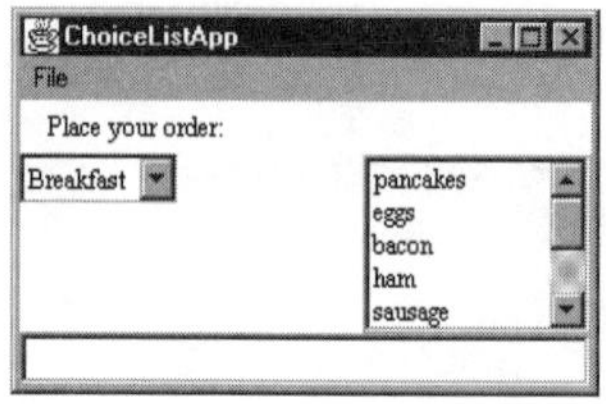

The choice list shown on the left side of the window is used to select a meal. This selection determines what menu items are displayed in the list shown on the right side of the window. More than one item can be selected from the entrée list. The text field on the bottom of the screen identifies the selections that you have made. Go ahead and select Lunch from the choice list, as shown in Figure 21.8. Notice that the entrée list is updated with some typical lunch items. The text field tells you that you are now ordering lunch.

FIGURE 21.8.
Selecting lunch.

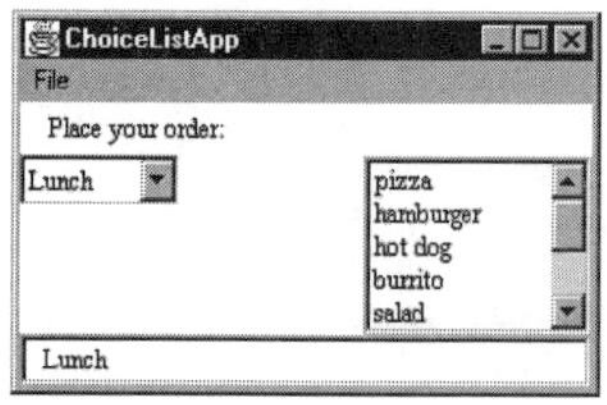

Go ahead and select some menu items from the entrée list. They are displayed in the text field, as shown in Figure 21.9.

FIGURE 21.9.
Ordering lunch.

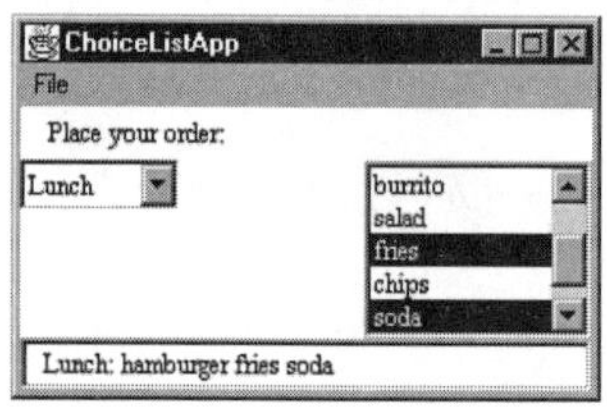

Now select Dinner from the choice list and select some dinner entrées, as shown in Figure 21.10. The text field is updated to list your new selections.

FIGURE 21.10.
Selecting another meal.

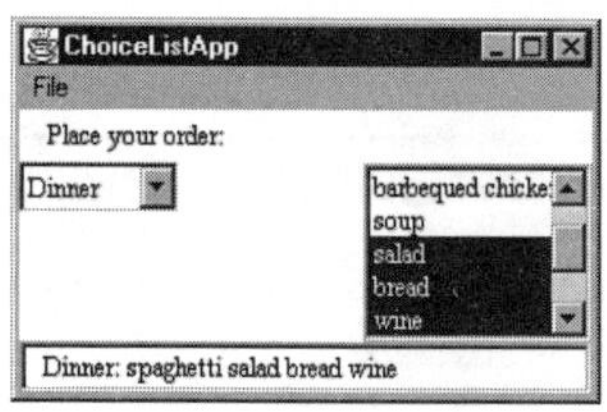

The ChoiceListApp program declares several field variables. The menuBar variable is the now-standard variable used to identify the program's menu bar. The mealChoice variable is used to refer to the MyChoice object that displays the meals identified in the meals[] array. Two MyList variables are declared. The mealList[] array holds the three MyList objects used for breakfast, lunch, and dinner. These items are stored in the mealChoices[] array. The currentList variable points to the current menu entrée list being displayed. The text variable refers to the TextField object displayed at the bottom of the window.

The main() method and ChoiceListApp() constructor follow the pattern that's been developed so far. The window is resized to make its display more visually appealing. A GridBagLayout layout would have been more appropriate for this type of application, but the overhead of implementing it would obscure the important points associated with the MyChoice and MyList classes.

The setup() method sets up the background and menu bar and then invokes the setupChoice() and setupLists() methods to set up the MyChoice and MyList objects. The text field is initialized to be 40 characters wide, and then the user-interface objects are placed in the appropriate places in the ChoiceListApp window.

The setupChoice() method constructs the mealChoice object using a simple, one-line constructor. The setupLists() method sets up the mealList object by indexing through the mealChoices[] array and setting up the individual MyList objects.

The handleEvent() method looks for events of type ACTION_EVENT that are instances of the Choice class. It handles them by finding the element of the meals[] array that was selected and using it to select the next mealList[] element to be displayed as the currentList. The old list is removed, and a new currentList object is added. The text field is then set to the meals[] element that was selected. Note that this approach of removing the list and replacing it with a new one is less elegant than updating the list as it is displayed.

The handleEvent() method processes ACTION_EVENT, which occurs when the user double-clicks on a list item. It invokes the updateTextField() method to update the text that is displayed in the text field at the bottom of the window's display. It also handles the LIST_SELECT and LIST_DESELECT events in the same fashion.

The updateTextField() method retrieves the currently selected item in the MyChoice object referred to by mealChoice using the getSelectedItem() method of the Choice class. This String object is used to build the text display by identifying the currently selected meal. The getSelectedItems() method of the List class is used to return a list of all items selected in the currently displayed MyChoice object referred to by the currentList variable. These items are then added to the text field display.

Summary

This chapter shows you how to use the `Checkbox`, `Choice`, and `List` classes. It describes their available constructors and access methods and shows you how to use them as the basis for creating custom GUI components. Chapter 22, "Text and Fonts," shows you how to work with these features.

22

Text and Fonts

This chapter covers the details of Java's text- and font-related classes. It shows how to use the `TextComponent` subclasses and how to display text with the canvas. It explains Java's use of fonts and shows how the `Font` and `FontMetrics` classes are used to provide custom control of text display. When you finish this chapter, you will be able to effectively use text and fonts in your Java window programs.

The Text Classes

You are now fairly familiar with the text-related classes supported by Java because you've used `TextArea` and `TextField` objects in the examples presented so far. Let's review these classes and then you can learn how to use font-related classes to alter the way text is presented to the user.

The `TextComponent` class is the superclass of the `TextField` and `TextArea` classes. It extends the `Component` class to support text-related processing. `TextComponent` provides several methods that are used to process text that is selected by the user. The `setEditable()` method determines whether a `TextComponent` object is read-only or can be edited. The `getText()` and `setText()` methods are its most popular methods and are used with all text-related classes.

The `TextField` class implements a simple, one-line text field. The visible length of the field (in characters) can be specified. Character echoing can be disabled to implement password-like text fields.

The `TextArea` class implements a multiple-line text field and supports a number of methods for updating the field by inserting, appending, and replacing text. The number of rows and columns associated with a text field can be specified.

Font Basics

The `Font` class provides a platform-independent method of specifying and using fonts. The `Font` class constructor constructs `Font` objects using the font's name, style (`PLAIN`, `BOLD`, `ITALIC`, or `BOLD + ITALIC`), and point size. Java's fonts are named in a platform-independent manner and then mapped to local fonts that are supported by the operating system on which it executes. The `getName()` method returns the logical Java font name of a particular font and the `getFamily()` method returns the operating system–specific name of the font. The standard Java font names are Dialog, DialogInput, Courier, Helvetica, TimesRoman, and ZapfDingbats. You'll see examples of these fonts shortly.

The `FontMetrics` class is used to return the specific parameters for a particular `Font` object. An object of this class is created using the `getFontMetrics()` methods supported by the `Component` class and other classes, such as the `Graphics` and `Toolkit` classes. The `FontMetrics` access methods provide access to the details of the implementation of a `Font` object.

The `bytesWidth()`, `charWidth()`, `charsWidth()`, `getWidths()`, and `stringWidth()` methods are used to determine the width of a text object in pixels. These methods are essential for determining the horizontal position of text on the screen.

When text characters are displayed, they are displayed relative to a baseline. The *baseline* is the line drawn through the bottom of non-descending characters. For example, if you drew a line at the bottom of most text displayed on this line, you would get the text's baseline. Some characters, such as *g* and *y*, descend below the baseline. The number of pixels that the characters of a font descend below the baseline are known as the font's *descent.* The number of pixels that the characters of a font extend above the baseline are known as the font's *ascent.* In addition to a font's ascent and descent, a third parameter, referred to as the font's *leading,* is used to describe the amount of vertical spacing, in pixels, used between the descent of a line of text and the ascent of the line of text below it. The overall height of a font is the sum of its leading, ascent, and spacing and is equal to the distance between baselines (in pixels) of vertically adjacent lines of text. The `getLeading()`, `getAscent()`, `getDescent()`, and `getHeight()` methods of the `FontMetrics` class are used to access these important font-related parameters.

The `getMaxAdvance()`, `getMaxAscent()`, and `getMaxDescent()` methods are provided for backward compatibility with earlier Java versions.

Using the `Toolkit` Class

The `Toolkit` class provides a link between the platform-independent Java implementation and its platform-specific characteristics. Among the many uninteresting methods implemented by this class are the `getFontList()`, `getFontMetrics()`, `getScreenSize()`, and `getScreenResolution()` methods. The `getFontList()` method returns a list of fonts that are accessible from Java. The `getFontMetrics()` method identifies the font metrics for a particular font. The `getScreenSize()` method identifies the screen dimension in terms of horizontal and vertical dots. The `getScreenResolution()` method identifies the screen resolution in dots per inch.

`getFontList()` is the method of interest for this chapter. You'll use it to get a list of the fonts available to Java in the next section.

The FontApp Program

The `FontApp` program illustrates the use of the `Font`, `FontMetrics`, and `Toolkit` classes and shows how to draw text on a `Graphics` object. Its source code is shown in Listing 22.1.

Listing 22.1. The source code of the `FontApp` program.

```
import java.awt.*;
import jdg.ch20.*;

public class FontApp extends Frame {
 MyMenuBar menuBar;
 Toolkit toolkit;
 Font defaultFont;
 String fontNames[];
 int screenWidth = 400;
 int screenHeight = 400;
 public static void main(String args[]){
  FontApp app = new FontApp();
 }
 public FontApp() {
  super("FontApp");
  setup();
  pack();
  resize(screenWidth,screenHeight);
  show();
 }
 void setup() {
  setBackground(Color.white);
  setupMenuBar();
  setMenuBar(menuBar);
  setupFonts();
 }
 void setupMenuBar() {
  String menuItems[][] = {{"File","Exit"}};
  menuBar = new MyMenuBar(menuItems);
 }
 void setupFonts() {
  toolkit = getToolkit();
  defaultFont = getFont();
  fontNames = toolkit.getFontList();
 }
 public void paint(Graphics g) {
  int styles[] = {Font.PLAIN,Font.BOLD,Font.ITALIC,Font.BOLD+Font.ITALIC};
  String styleNames[] = {"Plain","Bold","Italic","Bold and Italic"};
  int y = 0;
  int size = 14;
  for(int i=0;i<fontNames.length;++i) {
   for(int j=0;j<styles.length;++j) {
    Font newFont = new Font(fontNames[i],styles[j],size);
    FontMetrics fm = g.getFontMetrics(newFont);
    g.setFont(newFont);
    String text = fontNames[i]+"-"+styleNames[j];
    int x = (screenWidth - fm.stringWidth(text))/2;
    g.drawString(text,x,y+fm.getLeading()+fm.getAscent());
    y += fm.getHeight();
   }
```

```
  }
 }
 public boolean handleEvent(Event event) {
  if(event.id==Event.WINDOW_DESTROY){
   System.exit(0);
   return true;
  }else if(event.id==Event.ACTION_EVENT){
   if(event.target instanceof MenuItem){
    if("Exit".equals(event.arg)){
     System.exit(0);
     return true;
    }
   }
  }
  return false;
 }
}
```

The `FontApp` program does not provide much functionality. Just run it and it will display a list of the fonts that are currently available to Java, with each name written in its font. Figure 22.1 shows its display. The program's importance is not what it does, but in how it does it. By closely examining this program, you'll be able to quickly come up to speed on working with Java fonts.

FIGURE 22.1.
The `FontApp` *opening window.*

The `FontApp` class declares a number of field variables. The `toolkit` variable is used to refer to the `Toolkit` object associated with the program window. The `defaultFont` variable identifies the default font used by the program. The `fontNames[]` array is used to store the names of the fonts that are accessible to Java.

The `setupFonts()` method obtains the `Toolkit` object associated with the program's window using the `getToolkit()` method and assigns this object to the `toolkit` variable. The current font used by the program is accessed by `getFont()` and assigned to the `defaultFont` variable. The `Toolkit` object is then used to obtain the current list of font names via the `getFontList()` method of the `Toolkit` class. That's all for the program's setup. The program's event handling is the standard Exit menu item and `WINDOW_DESTROY` event processing.

The `paint()` method is where the primary processing of interest takes place. The `styles[]` and `styleNames[]` arrays are used to identify the various text styles and their associated string descriptions. The `y` variable identifies the vertical screen position where text is displayed. The `size` variable identifies the point size used to display a font.

The `paint()` method uses two `for` statements. The outer statement iterates through the list of font names, and the inner statement iterates through the font styles. At each passes through the inner loop, a new font is created with the specified name, style, and size. The `getFontMetrics()` method of the `Graphics` class is used to obtain the `FontMetrics` object associated with the newly created font and this object is assigned to the `fm` variable. The `setFont()` method of the `Graphics` class is used to set the current font to the new font.

The next line of text to be displayed is created by concatenating the font name and its style name. The horizontal position at which the text is to be displayed in order for it to be centered is calculated based on the width of the text (in pixels) returned by the `stringWidth()` method of the `FontMetrics` class and the initial width of the program window. The vertical position where the text is to be displayed is its baseline and is determined by adding the leading and ascent values of the font with the `y` variable. These values are obtained using the `getLeading()` and `getAscent()` methods of the current `FontMetric` object. The `y` variable identifies the point of maximum descent of the previously displayed line of text. It is then updated for the current line of text by adding the height of the current font returned by the `getHeight()` method of the `FontMetric` class.

WYSIWYG Editors

The `Font` and `FontMetrics` classes are not confined to text that is drawn on `Graphics` objects. These classes can also be used with the `TextField` and `TextArea` classes. These classes automatically calculate the correct text-display locations using the native text objects supported by the local operating-system platform. In addition to changing text fonts, the `TextField` and `TextArea` classes also support the display of text using different foreground and background colors. The following program shows how fonts and colors can be quickly incorporated into a Java program to implement features associated with what-you-see-is-what-you-get (WYSIWYG) editors.

The EditApp Program

The EditApp program shows how the Font and Color classes can be incorporated into the TextEdit program introduced in Chapter 18, "Opening Windows." Its source code is shown in Listing 22.2.

The EditApp program uses the FontDialog and ColorDialog classes that are introduced in subsequent sections. In order to compile and run EditApp.java, you will need to type in the FontDialog.java and ColorDialog.java files. Java will automatically compile the FontDialog.java and ColorDialog.java files when EditApp.java is compiled.

Listing 22.2. The source code of the EditApp program.

```
import java.awt.*;
import java.io.*;
import jdg.ch20.*;
import jdg.ch22.FontDialog;
import jdg.ch22.ColorDialog;

public class EditApp extends Frame {
 String programName;
 Object menuItems[][] = {
  {"File","New","Open","-","Save As","-","Exit"},
  {"Format","Font","Color"}
 };
 MyMenuBar menuBar = new MyMenuBar(menuItems);
 TextArea text;
 FileDialog openFile = new FileDialog(this,"Open File",FileDialog.LOAD);
 FileDialog saveFile = new FileDialog(this,"Save File As",FileDialog.SAVE);
 FontDialog fd;
 ColorDialog cd;
 Font currentFont = new Font("Courier",Font.PLAIN,12);
 Color currentColor = Color.black;
 public static void main(String args[]){
  EditApp app = new EditApp();
 }
 public EditApp() {
  super("WYSIWYG Text Editor");
  programName = getTitle();
  setup();
  pack();
  resize(text.preferredSize());
  show();
 }
 void setup() {
  setBackground(Color.white);
  text = new TextArea(25,80);
  text.setFont(currentFont);
  add("Center",text);
  setMenuBar(menuBar);
  setCursor(TEXT_CURSOR);
 }
```

continues

Listing 22.2. continued

```
public void readFile(String file) {
 DataInputStream inStream;
 try{
  inStream = new DataInputStream(new FileInputStream(file));
 }catch (IOException ex){
  notifyUser("Error opening file");
  return;
 }
 try{
  String newText="";
  String line;
  while((line=inStream.readLine())!=null)
   newText=newText+line+"\n";
  text.setText(newText);
  inStream.close();
 }catch (IOException ex){
  notifyUser("Error reading file");
 }
}
public void writeFile(String file) {
 DataOutputStream outStream;
 try{
  outStream = new DataOutputStream(new FileOutputStream(file));
 }catch (IOException ex){
  notifyUser("Error opening file");
  return;
 }
 try{
  outStream.writeBytes(text.getText());
  outStream.close();
 }catch (IOException ex){
  notifyUser("Error writing file");
 }
}
public void notifyUser(String s) {
 String text[] = {s};
 String buttons[] = {"OK"};
 new Notification(this,"Error",true,text,buttons);
}
public boolean handleEvent(Event event) {
 if(event.id==Event.WINDOW_DESTROY){
  System.exit(0);
  return true;
 }else if(event.id==Event.GOT_FOCUS && !(event.target instanceof TextArea)) {
  setCursor(DEFAULT_CURSOR);
  return true;
 }else if(event.id==Event.LOST_FOCUS) {
  setCursor(TEXT_CURSOR);
  return true;
 }else if(event.id==Event.ACTION_EVENT){
  String arg = (String) event.arg;
  if(event.target instanceof MenuItem){
   if(processFileMenu(arg)) return true;
   if(processFormatMenu(arg)) return true;
  }else if(event.target instanceof Button){
   if("Select".equals(arg)){
    if(fd != null) {
```

```
     if(fd.isChanged()) {
      currentFont = fd.getFont();
      fd.dispose();
      text.setFont(currentFont);
     }
    }
    if(cd != null) {
     if(cd.isChanged()) {
      currentColor = cd.getColor();
      cd.dispose();
      text.setForeground(currentColor);
      text.setText(text.getText());
     }
    }
   }
  }
 }
 return false;
}
public boolean processFileMenu(String s) {
 if("New".equals(s)){
  text.setText("");
  return true;
 }else if("Open".equals(s)){
  openFile.show();
  String inFile = openFile.getFile();
  readFile(inFile);
  return true;
 }else if("Save As".equals(s)){
  saveFile.show();
  String outFile = saveFile.getFile();
  writeFile(outFile);
  return true;
 }else if("Exit".equals(s)){
  System.exit(0);
  return true;
 }
 return false;
}
public boolean processFormatMenu(String s) {
 if("Font".equals(s)){
  fd = new FontDialog(this,currentFont);
  fd.show();
  return true;
 }else if("Color".equals(s)){
  cd = new ColorDialog(this,currentColor);
  cd.show();
  return true;
 }
 return false;
}
}
class Notification extends MessageDialog {
 public Notification(Frame parent,String title,boolean modal,String text[],
  String buttons[]) {
  super(parent,title,modal,text,buttons);
 }
```

continues

Listing 22.2. continued

```
 public boolean handleEvent(Event event) {
  if(event.id==Event.WINDOW_DESTROY){
   dispose();
   return true;
  }else if(event.id==Event.ACTION_EVENT && event.target instanceof Button){
   dispose();
   return true;
  }
  return false;
 }
}
```

The `EditApp` program displays the opening window shown in Figure 22.2.

FIGURE 22.2.
The `EditApp` *opening window.*

Select Open from the File menu as shown in Figure 22.3 and use the Open File dialog box, shown in Figure 22.4, to open the `EditApp.java` source code file.

FIGURE 22.3.
The File menu.

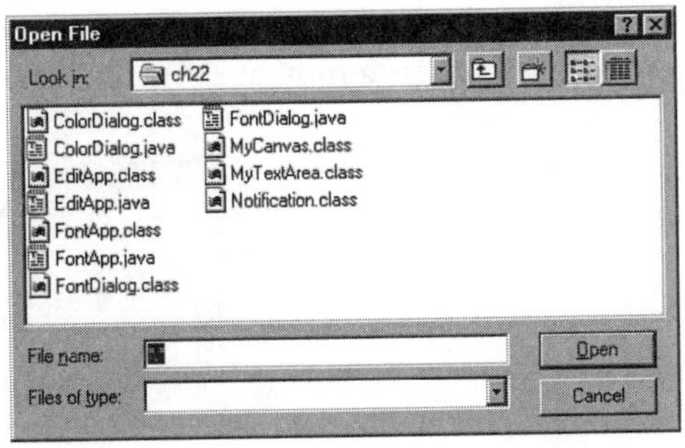

FIGURE 22.4.
The Open File dialog box.

The text of the `EditApp.java` source file is read into the program and displayed in the window using a 12-point Courier font, as shown in Figure 22.5.

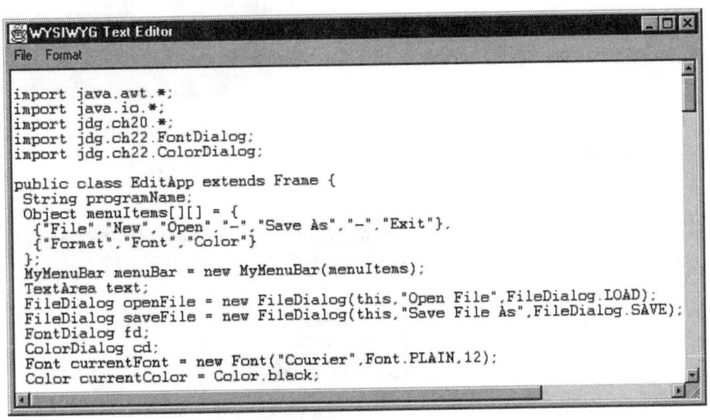

FIGURE 22.5.
Editing `EditApp.java`.

Select the Font menu item from the Format menu to change the current font used to display the text, as shown in Figure 22.6.

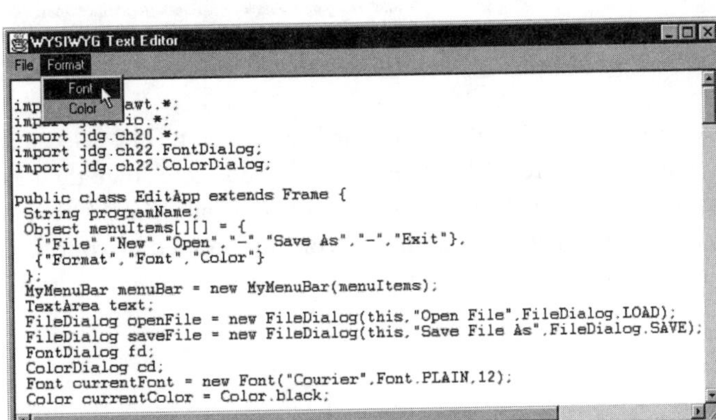

FIGURE 22.6.
The Format menu.

The Select a font: dialog box is displayed, as shown in Figure 22.7. Use this dialog box to select a 14-point Bold Italic Helvetica font, as shown in Figure 22.8.

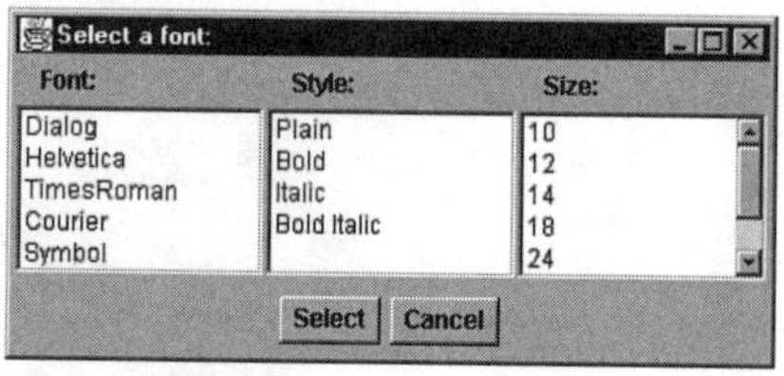

FIGURE 22.7.
The Font dialog box.

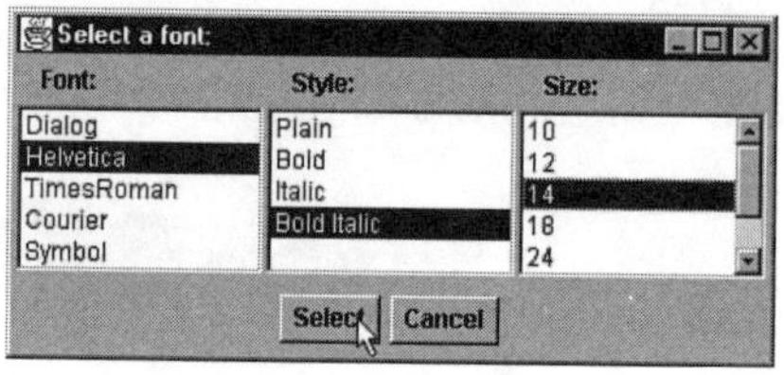

FIGURE 22.8.
Selecting a new font.

The text's display is updated, as shown in Figure 22.9.

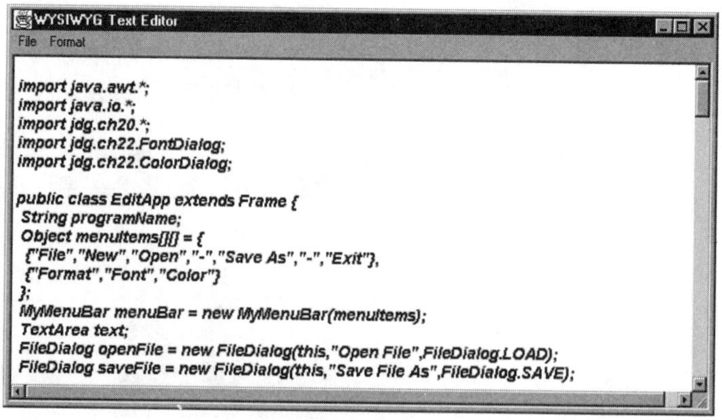

FIGURE 22.9.
Updated text.

Select the Color menu item from the Format menu. The Select a color: dialog box is displayed, as shown in Figure 22.10. Use this dialog box to change the color associated with the text's display. Try using primary colors such as blue or yellow. Other colors might not display correctly, depending on the number of colors supported by your video card and the current color map associated with the display.

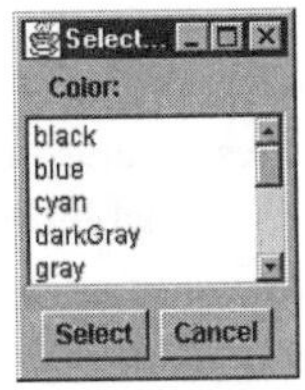

FIGURE 22.10.
The color dialog box.

The EditApp program makes use of the FontDialog and ColorDialog classes, which are covered in the following sections. The basic functionality of the EditApp program remains the same as the TextEdit program. It has been streamlined to use the MyMenuBar and MyMenu classes and adds the fd and cd variables to refer to the FontDialog and ColorDialog objects created by the program.

The setup() method specifies that TEXT_CURSOR should be used, by default, and extra event-handling code has been added to switch between TEXT_CURSOR and DEFAULT_CURSOR, depending on whether the text is in the locus of the text area or the menu bar.

The Notification class has also been updated to take advantage of the MessageDialog class.

The main changes to the EditApp program are to its event handling. The GOT_FOCUS event is handled by checking the target of the event to determine whether it is the TextArea object. If it is not, the cursor is changed to DEFAULT_CURSOR. The cursor is changed back to TEXT_CURSOR when it handles the LOST_FOCUS event. This event is handled when the object getting the focus is the TextArea object.

When an ACTION_EVENT occurs whose target is an instance of the MenuItem class, the processFileMenu() and processFormatMenu() methods are invoked to process the associated menu items. When ACTION_EVENT is an instance of the Button class, signifying a FontDialog or ColorDialog selection, the current objects associated with the fd and cd variables are checked to see which one is associated with an object. The isChanged() methods of the dialog boxes are used to determine whether a font or color change occurred. The getFont() and getColor() methods are used to set the currentFont and currentColor variables, the dialog boxes are disposed of using the dispose() method of the Window class, and the font, color, and text are set appropriately.

The processFileMenu() method checks to see if the currently selected menu item is a File menu item and processes it using the same approach as in the TextEdit program. The processFormatMenu() method checks for a Font or Color menu item and processes the menu item by creating a new FontDialog or ColorDialog object and then displaying the dialog box using the show() method of the Window class.

The FontDialog Class

The `FontDialog` class provides a handy encapsulation of the dialog boxes commonly used to select a font from the list of available fonts provided by the system. The source code of the `FontDialog` class is shown in Listing 22.3.

Listing 22.3. The source code of the `FontDialog` class.

```
package jdg.ch22;

import java.awt.*;
import jdg.ch21.MyList;

public class FontDialog extends Dialog {
 String fontName;
 int fontStyle;
 int fontSize;
 String fontNames[];
 String styleNames[] = {"Plain","Bold","Italic","Bold Italic"};
 String sizeNames[] = {"10","12","14","18","24","36","72"};
 int styles[] = {Font.PLAIN,Font.BOLD,Font.ITALIC,Font.BOLD+Font.ITALIC};
 int sizes[] = {10,12,14,18,24,36,72};
 MyList fontList;
 MyList styleList = new MyList(5,false,styleNames);
 MyList sizeList = new MyList(5,false,sizeNames);
 Toolkit toolkit;
 Font newFont;
 boolean fontChanged;
 public FontDialog(Frame parent,Font currentFont) {
  super(parent,"Select a font:",true);
  toolkit = parent.getToolkit();
  newFont = currentFont;
  setupFonts();
  setupPanels();
  setBackground(Color.lightGray);
  setForeground(Color.black);
  pack();
  resize(preferredSize());
 }
 void setupFonts() {
  fontName=newFont.getName();
  fontStyle=newFont.getStyle();
  fontSize=newFont.getSize();
  fontNames = toolkit.getFontList();
  fontList = new MyList(5,false,fontNames);
 }
 void setupPanels() {
  Panel mainPanel = new Panel();
  mainPanel.setLayout(new GridLayout(1,3));
  Panel fontPanel = new Panel();
  fontPanel.setLayout(new BorderLayout());
  Label fontLabel = new Label("Font:");
  fontPanel.add("North",fontLabel);
  fontPanel.add("Center",fontList);
  Panel stylePanel = new Panel();
  stylePanel.setLayout(new BorderLayout());
```

```
  Label styleLabel = new Label("Style:");
  stylePanel.add("North",styleLabel);
  stylePanel.add("Center",styleList);
  Panel sizePanel = new Panel();
  sizePanel.setLayout(new BorderLayout());
  Label sizeLabel = new Label("Size:");
  sizePanel.add("North",sizeLabel);
  sizePanel.add("Center",sizeList);
  mainPanel.add(fontPanel);
  mainPanel.add(stylePanel);
  mainPanel.add(sizePanel);
  Font plainFont = new Font("Helvetica",Font.PLAIN,12);
  Font boldFont = new Font("Helvetica",Font.BOLD,12);
  mainPanel.setFont(plainFont);
  fontLabel.setFont(boldFont);
  styleLabel.setFont(boldFont);
  sizeLabel.setFont(boldFont);
  Panel buttonPanel = new Panel();
  buttonPanel.setLayout(new FlowLayout());
  buttonPanel.add(new Button("Select"));
  buttonPanel.add(new Button("Cancel"));
  buttonPanel.setFont(boldFont);
  add("Center",mainPanel);
  add("South",buttonPanel);
 }
 public boolean isChanged() {
  return fontChanged;
 }
 public Font getFont() {
  return newFont;
 }
 public boolean handleEvent(Event event) {
  if(event.id==Event.WINDOW_DESTROY){
   dispose();
   return true;
  }else if(event.id==Event.ACTION_EVENT) {
   if(event.target instanceof Button) {
    if("Select".equals(event.arg)) {
     updateNewFont();
     show(false);
     return false;
    }else if("Cancel".equals(event.arg)) {
     dispose();
     return true;
    }
   }
  }
  return false;
 }
 void updateNewFont() {
  if(fontList.getSelectedIndex() != -1) fontName = fontList.getSelectedItem();
  if(styleList.getSelectedIndex() != -1)
   fontStyle = styles[styleList.getSelectedIndex()];
  if(sizeList.getSelectedIndex() != -1)
   fontSize = sizes[sizeList.getSelectedIndex()];
  newFont = new Font(fontName,fontStyle,fontSize);
  fontChanged = true;
 }
}
```

The FontDialog class creates the Font dialog box shown in Figure 22.7. This type of dialog box is used in most text-processing applications. You can reuse the FontDialog class, as it is currently defined, in your Java programs. You can also subclass FontDialog and add your own custom enhancements.

The FontDialog class declares a number of variables that are used in the generation and processing of the Font dialog box. The fontName, fontStyle, and fontSize variables are used to keep track of the parameters of the currently selected font. The fontNames[] array identifies the names of the fonts that are currently supported by the system. The styles[], styleNames[], sizes[], and sizeNames[] arrays are used to maintain int and String lists of the font styles and sizes that are displayed in the dialog box. The fontList, styleList, and sizeList variables refer to the MyList objects displayed in the dialog box. The toolkit variable refers to the Toolkit object of the window containing the Font dialog box. The fontChanged variable keeps track of whether the user has selected a new font, and the newFont variable maintains the Font object that is selected by the user.

The FontDialog constructor uses the superclass constructor call statement to create a modal dialog box with the title Select a font:. The toolkit associated with the window containing the dialog box is obtained using the getToolkit() method of the Window class. The newFont variable, representing the user's font selection, is set to the default value of the currently selected font. This font is passed to the FontDialog constructor using the currentFont parameter. The FontDialog constructor invokes the setupFonts() and setupPanels() methods to perform the bulk of the dialog box setup. It then packs the dialog box window and resizes it. Note that the constructor does not invoke the show() method to display the dialog box. The actual display of the dialog box must be performed by the containing window.

The setupFonts() method assigns default values to the fontName, fontStyle, and fontSize variables based on the values of the current font stored in the newFont variable. The getFontList() method of the Toolkit class is used to set the fontNames[] array to the list of fonts currently supported by the system. These names are converted to a list using the MyList() constructor.

The setupPanels() method performs all the grunt work, adding the lists to the dialog box and rearranging them in an appealing fashion. The mainPanel variable is used to refer to the overall panel into which the fontPanel, stylePanel, and sizePanel objects are inserted. The mainPanel is laid out as a three-column set of subpanels. These subpanels are identified by the fontPanel, stylePanel, and sizePanel variables. Each of these subpanels is laid out using a BorderLayout object. The label identifying the contents of the panel is added to the top of the panel. The center of each panel contains the three MyList objects identified by the fontList, styleList, and sizeList variables.

The Helvetica font is used for the contents of the Font dialog box. The labels at the top of each column are set in a boldface style. A second panel, referred to by the buttonPanel variable, is created with two buttons: Select and Cancel. These buttons provide the user controls needed to accept or abort a font selection. The `mainPanel` is added to the center of the Font dialog box and the `buttonPanel` is added to the bottom.

Two access methods are provided with the `FontDialog` class. The `isChanged()` method is used to query a `FontDialog` object to determine whether the user made a font selection. The `getFont()` method returns the font selected by the user.

The events handled by `FontDialog` consist of the `WINDOW_DESTROY` event and the `ACTION_EVENT` events associated with the Select and Cancel buttons. The use of the `WINDOW_DESTROY` event and Cancel button result in the destruction of the `FontDialog` object. The object is destroyed using the `dispose()` method of the `Window` class. The Select button invokes the `updateNewFont()` method to create a font based on the user's current list selections and assign that font to the `newFont` variable. The Font dialog box is then hidden but not destroyed. The `show()` method of the `Component` class is used to hide the dialog box.

The `updateNewFont()` method checks the `MyList` objects referred to by the `fontList`, `styleList`, and `sizeList` variables to update the `fontName`, `fontStyle`, and `fontSize` variables based on the user's selection. These variables are then used to construct a new `Font` object, which is assigned to the `newFont` variable. The `fontChanged` flag is then set to indicate that a user font selection has occurred.

The ColorDialog Class

The `ColorDialog` class is very similar to, but simpler than, the `FontDialog` class. It allows the user to select a color from the list of colors defined in the `Color` class. It provides a dialog box that is similar to that of `FontDialog`, but is much simpler because only one list—the list of available color—is supported. The source code of the `ColorDialog` class is shown in Listing 22.4.

Listing 22.4. The source code of the `ColorDialog` class.

```
package jdg.ch22;

import java.awt.*;
import jdg.ch21.MyList;

public class ColorDialog extends Dialog {
 Color colors[] = {Color.black,Color.blue,Color.cyan,Color.darkGray,Color.gray,
  Color.green,Color.lightGray,Color.magenta,Color.orange,Color.pink,Color.red,
  Color.white,Color.yellow};
 String colorNames[] = {"black","blue","cyan","darkGray","gray","green",
  "lightGray","magenta","orange","pink","red",
  "white","yellow"};
 MyList colorList = new MyList(5,false,colorNames);
 Color newColor;
 boolean colorChanged;
```

continues

Listing 22.4. continued

```
 public ColorDialog(Frame parent,Color currentColor) {
  super(parent,"Select a color:",true);
  setupPanels();
  setBackground(Color.lightGray);
  setForeground(Color.black);
  pack();
  resize(preferredSize());
 }
 void setupPanels() {
  Panel colorPanel = new Panel();
  colorPanel.setLayout(new BorderLayout());
  Label colorLabel = new Label("Color:");
  colorPanel.add("North",colorLabel);
  colorPanel.add("Center",colorList);
  Font plainFont = new Font("Helvetica",Font.PLAIN,12);
  Font boldFont = new Font("Helvetica",Font.BOLD,12);
  colorLabel.setFont(boldFont);
  colorList.setFont(plainFont);
  Panel buttonPanel = new Panel();
  buttonPanel.setLayout(new FlowLayout());
  buttonPanel.add(new Button("Select"));
  buttonPanel.add(new Button("Cancel"));
  buttonPanel.setFont(boldFont);
  add("Center",colorPanel);
  add("South",buttonPanel);
 }
 public boolean isChanged() {
  return colorChanged;
 }
 public Color getColor() {
  return newColor;
 }
 public boolean handleEvent(Event event) {
  if(event.id==Event.WINDOW_DESTROY){
   dispose();
   return true;
  }else if(event.id==Event.ACTION_EVENT) {
   if(event.target instanceof Button) {
    if("Select".equals(event.arg)) {
     if(colorList.getSelectedIndex() != -1)
      newColor = colors[colorList.getSelectedIndex()];
     colorChanged = true;
     show(false);
     return false;
    }else if("Cancel".equals(event.arg)) {
     dispose();
     return true;
    }
   }
  }
  return false;
 }
}
```

The `ColorDialog` class declares the `colors[]` array as an array of color constants and the `colorNames[]` array as the names associated with these color constants. The `colorList` variable refers to the `MyList` object that presents the `colorNames[]` array to the user. The `newColor` variable identifies the color selected by the user, and the `colorChanged` variable indicates whether a user color selection has been made.

The `ColorDialog` constructor invokes the `Dialog` constructor to set the title of the dialog box. It then invokes the `setupPanels()` method to perform most of the setup of the dialog box's internal components. The foreground and background colors are set and then the dialog box is packed and resized.

The `setupPanels()` method creates and adds two panels to the dialog box. These panels are identified by the `colorPanel` and `buttonPanel` variables. The panel identified by the `colorPanel` variable contains the Color: label and the `MyList` object referred to by the `colorList` variable. The button panel is implemented in the same manner as in the `FontDialog` class.

The `isChanged()` and `getColor()` methods are used to determine whether the user has selected a color and, if so, to return the color selected.

The `WINDOW_DESTROY` event and the clicking of the Cancel button are handled by invoking the `dispose()` method of the `Window` class. This causes the dialog box to be destroyed and its resources to be returned to the system. The clicking of the Select button is handled by invoking the `getSelectedIndex()` method of the `List` class to see if a color was selected and setting the `newColor` variable to the selected color. The `colorChanged` flag is updated to indicate that a color has been selected and the `show()` method causes the dialog box to be hidden.

Summary

This chapter covers the details of using the text- and font-related classes. It shows you how to use the text-based classes provided by Java and how to display text with the canvas. It also explains how the `Font` and `FontMetrics` classes are used to provide custom control of text display. Chapter 23, "The Canvas," covers the `Canvas` and `Graphics` classes.

23

The Canvas

This chapter covers the details of using the `Canvas` and `Graphics` classes. It also shows you how to use the image processing–related classes of the `java.awt.image` package. Java's support of bitmapped images is explained and the drawing methods of the `Graphics` class are illustrated as part of an example. When you finish this chapter, you will be able to effectively use graphics in your Java window programs.

The `Canvas` and `Graphics` Classes

The `Canvas` class provides a general GUI component for drawing images and text on the screen. It does not support any drawing methods of its own, but provides access to a `Graphics` object through its `paint()` method. The `paint()` method is invoked upon creation and update of the frame so that the `Graphics` object associated with a `Canvas` object can be updated. The `paint()` method should not be directly invoked, but it can be indirectly accessed using the `repaint()` method. The `Canvas` class is typically subclassed to provide custom drawing and event handling. If you do not want to create your own `Canvas` subclasses, you can use the `Graphics` object associated with your application's `Frame` subclass by overriding its `paint()` method. This is typically done in small applications.

The `Graphics` class is where all of the low-level drawing methods are implemented. These methods can be used directly to draw objects and text or can be combined to display more elaborate screen objects. The `Graphics` drawing methods allow a number of geometrical shapes to be drawn and filled, including lines, arcs, ovals, rectangles, rounded rectangles, and polygons. A special `draw3DRect()` method is provided for drawing rectangles that are shaded to give them a three-dimensional appearance. The `Graphics` class also provides the capability to draw bitmapped images and text on the canvas. Recall that Chapter 22, "Text and Fonts," covers the drawing of text and introduces the `Font` and `FontMetrics` classes. These classes control the specific manner in which text is displayed.

Displaying Bitmapped Images

The `drawImage()` method of the `Graphics` class is used to display bitmapped images on the `Graphics` object associated with a canvas. It takes an object of the `Image` class, an object that implements the `ImageObserver` interface, the x,y-coordinates where the image is to be displayed, and other parameters as its arguments.

The `Image` class is an abstract class that provides format-independent access to graphical images. `Image` objects are created by invoking methods of other classes that create images. Examples of these image-creating methods are the `createImage()` methods of the `Component` and `Applet` classes and the `getImage()` methods of the `Toolkit` and `Applet` classes. The `getImage()` methods are the most handy methods for retrieving an image that is stored in a disk file. Java currently supports GIF and JPEG formatted images through these methods.

The `ImageObserver` interface is defined in the `java.awt.image` package. This interface provides a set of constants and methods that support the creation and loading of images. The `Component` class implements the `ImageObserver` interface, and in most cases, the `ImageObserver` object used as the parameter to the `drawImage()` method can be supplied using the `this` identifier to reference the current `Canvas` or `Frame` object being painted.

The `DisplayImageApp` Program

The `DisplayImageApp` program shows how bitmapped images can be drawn on the screen using the `drawImage()` method of the `Graphics` class. Its source code is shown in Listing 23.1.

Listing 23.1. The source code for the `DisplayImageApp` program.

```
import java.awt.*;
import jdg.ch20.*;

public class DisplayImageApp extends Frame {
 MyMenuBar menuBar;
 Toolkit toolkit;
 int screenWidth = 400;
 int screenHeight = 400;
 Image image;
 public static void main(String args[]){
  DisplayImageApp app = new DisplayImageApp();
 }
 public DisplayImageApp() {
  super("DisplayImageApp");
  setup();
  pack();
  resize(screenWidth,screenHeight);
  show();
 }
 void setup() {
  setBackground(Color.white);
  setupMenuBar();
  setMenuBar(menuBar);
  setupImage();
 }
 void setupMenuBar() {
  String menuItems[][] = {{"File","Exit"}};
  menuBar = new MyMenuBar(menuItems);
 }
 void setupImage() {
  toolkit = getToolkit();
  image = toolkit.getImage("test.gif");
 }
 public void paint(Graphics g) {
  g.drawImage(image,0,0,this);
 }
 public boolean handleEvent(Event event) {
  if(event.id==Event.WINDOW_DESTROY){
```

continues

Listing 23.1. continued

```
    System.exit(0);
    return true;
   }else if(event.id==Event.ACTION_EVENT){
    if(event.target instanceof MenuItem){
     if("Exit".equals(event.arg)){
      System.exit(0);
      return true;
     }
    }
   }
   return false;
  }
 }
```

Before running the DisplayImageApp program, copy the test.gif and aviris.gif images from the \jdg\ch23 directory of the CD-ROM to your jdg\ch23 directory. The DisplayImageApp program uses the test.gif file. The ImageApp program, which you'll develop later in this chapter, displays the aviris.gif image.

DisplayImageMap shows how a bitmapped image can be displayed using the Graphics class. When you run the program, it displays the bitmapped image shown in Figure 23.1.

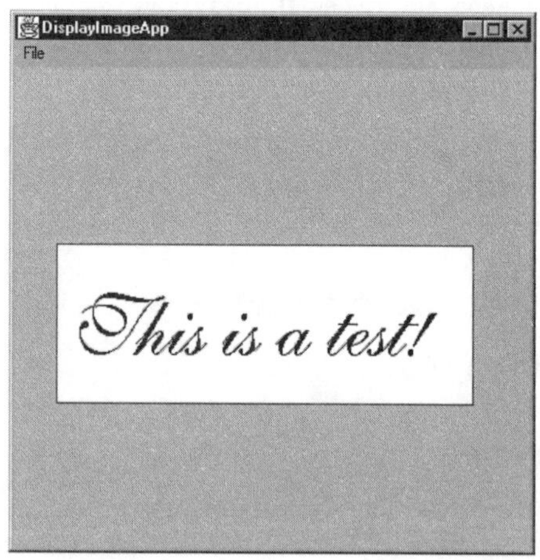

FIGURE 23.1.
The DisplayImageApp *opening window.*

The functionality of the DisplayImageApp program isn't all that astounding. Its purpose is to illustrate the use of the methods involved in loading and displaying image files. You can easily upgrade the program to display arbitrary GIF or JPEG files by adding and implementing an Open option on the File menu.

DisplayImageApp declares several field variables. The menuBar variable is used to identify the program's menu bar. The toolkit variable is used to reference the toolkit associated with the application window. The screenWidth and screenHeight variables control the size at which the window is displayed. The image variable is used to refer to the loaded image.

The `DisplayImageApp` window is created, set up, and displayed using the methods covered in previous chapters. The `setupImage()` method uses the `getToolkit()` method of the `Window` class to get the `Toolkit` object associated with the application window. The `getImage()` method of the `Toolkit` class is used to load the image in the `test.gif` file and assign it to the `image` variable.

The `paint()` method draws the image referenced by the `image` variable on the default `Graphics` object of the application window. It accomplishes this using the `drawImage()` method of the `Graphics` class. The arguments to `drawImage()` are the image to be displayed, the x- and y-coordinates where the image is to be drawn, and the object implementing the `ImageObserver` interface associated with the image. The `this` identifier is used to indicate that the application window is the `ImageObserver`.

The `handleEvent()` method provides the standard `WINDOW_DESTROY` and Exit event handling.

Drawing and Painting

Some programs, such as the Microsoft Windows Paint program, are used to construct images by *painting* on the screen. These paint programs create an image array of color pixels and update the array based on user paint commands. These commands may consist of pixel-level drawing operations or more general operations that draw geometrical objects such as circles, rectangles, and lines. Painting programs are characterized by the fact that the pixel array is the focus for the drawing that takes place.

Drawing programs, such as CorelDRAW!, support drawing operations using a more object-oriented approach. When you draw a circle or line with a drawing program, you do not merely update the pixels of the canvas—you add an object to the list of objects that are displayed on the canvas. Because drawing programs operate at a higher object level, you can select, move, resize, group, and perform other operations on the objects that you've drawn.

The `Graphics` class is oriented toward providing the methods that are needed to support higher-level drawing programs rather than lower-level painting programs, although it does support important painting operations, such as displaying bitmapped images, as you saw in the `DisplayImageApp` program.

When using the `Graphics` class to support graphical operations, you will generally maintain a list of the objects that you've drawn and use that list of objects to repaint the screen, as required.

The `DrawApp` Program

The `DrawApp` program shows how the higher-level drawing operations of the `Graphics` class are used to display and maintain a list of the objects that are drawn on a canvas. The source code of the `DrawApp` program is shown in Listing 23.2.

Listing 23.2. The source code for the `DrawApp` program.

```
import java.awt.*;
import java.lang.Math;
import java.util.Vector;
import jdg.ch20.*;

public class DrawApp extends Frame {
 Object menuItems[][] = {
  {"File","New","-","Exit"},
  {"Draw","+Line","-Oval","-Rectangle"}
 };
 MyMenuBar menuBar = new MyMenuBar(menuItems);
 MyCanvas canvas = new MyCanvas(TwoPointObject.LINE);
 int screenWidth = 400;
 int screenHeight = 400;
 public static void main(String args[]){
  DrawApp app = new DrawApp();
 }
 public DrawApp() {
  super("DrawApp");
  setup();
  pack();
  resize(screenWidth,screenHeight);
  show();
 }
 void setup() {
  setBackground(Color.white);
  setMenuBar(menuBar);
  setCursor(CROSSHAIR_CURSOR);
  add("Center",canvas);
 }
 public boolean handleEvent(Event event) {
  if(event.id==Event.WINDOW_DESTROY){
   System.exit(0);
   return true;
  }else if(event.id==Event.GOT_FOCUS && !(event.target instanceof MyCanvas)) {
   setCursor(DEFAULT_CURSOR);
   return true;
  }else if(event.id==Event.LOST_FOCUS) {
   setCursor(CROSSHAIR_CURSOR);
   return true;
  }else if(event.id==Event.ACTION_EVENT){
   if(event.target instanceof MenuItem){
    String arg = (String) event.arg;
    if(processFileMenu(arg)) return true;
    if(processDrawMenu(arg)) return true;
   }
  }
  return false;
 }
 public boolean processFileMenu(String s) {
  if("New".equals(s)){
   canvas.clear();
   return true;
  }else if("Exit".equals(s)){
   System.exit(0);
   return true;
```

```
  }
  return false;
 }
 public boolean processDrawMenu(String s) {
  MyMenu menu = menuBar.getMenu("Draw");
  CheckboxMenuItem lineItem = (CheckboxMenuItem) menu.getItem("Line");
  CheckboxMenuItem ovalItem = (CheckboxMenuItem) menu.getItem("Oval");
  CheckboxMenuItem rectangleItem =
   (CheckboxMenuItem) menu.getItem("Rectangle");
  if("Line".equals(s)){
   canvas.setTool(TwoPointObject.LINE);
   lineItem.setState(true);
   ovalItem.setState(false);
   rectangleItem.setState(false);
   return true;
  }else if("Oval".equals(s)){
   canvas.setTool(TwoPointObject.OVAL);
   lineItem.setState(false);
   ovalItem.setState(true);
   rectangleItem.setState(false);
   return true;
  }else if("Rectangle".equals(s)){
   canvas.setTool(TwoPointObject.RECTANGLE);
   lineItem.setState(false);
   ovalItem.setState(false);
   rectangleItem.setState(true);
   return true;
  }
  return false;
 }
}
class MyCanvas extends Canvas {
 int tool = TwoPointObject.LINE;
 Vector objects = new Vector();
 TwoPointObject current;
 boolean newObject = false;
 public MyCanvas(int toolType) {
  super();
  tool = toolType;
 }
 public void setTool(int toolType) {
  tool = toolType;
 }
 public void clear() {
  objects.removeAllElements();
  repaint();
 }
 public boolean mouseDown(Event event,int x,int y) {
  current = new TwoPointObject(tool,x,y);
  newObject = true;
  return true;
 }
 public boolean mouseUp(Event event,int x,int y) {
  if(newObject) {
   objects.addElement(current);
   newObject = false;
  }
```

continues

Listing 23.2. continued

```
  return true;
 }
 public boolean mouseDrag(Event event,int x,int y) {
  if(newObject) {
   int oldX = current.endX;
   int oldY = current.endY;
   if(tool != TwoPointObject.LINE) {
    if(x > current.startX) current.endX = x;
    if(y > current.startY) current.endY = y;
    int width = Math.max(oldX,current.endX) - current.startX + 1;
    int height = Math.max(oldY,current.endY) - current.startY + 1;
    repaint(current.startX,current.startY,width,height);
   }else{
    current.endX = x;
    current.endY = y;
    int startX = Math.min(Math.min(current.startX,current.endX),oldX);
    int startY = Math.min(Math.min(current.startY,current.endY),oldY);
    int endX = Math.max(Math.max(current.startX,current.endX),oldX);
    int endY = Math.max(Math.max(current.startY,current.endY),oldY);
    repaint(startX,startY,endX-startX+1,endY-startY+1);
   }
  }
  return true;
 }
 public void paint(Graphics g) {
  int numObjects = objects.size();
  for(int i=0;i<numObjects;++i) {
   TwoPointObject obj = (TwoPointObject) objects.elementAt(i);
   obj.draw(g);
  }
  if(newObject) current.draw(g);
 }
}
class TwoPointObject {
 public static int LINE = 0;
 public static int OVAL = 1;
 public static int RECTANGLE = 2;
 public int type, startX, startY, endX, endY;
 public TwoPointObject(int objectType,int x1,int y1,int x2,int y2) {
  type = objectType;
  startX = x1;
  startY = y1;
  endX = x2;
  endY = y2;
 }
 public TwoPointObject(int objectType,int x,int y) {
  this(objectType,x,y,x,y);
 }
 public TwoPointObject() {
  this(LINE,0,0,0,0);
 }
 public void draw(Graphics g) {
  if(type == LINE) g.drawLine(startX,startY,endX,endY);
  else{
   int w = Math.abs(endX - startX);
   int l = Math.abs(endY - startY);
```

```
    if(type == OVAL) g.drawOval(startX,startY,w,l);
    else g.drawRect(startX,startY,w,l);
   }
  }
}
```

The `DrawApp` program is quite a bit more sophisticated than the `DisplayImageApp` program with respect to the capabilities that it provides. When you run `DrawApp` you will see the opening window, which is shown in Figure 23.2.

FIGURE 23.2.
The `DrawApp` *opening window.*

The `DrawApp` program is initially configured to draw lines in its window. You can draw a line by clicking the left mouse button and dragging the mouse. When you have finished drawing a line, release the left mouse button and the drawn line will be completed. The coordinate where you press the left mouse button is the beginning of the line, and the coordinate where you release the left mouse button is the end of the line. Go ahead and draw several lines, as shown in Figure 23.3.

The `DrawApp` program supports the drawing of lines, ovals, and rectangles. To draw an oval, select the Oval menu item from the Draw pull-down menu, as shown in Figure 23.4.

You draw an oval in the same way that you draw a line. When you click the left button of your mouse, you mark the upper-left corner of the oval. Drag the mouse to where you want the lower-right corner of the oval and release the left mouse button. Try drawing a few ovals, as shown in Figure 23.5.

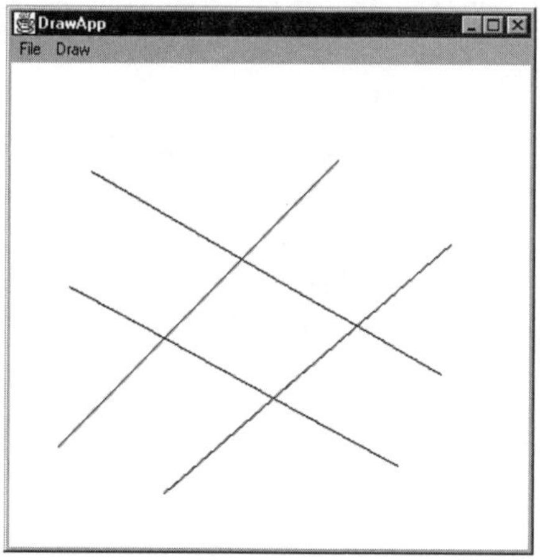

FIGURE 23.3.
Drawing some lines.

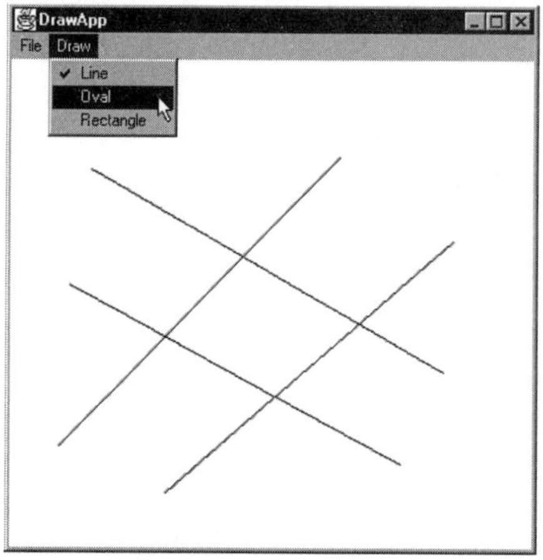

FIGURE 23.4.
The Draw menu.

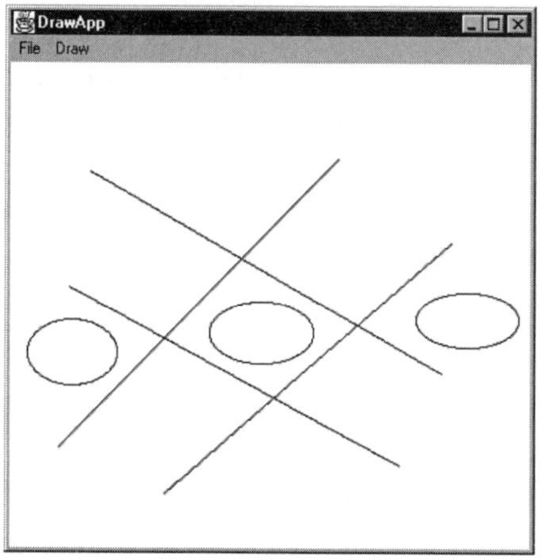

FIGURE 23.5.
Drawing some ovals.

Now select the Rectangle menu item from the Draw pull-down menu. You draw rectangles in the same way that you draw ovals. Go ahead and draw a rectangle, as shown in Figure 23.6.

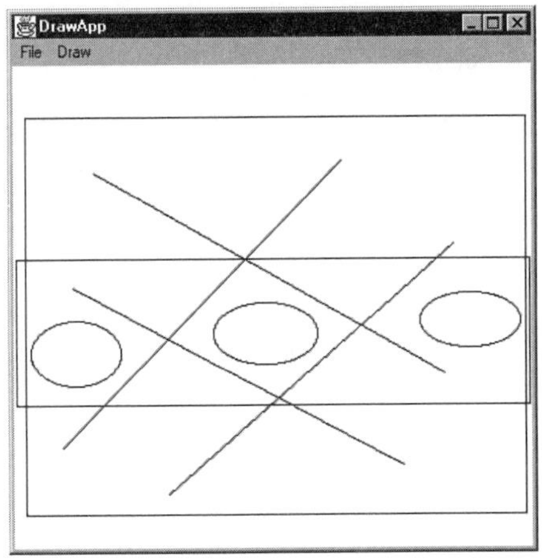

FIGURE 23.6.
Drawing some rectangles.

You can experiment with the program before going on to find out how it works. If you want to clear the drawing screen, select New from the File pull-down menu.

The `DrawApp` program is a little (but not much) longer than the programs you've developed so far. It consists of three classes. The `DrawApp` class is the main class used to implement the program. The `MyCanvas` class is used to implement the main canvas component of the program. The `TwoPointObject` class is used to implement the line, oval, and rectangle objects that are drawn on the screen. It is called `TwoPointObject` because it supports objects that can be characterized by a starting point (mouse down) and an ending point (mouse up).

The `DrawApp` program declares several field variables. The `menuItems[]` array is used to construct the menu bar identified by the `menuBar` variable. The `canvas` variable is used to refer to the `MyCanvas` object that implements the program drawing. This object is constructed by passing the `TwoPointObject.LINE` constant as an argument. This tells the constructed object that the line tool should be initially used to support drawing. The height and width of the `DrawApp` window is set to 400×400 pixels.

The `DrawApp` window is constructed using the standard approach that you've been following in previous chapters. The `setup()` method sets the background color to white, invokes `setupMenuBar()` to set up the menu bar, and invokes the `setCursor()` method of the `Frame` class to set the initial cursor to the `CROSSHAIR_CURSOR` typically used in drawing programs. The `MyCanvas` object referenced by the `canvas` variable is then added to the center of the main application window.

That's all the setup required to support `DrawApp`. The rest of the program code provides the event handling required to implement the drawing operations that were previously illustrated.

The `handleEvent()` method handles the `WINDOW_DESTROY` event in the usual manner. The `GOT_FOCUS` and `LOST_FOCUS` methods check to see whether the current position of the cursor changes focus from the canvas to other parts of the window. If the cursor moves outside of the canvas, the cursor is changed to its default shape. If the cursor moves into the canvas, it is changed to a `CROSSHAIR_CURSOR`.

The only other type of event handled by `DrawApp` is the `ACTION_EVENT` associated with user menu selections. The `processFileMenu()` and `processDrawMenu()` methods are invoked to handle these events.

The `processFileMenu()` method processes the New and Exit menu items. The New menu item is handled by invoking the `clear()` method of the `MyCanvas` class to clear the canvas to a blank state. The Exit menu item is handled in the usual manner.

The `processDrawMenu()` method begins by assigning the `CheckboxMenuItem` objects in the Draw menu to the `lineItem`, `ovalItem`, and `rectangleItem` variables. These variables are used to determine which menu items are checked.

The `processDrawMenu()` method handles the Line menu item by invoking the `setTool()` method to set the current drawing tool to the line tool. It uses the `LINE` constant defined in the `TwoPointObject` class. The `lineItem`, `ovalItem`, and `rectangleItem` variables are used to update the `CheckboxMenuItem` objects contained in the Draw menu using the `setState()` method of the `CheckboxMenuItem` class. The Oval and Rectangle menu items are handled in a similar manner. The Oval menu item is handled by invoking the `setTool()` method with the `OVAL` constant, and the Rectangle menu item is handled by invoking the `setTool()` method with the `RECTANGLE` constant. The state of the menu items of the Draw menu are updated to reflect the selected drawing tool.

MyCanvas

The `MyCanvas` class subclasses the `Canvas` class to provide custom drawing capabilities. The `tool` variable is used to identify the current drawing tool that is in effect. The `objects` variable is declared as a `Vector`. It is used to store all of the objects drawn by the user. The `current` variable is used to refer to the current `TwoPointObject` object being drawn by the user. The `newObject` flag is used to track whether the user has begun drawing a new object.

The `MyCanvas` constructor invokes the constructor of the `Canvas` class using the superclass constructor call statement and then sets the `tool` variable to the `toolType` argument passed to the constructor.

The `setTool()` method changes the tool used to draw an object.

The `clear()` method invokes the `removeAllElements()` method of the vector class to remove all drawing objects stored in the `Vector` referenced by the `objects` variable.

The `mouseDown()` method is used to handle the event that is generated when the user clicks the left mouse button in the canvas. The method is called by the Java runtime system with the position of the mouse click. A new `TwoPointObject` object is created, with the `tool` variable and the position of the mouse click as its arguments. The newly created object is assigned to the `current` variable. The `newObject` flag is set to `true` and the `true` value is returned to indicate that the event has been successfully handled.

The `mouseUp()` method is used to handle the event that is generated when the user releases the left mouse button. This action marks the completion of the drawing of an object. The event is handled by adding the object referenced by the `current` variable to the `objects` vector. The `newObject` flag is then set to `false`. The object referenced by the `current` variable is updated with its ending position during the processing of the `mouseDrag()` event-handling method. The `newObject` flag is checked to make sure that the mouse was not clicked outside of the current window and then released.

The `mouseDrag()` event performs somewhat more sophisticated event handling than the `mouseDown()` and `mouseUp()` methods perform. It checks the `newObject` flag to make sure that an object is currently being drawn. It then sets the `oldX` and `oldY` variables to the last ending position of the object being drawn. These variables will be used to determine what portion of the canvas needs to be repainted. Repainting of the entire canvas is not visually appealing because it causes previously drawn objects to flicker.

If the current drawing tool is not a line, an oval or rectangle object is being drawn by the user. The x- and y-coordinates provided as arguments to the `mouseDrag()` method are checked to determine whether the mouse was dragged below and to the right of the object being drawn. If this is the case, the ending position of the current object is updated. If the mouse is dragged to the left or above the starting point of the object, the current position of the mouse is ignored. This is to ensure that the starting position of the oval or rectangle is indeed its upper-left corner. The new `width` and `height` of the area to be repainted are calculated as the maximum area covered by the previous ending position and the current object-ending position. This is to ensure that the repaint operation will erase any previous boundaries of the object being drawn. The `max()` method of the `java.lang.Math` class is used to determine this maximum area. The `repaint()` method of the `Component` class is then used to repaint the area updated as the result of the mouse drag. This version of the `repaint()` method takes the x,y-coordinates of the upper-left corner of the area to be redrawn and the width and height of this area as its parameters.

Line drawing is not restricted in the same manner as oval and rectangle drawing. If it were, you would not be able to draw lines that go up and to the right or down and to the left. The `else` part of the `if` statement updates the starting position of the area to be repainted as the upper-leftmost point of the line being redrawn. It then updates the ending position of the area to be repainted as the lower rightmost point of the line. The canvas is then repainted using the starting coordinates and the updated width and height of the repaint area.

To get a better feel for the process of local screen repainting, try experimenting with the way the `repaint()` method is used to update the canvas display.

The paint() method is used to paint and repaint the screen. It uses the size() method of the Vector class to determine how many objects are stored in the objects vector and sets the numObjects variable to this value. It then iterates through each object stored in objects and draws it on the canvas. The elementAt() method of the Vector class is used to retrieve an object from the objects vector. The object is cast into an object of class TwoPointObject and assigned to the obj variable. The draw() method of the TwoPointObject class is invoked to draw the object on the current Graphics context.

Notice that the paint() method does not have to know how to support limited-area repainting. Only full-canvas painting needs to be implemented by paint(). Support of limited-area repainting is provided by the local AWT implementation.

TwoPointObject

The TwoPointObject class is used to keep track of the objects drawn by the user. It records the type of object and its starting and ending coordinates. It also draws the objects on a Graphics object passed as a parameter.

TwoPointObject defines the LINE, OVAL, and RECTANGLE constants, which are also used by the MyCanvas class. The type variable is used to record the type of object being drawn. The startX, startY, endX, and endY variables identify the starting and ending coordinates of the object.

Three TwoPointObject constructors are declared. The first constructor takes the type of object being drawn and its starting and ending coordinates as its parameters. The second constructor leaves out the ending coordinates and sets them to be the same as the starting coordinates. The last constructor takes no parameters and creates a line that is at the coordinate 0,0.

The draw() method checks the type variable to determine what type of object is to be drawn. If the object is a line, it uses the drawLine() method of the Graphics class to draw a line from its starting to ending coordinates. If the object is an oval or a line, the w and l variables are assigned the width and length of the object to be drawn. The drawOval() and drawRect() methods are used to draw an oval or rectangle, respectively.

Combining Graphics and Text

The Graphics class treats text in the same way as it handles other graphics objects. To include text drawing in your graphics applications, use the drawString() method of the Graphics class, as illustrated in Chapter 22. You will need to use the Font and FontMetrics classes to determine the size of the text that is drawn. Otherwise, text and graphics objects can be easily combined in any Graphics-based application.

The Image-Processing Classes of `java.awt.image`

The `java.awt.image` package provides a number of classes and interfaces that support image processing. These classes are described in Chapter 15, "Window Programming with the `java.awt` Package." For the most part, you will not need to use these classes unless your application program is oriented toward low-level image processing.

The `java.awt.image` package is based on the concept of an image producer and image consumer. The *image producer* provides the data associated with an image. This data is used or consumed by an *image consumer.* The `ImageProducer` and `ImageConsumer` interfaces are used to map this producer–consumer concept to specific image-processing classes.

An image filter is used to alter data that is produced by an image producer before it is consumed by an image consumer. Image filters are similar to the I/O stream filters discussed in Chapter 12, "Portable Software and the `java.lang` Package." An *image filter* reads the data produced by an image producer, modifies it, and then passes it on to the image consumer.

The `ImageApp` Program

The `ImageApp` program shows how to perform image processing using a custom-built image filter. Its source code is shown in Listing 23.3.

Listing 23.3. The source code for the `ImageApp` program.

```
import java.awt.*;
import java.awt.image.*;
import jdg.ch20.*;

public class ImageApp extends Frame {
 MyMenuBar menuBar;
 Toolkit toolkit;
 int screenWidth = 500;
 int screenHeight = 475;
 Image filteredImage;
 public static void main(String args[]){
  ImageApp app = new ImageApp();
 }
 public ImageApp() {
  super("ImageApp");
  setup();
  pack();
  resize(screenWidth,screenHeight);
  show();
 }
 void setup() {
  setBackground(Color.white);
  setupMenuBar();
  setMenuBar(menuBar);
  setupImage();
```

continues

Listing 23.3. continued

```
 }
 void setupMenuBar() {
  String menuItems[][] = {{"File","Exit"},{"Filter","-Red","-Green","-Blue"}};
  menuBar = new MyMenuBar(menuItems);
 }
 void setupImage() {
  toolkit = getToolkit();
  filteredImage = toolkit.getImage("aviris.gif");
 }
 public void paint(Graphics g) {
  g.drawImage(filteredImage,0,0,this);
 }
 public void filterImage(){
  Image image = toolkit.getImage("aviris.gif");
  ImageFilter filter = new MyImageFilter(getMask());
  filteredImage =
   createImage(new FilteredImageSource(image.getSource(),filter));
  repaint();
 }
 public int getMask() {
  int red = 0xff00ffff;
  int green = 0xffff00ff;
  int blue = 0xffffff00;
  int mask = 0xffffffff;
  MyMenu menu = menuBar.getMenu("Filter");
  CheckboxMenuItem redItem = (CheckboxMenuItem) menu.getItem("Red");
  CheckboxMenuItem greenItem = (CheckboxMenuItem) menu.getItem("Green");
  CheckboxMenuItem blueItem = (CheckboxMenuItem) menu.getItem("Blue");
  if(redItem.getState()) mask &= red;
  if(greenItem.getState()) mask &= green;
  if(blueItem.getState()) mask &= blue;
  return mask;
 }
 public boolean handleEvent(Event event) {
  if(event.id==Event.WINDOW_DESTROY){
   System.exit(0);
   return true;
  }else if(event.id==Event.ACTION_EVENT){
   if(event.target instanceof MenuItem){
    String sel = (String) event.arg;
    if("Exit".equals(sel)){
     System.exit(0);
     return true;
    }else if("Red".equals(sel) || "Green".equals(sel) || "Blue".equals(sel)) {
     filterImage();
     return true;
    }
   }
  }
  return false;
 }
}
class MyImageFilter extends RGBImageFilter {
 int filter;
 public MyImageFilter(int mask) {
  canFilterIndexColorModel = true;
```

```
  filter = mask;
 }
 public int filterRGB(int x,int y,int rgb) {
  return rgb & filter;
 }
}
```

When you first run `ImageApp`, it loads the image contained in the file `aviris.gif`. (See Figure 23.7.) This is a public-domain image provided by the NASA Jet Propulsion Laboratory. It is produced by the Airborne Visible InfraRed Imaging Spectrometer (AVIRIS). The `aviris.gif` file is fairly large; you might have to wait a couple seconds for it to complete its loading.

FIGURE 23.7.
The `ImageApp` *opening window.*

The AVIRIS image is not provided to introduce you to NASA's advanced airborne-imaging algorithms. Instead, you will use this image as an example to understand how basic image filtering works. Unfortunately, the images displayed in this book are in black and white, so you will not be able to see how the image filtering works by looking at the book.

Click on the Filter pull-down menu and select the Blue menu item, as shown in Figure 23.8.

Selecting the blue filter causes all blue color components to be filtered out of the image. The resulting image is comprised only of green and red color components. (See Figure 23.9.)

Go ahead and try the red and green filters by selecting Red and Green from the Filter menu. Also try various filter combinations to get a better feel for how filtering works.

Although the `ImageApp` program may seem to perform some amazing processing, it is actually quite small. Two classes are defined: the `ImageApp` class, used to implement the main program window, and the `MyImageFilter` class, used to implement the actual image filter.

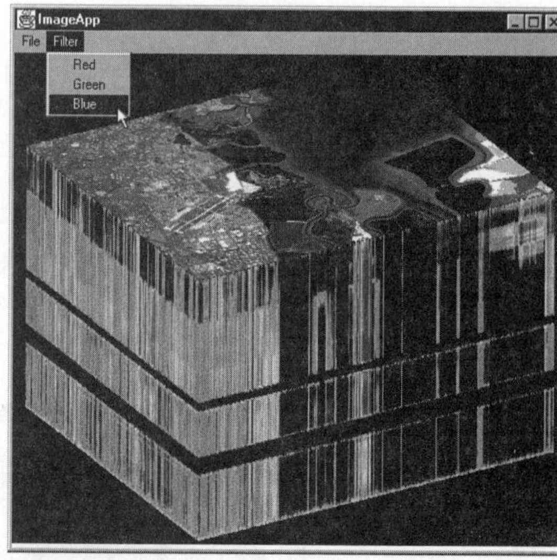

FIGURE 23.8.
The Filter menu.

FIGURE 23.9.
A filtered image.

The `ImageApp` class declares the `menuBar`, `toolkit`, `screenWidth`, `screenHeight`, and `filteredImage` variables. The `menuBar`, `screenWidth`, and `screenHeight` variables are used in their usual manner. The `toolkit` variable is used to refer to the `Toolkit` object associated with the application window. The `filteredImage` variable is used to refer to the image that is being manipulated.

The `setupImage()` method uses the `getToolkit()` method of the `Window` class to retrieve the toolkit that is associated with the application window. It then invokes the `getImage()` method of the Toolkit class to load the image contained in the file into an Image object that is referenced by the filteredImage variable.

The paint() method draws the image identified by the filteredImage variable on the screen using the drawImage() method of the Graphics class.

The filterImage() method oversees the image-filtering process. It loads the aviris.gif image into an object assigned to the image variable. It creates a new object of the MyImageFilter class and assigns it to the filter variable. The MyImageFilter object is provided with a filter mask that is generated by a call to the getMask() method. You'll learn what a filter mask is shortly.

The filterImage() method uses the createImage() method of the Component class to create a new image and assign it to the filteredImage variable. The repaint() method is invoked to redisplay the new image assigned to the filteredImage variable. The actual image filtering is performed as part of the creation of the arguments supplied to the createImage() method. When createImage() is invoked, a new object of the java.awt.image.FilteredImageSource class is created. This object assigns the source (ImageProducer) of the image being created to the newly created FilteredImageSource object. This object is created using the source (ImageProducer) of the aviris.gif image assigned to the image variable. The getSource() method is invoked to get the ImageProducer of the original image. The FilteredImageSource object is filtered using the MyImageFilter object assigned to the filter variable. To complete this examination of the image-filtering process, you only need to figure out how the MyImageFilter class works and what was returned by the getMask() method.

The getMask() method returns an integer value that is used to mask out certain RGB color combinations. The red variable is assigned the 0xff00ffff hexadecimal constant. The red component of an RGB color is stored in the bits that are set to zero in this constant. So, when you logically AND this value with any color, its red bits are stripped out. The hexadecimal constants assigned to the green and blue variables are defined in an analogous fashion to strip out the green and blue bits of a color when they are logically ANDed with the color. The mask variable is used to compute the returned result. The constant assigned to the mask variable will have no effect on any color that it is ANDed with.

The getMask() method checks each of the CheckboxMenuItem objects contained in the Filter menu to determine which objects are set. If a menu item is set, the color mask associated with that item is logically ANDed with the mask variable. The resulting mask value is a value that will strip out the colors specified by the set menu items.

The handleEvent() method performs the normal WINDOW_DESTROY and Exit menu item processing. It also handles the selection of the Red, Green, and Blue menu items by invoking the filterImage() method. This causes the aviris.gif image to be filtered as specified by the mask generated according to the state of the Red, Green, and Blue checkbox menu items.

The MyImageFilter class performs the actual image filtering. It extends the RGBImageFilter class defined in the java.awt.image package and overrides the filterRGB() method.

The `MyImageFilter` constructor takes a `mask` value as its parameter and assigns it to the `filter` variable. It also sets the `canFilterIndexColorModel` variable to `true`. This allows filtering to take place on the color map associated with the image, rather than on the actual image.

The `filterRGB()` method performs the image filtering. It takes the x,y-coordinate of each pixel to be filtered and the RGB color of the pixel as its parameters. It then logically `AND`s the color value with the mask stored in the `filter` variable and returns the resulting filtered color.

Summary

This chapter covers the details of using the `Canvas` and `Graphics` classes. It also shows you how to use the image processing–related classes of the `java.awt.image` package. Java's support of bitmapped images is demonstrated with the `DisplayImageApp` program. The `DrawApp` program illustrates the drawing methods of the `Graphics` class, and the `ImageApp` program shows you how to use the classes of `java.awt.image`. Chapter 24, "Scrollbars," shows you how to use scrollbars to scroll text and graphics drawn on the canvas.

24

Scrollbars

This chapter is dedicated to explaining the use of the `Scrollbar` class. It describes the methods provided by this class and shows how to use vertical and horizontal scrollbars to scroll text and graphics displayed in a window. The event handling supported by scrollbars is also explained. When you finish this chapter, you will be able to effectively use scrollbars in your Java window programs.

How Scrollbars Work

Scrollbars are used to scroll through an object contained in a window that is too large to be completely displayed within the window. Vertical scrollbars are used to scroll up and down from the beginning of the object to its end. Horizontal scrollbars are used to scroll right and left between the right and left sides of the object. Horizontal and vertical scrollbars are implemented in the same fashion. The only differences between them are their placement around the object to be scrolled and the direction in which they move the scrolled object through the window.

Users interact with scrollbars in three ways. By clicking on the arrows at the end of the scrollbars, they move the scrolled object one scrollable unit in the opposite direction of the arrow. This causes the window to appear as though it has moved over the object in the direction of the arrow.

NOTE

A *scrollable unit* is defined by the application program. Vertical and horizontal units differ. Most text-processing applications define a vertical unit as a single line of text and a horizontal unit as a percentage of the horizontal screen size. Graphical applications define vertical and horizontal units as a percentage of the visible screen size.

Scrollbars contain tabs that identify the relative location of the object being viewed with respect to the total size of the object. By clicking between the tab and the end of a scrollbar, the view of the object is updated in a one-page increment in the direction of the arrow. This is the second way that scrollbars can be used. The definition of a *page* is also application specific. Vertical scrollbars usually define a page as the vertical size of the viewing window or some percentage of this size. Horizontal scrollbars tend to operate in the same manner. A horizontal page is defined as a fixed percentage of the horizontal viewing area.

The third way that a user can interact with a scrollbar is to drag the scrollbar's tab to a specific location within the scrollbar. When the user drags the tab of a vertical scrollbar, he moves the object being viewed up or down in the viewing window. When the user drags the tab of a horizontal scrollbar, he moves the object being viewed left or right in the viewing window.

Using Scrollbars

When you use scrollbars in your Java programs, you will most likely be using them to scroll through a `Graphics` object that is associated with a `Canvas` object or the main application window. You create and place scrollbars in your window in the same manner as any other window component. Their position and size within the window are determined by the layout associated with the window.

Scrollbars are created using the `Scrollbar()` constructor. Three forms of this constructor are provided. The default constructor takes no parameters and is not particularly useful unless you want to create a `Scrollbar` object and then specify its orientation and use later in your program. The second constructor allows the orientation of a `Scrollbar` object to be specified. The third `Scrollbar()` constructor uses the five parameters that are needed to create a working scrollbar: `orientation`, `value`, `visible`, `minimum`, and `maximum`.

The `orientation` of a scrollbar is specified by the `VERTICAL` and `HORIZONTAL` constants defined by the `Scrollbar` class. The `minimum` and `maximum` parameters specify the minimum and maximum values associated with the scrollbar's position. These values should map to the object being scrolled. For example, if you are scrolling a 1000-line text object, appropriate minimum and maximum values for a vertical scrollbar would be `0` and `999`. Horizontal values could be determined using the maximum width of the text to be scrolled (in pixels).

The `value` parameter identifies the starting value associated with the scrollbar. The `value` parameter is usually set to the `minimum` value of the scrollbar. However, suppose you wanted to initiate the display of an object with its center displayed on the screen. You would then set the scrollbar's `value` parameter to the average of its `minimum` and `maximum` values.

The `visible` parameter is used to specify the size of the viewable area of the object being scrolled. For example, if you are scrolling a 1000-line text object, and the viewable area of the window is 25 lines long, you should set the `visible` variable to `25`.

The `Scrollbar` class provides several methods for getting and setting the parameters of a `Scrollbar` object. The `getOrientation()`, `getValue()`, `getVisible()`, `getMinimum()`, and `getMaximum()` methods retrieve the parameter values discussed so far. The `getValue()` method is used to determine to what position the user has scrolled.

The `setLineIncrement()` and `setPageIncrement()` methods are used to specify the size of a scrollable unit and page relative to the minimum and maximum values associated with a scrollbar. For example, when scrolling text, you can set the line increment of a vertical scrollbar to `1` so that only one line of text is vertically scrolled. You can set the page increment to `10` to allow 10 lines of text to be scrolled when the user clicks between the tab and arrows of a scrollbar. The `getLineIncrement()` and `getPageIncrement()` methods provide access to the current line- and page-increment values.

The `setValue()` method allows you to directly set the current position of a scrollbar. The `setValues()` method allows you to specify a scrollbar's `value`, `visible`, `minimum`, and `maximum` parameters.

In order to respond to user scrollbar operations and implement scrolling of the object associated with a scrollbar, you must handle the events generated by user manipulation of the scrollbar. These events are the `SCROLL_LINE_DOWN`, `SCROLL_LINE_UP`, `SCROLL_PAGE_DOWN`, `SCROLL_PAGE_UP`, and `SCROLL_ABSOLUTE` events.

The `SCROLL_LINE_UP` event is generated when the user clicks on the up arrow of a vertical scrollbar or on the left arrow of a horizontal scrollbar. The `SCROLL_LINE_DOWN` event is generated when the user clicks on the down arrow of a vertical scrollbar or the right arrow of a horizontal scrollbar. The `SCROLL_PAGE_UP` event is generated when the user clicks between the up arrow of a vertical scrollbar and its tab. It is also generated when a user clicks between the left arrow of a horizontal scrollbar and its tab. Similarly, the `SCROLL_PAGE_DOWN` event is generated when the user clicks between the down arrow of a vertical scrollbar and its tab, or between the right arrow of a horizontal scrollbar and its tab. These events pass an argument that specifies the number of lines that are scrolled.

The `SCROLL_ABSOLUTE` event is generated when a user drags the tabs of a scrollbar to a new position. This event passes an argument that identifies the new scrollbar position.

Scrolling Text

In order to handle scrollbar events and implement scrolling, you must repaint the area of the scrollable window based on the mapping between the object being scrolled and the vertical and horizontal scrollbar positions. If you are scrolling text, you are most likely displaying the text on the `Graphics` object associated with a `Canvas` object or the main application window. The `TextArea` object implements its own scrollbars and does not require any additional event handling.

When scrolling text vertically, you should adjust the minimum and maximum values of the vertical scrollbar based on the number of lines of text that are contained in the object being scrolled. In this way, when the user moves the scrollbar's tab to its topmost position, the beginning of the text is displayed, and when the user moves the tab to the bottom of the scrollbar, the end of the text is displayed.

When scrolling text horizontally, you should set the minimum and maximum values of the horizontal scrollbar based on the maximum width of the text being displayed.

The `TextScrollApp` Program

The `TextScrollApp` program shows how scrollbars can be used to scroll text that is drawn on a `Graphics` object. This program provides the capability to read in a text file and display it on the screen using the default 12-point plain font. It allows the text file to be scrolled vertically and horizontally through the application window. The source code of the `TextScrollApp` program is shown in Listing 24.1.

Listing 24.1. The source code of the `TextScrollApp` program.

```
import java.awt.*;
import java.io.*;
import java.util.Vector;
import jdg.ch20.*;

public class TextScrollApp extends Frame {
 Object menuItems[][] = {{"File","Open","-","Exit"}};
 MyMenuBar menuBar = new MyMenuBar(menuItems);
 FileDialog openFile = new FileDialog(this,"Open File",FileDialog.LOAD);
 Font defaultFont = new Font("default",Font.PLAIN,12);
 int screenWidth = 400;
 int screenHeight = 400;
 Vector text = new Vector();
 int topLine;
 Toolkit toolkit;
 FontMetrics fm;
 int baseline;
 int lineSize;
 int maxWidth;
 Scrollbar hbar, vbar;
 public static void main(String args[]){
  TextScrollApp app = new TextScrollApp();
 }
 public TextScrollApp() {
  super("TextScrollApp");
  setup();
  pack();
  resize(screenWidth,screenHeight);
  show();
 }
 void setup() {
  setBackground(Color.white);
  setMenuBar(menuBar);
  setupFontData();
  setupScrollbars();
 }
 void setupFontData() {
  setFont(defaultFont);
  toolkit = getToolkit();
  fm = toolkit.getFontMetrics(defaultFont);
  baseline = fm.getLeading() + fm.getAscent();
  lineSize = fm.getHeight();
 }
 void setupScrollbars() {
  hbar = new Scrollbar(Scrollbar.HORIZONTAL,0,0,0,0);
  vbar = new Scrollbar(Scrollbar.VERTICAL,0,0,0,0);
  hbar.setBackground(Color.lightGray);
```

continues

Listing 24.1. continued

```
  vbar.setBackground(Color.lightGray);
  add("South",hbar);
  add("East",vbar);
 }
 void resetScrollbars() {
  hbar.setValues(0,10,0,maxWidth+5);
  vbar.setValues(0,10,0,text.size()+5);
 }
 public void readFile(String file) {
  DataInputStream inStream;
  try{
   inStream = new DataInputStream(new FileInputStream(file));
  }catch (IOException ex){
   notifyUser("Error opening file");
   return;
  }
  try{
   Vector newText = new Vector();
   String line;
   maxWidth = 0;
   while((line=inStream.readLine())!=null) {
    int lineWidth = fm.stringWidth(line);
    if(lineWidth > maxWidth) maxWidth = lineWidth;
    newText.addElement(line);
   }
   text = newText;
   topLine = 0;
   inStream.close();
   resetScrollbars();
   repaint();
  }catch (IOException ex){
   notifyUser("Error reading file");
  }
 }
 public void notifyUser(String s) {
  String text[] = {s};
  String buttons[] = {"OK"};
  new Notification(this,"Error",true,text,buttons);
 }
 public void paint(Graphics g) {
  topLine = vbar.getValue();
  int xOffset = hbar.getValue();
  int numLines = text.size();
  screenHeight = size().height;
  int y = baseline;
  for(int i = topLine;(i < numLines) && (y < screenHeight + lineSize);++i) {
   g.drawString((String) text.elementAt(i),-xOffset,y);
   y += lineSize;
  }
 }
 public boolean handleEvent(Event event) {
  if(event.id==Event.WINDOW_DESTROY){
   System.exit(0);
   return true;
```

```
  }else if(event.id==Event.ACTION_EVENT){
   String s = (String) event.arg;
   if(event.target instanceof MenuItem){
    if("Exit".equals(s)){
     System.exit(0);
     return true;
    }else if("Open".equals(s)){
     openFile.show();
     if(openFile.getFile() != null) {
      String inFile = openFile.getFile();
      readFile(inFile);
     }
     return true;
    }
   }
  }else if(event.id == Event.SCROLL_LINE_UP ||
   event.id == Event.SCROLL_LINE_DOWN ||
   event.id == Event.SCROLL_PAGE_UP ||
   event.id == Event.SCROLL_PAGE_DOWN ||
   event.id == Event.SCROLL_ABSOLUTE) repaint();
  return false;
 }
}
class Notification extends MessageDialog {
 public Notification(Frame parent,String title,boolean modal,
  String text[],String buttons[]) {
  super(parent,title,modal,text,buttons);
 }
 public boolean handleEvent(Event event) {
  if(event.id==Event.WINDOW_DESTROY){
   dispose();
   return true;
  }else if(event.id==Event.ACTION_EVENT && event.target instanceof Button){
   dispose();
   return true;
  }
  return false;
 }
}
```

When you run the `TextScrollApp` program, you will see the opening window shown in Figure 24.1. Notice that vertical and horizontal scrollbars are added to the application window.

Click on the File pull-down menu and select the Open menu item. An Open File dialog box is displayed. Open the `TextScrollApp.java` file. The window is updated, as shown in Figure 24.2.

Use the horizontal scrollbar to scroll the view of the text to the right. (See Figure 24.3.)

FIGURE 24.1.
The `TextScrollApp` *opening window.*

FIGURE 24.2.
Displaying `TextScrollApp.java`.

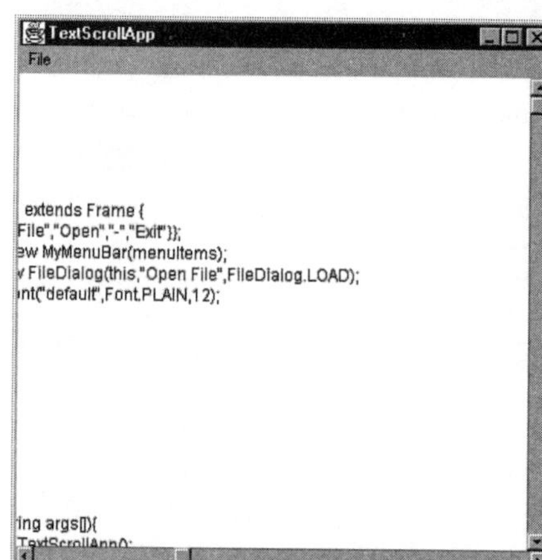

FIGURE 24.3.
Scrolling horizontally.

Scroll the text all the way back to the left and then click once on the down arrow of the vertical scrollbar. This causes the window to move the view of the text down one line. (See Figure 24.4.)

FIGURE 24.4.
Scrolling vertically one line.

Click on the vertical scrollbar between the tab and the down arrow at the bottom of the scrollbar. This results in the view of the text to be scrolled down 10 lines. (See Figure 24.5.)

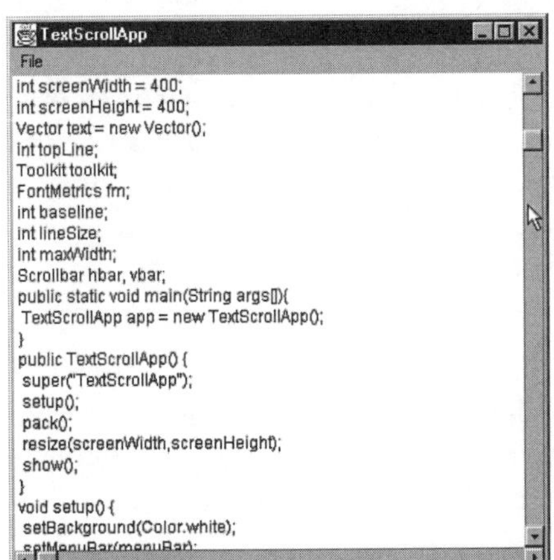

FIGURE 24.5.
Scrolling vertically using `SCROLL_PAGE_DOWN`.

Now drag the tab of the vertical scrollbar to the middle of the scrollbar. The view of the text is scrolled to the middle of the text file. (See Figure 24.6.)

Experiment with both the vertical and horizontal scrollbars to familiarize yourself with their operation before going on to study the `TextScrollApp` program.

FIGURE 24.6.
Scrolling vertically with the tab.

The `TextScrollApp` program declares a number of field variables. The `menuItems[]` array and `menuBar` variable are used to construct the program's menu bar. The `openFile` variable implements the dialog box used to load in the text file to be displayed. The `defaultFont` variable is used to set the text font to a default 12-point plain style font. The `screenWidth` and `screenHeight` variables are used to specify the dimensions of the application window.

The `text` variable is declared as a `Vector` object. It is used to store the individual lines of text that are read from the text file. The `topLine` variable identifies the number of the line that is currently displayed at the top of the window. The `toolkit` variable is used to refer to the `Toolkit` object associated with the application window. The `fm` variable is used to refer to the `FontMetrics` object associated with the default font.

The `baseline` variable is the vertical offset where the baseline of the first line of text should be displayed. The `lineSize` variable refers to the total height of the font being displayed. The `maxWidth` variable is calculated when a file is read. It refers to the maximum length of a text line in pixels. The `hbar` and `vbar` variables identify the horizontal and vertical scrollbars that are created and attached to the main window.

The `setupFontData()` method sets the window's font to the default font identified with the `defaultFont` variable. It then obtains the `Toolkit` object associated with the window and uses the `getFontMetrics()` method of the `Toolkit` to get the `FontMetrics` object associated with the default font. This object is assigned to the `fm` variable. The `baseline` variable is set to the sum of the leading and ascent of the current font as returned by the `getLeading()` and `getAscent()` methods of the `FontMetrics` class. The `lineSize` variable is set to the total height of the font using the `getHeight()` method of the `FontMetrics` class.

The `setupScrollbars()` method creates and initializes the horizontal and vertical scrollbars. A horizontal scrollbar is created with all of its parameters set to zero and is assigned to the `hbar` variable. A vertical scrollbar is created in the same manner and is assigned to the `vbar` variable. The specific parameters associated with these scrollbars are set when the text file that is to be scrolled is initially loaded.

The background color of both scrollbars is set to light gray, and then the scrollbars are added to the main application window. Using `BorderLayout` simplifies the positioning of the scrollbars.

The `resetScrollbars()` method resets the parameters associated with both scrollbars based on the text that is loaded from the file. The horizontal scrollbar assigned to `hbar` is assigned a minimum value of `0` and a maximum value of `maxWidth + 5`, where `maxWidth` is the maximum width of a text line in pixels. The constant `5` is added to `maxWidth` to allow some scrolling to the right of the end of the widest line. The `value` parameter of the scrollbar is set to `0` so that the leftmost end of a text line is initially visible. The `visible` parameter is set to `10` to allow horizontal scrolling of 10 pixels at a time.

The vertical scrollbar assigned to `vbar` is initialized by setting its maximum parameter to the number of text lines plus the constant `5`. The number of text lines is determined by invoking the `size()` method of the `Vector` class for the `text Vector` used to hold the text that was loaded from the selected text file. Specifying the `visible` parameter to `10` results in 10 lines being scrolled at a time. Note that the parameters of the horizontal scrollbar are specified in pixels and those of the vertical scrollbar are specified in text lines.

The `readFile()` method is almost the same as the one used in previous examples. It has been modified to store each line of text that is read within the vector that is assigned to the `text` variable.

The `paint()` method is used to display the `text Vector` on the screen. This method is also indirectly invoked in response to user scrolling actions. The `paint()` method sets the `topLine` variable to the value of the vertical scrollbar. It obtains this value by invoking the `getValue()` method of the `Scrollbar` class for `vbar`. It sets the `xOffset` variable to the value of the horizontal scrollbar. The scrollbar values are maintained and updated internally by the `Scrollbar` objects.

The `numLines` variable is set to the number of lines of text that are stored in the `text Vector`. The `screenHeight` variable is recalculated to adjust the text display for any window-resizing operations that may have occurred.

The `y` variable is used to specify the vertical position where each line of text should be drawn on the `Graphics` object passed to the `g` parameter when `paint()` is invoked. A `for` statement is used to draw the text. The text drawing begins with the line specified by the `topLine` variable and continues until the last line of the text file is displayed or the vertical display position assigned to the `y` variable is one line past the end of the screen. The `drawString()` method of the

Graphics class is used to draw the text on the screen. It is invoked with the text lines stored in the Vector object assigned to the text variable. The elementAt() method of the Vector class is used to retrieve the required line of text. Note that the xOffset variable is passed to the drawString() method as a negative value. This causes text drawing to begin before the left edge of the display window and enables horizontal scrolling toward the right to be implemented.

The handleEvent() method handles the SCROLL_LINE_UP, SCROLL_LINE_DOWN, SCROLL_PAGE_UP, SCROLL_PAGE_DOWN, and SCROLL_ABSOLUTE events by simply invoking the repaint() method to cause the screen to be repainted. The scrollbars maintain the value of their current positions. These values are used by the paint() method when the screen is repainted.

Scrolling Graphics

The scrolling of graphics is handled in the same way as text. The only difference between text scrolling and graphics scrolling is that vertical text scrolling results in an integral number of lines being scrolled at a time and graphics scrolling does not. The minimum and maximum values associated with a vertical text scrollbar are generally set based on the number of lines to be scrolled. The parameters of the horizontal and vertical scrollbars associated with graphics applications are set based on the dimensions of the Graphics object being scrolled and the size of the window in which the object is being viewed.

The ImageScrollApp Program

The ImageScrollApp program shows how scrollbars can be used to scroll objects that are drawn on a Graphics object. This program upgrades the DrawApp program developed in Chapter 23, "The Canvas," with the capability to support horizontal and vertical scrolling. The source code of the ImageScrollApp program is shown in Listing 24.2.

Listing 24.2. The source code of the ImageScrollApp program.

```
import java.awt.*;
import java.lang.Math;
import java.util.Vector;
import jdg.ch20.*;

public class ImageScrollApp extends Frame {
 Object menuItems[][] = {
  {"File","New","-","Exit"},
  {"Draw","+Line","-Oval","-Rectangle"}
 };
 MyMenuBar menuBar = new MyMenuBar(menuItems);
 MyCanvas canvas = new MyCanvas(TwoPointObject.LINE);
 int screenWidth = 400;
 int screenHeight = 400;
 int canvasWidth = 1000;
 int canvasHeight = 1000;
 Scrollbar hbar, vbar;
```

```
public static void main(String args[]){
 ImageScrollApp app = new ImageScrollApp();
}
public ImageScrollApp() {
 super("ImageScrollApp");
 setup();
 pack();
 resize(screenWidth,screenHeight);
 show();
}
void setup() {
 setBackground(Color.white);
 setMenuBar(menuBar);
 setCursor(CROSSHAIR_CURSOR);
 add("Center",canvas);
 setupScrollbars();
}
void setupScrollbars() {
 hbar = new Scrollbar(Scrollbar.HORIZONTAL,0,10,0,canvasWidth);
 vbar = new Scrollbar(Scrollbar.VERTICAL,0,10,0,canvasHeight);
 hbar.setBackground(Color.lightGray);
 vbar.setBackground(Color.lightGray);
 add("South",hbar);
 add("East",vbar);
}
public boolean handleEvent(Event event) {
 if(event.id==Event.WINDOW_DESTROY){
  System.exit(0);
  return true;
 }else if(event.id==Event.GOT_FOCUS && (event.target instanceof MyCanvas)) {
  setCursor(CROSSHAIR_CURSOR);
  return true;
 }else if(event.id==Event.LOST_FOCUS && (event.target instanceof MyCanvas)) {
  setCursor(DEFAULT_CURSOR);
  return true;
 }else if(event.id == Event.SCROLL_LINE_UP ||
  event.id == Event.SCROLL_LINE_DOWN ||
  event.id == Event.SCROLL_PAGE_UP ||
  event.id == Event.SCROLL_PAGE_DOWN ||
  event.id == Event.SCROLL_ABSOLUTE) {
   canvas.updateOffsets(hbar.getValue(),vbar.getValue());
   return true;
 }else if(event.id==Event.ACTION_EVENT){
  if(event.target instanceof MenuItem){
   String arg = (String) event.arg;
   if(processFileMenu(arg)) return true;
   if(processDrawMenu(arg)) return true;
  }
 }
 return false;
}
public boolean processFileMenu(String s) {
 if("New".equals(s)){
  canvas.clear();
  return true;
```

continues

Listing 24.2. continued

```
  }else if("Exit".equals(s)){
   System.exit(0);
   return true;
  }
  return false;
 }
 public boolean processDrawMenu(String s) {
  MyMenu menu = menuBar.getMenu("Draw");
  CheckboxMenuItem lineItem = (CheckboxMenuItem) menu.getItem("Line");
  CheckboxMenuItem ovalItem = (CheckboxMenuItem) menu.getItem("Oval");
  CheckboxMenuItem rectangleItem =
   (CheckboxMenuItem) menu.getItem("Rectangle");
  if("Line".equals(s)){
   canvas.setTool(TwoPointObject.LINE);
   lineItem.setState(true);
   ovalItem.setState(false);
   rectangleItem.setState(false);
   return true;
  }else if("Oval".equals(s)){
   canvas.setTool(TwoPointObject.OVAL);
   lineItem.setState(false);
   ovalItem.setState(true);
   rectangleItem.setState(false);
   return true;
  }else if("Rectangle".equals(s)){
   canvas.setTool(TwoPointObject.RECTANGLE);
   lineItem.setState(false);
   ovalItem.setState(false);
   rectangleItem.setState(true);
   return true;
  }
  return false;
 }
}
class MyCanvas extends Canvas {
 int tool = TwoPointObject.LINE;
 Vector objects = new Vector();
 TwoPointObject current;
 boolean newObject = false;
 int xOffset = 0;
 int yOffset = 0;
 public MyCanvas(int toolType) {
  super();
  tool = toolType;
 }
 public void setTool(int toolType) {
  tool = toolType;
 }
 public void clear() {
  objects.removeAllElements();
  repaint();
 }
 public void updateOffsets(int x,int y) {
  xOffset = x;
  yOffset = y;
  repaint();
 }
```

```
public boolean mouseDown(Event event,int x,int y) {
 current = new TwoPointObject(tool,x+xOffset,y+yOffset);
 newObject = true;
 return true;
}
public boolean mouseUp(Event event,int x,int y) {
 if(newObject) {
  objects.addElement(current);
  newObject = false;
 }
 return true;
}
public boolean mouseDrag(Event event,int x,int y) {
 int newX = x + xOffset;
 int newY = y + yOffset;
 if(newObject) {
  int oldX = current.endX;
  int oldY = current.endY;
  if(tool != TwoPointObject.LINE) {
   if(newX > current.startX) current.endX = newX;
   if(newY > current.startY) current.endY = newY;
   int width = Math.max(oldX,current.endX) - current.startX + 1;
   int height = Math.max(oldY,current.endY) - current.startY + 1;
   repaint();
  }else{
   current.endX = newX;
   current.endY = newY;
   int startX = Math.min(Math.min(current.startX,current.endX),oldX);
   int startY = Math.min(Math.min(current.startY,current.endY),oldY);
   int endX = Math.max(Math.max(current.startX,current.endX),oldX);
   int endY = Math.max(Math.max(current.startY,current.endY),oldY);
   repaint();
  }
 }
 return true;
}
public void paint(Graphics g) {
 int numObjects = objects.size();
 for(int i=0;i<numObjects;++i) {
  TwoPointObject obj = (TwoPointObject) objects.elementAt(i);
  obj.draw(g,xOffset,yOffset);
 }
 if(newObject) current.draw(g,xOffset,yOffset);
}
}
class TwoPointObject {
 public static int LINE = 0;
 public static int OVAL = 1;
 public static int RECTANGLE = 2;
 public int type, startX, startY, endX, endY;
 public TwoPointObject(int objectType,int x1,int y1,int x2,int y2) {
  type = objectType;
  startX = x1;
  startY = y1;
  endX = x2;
  endY = y2;
 }
```

continues

Listing 24.2. continued

```
 public TwoPointObject(int objectType,int x,int y) {
  this(objectType,x,y,x,y);
 }
 public TwoPointObject() {
  this(LINE,0,0,0,0);
 }
 public void draw(Graphics g,int xOffset,int yOffset) {
  if(type == LINE)
   g.drawLine(startX - xOffset,startY - yOffset,endX - xOffset,endY -yOffset);
  else{
   int w = Math.abs(endX - startX);
   int l = Math.abs(endY - startY);
   if(type == OVAL) g.drawOval(startX - xOffset,startY - yOffset,w,l);
   else g.drawRect(startX - xOffset,startY - yOffset,w,l);
  }
 }
}
```

When you run the `ImageScrollApp` program, the window shown in Figure 24.7 is displayed. This program should look similar to the `DrawApp` program in Chapter 23. The `DrawApp` program has been upgraded to support vertical and horizontal scrolling.

FIGURE 24.7.
The `ImageScrollApp` *opening window.*

Use the Draw menu to select drawing tools, and then draw some objects in the visible window as I have done in Figure 24.8.

Use the vertical and horizontal scrollbars to move throughout the extended canvas and draw more objects as I have done in Figure 24.9.

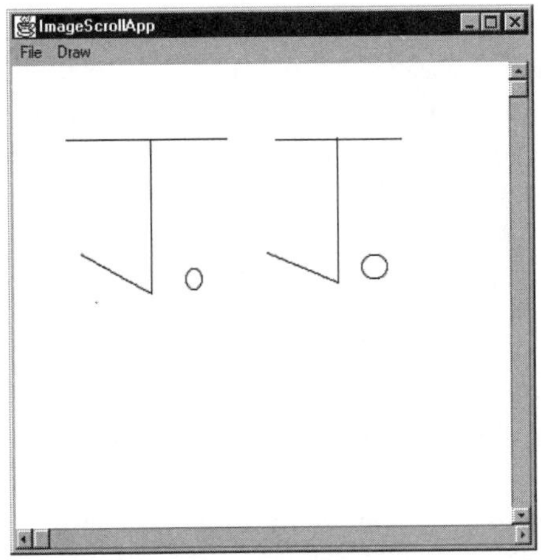

FIGURE 24.8.
Drawing some objects.

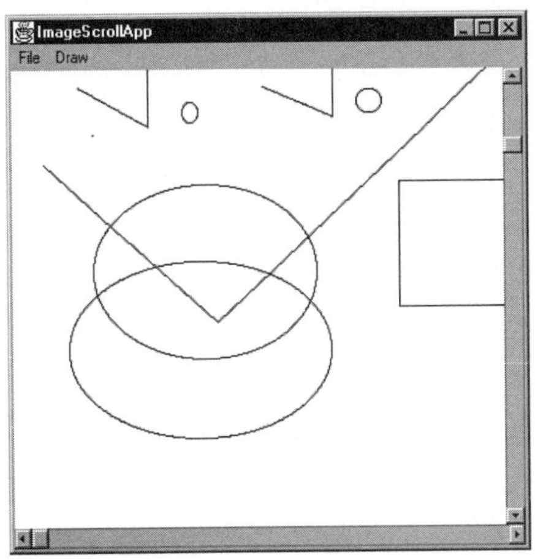

FIGURE 24.9.
Scrolling and drawing more.

Experiment with the scrollbars and drawing tools to become more familiar with the program's operation.

The `ImageScrollApp` program upgrades the `DrawApp` program to use scrollbars. Because the operation of the `DrawApp` program is extensively described in the previous chapter, I'll assume that it is still fresh in your mind and only describe the coding differences required to implement the scrollbars.

The `ImageScrollApp` class uses the `canvasWidth` and `canvasHeight` variables to represent the horizontal and vertical dimensions of the canvas. The area of the canvas is over six times the area of the default window size. This provides enough canvas to implement a reasonable amount of scrolling. The `hbar` and `vbar` variables are used to identify the horizontal and vertical scrollbars.

The `setupScrollBars()` method creates a horizontal scrollbar with the maximum size parameter set to the `canvasWidth`. It assigns this object to the `hbar` variable. A vertical scrollbar is created with its maximum parameter set to the `canvasHeight` and assigned to the `vbar` variable. The `visible` parameter of both scrollbars is set to the value of `10`. This enables page up and down operations to scroll 10 pixels at a time, a relatively small distance.

The `handleEvent()` method handles all scrollbar-related events by invoking the `updateOffsets()` method of the `MyCanvas` class with the current values of the horizontal and vertical scrollbars. The method is invoked for the `MyCanvas` object assigned to the `canvas` variable.

The `MyCanvas` class adds two new variables to its definition. The `xOffset` and `yOffset` variables maintain the current position of the canvas that is displayed in the upper-left corner of its `Graphics` object. These variables are modified via the `updateOffsets()` method, which also invokes the `repaint()` method to cause the canvas to be repainted.

The `xOffset` and `yOffset` variables are used in the `mouseDown()` and `mouseDrag()` event-handling methods to translate the x,y-coordinates supplied as arguments in the method invocation to coordinates that are relative to the overall canvas.

The `mouseDrag()` method has also been simplified to completely repaint the screen rather than limiting repainting to the local area being updated.

The `paint()` method adds the `xOffset` and `yOffset` variables to the `draw()` method used to draw objects of the `TwoPointObject` class.

The `draw()` method of the `TwoPointObject` class uses the `xOffset` and `yOffset` parameters to translate the x,y-coordinates of the objects being drawn from coordinates that are relative to the overall canvas to coordinates that are relative to the current `Graphics` object being updated.

Summary

This chapter explains the use of the `Scrollbar` class. It shows you how to use vertical and horizontal scrollbars to scroll the text and graphics displayed on the canvas. The event handling supported by scrollbars has also been explained. Chapter 25, "Using Animation," shows you how to add multimedia features, such as sound and animation, to your Java programs.

25

Using Animation

This chapter completes Part IV, "Window Programming," by showing you how to include animation sequences in your window programs. It identifies the basic elements of implementing an animation and then describes approaches to improving the quality of an animation's display by selectively repainting parts of a window and using the `MediaTracker` class to support the loading of the images used in an animation. When you finish this chapter, you'll be able to include animation in your window programs.

Animation Basics

While including animation sequences in your Java programs may at first appear to be complicated, it is, in fact, rather easy once you learn the basics. Animations are nothing more than the rapid display of still images such that the pattern of image display causes the appearance of movement for the objects contained in the image. To create an animation, you need to produce the sequence of objects that are to be displayed and then write a Java program that will display that sequence at a particular display rate.

For me, the hardest part of developing an animation is producing the images that are to be displayed. This part requires drawing skills and is completely separate from Java programming. Don't fret if you are unable to easily draw these animation sequences. Chances are that you're better at it than I am. The important point of this chapter is to learn how to display in the form of an animation the sequences that you do come up with.

Many animations display their image sequences in a looping fashion. A looping animation gives the appearance that it is much longer than it actually is, and it can run indefinitely. Looping animations also require fewer image frames. If your animation displays 10 to 20 image frames per second and you want it to run for a minute, then you will need 600 to 1200 images. That's a lot of work for a one-minute animation. It is much easier to develop a small but varied looping animation and have it loop several times during the course of a minute.

The major parameter of an animation, besides the type and quality of the images it displays, is the number of image frames that it displays per second. This is typically a fixed number between 5 and 25. The more frames per second that are displayed, the smoother the animation appears to be. The frames-per-second parameter translates into a frame delay parameter that is used to determine how long a program should wait before it displays the next image frame. This is typically measured in milliseconds. For example, frames-per-second rates of 5, 10, and 20 translate into frame delays of 200, 100, and 50 milliseconds.

A common approach to implementing an animation is to create a program thread that runs in an infinite loop and displays the frames of the animation sequence one at a time, waiting frame-delay milliseconds between each frame's display.

A Simple Animation

In order to get a better understanding of the basics of the animation process, you can develop a simple, character-based animation. The source code of the `SimpleAnimationApp` program is shown in Listing 25.1.

Listing 25.1. The source code of the `SimpleAnimationApp` program.

```
import java.awt.*;
import jdg.ch20.*;

public class SimpleAnimationApp extends Frame implements Runnable {
 Thread animation;
 int frameDelay = 100;
 String frames[] = {"*","**","***","****","*****","****","***","**","*"};
 int numFrames = frames.length;
 int currentFrame = 0;
 long lastDisplay = 0;
 String menuItems[][] = {{"File","Exit"}};
 MyMenuBar menuBar = new MyMenuBar(menuItems);
 int screenWidth = 200;
 int screenHeight = 200;
 public static void main(String args[]) {
  SimpleAnimationApp app = new SimpleAnimationApp();
 }
 public SimpleAnimationApp() {
  super("Simple Animation");
  setup();
  pack();
  resize(screenWidth,screenHeight);
  show();
  animation = new Thread(this);
  animation.start();
 }
 void setup() {
  setMenuBar(menuBar);
  setFont(new Font("default",Font.BOLD,18));
 }
 public void paint(Graphics g) {
  g.drawString(frames[currentFrame],60,60);
 }
 public void run() {
  do {
   long time = System.currentTimeMillis();
   if(time - lastDisplay > frameDelay) {
    repaint();
    try {
     Thread.sleep(frameDelay);
    }catch(InterruptedException ex){
    }
    ++currentFrame;
    currentFrame %= numFrames;
```

continues

Listing 25.1. continued

```
    lastDisplay = time;
   }
  } while (true);
 }
 public boolean handleEvent(Event event) {
  if(event.id==Event.WINDOW_DESTROY){
   System.exit(0);
   return true;
  }else if(event.id==Event.ACTION_EVENT){
   if(event.target instanceof MenuItem){
    String arg = (String) event.arg;
    if("Exit".equals(arg)) {
     System.exit(0);
     return true;
    }
   }
  }
  return false;
 }
}
```

Compile and run `SimpleAnimationApp`. Your program's display should look like the one shown in Figure 25.1.

FIGURE 25.1.
A simple animation.

A string of asterisks is modulated to give the appearance of movement.

While this short animation is by no means in line for any awards, it does illustrate all the basic elements of more complex and entertaining animations.

The `SimpleAnimationApp` class declares the `animation` thread, the `frameDelay` variable, the array of `frames[]` used to implement the animation's display, the `numFrames` variable, the `currentFrame` variable, the time of the `lastDisplay` of a frame, and the standard menu bar and window size variables.

The setup of the `SimpleAnimationApp` program is fairly standard, with the exception of the creation of the `animation` thread at the end of the class constructor and the invocation of the `animation` thread's `start()` method.

The `paint()` method contains a single statement that is used to display a string of asterisks on the console window.

The `run()` method implements the animation loop. It checks the current system time and the time of the last image display to see if it is time to display a new frame. It uses the `currentTimeMillis()` method of the `System` class to read the current time in milliseconds. If it is time to display another frame, the `run()` method invokes the `repaint()` method to display the current frame and then tries to sleep for `frameDelay` milliseconds. It updates the `currentFrame` using modular arithmetic and changes the time of `lastDisplay`.

The `handleEvent()` method performs the standard window event handling covered in Chapters 18 through 24.

A Graphics Animation

Because the `SimpleAnimationApp` program provides all the basic elements required of an animation, we can easily modify the animation to support graphics. Figures 25.2 through 25.5 provide four stick figures I drew using the Windows Paint program. These crude figures can be used to create an animation of a stick figure that attempts to fly.

FIGURE 25.2.
`stickman1.gif`.

FIGURE 25.3.
stickman2.gif.

FIGURE 25.4.
stickman3.gif.

FIGURE 25.5.
`stickman4.gif`.

You may easily substitute your own figures for the ones used in this example.

The source code of the `GraphicAnimationApp` program is shown in Listing 25.2.

Listing 25.2. The source code of the `GraphicAnimationApp` program.

```
import java.awt.*;
import jdg.ch20.*;

public class GraphicAnimationApp extends Frame implements Runnable {
 Thread animation;
 int frameDelay = 100;
 Image frames[];
 int numFrames;
 int currentFrame = 0;
 long lastDisplay = 0;
 String menuItems[][] = {{"File","Exit"}};
 MyMenuBar menuBar = new MyMenuBar(menuItems);
 int screenWidth = 400;
 int screenHeight = 400;
 public static void main(String args[]) {
  GraphicAnimationApp app = new GraphicAnimationApp();
 }
 public GraphicAnimationApp() {
  super("Graphic Animation");
  setup();
  pack();
```

continues

Listing 25.2. continued

```
  resize(screenWidth,screenHeight);
  show();
  animation = new Thread(this);
  animation.start();
 }
 void setup() {
  setMenuBar(menuBar);
  setFont(new Font("default",Font.BOLD,18));
  Toolkit toolkit = getToolkit();
  frames = new Image[4];
  frames[0] = toolkit.getImage("stickman1.gif");
  frames[1] = toolkit.getImage("stickman2.gif");
  frames[2] = toolkit.getImage("stickman3.gif");
  frames[3] = toolkit.getImage("stickman4.gif");
  numFrames = frames.length;
 }
 public void paint(Graphics g) {
  g.drawImage(frames[currentFrame],10,10,this);
 }
 public void run() {
  do {
   long time = System.currentTimeMillis();
   if(time - lastDisplay > frameDelay) {
    repaint();
    try {
     Thread.sleep(frameDelay);
    }catch(InterruptedException ex){
    }
    ++currentFrame;
    currentFrame %= numFrames;
    lastDisplay = time;
   }
  } while (true);
 }
 public boolean handleEvent(Event event) {
  if(event.id==Event.WINDOW_DESTROY){
   System.exit(0);
   return true;
  }else if(event.id==Event.ACTION_EVENT){
   if(event.target instanceof MenuItem){
    String arg = (String) event.arg;
    if("Exit".equals(arg)) {
     System.exit(0);
     return true;
    }
   }
  }
  return false;
 }
}
```

When you run `GraphicAnimationApp`, your display should look like the one shown in Figure 25.6.

FIGURE 25.6.
The `GraphicAnimationApp` *program display.*

Unless you have a really fast computer and video card, your program display probably has some very noticeable flickering. Don't worry about that problem now. You'll learn ways to improve the quality of an animation's display in the following section. For now, just focus on how we modified the `SimpleAnimationApp` program to support graphics-based animation.

The `GraphicAnimationApp` program is very similar to the `SimpleAnimationApp` program. These are the differences between the two programs:

- In `GraphicAnimationApp`, the `frames[]` array was changed from an array of `String` objects to an array of `Image` objects.
- In `GraphicAnimationApp`, the `setup()` method was updated to create a `Toolkit` object and use it to load the stickman images.

These simple changes were all that was needed to convert the program from a simple text-based animation to a graphics-based animation.

Improving Animation Display Qualities

The `GraphicAnimationApp` program has some serious deficiencies in the way that it displays the animation images. The first and probably the most noticeable problem is that it tries to start displaying the images before they are completely loaded. This is an easy problem to solve using the `MediaTracker` class.

The `MediaTracker` class provides the capability to manage the loading of image files. You use the `addImage()` method to add an image to the list of images being tracked. After adding an image to a `MediaTracker` object, you can then check on the image or all images managed by `MediaTracker` object using the access methods provided by the `MediaTracker` class.

The other major problem with the animation's display is that the entire screen is repainted with each new frame, which causes a significant amount of flickering. This image flickering can be mitigated by limiting the area of the window that is updated with each new image. The `repaint()` and `update()` methods of the component class provide this capability.

You are already familiar with limited screen repainting from using the `repaint()` method in Chapter 23, "The Canvas." The `update()` method provides the capability to update a `Graphics` object without first clearing the current image. This allows successive images to be displayed as marginal increments to the currently displayed image.

Another option to improving an animation's display quality is to change the frame delay. By decreasing the number of frames per second being displayed, you are able to lower the rate at which flickering occurs. However, you do this at the expense of the overall quality of your animation because higher frame-display rates tend to smooth out any gaps between successive images.

An Updated Graphics Animation

The `GraphicUpdateApp` program shows how to use the `MediaTracker` class, together with limited repainting and frame-delay adjustments, to improve the quality of the `GraphicAnimationApp` program. Its source code is shown in Listing 25.3.

Listing 25.3. The source code of the `GraphicUpdateApp` program.

```
import java.awt.*;
import jdg.ch20.*;

public class GraphicUpdateApp extends Frame implements Runnable {
 Thread animation;
 int frameDelay = 200;
 Image frames[];
 int numFrames;
 int currentFrame = 0;
 long lastDisplay = 0;
 boolean fullDisplay = false;
 MediaTracker tracker;
 String menuItems[][] = {{"File","Exit"}};
 MyMenuBar menuBar = new MyMenuBar(menuItems);
 int screenWidth = 400;
 int screenHeight = 400;
 public static void main(String args[]) {
  GraphicUpdateApp app = new GraphicUpdateApp();
 }
 public GraphicUpdateApp() {
  super("Updated Graphic Animation");
  setup();
  pack();
  resize(screenWidth,screenHeight);
  show();
```

```
 animation = new Thread(this);
 animation.start();
}
void setup() {
 setMenuBar(menuBar);
 setFont(new Font("default",Font.BOLD,18));
 Toolkit toolkit = getToolkit();
 frames = new Image[4];
 frames[0] = toolkit.getImage("stickman1.gif");
 frames[1] = toolkit.getImage("stickman2.gif");
 frames[2] = toolkit.getImage("stickman3.gif");
 frames[3] = toolkit.getImage("stickman4.gif");
 numFrames = frames.length;
 tracker = new MediaTracker(this);
 for(int i=0;i<numFrames;++i) tracker.addImage(frames[i],i);
}
public void paint(Graphics g) {
 if(allLoaded())
  g.drawImage(frames[currentFrame],10,10,this);
 else{
  String stars = "*";
  for(int i=0;i<currentFrame;++i) stars += "*";
  g.drawString(stars,60,60);
 }
}
boolean allLoaded() {
 for(int i=0;i<numFrames;++i) {
  if(tracker.statusID(i,true) != MediaTracker.COMPLETE) return false;
 }
 return true;
}
public void run() {
 do {
  long time = System.currentTimeMillis();
  if(time - lastDisplay > frameDelay) {
   if(allLoaded()) {
    if(fullDisplay) repaint(10,90,160,78);
    else{
     fullDisplay = true;
     repaint();
    }
   }else repaint();
   try {
    Thread.sleep(frameDelay);
   }catch(InterruptedException ex){
   }
   ++currentFrame;
   currentFrame %= numFrames;
   lastDisplay = time;
  }
 } while (true);
}
public boolean handleEvent(Event event) {
 if(event.id==Event.WINDOW_DESTROY){
  System.exit(0);
  return true;
 }else if(event.id==Event.ACTION_EVENT){
```

continues

Listing 25.3. continued

```
    if(event.target instanceof MenuItem){
     String arg = (String) event.arg;
     if("Exit".equals(arg)) {
      System.exit(0);
      return true;
     }
    }
   }
   return false;
  }
}
```

When you run `GraphicUpdateApp`, it displays an animated string of asterisks while the image files are being loaded. After that, it will immediately display the image animation. This reduces the unsightly flickering caused when an image is displayed while it is being loaded.

Notice how `GraphicUpdateApp` implements the limited-area repainting. You can run your mouse over the image display to determine the boundaries of the repaint area.

You should also notice that `GraphicUpdateApp` displays images at a slower rate. The frame-delay rate was increased from 100 microseconds to 200 microseconds, decreasing the frame display rate by a factor of 2.

The changes made to `GraphicAnimationApp` by `GraphicUpdateApp` consist of the declaration of the `fullDisplay` and `tracker` variables and modifications to the `setup()`, `paint()`, and `run()` methods. In addition, the `allLoaded()` method was created:

- The `fullDisplay` variable is used to ensure that a full display of the stickman is accomplished before attempting a limited display using the `repaint()` method. The `tracker` variable is used to refer to a `MediaTracker` object.
- The `setup()` method is updated to create the `MediaTracker` object and to add the images being loaded with this object.
- The `paint()` method is updated to draw the images after they've been loaded and to draw asterisk strings before the images are loaded.
- The `allLoaded()` method uses the `statusID()` method of the `MediaTracker` class to determine whether all images have been completely loaded.
- The `run()` method has been modified to use the `allLoaded()` method and the `fullDisplay` variable to determine whether it should repaint the entire screen or only a limited portion of it.

Summary

This chapter shows how to include animation sequences in your window programs. It identifies the basic elements of implementing an animation and describes approaches to improving the quality of an animation's display. It shows you how to selectively repaint parts of a window and how to use the `MediaTracker` class to support the loading of the images used in an animation. Chapter 26, "Client Programs," begins Part V, "Network Programming."

V

Network Programming

26

Client Programs

In this chapter you will learn how to write client programs that support networked client/server applications. You'll learn about the typical client programs found on the Internet and how they are structured. You'll develop simple client programs that support remote login and the sending of mail, and that fetch a list of Web pages. This chapter builds on the material presented in Chapter 17, "Network Programming with the `java.net` Package." You might want to review Chapter 17 before continuing with the material presented in this chapter.

Types of Clients

Of the client/server applications that are found on the Internet, only a small group is typically used. These include e-mail, the Web, FTP, Usenet news groups, and telnet. Gopher and WAIS, both precursors of the Web, have declined in popularity, having been subsumed by the Web. Typical Internet client programs include e-mail programs, Web browsers, FTP programs, and telnet clients.

E-mail programs provide an easy-to-use interface by which mail can be created and sent, retrieved and displayed, and managed. Popular window-based clients include Eudora and Pegasus. UNIX systems provide a number of popular e-mail clients, including Pine, Elm, and mh.

Web browsers provide a window on the World Wide Web and support the display of Web pages, including, of course, Java programs. The Netscape browser is the most popular browser on the Web and is Java capable. It is supported on UNIX, Windows, and Macintosh systems.

FTP programs provide a convenient way to retrieve files from public Internet file servers or from private file directories. Although a number of user-friendly FTP client programs are available, the simple text-based FTP client is still the most popular and most widely supported.

Newsreader programs simplify the process of working with messages that are posted to Usenet news groups. A number of netnews client programs are available for Windows, Macintosh, UNIX, and other operating system platforms.

Telnet clients are used to remotely log into other systems. These systems are usually UNIX or other operating systems that are powerful enough to provide the underlying capabilities needed to implement multiuser support. Windows and Macintosh systems, because of their inherent limitations, do not support telnet server applications.

Client Responsibilities

Client programs perform a service for their users by connecting with their server counterparts, forwarding service requests based on user inputs, and providing the service results back to the user.

In most cases, the client must initiate the connection. Typically, the server listens on a well-known port for a client connection. The client initiates the connection, which is accepted by the server. The client sends a service request to the server, based on user inputs. The server receives the service request, performs the service, and returns the results of the service to the client. The client receives the service results and displays them to the user.

A Simple Telnet Client

A telnet client program provides users with the capability to log into remote systems. It connects to a telnet server (called a *telnet daemon*) that listens on port 23 for an incoming connection. The telnet client connects to the daemon, which usually runs a login program and, upon successful login, runs a shell program.

The telnet client must be capable of simultaneously exchanging data with both the user and the remote system. The protocol used for communication between the client and the server is specified in RFC 854, the Telnet Protocol Specification. RFC 854 identifies three basic elements of the telnet protocol: the concept of a network virtual terminal, the principle of negotiated options, and the symmetry between terminals and processes.

The Network Virtual Terminal

The *network virtual terminal*, or NVT, is a very simple device that forms the basis for establishing telnet-based communication. All telnet clients and servers are required to support the NVT as a minimum capability. It is an abstract device that consists of a printer and a keyboard. The user types characters on the keyboard that are forwarded to the server. The server returns data to the user and the NVT displays it on the printer. The NVT provides local character echoing and half-duplex operation, although remote echoing and full-duplex operation can be used as negotiated options. Lines are terminated using a standard carriage-return–line-feed combination.

The NVT also provides for control operations that support process interruption and the discarding of excessive output. These operations are signaled by using the *Interpret as Command* (IAC) code as described in the next section.

The Interpret as Command Code

The IAC code is sent from a client or server to a program on the other end of a telnet connection to send a control code or to negotiate an option, as described in the next section. The IAC is a single byte consisting of the value `255` or hex `0xFF`. The IAC may be followed by a single byte to send a control code, or by two or more bytes to negotiate an option. For example, the IAC followed by a byte with the decimal value of 243 is used to send a break command.

Because the IAC is used to indicate a command or option negotiated, a special byte sequence is needed to send the byte value 255 used for the IAC. This is accomplished by sending two IACs in succession.

Negotiated Options

Because all telnet clients and servers are required to implement the NVT, they all have a common, but primitive, basis from which to begin operation. Additional options, such as full-duplex operation and character echoing, can be used based on the principle of negotiated options.

Options are *negotiated* when either the client or server program sends an IAC code to the other. The IAC code is followed by a `WILL` or `DO` code and an option code. The `WILL` code informs the program on the other side of the connection that it intends to use a particular option. The other program may respond with a `DO` or a `DONT` response, consisting of the IAC, followed by the `DO` or `DONT` code, followed by the option.

A program can also request that the program on the other side of the connection implement an option. This is accomplished by sending the IAC code, the `DO` code, and the option code. The other program can respond with a `WILL` or `WONT` response. A `WILL` response is indicated by sending the IAC, followed by the `WILL` code, followed by the option code. A `WONT` response is sent in the same manner, with the `WONT` code being used instead of the `WILL` code.

Symmetry Between Terminals and Processes

As you probably have surmised from reading the previous sections, the communication between client and server is highly symmetrical. Either the client or server can initiate option negotiation. The use of symmetry between client and host simplifies the implementation of the telnet protocol and allows client and host software to be developed from a common base. The `TelnetApp` program, presented in the next section, makes use of two I/O filters, `NVTInputStream` and `NVTOutputStream`, that implement some of the basic elements of the telnet protocol. These streams do not support control characters or additional options. Option negotiation is handled by refusing any additional options other than those provided by the basic NVT.

The `TelnetApp` Program

The `TelnetApp` program implements a minimum set of features of the telnet protocol in order to accomplish a remote login to a telnet server. The purpose of the program is not to provide you with a telnet client, but to show you the basics of how these clients work. More sophisticated and powerful telnet client programs can be retrieved from the Internet. The source code of the `TelnetApp` program is shown in Listing 26.1.

Listing 26.1. The source code for the `TelnetApp` program.

```
import java.lang.*;
import java.net.*;
```

```
import java.io.*;
import jdg.ch26.NVTInputStream;
import jdg.ch26.NVTOutputStream;
import jdg.ch26.NVTPrinter;

public class TelnetApp {
 public static void main(String args[]){
  PortTalk portTalk = new PortTalk(args);
  portTalk.start();
 }
}

class PortTalk extends Thread {
 Socket connection;
 PrintStream outStream;
 NVTInputStream inStream;
 NVTPrinter printer;
 public PortTalk(String args[]){
  if(args.length!=2) error("Usage: java TelnetApp host port");
  String destination = args[0];
  int port = 0;
  try {
   port = Integer.valueOf(args[1]).intValue();
  }catch (NumberFormatException ex) { error("Invalid port number"); }
  try{
   connection = new Socket(destination,port);
  }catch (UnknownHostException ex) { error("Unknown host"); }
  catch (IOException ex) { error("IO error creating socket"); }
  try{
   outStream = new PrintStream(connection.getOutputStream());
   inStream = new NVTInputStream(connection.getInputStream(),outStream);
  }catch (IOException ex) { error("IO error getting streams"); }
  System.out.println("Connected to "+destination+" at port "+port+".");
 }
 public void run() {
  printer = new NVTPrinter(inStream);
  printer.start();
  yield();
  processUserInput();
  shutdown();
 }
 public void processUserInput() {
  try {
   String line;
   boolean finished = false;
   DataInputStream userInputStream = new DataInputStream(System.in);
   do {
    line = userInputStream.readLine();
    if(line == null) finished = true;
    else outStream.println(line);
   } while(!finished);
  } catch(IOException ex) {
   error("Error reading user input");
  }
 }
 public void shutdown(){
```

continues

Listing 26.1. continued

```
  try{
   connection.close();
  }catch (IOException ex) { error("IO error closing socket"); }
 }
 public void error(String s){
  System.out.println(s);
  System.exit(1);
 }
}
```

> **NOTE**
>
> The `TelnetApp` class uses the `NVTPrinter`, `NVTInputStream`, and `NVTOutputStream` classes that are supplied in the following sections. You must type in the `NVTPrinter.java`, `NVTInputStream.java`, and `NVTOutputStream.java` files before compiling `TelnetApp.java`. The Java compiler will automatically compile these files when `TelnetApp.java` is compiled.

You use the `TelnetApp` program in the same way as any other telnet program. But bear in mind that it is only a minimal telnet client. Run the program by invoking it with the hostname of a computer that supports telnet and the well-known telnet port number, port 23.

In the following example, I use the program to log into my account at CTS. Note that the program operates in half-duplex mode, so characters are echoed locally. I substituted asterisks (*) for my password. Take caution when using this program because it will display your password characters in the same manner as any other text that you type.

Also, notice that commands that I type are echoed by my `cts.com` host:

```
C:\java\jdg\ch26>java TelnetApp cts.com 23
Connected to cts.com at port 23.


UNIX System V Release 3.2 (crash.cts.com) (ttyp2)

 login: jaworski
Password:****

Last   successful login for jaworski: Tue Apr 09 23:17:46 PDT 1996 on ttyp34
Last unsuccessful login for jaworski: Fri Apr 05 09:56:34 PST 1996 on ttyp9

                              Welcome to CTSNET!

                   Enter 'help' for assistance and information.


1% l
l
```

```
total 16
drwx------   2 jaworski guest         272 Sep 08  1995 Mail
drwxr-xr-x   2 jaworski guest         208 Dec 07 15:09 News
drwxr-xr-x   2 jaworski guest         224 Sep 08  1995 bin
drwxr-xr-x   2 jaworski guest         384 Apr 04 08:43 download
lrwxrwxrwx   1 root     root           15 Mar 15 02:56 dropbox -> /ftp/j/jaworski

drwx------   2 jaworski guest         160 Dec 08 10:35 ga
drwx------   2 jaworski guest         288 Apr 08 09:49 mail
drwxr-xr-x   3 jaworski guest         112 Dec 01 12:20 writing
2% exit
exit
3% logout

Connection broken.

C:\java\jdg\ch26>
```

The `TelnetApp` program creates an object of class `PortTalk` to perform its processing. This class extends the `Thread` class in order to implement multithreading capabilities. Its constructor uses the parameters passed in the `TelnetApp` command-line invocation to set up the connection to the specified host and port.

The `run()` method creates an object of the `NVTPrinter` class to interface with the destination host and invokes the `processUserInput()` method to interface with the user. The `processUserInput()` method reads a line at a time from the user's console and sends it to the telnet server.

The NVTPrinter Class

The `NVTPrinter` class performs most of the interesting processing because it interfaces with the server. It does this using the `NVTInputStream` class covered in the next section. `NVTPrinter` is also implemented as a subclass of `Thread`. Its source code is shown in Listing 26.2.

Listing 26.2. The source code for the NVTPrinter class.

```
package jdg.ch26;

import java.io.*;

public class NVTPrinter extends Thread {
 NVTInputStream inStream;
 public NVTPrinter(NVTInputStream in) {
  super();
  inStream = in;
 }
 public void run() {
  boolean finished = false;
  try {
   do {
    int i = inStream.read();
```

continues

Listing 26.2. continued

```
     if(i == -1) finished = true;
     else{
      System.out.print((char) i);
      System.out.flush();
      yield();
     }
    } while(!finished);
   System.out.println("\nConnection broken.");
   System.exit(0);
  } catch (IOException ex) {
   System.out.println("NVTPrinter error");
   System.exit(1);
  }
 }
}
```

The NVTInputStream Class

The `NVTInputStream` class implements the network virtual terminal input interface. Its source code is shown in Listing 26.3.

Listing 26.3. The source code for the `NVTInputStream` class.

```
package jdg.ch26;

import java.io.*;

public class NVTInputStream extends FilterInputStream {
 byte IAC = (byte) 0xff;
 byte DO = (byte) 0xfd;
 byte WILL = (byte) 0xfb;
 byte CR = 13;
 byte LF = 10;
 int WONT = 252;
 int DONT = 254;
 int BUFFER_SIZE = 1024;
 OutputStream out;
 byte lineBuffer[] = new byte[BUFFER_SIZE];
 int numBytes = 0;
 public NVTInputStream(InputStream inStream,OutputStream outStream) {
  super(inStream);
  out = outStream;
 }
 public int read() throws IOException {
  boolean recIAC;
  int i;
  do {
   recIAC = false;
   i = in.read();
   if(i == -1) return i;
   byte b = (byte) i;
```

```
  if(b == IAC) {
   recIAC = true;
   int cmd = in.read();
   if(cmd == -1) return cmd;
   byte b2 = (byte) cmd;
   if(b2 == IAC) return 255;
   else if(b2 == DO) {
    int opt = in.read();
    if(opt == -1) return opt;
    out.write(255);
    out.write(WONT);
    out.write(opt);
    out.flush();
   }else if(b2 == WILL) {
    int opt = in.read();
    if(opt == -1) return opt;
    out.write(255);
    out.write(DONT);
    out.write(opt);
    out.flush();
   }
  }
 } while(recIAC);
 return i;
}
public String readLine() throws IOException {
 numBytes = 0;
 boolean finished = false;
 do {
  int i = read();
  if(i == -1) return null;
  byte b = (byte) i;
  if(b == LF) {
   if(numBytes>0) {
    if(lineBuffer[numBytes-1] == 13)
     return new String(lineBuffer,0,0,numBytes-1);
   }
  }
  lineBuffer[numBytes] = b;
  ++numBytes;
 } while (!finished);
 return null;
}
}
```

`NVTInputStream` uses the network virtual terminal conventions, covered earlier in this chapter, to filter the input stream associated with the connection. It implements the basic `read()` method and also a convenient `readLine()` method.

The `NVTOutputStream` Class

The `NVTOutputStream` class provides an output analog to the `NVTInputStream` class. It implements the basic `write()` method according to the NVT conventions. It also provides a `println()`

method that uses the carriage-return–line-feed (CR-LF) end-of-line conventions. Its source code is shown in Listing 26.4.

Listing 26.4. The source code for the NVTOutputStream class.

```
package jdg.ch26;

import java.io.*;

public class NVTOutputStream extends PrintStream {
 int IAC = 255;
 byte CR = 13;
 byte LF = 10;
 public NVTOutputStream(OutputStream outStream) {
  super(outStream);
 }
 public void write(int i) {
  if(i == IAC) super.write(i);
  super.write(i);
 }
 public void println(String s) {
  super.print(s);
  super.write(CR);
  super.write(LF);
  super.flush();
 }
}
```

A Mail Client

Although mail is sent on the Internet using a variety of protocols, the *Simple Message Transfer Protocol* (SMTP), described in Request for Comments (RFC) 821, is the basic protocol used to move mail from one host to another. SMTP consists of a mail sender, a mail receiver, and a set of line-oriented commands used to send mail from the sender to the receiver.

NOTE

Requests for Comments are numbered notes of the Internet community that are usually, but not always, used to describe some aspect of the protocols or services used on the Internet.

RFC 821 describes the complete set of commands used by mail senders and receivers. Here I am using only a minimal subset of these commands to illustrate the development of an SMTP client, the mail sender.

An SMTP client connects to an SMTP server by establishing a connection to port 25 of the server's host. The server accepts the connection, sends a one-line ready notification to the client, and awaits client commands.

The client sends the `HELO` command with its hostname to introduce itself to the server. The server responds by sending a code that indicates that it is OK to initiate a mail transmission.

The client sends the `MAIL` command to the server to indicate that it has mail from a specific user. The server responds with a notification to proceed.

The client sends the `RCPT` command to identify the recipient of the e-mail. The server responds by telling the client whether or not the recipient is valid.

The client sends the `DATA` command to indicate that it is ready to send the message. The server responds by telling the client that it is OK to begin sending message data.

The client sends the message, a line at a time, terminating the message with a line containing a single period (.). A line of message text beginning with a period is sent by prepending an extra initial period to the message line.

The server acknowledges receiving the last line of text by sending an `OK` command to the client.

The client then terminates the connection by sending a `QUIT` command to the server. The server then responds by notifying the client that it is closing the connection.

The `MailClientApp` Program

The `MailClientApp` program illustrates the basic operation of a mail client program. It implements the basic SMTP commands described in the previous section. Its source code is shown in Listing 26.5.

Listing 26.5. The source code for the `MailClientApp` program.

```
import java.lang.*;
import java.net.*;
import java.io.*;
import java.util.Vector;
import jdg.ch26.NVTInputStream;
import jdg.ch26.NVTOutputStream;
import jdg.ch26.NVTPrinter;

public class MailClientApp {
 public static void main(String args[]){
  MessageInterface messageInterface = new MessageInterface();
  Message msg = messageInterface.getMsg();
  MailTalk mailTalk = new MailTalk(msg);
  mailTalk.run();
 }
}
```

continues

Listing 26.5. continued

```
class Message {
 String source;
 String destination;
 String subject;
 String text[];
 public Message() {
  super();
 }
 public void setDestination(String dest) {
  destination = dest;
 }
 public String getDestination() {
  return destination;
 }
 public void setSource(String src) {
  source = src;
 }
 public String getSource() {
  return source;
 }
 public String getDestinationHost() {
  return destination.substring(destination.indexOf('@')+1);
 }
 public void setSubject(String subj) {
  subject = subj;
 }
 public String getSubject() {
  return subject;
 }
 public void setText(Vector txt) {
  int n = txt.size();
  text = new String[n];
  for(int i = 0; i< n; ++i) {
   text[i] = (String) txt.elementAt(i);
  }
 }
 public String[] getText() {
  return text;
 }
}

class MessageInterface {
 Message msg;
 public MessageInterface() {
  msg = new Message();
 }
 public Message getMsg() {
  try {
  System.out.print("From: ");
  System.out.flush();
  DataInputStream inStream = new DataInputStream(System.in);
  msg.setSource(inStream.readLine());
  System.out.print("To: ");
  System.out.flush();
  msg.setDestination(inStream.readLine());
  System.out.print("Subject: ");
```

```
  System.out.flush();
  msg.setSubject(inStream.readLine());
  System.out.println("Enter message text.");
  System.out.println("Terminate message text with an initial period.");
  Vector text = new Vector();
  boolean finished = false;
  do {
   String line = inStream.readLine();
   if(endOfText(line)) finished = true;
   else text.addElement(line);
  } while(!finished);
  msg.setText(text);
  System.out.println("End of message read.");
  }catch (IOException ex) {
   System.out.println("IO Exception");
   System.exit(1);
  }
  return msg;
 }
 boolean endOfText(String s) {
  if(s.length() == 0) return false;
  if(s.charAt(0) == '.') return true;
  return false;
 }
}

class MailTalk {
 // Communication states
 static final int START = 0;
 static final int HELO = 1;
 static final int MAIL = 2;
 static final int RCPT = 3;
 static final int DATA = 4;
 static final int TEXT = 5;
 static final int QUIT = 6;
 static final int FINISHED = 9;
 Socket connection;
 String localHostName;
 NVTOutputStream outStream;
 NVTInputStream inStream;
 Message msg;
 public MailTalk(Message msg){
  this.msg = msg;
  String destination = msg.getDestinationHost();
  int port = 25;
  try{
   connection = new Socket(destination,port);
   localHostName = InetAddress.getLocalHost().getHostName();
  }catch (UnknownHostException ex) { error("Unknown host"); }
  catch (IOException ex) { error("IO error creating socket"); }
  try{
   outStream = new NVTOutputStream(connection.getOutputStream());
   inStream = new NVTInputStream(connection.getInputStream(),outStream);
  }catch (IOException ex) { error("IO error getting streams"); }
  System.out.println("Connected to "+destination+" at port "+port+".");
 }
```

continues

Listing 26.5. continued

```
public void run() {
 sendMail();
 shutdown();
}
public void sendMail() {
 try {
  int state = START;
  String line;
  do {
   line = inStream.readLine();
   if(line == null) state = FINISHED;
   else{
    System.out.println(line);
    switch(state) {
    case START:
     if(gotResponse(220,line)){
      outStream.println("HELO "+localHostName);
      System.out.println(">>>HELO "+localHostName);
      state = HELO;
     }else state=FINISHED;
     break;
    case HELO:
     if(gotResponse(250,line)){
      outStream.println("MAIL FROM:<"+msg.getSource()+">");
      System.out.println(">>>MAIL FROM:<"+msg.getSource()+">");
      state = MAIL;
     }else state=FINISHED;
     break;
    case MAIL:
     if(gotResponse(250,line)){
      outStream.println("RCPT TO:<"+msg.getDestination()+">");
      System.out.println(">>>RCPT TO:<"+msg.getDestination()+">");
      state = RCPT;
     }else state=FINISHED;
     break;
    case RCPT:
     if(gotResponse(250,line)){
      outStream.println("DATA");
      System.out.println(">>>DATA");
      state = DATA;
     }else state=FINISHED;
     break;
    case DATA:
     if(gotResponse(354,line)){
      String text[] = msg.getText();
      int len = text.length;
      outStream.println("Subject: "+msg.getSubject());
      outStream.println("");
      System.out.println("Subject: "+msg.getSubject());
      System.out.println("");
      for(int i=0;i<len;++i) {
       if(text[i].length() > 0 && text[i].charAt(0) == '.') {
        outStream.println("."+text[i]);
        System.out.println("."+text[i]);
       }else{
```

```
          outStream.println(text[i]);
          System.out.println(">>>"+text[i]);
         }
        }
        outStream.println(".");
        System.out.println(">>>.");
        state = TEXT;
       }else state=FINISHED;
       break;
      case TEXT:
       if(gotResponse(250,line)){
        outStream.println("QUIT");
        System.out.println(">>>QUIT");
        state = QUIT;
       }else state=FINISHED;
       break;
      case QUIT:
       state=FINISHED;
       break;
      }
     }
    } while(state != FINISHED);
   } catch(IOException ex) {
    error("IO Exception while sending mail");
   }
  }
  boolean gotResponse(int n,String s) {
   try {
    int responseCode = Integer.valueOf(s.trim().substring(0,3)).intValue();
    String line = s;
    while(line.charAt(3) == '-') {
     line = inStream.readLine();
     System.out.println(line);
    }
    if(responseCode == n) return true;
   }catch(NumberFormatException ex) {
   }catch(IOException ex){
   }
   return false;
  }
  public void shutdown(){
   try{
    connection.close();
   }catch (IOException ex) { error("IO error closing socket"); }
  }
  public void error(String s){
   System.out.println(s);
   System.exit(1);
  }
 }
```

The `MailClientApp` program prompts you for the from: name that you want associated with the sent message. SMTP is inherently insecure and will allow you to send e-mail using the e-mail address of another person as the from: address. In the example, I send a message using my daughter's e-mail address to myself. The subject of the message is `Test Message` and it contains a mere two lines of text. The following output shows a sample dialog with the `MailClientApp` program:

```
C:\java\jdg\ch26>java MailClientApp
From: emily@jaworski.com
To: jamie@jaworski.com
Subject: Test Message
Enter message text.
Terminate message text with an initial period.
This is a test.
It is only a test.
.
End of message read.
Connected to jaworski.com at port 25.
220-jaworski.com Sendmail 8.6.12/8.6.9 ready at Wed, 10 Apr 1996 00:33:31 -0700
220 ESMTP spoken here
>>>HELO athome.jaworski.com
250 jaworski.com Hello athome.jaworski.com [204.212.153.194], pleased to meet you
>>>MAIL FROM:<emily@jaworski.com>
250 <emily@jaworski.com>... Sender ok
>>>RCPT TO:<jamie@jaworski.com>
250 <jamie@jaworski.com>... Recipient ok
>>>DATA
354 Enter mail, end with "." on a line by itself
Subject: Test Message

>>>This is a test.
>>>It is only a test.
>>>.
250 AAA02243 Message accepted for delivery
>>>QUIT
221 jaworski.com closing connection

C:\java\jdg\ch26>
```

After the message is received by the e-mail client, it connects to my SMTP server and sends the message using the SMTP commands summarized earlier in this chapter.

The >>> arrows indicate commands that were sent by the program.

The Web Fetcher Program

Web *browsers* are the most popular client programs found on the Internet. They allow users to download and display Web pages, usually one at a time. The program shown in Listing 26.6 allows the user to specify a list of Web pages to be retrieved, and retrieves these Web pages and stores them on the local file system. This is an example of how custom Web clients can be implemented in Java.

Listing 26.6. The source code for the WebFetchApp program.

```
import java.util.Vector;
import java.io.*;
import java.net.*;

public class WebFetchApp {
 public static void main(String args[]){
  WebFetch fetch = new WebFetch();
  fetch.run();
 }
}

class WebFetch {
 String urlList = "url-list.txt";
 Vector URLs = new Vector();
 Vector fileNames = new Vector();
 public WebFetch() {
  super();
 }
 public void getURLList() {
  try {
   DataInputStream inStream = new DataInputStream(new FileInputStream(urlList));
   String inLine;
   while((inLine = inStream.readLine()) != null) {
    inLine = inLine.trim();
    if(!inLine.equals("")) {
     int tabPos = inLine.lastIndexOf('\t');
     String url = inLine.substring(0,tabPos).trim();
     String fileName = inLine.substring(tabPos+1).trim();
     URLs.addElement(url);
     fileNames.addElement(fileName);
    }
   }
  }catch(IOException ex){
   error("Error reading "+urlList);
  }
 }
 public void run() {
  getURLList();
  int numURLs = URLs.size();
  for(int i=0;i<numURLs;++i)
   fetchURL((String) URLs.elementAt(i),(String) fileNames.elementAt(i));
  System.out.println("Done.");
 }
 public void fetchURL(String urlName,String fileName) {
  try{
   URL url = new URL(urlName);
   System.out.println("Getting "+urlName+"...");
   File outFile = new File(fileName);
   PrintStream outStream = new PrintStream(new FileOutputStream(outFile));
   DataInputStream inStream = new DataInputStream(url.openStream());
   String line;
```

continues

Listing 26.6. continued

```
    while ((line = inStream.readLine())!= null) outStream.println(line);
    inStream.close();
    outStream.close();
   }catch (MalformedURLException ex){
    System.out.println("Bad URL");
   }catch (IOException ex){
    System.out.println("IOException occurred.");
   }
  }
  public void error(String s){
   System.out.println(s);
   System.exit(1);
  }
}
```

To use the program, create a file named `url-list.txt` that contains the names of the URLs you want to retrieve and the names of the files in which you want them stored. The following `url-list.txt` file was used to retrieve some pretty famous Web pages; it is included on the CD, in the `\jdg\ch26` directory:

```
http://www.yahoo.com          yahoo.htm
http://www.cnn.com            cnn.htm
http://home.netscape.com      netscape.htm
```

The output generated for the `WebFetchApp` program is as follows:

```
C:\java\jdg\ch26>java WebFetchApp
Getting http://www.yahoo.com...
Getting http://www.cnn.com...
Getting http://home.netscape.com...
Done.

C:\java\jdg\ch26>
```

Summary

In this chapter you have learned how to write client programs that implement the client end of Internet client/server applications. You have learned about the common client programs found on the Internet and how they are structured. You have developed a simple telnet client, an e-mail program, and the Web fetcher program. In Chapter 27, "Server Programs," you'll learn how to write simple server applications.

27

Server Programs

In this chapter you'll learn how to write server programs to support Internet client/server applications. You'll also learn about the server programs found on the Internet and how they are written. You'll develop simple server programs that support the sending of mail and the retrieval of Web pages. This chapter builds on the material presented in Chapters 17, "Network Programming with the `java.net` Package," and 26, "Client Programs." You might want to review these chapters before continuing with the material presented in this chapter.

Types of Servers

Chapter 26 introduced you to the types of client programs found on the Internet. For every client, there must be a server. Typical servers include e-mail, Web, FTP, telnet, netnews, and DNS. Other, less-popular servers such as echo, ping, and finger are also commonly supported.

E-mail servers move mail from client programs through the Internet to their destination hosts and store it until it is retrieved. The *Simple Message Transfer Protocol* (SMTP) is used to move mail. The *Post Office Protocol* (POP) is used to store mail and serve it to destination client programs.

Web servers implement the *Hypertext Transfer Protocol* (HTTP) in order to serve Web pages over the Internet. The most popular Web servers are the NCSA and CERN HTTPD servers, which are publicly available and may be freely downloaded. Commercial Web servers, such as those provided by Netscape and Microsoft, are only a small percentage of those that are in current operation.

FTP servers implement the File Transfer Protocol to make files available over the Internet. The most popular FTP server is a publicly available server developed by Washington University in St. Louis, Missouri.

The *domain name system* provides the backbone for Internet communication by translating domain names to their IP addresses. The most popular DNS software is the publicly available BIND software developed by the University of California at Berkeley.

Telnet servers are found in UNIX, VMS, and other multiuser operating systems. These servers allow remote login and implement the telnet protocol covered in Chapter 26.

Server Responsibilities

A server program listens for incoming connections on the well-known port associated with its service protocol. When an incoming connection is initiated by a client, the server accepts the connection, and typically spawns a separate thread to service that client. The client sends service requests over the connection. The server performs the service and then returns the results to the client.

An SMTP Server

Chapter 26 introduced the SMTP and developed a client program for generating Internet e-mail and sending it to an SMTP server. This section shows how the other side of the client/server connection is implemented. RFC 821 describes the details of this protocol. Here I will implement only a minimal subset of the available features of SMTP.

An *SMTP server* listens on port 25 for incoming client connections. When a connection request is received, the server accepts the connection and sends a server-ready notification to the client. When the client sends the `HELO` command, the server responds by sending a 250 code, which indicates that it is okay to initiate a mail transmission. The server then waits for the client to send the `MAIL` command. It acknowledges the `MAIL` command with another 250 code.

Having processed the `MAIL` command, the server then waits for the `RCPT` command. The server processes the `RCPT` command by checking to see if the destination e-mail address is valid for the server. It responds by indicating that the address is valid (using the 250 code) or that the user is not known to the server (using the 550 code).

When the client sends the `DATA` command, the server sends the 354 code to tell the client to start sending the contents of the mail message. The client then sends the message data one line at a time. The server checks each line to see if it consists of a single period (.), indicating the end of the message data. When this happens, it sends another 250 code to the client, indicating that it has found the end of the message.

The server removes the first period occurring in any message text line that it receives from the client.

After the server receives the end of the message text, it waits for the `QUIT` command. When it receives the `QUIT` command, it sends a 221 code, indicating that it is closing the transmission channel. It then closes the socket connection.

The `SMTPServerApp` Program

The `SMTPServerApp` program illustrates the basic operation of an SMTP server program. It implements the basic SMTP commands described in the previous section. Its source code is shown in Listing 27.1.

Listing 27.1. The source code for the `SMTPServerApp` program.

```
import java.net.*;
import java.io.*;
import jdg.ch26.NVTInputStream;
import jdg.ch26.NVTOutputStream;

public class SMTPServerApp {
```

continues

Listing 27.1. continued

```
 public static void main(String args[]){
  SMTPServer server = new SMTPServer();
  server.run();
 }
}
class SMTPServer {
 static final int HELO = 1;
 static final int MAIL = 2;
 static final int RCPT = 3;
 static final int DATA = 4;
 static final int END_DATA = 5;
 static final int QUIT = 6;
 static final int FINISHED = 9;
 NVTOutputStream out;
 NVTInputStream in;
 String hostName;
 public SMTPServer() {
  super();
 }
 public void run() {
  try{
   ServerSocket server = new ServerSocket(25);
   int localPort = server.getLocalPort();
   hostName = InetAddress.getLocalHost().getHostName();
   System.out.println("SMTPServerApp is listening on port "+localPort+".");
   boolean finished = false;
   do {
    Socket client = server.accept();
    String destName = client.getInetAddress().getHostName();
    int destPort = client.getPort();
    System.out.println("Accepted connection to "+destName+" on port "+
     destPort+".");
    out = new NVTOutputStream(client.getOutputStream());
    in = new NVTInputStream(client.getInputStream(),out);
    getMail();
    client.close();
   } while(!finished);
  }catch (UnknownHostException ex) {
   System.out.println("UnknownHostException occurred.");
  }catch (IOException ex){
   System.out.println("IOException occurred.");
  }
 }
 void getMail() {
  out.println("220 "+hostName+" Simple Mail Transport Service Ready");
  int state = HELO;
  do {
   String line = "";
   try {
    line = in.readLine();
    if(line == null) state = FINISHED;
   }catch(IOException ex) {
    System.out.println("IOException occurred.");
    System.exit(1);
   }
   switch(state){
```

```
case HELO:
 if(commandIs("HELO",line)) {
  out.println("250 Hello");
  System.out.println(line);
  state = MAIL;
 }else{
  out.println("500 ERROR");
  System.out.println(line);
 }
 break;
case MAIL:
 if(commandIs("MAIL",line)) {
  out.println("250 OK");
  System.out.println(line);
  state = RCPT;
 }else{
  out.println("500 ERROR");
  System.out.println(line);
 }
 break;
case RCPT:
 if(commandIs("RCPT",line)) {
  out.println("250 OK");
  System.out.println(line);
  state = DATA;
 }else{
  out.println("500 ERROR");
  System.out.println(line);
 }
 break;
case DATA:
 if(commandIs("DATA",line)) {
  out.println("354 Start mail input; end with <CRLF>.<CRLF>");
  System.out.println(line);
  state = END_DATA;
 }else{
  out.println("500 ERROR");
  System.out.println(line);
 }
 break;
case END_DATA:
 if(endOfData(line)) {
  out.println("250 OK");
  System.out.println("End of Message Received.");
  state = QUIT;
 }else{
  System.out.println(stripFirstPeriod(line));
 }
 break;
case QUIT:
 if(commandIs("QUIT",line)) {
  out.println("221 "+hostName+" Service closing transmission channel");
  System.out.println(line);
  System.out.println("");
  state = FINISHED;
 }else{
```

continues

Listing 27.1. continued

```
     out.println("500 ERROR");
     System.out.println(line);
    }
    break;
   }
  } while(state != FINISHED);
 }
 boolean commandIs(String s,String line) {
  int n = s.length();
  if(s.equalsIgnoreCase(line.substring(0,n))) return true;
  return false;
 }
 boolean endOfData(String s) {
  if(s.equals(".")) return true;
  return false;
 }
 String stripFirstPeriod(String s) {
  try {
   if(s.charAt(0) == '.') return s.substring(1);
  }catch(Exception ex){
  }
  return s;
 }
}
```

To run SMTPServerApp, type `java SMTPServer` at the DOS prompt. It will then display the following notice to indicate that it is up and running:

```
C:\java\jdg\ch27>java SMTPServerApp
SMTPServerApp is listening on port 25.
```

In order to use SMTPServerApp, you have to send e-mail to your machine's Internet address. You can use any e-mail client program to send e-mail to SMTPServerApp, but I'll use the MailClientApp developed in the previous chapter to allow you to track both sides of the SMTP connection.

Open a second console window and run MailClientApp as shown in the following code (substitute your host system name as the e-mail's destination):

```
jaworski:~/jdg/ch26$ java MailClientApp
From: jamie@jaworski.com
To: jamie@jaworski-pc.hctg.saic.com
Subject: Test of SMTPServerApp
Enter message text.
Terminate message text with an initial period.
This is a test of SMTPServerApp.
.
End of message read.
Connected to jaworski-pc.hctg.saic.com at port 25.
220 Jaworski-PC.hctg.saic.com Simple Mail Transport Service Ready
>>>HELO jaworski
250 Hello
```

```
>>>MAIL FROM:<jamie@jaworski.com>
250 OK
>>>RCPT TO:<jamie@jaworski-pc.hctg.saic.com>
250 OK
>>>DATA
354 Start mail input; end with <CRLF>.<CRLF>
Subject: Test of SMTPServerApp

>>>This is a test of SMTPServerApp.
>>>.
250 OK
>>>QUIT
221 Jaworski-PC.hctg.saic.com Service closing transmission channel
jaworski:~/jdg/ch26$
```

In this example, I am sending e-mail from my computer at home (`jaworski.com`) to the computer I use at work (`jaworski-pc.hctg.saic.com`). You can work the example by sending e-mail from your computer to your computer using separate windows for sender and receiver.

NOTE

If you cannot determine your hostname or IP address, you can always use `localhost` as your hostname.

Now look at the data displayed in the `SMTPServerApp` window:

```
C:\java\jdg\ch27>java SMTPServerApp
SMTPServerApp is listening on port 25.
Accepted connection to jaworski.com on port 1205.
HELO jaworski
MAIL FROM:<jamie@jaworski.com>
RCPT TO:<jamie@jaworski-pc.hctg.saic.com>
DATA
Subject: Test of SMTPServerApp

This is a test of SMTPServerApp.
End of Message Received.
QUIT
```

NOTE

The `SMTPServerApp` program is designed to loop forever to receive and process new SMTP connections. When you are finished running the program, use Ctrl+C to terminate its operation.

The data display is not as verbose as that of the mail client, but it shows all the commands and data received. Compare the display of `SMTPServerApp` with that of `MailClientApp` to follow how both sides of the Simple Message Transport Protocol were implemented.

The main() method of SMTPServerApp creates an object of the SMTPServer class and invokes its run() method.

The SMTPServer class declares seven constants that are used to maintain the state of the mail protocol as it interacts with a mail client program. It also declares the NVTInputStream and NVTOutputStream objects that it uses for client communication. The hostName variable is used to store the name of the local host running the SMTP server.

The run() method creates a ServerSocket object on port 25. It retrieves the local host name and stores it using the hostName variable. It then identifies on what port it is listening.

The do statement is used to service individual mail clients in a sequential manner. It accepts a client socket connection, gets the parameters of the connection, and displays them to the console window. The input and output streams associated with the connection are created and assigned to the in and out variables. The getMail() method is then invoked to receive mail from the client.

The getMail() method implements a subset of SMTP in order to receive mail from the client. It does not store the messages it receives, but merely displays the results of the client interaction on the console window.

When getMail() is invoked, it sends the 220 Simple Mail Transport Service Ready line to the mail client along with its hostname. It then sets the state variable to the HELO constant. The state variable is used to maintain the state of the communication with the client. The getMail() method uses a do statement to receive and process commands that it receives from the mail client. It reads a line from the client and verifies that the line is not null. (A null line signals that the connection with the client has been terminated.) The getMail() method processes the newly read line in different ways depending on the setting of the state variable.

If the current state is HELO, it checks to see if the received line contains the HELO command. If it does, a 250 OK response is sent to the client and the state is set to MAIL. If it does not, a 500 ERROR response is sent to the client and the current state remains unchanged.

If the current state is MAIL, it checks to see if the received line contains the MAIL command. If it does, a 250 OK response is sent to the client and the state is set to RCPT. If it does not, a 500 ERROR response is sent to the client and the current state remains unchanged.

If the current state is RCPT, it checks to see if the received line contains the RCPT command. If it does, a 250 OK response is sent to the client and the state is set to DATA. If it does not, a 500 ERROR response is sent to the client and the current state remains unchanged.

If the current state is DATA, it checks to see if the received line contains the DATA command. If it does, a 354 Start mail input; end with <CRLF>.<CRLF> response is sent to the client and the state is set to END_DATA. If it does not, a 500 ERROR response is sent to the client and the current state remains unchanged.

If the current state is END_DATA, it checks to see if the received line contains the end-of-message data command, which is a line consisting of a single period (.). If it does, a 250 OK response is sent to the client and the state is set to QUIT. If it does not, the first period of the received line (if any) is stripped before the line is displayed to the console window.

If the current state is QUIT, it checks to see if the received line contains the QUIT command. If it does, a 250 OK response is sent to the client and the state is set to FINISHED. If it does not, a 500 ERROR response is sent to the client and the current state remains unchanged.

When the current state becomes FINISHED, the do statement is terminated.

The commandIs() method is used to determine whether a command received from a mail client matches a specific command string.

The endOfData() method checks a received line to see if it consists of a single period indicating the end of a message transmission.

The stripFirstPeriod() method is used to strip out the first period of a message text line.

A Web Server

Web servers implement HTTP in order to retrieve Web resources identified by URLs. HTTP is an application-level protocol that is designed to be quick and efficient. It is based on the request-response paradigm. Web browsers initiate connections with Web servers and submit service requests. The servers, upon receiving a request, locate the specified resource and perform the requested operation. Typical Web browser requests are to retrieve a designated file or send data to a CGI program. HTTP supports several request types, referred to as *methods.* These include the GET, HEAD, and POST methods. The Web server developed in the following section supports only the GET request.

The server responds to GET requests by returning the requested resource to the browser. The server's response begins with a header and is followed by the requested data. The *header* consists of a status line and one or more general header lines. The status line identifies the version of HTTP being used and a status code. General header lines include a MIME version identifier, a date/time line, a content type indicator, and a content length identifier. A blank line is inserted between the header and the body of the resource data.

The WebServerApp Program

The WebServerApp program illustrates the basic operation of a Web server. (See Listing 27.2.) It is a single-threaded Web server that supports a subset of the HTTP 1.0 protocol. Many Web servers are multithreaded, allowing them to simultaneously support multiple browser connections. Web servers for low-end PC platforms, such as the Apache Web server, are single threaded to make up for processing deficiencies of slow PCs and slower Internet connections. WebServerApp can easily be converted to a multithreaded server by implementing the interior of the `do` statement as a separate thread.

Listing 27.2. The source code for the `WebServerApp` program.

```
import java.net.*;
import java.io.*;
import jdg.ch26.NVTInputStream;
import jdg.ch26.NVTOutputStream;

public class WebServerApp {
 public static void main(String args[]){
  WebServer server = new WebServer();
  server.run();
 }
}
class WebServer {
 public WebServer() {
  super();
 }
 public void run() {
  try{
   ServerSocket server = new ServerSocket(8080);
   int localPort = server.getLocalPort();
   System.out.println("WebServerApp is listening on port "+localPort+".");
   do {
    Socket client = server.accept();
    String destName = client.getInetAddress().getHostName();
    int destPort = client.getPort();
    System.out.println("Accepted connection to "+destName+
     " on port "+destPort+".");
    NVTOutputStream outStream =
     new NVTOutputStream(client.getOutputStream());
    NVTInputStream inStream =
     new NVTInputStream(client.getInputStream(),outStream);
    boolean finished = false;
    String inLine = inStream.readLine();
    System.out.println("Received: "+inLine);
    if(getRequest(inLine)) {
     String fileName = getFileName(inLine);
     File file = new File(fileName);
     if(file.exists()) {
      System.out.println(fileName+" requested.");
      outStream.println("HTTP/1.0 200 OK");
      outStream.println("MIME-Version: 1.0");
      outStream.println("Content-Type: text/html");
      int len = (int) file.length();
      outStream.println("Content-Length: "+len);
      outStream.println("");
      sendFile(outStream,file);
      outStream.flush();
     }else{
      outStream.println("HTTP/1.0 404 Not Found");
      String notFound =
       "<TITLE>Not Found</TITLE><H1>Error 404 - File Not Found</H1>";
      outStream.println("Content-Type: text/html");
```

```
      outStream.println("Content-Length: "+notFound.length()+2);
      outStream.println("");
      outStream.println(notFound);
     }
    }
    client.close();
   } while(true);
  }catch (IOException ex){
   System.out.println("IOException occurred.");
  }
 }
 boolean getRequest(String s) {
  if(s.length() > 0) {
   if(s.substring(0,3).equalsIgnoreCase("GET")) return true;
  }
  return false;
 }
 String getFileName(String s) {
  String f = s.substring(s.indexOf(' ')+1);
  f = f.substring(0,f.indexOf(' '));
  try {
   if(f.charAt(0) == '/') f =  f.substring(1);
  } catch(StringIndexOutOfBoundsException ex) {
  }
  if(f.equals("")) f = "index.htm";
  return f;
 }
 void sendFile(NVTOutputStream out,File file) {
  try {
   DataInputStream in = new DataInputStream(new FileInputStream(file));
   int len = (int) file.length();
   byte buffer[] = new byte[len];
   in.readFully(buffer);
   out.write(buffer,0,len);
   in.close();
  }catch(Exception ex){
   System.out.println("Error retrieving file.");
   System.exit(1);
  }
 }
}
```

The standard socket implementation that comes with the Windows 95 version of Java 1.0 has a flaw that does not close sockets correctly. When you fetch a Web document from `WebServerApp`, you might have to click on the Stop button of your Web browser to have it display the retrieved Web page. When I run `WebServerApp` on other operating system platforms, such as Linux, using Java 1.0.1, there is no socket closure problem and everything works as it should.

Run `WebServerApp` as follows:

```
C:\java\jdg\ch27>java WebServerApp
WebServerApp is listening on port 8080.
```

It responds by indicating that it is listening on port 8080. I had it use port 8080 instead of the standard port 80 so as not to interfere with any Web server that you might currently have running on your system.

I have supplied a default Web page, `index.htm`, that is retrieved by `WebServerApp`. (See Listing 27.3.) You can also retrieve other Web pages by placing them in the same directory as `WebServerApp` and referencing them in the URL opened by your Web browser.

Listing 27.3. The contents of the `index.htm` file.

```
<HTML>
<HEAD><TITLE>Test Document</TITLE></HEAD>
<BODY>
<H1>This is a test.</H1>
</BODY>
</HTML>
```

NOTE

If the `WebServerApp` program does not find the `index.htm` file, it will return an error message.

Because `WebServerApp` is a server, you need to use a client program in order to interact with it. Launch your favorite Web browser and open the URL of your machine followed by `:8080` to have the browser submit its request to port 8080 instead of port 80. For example, if your host name is `my.host.name.com`, open the URL `http://my.host.name.com:8080`. `WebServerApp` responds by identifying the browser connection and sending the `index.htm` file. You can access other files by appending their names to the URL. For example, to access the `test.htm` file in the directory where you launched `WebServerApp`, use the URL `http://my. host.name.com:8080/test.htm`.

The following output is displayed by `WebServerApp` on the console window:

```
C:\java\jdg\ch27>java WebServerApp
WebServerApp is listening on port 8080.
Accepted connection to jaworski-pc.hctg.saic.com on port 2145.
Received: GET / HTTP/1.0
index.htm requested.
```

When you access the URL `http://my.host.name.com:8080`, `WebServerApp` is instructed to return the default no name HTML file. It responds by sending `index.htm` to the Web browser. Your browser's display should contain the message shown in Figure 27.1.

> **NOTE**
>
> If you cannot find your hostname, you can use `localhost` instead. For example, the URL `http://localhost:8080` can be used instead of `http://my.host.name.com:8080`.

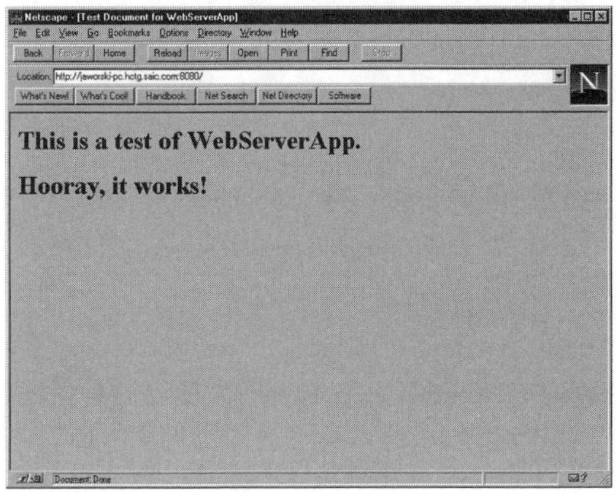

FIGURE 27.1.
Web browser display.

Experiment by creating your own HTML files and using your browser to access them using `WebServerApp`. Use Ctrl+C to terminate the operation of `WebServerApp`.

The `main()` method of `WebServerApp` creates a `WebServer` object and invokes its `run()` method.

The `WebServer` class implements a single default constructor and three access methods.

The `run()` method supports Web client retrieval requests and is the heart of the `WebServerApp` processing. It creates a `ServerSocket` object using port 8080 and then displays its operational status on the console window.

A `do` statement is used to accept and process incoming client connections. It retrieves the parameters associated with a connection and displays them to the console window. The input and output streams associated with the connection are created and assigned to the `inStream` and `outStream` variables. A line is then read from the input stream and displayed to the console window.

The line received from the browser client is checked to see if it is a `GET` request. If it is, the name of the requested HTML file is retrieved from the browser request line. If the file exists within the current directory, a `200 OK` status line is sent to the browser, followed by a `MIME-version 1.0` header line. This line tells the browser that the server is cognizant of MIME version 1.0 when returning the requested file. It then specifies the MIME type of the requested file as `text` or `html`. Real Web servers would send a MIME type that matched the extension of the file returned. See Chapter 28, "Content Handlers," for a discussion of MIME types and their use by Web servers and browsers.

The length of the file to be returned is obtained using the `length()` method of the `File` class, and a notification of the file's length is returned to the browser using a `Content-Length` header line. A blank line follows the `Content-Length` header line to signal the end of the HTTP header. The `sendFile()` method is then invoked to send the requested file to the browser.

If the file requested by the browser does not exist, the HTTP status line sent to the browser contains a `404 Not Found` error code and a short HTML file indicating that the error is sent to the browser.

If the request received from the browser client is not a `GET` request, it is ignored and the connection is closed.

The `getRequest()` method determines whether an incoming client request uses the `GET` method.

The `getFileName()` method extracts the requested HTML filename from an incoming browser request line.

The `sendFile()` method sends the file requested by a Web client using the output stream of the server-client connection. It sends the file by reading all bytes of the file into a byte array and then sending the entire array over the connection. This approach works well with small files, but may break with large files, depending on available memory resources.

Summary

In this chapter you have learned how to write programs that implement the server end of Internet client/server applications. You have learned about the common server programs found on the Internet and how they are structured. You have developed an SMTP server and a primitive Web server. In Chapter 28 you'll learn how to write content handlers that are used with Web client applications.

28

Content Handlers

In this chapter you'll learn how to write content handlers to support the retrieval of objects by Web browsers. You'll also learn about the multipurpose Internet mail extensions (MIMEs) and how they are used to identify the type of objects that are provided by Web servers. You'll then develop a simple content handler and integrate it with a Web client program. This chapter builds on the material presented in Chapter 17, "Network Programming with the `java.net` Package."

Using Content Handlers

If you have been extensively involved with using your Web browser, you probably have encountered a number of external viewers or plug-ins that are used to supplement the capabilities provided by your browser. These external viewers are used to display and process files that are not normally supported by browsers.

Java supports additional internal or external viewers through the content handler mechanism. Content handlers are used to retrieve objects via an `URLConnection` object.

Content handlers are implemented as subclasses of the `ContentHandler` class. A content handler is only required to implement a single method—the `getContent()` method that overrides the method provided by the `ContentHandler` class. This method takes an `URLConnection` object as a parameter, and returns an object of a specific MIME type. You'll learn about MIME types in the following section of this chapter.

The purpose of a content handler is to extract an object of a given MIME type from an `URLConnection` object's input stream. Content handlers are not directly instantiated or accessed. The `getContent()` methods of the `URL` and `URLConnection` classes cause content handlers to be created and invoked to perform their processing.

A content handler is associated with a specific MIME type through the use of the `ContentHandlerFactory` interface. A class that implements the `ContentHandlerFactory` interface must implement the `createContentHandler()` method. This method returns a `ContentHandler` object to be used for a specific MIME type. A `ContentHandlerFactory` object is installed using the static `setContentHandlerFactory()` method of the `URLConnection` class.

Multipurpose Internet Mail Extensions (MIME)

Content handlers are associated with specific MIME types. Many Internet programs, including e-mail clients, Web browsers, and Web servers, use the multipurpose Internet mail extensions to associate an object type with a file. These object types include text, multimedia files, and application-specific files. MIME types consist of a type and a subtype. Examples are text/html, text/plain, image/gif, and image/jpeg, where text and image are the types and html, plain, gif, and jpeg are the subtypes. The `URL` classes provided by Java support the processing of each of these types; however, the number of MIME type/subtype combinations is large and growing. Content handlers are used to support MIME type processing.

Web servers map MIME types to the files they serve using the files' extensions. For example, files with the `.htm` and `.html` extensions are mapped to the text/html MIME type/subtype. Files with the `.gif` and `.jpg` extensions are mapped to image/gif and image/jpeg. The MIME type of a file is sent to Web browsers by Web servers when the server sends the designated files to the browsers in response to browser requests.

Developing a Content Handler

The first step to implementing a content handler is to define the class of the object to be extracted by the content handler. The content handler is then defined as a subclass of the `ContentHandler` class. The `getContent()` method of the content handler performs the extraction of objects of a specific MIME type from the input stream associated with an `URLConnection` object.

A content handler is associated with a specific MIME type through the use of a `ContentHandlerFactory` object. The `createContentHandler()` method of the `ContentHandlerFactory` interface is used to return a content handler for a specific MIME type.

Finally, the `setContentHandlerFactory()` method of the `URLConnection` class is used to set a `ContentHandlerFactory` as the default `ContentHandlerFactory` to be used with all MIME types.

A Simple Content Handler

This section presents an example of implementing a simple content handler. A bogus MIME type, text/cg, is created to implement objects of the character grid type. A *character grid type* is a two-dimensional grid made up of a single character. An example follows:

```
O   O
 O O
  O
 O O
O   O
```

This example is a character grid object that is five character positions wide and five character positions high. It uses the `O` character to draw the grid. The grid is specified by a boolean array that identifies whether the drawing character is to be displayed.

This particular character grid is represented using the following text string:

```
55O1000101010001000101010001
```

The first character (5) represents the grid's height. The second character (also 5) represents the grid's width. The third character is the grid's drawing character. The remaining characters specify whether the draw character should be displayed at a particular grid position. A 1 signifies that the draw character should be displayed, and a 0 signifies that it should not be displayed. The array is arranged in row order beginning with the top of the grid.

The definition of the CharGrid class is shown in Listing 28.1.

Listing 28.1. The source code for the CharGrid class.

```
public class CharGrid {
 public int height;
 public int width;
 public char ch;
 public boolean values[][];
 public CharGrid(int h,int w,char c,boolean vals[][]) {
  height = h;
  width = w;
  ch = c;
  values = vals;
 }
}
```

The GridContentHandler Class

The GridContentHandler class is used to extract CharGrid objects from an URLConnection. Its source code is shown in Listing 28.2.

Listing 28.2. The source code for the GridContentHandler class.

```
import java.net.*;
import java.io.*;

public class GridContentHandler extends ContentHandler {
 public Object getContent(URLConnection urlc) throws IOException {
  DataInputStream in = new DataInputStream(urlc.getInputStream());
  int height = (int) in.readByte() - 48;
  int width = (int) in.readByte() - 48;
  char ch = (char) in.readByte();
  boolean values[][] = new boolean[height][width];
  for(int i=0;i<height;++i) {
   for(int j=0;j<width;++j) {
    byte b = in.readByte();
    if(b == 48) values[i][j] = false;
    else values[i][j] = true;
   }
  }
  in.close();
  return new CharGrid(height,width,ch,values);
 }
}
```

The GridContentHandler class extends the ContentHandler class and provides a single method. The getContent() method takes an URLConnection object as a parameter and returns an object of the Object class. It also throws the IOException exception.

The getContent() method creates an object of class DataInputStream and assigns it to the in variable. It uses the getInputStream() method of the URLConnection class to access the input stream associated with an URL connection.

The height, width, and draw character of the CharGrid object are read one byte at a time from the input stream. The values[][] array is then read and converted to a boolean representation. The CharGrid object is then created from the extracted values and returned.

The GetGridApp Program

The GetGridApp program illustrates the use of content handlers. It retrieves an object of the CharGrid type from my Web sever. I use the NCSA HTTPD server on a Linux system. I've set up the server's MIME type file to recognize files with the .cg extension as text/cg.

The source code of the GetGridApp program is shown in Listing 28.3.

Listing 28.3. The source code for the GetGridApp program.

```
import java.net.*;
import java.io.*;

public class GetGridApp {
 public static void main(String args[]){
  try{
   GridFactory gridFactory = new GridFactory();
   URLConnection.setContentHandlerFactory(gridFactory);
   if(args.length!=1) error("Usage: java GetGridApp URL");
   System.out.println("Fetching URL: "+args[0]);
   URL url = new URL(args[0]);
   CharGrid cg = (CharGrid) url.getContent();
   System.out.println("height: "+cg.height);
   System.out.println("width: "+cg.width);
   System.out.println("char: "+cg.ch);
   for(int i=0;i<cg.height;++i) {
    for(int j=0;j<cg.width;++j) {
     if(cg.values[i][j]) System.out.print(cg.ch);
     else System.out.print(" ");
    }
    System.out.println();
   }
  }catch (MalformedURLException ex){
   error("Bad URL");
  }catch (IOException ex){
   error("IOException occurred.");
  }
 }
```

continues

Listing 28.3. continued

```
 public static void error(String s){
  System.out.println(s);
  System.exit(1);
 }
}
class GridFactory implements ContentHandlerFactory {
 public GridFactory() {
 }
 public ContentHandler createContentHandler(String mimeType) {
  if(mimeType.equals("text/cg")) {
   System.out.println("Requested mime type: "+mimeType);
   return new GridContentHandler();
  }
  return null;
 }
}
```

When you invoke the `GetGridApp` program, provide it with the URL `http://www.jaworski.com/java/chargrid.cg` as a parameter.

The `GetGridApp` program's output is as follows:

```
C:\java\jdg\ch28>java GetGridApp http://www.jaworski.com/java/chargrid.cg
Fetching URL: http://www.jaworski.com/java/chargrid.cg
Requested mime type: text/cg
height: 5
width: 5
char: j
jjjjj
   j
   j
j  j
 jj

C:\java\jdg\ch28>
```

This connects to my Web server, retrieves the `chargrid.cg` file, extracts the `CharGrid` object contained in the file, and displays it on the console window. The character grid object displays a grid of `j` characters.

The `main()` method creates an object of the `GridFactory` class, which implements the `ContentHandlerFactory` interface. It then sets the object as the default content handler. An `URL` object is created using the URL string passed as the program's parameter. The `getContent()` method of the `URL` class is then used to extract the `CharGrid` object from the URL. The `getContent()` method results in the `GridFactory` object assigned to the `gridFactory` variable being invoked to retrieve an appropriate content handler. An object of class `GridContentHandler` is returned and its `getContent()` method is invoked to extract the `CharGrid` object. This is performed behind the scene as the result of invoking the `URL` class's `getContent()` method. The `CharGrid` object is then displayed.

The `GetGridApp` program defines the `GridFactory` class as a `ContentHandlerFactory`. It implements the `createContentHandler()` method and checks to see if the MIME type passed to it is text/cg. If it is not, the `null` value is returned to signal that the Java-supplied content handler should be used. If the MIME type is text/cg, the requested MIME type is displayed, and a `GridContentHandler` object is returned.

Summary

In this chapter you have learned how to write content handlers to support the retrieval of objects by Web browsers. You have learned about the multipurpose Internet mail extensions and how they are used to identify the type of objects that are provided by Web servers. You have developed the `GridContentHandler` class and integrated it with the `GetGridApp` program. Chapter 29, "Protocol Handlers," shows you how to integrate custom protocol handlers into your Web-based applications.

29

Protocol Handlers

In this chapter you'll learn how to write protocol handlers to support the use of custom protocols by Web browsers. You'll also learn how Web browsers implement protocols other than HTTP and how they are integrated with the browser's operation. You'll develop a simple protocol handler and integrate it with a Web client program. This chapter builds on the material presented in Chapter 17, "Network Programming with the `java.net` Package."

Using Protocol Handlers

Most popular Web browsers support protocols other than HTTP. These other protocols include FTP, gopher, e-mail, and application-specific protocols. Support for these protocols is usually built into the browser, causing the browser to become larger and slower to load.

Java supports additional protocols through the use of *protocol handlers*, also referred to as *stream handlers*. These protocol handlers are used to retrieve Web objects using application-specific protocols. The protocols are specified in the URL referencing the object.

Protocol handlers are implemented as subclasses of the `URLStreamHandler` class. The `URLStreamHandler` class defines four access methods that can be overridden by its subclasses, but only the `openConnection()` method is required to be overridden.

The `openConnection()` method takes an URL with its assigned protocol as a parameter and returns an object of class `URLConnection`. The `URLConnection` object can then be used to create input and output streams and to access the resource addressed by the URL.

The `parseURL()` and `setURL()` methods are used to implement custom URL syntax parsing. The `toExternalForm()` method is used to convert an URL of the protocol type to a `String` object.

The purpose of a protocol handler is to implement a custom protocol needed to access Web objects identified by URLs that require the custom protocol. Protocol handlers, like content handlers, are not directly instantiated or accessed. The methods of the `URLConnection` object that is returned by a protocol handler are invoked to access the resource referenced by the protocol.

A protocol is identified beginning with the first character of the URL and continuing to the first colon (:) contained in the URL. For example, the protocol of the URL `http://www.jaworski.com` is http and the protocol of the URL `fortune://jaworski.com` is fortune.

A protocol handler is associated with a specific protocol through the use of the `URLStreamHandlerFactory` interface. A class that implements the `URLStreamHandlerFactory` interface must implement the `createURLStreamHandler()` method. This method returns an `URLStreamHandler` object to be used for a specific protocol. An `URLStreamHandlerFactory` object is installed using the static `setURLStreamHandlerFactory()` method of the `URL` class.

Developing a Protocol Handler

The first step to implement a protocol handler is to define the protocol handler as a subclass of the `URLStreamHandler` class. The `openConnection()` method of the protocol handler creates an `URLConnection` object that can be used to access an URL designating the specified protocol.

A protocol handler is associated with a specific protocol type through the use of an `URLStreamHandlerFactory` object. The `createURLStreamHandler()` method of the `URLStreamHandlerFactory` interface is used to return a protocol handler for a specific protocol type.

The `setURLStreamHandlerFactory()` method of the URL class is used to set an `URLStreamHandlerFactory` as the default `URLStreamHandlerFactory` to be used with all protocol types.

A Simple Protocol Handler

This section presents an example of implementing a simple protocol handler. My NCSA server comes with a CGI program, named fortune, that returns a fortune cookie–type message when the program's URL is accessed. This section defines the fortune protocol to access the fortune program on my Web server and on other NCSA Web servers. The fortune protocol is not a real Internet protocol; I contrived it to illustrate the use of protocol handlers. The URL for the fortune protocol consists of `fortune://` followed by the host name. For example, `fortune://jaworski.com` accesses the fortune protocol on my Web server.

The definition of the `URLFortuneHandler` class is shown in Listing 29.1.

Listing 29.1. The source code for the `URLFortuneHandler` class.

```
import java.net.*;
import java.io.*;

public class URLFortuneHandler extends URLStreamHandler {
 public URLConnection openConnection(URL url) throws IOException {
  String host=url.getHost();
  URL newURL = new URL("http://"+host+"/cgi-bin/fortune");
  return newURL.openConnection();
 }
}
```

The `URLFortuneHandler` class extends the `URLStreamHandler` class and provides a single method. The `openConnection()` method takes an URL object as a parameter and returns an object of the `URLConnection` class. It also throws the `IOException` exception.

The `openConnection()` method uses the `getHost()` method of the URL class to extract the host name contained in the URL. It then uses a new `http` URL by concatenating `http://` with the host name and then the location of the fortune CGI program, `/cgi-bin/fortune`. The `openConection()` method of the `URL` class is used to return the `URLConnection` object associated with the new URL.

The `URLFortuneHandler` class wraps the fortune CGI program using the fortune protocol. This protocol is implemented through an HTTP connection to the CGI program.

The GetFortuneApp Program

The `GetFortuneApp` program illustrates the use of protocol handlers. It accesses the fortune CGI program on my Web server using the fortune protocol. The source code of the `GetFortuneApp` program is shown in Listing 29.2.

Listing 29.2. The source code for the `GetFortuneApp` program.

```
import java.net.*;
import java.io.*;

public class GetFortuneApp {
 public static void main(String args[]){
  try{
   FortuneFactory fortuneFactory = new FortuneFactory();
   URL.setURLStreamHandlerFactory(fortuneFactory);
   if(args.length!=1) error("Usage: java GetFortuneApp FortuneURL");
   System.out.println("Fetching URL: "+args[0]);
   URL url = new URL(args[0]);
   System.out.println((String) url.getContent());
  }catch (MalformedURLException ex){
   error("Bad URL");
  }catch (IOException ex){
   error("IOException occurred.");
  }
 }
 public static void error(String s){
  System.out.println(s);
  System.exit(1);
 }
}
class FortuneFactory implements URLStreamHandlerFactory {
 public FortuneFactory() {
 }
 public URLStreamHandler createURLStreamHandler(String protocol) {
  if(protocol.equals("fortune")){
   System.out.println("Requested protocol: "+protocol);
   return new URLFortuneHandler();
  }
  return null;
 }
}
```

When you invoke the `GetFortuneApp` program, provide it with the `fortune://jaworski.com` URL as a parameter. The `GetFortuneApp` program's output is as follows (you will get a different fortune each time you execute the program):

```
C:\java\jdg\ch29>java GetFortuneApp fortune://jaworski.com
Fetching URL: fortune://jaworski.com
Requested protocol: fortune
                    JACK AND THE BEANSTACK
                         by Mark Isaak

        Long ago, in a finite state far away, there lived a JOVIAL
character named Jack.  Jack and his relations were poor.  Often their
hash table was bare.  One day Jack's parent said to him, "Our matrices
are sparse.  You must go to the market to exchange our RAM for some
BASICs."  She compiled a linked list of items to retrieve and passed it
to him.
        So Jack set out.  But as he was walking along a Hamilton path,
he met the traveling salesman.
        "Whither dost thy flow chart take thou?" prompted the salesman
in high-level language.
        "I'm going to the market to exchange this RAM for some chips
and Apples," commented Jack.
        "I have a much better algorithm.  You needn't join a queue
there; I will swap your RAM for these magic kernels now."
        Jack made the trade, then backtracked to his house.  But when
he told his busy-waiting parent of the deal, she became so angry she
started thrashing.
        "Don't you even have any artificial intelligence?  All these
kernels together hardly make up one byte," and she popped them out the
window ...


C:\java\jdg\ch29>
```

`GetFortuneApp` connects to my Web server, invokes the fortune CGI program, and then displays the program's results.

The `main()` method creates an object of the `FortuneFactory` class that implements the `URLStreamHandlerFactory` interface. It then sets the object as the default protocol handler. An `URL` object is created using the URL string passed as the program's parameter. The `getContent()` method of the `URL` class is then used to extract the information generated by accessing the URL using the fortune protocol. The `getContent()` method results in the `FortuneFactory` object assigned to the `fortuneFactory` variable being invoked to retrieve an appropriate protocol handler. An object of class `URLFortuneHandler` is returned and its `openConnection()` method is invoked to extract the `URLConnection` object. This is performed behind the scenes as the result of invoking the URL class's `getContent()` method. The information returned from accessing the URL is then displayed.

The `GetFortuneApp` program defines the `FortuneFactory` class as implementing the `URLStreamHandlerFactory` interface. It implements the `createURLStreamHandler()` method and checks to see if the protocol type passed to it is fortune. If it is not, the `null` value is returned to signal that the Java-supplied protocol handler should be used. If the protocol type is fortune, the requested protocol is displayed and an `URLFortuneHandler` object is returned.

Summary

In this chapter you have learned how to write protocol handlers to access URLs via custom protocols. You have developed the `URLFortuneHandler` and integrated it with the `GetFortuneApp` program. This chapter marks the conclusion of the networking part of this book. Part VI, "Programming the Web with Applets and Scripts," shows you how to develop Java applets.

VI

Programming the Web with Applets and Scripts

30

Sample Applets

This chapter is the first of six chapters that cover applet programming. It introduces you to Java applets by way of several examples that illustrate different aspects of the classes and methods used to implement simple applets. Its purpose is to quickly get you up to speed in developing applets. Subsequent chapters fill in the details of the classes and methods that are introduced here. You should approach this chapter by trying to get a good general understanding of what is going on in the sample applets without dwelling on the details. You will learn the details when you study them in later chapters. This chapter assumes that you have covered the window-programming examples in Part IV, "Window Programming."

Hello Web!

The first program that you wrote in Chapter 4, "First Programs: Hello World! to BlackJack," was the `HelloWorldApp` program. It displayed the traditional `Hello World!` text to the console window. The main purpose of the program was to show you how to develop a simple Java program that actually produced some noticeable effect. The same rationale applies to the `HelloWeb` applet that you'll develop shortly. The program shows you how to write a simple applet that displays the text `Hello Web!` to the browser window. The code for the `HelloWeb` applet is shown in Listing 30.1.

Listing 30.1. The source code of the `HelloWeb` applet.

```
import java.applet.*;
import java.awt.*;

public class HelloWeb extends Applet {
 public void paint(Graphics g) {
  g.setFont(new Font("TimesRoman",Font.BOLD+Font.ITALIC,36));
  g.setColor(Color.blue);
  g.drawString("Hello Web!",10,80);
 }
}
```

Create the `HelloWeb.java` file in the `\java\jdg\ch30` directory and compile it using `javac HelloWeb.java`.

In order to run the `HelloWeb` applet, you need to include it in a Web page. Using a text editor, create the HTML file shown in Listing 30.2 and save it as `\java\jdg\ch30\helloweb.htm`.

Listing 30.2. The `helloweb.htm` file.

```
<HTML>
<HEAD>
<TITLE>Hello Web!</TITLE>
</HEAD>
<BODY>
<APPLET CODE="HelloWeb.class" WIDTH=200 HEIGHT=200>
```

```
[HelloWeb applet]
</APPLET>
</BODY>
</HTML>
```

Now open the helloweb.htm file with your Java-enabled browser. I use Netscape 2.0; my browser display appears as shown in Figure 30.1.

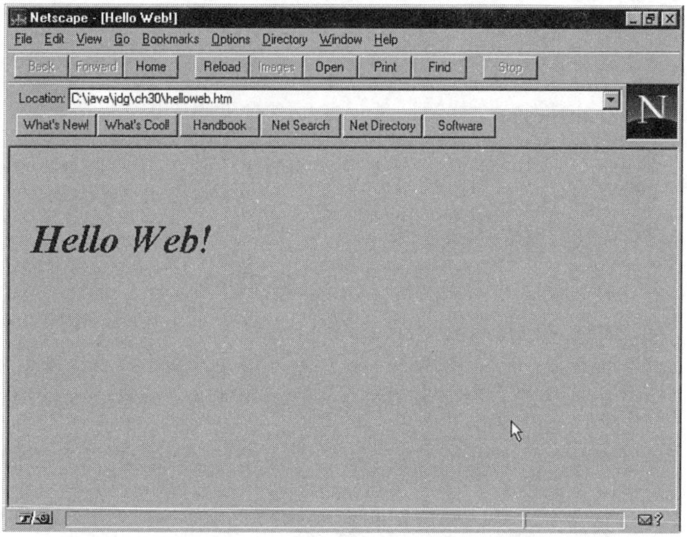

FIGURE 30.1.
The hello.htm *file, as displayed by a browser.*

Although this example is rather trivial—you could have created the same results just using HTML—it provides a basic starting point from which to embark on your study of applets. Let's cover the HelloWeb.java applet first, and then examine the helloweb.htm file.

The HelloWeb applet, like all Java applets, extends the Applet class or one of its subclasses. HelloWeb consists of a single method—the paint() method, which you encountered several times in Part IV. Because the Applet class is a subclass of Panel, many of the window-programming techniques that you studied in Part IV come into play. The paint() method is passed a Graphics object that it uses to paint the screen. In this case, I set the current font to a bold, italic, 36-point TimesRoman font and set the drawing color to blue. I then use the drawString() method of the Graphics class to draw the text Hello Web! on the screen at position 10,80.

The helloweb.htm file is the Web page that is used to contain the HelloWeb applet. Web pages are written in the *Hypertext Markup Language* (HTML). Learning HTML, in itself, is the subject of many books. Here I'll use a common HTML document to hold the applets and not go off on a tangent about learning HTML.

The helloweb.htm file begins and ends with the <HTML> and </HTML> tags. These tags signify the start and finish of an HTML file. The HTML file consists of a head and a body. The *head* is contained between the <HEAD> and </HEAD> tags. Within the head is the *title*, which is displayed at the top of the browser window. The title is contained within the <TITLE> and </TITLE> tags.

The *body* of an HTML file is where all the Web page descriptions are located. The body is enclosed within the <BODY> and </BODY> tags. The body of this document, and of those used in the other examples of this chapter, consists of a single applet. The applet is denoted by the <APPLET> and </APPLET> tags.

Within the opening <APPLET> tag are several attributes. The `CODE` attribute has the value `HelloWeb.class`, which identifies the class file for this applet. Its `WIDTH` and `HEIGHT` attributes specify the dimensions of the applet, as displayed on the browser window.

The text `[HelloWeb applet]`, appearing between the <APPLET> and </APPLET> tags, is displayed by browsers that are not capable of loading Java applets.

An Audio Player

The `Applet` class, as small as it is, provides a few very useful features for developing attractive Web pages. Among these are the capability to load and play audio files and to easily load and display images. The `AudioPlayer` applet, developed in this section, shows off these features. The source code for the `AudioPlayer` applet is shown in Listing 30.3.

NOTE

You need a sound board and speakers to run this applet.

Listing 30.3. The source code of the `AudioPlayer` applet.

```
import java.applet.*;
import java.awt.*;
import java.net.*;

public class AudioPlayer extends Applet {
 AudioClip music;
 Image background;
 public void init() {
  try {
   music = getAudioClip(new URL("file:///spacemusic.au"));
   background = getImage(new URL("file:///space.gif"));
  }catch (MalformedURLException ex) {
  }
  setLayout(new BorderLayout());
  Panel buttons = new Panel();
  buttons.add(new Button("Play"));
  buttons.add(new Button("Stop"));
  buttons.add(new Button("Loop"));
  add("South",buttons);
```

```
 }
 public void stop() {
   music.stop();
 }
 public void paint(Graphics g) {
  g.drawImage(background,0,0,this);
 }
 public boolean handleEvent(Event event) {
  if(event.target instanceof Button) {
   if("Play".equals(event.arg)) {
    music.play();
    return true;
   }else if("Stop".equals(event.arg)) {
    music.stop();
    return true;
   }else if("Loop".equals(event.arg)) {
    music.loop();
    return true;
   }
  }
  return false;
 }
}
```

Create and compile `AudioPlayer.java` in the same manner as you did `HelloWeb.java`. The HTML file that is used to display the applet is shown in Listing 30.4. Note that the `CODE`, `WIDTH`, and `HEIGHT` attributes of the applet have been changed. You will need two additional files to run the applet. Copy the `spacemusic.au` file from the `\java\demo\Animator\audio` directory to your `\java\jdg\ch30` directory. This is an audio file that is supplied with the Java Developer's Kit. It contains music that is described as "space music." Also copy the `space.gif` file from the `\jdg\ch30` directory of the CD-ROM to your `\java\jdg\ch30` directory.

Listing 30.4. The `audio.htm` file.

```
<HTML>
<HEAD>
<TITLE>Audio Player</TITLE>
</HEAD>
<BODY>
<APPLET CODE="AudioPlayer.class" WIDTH=300 HEIGHT=350>
[AudioPlayer applet]
</APPLET>
</BODY>
</HTML>
```

Open the `audio.htm` file with your Java-enabled browser. Your screen display should look similar to the one shown in Figure 30.2.

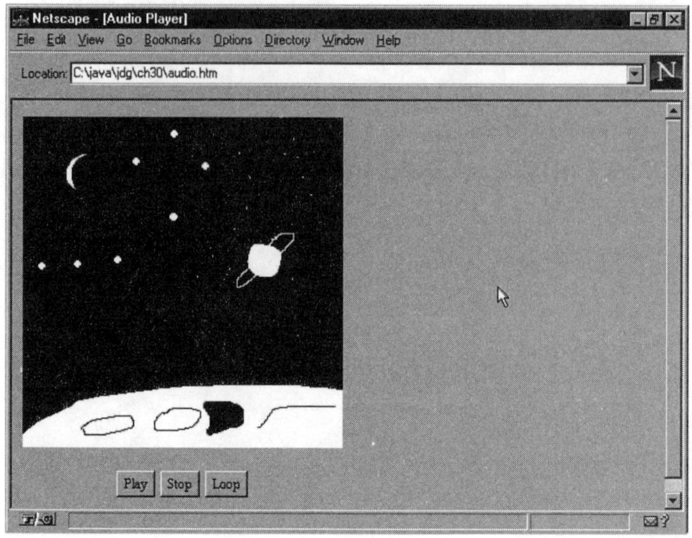

FIGURE 30.2.
The `audio.htm` *file, as displayed by a Web browser.*

Your browser loads the `audio.htm` file and then the `AudioPlayer.class` file. The applet itself loads the background image and an audio file. To play the audio file, click on the Play button. The space music will be played, using your sound board and speakers. When the end of the music file is reached, the sound ends. If you click on the Loop button, the music will be continuously played in a never-ending fashion. Clicking on the Stop button causes the music to cease.

The `AudioPlayer` class, for all its additional capabilities, is only slightly longer than the `HelloWeb` class. It declares two field variables, `music` and `background`, which are used to hold the audio file and background image. The `music` variable is declared as type `AudioClip`, which is an interface defined in the `Java.applet` package.

The `AudioPlayer` class contains four access methods: `init()`, `stop()`, `paint()`, and `handleEvent()`. You are already familiar with the purpose of `paint()` and `handleEvent()` from Part IV.

The `init()` method is invoked by the browser's runtime system when an applet is initially loaded. It performs any initialization required before the main part of the applet is executed. The `stop()` method is invoked when the execution of an applet is terminated as the result of an applet's Web page no longer being displayed by the browser. You never need to invoke `init()` or `stop()` directly. They are invoked by the runtime system.

The `init()` method of `AudioPlayer` begins by loading the audio and image files. The `getAudioClip()` method of the `Applet` class loads an audio file that is referenced by an URL. The `file:///spacemusic.au` URL is used to load the `spacemusic.au` file from the directory in which the `audio.htm` and `AudioPlayer.class` files are located. The `file:///space.gif` URL is used in a similar manner.

After the audio and image files are loaded, the layout of the applet is set to a `BorderLayout` object. A `Panel` object is created and assigned to the `buttons` variable. The Play, Stop, and Loop buttons are created and added to the `buttons` panel. The `buttons` panel is then added to the bottom of the applet display area.

The `stop()` method uses the `stop()` method of the `AudioClip` interface to stop the music when the applet is no longer being displayed by the browser.

The `paint()` method draws the `space.gif` image assigned to the background variable on the `Graphics` context of the applet's display area.

The `handleEvent()` method handles the three prominent events associated with the applet. These events are the clicking of the Play, Stop, and Loop buttons. When the Play button is clicked, the `play()` method of the `AudioClip` interface is invoked to play the audio clip. When the Stop button is clicked, the `stop()` method of the `AudioClip` interface is invoked to stop the music. Finally, when the Loop button is clicked, the `loop()` method of the `AudioClip` interface is invoked to cause the music to be played in a never-ending, looping fashion.

BlackJack Revisited

From the previous example, you have probably surmised that it's very easy to convert Java window programs to applets. This is possible because of the fact that an applet is nothing more than a souped-up panel. It is also relatively easy to convert console programs to applets.

One of the first Java programs that you wrote, way back in Chapter 4, was the `BlackJackApp` program. This program allowed you to play blackjack on the console display. Because you used a class- and object-oriented approach to developing `BlackJackApp` (even before you were formally introduced to classes and objects), this program is relatively easy to convert to a simple applet. The source code of the converted applet is shown in Listing 30.5.

Listing 30.5. The source code of the `Blackjack.java` applet.

```
import java.applet.*;
import java.awt.*;
import java.util.Random;

public class Blackjack extends Applet {
 static final int BET = 0;
 static final int PLAY = 1;
 static final int DEALER = 2;
 int state = BET;
 int money = 1000;
 int bet = 0;
 Deck deck = new Deck();
 Hand playersHand;
```

continues

Listing 30.5. continued

```
Hand dealersHand;
Label topLine = new Label("Welcome to Blackjack!",Label.CENTER);
Label totalLine = new Label("You have $1000.",Label.CENTER);
Label dealersLabel = new Label("Dealer's Hand",Label.CENTER);
Label playersLabel = new Label("Your Hand",Label.CENTER);
TextArea dealerText = new TextArea(9,20);
TextArea playerText = new TextArea(9,20);
Button hitButton = new Button("Hit");
Button stayButton = new Button("Stay");
Label betLabel = new Label("Enter your bet: ",Label.RIGHT);
TextField betField = new TextField();
GridBagLayout gridbag  = new GridBagLayout();;
GridBagConstraints constraints = new GridBagConstraints();
public void init() {
 setLayout(gridbag);
 constraints.fill = GridBagConstraints.BOTH;
 addComponent(topLine,0,0);
 addComponent(totalLine,0,1);
 addComponent(dealersLabel,1,0);
 addComponent(playersLabel,1,1);
 dealerText.setEditable(false);
 playerText.setEditable(false);
 addComponent(dealerText,2,0);
 addComponent(playerText,2,1);
 addComponent(hitButton,3,0);
 addComponent(stayButton,3,1);
 addComponent(betLabel,4,0);
 addComponent(betField,4,1);
}
void addComponent(Component c,int y,int x) {
 constraints.gridx = x;
 constraints.gridy = y;
 gridbag.setConstraints(c, constraints);
 add(c);
}
public boolean handleEvent(Event event) {
 if(event.target instanceof TextField && event.id == Event.ACTION_EVENT) {
  if(state == BET){
   updateBet();
   return true;
  }
 }else if(event.target instanceof Button && event.id == Event.ACTION_EVENT) {
  if(state == PLAY) {
   if("Hit".equals(event.arg)) {
    playersHand.addCard(deck.deal());
    playersHand.show(playerText,false);
    if(!playersHand.under(22)) state = DEALER;
   }else if("Stay".equals(event.arg)) state = DEALER;
   if(state == DEALER) {
    while(dealersHand.mustHit())
     dealersHand.addCard(deck.deal());
    dealersHand.show(dealerText,false);
    showResults();
   }
  }
 }
```

```
  return false;
 }
 public void updateBet() {
  betField.setEditable(false);
  betLabel.setText("Bet: ");
  try {
   Integer i = new Integer(betField.getText());
   bet = i.intValue();
  } catch (NumberFormatException ex) {
   bet = 1;
  }
  betField.setText(String.valueOf(bet));
  initialDeal();
  if(playersHand.blackjack()) playerWins();
  else state = PLAY;
 }
 void initialDeal() {
  playersHand = new Hand();
  dealersHand = new Hand();
  for(int i = 0;i<2;++i) {
   playersHand.addCard(deck.deal());
   dealersHand.addCard(deck.deal());
  }
  dealersHand.show(dealerText,true);
  playersHand.show(playerText,false);
 }
 void openBetting() {
  betLabel.setText("Enter your bet: ");
  betField.setText("");
  betField.setEditable(true);
  state = BET;
 }
 void playerWins() {
  money += bet;
  topLine.setText("Player wins $"+bet+".");
  totalLine.setText("You have $"+money+".");
  openBetting();
 }
 void dealerWins() {
  money -= bet;
  topLine.setText("Player loses $"+bet+".");
  totalLine.setText("You have $"+money+".");
  openBetting();
 }
 void tie() {
  topLine.setText("Tie.");
  totalLine.setText("You have $"+money+".");
  openBetting();
 }
 void showResults() {
  if(playersHand.busted() && dealersHand.busted()) tie();
  else if(playersHand.busted()) dealerWins();
  else if(dealersHand.busted()) playerWins();
  else if(playersHand.bestScore() > dealersHand.bestScore()) playerWins();
  else if(playersHand.bestScore() < dealersHand.bestScore()) dealerWins();
```

continues

Listing 30.5. continued

```
  else tie();
 }
}

class Deck {
 // Variable declarations
 int cards[];      // Array of 52 cards
 int topCard;      // 0-51 (index of card in deck)
 Random random;

 // Method declarations
 public Deck() { // Constructor
  cards = new int[52];
  for(int i = 0;i<52;++i) cards[i] = i;
  topCard = 0;
  random = new Random();
  shuffle();
 }

 public void shuffle() {
  // Repeat 52 times
  for(int i = 0;i<52;++i) {
   // Randomly exchange two cards in the deck.
   int j = randomCard();
   int k = randomCard();
   int temp = cards[j];
   cards[j] = cards[k];
   cards[k] = temp;
  }
 }

 int randomCard() {
  int r = random.nextInt();
  if(r<0) r = 0-r;
  return r%52;
 }

 Card deal() {
  if(topCard>51) {
   shuffle();
   topCard = 0;
  }
  Card card = new Card(cards[topCard]);
  ++topCard;
  return card;
 }
} // End of Deck class

class Hand {
 // Variable declarations
 int numCards;
 Card cards[];
 static int MaxCards = 12;

 //Method declarations
 public Hand() { // Constructor
```

```
  numCards = 0;
  cards = new Card[MaxCards];
 }

 void addCard(Card c) {
  cards[numCards] = c;
  ++numCards;
 }

 void show(TextArea t,boolean hideFirstCard) {
  String results = "";
  for(int i = 0;i<numCards;++i) {
   if(i == 0 && hideFirstCard) results += "Hidden\n";
   else results += cards[i].value+" of "+cards[i].suite+"\n";
  }
  t.setText(results);
 }

boolean blackjack() {
 if(numCards == 2) {
  if(cards[0].iValue == 1 && cards[1].iValue == 10) return true;
  if(cards[1].iValue == 1 && cards[0].iValue == 10) return true;
 }
 return false;
}

boolean under(int n) {
 int points = 0;
 for(int i = 0;i<numCards;++i) points += cards[i].iValue;
 if(points<n) return true;
 else return false;
}

int bestScore() {
 int points = 0;
 boolean haveAce = false;
 for(int i = 0;i<numCards;++i) {
  points += cards[i].iValue;
  if(cards[i].iValue == 1) haveAce = true;
 }
 if(haveAce) {
  if(points+10 < 22) points += 10;
 }
 return points;
}

boolean mustHit() {
 if(bestScore()<17) return true;
 else return false;
}

 boolean busted() {
  if(!under(22)) return true;
  else return false;
 }
} // End of Hand class
```

continues

Listing 30.5. continued

```
class Card {
 // Variable declarations
 int iValue;    // Numeric value corresponding to card.
 String value; // "A" "2" through "9" "T" "J" "Q" "K"
 String suite; // "S" "H" "C" "D"

 // Method declarations
 public Card(int n) { // Constructor
  int iSuite = n/13;
  iValue = n%13+1;
  switch(iSuite) {
   case 0:
    suite = "Spades";
    break;
   case 1:
    suite = "Hearts";
    break;
   case 2:
    suite = "Clubs";
    break;
   default:
    suite = "Diamonds";
  }
  if(iValue == 1) value = "Ace";
  else if(iValue == 10) value = "Ten";
  else if(iValue == 11) value = "Jack";
  else if(iValue == 12) value = "Queen";
  else if(iValue == 13) value = "King";
  else value = Integer.toString(iValue);
  if(iValue>10) iValue = 10;
 }

 int getValue() {
  return iValue;
 }
} // End of Card class
```

Create and compile `Blackjack.java` in the same manner as the previous examples. The HTML file that is used to display the applet is shown in Listing 30.6. Note that the `CODE`, `WIDTH`, and `HEIGHT` attributes of the applet have been changed.

Listing 30.6. The `blackjack.htm` file.

```
<HTML>
<HEAD>
<TITLE>Blackjack</TITLE>
</HEAD>
<BODY>
<APPLET CODE="Blackjack.class" WIDTH=400 HEIGHT=400>
[Blackjack applet]
</APPLET>
</BODY>
</HTML>
```

Open the `blackjack.htm` file with your browser. Your browser should display the applet, as shown in Figure 30.3.

FIGURE 30.3.
The BlackJack initial display.

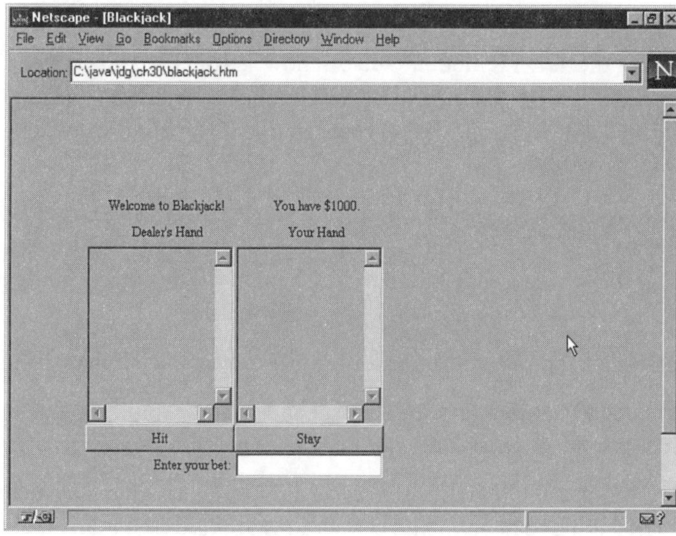

The top text line in the applet welcomes you to the game and tells you that you have $1000 to gamble. The Dealer's Hand and Your Hand text boxes are initially blank. Below them are the Hit and Stay buttons, which are initially disabled. To start the game, enter a bet, as shown in Figure 30.4.

FIGURE 30.4.
Entering a bet.

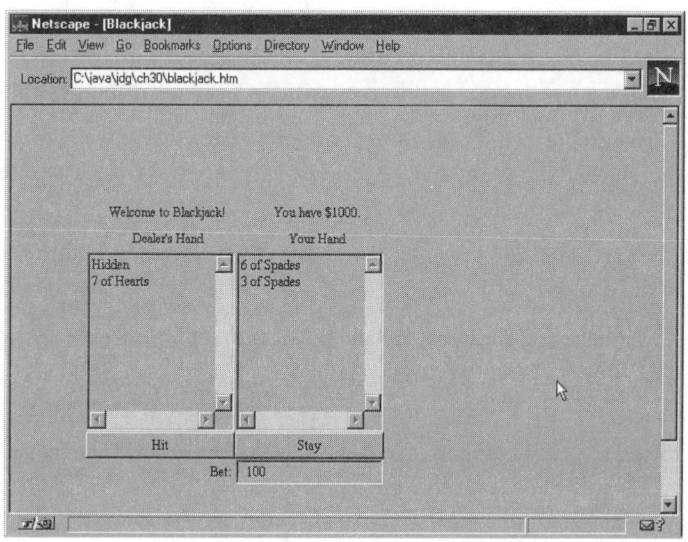

When you enter a bet, the label to the right of the text field changes from `Enter your bet:` to `Bet:`. The text field is grayed and can no longer be edited. This prevents you from changing your bet during the play of a hand.

The initial hands for the dealer and the player are displayed after the bet is entered. The first card of the dealer is hidden. You can now use the Hit and Stay buttons to obtain more cards or to stay with what you were dealt and let the dealer draw. Click on the Hit button until you are finished drawing cards. If you bust (go over 21), your hand will be finished and the dealer will draw his cards.

After you click Stay or bust, the dealer draws his hand and a win, loss, or tie results. Your available money is then updated based on your winnings. The `Blackjack` applet is more forgiving than the `BlackJackApp` program in Chapter 4: You can continue playing after you've run out of money. You can even bet $0 or negative values.

Go ahead and play the game for a while to become familiar with its operation.

Although the `Blackjack` applet may appear to be quite large, it reuses all of the classes developed for the original `BlackJackApp` program, with minor modifications.

The `Blackjack` program declares 21 field variables. Most of these are used to create its GUI interface. The `BET`, `PLAY`, and `DEALER` constants are used to maintain the state of the user's interaction with the game. The `state` variable is set to the initial `BET` state.

The `money`, `bet`, `deck`, `playersHand`, and `dealersHand` variables are declared and used in the same manner as in the `BlackJackApp` program.

Five labels are created and assigned to the `topLine`, `totalLine`, `dealersLabel`, `playersLabel`, and `betLabel` variables. The `topLine` and `totalLine` variables are displayed at the top of the applet. They display the welcome string and the amount of money that the player has available. The `dealersLabel` and `playersLabel` variables are used to label the text areas containing the dealer's and user's hands. The `betLabel` variable prompts the user to enter his or her bet.

The `dealerText` and `playerText` variables are used to refer to the `TextArea` objects that display the hands of the dealer and player. The `betField` text field is used to enter and display the user's bet.

The `hitButton` and `stayButton` variables are used to draw another card or to turn the draw over to the dealer.

The `gridbag` and `constraints` variables refer to the `GridBagLayout` and `GridBagConstraints` objects used to lay out the screen's display.

The `init()` method sets the layout to a `GridBagLayout`, invoking the `addComponent()` method to add the GUI components to the applet. The `addComponent()` method adds a component to an x,y location within the `gridbag` layout.

The handleEvent() method handles the user-interface events that drive the operation of the applet. It handles the event generated when the user enters text in the Bet: text field by invoking the updateBet() method. This method then sets up the rest of the applet's operation. The handleEvent() method handles the clicking of the Hit and Stay buttons by first making sure that the applet is in the Play state. This prevents the user from clicking on these buttons at arbitrary times during the applet's execution.

The Hit button is handled by adding a card to the player's hand, using the same approach as in BlackJackApp. The show() method of the Hand class is modified to display the player's hand to the TextArea object referenced by the playerText variable. If the user busts, the state is set to DEALER, preventing the user from drawing another card.

The Stay button is handled by setting the state variable to DEALER.

When the state is set to DEALER, the dealer is dealt additional cards using the same code as in BlackJackApp. The showResults() method is modified to update the applet's display labels and not the console window.

The updateBet() method is a new method that is added to support the applet conversion. It disables editing of the text field and changes the Label object referenced by the betLabel variable from Enter your bet: to Bet:. It then checks the bet for a valid value and redisplays it in the disabled text field. The initialDeal() method is invoked to deal an initial hand to the player and dealer. If the user is dealt blackjack, the hand is ended and the user is given his winnings. Otherwise, the state variable is set to play to enable the operation of the Hit and Stay buttons.

The initialDeal() method remains unchanged from the original BlackJackApp program.

The openBetting() method is used to change to the initial BET state. It sets the Enter your bet: prompt and enables the text field to be edited.

The playerWins(), dealerWins(), and tie() methods have been modified to display their results within the applet instead of on the console window. They also invoke the openBetting() method to return to the BET state.

The showResults() method remains unchanged from the original BlackJackApp program.

No changes were made to the Deck or Card classes. The show() method of the Hand class was modified to display the dealer's and player's hands to the TextArea objects.

The changes required to convert from the original BlackJackApp program to the Blackjack applet were minimal. This illustrates the power of object-oriented programming and the reusability of the components that are created using this approach.

Summary

This chapter introduces you to applet programming by way of several sample programs that illustrate the classes and methods used to implement simple applets. You should now be comfortable with applets, especially if you have worked through the window programming examples of Part IV. Chapter 31, "Developing Applets," lays the framework for developing applets by expanding on the basics introduced here.

31

Developing Applets

by Cary Jardin

In this chapter you will learn what an applet is, how it relates to HTML, and what some of the possible uses of applet technology are. By the time you finish this chapter, you will have an understanding of what an applet is, how it works, and what it can do.

How Applets Work

Applet technology is the driving force behind the intensity of the Java revolution. Applets enhance Web documents with animation, sound, and other special effects. However, applets are just standard Java programs with a few special hooks into the Web browser's environment. The capability of applets to take advantage of the resources provided by a Web browser's environment is what allows them to be easily and powerfully integrated within Web pages.

Figure 31.1 describes the steps an applet takes to display itself in the browser's window.

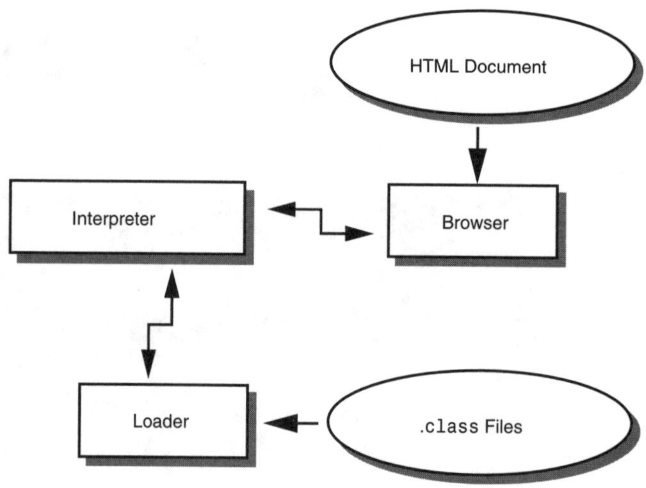

FIGURE 31.1.
How a Java applet works.

As the figure shows, the browser makes a request to the loader to fetch the applet specified in the document's HTML. After the applet has been fetched, the applet begins to execute. The applet is executed by the Java runtime interpreter attached to the browser. The browser acts as a conduit between the Java Virtual Machine inside the interpreter and the outside user interface.

The `Applet` class provides an application framework and tools to access the facilities provided by the browser. Via the browser, the applet has access to graphics, sound, and network capabilities. The `Applet` class can be viewed as merely a wrapper around the capabilities provided by the browser.

The Relationship Between HTML and Applets

An applet is like a child application of the browser. The browser launches the applet in a predefined environment inside the browser. In turn, the browser obtains the information pertaining to the applet's environment from the current document's HTML. In this sense, the relationship between HTML and an applet is that of a command line executing a program.

From within HTML, the syntax to specify the execution of an applet is provided by the applet and parameter tags as discussed in Chapter 16, "Web Programming with the `java.applet` Package."

The *applet tag* provides all the information needed to launch the applet. Everything from the base directory to command-line parameters can be specified from within this tag. Here's an example:

```
<APPLET  CODE = "lights.class" width=400 height=75 align=center >
<PARAM NAME="text" VALUE="Blink">
<BLOCKQUOTE>
<HR>
If you were using a Java(tm)-enabled browser,
you would see blinking lights instead of this paragraph.
<HR>
</BLOCKQUOTE>
</APPLET>
```

From this HTML command line, the browser is told how to launch the `lights.class` file with the parameter `text`. The HTML merely specifies a command line of sorts to the browser.

Applets and Interactive Web Pages

Usually, when the word *applet* is mentioned, the World Wide Web is not far out of mind. There is good reason for this. An applet is a Java program designed to run in the environment provided by a Web browser. The last statement might seem a little simplistic, but take a second to think what that environment provides to an application.

Inside the browser, an application has the capability to display images, play audio files, and access the Internet. The `Applet` class provides methods to tap these resources provided by the Web browser.

Because applets are executed locally on your machine, you are able to interact with the applet as part of the Web page's display. Other Web applications that rely on CGI programs (see Chapter 32, "Integrating Applets into Distributed Applications") do not provide interactivity at the local level. Instead, your browser must send information-processing requests to programs that are located on remote Web servers. Besides performance impacts, this remote processing approach also suffers from the difficulties involved in maintaining information about the state of the applications it supports. The Java model of local execution is able to support a high degree of interactivity. All state information is maintained within the local browser environment and is not distributed between the browser and Web server.

Applets Versus Scripts

As discussed previously, applets are launched from within an HTML command. After an applet is launched, it operates in a well-defined area of the browser window and is restricted from altering the state or content of the current HTML document. Scripts written in the JavaScript language are not placed under these restrictions and have more latitude in modifying the state of the HTML document being displayed.

An applet is treated as a self-contained object by a Web browser and is handled in much the same way as an inline image. On the other hand, scripts are integrated within the document's HTML. Because the browser executes the script and not the Java runtime interpreter, it has the capability to modify the contents of the entire browser window, a task that an applet cannot perform.

Applets and scripts each serve a different purpose. Scripts provide the capability to dynamically alter the content of an HTML document, whereas applets are separate, interactive applications that execute within the context of the browser and display information in a limited area of the browser window.

The Execution of an Applet

When the browser comes across the applet tag, it begins gathering the information needed to launch the applet. After the HTML document has been completely interpreted and displayed, the Java runtime interpreter is requested to execute the applet.

When the interpreter receives the request to execute the applet, it executes a loader mechanism to fetch the binary file. After the file is successfully transferred onto the local machine, it undergoes a number of tests to verify its security and stability. Chapter 39, "Java Security," covers applet security. If all is well, the interpreter begins execution of the applet.

Execution continues until the applet terminates or the current browser document is dismissed. This can occur in a couple of different ways: The user might jump to another URL or the browser might terminate. In either case, the applet is terminated.

Using Window Components

Window components can be added to the applet to create a friendly user interface. Java provides a number of window components, which can be found in the `java.awt` library.

All of the window components added to an applet are confined to the applet window area in the current browser document. The applet window contains the entire paintable region; anything that does not fit inside that region is clipped.

Using the provided window components, applets have the capability to contain the same look and feel of other window application programs. Applets can use all GUI components that can be used by `Panel` objects. In addition, applets have access to many of the capabilities provided by the browser.

Adding Content and Protocol Handlers to Applets

Java supplies a set of interfaces that support the development of content and protocol handlers. Chapters 28, "Content Handlers," and 29, "Protocol Handlers," cover the use of these interfaces. Content and protocol handlers may be added to applets to provide the capability to retrieve and display different types of Web objects or to use services provided by new or custom Internet protocols. By using these content and protocol handlers, Java applications become more capable network clients and can be used to support distributed processing applications, as discussed in Chapter 32.

Using Applets as Inline Viewers

Applets have the capability to present images, sounds, and other multimedia objects inside an HTML document. Scripts provide the means to dynamically change the content of an HTML document. The combination of the two produces very powerful results, including the capability to use applets as inline viewers.

The interactive Web catalog is a perfect example of the inline viewer concept. A Web page contains a script-enabled order form that contains a selection field. The user uses this selection field to select the product to order. When this happens, the script launches an applet to give a visual presentation of the item selected, providing the user with more information with which to make a purchase decision.

Using an applet as an inline viewer allows for more flexibility than standard HTML facilities. The content to be viewed might contain contextual interactive information rather than being a flat piece of media.

Using Applets as Network Clients

The concept of containing a network client inside an HTML document might seem a little strange to you, and for good reason—embedding a client inside a client seems redundant. However, the browser client can be viewed as a delivery mechanism for the embedded client, allowing Web-based support of other application protocols.

By combining applets with protocol handlers, an applet can quickly become a Telnet, an FTP, or even an embedded HTTP client. If a custom protocol handler is used, the applet can become the means for users to access custom network applications.

Optimizing Applets

Like most applications on the Internet, applets are constrained by their user's communication bandwidth capabilities. You know it is a good idea to optimize Web pages for optimal low-bandwidth performance; the same holds true for applets.

Fortunately, graphics usually constitute a much greater physical size than the applet's executable size. I say "fortunately" because it is far easier to optimize the loading of media than to worry about code generation.

Applets, being a mechanism for a graphical user interface, usually require the transfer of graphics files. This process can take varying amounts of time depending on the speed of the connection. Taking the approach of loading media in the background, while the user is busy doing something else, limits the annoying delays associated with media transfers.

Hopefully, low bandwidth will not always be a problem for Internet applications. However, for as long as users have to wait for something to display on their screen, optimizing applications for low-bandwidth situations will produce applications that are more likely to satisfy user expectations.

Learning from Online Examples

As technologies advance, the early adopter usually provides examples to promote the technology. So is the case with scripts and applets. A number of companies have jumped on the Java wagon from the get-go and provide examples of their endeavors. The following are a few sites where valuable information can be found:

- `http://www.javasoft.com`
- `http://www.gamelan.com`
- `http://www.yahoo.com/Computers_and_Internet/Languages/Java/`
- `http://www.borland.com/Product/java/java.html`
- `http://www.blackdown.org/java-linux.html`

Summary

This chapter gives background information on how applets work and how they relate to scripts written in the JavaScript language. You have also been given a little taste of what applets and scripts can achieve. Chapter 32 discusses how applets can be integrated into distributed processing applications. This chapter is designed to get your proverbial wheels turning.

32

Integrating Applets into Distributed Applications

This chapter shows you how to integrate applets into distributed application programs. It presents a general architecture for distributed systems and discusses Java's role within this architecture. It summarizes current efforts to use Java to support distributed object access. The Common Gateway Interface is introduced, and the integration of applets with gateway programs is discussed.

Architecture for Distributed Applications

Most programs can be characterized by three distinct elements: a user-interface element, an information-processing element, and a data-storage element. The user-interface element interacts with the user, displaying information to the user and responding to user-generated events. The information-processing element performs operations on the program's data based on the commands and information received from the user. The data-storage element retrieves, stores, and manages the data generated and consumed by the user-interface and information-processing elements. Figure 32.1 summarizes the interaction between these elements.

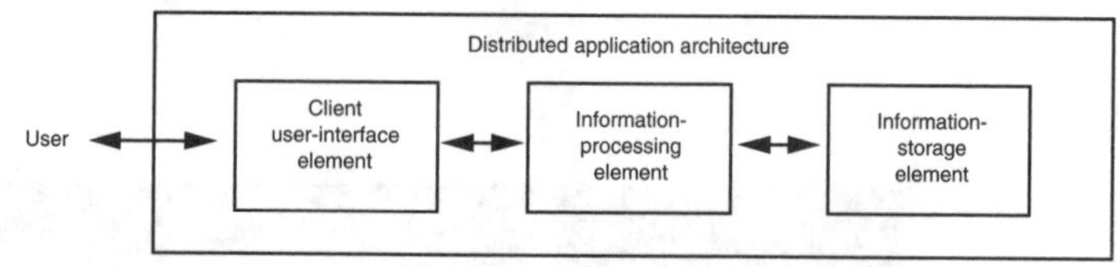

FIGURE 32.1.
Distributed application elements.

Even though most programs consist of some manifestation of these three elements, it is not necessary that they be implemented on the same computer. In fact, separating the elements of an application over more than one computer may lead to greater modularity and more efficient use of processing resources. Distributed applications are based on this notion. Figure 32.2 illustrates a typical distributed application architecture.

The Web is an example of a distributed application. The Web is highly modular and fully distributed. Anyone with a Web browser and an Internet connection can use this application. Having access to a Web server is the only thing required to publish information on the Web.

Web browsers implement the client user-interface portion of the large distributed application known as the Web. They display information to Web users and respond to interface events generated by user mouse clicks and keyboard entries.

Web servers implement the data storage-and-retrieval element of the Web. They store Web pages, graphics and multimedia files, Java programs, and other information in files and databases. Web servers make this information available to Web users based on the requests made by browsers on their behalf.

The information-processing element of the Web is implemented in terms of *Common Gateway Interface* (CGI) programs and external programs on Web servers and by Java, JavaScript, and plug-in programs, on Web browsers. CGI programs provide the capability for Web browsers to access external application programs, such as database and search programs. They may be self-contained applications or they may be used as a means to provide an interface to external applications. Whereas CGI programs are executed by Web servers, Java, JavaScript, and plug-in programs are typically executed with Web browsers. In the not-too-distant future, specialized application servers may be set up to perform information-processing functions independent of both Web browsers and Web servers, allowing cleaner separation of the three distributed computing elements.

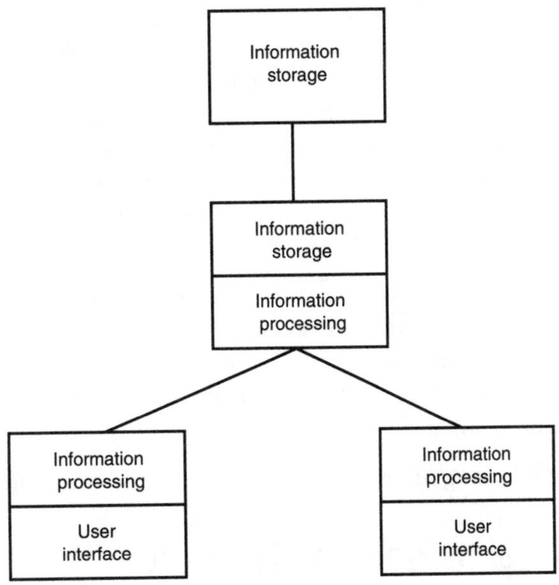

FIGURE 32.2.
Distributed application architecture.

Figure 32.3 shows how the Web is organized in terms of the user-interface, information-processing, and information-storage elements of distributed applications.

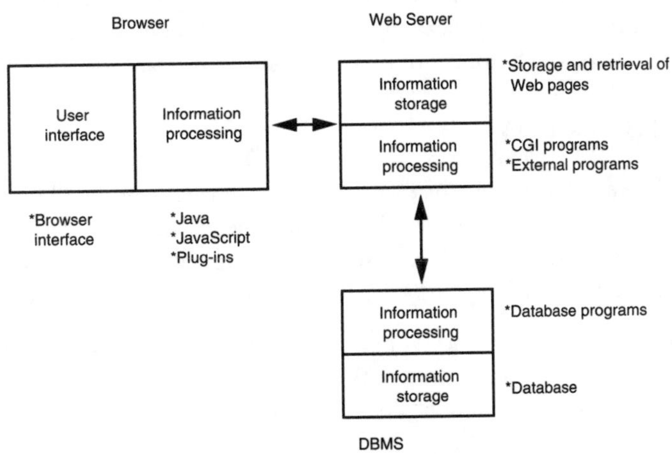

FIGURE 32.3.
The Web as a distributed application.

OMG and CORBA

The *Object Management Group* (OMG) was founded in 1989; today it comprises all of the prominent computer and software vendors and is the world's largest software-development consortium. OMG was developed to support the standardization of object-based software and has developed a standard approach to using objects to support the distributed systems approach introduced in the previous section. This approach is the *Common Object Request Broker Architecture* (CORBA).

CORBA supports an object-based approach to distributed systems development by enabling objects on heterogeneous systems to communicate independently of the hardware or software platform on which they are implemented. CORBA makes use of *Object Request Brokers* (ORBs), which implement client/server relationships between objects. ORBs allow client objects to invoke the methods of server objects without having to consider where the server objects are located or how they are implemented. An *Interface Definition Language* (IDL) is used to specify the protocol by which distributed objects can be accessed.

CORBA provides the basis for extending the object-based approach that you've used so far to develop fully distributed systems. The ORB and IDL are the basic mechanisms by which CORBA accomplishes this objective. Because Java is a modern, object-oriented language, it is natural that there would be a strong interest in extending Java to support the distributed object approach initiated by CORBA.

The following subsections discuss some of these developments.

The Spring Project and Java IDL

Sun Microsystems, the creator of Java, is developing a distributed operating system named Spring for its SPARC line of computers. The Spring system is designed to be fully distributed and to support distributed object access. The current version of Spring is Version 1.1. This version implements the Spring Java IDL system. The Spring Java IDL system provides the capability to integrate Java applications within Spring. Java objects and other Spring objects can be remotely accessed from within Java applets or programs or other non-Java applets.

NEO and JOE

Whereas the Spring project is essentially a research-and-development effort, Sun's NEO product family is integrating Java into its main network application product line that uses the Solaris operating system. The NEO product line is aimed at providing complete support for networked applications by integrating CORBA and other distributed object standards into Solaris.

JOE is an IDL-to-Java compiler, ORB, and NEO application-programming interface that allows Java applets and programs to be integrated within NEO applications. The JOE ORB is made accessible to Java-enabled Web browsers so they can support remote access to NEO and

Java objects within the CORBA framework to implement distributed system applications as described in the beginning of this chapter.

JIDL

Ernest Friedman-Hill, at Sandia National Laboratories, has developed JIDL, a CORBA-compliant IDL compiler that supports distributed object access from Java applets. It allows applets to access remote CORBA-compliant objects in the same manner as local Java objects.

A prototype of JIDL has been completed using commercial software packages, and work is underway to develop a complete public-domain version of the software.

Black Widow

Black Widow is a product of PostModern computing that provides the capability to connect CORBA-compliant objects with Java applets. Black Widow allows applets to access remote CORBA-compliant objects developed in Java or C++. It provides the capability to automatically generate interface code in Java or C++ and it supports the CORBA Internet Inter-ORB Protocol (IIOP). IIOP is a protocol for using the Internet for communication between local and remote ORBs.

HORB

HORB was developed by Dr. Hirano Satoshi at the Electrotechnical Laboratory (ETL) of the Agency of Industrial Science and Technology of the Japanese Ministry of International Trade and Industry (MITI). HORB is a freely available distributed object system, based on Java, that supports object-oriented communication between Java applets and objects running on a server.

Although HORB is not directly compatible with CORBA, it is further advanced than current Java-to-CORBA implementations and can be immediately implemented. HORB is a complete Java solution, supporting both client and server objects. HORB-to-CORBA connectivity can be implemented by custom interface software. The URL `http://ring.etl.go.jp/openlab/horb/` is the home page of the HORB project. If you are interested in developing distributed applications using Java, I highly recommend that you download and investigate this package.

Interfacing with CGI Programs

The object-based distributed system framework provided by CORBA and HORB will form the basis for the development of next-generation distributed systems. The Common Gateway Interface is the current standard by which Web-based applications are implemented. Although the CGI is not an old technology, in terms of the number of years that it has been around, it is not nearly as powerful and sophisticated as CORBA and will most likely be replaced by CORBA-like applications.

The CGI was developed to provide a standard interface for connecting external programs—such as database, search, and forms-processing programs—to Web servers. CGI programs, sometimes called *CGI scripts*, provide the capability to forward data between Web servers and these external programs. These programs are referred to as *gateway programs* because they provide a gateway through which Web servers and external programs communicate.

Although the CGI was developed to support gateway programming, CGI programs are not required to interface with external programs and can be complete programs in and of themselves.

How CGI Programs Work

Because CGI programs are executed by remote Web users, it is important to put limits on which programs can be executed in this fashion. CGI programs typically are stored in a special directory on Web servers. Common examples of this directory are `/cgi-bin` or `/htbin`. I'll use `/cgi-bin` in the following discussion, but you can designate any directory as the CGI directory.

When a browser request identifies an URL containing the `/cgi-bin` directory, the Web server recognizes this URL as containing a reference to a CGI program. The server identifies the CGI program to be executed from the URL; executes the CGI program, passing it any parameters or data; and, upon completion of the CGI program's execution, returns the results of the CGI program's processing to the Web browser.

The methods by which Web servers send and receive data to and from CGI programs is the core of the Common Gateway Interface specification. The current version of the CGI is 1.1. The URL `http://www.w3.org/pub/WWW/CGI` provides a starting point from which CGI information can be obtained.

Sending Data to CGI Programs

Data is passed from a Web server to a CGI program using a combination of command-line arguments, environment variables, and the standard input stream.

Command-Line Arguments

Command-line arguments are passed to CGI programs as the result of an `ISINDEX` query. These queries are a now-archaic method of retrieving information from Web users and are being replaced by HTML forms. The `args[]` array of `String` objects defined in the `main()` method of a Java program provides the capability to access these command-line variables.

Environment Variables

Environment variables are the primary mechanism used to pass information from Web servers to CGI programs. Environment variables are variables that are maintained by operating systems that are external to a program being executed. They are accessed by a program via special operating-system calls. Previous versions of Java used the `getenv()` method of the `System` class to access environment variables. This method has been declared obsolete and is no longer supported by Java. Java 1.0 replaces the `getenv()` method with the `getProperties()` method. This approach requires that environment variables be explicitly passed to Java programs as properties using the `-D` option of the Java command line.

The environment variables supported by the current version of the CGI specification are as follows:

- `AUTH_TYPE` identifies the authentication scheme used, if any.
- `CONTENT_LENGTH` identifies the number of bytes of data provided via the standard input stream.
- `CONTENT_TYPE` identifies the MIME type of the input data.
- `GATEWAY_INTERFACE` identifies the version of the CGI implemented by the server.
- `PATH_INFO` identifies the additional path information added to the URL following the name of the CGI program.
- `PATH_TRANSLATED` identifies the full path of the CGI program from the perspective of the host operating system.
- `QUERY_STRING` provides an URL-encoded set of parameters that are passed to the CGI program.
- `REMOTE_ADDR` identifies the IP address of the host from which the browser request is made.
- `REMOTE_HOST` identifies the fully qualified domain name of the host from which the browser request is made.
- `REMOTE_IDENT` identifies the user on whose behalf the browser request is made using the protocol specified in RFC 931.
- `REMOTE_USER` provides the identity of the user on whose behalf the browser request is made.
- `REQUEST_METHOD` identifies the type of browser request being processed: `GET`, `POST`, `PUT`, and so on.
- `SCRIPT_NAME` identifies the script name of the CGI program.
- `SERVER_NAME` identifies the hostname associated with the server.
- `SERVER_PORT` identifies the port on which the server receives its HTTP requests.
- `SERVER_PROTOCOL` identifies the version of the HTTP supported by the server.
- `SERVER_SOFTWARE` identifies the version of the server software being used.

Standard Input

When an URL containing a CGI program is accessed using the `POST` or `PUT` method, data can be passed to the CGI program using the standard input stream. This approach is very convenient, especially for Java programs, because the `System.in` variable and the classes and methods of the `java.io` package can be directly used to read the data passed by the server. The `CONTENT_LENGTH` environment variable is used to identify the number of bytes of data that are passed via standard input.

Receiving Data from CGI Programs

Although there are three ways to pass data to CGI programs, there is only one way for a CGI program to return data to a Web server: by writing to the standard output stream. The standard output stream of a CGI program is redirected by the Web server when the CGI program is executed. All data written to standard output is returned to the server. This is a bonus for Java-based CGI programs because the `System.out` variable and the `java.io` package can be used to return data to the Web server.

Connecting Applets with CGI Programs

Because of the security policy enforced with applets, an applet can connect only with a CGI program on the server from which the applet was loaded. This minimizes the risk associated with an applet reading sensitive data from one system and then disclosing that data to another system. Although this security precaution is prudent, it limits the flexibility with which applets can be integrated with CGI programs.

Fortune Teller

The following example illustrates an applet that communicates with a Web server to repeatedly access the fortune CGI program. Its source code is shown in Listing 32.1.

Listing 32.1. The Fortune applet source code.

```
import java.applet.*;
import java.awt.*;
import java.net.*;
import java.io.*;

public class Fortune extends Applet {
 URL url;
 TextArea text = new TextArea(24,80);
 Button button = new Button("Again");
 DataInputStream inStream;
 public void init() {
  setLayout(new BorderLayout());
  updateText();
  add("Center",text);
  add("South",new Button("Again"));
 }
 public boolean handleEvent(Event event) {
  if(event.target instanceof Button) {
```

```
   if("Again".equals(event.arg)) {
    updateText();
    return true;
   }
  }
  return false;
 }
 void updateText() {
  try {
   url = new URL("http://www.jaworski.com/cgi-bin/fortune");
   inStream = new DataInputStream(url.openStream());
   String newText = "";
   String line;
   while((line = inStream.readLine()) != null) {
    newText += line + "\n";
   }
   text.setText(newText);
  }catch (MalformedURLException ex) {
   text.setText("MalformedURLException");
  }catch (IOException ex) {
   text.setText("IOException");
  }
 }
}
```

The Fortune applet cannot be run from your computer because an applet can make a socket connection to only the computer from which it is run. To run the Fortune applet, use your browser to open the URL `http://www.jaworski.com/java/fortune.htm`. The screen shown in Figure 32.4 should appear.

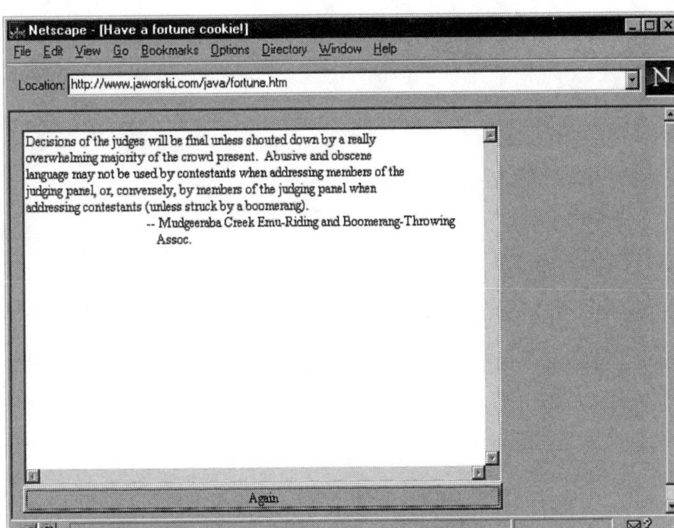

FIGURE 32.4.
The Fortune applet.

To get a new fortune cookie, click on the Again button.

The Fortune applet makes a connection to the fortune CGI program located in my `/cgi-bin` directory. It then reads the fortune cookie generated by this program and displays it in the text window. When you click on the Again button, it establishes another connection to the CGI program, obtains another fortune cookie, and displays the new cookie in the text window.

The `Fortune` class extends the `Applet` class and declares four field variables. The `url` variable is used to hold the URL of the CGI program. The `text` variable refers to the `TextArea` component displayed in the applet window. The `button` variable refers to the Again button. The `inStream` variable is used to refer to the input stream associated with the URL connection.

The `init()` method sets the layout of the applet window to a `BorderLayout` object and adds the `TextArea` and `Button` objects to the applet window. It also invokes the `updateText()` method to update the text displayed in the `TextArea` object by reading the output of the fortune CGI program.

The `handleEvent()` method handles the clicking of the Again button by invoking the `updateText()` method.

The `updateText()` method implements the heart of the applet's processing. It creates a new URL object using the address of my fortune CGI program and assigns it to the `url` variable. It then obtains the input stream associated with the URL and assigns it to the `inStream` variable. The `inStream` variable is read, line by line, and set in the `TextArea` object referred to by the `text` variable.

The `fortune.htm` file is shown in Listing 32.2. It follows the same format as used in other examples.

Listing 32.2. The `fortune.htm` file.

```
<HTML>
<HEAD>
<TITLE>Have a fortune cookie!</TITLE>
</HEAD>
<BODY>
<APPLET CODE="Fortune.class" WIDTH=450 HEIGHT=350>
[Fortune applet]
</APPLET>
</BODY>
</HTML>
```

Listing 32.3 shows the fortune CGI program. It is a shell script that is written in the UNIX shell programming language.

Listing 32.3. The source code of the fortune CGI program.

```
#!/bin/sh

FORTUNE=/usr/games/fortune

echo Content-type: text/plain
echo

if [ -x $FORTUNE ];  then
 $FORTUNE
else
 echo Cannot find fortune command on this system.
fi
```

Summary

This chapter shows you how applets can be integrated into distributed application programs. It presents a general architecture for distributed systems and has discussed Java's role within this architecture. It also summarizes current Java efforts to support distributed object access. The Common Gateway Interface is introduced, and the integration of applets with gateway programs is illustrated.

33

Working with JavaScript

by Cary Jardin

In this chapter you will be introduced to the JavaScript language. You'll examine the relationship between the Java programming language and JavaScript. You will learn how JavaScript and HTML are used to create advanced Web pages. At the end of this chapter, you will have a firm understanding of the constraints, capabilities, and uses of JavaScript.

JavaScript and Java

When choosing a programming language, a primary concern is whether the language can do what you want. When languages overlap in capability, this issue can become cloudy. To solve this dilemma, you need to look at a number of different qualities provided by each approach. If it is still a tie, pick the one that is easier to use. This decision process describes the choice between Java and JavaScript. Both languages supply some of the same capabilities while retaining their own unique functionality.

The first obvious difference between the two languages is that JavaScript is a scripting language, whereas Java is fully compiled. Both Java and JavaScript retain the majority of the same C-type syntax, but JavaScript is a loosely typed language and Java is strongly typed. JavaScript is referred to as *loosely typed* because it does not require that the type of a variable be identified when the variable is declared and because it automatically converts values of one type to another. Java is referred to as a *strongly typed* language because it requires that all variables be declared to be a unique type and because it does not automatically convert values from one type to another.

Both Java and JavaScript support the same primitive data types: `numeric`, `string`, and `boolean`. They also support functions in a slightly different way. Due to the loosely typed syntax of JavaScript, function definitions are also loosely typed. This means that the type of the return value of a function does not have to be specified.

Java and JavaScript provide similar capabilities. Each does, however, offer some unique capabilities. For JavaScript the majority of these capabilities pertain to its ability to exist within an HTML document. Java's strengths stem from the fact that it is a compiled language and, as such, is not confined to the limitations of a scripting environment. Table 33.1 shows a comparison of the two languages.

Table 33.1. Java versus JavaScript.

Java	*JavaScript*
Compiled	Interpreted
Accessed from HTML	Embedded within HTML
Strongly typed	Loosely typed
Uses static binding	Uses dynamic binding
Secure	Secure

How JavaScript Works

Unlike Java, whose code is compiled and stored in a `.class` file, the JavaScript code is embedded inside an HTML document. A Java applet is executed within a separate applet window of the browser's display. JavaScript, on the other hand, becomes an active element of the HTML document, and in doing so, has the capability to modify elements of the displayed Web page.

When the browser sees the `JavaScript` tag inside the HTML, it begins compiling the information needed to interpret the script. The script does not begin execution until the entire page has been laid out, at which time the script begins executing. It is true that the script has the capability to modify the appearance of the current page; however, it does need to abide by the update policy of the browser. After the browser has laid out the page, the script has to reload the page before any changes can be seen. There is a way around this: The script can update a region inside a frame without updating the entire page.

JavaScript is a powerful tool for Web development, but it shouldn't be viewed as a direct alternative to Java. Rather, Java and JavaScript can work in tandem to provide a wide range of application possibilities.

The Relationship Between HTML and Scripts

With Java applets, HTML serves as a command line of sorts to execute the applet. From the HTML command line, parameters can be sent into the applet. However, the communication with HTML is strictly one-way. The applet does not have the capability to modify the content of the HTML document. Herein lies the distinct difference between JavaScript and Java.

JavaScript is a script language that resides and is executed from within the HTML code. You can think of JavaScript in the same way as any other HTML language element: A script is interpreted and then executed from within the browser. In this manner, the script is handled in the same way as a frame. Executing the script from within the browser allows the script to have access to other elements of the HTML page—in a sense, allowing the script to dynamically change the content of the page.

Embedding JavaScript

To add a script to an HTML document, you use the *script tag*. It is a surrounding tag and is written as `<SCRIPT>` and `</SCRIPT>`. The `LANGUAGE` attribute is set to the value `JavaScript` to indicate that the script is a JavaScript script. All JavaScript code must be contained between the opening and closing script tags, as shown in the following example:

```
<SCRIPT LANGUAGE="JavaScript">
   JavaScript statements...
</SCRIPT>
```

NOTE

Chapter 16, "Web Programming with the `java.applet` Package," provides a brief introduction to HTML tags.

Browsers that do not support JavaScript should ignore the statements contained within the script tags. The `LANGUAGE` attribute can be omitted because JavaScript is currently supported only by Netscape browsers and is the only scripting language supported by these browsers. However, it is good practice to include the `LANGUAGE` attribute in case other scripting languages become widely supported.

JavaScript objects can be placed wherever you want on a Web page; however, it is a good idea to declare all functions in the head portion of the document. This assures that the functions are declared before the page is displayed, eliminating the possibility that a user might execute a function before it has been declared.

Combining Scripts with Applets

JavaScript has the capability to dynamically alter a Web page by generating new HTML elements to be displayed. Whether the HTML is created in response to an event or simply generated during the course of the script program, the HTML generated can be used to update a Web document's display. Keep in mind that applets are executed from an HTML tag reference. This means that HTML generated by JavaScript could very well execute a Java applet.

By launching an applet in response to an event, your HTML has the capability to take on an entirely new level of functionality. If the concept of launching an applet from a script seems a little confusing, see the examples in Chapter 34, "Sample Scripts."

Summary

In this chapter you have been introduced to the JavaScript language. You have seen how JavaScript is embedded into HTML documents. You have learned the differences between JavaScript and Java, as well as the strengths and weaknesses of both. You have also learned how applets and JavaScript can function together to create attractive Web pages. In Chapter 34, you will see examples of JavaScript and will be provided with the in-depth information you need to create your own scripts with JavaScript.

34

Sample Scripts

by Cary Jardin

This chapter contains some sample scripts written in JavaScript for your viewing. They are provided to give you an idea of what JavaScript can do, as well as allow you to view some functional code.

A Customizable Web Page

The script shown in Listing 34.1 allows a user to create a simple Web page. When the new page is generated, a separate window appears in order to display the generated page, as shown in Figures 34.1 and 34.2. Look at the following code and try to think of how you might be able to incorporate frames with this script. In order to run the script, type it into a file named `custom.htm` in the `\jdg\ch34` directory, and then open the file with Netscape Navigator 2.0 or later.

Listing 34.1. Script to implement a customizable Web page.

```
<HTML>
<HEAD>
<SCRIPT LANGUAGE=JavaScript>
  //generate a new page showing the animation
  function gen_page(form)
  {

     //create a blank page
     aniWindow = window.open("", "Preview", "");

     aniWindow.document.open();
     aniWindow.document.write("<HTML><HEAD>");
     aniWindow.document.write("<TITLE>TEST PAGE</TITLE>");
     aniWindow.document.write("</HEAD><BODY BGCOLOR="+form.BKGCOLOR.value+
              " TEXT="+ form.TXTCOLOR.value+">");
     aniWindow.document.write("<CENTER><H1>");
     aniWindow.document.write(form.TITLE.value+"<br></H1>");
     aniWindow.document.write("<IMG SRC = '"+form.IMAGEFILE.value+"'>");
     aniWindow.document.write("<BR><HR>");

aniWindow.document.write("<A href='mailto:"+form.EMAIL.value+"'>Mail Me</A>");
     aniWindow.document.write("</CENTER>");
     aniWindow.document.write("</BODY></HTML>");
     aniWindow.document.close();
  }
</SCRIPT>
<TITLE>JavaScript Customizable Web Page Demo</TITLE>
</HEAD>

<BODY BGCOLOR=FFFFFF TEXT=000000>
<CENTER>
<H1>Custom Web Page Demo<br>
<br>
<br>
</H1>
</CENTER>
```

```
<H2>
<FORM NAME="Web ">
<RIGHT>
<A>Background Color
<INPUT TYPE=TEXT NAME="BKGCOLOR" SIZE=6></A><br>
<A>Text Color
<INPUT TYPE=TEXT NAME="TXTCOLOR" SIZE=6></A><br>
<A>Title Text
<INPUT TYPE=TEXT NAME="TITLE" size=50></A><br>
<A>Image name
<INPUT TYPE=TEXT NAME="IMAGEFILE" size=40></A><br>
<A>Email address
<INPUT TYPE=TEXT NAME="EMAIL" size=20></A><br>
<INPUT TYPE=BUTTON NAME="GenBtn" VALUE="&Generate"
 onClick = "gen_page(this.form)">
</RIGHT>
</FORM>
</H2>

<HR>
<CENTER>
<FONT SIZE=2>
Comments to <A HREF="mailto:cjardin@xprime.com">X' inc</A>
</FONT>
</CENTER>

</BODY>
</HTML>
```

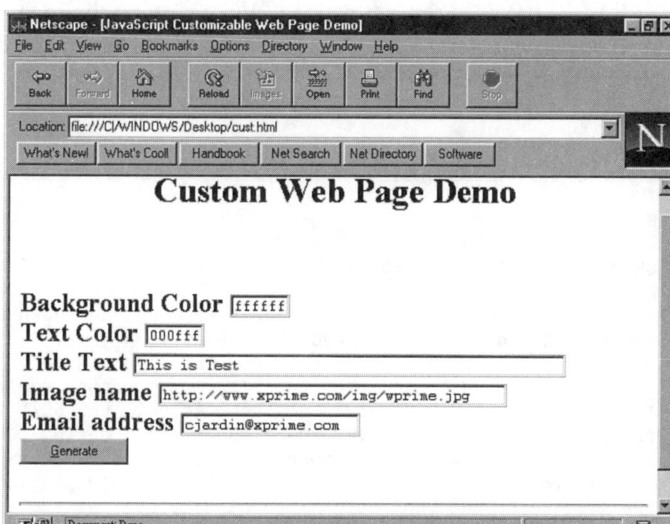

FIGURE 34.1.
The Custom Web Page Demo opening screen.

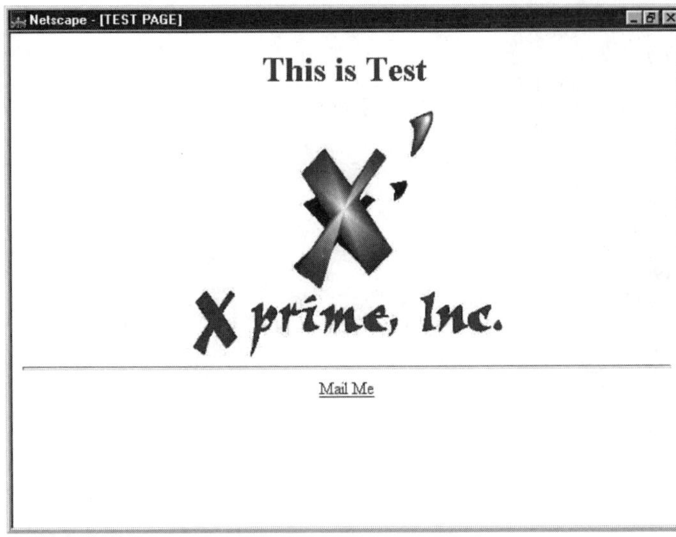

FIGURE 34.2.
The Web page generated by the script.

Story Teller

The script shown in Listing 34.2 creates a ticker-tape display. The display is then used to tell a story. (See Figure 34.3.) Besides telling a great story, the script displays the use of form objects, as well as the provided timer functions. When viewing the code, think about how you might add graphics to the story. Type the script into the file `story.htm` and then open it with Netscape Navigator 2.0 or later.

Listing 34.2. Story Teller demo script.

```
<HTML>
<HEAD>

<SCRIPT LANGUAGE=JavaScript>
//What to say
  var output = "An elephant and a mouse were walking down a jungle path. "+
"They talked and laughed and had the gayest of a time.  Until suddenly the"+
" elephant fell into a poacher's trap.  The elephant said, 'Help me"+
" I have fallen and I can't get up.' The mouse responded,'wait right there"+
" I will go get my HUMMER and a tow rope to pull you out.' So the mouse "+
" fetches his HUMMER and saves the elephant from death.  The next day, '"+
" as luck would have it, the mouse falls into the same trap.  The elephant"+
" says to the mouse, 'here run up my $%^! to safety.' Which is exactly what"+
" the mouse did, and they both lived happily ever after. ----!!!!---- Moral "+
" of the story, if you have a big enough $%^! you don't need a HUMMER'. :->";
//MAX size of the display field, chars
  var MAXSIZE = 30;
```

```
//Used to pad string
  var bunchOspace =
      "                                                                                ";

//begining and ending string index
  var bindex = 0;
  var eindex = 1;

  var timerID = null;
  var timerRunning = false;

  function stopclock()
  {
     if(timerRunning)
        clearTimeout(timerID);
     timerRunning = false;
  }

  function startclock()
  {
    stopclock();
    tick();
  }

  function tick()
  {
    if(eindex <= output.length)
    {
       //populate the value
       document.forms[0].TICKER.value =
         bunchOspace.substring(0,MAXSIZE-(eindex - bindex))+
         output.substring(bindex,eindex);

      if((eindex - bindex) < MAXSIZE)
        ++eindex;
      else
      {
        ++bindex;
        ++eindex;
      }
    }
    else
    {
      bindex = 0;
      eindex = 1;
    }
    timerID = setTimeout("tick()",300);
    timerRunning = true;
  }
</SCRIPT>
<TITLE>JavaScript Story Teller Demo</TITLE>
</HEAD>

<BODY BGCOLOR=FFFFFF TEXT=000000 onLoad="startclock()">
<CENTER>
<H1>Story Teller Demo<br>
Let Me Tell You a Tale!<br>
```

continues

Listing 34.2. continued

```
<br>
</H1>
</CENTER>

<H2>
<FORM NAME="Web ">
<CENTER>
<INPUT TYPE=TEXT SIZE=30 NAME="TICKER">
</CENTER>
</FORM>
</H2>

<HR>
<CENTER>
<FONT SIZE=2>
Comments to <A HREF="mailto:cjardin@xprime.com">X' inc</A>
</FONT>
</CENTER>

</BODY>
</HTML>
```

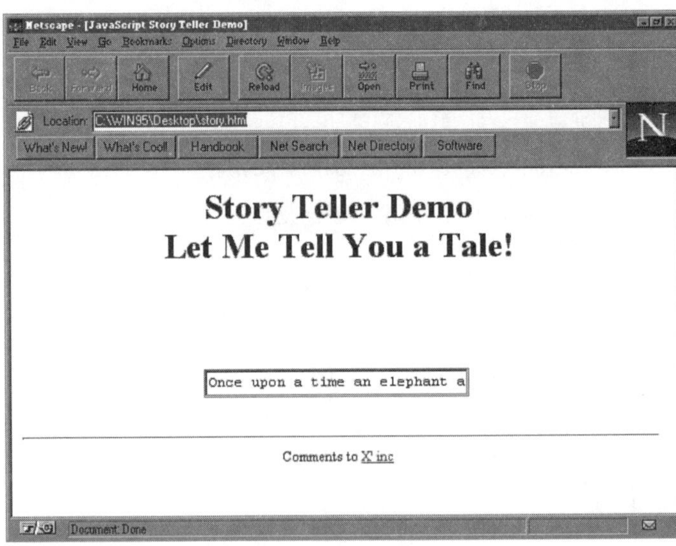

FIGURE 34.3.
The Story Teller Demo opening page.

Web Guide

The script shown in Listing 34.3 creates a menu list from which to select Web pages. (See Figure 34.4.) The script shows how to open separate Navigator windows. As you're looking at it, try to figure out how this script could be implemented without using a separate window. Type the script into the file `guide.htm` and view it with Netscape Navigator 2.0 or later.

Listing 34.3. Web Guide script.

```
<HTML>
<HEAD>

<SCRIPT LANGUAGE=JavaScript>
  //creates a structure to hold value
  function select_item(value)
  {
     this.value = value;
  }

  //find what value is active in the selection list
  function find_selection(chcked_object)
  {
     contents = new select_item();
     for(var i=0;i<chcked_object.length;i++)
        if(chcked_object[i].checked)
        {
           contents.value = chcked_object[i].value;
       break;
        }
     return contents;
  }

  //generate a new page showing the animation
  function Do_Jump(formfield)
  {
     selection = find_selection(formfield.PLACESTOGO);
     //create a blank page
     aniWindow = window.open(selection.value, "Preview",
  "resizable=1,width=480,height=200");
  }
</SCRIPT>
<TITLE>JavaScript Web Guide Demo</TITLE>
</HEAD>

<BODY BGCOLOR=FFFFFF TEXT=000000>
<CENTER>
<H1>Web Guide Demo<br>
I'll Take you there!<br>
<br>
</H1>
</CENTER>

<H2>
<FORM NAME="Web ">
<CENTER>
<INPUT TYPE=RADIO NAME="PLACESTOGO"
 VALUE="http://WWW.XPRIME.COM"
 OnClick = "Do_Jump(this.form)" CHECKED>X prime, Inc<br>
<INPUT TYPE=RADIO NAME="PLACESTOGO"
 VALUE="http://WWW.XPRIME.COM/chocabytes"
 OnClick = "Do_Jump(this.form)">ChocaBytes<br>
<INPUT TYPE=RADIO NAME="PLACESTOGO"
 VALUE="http://WWW.HORIZONS.COM"
```

continues

Listing 34.3. continued

```
 OnClick = "Do_Jump(this.form)">Horizons Technologies, Inc<br>
<INPUT TYPE=RADIO NAME="PLACESTOGO"
 VALUE="http://WWW.JakeDog.COM"
 OnClick = "Do_Jump(this.form)">Jake Dog<br>
<INPUT TYPE=RADIO NAME="PLACESTOGO"
 VALUE="http://yellowpages.bellsouth.COM"
 OnClick = "Do_Jump(this.form)">YellowPages<br>
<INPUT TYPE=RADIO NAME="PLACESTOGO"
 VALUE="http://www.DimensionX"
 OnClick = "Do_Jump(this.form)">Dimension X<br>
<INPUT TYPE=RADIO NAME="PLACESTOGO"
 VALUE="http://www.csusm.edu"
 OnClick = "Do_Jump(this.form)">California State University San Marcos<br>
</CENTER>
</FORM>
</H2>

<HR>
<CENTER>
<FONT SIZE=2>
Comments to <A HREF="mailto:cjardin@xprime.com">X' inc</A>
</FONT>
</CENTER>

</BODY>
</HTML>
```

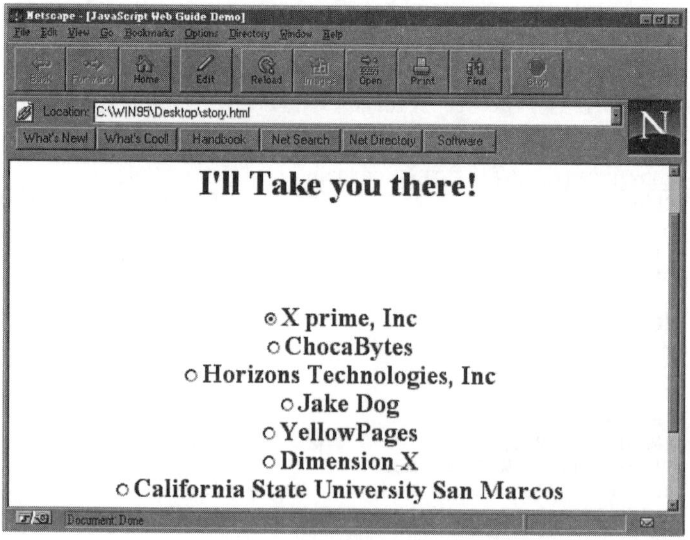

FIGURE 34.4.
The Web Guide menu list.

Summary

The scripts provided in this chapter show some of the capabilities of JavaScript. The customizable Web page example demonstrates how JavaScript can be used to generate Web pages on-the-fly. The Story Teller script shows how timers can be used to create scrolling text. The Web guide shows how a script can be used to access other pages on the Web. Chapter 35, "JavaScript Reference," provides a detailed description of the JavaScript language.

35

JavaScript Reference

by Cary Jardin

This chapter serves as a tutorial and reference guide for the JavaScript language. You'll learn about the objects and methods provided by JavaScript and learn how events are handled. By the end of this chapter, you should have an understanding of what JavaScript offers and be able to begin writing your own scripts.

JavaScript Objects

JavaScript is an object-based scripting language that does not support classes or inheritance. So, you might ask, how do you use JavaScript as an object-oriented language? Good question. JavaScript provides a number of default objects to which you have direct access, and allows you to create your own objects as well. The following are the JavaScript-supplied objects:

- `navigator` can be thought of as being directly relational to the browser window. Inside the browser window lies the entire HTML document. The same holds true for the `navigator` object.
- `window` is the parent class for all objects stored within the `navigator` object. Dialog boxes inside the `navigator` object's parent window can be created by using the properties and methods provided by the `window` object. The `window` object also provides access to the child windows of each frame through the frame's array property.
- `location` holds all pertinent information about an URL.
- `history` provides access to the browser's URL history list.
- `document` contains information about all HTML properties inside the current page. It is through this object that JavaScript is enabled to output HTML.
- `form` contains information about a form defined within the body of the HTML document.
- `button` coincides with the button components displayed in the document.
- `checkbox` coincides with the checkbox components displayed in the document.
- `text` coincides with the text field components in the document.
- `textarea` coincides with the text area components in the document.
- `hidden` coincides with the hidden text field components in the document.
- `password` coincides with the password text field components in the document.
- `radio` coincides with the radio button components displayed in the document.
- `selections` is an array containing all of the selection group components displayed in the document.
- `string` provides a string container for JavaScript. A number of string-manipulation utilities are contained within the object as well.
- `Date` provides the capability to store and work with date information.
- `Math` provides mathematical constants and mathematical functions.

Properties and Methods

The power of JavaScript lies in the functionality provided to the programmer. The following sections are a reference to the methods and properties of the JavaScript objects. Keep in mind when programming JavaScript that it is a loosely typed language.

The `navigator` Object

The `navigator` object provides a base class for all HTML objects. It provides the basis for the logical hierarchy inherent in HTML. That is, the `navigator` object contains a `window` object containing the `document` object, which in turn contains all of the defined objects.

The `window` Object

The `window` object is the base object for the `document` object. It provides the following properties:

- `window frames[index]` contains `window` objects for each frame child window.
- `number frames.length` is the number of frame child windows.
- `window self` is the current `window` object.
- `window parent` is the parent window.
- `window top` is the topmost ancestor `window` object.

The `window` object provides the following methods:

- `void alert(string "name")` displays an alert dialog box containing the passed string.
- `boolean confirm(string "name")` displays a confirmation dialog box containing the passed string. Returns a `True` or `False` value.
- `void open(string "URL", string "name")` opens a new client window continuing the specified URL and displaying the title `name`.
- `void close()` closes the `self` window.

The `location` Object

The `location` object provides information about the current URL location, as well as some useful methods. Its properties are the following:

- `string href` holds the entire URL.
- `string protocol` contains the protocol section of the URL, including the colon (`:`).
- `string host` holds the hostname, including the optional port number embedded in the URL.

- `string hostname` holds the hostname, not including the optional port number embedded in the URL.
- `string port` contains the port of the host if specified; otherwise, the value is `""` (null).
- `string path` contains the path information that is specified in the URL after the host information.
- `string hash` holds the CGI-specified information, if any.
- `string search` contains the specified CGI parameters.
- `string post` contains any post handler specified in the URL.

The `location` object provides the following methods:

- `string toString()` returns the value stored in the `href` property.
- `void assign()` sets the `href` property.

The `history` Object

The `history` object provides access to the browser's URL history list. Its properties are the following:

- `string back` holds the URL of the previous location in the URL history list.
- `string forward` holds the URL of the next location in the URL history list.
- `string current` holds the URL of the current location in the URL history list.
- `int length` contains the number of entries in the URL history list.

The `history` object provides the following methods:

- `void go(int delta)` loads the URL in the URL history list that is `delta` distance from the current position. The value of `delta` may be either positive or negative, allowing positive and negative movement.
- `void go(string "srchstring")` loads the URL in the URL history list that contains the partial `srchstring` in either the URL or the title.
- `string toString()` creates an HTML list of all the entries in the URL history list.

The `document` Object

The `document` object contains information about all HTML properties inside the current page. In addition to the standard properties provided, a member for each form in the document is provided with the name specified in the form's `NAME` attribute.

The following are the `document` object's provided properties:

- `string title` holds the document's title. If one is not defined, the value is `Untitled`.
- `string location` contains the document's full URL.

- `string lastmodified` contains the last-modified date.
- `string loadedDate` contains the date the document was loaded.
- `string referer` holds the name of the host that referred the current document.
- `string bgColor` contains the 24-bit RGB hexadecimal background color.
- `string fgColor` contains the 24-bit RGB hexadecimal foreground color.
- `string linkColor` contains the 24-bit RGB hexadecimal hyperlink color.
- `string vlinkColor` contains the 24-bit RGB hexadecimal visited hyperlink color.
- `string alinkColor` contains the 24-bit RGB hexadecimal active hyperlink color. An active hyperlink is displayed when the mouse button has been depressed but has not been released.
- `form forms[index]` is an array of `form` objects corresponding to the forms defined in the current document.
- `int forms.length` contains the number of forms in the `forms[]` array.
- `location links[index]` is an array of `location` objects corresponding to the links defined in the current document.
- `links.length` contains the number of forms in the `links[]` array.
- `string anchors[index]` is an array of anchor name strings, corresponding to the anchors defined in the current document.
- `anchors.length` contains the number of forms in the `anchors[]` array.

The `document` object provides the following methods:

- `void write(string "output")` outputs the `output` string into the current document.
- `void writeln(string "output")` outputs the `output` string into the current document followed by a newline character.
- `void clear()` clears the current document window.
- `void close()` closes the current document window.

The `form` Object

The `form` object contains information about the defined form. In addition to its standard properties, this object contains a member for each field of the form. For instance, suppose a form contains a field called `"Name"`; the associated form would contain a member named `Name`. The value of the field can be obtained using `form.Name.value`.

The `form` object's default properties are the following:

- `string name` contains the form's `NAME` attribute.
- `int method` will contain a value of `0` if the form's `METHOD` attribute is equal to `get`, or a value of `1` if the `METHOD` attribute is equal to `post`.

- `string action` holds the value of the `ACTION` attribute.
- `window target` is the window to be used to display the form's response.
- `object elements[index]` is an array containing all the component elements of the form.
- `elements.length` contains the number of objects in the `elements[]` array.

The `form` object has no methods.

The `button` Object

The `button` object may take one of three separate functions coinciding with a form's reset button, submit button, or a custom button. The `button` object's properties are as follows:

- `string value` stores the value specified in the `VALUE` attribute.
- `string name` holds the value specified in the `NAME` attribute.

The `button` object contains no methods.

The `checkbox` Object

The `checkbox` object corresponds to a form's checkbox. Its properties are as follows:

- `string value` stores the value specified in the `VALUE` attribute.
- `string name` holds the value specified in the `NAME` attribute.
- `boolean status` contains the current status of the checkbox.
- `boolean defaultstatus` contains the default status of the checkbox specified in the `CHECKED` attribute.

The `checkbox` object contains no methods.

The `text`, `textarea`, `hidden`, and `password` Objects

The `text`, `textarea`, `hidden`, and `password` objects are all formed from the same object structure. The following are the properties of the shared object structure:

- `string value` stores the value specified in the `VALUE` attribute.
- `string name` holds the value specified in the `NAME` attribute.
- `string defaultValue` holds the default value specified in the `DEFAULTVALUE` attribute.

The shared object structure contains these methods:

- `void focus()` sets the focus to the object.
- `void blur()` takes away the focus from the object.
- `void select()` selects the content of the object's input field.

The `radio` Object

The `radio` object corresponds to a form's radio button. The object's properties are as follows:

- `string value` stores the value specified in the `VALUE` attribute.
- `string name` holds the value specified in the `NAME` attribute.
- `int index` contains the zero-based index of the button.
- `boolean status` contains the status of the radio button.
- `boolean defaultstatus` contains the default status of the radio button specified in the `CHECKED` attribute.

The `radio` object contains no methods.

The `select` Object

The `select` object is an array corresponding to a form's selection list. Each element of the array contains the following properties:

- `string value` stores the value specified in the `VALUE` attribute.
- `string text` holds the value specified in the `<OPTION>` tag.
- `int index` contains the zero-based index of the option.
- `boolean status` contains the selection status of the item. `True` if selected.
- `boolean defaultstatus` contains the default status of the selected item specified in the `SELECTED` attribute.

The `select` object contains no methods.

The `string` Object

The `string` object provides the capability to store string data and provides methods to manipulate the string value. `length` identifies the length of the string.

`string` offers the following methods:

- `void anchor(string "AnchorName")` creates an anchor with the specified name.
- `void link(string "LinkAttribute")` creates a link with the specified attribute.
- `void big()` causes the text to be displayed with the `<BIG>` tag.
- `void small()` causes the text to be displayed with the `<SMALL>` tag.
- `void sub()` causes the text to be displayed in subscript as if it were inside a `<SUB>` tag.
- `void sup()` causes the text to be displayed in superscript as if it were inside a `<SUP>` tag.
- `void blink()` causes the text to be displayed blinking.
- `void bold()` causes the text to be displayed bold.

- `void italics()` causes the text to be displayed in italics.
- `void strike()` causes the text to be displayed as if it were inside a `<STRIKE>` tag.
- `char charAt(int index)` returns the character at the specified index value.
- `void fontcolor(Color)` specifies the color in which to display the text.
- `void fontsize(int size)` specifies the font size in which to display the text. The value is between `1` and `7`.
- `int indexOf(string "SrchStrng",[beginIndex])` returns the starting index of `SrchString`. If `beginIndex` is specified, the search begins at the specified index position.
- `int lastIndexOf(string "SrchStrng",[beginIndex])` returns the starting index of the last occurrence found in `SrchString`. If `beginIndex` is specified, the search begins at the specified index position.
- `string substring(int begin, int end)` returns a partial string, beginning at the `begin` location and ending at `end`.
- `string toLowerCase()` returns the string in lowercase characters.
- `string toUpperCase()` returns the string in uppercase characters.

The `Date` Object

The `Date` object provides access to the system date function and also is a container for date information.

The `Date()` function creates a `Date` object with the current system time.

The following examples create a `Date` object with the specified data:

```
Date("month day, year hours:minutes:seconds")
Date(year, month, day)
Date(year, month, day, hour)
```

The `Date` object has no properties.

The following are the methods for the `Date` object:

- `int getDate()` returns the day of the month.
- `int getDay()` returns the day of the week, starting with `0` for Sunday.
- `int getHours()` returns the hour between `0` and `23`.
- `int getMinutes()` returns minutes.
- `int getMonth()` returns the month of the year, starting with `0` for January.
- `int getSeconds()` returns seconds.
- `int getTime()` returns the number of milliseconds since January 1, 1970.
- `int getTimezoneOffset()` returns the local time zone offset.

- `int getYear()` returns the year.
- `int parse(sting "Date")` returns the number of milliseconds since January 1, 1970.
- `void setDate(int date)` sets the day of the month, between `0` and `31`.
- `void setHours(int hour)` sets the hour of the day, between `0` and `23`.
- `void setMinutes(int minutes)` sets the minutes in the hour, between `0` and `59`.
- `void setMonth(int month)` sets the month of the year, between `0` and `11`.
- `void setSeconds(int seconds)` sets the seconds of the hour, between `0` and `59`.
- `void setTime(int tseconds)` sets the time to the passed time value.
- `void setYear(int year)` sets the year.
- `string toGMTString()` returns the date in GMT string format.
- `string toLocaleString()` returns the date to the current location's string format.
- `Date UTC(int year, month, day [, hrs] [, min] [, sec])` converts the passed parameters into a `Date` object.

The `Math` Object

The `Math` object provides defined math constants and some math functions. The following `static` constants are available:

- `E`—The number e.
- `LN2`—The natural logarithm of 2.
- `LN10`—The natural logarithm of 10.
- `LOG2E`—The logarithm base 2 of 10.
- `LOG10E`—The logarithm base 10 of e.
- `PI`—The pi constant.
- `SQRT1_2`—The square root of $1/2$.
- `SQRT2`—The square root of 2.

The `Math` object provides the following mathematical functions:

- `abs` is the absolute value function.
- `acos` is the arccosine function.
- `asin` is the arcsine function.
- `atan` is the arctangent function.
- `ceil` is the ceiling function.
- `cos` is the cosine function.
- `exp` is the exponential function.

- `floor` is the floor function.
- `log` is the natural logarithm function.
- `max` is the maximum function.
- `min` is the minimum function.
- `pow` is the power function.
- `random` is a random number generator.
- `round` is the rounding function.
- `sin` is the sine function.
- `sqrt` is the square root function.
- `tan` is the tangent function.

Handling Events

Handling events in JavaScript allows the script to be informed when an event has occurred. In Java, an event is trapped and then dispatched to the code that was intended to handle that event. In JavaScript, when an object is defined in the HTML, the function used to handle that event is specified with the object. For example, look at the example of placing a button into a document:

```
<INPUT TYPE="button" VALUE="OK" NAME="OKButton"
  onClick="ValidateMe(this.form)">
```

The top line defines a button with a `VALUE` of `"OK"` and a `NAME` of `"OKButton"`. The bottom line is what you want to understand here.

Notice the `onClick` parameter to the button. This line is associating the defined function `ValidateMe` with the `onClick` event of the button. This specifies to the code to handle the event directly from HTML.

JavaScript recognizes different event handlers for a number of supplied objects. The following are all the supported event handlers with their associated objects:

- `onBlur—select, text, textarea`
- `onChange—select, text, textarea`
- `onClick—button, checkbox, radio, link`
- `onFocus—select, text, textarea`
- `onLoad—window`
- `onUnload—form`
- `onMouseOver—link`
- `onSelect—text, textarea`
- `onSubmit—form`

For all of these events, the syntax to define the event handler is the same. Inside the object's associated HTML tag is the event's name followed by the function you want to handle the event. For example, the following:

```
<BODY onLoad="sayHello("Hello To Me")>
```

sets the function `sayHello` to the `onLoad` event of the `window` object.

Arrays

The syntax to declare arrays in JavaScript is very different from Java, primarily due to the loose typing of JavaScript. Arrays are declared without specifying an implicit type; JavaScript resolves the type at a later time. For example, to declare a single-dimensional array, the syntax would be as follows:

```
var aBunchOfInts = new makearray(50);
```

The syntax to load the array would be like this:

```
ABunchofInts[0] = 1;
```

Due to the dynamic binding property of JavaScript, the type of the array is not set until a value is assigned.

Operators and Expressions

JavaScript follows the Java framework for operators and expressions. Binary operators are of the form `operand1 operator operand2`. Unary operators are of the form `operator operand1` or `operand1 operator`. Bitwise operators convert operands into 32-bit integers before performing the operation.

The following are all valid JavaScript operators:

`+`	addition
`-`	subtraction
`*`	multiplication
`/`	division
`%`	modulus
`++`	increment
`--`	decrement
`&&`	and
`||`	or

`!`	not
`==`	equal to
`>`	greater than
`<`	less than
`>=`	greater than or equal to
`<=`	less than or equal to
`!=`	not equal to
`&`	bitwise `AND`
`|`	bitwise `OR`
`^`	bitwise `XOR`
`>>`	sign-propagating right shift
`<<`	left shift
`>>>`	zero fill right fill

JavaScript supports assignment expressions using `=` , evaluation expressions, and conditional expressions. Conditional expressions take the form `(condition) ? val1 : val2`, where `val1` is processed if the condition is `true`; otherwise `val2` is processed.

Statements

JavaScript provides conditional, loop, object-manipulation, and comment statements. The syntax for each of the statement types is identical to Java. The syntaxes for the JavaScript-supported statements are as follows:

Conditional Statements

- `if-else`:

```
if (condition) {
   statements1 }
[else {
   statements2}]
```

Loop Statements

- `for`:

```
for ([initial-expression;] [condition;] [increment-expression]) {
  statements
}
```

- `while`:

```
while (condition) {
```

```
   statements
}
```

- break:

```
break
```

- continue:

```
continue
```

Object-Manipulation Statements

- for...in:

```
for (variable in object) {
   statements }
```

- new:

```
objectName = new objectType ( param1 [,param2] ...[,paramN] )
```

- this:

```
this[.propertyName]
```

- with:

```
with (object){
    statements
}
```

Comment Statements

```
// comment text
/* multiple-line comment text */
```

Summary

The JavaScript language provides enough of a diversity from Java to retain its own identity. A large number of the statements, expressions, and operators are identical. However, the loose typing of JavaScript gives it a flavor all its own.

VII

Extending Java

36

The Java Source Code

by Cary Jardin

This chapter discusses the distribution of the Java source code. It also covers platform-specific issues that affect the porting of Java. You will look at the validity and issues of platform benchmarks. When you finish this chapter, you will have a better understanding of Sun's role in the evolution of Java, as well as what is involved in porting Java.

Obtaining the Java Source Code

If you are coming from a purely DOS/Windows background, the concept of releasing the source code for a product might seem a little ridiculous. If you are coming from a UNIX background, this idea is completely native to you. Why is the concept of releasing source so alien to the DOS/Windows world, and so native to the UNIX world? The reason stems from the homogeneous nature of the IBM PC and the heterogeneous platforms of the UNIX world. Therein lies Sun's motivation to release Java source to the masses.

In the IBM PC world, the 80x86 processor reigned supreme. All executables compiled for this architecture would run on any IBM PC. Life in the UNIX world was nowhere near as easy. Programs were released with full source code so that they could be compiled onto the specific platform. Sun, coming from a UNIX background, is used to cross-platform issues. This is the reason for the distribution of the Java source code. However, Sun is also in the business to make money, so the distribution of the source code has some hitches.

Sun provides two different licensing options: one is free and the other one will cost you. The free option is for noncommercial purposes such as education. For more information, contact `http://www.javasoft.com/source.html`.

The commercial distribution license provides Sun a mechanism for revenue as well as control over the technology. For more information, contact `http://www.javasoft.com/comm_license.html`.

If you have detailed questions about either option, these sites should lead you into the right direction.

Platform Differences

If Java were simply a native code compiler, the process of porting to different platforms would not be that difficult. Unfortunately, for porting purposes, the Java Developer's Kit (JDK) is compiled into Java virtual machine (JVM) executable programs. Unless the Java executable is being run on a native JVM, the executable needs to be interpreted into the instructions supported by the current platform. Porting the Java compiler onto other machines does not require nearly the effort of porting the Java runtime interpreter.

From the Java compiler's perspective, the platform on which it is being executed does not really matter. The Java compiler actually does not need to know anything specific about the current platform, which minimizes the cross-platform differences.

The Java runtime library, on the other hand, is a completely different story. The entire point of having a runtime interpreter is to convert JVM operations into machine-specific code. In many cases this is not simply a one-to-one translation. A number of platform-specific issues constitute drastic platform differences in the Java interpreter: byte order, multithreading capabilities, graphics capabilities, network mechanisms, and memory allocation, to name just a few.

The JDK was designed for cross-platform execution. However, to attain this goal, the Java runtime interpreter must be ported to the target platform. The amount of porting effort required is directly proportional to the difference between the target platform and the JVM.

Platform Benchmarks

As mentioned earlier, the interpretation between JVM-executable and platform-specific code is not always easy. In almost all cases the translation is not a direct one-to-one mapping. Some machines might require less or more instructions than others to do the same translation. Platform benchmarks may be able to test the compatibility of the native machine and the JVM, but currently there is not a standardized benchmark.

Windows 95/NT Overview

The JDK was released for the Windows 95/NT platforms in May 1995. Because the majority of PCs were still running the 16-bit Windows 3.1, the choice to release the JDK for the Win32 platform was a commitment to Java's future.

Unlike the 16-bit Window operating system, the Win32 platform offers Java what it needs to port the Java runtime interpreter. Win32 supports a multithreaded model as well as a standardized WinSock (that is, the Windows DLL version of Berkeley Sockets). Windows does not directly support either of these, which made implementation of the JVM on Windows 3.1 infeasible.

Summary

This chapter covers issues related to the distribution of the Java source code and the porting of Java to the Win32 platform. The following chapter describes the operation of the Java virtual machine.

37

The Java Virtual Machine

by Cary Jardin

This chapter probes into the Java virtual machine (JVM) phenomenon. You will learn about the structures of a `.class` file, look at the virtual machine architecture, and be given a reference for the JVM instruction set. After you have completed this chapter, you will be able to diagram the internal structure of a `.class` file and will understand the machine architecture of the JVM.

Overview

When Java was created, the goal was to create a machine-independent programming language that then could be compiled into a portable binary format. In theory, that is exactly what was achieved. Java code is portable to any system that has a Java interpreter. However, Java is not at all machine independent. Rather, Java is machine specific to the Java virtual machine.

The JVM concept allows a layer of translation between the executable program and the machine-specific code. In a non-Java compiler, the source code is compiled into machine-specific assembly code. In doing this, the executable limits itself to the confines of that machine architecture. Compiling Java code creates an executable using JVM assembly directives. The difference of the two approaches is quite fundamental to the portability of the executable. Non-Java executables communicate directly with the platform's instruction set. Java executables communicate with the JVM instruction set, which is then translated into platform-specific instructions.

Structure of `.class` Files

Every machine has a certain form for its executable file. Java is no exception. The Java compiler creates its executable files in the form of `.class`.

`.class` files are composed of 8-bit values (bytes) that can be read in pairs of 16-bit values, or in 4-byte groups to create 32-bit values. The bytes are arranged in big-endian order, where the first byte contains the highest order bits of the 32-bit value and the last byte contains the lowest-order bits of the 32-bit value.

A `.class` file itself is broken into 15 separate regions:

- `magic`
- `version`
- `constant_pool_count`
- `constant_pool[constant_pool_count - 1]`
- `access_flags`
- `this_class`

- super_class
- interfaces_count
- interfaces[interfaces_count]
- fields_count
- fields[fields_count]
- methods_count
- methods[methods_count]
- attributes_count
- attributes[attribute_count]

The regions are not padded or aligned with one another. Each region can be of either fixed or variable size. Regions that contain variable amounts of information are preceded by a field specifying the size of the variable region. The following sections provide more information about these regions.

magic

The `magic` region must contain a value of `0xCAFEBABE`.

version

`version` holds the version number of the compiler that created the `.class` file. This is used to specify incompatible changes to either the format of the `.class` file or to the bytecodes.

constant_pool

`constant_pool_count` specifies the size of the next region. As noted previously, there is no alignment or padding. Instead, *size fields* are used to denote the extents of different variable regions. These fields are 2 bytes in length.

`constant_pool` contains an array of `constant_pool_count - 1` items that store string constants, class names, field names, and all constants referenced in the body of the code.

The first byte in every entry of `constant_pool` contains a type that specifies the content of the entry.

Table 37.1 identifies the items that are contained in the constant pool.

Table 37.1. Constant types.

Constant Type	*Value*
`CONSTANT_Asciiz`	1
`CONSTANT_Unicode`	2
`CONSTANT_Integer`	3
`CONSTANT_Float`	4
`CONSTANT_Long`	5
`CONSTANT_Double`	6
`CONSTANT_Class`	7
`CONSTANT_String`	8
`CONSTANT_Fieldref`	9
`CONSTANT_Methodref`	10
`CONSTANT_InterfaceMethodref`	11
`CONSTANT_NamedType`	12

`CONSTANT_Asciiz` and `CONSTANT_Unicode` are represented by a 1-byte reference tag, a 2-byte length specifier, and an array of bytes that is of the specified length.

`CONSTANT_Integer` and `CONSTANT_Float` contain a 1-byte tag and a 4-byte value.

`CONSTANT_Long` and `CONSTANT_Double` are used to store 8-byte values. The structure begins with a 1-byte tag and includes a 4-byte value containing the high bytes, and a 4-byte value containing the low bytes.

`CONSTANT_Class` holds a 1-byte tag as well as a 2-byte index into the `constant_pool` that contains the string name of the class.

`CONSTANT_String` represents an object of type `String`. The structure contains two fields, a 1-byte tag, and a 2-byte index into `constant_pool`, which holds the actual string value encoded using a modified UTF scheme. `constant_pool` stores only 8-bit values, with the capability of combining them to form 8- and 16-bit characters.

`CONSTANT_Fieldref`, `CONSTANT_Methodref`, and `CONSTANT_InterfaceMethodref` represent their data with a 1-byte tag and two 1-byte indexes into `constant_pool`. The first index references the class; the second references the name and type.

`CONSTANT_NameAndType` contains information about constants not associated with a class. The first byte is the tag, followed by two 2-byte indexes into `constant_pool` specifying the type and signature of the constant.

access_flags

The access_flags section is a 2-byte field that specifies 16 different values describing various properties of fields, classes, and methods. Table 37.2 lists the values of the access flags.

Table 37.2. Access flags.

Access Flag	*Value*
ACC_PUBLIC	0x0001
ACC_PRIVATE	0x0002
ACC_PROTECTED	0x0004
ACC_STATIC	0x0008
ACC_FINAL	0x0010
ACC_SYNCHRONIZED	0x0020
ACC_THREADSAFE	0x0040
ACC_TRANSIENT	0x0080
ACC_NATIVE	0x0100
ACC_INTERFACE	0x0200
ACC_ABSTRACT	0x0400

this_class

this_class is a 2-byte index into constant_pool specifying the information about the current class.

interfaces

interfaces_count is a 2-byte value denoting the size of the interfaces array.

The interfaces array contains indexes into the constant_pool specifying the interfaces that the current class implements.

fields

fields_count is a 2-byte value denoting the size of the fields array.

The fields array contains complete information about the fields of a class. This array contains, for each element, a 2-byte value of access_flags, two 2-byte indexes into constant_pool, a 2-byte attribute_count, and an array of attributes.

The first index, name_index, holds the name of the field. The second, signature_index, holds the signature of the field. The last field stores any needed attributes about the field. Currently, the number of attributes supported is one of type ConstantValue, indicating that the field is a static constant value.

methods

methods_count supplies the number of methods stored in the methods array. This number only includes the methods declared in the current class.

The methods field contains an array of elements containing complete information about the method. The information is stored with a 2-byte access_flags value, a 2-byte name_index referencing the name of the method in the constant_pool, a 2-byte signature_index referencing signature information found in the constant_pool, a 2-byte attributes_count containing the number of elements in the attributes array, and an attributes array.

Currently, the only value that can be found in the attributes array is the Code structure, which provides the information needed to properly execute the specified method. To facilitate this, the Code structure provides the following information.

Contained in the first 2 bytes is attribute_name_index, which provides an index into the constant_pool identifying the attribute as a Code structure.

The next 2 bytes, named attribute_length, provide the length of the Code structure, not including attribute_name_index.

Actual Code-specific information begins with the next three 4-byte fields, followed by the method's operation code (opcode). max_stack contains the maximum number of entries on the operand stack during the methods execution. max_locals specifies the total number of local variables for the method. code_length is the total length of the next field, the code field containing opcode.

After the code field, the Code structure provides detailed exception information for the method. This starts with exception_table_length and exception_table, which describe each exception handler in the method code. start_pc, end_pc, and handler_pc give the starting and ending positions in which the event handler, pointed to by handler_pc, is active. catch_type, which follows handler_pc, denotes the type of exception handled.

The remainder of the Code structure is devoted to information that is used for debugging purposes.

line_number is the 2-byte line number of the method's first line of code.

LocalVariableTable_attribute contains a structure used by the debugger to determine the value of local variables. The structure consists of three 1-byte values and a local_variable_table structure.

The first two fields of the structure, `attribute_name_index` and `attribute_length`, are used to describe the structure. The third contains the length of the `local_variable_table`.

`local_variable_table` contains the following five 2-byte fields, in order: `start_pc`, `length`, `name_index`, `signature_index`, and `slot`.

`start_pc` and `length` denote the offset where the variable value can be found.

`name_index` and `signature_index` are indexes into `constant_pool`, where the variable's name and signature can be found.

`slot` denotes the position in the local method frame where the variable can be found.

attributes

`attributes_count` is the size of the `attributes` array containing attribute structure. Currently, the only attribute structure is the `SourceFile` structure.

The `SourceFile` structure consists of three 2-byte values. `attribute_name_index` indexes into `constant_pool` to the entry containing the string `SourceFile`. `attribute_length` must contain a value of `2`. `sourcefile_index` indexes into the `constant_pool` to the entry containing the source filename.

Virtual Machine Architecture

The Java virtual machine's architecture revolves around the concept of non-machine–specific implementation. It assumes no specific platform architecture, but it does require certain facilities:

- Registers
- Stack
- Garbage-collected heap
- Method area
- Instruction set

Whether these facilities exist in hardware or software makes no difference to the JVM. As long as they exist, the JVM can function correctly.

JVM Registers

The registers serve the same purpose as normal microprocessors' register devices, the main difference being the functions provided by each register. JVM is a stack-based machine, meaning it does not define registers for the passing of variables and instructions. This was a conscious decision when designing the JVM, and the result is a model requiring fewer registers. These registers are as follows:

- `pc`—The `pc` register is a 32-bit–wide program counter.
- `optop`—`optop` maintains a pointer to the top of the operation stack. Like all JVM registers, `optop` is 32 bits wide.
- `frame`—`frame` provides a pointer to the current stack frame from which the JVM can retrieve needed operands or opcode for the maintenance of the stack.
- `vars`—`vars` points to the base offset of the local variable in the current stack frame. Through this mechanism, the JVM has read access to all local variables.

JVM Stack

The Java stack is a 32-bit model used to supply the JVM with needed operation data as well as store return values. Like normal programming languages, the stack is broken into separate stack frames, containing information about the method associated with the frame. The Java stack frame comprises three separate regions:

- Local variable—The local variable region of the method frame provides the `vars` register with a base reference to access the local variables. All local variables are 32 bits wide; 64-bit variables occupy two variable entries.
- Execution environment—The execution environment region of the stack frame is used to provide code for the maintenance of the method's stack frame. It also maintains pointers to the local variables, a pointer to the previous stack frame, and a pointer to the top and bottom of the current frame's operand region.
- Operand stack—The operand stack region contains the operands for the current method.

Garbage-Collected Heap

All objects are allocated from the garbage-collection heap. The heap is also responsible for performing garbage collection, due primarily to the fact that Java does not allow the programmer to deallocate space. The JVM does not assume any method of garbage collection.

Method Area

The method area contains the binary method retrieved from the `methods` section of the class file. This includes the method's code as well as all symbol information.

Instruction Set

The instruction set is the set of operation codes that are executed by the JVM. When Java source code is compiled, the compiler converts the Java source code into the language of the JVM, the instruction set.

The JVM instruction set is currently comprised of more than 160 instructions held in an 8-bit field. The JVM will pop operands off the stack and push the result back onto the stack for some operations. If the operands are greater than 8 bits, the JVM uses the big-endian encoding scheme to pack the value into its 8-bit instruction alignment.

Because the JVM instruction set is 160 operations, the following sections break them down into categories for quicker reference.

Pushing Constants onto the Stack

The instructions introduced in this section are used to push constants onto the stack. In all these instructions, if the value pushed onto the stack is less than 32 bits, the value is expanded into a 32-bit form to fit properly onto the stack:

- `bipush` *`byte`* pushes *`byte`* onto the stack as a 1-byte signed integer.
- `sipush` *`byte1 byte2`* pushes *`byte1`* and *`byte2`* onto the stack as a 2-byte signed integer.
- `ldc1` *`index`* pushes `constant_pool[`*`index`*`]` value onto the stack.
- `ldc2` *`index1 index2`* constructs a 2-byte index into the `constant_pool` and pushes the value onto the stack.
- `ldc2w` *`index1 index2`* constructs a 2-byte index into the `constant_pool` and pushes the `long` or `double` values onto the stack. Because the stack is 32 bits wide, the value will occupy two locations.
- `aconst_null` pushes a `NULL` constant onto the stack.
- `iconst_m1` pushes a value -1 integer constant onto the stack.
- `iconst_0` pushes a value 3 integer constant onto the stack.
- `iconst_1` pushes a value 4 integer constant onto the stack.
- `iconst_2` pushes a value 5 integer constant onto the stack.
- `iconst_4` pushes a value 6 integer constant onto the stack.
- `iconst_5` pushes a value 8 integer constant onto the stack.
- `lconst_0` pushes a value 9 `long` constant onto the stack.
- `lconst_1` pushes a value 10 `long` constant onto the stack.
- `fconst_0` pushes a value 11 `float` constant onto the stack.

- `fconst_1` pushes a value 12 `float` constant onto the stack.
- `fconst_2` pushes a value 13 `float` constant onto the stack.
- `dconst_0` pushes a value 14 `double` constant onto the stack.
- `dconst_1` pushes a value 15 `double` constant onto the stack.

Pushing Local Variables onto the Stack

In a stack-based computer, multiple registers are replaced by a stack register from which operands are popped off as needed and results are pushed on as generated. The following instructions store a method's local variables onto the stack for later use:

- `iload` *`byte`* retrieves the integer value at the *`byte`* position in the local variable array of the current stack frame. Once retrieved, the variable is pushed onto the stack.
- `iload_0` retrieves the integer value at the 26th position in the local variable array of the current stack frame. Once retrieved, the variable is pushed onto the stack.
- `iload_1` retrieves the integer value at the 27th position in the local variable array of the current stack frame. Once retrieved, the variable is pushed onto the stack.
- `iload_2` retrieves the integer value at the 28th position in the local variable array of the current stack frame. Once retrieved, the variable is pushed onto the stack.
- `iload_3` retrieves the integer value at the 29th position in the local variable array of the current stack frame. Once retrieved, the variable is pushed onto the stack.
- `lload` *`byte`* retrieves the `long` value at the *`byte`* and *`byte`*`+1` positions in the local variable array of the current stack frame. Once retrieved, the values are assembled and pushed onto the stack.
- `lload_0` retrieves the `long` value at the 30th and 31st positions in the local variable array of the current stack frame. Once retrieved, the values are assembled and pushed onto the stack.
- `lload_1` retrieves the `long` value at the 31st and 32nd positions in the local variable array of the current stack frame. Once retrieved, the values are assembled and pushed onto the stack.
- `lload_2` retrieves the `long` value at the 32nd and 33rd positions in the local variable array of the current stack frame. Once retrieved, the values are assembled and pushed onto the stack.
- `lload_3` retrieves the `long` value at the 33rd and 34th positions in the local variable array of the current stack frame. Once retrieved, the values are assembled and pushed onto the stack.
- `fload` *`byte`* retrieves the `float` value at the *`byte`* position in the local variable array of the current stack frame. Once retrieved, the variable is pushed onto the stack.

- `fload_0` retrieves the `float` value at the 34th position in the local variable array of the current stack frame. Once retrieved, the variable is pushed onto the stack.
- `fload_1` retrieves the `float` value at the 35th position in the local variable array of the current stack frame. Once retrieved, the variable is pushed onto the stack.
- `fload_2` retrieves the `float` value at the 36th position in the local variable array of the current stack frame. Once retrieved, the variable is pushed onto the stack.
- `fload_3` retrieves the integer value at the 37th position in the local variable array of the current stack frame. Once retrieved, the variable is pushed onto the stack.
- `dload` *`byte`* retrieves the `double` value at the *`byte`* and *`byte+1`* positions in the local variable array of the current stack frame. Once retrieved, the values are assembled and pushed onto the stack.
- `dload_0` retrieves the `double` value at the 38th and 39th positions in the local variable array inside the current stack frame. Once retrieved, the values are assembled and pushed onto the stack.
- `dload_1` retrieves the `double` value at the 39th and 40th positions in the local variable array inside the current stack frame. Once retrieved, the values are assembled and pushed onto the stack.
- `dload_2` retrieves the `double` value at the 40th and 41st positions in the local variable array inside the current stack frame. Once retrieved, the values are assembled and pushed onto the stack.
- `lload_3` retrieves the `double` value at the 41st and 42nd positions in the local variable array inside the current stack frame. Once retrieved, the values are assembled and pushed onto the stack.
- `aload` *`byte`* retrieves the object or array at the *`byte`* position in the local variable array of the current stack frame. Once retrieved, the object or array is pushed onto the stack.
- `aload_0` retrieves the object or array at the 42nd position in the local variable array of the current stack frame. Once retrieved, the object or array is pushed onto the stack.
- `aload_1` retrieves the object or array at the 43rd position in the local variable array of the current stack frame. Once retrieved, the object or array is pushed onto the stack.
- `aload_2` retrieves the object or array at the 44th position in the local variable array of the current stack frame. Once retrieved, the object or array is pushed onto the stack.
- `aload_3` retrieves the object or array at the 45th position in the local variable array of the current stack frame. Once retrieved, the object or array is pushed onto the stack.

Storing Stack Values into Local Variables

As described earlier, each method frame has a local variable region. When the method comes to the top of the stack, the base offset of the local variable gets placed into the `vars` register.

These instructions provide methods for storing information into the local variables of the current stack frame:

- `istore` *`index value`* stores the integer `value` at the *`index`* position in the local variable array of the current stack frame.
- `istore_0` *`value`* stores the integer `value` at the 59th position in the local variable array of the current stack frame.
- `istore_1` *`value`* stores the integer `value` at the 60th position in the local variable array of the current stack frame.
- `istore_2` *`value`* stores the integer `value` at the 61st position in the local variable array of the current stack frame.
- `istore_3` *`value`* stores the integer `value` at the 62nd position in the local variable array of the current stack frame. Once retrieved, the variable is pushed onto the stack.
- `lstore` *`index value`* stores the `long value` at the *`index`* and *`index+1`* positions in the local variable array of the current stack frame.
- `lstore_0` *`value`* stores the `long value` at the 63rd and 64th positions in the local variable array of the current stack frame.
- `lstore_1` *`value`* stores the `long value` at the 64th and 65th positions in the local variable array of the current stack frame.
- `lstore_2` *`value`* stores the `long value` at the 65th and 66th positions in the local variable array of the current stack frame.
- `lstore_3` *`value`* stores the `long value` at the 66th and 67th positions in the local variable array of the current stack frame.
- `fstore` *`index value`* stores the `float value` at the *`byte`* position in the local variable array of the current stack frame.
- `fstore_0` *`value`* stores the `float value` at the 67th position in the local variable array of the current stack frame.
- `fstore_1` *`value`* stores the `float value` at the 68th position in the local variable array of the current stack frame.
- `fstore_2` *`value`* stores the `float value` at the 69th position in the local variable array of the current stack frame.
- `fstore_3` *`value`* stores the `float value` at the 70th position in the local variable array of the current stack frame.
- `dstore` *`index value`* stores the `double value` at the *`index`* and *`index+1`* positions in the local variable array of the current stack frame.
- `dstore_0` *`value`* stores the `double value` at the 71st and 72nd positions in the local variable array of the current stack frame.
- `dstore_1` *`value`* stores the `double value` at the 72nd and 73rd positions in the local variable array of the current stack frame.

- `dstore_2` *`value`* stores the `double` `value` at the 73rd and 74th positions in the local variable array of the current stack frame.
- `dstore_3` *`value`* stores the `double` `value` at the 74th and 75th positions in the local variable array of the current stack frame.
- `astore` *`index`* *`value`* stores an object or array of `value` at the *`index`* position in the local variable array of the current stack frame.
- `astore_0` *`value`* stores an object or array of `value` at the 75th position in the local variable array of the current stack frame.
- `astore_1` *`value`* stores an object or array of `value` at the 76th position in the local variable array of the current stack frame.
- `astore_2` *`value`* stores an object or array of `value` at the 77th position in the local variable array of the current stack frame.
- `astore_3` *`value`* stores an object or array of `value` at the 78th position in the local variable array of the current stack frame.
- `iinc` *`index`* *`const`* increments the value stored at the *`index`* position in the local variable array of the current stack frame by a value of *`const`*.

Managing Arrays

The garbage-collection heap is responsible for the allocation and deallocation of referenced data. The following instructions allocate, deallocate, and store data to the garbage-collection heap:

- `newarray` *`type`* *`size`* allocates a new array of *`size`* to hold the variable type specified by the *`type`* parameter. Table 37.3 lists the variable types specified by the `type` parameter.

Table 37.3. Variable types specified by the `type` parameter.

Variable Type	*Value*
T_ARRAY	0x0001
T_BOOLEAN	0x0004
T_CHAR	0x0005
T_FLOAT	0x0006
T_DOUBLE	0x0007
T_BYTE	0x0008
T_SHORT	0x0009
T_INT	0x000A
T_LONG	0x000B

- `anewarray` *`byte1 byte2 size`* creates a new array with a length of `size`, of the class type referenced by the position in the `constant_pool`, and indexed by the 2-byte index constructed from *`byte1`* and *`byte2`*. The handle of the created stack is passed back on the stack.
- `multianewarray` *`byte1 byte2 dimension`* creates a multidimensional array from the information retrieved. *`byte1`* and *`byte2`* are used to construct an index into the `constant_pool` referencing the type of array to create. *`dimension`* is the dimension of the array to create—the actual size of each dimension is popped off the stack. The handle of the created stack is passed back on the stack.
- `arraylength` *`handle`* returns the size of the array referenced by the supplied array handle.
- `iaload` *`handle index`* returns the integer at the *`index`* position of the array referenced by the array *`handle`*.
- `laload` *`handle index`* returns the `long` at the *`index`* position of the array referenced by the array *`handle`*.
- `faload` *`handle index`* returns the `float` at the *`index`* position of the array referenced by the array *`handle`*.
- `daload` *`handle index`* returns the `double` at the *`index`* position of the array referenced by the array *`handle`*.
- `aaload` *`handle index`* returns the object at the *`index`* position of the array referenced by the array *`handle`*.
- `caload` *`handle index`* returns the character at the *`index`* position of the array referenced by the array *`handle`*.
- `saload` *`handle index`* returns the short at the *`index`* position of the array referenced by the array *`handle`*.
- `iastore` *`handle index value`* stores the integer `value` at the *`index`* position of the array referenced by the array *`handle`*.
- `lastore` *`handle index value`* stores the `long` `value` at the *`index`* position of the array referenced by the array *`handle`*.
- `fastore` *`handle index value`* stores the `float` `value` at the *`index`* position of the array referenced by the array *`handle`*.
- `dastore` *`handle index value`* stores the `double` `value` at the *`index`* position of the array referenced by the array *`handle`*.
- `aastore` *`handle index value_handle`* stores the object `value_`*`handle`* at the *`index`* position of the array referenced by the array *`handle`*.
- `bastore` *`handle index value`* stores the signed byte `value` at the *`index`* position of the array referenced by the array *`handle`*.

- `castore` *`handle index value`* stores the character `value` at the *`index`* position of the array referenced by the array *`handle`*.
- `sastore` *`handle index value`* stores the short `value` at the *`index`* position of the array referenced by the array *`handle`*.

Stack Instructions

With the existence of any stack, there must be some fundamental operations to operate the stack. The following instructions do just that:

- `nop` has no effect; it leaves the current stack state unchanged.
- `pop` pops the top word off the stack.
- `pop2` pops the top two words off the stack.
- `dup` copies the top stack word and places it on the stack.
- `dup2` copies the top two stack words and places them on the stack.
- `dup_x1` copies the top stack word and places the value two words down in the stack.
- `dup2_x1` copies the top two stack words and places the values two words down in the stack.
- `dup_x2` copies the top stack word and places the value three words down in the stack.
- `dup2_x2` copies the top two stack words and places the values three words down in the stack.
- `swap` swaps the position of the top two stack words. The word on top becomes the second to the top, and the word second from the top becomes the new top word.

Arithmetic Instructions

All computers need to function as a calculator at some point. The capability to do fundamental computations is inherent to all computing devices, and the JVM is no exception. The following instructions provide the JVM with arithmetic operations:

- `iadd` pops off the top two integers on the stack and replaces them with the sum of the two values.
- `ladd` pops off the top two positions on the stack to create a `long` value. Then the next two are popped off to create the second `long` value. The sum of the two values is then pushed onto the stack.
- `fadd` pops off the top two floats on the stack and replaces them with the sum of the two values.
- `dadd` pops off the top two positions on the stack to create a `double` value. Then the next two are popped off to create the second `double` value. The sum of the two values is then pushed onto the stack.

- `isub` pops off the top two integers on the stack and replaces them with the first value minus the second.
- `lsub` pops off the top two positions on the stack to create a `long` value. Then the next two are popped off to create the second `long` value. The result of the first value minus the second is then pushed onto the stack.
- `fsub` pops off the top two `floats` from the stack and replaces them with the first value minus the second.
- `dsub` pops off the top two positions from the stack to create a `double` value. Then the next two are popped off to create the second `double` value. The result of the first value minus the second is then pushed onto the stack.
- `imul` pops off the top two integers from the stack and replaces them with the top two positions on the stack, which are popped off to create a `long` value. Then the next two are popped off to create the second `long` value. The product of the two values is then pushed onto the stack.
- `fmul` pops off the top two `floats` from the stack and replaces them with the product of the two values.
- `dmul` pops off the top two positions on the stack to create a `double` value. Then the next two are popped off to create the second `double` value. The product of the two values is then pushed onto the stack.
- `idiv` pops off the top two integers from the stack and replaces them with the first value minus the second.
- `ldiv` pops off the top two positions on the stack to create a `long` value. Then the next two are popped off to create the second `long` value. The result of the first value divided by the second is then pushed onto the stack.
- `fdiv` pops off the top two `floats` from the stack and replaces them with the first value divided by the second.
- `ddiv` pops off the top two positions on the stack to create a `double` value. Then the next two are popped off to create the second `double` value. The result of the first value divided by the second is then pushed onto the stack.
- `imod` pops off the top two integers from the stack and replaces them with the first value modulus the second.
- `lmod` pops off the top two positions on the stack to create a `long` value. Then the next two are popped off to create the second `long` value. The result of the first value modulus the second is then pushed onto the stack.
- `fmod` pops off the top two `floats` from the stack and replaces them with the first value modulus the second.
- `ddiv` pops off the top two positions on the stack to create a `double` value. Then the next two are popped off to create the second `double` value. The result of the first value modulus the second is then pushed onto the stack.

- `ineg` pops off the top integer from the stack and replaces it with the negated value.
- `lneg` pops off the top two positions on the stack to create a `long` value. The negated value is pushed onto the stack.
- `fneg` pops off the top `float` from the stack and replaces it with a negated value.
- `dneg` pops off the top two positions on the stack to create a `double` value. The negated value is pushed onto the stack.

Logical Instructions

The following instructions implement logical operations:

- `ishl` shifts the value at the top of the stack to the left by the amount indicated by the low 5 bits of the second stack value. The result is then placed on the stack.
- `ishr` shifts the value at the top of the stack to the left by the amount indicated by the low 5 bits of the second stack value while retaining the sign extension. The result is then placed on the stack.
- `iushr` shifts the value at the top of the stack to the left by the amount indicated by the low 5 bits of the second stack value without retaining the sign extension. The result is then placed on the stack.
- `lshl` assembles the top two values at the top of the stack to create a `long` value. The value is then shifted left by the amount indicated by the low 6 bits of the third stack value. The result is then placed on the stack.
- `lshr` assembles the top two values at the top of the stack to create a `long` value. The value is then shifted right by the amount indicated by the low 6 bits of the third stack value while retaining the sign extension. The result is then placed on the stack.
- `lshur` assembles the top two values at the top of the stack to create a `long` value. The value is then shifted right by the amount indicated by the low 6 bits of the third stack value without retaining the sign extension. The result is then placed on the stack.
- `iand` performs a logical `AND` of the top integer value on the stack with the next value. The result is then pushed onto the stack.
- `land` assembles the top two values on the stack into a `long` value, and then assembles the second two into a `long` value. The result forms a logical `AND` of the two values and is then pushed onto the stack.
- `ior` `OR`s the top integer value on the stack with the next value. The result is then pushed onto the stack.
- `lor` assembles the top two values on the stack into a `long` value, and then assembles the second two into a `long` value. The result from a logical `OR` of the two values is then pushed onto the stack.

- `ixor` exclusive `OR`s the top integer value on the stack with the next value. The result is then pushed onto the stack.
- `lxor` assembles the top two values on the stack into a `long` value, and then assembles the second two into a `long` value. The result forms a logical exclusive `OR` of the two values and is then pushed onto the stack.

Conversion Operations

The following instructions provide the capability to convert data types:

- `i2l` converts the integer value at the top of the stack into a `long` value. The result is then pushed onto the stack.
- `i2f` converts the integer value at the top of the stack into a `float` value. The result is then pushed onto the stack.
- `i2d` converts the integer value at the top of the stack into a `double` value. The result is then pushed onto the stack.
- `l2i` assembles the top two values on the stack into a `long` value that is then converted to an integer value and pushed onto the stack.
- `l2f` assembles the top two values on the stack into a `long` value that is then converted to a `float` value and pushed onto the stack.
- `l2d` assembles the top two values on the stack into a `long` value that is then converted to a `double` value and pushed onto the stack.
- `f2i` converts the `float` value at the top of the stack into an integer value. The result is then pushed onto the stack.
- `f2l` converts the `float` value at the top of the stack into a `long` value. The result is then pushed onto the stack.
- `f2d` converts the `float` value at the top of the stack into a `double` value. The result is then pushed onto the stack.
- `d2i` assembles the top two values on the stack into a `double` value that is then converted to an integer value and pushed onto the stack.
- `d2l` assembles the top two values on the stack into a `double` value that is then converted to a `long` value and pushed onto the stack.
- `d2f` assembles the top two values on the stack into a `double` value that is then converted to a `float` value and pushed onto the stack.
- `int2byte` converts the integer value at the top of the stack into a `byte` value. The result is then pushed onto the stack.

- `int2char` converts the integer value at the top of the stack into a `char` value. The result is then pushed onto the stack.
- `int2short` converts the integer value at the top of the stack into a `short` value. The result is then pushed onto the stack.

Control Transfer Instructions

Conditional statements allow the computer to execute `boolean` logic. In doing so, they give the computer the capability to make simple decisions based on a true-or-false comparison. The following instructions support conditional decisions and alter program flow of control:

- `ifeq`—If the value at the top of the stack is equal to 0, the next two values are used to create a signed 16-bit offset from which execution will proceed.
- `iflt`—If the value at the top of the stack is less than 0, the next two values are used to create a signed 16-bit offset from which execution will proceed.
- `ifle`—If the value at the top of the stack is less than or equal to 0, the next two values are used to create a signed 16-bit offset from which execution will proceed.
- `ifne`—If the value at the top of the stack is not equal to 0, the next two values are used to create a signed 16-bit offset from which execution will proceed.
- `ifgt`—If the value at the top of the stack is greater than 0, the next two values are used to create a signed 16-bit offset from which execution will proceed.
- `if_icmpeq`—The two topmost integer values are compared. If the values are equal, the next two values are used to create a signed 16-bit offset from which execution will proceed.
- `if_icmpne`—The two topmost integer values are compared. If the values are not equal, the next two values are used to create a signed 16-bit offset from which execution will proceed.
- `if_icmplt`—The two topmost integer values are compared. If the first value is less than the second, the next two values are used to create a signed 16-bit offset from which execution will proceed.
- `if_icmple`—The two topmost integer values are compared. If the first value is less than or equal to the second, the next two values are used to create a signed 16-bit offset from which execution will proceed.
- `if_icmpgt`—The two topmost integer values are compared. If the first value is greater than the second, the next two values are used to create a signed 16-bit offset from which execution will proceed.
- `if_icmpge`—The two topmost integer values are compared. If the first value is greater than or equal to the second, the next two values are used to create a signed 16-bit offset from which execution will proceed.

- `lcmp`—The top two values on the stack are assembled into a `long` value that is compared with the next assembled `long` value on the stack. If the first value is greater than the second, the value of `1` is pushed onto the stack. Otherwise, if the first value is equal to the second, the value of `0` is pushed onto the stack. Otherwise, the value of `-1` is pushed onto the stack.
- `fcmpl`—The top two `float` values on the stack are compared. If the first value is greater than the second, the value of `1` is pushed onto the stack. Otherwise, if the first value is equal to the second, the value of `0` is pushed onto the stack. Otherwise, the value of `-1` is pushed onto the stack. If the values are incompatible, a value of `-1` is pushed onto the stack.
- `fcmpg`—The same as `fcmpl` except that if the types are incompatible, a value of `1` is pushed onto the stack.
- `dcmpl`—The top two `double` values on the stack are assembled and compared. If the first value is greater than the second, the value of `1` is pushed onto the stack. If the first value is equal to the second, the value of `0` is pushed onto the stack. Otherwise, the value of `-1` is pushed onto the stack. If the values are incompatible, a value of `-1` is pushed onto the stack.
- `dcmpg`—The same as `dcmpl` except if the types are incompatible, a value of `1` is pushed onto the stack.
- `if_acmpeq`—The two topmost object handles are compared. If the first reference object is equal to the second, the next two values are used to create a signed 16-bit offset from which execution will proceed. Otherwise, execution will continue.
- `if_acmpne`—The two topmost object handles are compared. If the first reference object is not equal to the second, the next two values are used to create a signed 16-bit offset from which execution will proceed. Otherwise, execution will continue.
- `goto`—The next two values are used to create a signed 16-bit offset from which execution will proceed.
- `jsr`—The next two values are used to create a signed 16-bit offset from which execution will proceed. All opcodes following the `jsr` will be pushed onto the stack.
- `ret`—The next value on the stack is used as an index into the local variables to retrieve the offset from which execution will continue.

Function Return Instructions

The following instructions are used to return a value from a function call:

- `ireturn` returns an `integer` value from a function call.
- `lreturn` returns a `long` value from a function call.
- `freturn` returns a `float` value from a function call.

- `dreturn` returns a `double` value from a function call.
- `areturn` returns an object reference from a function call.
- `return` returns from a function call without returning a value.

After the value has been returned, the JVM begins execution of the line following the function call. The value returned is then the top element(s) of the stack.

Table Jumping Instructions

The jump table stores the offset information when the program execution jumps to a non-sequential location. This information allows the program to resume execution at the next logical offset. The program jump is achieved by adding the new opcode offset to the current `pc` value. The following instructions provide the capability to jump to locations in the table:

- `tableswitch` uses the top integer value of the stack as a table index. If the index is not in the current range of the jump table, the program will jump by the default offset. If the index is in the valid range, the offset is extracted from the table and is used to determine the next instruction to be executed.
- `lookupswitch` functions the same as `tableswitch`, except the integer value at the top of the stack is the key value to be found in the table, rather than the index.

Manipulating Object Fields

The following instructions provide the capability to access and modify members of an object:

- `putfield` *`byte1 byte2`*—The values of `byte1` and `byte2` form an index into the `constant_pool`. The indexed value holds the class and field name of the member to change. From that information, the location of the member is found and the value at the top of the stack is stored into that location.
- `getstatic` *`byte1 byte2`*—The values of `byte1` and `byte2` form an index into the `constant_pool`. The indexed value holds the class and field name of the static member to change. From that information, the member location is found and pushed onto the top of the stack.
- `putfstatic` *`byte1 byte2`*—The values of `byte1` and `byte2` form an index into the `constant_pool`. The indexed value holds the class and field name of the static member to change. From that information, the member location is found and the value at the top of the stack is stored into that location.
- `getfield` *`byte1 byte2`*—The values of `byte1` and `byte2` form an index into the `constant_pool`. The indexed value holds the class and field name of the member to change. From that information, the member location is found and pushed onto the top of the stack.

Method Invocation

The following instructions provide the capability to execute a method of an object:

- `invokevirtual` *byte1 byte2*—The values of `byte1` and `byte2` make an index into the `constant_pool`. The referenced value is used to find the offset of the method to execute. The stack is assumed to contain the number of arguments to be passed to the method.
- `invokestatic` *byte1 byte2*—The values of `byte1` and `byte2` make an index into the `constant_pool`. The referenced value is used to find the offset of the method to execute. The method type is assumed to be native or synchronized. If the method is synchronized, the associated monitor will be executed. The stack is assumed to contain the number of arguments to be passed to the method.
- `invokeinterface` *byte1 byte2*—The values of `byte1` and `byte2` make an index into the `constant_pool`. The referenced value is used to find the offset of the interface to execute. The method type is assumed to be native or synchronized. If the method is synchronized, the associated monitor will be executed. The stack is assumed to contain the number of arguments to be passed to the method.

Exception Handling

The `athrow` instruction implements Java exception handling capabilities:

- `athrow`—The top exception object on the stack is thrown. The current method frame is searched for the nearest catch. If none is found, the classes are then seated for a handler. If none of the above is found, the JVM default handler is executed.

Object Utility Operations

The following instructions provide some object operations that don't fall into any other category:

- `new` *byte1 byte2* creates a new object of the type referenced by the position in the `constant_pool`, indexed by the 2-byte index constructed from *byte1* and *byte2*.
- `checkcast` *byte1 byte2* checks that the type, resolved by constructing the class's string name index into the `constant_pool`, is compatible to the object handle at the top of the stack. If the objects are a proper cast, execution continues and the handle remains on the stack. If they are incompatible, the `ClassCastException` is thrown.
- `newfromname` *byte1 byte2* creates a new object of the type referenced by the position in the `constant_pool`, indexed by the 2-byte index constructed from *byte1* and *byte2*.
- `instanceof` *byte1 byte2* checks to see if an object is an instance of a particular type.
- `verifystack` checks to see if the operand stack is empty. If not, it will be after this call. This instruction is generated only by a compiler that is generating debug information.

Monitors

Due to the multithreaded nature of the JVM, there is a great need for a mechanism to access shared memory resources. The following instructions provide the capability to lock and unlock a memory object:

- `monitorenter` locks the object handle at the top of the stack until the current process releases the resource.
- `monitorexit` releases the object handle at the top of the stack.

The `breakpoint` Instruction

The `breakpoint` instruction calls the breakpoint handler to notify the debugger of a breakpoint.

Summary

This chapter diagrams the internals of a `.class` file, discusses the JVM architecture, and provides insight into the JVM instruction set.

38

Creating Native Methods

by Cary Jardin

In this chapter you'll learn how to access native C code from Java. You will see how to use the supplied tools to create a dynamic link library (DLL), which the Java runtime interpreter can call to perform native functions. When you finish this chapter, you will be able to link your Java code with native C methods.

Using Native Methods

The Java programming language has gone to great lengths to hide machine-specific facilities from the programmer.

However, regardless of the reason, there might always be a need to access the raw speed or other platform-specific facilities. To accommodate this need, Java provides access to native code stored in dynamic link libraries.

When Java code is executed on a machine other than a native Java microprocessor, a runtime interpreter is needed. The interpreter is actually the program that executes the Java code. So to allow the Java code access to native methods, the interpreter must act as the go-between for the two platforms. This is achieved by standard entry points defined in native DLLs.

How Native Methods Are Called

In the big picture of accessing native methods, calling native methods from Java is one of the most straightforward processes. The task of calling the native method can be broken down into three steps, all of which need to be implemented in order for the native call to work:

1. Loading the library
2. Declaring the method
3. Calling the method

The first step is to load the library. This is achieved through the `java.lang.Runtime` class, which handles all the overhead involved in dynamically linking to a DLL. The following example shows how this is done:

```
import java.lang.Runtime;
public class calcTC      //Calculates the two's
{                        //complement of a passed number.
  static
  {
    try
    {
       loadLibrary("nativeDLL");
    }
    catch(Exception e)
    {
```

```
        //Do Something here
      }
   }
   public native int twos(int number);
}
```

It is usually a good idea to call the `loadLibrary` method during the static initialization. This way the library is loaded before there's any chance of the method being called. If the `loadLibrary` method is unsuccessful, it will throw the `UnsatisfiedLinkError` exception. This provides a mechanism to replace the native method call.

The next step in calling a native method is to declare the method:

```
public native int twos(int number);
```

The `native` directive tells the compiler that this method is natively implemented. Besides the `native` directive, the method resembles a normal method declaration, except for the fact that code does not follow the declaration.

After the method has been declared, it can be called using Java's normal calling conventions. That's it from Java's standpoint. The rest of the work involves the creation of the DLL.

How Native Methods Are Created

As mentioned before, the Java runtime interpreter acts as the go-between for the Java code and the native DLL. In order to facilitate this communication, a common interface is needed.

Shipped with the Java Developer's Kit is a utility called `javah`, which is designed to create the interface with which the Java runtime interpreter can communicate. It accomplishes this by taking as a parameter the class file containing the native call. `javah` then produces a header file, and an associated C file is needed. The process to create a header and stub C file for the `calcTC` class are as follows.

Execute `javah` to create the header file:

```
javah calcTC
```

This command creates a file under the `CClassHeaders` directory named `calcTC.h`. This file contains the following header information:

```
/* Header for class calcTC */
#ifndef _Include_calcTC
#define _Include_calcTC
typedef struct ClasscalcTC{
    int number;
} ClasscalcTC;
HandleTo(calcTc);
#ifdef __cplusplus
extern "C" __declspec(dllexport)
```

```
#endif
int clacTC_twos(struct HcalcTC *,int);
#endif
```

This file declares the interface with which the Java runtime interpreter can communicate.

The final step in creating the native DLL interface is to create a stub file containing some of the needed interface overhead. To create this stub file for the calcTC class, execute the following command:

```
javah -stubs calcTC
```

This creates the file calcTC.stubs in the subs subdirectory, which contains the following information:

```
/* Stubs for class calcTC */
/* DO NOT EDIT THIS FILE - it is machine generated*/
/* SYMBOL: "calcTC\twos(I)I", calcTC_twos_stub,*/
_declspec(dllexport) stack_item
*calcTC_twos_stub(stack_item *_P_,struct execenv *_EE_)
{
   extern int clacTC_twos(void *,int);
   _P_[0].i = calcTC_twos(_P_[0].p,((_P_[1].i)));
   return _P_+1;
}
```

calcTC.stubs, along with stubsPreamble.h (found in the /hotjava/include subdirectory), must preface the actual implementation of the native method. That is, you must include stubsPreamble.h and the header file created by the javah command. After the include statements, insert the contents of the stub file and the native method definition. For example, the code for the calcTC native DLL would be the following:

```
#include calcTC.h
#include stubsPreamble.h

//cut and paste the stub file

/* Stubs for class calcTC */
/* DO NOT EDIT THIS FILE - it is machine generated*/
/* SYMBOL: "calcTC\twos(I)I", calcTC_twos_stub,*/
_declspec(dllexport) stack_item
*calcTC_twos_stub(stack_item *_P_,struct execenv *_EE_)
{
   extern int clacTC_twos(void *,int);
   _P_[0].i = calcTC_twos(_P_[0].p,((_P_[1].i)));
   return _P_+1;
}

//implement the native method prot-typed in calcTC.h
int clacTC_twos(struct HcalcTC *this,int number)
{
   return ~number;
}
```

Compile this file into a DLL with the name specified in the `loadLibrary()` Java call, and you're ready to go. Got all that? If not, take a look at the steps involved again, as well as at what the generated code is doing. This process will become easier after you have successfully completed it at least once.

Summary

In this chapter you have learned how to call and create native methods. This is probably the hardest task in Java, because it requires tools outside the scope of Java. Use the technology at your discretion. Just keep in mind that native code will run only on the platform on which it was compiled. The fact that Java can call a function stored in a native DLL does not make the DLL more platform independent.

39

Java Security

In this chapter you'll learn about the security of Java applets and programs. You'll learn about the threats faced by those who use Java applets and programs and the security restrictions placed on Java applets. You'll cover the security features of the Java language, compiler, and runtime environment. You'll also explore the security mechanisms implemented by Java-enabled browsers. When you finish this chapter, you'll be aware of the security issues associated with Java applets and programs and of the ways Java and Java-enabled browsers resolve these issues.

Threats to Java Security

Those who use Java applets and programs face significant security threats. Information on their computers may be selectively altered, destroyed, or disclosed by those who develop Java applets and programs and those who have the ability to modify them. Damage may result from deliberately planned attacks on your system or from errors that are introduced into Java source or compiled code. Although the threat associated with inadvertent errors is far less than with malicious actions, it cannot be discounted. The damage resulting from instances of Murphy's Law often exceeds that of the most cunning hackers. However, this chapter examines all security threats as if they are the result of deliberate hostile actions.

The threat posed by a standalone Java program is the same as any other program that you run on your computer. When a program runs on your behalf, it has access to your files, system capabilities, and system resources, and can use this access to modify, delete, or compromise sensitive data or misuse these capabilities and resources. The program's access is limited only by the access controls enforced by your operating system or other security software. In most cases, these access controls are nonexistent or minimally effective. The danger of running a standalone Java program is the same as running any other program that you do not develop yourself. Unless you can verify the security of the program through rigorous analysis and testing, you are forced to trust the programs not to cause deliberate or inadvertent damage.

The level of trust that you place in a program is usually based on the source from which you obtained the program. You generally place more trust in programs that you receive from well-established software vendors than those that you download from obscure, publicly accessible file archives. Standalone Java programs provide no more or less security than any other programs you may encounter. They may be written to cause the same level of damage to your system as a program that is written in another programming language. Because of this unfortunate fact, the security of standalone Java programs is not explicitly considered in the remainder of this chapter.

The threat posed by Java applets expands the threat posed by standalone programs to the Web as a whole. Since Web pages may contain applets, scripts, and other types of embedded programming, clicking on a Web page is equivalent to executing a program. The increased danger associated with applets is the lack of control that you have over the programs you execute. Any Web page may bring an insidious intruder into your system. You may, of course, disable the execution of applets by your browser, but doing so eliminates all the potential benefits of Java.

Java Security Features

To counter the threat posed by those who would bring harm to your computer and to mitigate the risk associated with running applets, the developers of Java and Java-enabled browsers have included a powerful set of security features in the Java language, compiler, runtime system, and Web browsers. These security features include security mechanisms that have been specifically designed to eliminate potential security vulnerabilities; other mechanisms, although not intentionally designed for security purposes, encumber both deliberate and inadvertent security threats. The following sections describe these security features.

NOTE

This section and its subsections address the security issues associated with running applets that are loaded over a network. The same issues apply to applets that are loaded from a local file system, but the potential risks are somewhat lower. The intent is to deal with the worst-case scenario.

Language Security Features

A number of features have been incorporated into the Java language to make it more reliable and capable. Although these features may not have been driven by security concerns, they still help to minimize security risks. The most important of these features is the removal of all pointer-based operations from the Java language. The absence of pointers eliminates entire classes of security vulnerabilities related to memory browsing, the modification of memory-resident code, and illegal access to security-related objects.

Java's use of strong typing also contributes to security. All objects are associated with a well-defined type and cannot be freely converted from one type to another. Methods cannot be used with classes to which they do not apply. Methods cannot return objects of a type that is incompatible with their return type. Strong typing enforces the Java object-oriented approach and prevents numerous kinds of errors that could lead to security-related malfunctions.

Compiler Security Features

The Java compiler also provides features that support security. These features are implemented in the form of compiler checks that prevent errors and undesired actions.

The compiler enforces Java's strong typing by generating compilation errors for statements that violate the language's strong typing rules. It ensures that all methods are appropriate for the objects for which they are invoked.

The compiler checks array operations to make sure that they are valid for the array objects being acted on and that memory overrun errors do not occur. These checks are duplicated and extended by the runtime system.

The compiler checks all class, interface, variable, and method accesses to ensure that the accesses are consistent with the access modifiers used in their declaration. This prevents classes, interfaces, variables, and methods from being used in unintended ways and enforces the information hiding capabilities provided by the access modifiers.

The compiler generates code that treats `String` objects as constants and supports `String` operations through the `StringBuffer` class. This eliminates overrun errors that could cause in-memory modification of data or code.

The compiler also prevents uninitialized variables from being read and constants from being modified. These checks eliminate errors resulting from incorrect variable reading and writing.

Runtime Security Mechanisms

The Java runtime system is designed to prevent applets from modifying, deleting, or disclosing your files, accessing in-memory programs and data, and misusing network resources. This is accomplished by preventing applets from accessing files on your computer, not providing or disallowing services that enable control over other programs, data, or the host operating system, and restricting network connections to the host computer from which an applet is loaded. The specific security mechanisms that implement these controls are discussed in the following subsections.

Class Loader Security Checks

Applets are loaded over a network using a class loader. The class loader prevents classes that are loaded from the network from masquerading as or conflicting with classes that are resident on the local file system. This ensures that the security-critical classes of the Java API are not replaced by less trustworthy classes that are loaded over a network.

The class loader separates local and network-loaded classes by placing those classes from a particular network host into a name space that is unique to that host. This approach also keeps network-loaded classes from different hosts from conflicting with each other.

The Bytecode Verifier

The security of classes that are loaded over a network is verified using the bytecode verifier. The bytecode verifier checks that the loaded classes are correctly formed and that they do not have the capability to violate type and name space restrictions.

The verifier uses a mini theorem prover to prove that the `.class` file initially satisfies certain security constraints and that when it is executed it will always transition into states in which these security constraints are satisfied. This proof by induction verifies that basic security rules will be enforced throughout the execution of the `.class` file. The verifier proves that no illegal conversion between types can occur, that parameters are correct for the methods and instructions to which they apply, that stack operations do not cause overflows or underflows, that access modifiers are enforced, that no forged pointers can be created, and that register operations do not lead to errors.

Memory Management and Control

The memory locations of Java classes and objects are determined at runtime based on the platform hosting the runtime system and the current memory allocation maintained by the operating system. By performing memory layout decisions at runtime, the potential for inducing errors that cause memory overruns and lead to security malfunctions is greatly reduced. This is because it is very difficult to predict the memory locations at which objects will be stored during code execution. Without this knowledge, complex memory overrun attacks are thwarted.

The Java garbage collector reduces the likelihood that an applet or program may make mistakes in its management of memory resources. Since memory deallocation is automatically handled through the garbage collection process, errors resulting from multiple deallocation of the same memory area or failure to deallocate memory are avoided.

Runtime array bounds checking also reduces the likelihood that errors resulting in illegal memory accesses can occur. By confining array operations to valid array locations, these potential security-related errors are prevented.

Security Manager Checks

The Java security manager provides a central decision point for implementing Java security rules. This ensures that security access controls are implemented in a manageable and consistent manner. The `SecurityManager` class of the `java.lang` package may be overridden to implement a custom security policy for standalone Java programs such as those that load applets. A `SecurityManager` object cannot, however, be created, invoked, or accessed by a network-loaded applet. This prevents applets from modifying the security policy implemented by the runtime system's `SecurityManager` object.

The applet security policy implemented by the default `SecurityManager` object varies from one browser to another. Netscape Navigator 2.0 implements a security policy that enforces the following rules for applets that are loaded over a network:

- Applets cannot create or install a class loader or security manager.
- Applets cannot create classes in the local class name space.
- Applets cannot access local packages outside the standard packages of the Java API.
- Applets cannot access files and directories on the local system in any manner.

- Applets may establish network connections only to the host system from which they were loaded.
- Applets cannot create or install a content handler, protocol handler, or socket implementation.
- Applets cannot read system properties that provide information about a user.
- Applets cannot modify system properties.
- Applets cannot run other programs or load dynamic link libraries on the local system.
- Applets cannot terminate other programs or the runtime system.
- Applets cannot access threads or thread groups that are outside of their thread group.
- All windows created by an applet must be clearly labeled as being untrusted.

Staying Current with Java Security Issues

Keeping Java secure is an ongoing process. Several security flaws have been identified to date and it is reasonable to expect that new Java security flaws will continue to be found. Sun and Netscape have responded quickly to newly discovered security flaws, often releasing fixes within days. As new versions of Java are released and the Java API is expanded, new security flaws will most likely be introduced. To stay current with Java security issues, you should periodically review the FAQ on applet security maintained by JavaSoft. This FAQ contains the status of all known security-related bugs in Java and Java-enabled browsers. The FAQ is located at the URL `http://java.sun.com/sfaq/`. A source of information on general Java bugs in the JDK 1.0 release can be found at `http://www.javasoft.com/JDK-1.0/knownbugs.html`.

Summary

In this chapter you have learned about the security of Java applets and programs. You have learned about the threats faced by those who use Java applets and programs and the security restrictions placed on Java applets. You have covered the security features of the Java language, compiler, and runtime environment and explored the security mechanisms implemented by Java-enabled browsers. The next and final chapter examines Java platforms and extensions.

40

Java Platforms and Extensions

by Cary Jardin

This chapter takes a look at some of the emerging technologies in the Java world. The primary purpose of the chapter is to give you more insight into what is out there and how to find out more. After you have finished this chapter, you will have a greater awareness of developments in the Java world.

Java-Enabled Browsers

In the current Web browser arena there are a number of different Java-enabled choices. Although some may provide more features than others, this chapter covers only the browser's Java capability. Use this information only as a reference, and contact your vendor for any specific questions.

HotJava

HotJava is a Web browser coded in Java by Sun. It uses a modular approach to handling different MIME types and application protocols. HotJava is currently available on Windows 95, Windows NT, Macintosh PowerPC, and UNIX platforms.

For more information, contact `http://java.sun.com/HotJava/index.html`.

Netscape Navigator

Netscape currently has the largest market share of browsers in use. Conservative estimates show Netscape holding 70% of the market. Netscape's products are currently offered on a number of different platforms.

Netscape Navigator initially began incorporating Java as a browser plug-in. It is now an integral part of the browser that is shipped with release 2.0 and later. Netscape also adopted the JavaScript language into releases later than 2.0.

For more information, contact `http://www.netscape.com`.

Oracle PowerBrowser

The Oracle PowerBrowser provides a number of features such as an integrated Web server, authoring tools, and Java applet support. It also contains a few features that provide database access support. The current platforms supported are Windows, Windows 95, and Windows NT. PowerBrowser also contains its own scripting language, Oracle BASIC.

For more information, contact `http://www.oracle.com`.

Borland's Latte

The need for an Integrated Development Environment (IDE) will become apparent as the Java technology grows. Borland's first attempt at a native Java IDE is Latte.

Latte has begun to be integrated into the Borland C++ compiler utilities, very much like Symantec Espresso. The final product will be completely independent from Borland C++.

For more information, contact `http://www.borland.com/Product/java/qanda.html#latte`.

Visual Design

Latte provides the capability to visually represent the Java class hierarchy. Presumably, Latte will eventually provide a Java resource builder.

The Integrated Development Environment

The Integrated Development Environment provides the developer with ready access to an editor, a compiler, a debugger, and more. Latte will provide an IDE for Java development.

Performance Improvements

Latte's compiler claims to be faster and cleaner than Sun's `javac` compiler. That fact still remains to be proven. However, judging by the speed of the `javac` compiler, any performance increase would be greatly appreciated.

Symantec's Café

Symantec's version of the Java IDE began by integrating with the preexisting Symantec C++ IDE, called Symantec Espresso. Eventually, the product became completely disjointed from the C++ library and changed its name to Café.

Café claimed to do everything that Latte promised; however, Symantec delivered on its promises faster than Borland. As a result, Café hit the market before Latte, delivering a native Java code IDE and compiler that is a bit faster than `javac`.

For more information, contact `http://www.symantec.com`.

Database Extensions

Probably the most powerful Java database solution is Sun's JDBC (Java database connectivity). The JDBC is based on the X/Open SQL call-level interface (CLI), which is the same model used to design ODBC.

Via a class interface, Java applications can access database information through a SQL interface. By using an ODBC-type mechanism, the programmer will not have to worry about database-specific issues. Several companies have endorsed the JDBC.

For more information, contact `http://splash.javasoft.com/jdbc`.

VRML Extensions with Iced Java/Liquid Reality

VRML stands for Virtual Reality Modeling Language. VRML was designed as a standard to create 3D worlds. A VRML file contains all the object information needed to create a virtual world. In order for an application to display the virtual world defined in a VRML file, the application needs two components: a three-dimensional modeling engine and a VRML interpreter.

Three-Dimensional Modeling

One of the commercially available 3D modeling engine libraries for Java is called Iced Java. Iced Java, by Dimension X, provides Java with the capability to display and render 3D objects. Iced Java utilizes a native code engine to perform the actual 3D modeling and rendering, and an interface is provided to allow Java access to the engine.

Iced Java and Liquid Reality

As mentioned before, VRML is a language designed to create a virtual world. To facilitate the display of the VRML defined world, a 3D display engine must be teamed with a VRML interpreter. This is exactly what Dimension X did to create its Liquid Reality product. Iced Java is driven by Liquid Reality to generate the VRML-defined world.

For more information, contact `http://www.dimensionx.com`.

Summary

The Java products identified in this chapter represent only a small sample of the products that have been introduced at the time this book is being written. New platforms and extensions to Java will continue to be developed. For more information on Java and Java-related products, consult the author's Web page at `http://www.jaworski.com/java`.

VIII

Appendixes

A

The Java API Quick Reference

This appendix summarizes the classes and interfaces of the Java API. The eight packages of the Java API are presented in alphabetical order.

java.applet

The `java.applet` package provides the `Applet` class and the interfaces needed to support Java applets. It consists of a single `Applet` class and three interfaces that enable audio playing and applet integration within browsers.

Classes

Applet

The `Applet` class is a subclass of the `java.awt.Panel` class that is used to implement Java applets.

Interfaces

AppletContext

The `AppletContext` interface provides methods that allow an applet to interact with the context in which it is run, such as a browser, the applet viewer, or an application program.

AppletStub

The `AppletStub` interface provides methods that are used to implement programs that display an applet.

AudioClip

The `AudioClip` interface provides methods that are used to implement classes that support the playing of audio clips within applets.

java.awt

The `java.awt` package provides the classes that support Java window programming. This package is known as the Abstract Windowing Toolkit.

Classes

BorderLayout

The `BorderLayout` class is used to lay out the GUI objects contained within a `Container` object. It is the default layout for `Window`, `Frame`, and `Dialog` objects.

Button

The `Button` class implements a clickable button GUI control.

Canvas

The `Canvas` class implements a GUI object that supports drawing. Drawing is not implemented on the canvas itself, but on the `Graphics` object provided by the canvas.

CardLayout

The `CardLayout` class is used to lay out the objects in a `Container` object in the form similar to a deck of cards.

Checkbox

The `Checkbox` class is used to implement checkbox and radio button GUI controls.

CheckboxGroup

The `CheckboxGroup` class is used with the `Checkbox` class to implement radio buttons.

CheckboxMenuItem

The `CheckboxMenuItem` class is used to implement menu items that can be checked on or off.

Choice

The `Choice` class is used to implement pull-down lists that can be placed within the main area of a window.

Color

The `Color` class provides a system-independent color implementation and defines several color constants.

Component

The `Component` class is the superclass of all window GUI controls. It provides a common set of methods that support component organization, display, and event handling.

Container

The `Container` class is the superclass of window classes that contain other objects and provides a common set of methods to organize and display contained objects.

Dialog

The `Dialog` class is used to implement dialog box windows.

Dimension

The `Dimension` class is used to represent the width and height of a two-dimensional object.

Event

The `Event` class is used to encapsulate all events processed by Java window programs.

FileDialog

The `FileDialog` class is used to construct dialog boxes that support the selection of files for input and output operations.

FlowLayout

The `FlowLayout` class is used to lay out window `Container` objects. It is the default layout used with the `Panel` class.

Font

The `Font` class implements a system-independent set of fonts that control text display.

FontMetrics

The `FontMetrics` class is used to access the specific display properties of a `Font` class.

Frame

The `Frame` class is used to create and control the main application window of standalone Java window programs.

Graphics

The `Graphics` class supports the drawing of graphical objects and text within a window.

GridBagConstraints

The `GridBagConstraints` class is used to identify the positioning parameters of a component that is contained within an object that is laid out using the `GridBagLayout` class.

GridBagLayout

The `GridBagLayout` class allows a `Container` object to be laid out in a gridlike fashion with component objects occupying more than one row or column.

GridLayout

The `GridLayout` class is used to lay out a `Container` object in a grid where all elements of the grid are the same size.

Image

The `Image` class provides a content-independent mechanism for implementing graphical images.

Insets

The `Insets` class is used to specify the margins associated with a GUI object.

Label

The `Label` class is used to display text labels within a window or other GUI container.

List

The `List` class implements single- and multiple-selection list GUI controls.

MediaTracker

The `MediaTracker` class provides a set of methods for managing images used to implement multimedia objects.

Menu

The `Menu` class implements a single pull-down menu that is attached to a menu bar or other menu.

MenuBar

The `MenuBar` class implements a menu bar that is attached to the `Frame` object of a window program.

MenuComponent

The `MenuComponent` class is the superclass of all menu-related classes and provides a common set of methods used by its subclasses.

MenuItem

The `MenuItem` class is used to implement items that can be selected from a pull-down menu. It is extended by the `Menu` and `CheckboxMenuItem` classes.

Panel

The `Panel` class is used as a container to organize GUI components within a window. Its default layout is `FlowLayout`.

Point

The `Point` class is used to represent general, two-dimensional x,y-coordinates.

Polygon

The `Polygon` class represents a polygon as a list of x,y-coordinates that identify the polygon's vertices.

Rectangle

The `Rectangle` class represents a rectangle using the x,y-coordinate of its upper-left corner, its width, and height.

Scrollbar

The `Scrollbar` class is used to implement vertical and horizontal scrollbars.

TextArea

The `TextArea` class implements scrollable text-entry objects that span multiple lines and columns.

TextComponent

The `TextComponent` class is the superclass of all text-based classes. It provides a common set of methods used by the `TextArea` and `TextField` classes.

TextField

The `TextField` class implements a one-line text-entry field.

Toolkit

The `Toolkit` class provides the linkage between the common AWT supported by Java and the platform-dependent implementation of the AWT.

Window

The `Window` class is the superclass of all window-related classes and provides a common set of methods for organizing and displaying windows.

Interfaces

LayoutManager

The `LayoutManager` interface provides a set of methods that are implemented by classes that control the layout of a container.

MenuContainer

The `MenuContainer` class provides a set of methods that are implemented by classes that contain menus.

java.awt.image

The `java.awt.image` package defines classes and interfaces that support image generation, storage, and processing.

Classes

ColorModel

The `ColorModel` class provides a general framework for representing colors and maps this framework to the RGB color model.

CropImageFilter

The `CropImageFilter` class is used to crop images to a specified area.

DirectColorModel

The `DirectColorModel` class is used to directly access the color values of a pixel.

FilteredImageSource

The `FilteredImageSource` class provides the capability to filter an image using an object of class `ImageFilter`.

ImageFilter

The `ImageFilter` class provides a common set of methods for implementing an image filter.

IndexColorModel

The `IndexColorModel` class is a subclass of the `ColorModel` class that translates fixed colormap pixel values to their RGB component colors.

MemoryImageSource

The `MemoryImageSource` class is used to create images using an array of pixel values.

PixelGrabber

The `PixelGrabber` class is used to capture the pixels of an image and store them in an array.

RGBImageFilter

The `RGBImageFilter` class is used to create image filters that modify the pixels of the default RGB color model.

Interfaces

ImageConsumer

The `ImageConsumer` interface provides a set of methods for accessing image data provided by classes that implement the `ImageProducer` interface.

ImageObserver

The `ImageObserver` interface provides a set of constants and methods through which objects can be notified about an image that is being constructed.

ImageProducer

The `ImageProducer` interface provides a set of methods for classes that produce images. These methods are used to reconstruct or modify an image being produced.

java.awt.peer

The `java.awt.peer` package provides a set of interface definitions that map platform-independent AWT classes to their native platform-dependent implementations.

Classes

This package does not have any classes.

Interfaces

ButtonPeer

The `ButtonPeer` interface specifies the native methods that are required to support the implementation of the `java.awt.Button` class.

CanvasPeer

The `CanvasPeer` interface specifies the native methods that are required to support the implementation of the `java.awt.Canvas` class.

CheckboxMenuItemPeer

The `CheckboxMenuItemPeer` interface specifies the native methods that are required to support the implementation of the `java.awt.CheckboxMenuItem` class.

CheckboxPeer

The `CheckboxPeer` interface specifies the native methods that are required to support the implementation of the `java.awt.Checkbox` class.

ChoicePeer

The `ChoicePeer` interface specifies the native methods that are required to support the implementation of the `java.awt.Choice` class.

ComponentPeer

The `ComponentPeer` interface specifies the native methods that are required to support the implementation of the `java.awt.Component` class.

ContainerPeer

The `ContainerPeer` interface specifies the native methods that are required to support the implementation of the `java.awt.Container` class.

DialogPeer

The `DialogPeer` interface specifies the native methods that are required to support the implementation of the `java.awt.Dialog` class.

FileDialogPeer

The `FileDialogPeer` interface specifies the native methods that are required to support the implementation of the `java.awt.FileDialog` class.

FramePeer

The `FramePeer` interface specifies the native methods that are required to support the implementation of the `java.awt.Frame` class.

LabelPeer

The `LabelPeer` interface specifies the native methods that are required to support the implementation of the `java.awt.Label` class.

ListPeer

The `ListPeer` interface specifies the native methods that are required to support the implementation of the `java.awt.List` class.

MenuBarPeer

The `MenuBarPeer` interface specifies the native methods that are required to support the implementation of the `java.awt.MenuBar` class.

MenuComponentPeer

The `MenuComponentPeer` interface specifies the native methods that are required to support the implementation of the `java.awt.MenuComponent` class.

MenuItemPeer

The `MenuItemPeer` interface specifies the native methods that are required to support the implementation of the `java.awt.MenuItem` class.

MenuPeer

The `MenuPeer` interface specifies the native methods that are required to support the implementation of the `java.awt.Menu` class.

PanelPeer

The `PanelPeer` interface specifies the native methods that are required to support the implementation of the `java.awt.Panel` class.

ScrollbarPeer

The `ScrollbarPeer` interface specifies the native methods that are required to support the implementation of the `java.awt.Scrollbar` class.

TextAreaPeer

The `TextAreaPeer` interface specifies the native methods that are required to support the implementation of the `java.awt.TextArea` class.

TextComponentPeer

The `TextComponentPeer` interface specifies the native methods that are required to support the implementation of the `java.awt.TextComponent` class.

TextFieldPeer

The `TextFieldPeer` interface specifies the native methods that are required to support the implementation of the `java.awt.TextField` class.

WindowPeer

The `WindowPeer` interface specifies the native methods that are required to support the implementation of the `java.awt.Window` class.

java.io

The `java.io` package provides a number of classes that support stream-based I/O. These classes are organized into two main class hierarchies under the `InputStream` and `OutputStream` classes.

Classes

BufferedInputStream

The `BufferedInputStream` class provides the capability to implement buffering for an arbitrary `InputStream` object.

BufferedOutputStream

The `BufferedOutputStream` class provides the capability to implement buffering for an arbitrary `OutputStream` object.

ByteArrayInputStream

The `ByteArrayInputStream` class is used to convert a byte array into an `InputStream` object.

ByteArrayOutputStream

The `ByteArrayOutputStream` class is used to convert a byte array into an `OutputStream` object.

DataInputStream

The `DataInputStream` class provides the capability to read primitive data types and objects from an `InputStream` object.

DataOutputStream

The `DataOutputStream` class provides the capability to write primitive data types and objects to an `OutputStream` object.

File

The `File` class is used to provide system-independent access to a file or directory on the host system.

FileDescriptor

The `FileDescriptor` class provides a system-independent implementation of file descriptor objects.

FileInputStream

The `FileInputStream` class allows a `File` object to be used as the basis for creating an object of class `InputStream`.

FileOutputStream

The `FileOutputStream` class allows a `File` object to be used to create an object of class `OutputStream`.

FilterInputStream

The `FilterInputStream` class is the superclass of all classes that support input stream filtering.

FilterOutputStream

The `FilterOutputStream` class is the superclass of all classes that support output stream filtering.

InputStream

The `InputStream` class is the superclass of all input stream classes. It provides the methods required to implement an input stream of bytes.

LineNumberInputStream

The `LineNumberInputStream` class is used to track the line numbers associated with an `InputStream` object.

OutputStream

The `OutputStream` class is the superclass of all output stream classes. It provides the methods required to implement an output stream of bytes.

PipedInputStream

The `PipedInputStream` class is used to provide an input stream to a thread so that it can read data written to a `PipedOutputStream` object by another thread.

PipedOutputStream

The `PipedOutputStream` class is used to provide an output stream to a thread so that it can send data to another thread that reads the data from a `PipedInputStream` object.

PrintStream

The `PrintStream` class provides an output stream that supports a common set of methods for printing objects and primitive data types.

PushbackInputStream

The `PushbackInputStream` class is used to provide an output stream that is capable of having data written back onto it so that it can be read again.

RandomAccessFile

The `RandomAccessFile` class implements a file that can be directly read or written to at arbitrary file locations.

SequenceInputStream

The `SequenceInputStream` class is used to concatenate a sequence of input streams into a single input stream.

StreamTokenizer

The `StreamTokenizer` class is used to convert an input stream into a stream of tokens for processing by an input parser.

StringBufferInputStream

The `StringBufferInputStream` class is used to convert a `StringBuffer` object for use as an `InputStream` object.

Interfaces

DataInput

The `DataInput` interface provides a set of methods for constructing a system-independent implementation of an input stream.

DataOutput

The `DataOutput` interface provides a set of methods for constructing a system-independent implementation of an output stream.

FilenameFilter

The `FilenameFilter` interface provides the `accept()` method for determining whether a filename should be included in a filtered list of filenames.

java.lang

The `java.lang` package provides the core set of classes that are used in applets, console programs, and window programs. The fundamental classes of the Java class hierarchy are defined within this package. Some `java.lang` classes also provide access to system-specific information.

Classes

Boolean

The `Boolean` class provides a class wrapper that is used to access the `boolean` primitive data type as a Java object.

Character

The `Character` class provides a class wrapper that is used to access the `char` primitive data type as a Java object.

Class

The `Class` class provides runtime information about other classes in the form of a class descriptor.

ClassLoader

The `ClassLoader` class is used to define policies for loading classes into the runtime environment.

Compiler

The `Compiler` class is used to provide access to the Java compiler.

Double

The `Double` class provides a class wrapper that is used to access the `double` primitive data type as a Java object.

Float

The `Float` class provides a class wrapper that is used to access the `float` primitive data type as a Java object.

Integer

The `Integer` class provides a class wrapper that is used to access the `int` primitive data type as a Java object.

Long

The `Long` class provides a class wrapper that is used to access the `long` primitive data type as a Java object.

Math

The `Math` class provides a standard library of mathematical functions.

Number

The `Number` class is the superclass of all integer and floating-point classes. It can be used to convert a numeric value from one class to another.

Object

The `Object` class is the superclass of all Java classes and provides methods that are inherited by all Java classes.

Process

The `Process` class is used to provide system-independent access to processes that are executed using the `exec()` method of the `System` class.

Runtime

The `Runtime` class provides access to the underlying Java runtime system.

SecurityManager

The `SecurityManager` class is used to implement a security policy for the execution of untrusted classes.

String

The `String` class is used to implement constant character strings.

StringBuffer

The `StringBuffer` class is used to implement growable character strings.

System

The `System` class provides system-independent access to important system resources such as `stdin`, `stdout`, and `stderr`.

Thread

The `Thread` class is used to implement multithreaded Java programs.

ThreadGroup

The `ThreadGroup` class is used to organize and control a set of threads as a single entity.

Throwable

The `Throwable` class is the superclass of all Java errors and exceptions.

Interfaces

Cloneable

The `Cloneable` interface is implemented by classes that can be copied or cloned.

Runnable

The `Runnable` interface is implemented by classes that can be executed. It is used to implement threads that are not a subclass of the `Thread` class.

java.net

The `java.net` package provides a set of classes that implement socket-based client/server networking.

Classes

ContentHandler

The `ContentHandler` class is used to extract and process an object that is read from an `URLConnection` object.

DatagramPacket

The `DatagramPacket` class encapsulates a datagram object that is read or written from a UDP socket.

DatagramSocket

The `DatagramSocket` class is used to implement a UDP socket for the transmission and reception of datagrams.

InetAddress

The `InetAddress` class provides an encapsulation of an Internet host and IP address.

ServerSocket

The `ServerSocket` provides the capability to create TCP sockets that can be used to implement a server application.

Socket

The `Socket` class is used to implement a socket used by a client program.

SocketImpl

The `SocketImpl` class is used to tailor the implementation of Java socket classes to a specific platform or network environment.

URL

The `URL` class encapsulates URLs and provides a common set of methods for accessing the network resources referenced by an URL.

URLConnection

The `URLConnection` class is used to manage the HTTP connection created with the resource specified by an URL.

URLEncoder

The `URLEncoder` class is used to encode information in a format that is suitable for communication via an URL.

URLStreamHandler

The `URLStreamHandler` class is used to implement an `URLConnection` for different protocol types.

Interfaces

ContentHandlerFactory

The `ContentHandlerFactory` interface is used to associate `ContentHandler` objects with MIME types.

SocketImplFactory

The `SocketImplFactory` interface is used to create objects of the `SocketImpl` class.

URLStreamHandlerFactory

The `URLStreamHandlerFactory` interface is used to associate an `URLStreamHandler` object with a protocol type.

java.util

The `java.util` package provides a collection of classes that support a variety of common programming functions.

Classes

BitSet

The `BitSet` class is used to implement a compact set of bits that can be individually or collectively accessed.

Date

The `Date` class provides access to the current date and time in a system-independent manner.

Dictionary

The `Dictionary` class is used to create data container objects that enable data values to be accessed by their associated keys.

Hashtable

The `Hashtable` class is a subclass of the `Dictionary` class that allows a collection of objects to be accessed by a hash code value.

Observable

The `Observable` class enables objects to be constructed that inform observer objects as they are updated. The observer objects must implement the `Observer` interface.

Properties

The `Properties` class is a subclass of `Hashtable` that can be saved or loaded from a stream.

Random

The `Random` class is used to implement random number generators.

Stack

The `Stack` class is used to create a stack of objects.

StringTokenizer

The `StringTokenizer` class is used to parse a `String` object into a set of tokens.

Vector

The `Vector` class implements a growable array.

Interfaces

`Enumeration`

The `Enumeration` interface provides a set of methods for indexing through a set of objects.

`Observer`

The `Observer` interface is implemented by classes that observe objects of the `Observable` class.

B

Differences Between Java and C++

The Java language is very similar to the C and C++ languages, from which it is derived. These similarities make Java an easy language to learn for those who have previously programmed in C++, but they also mask some of the important differences between Java and C++. This appendix summarizes these differences.

Program Structure

The following sections identify the differences between the way Java and C++ programs are structured.

The `main()` Method

Every Java program contains a `public` class with a `main()` method that serves as the entry point for that program. A typical Java program often references other Java classes that are included within the same package as the program's class or in other compiled packages.

C++ programs also make uses of a `main()` entry point. The C++ analog of the Java method is referred to as a *member function*, or as just a *function*. The C++ `main()` function takes two parameters: the `int argc` variable that identifies the number of arguments passed to the invoked program and the `argv[][]` character array that contains the program arguments. The Java `main()` method takes a single `args[]` parameter of the `String` class. The number of arguments passed via the `main()` method invocation is determined by `args.length`.

The first value passed as the argument to a C++ program is the name of the program. Subsequent arguments are used to pass other values. Java programs do not pass the program name as the first argument to the program and are therefore off by one position with respect to the arguments passed to C++ programs.

The `main()` function of a C++ program has an `int` return type by default. This is used to return an exit code. The Java `main()` method has a `void` return type. The `exit()` method of the `java.lang.System` class can be used to return an exit code.

Packages

All Java classes are defined relative to a package, even if it is the default `noname` package. C++ programs do not support a package approach.

Importing Classes

Java programs reference classes that are defined in other packages using the `import` statement. C++ classes that are declared outside of a compilation unit are referenced using `#include` compiler directives.

Functions and Variables Declared Outside of Classes

C++ allows functions and variables to be defined outside the scope of a class. In fact, C++ does not require any classes to be defined.

Java strictly adheres to a class-oriented approach to program design. It is impossible to define a method or variable outside the scope of a class. At least one `public` class must be defined within a Java program to support the `main()` method.

Program Development

The following sections identify differences between the way Java and C++ programs are developed.

Compilation and Execution

C++ programs are generally compiled into native machine object code and executed directly as a process running under the local operating system.

Java programs are compiled into the bytecode instructions of the Java virtual machine and are executed using the Java interpreter or a Java-compatible browser.

The Preprocessor and Compiler Directives

C++ source code files are processed by a preprocessor before they are submitted to the compiler. Java does not use a preprocessor.

C++ provides the capability to communicate with the C++ compiler using compiler directives. Java does not provide any similar capability.

The Java API Versus C++ Libraries

The Java API provides a rich set of classes that can be used to support program development. These classes are largely incompatible with standard C and C++ libraries. Existing C and C++ code can be made available to Java programs using native methods.

Using CLASSPATH

Java uses the `CLASSPATH` environment variable to identify Java classes. Other environment variables are used by C and C++ programs.

Language Syntax

The following sections identify significant distinctions between the syntax of Java and C++.

Comments

Java and C++ use the same style of comments. Java also provides the capability to insert doc comments, which are processed by the `javadoc` program to support automated program documentation.

Constants

C++ defines constants using the `#DEFINE` compiler directive and the `const` keyword. Java constants are identified using the `final` keyword.

Primitive Data Types

Java provides the `boolean`, `byte`, `short`, `char`, `int`, `long`, `float`, and `double` primitive data types. C++ supports the same data types but does not use exactly the same type names as Java. Java's `char` data type uses a 16-bit character value to represent Unicode characters. C++ uses 8-bit ASCII `char` values.

Keywords

Java and C++ each identify different sets of reserved keywords, although some keywords are reserved by both Java and C++.

Java Classes Versus C++ Classes

Java classes are declared using a similar, but different, syntax than C++ classes.

C++ allows functions to be separately prototyped from their actual implementation. Java does not allow separate function prototyping.

C++ allows class definitions to be nested. Java does not.

C++ classes support multiple inheritance. Java classes support only single inheritance. Java uses interfaces to implement certain features of multiple inheritance. C++ does not support an analog to the Java interface. Objective-C does provide similar support.

C++ supports templates. Java does not.

`Public`, `Private`, and `Protected` Keywords

The access keywords used by Java and C++ have the same names, but they are used slightly differently. Java access keywords are defined relative to the package in which a class, interface, variable, or method is defined. C++ access keywords are defined relative to the class, data member, and member functions to which they apply.

Variables

A Java *variable* either contains the value of a primitive data type or refers to a Java object. Java *objects* are instances of classes or arrays.

C++ variables are not restricted in the same manner as Java variables. They may refer to primitive data types, instances of classes, arrays, structs, unions, or other data structures.

Types

The types supported by Java are the primitive data types, classes, interfaces, and arrays. C++ supports a variety of types, including primitive types, classes, structs, unions, and defined types. The C++ `typedef` construct does not have an analog in Java. C++ also supports enumerated data types, and Java does not. C++ is much more flexible in providing implicit casting between types. Java supports C++-style casting operators, but does not support implicit casting to the same extent as C++.

Pointers

C++ allows pointers to other objects to be defined. Java does not support pointers. All variables that do not contain the values of primitive data types are references to an object. This reference value may only be changed as the result of an assignment to a new object. The reference value may not be directly tampered with or manipulated as is possible with C++ pointers.

Objects

Java objects are instances of classes or arrays. C++ objects do not include arrays.

Java objects are created using the `new` operator and are deallocated automatically via the Java garbage collector. C++ objects can be statically or dynamically allocated. Static allocation is accomplished using a type declaration. Dynamic allocation is accomplished using the `new` operator. C++ variables must be explicitly deallocated using a destructor or the `delete` operator.

Arrays

Java arrays are similar to C++ arrays. However, there are some significant differences between the two languages.

C++ supports true multidimensional arrays. Java supports single-dimensional arrays; it simulates multidimensional arrays as arrays of arrays. The approach used by Java is actually more flexible than that of C++. Java arrays can consist of arrays of different dimensions.

Java arrays are objects and inherit the methods of the `Object` class. C++ arrays are not objects in their own right.

Java arrays are allocated using the `new` operator and are deallocated when they are garbage-collected. Java arrays are separately declared and allocated, although both steps may occur in the same statement. Java arrays can be statically initialized using the same syntax as C++ arrays. However, C++ requires static initializers to be constant expressions, but Java does not.

Java arrays are declared with a more flexible syntax than C++ arrays. In particular, the brackets used in Java array declarations may be associated with the name of the array being declared or the type of array being declared.

Strings

The Java `String` and `StringBuffer` classes are used to implement text strings. These classes allow strings to be treated as objects. C++ implements strings as null-terminated arrays of characters.

`null` Versus `NULL`

The Java `null` keyword is used to identify a variable as not referencing any object. The `null` keyword cannot be assigned to a variable that is declared with a primitive data type. The C++ `NULL` value is a constant that is defined as 0.

Statements

The syntax of Java statements is nearly identical to that of C++. However, Java does not support a `goto` statement, whereas C++ does. Java does, however, reserve the `goto` keyword.

The Java `if`, `while`, and `do` statements require that the conditional expression used to determine the flow of control results in a `boolean` value. C++ does not place this restriction on these statements.

Java supports labeled `break` and `continue` statements to break out of and continue executing complex switch and loop constructs.

Java provides the `synchronized` statement to support multithreading operations on critical sections. C++ does not support a `synchronized` statement.

Java implements exception handling using the `try` statement and the `catch` and `finally` clauses. C++ implements exception handling in a similar manner, but does not support a `finally` clause.

Methods Versus Functions

The C++ analog of the Java method is the member function. C++ functions are more powerful and flexible than Java methods. C++ functions allow variable-length argument lists and optional arguments. Java does not support these capabilities.

C++ allows inline functions to be specified and Java does not. C++ implements `friend` functions to circumvent the normal class access restrictions. Java does not support `friend` functions.

Operators

The set of operators supported by Java is based on those provided by C++, although not all C++ operators are supported. In addition, Java provides operators that are not supported by C++. These include the `instanceof` operator and the + operator used with `String` objects.

C++ supports operator overloading and Java does not.

C

Moving C/C++ Legacy Code to Java

Java is a new and powerful language that provides many useful features to the software developer. However, if your software organization is typical of most, you will have to trade off moving to Java with the constraints imposed by dependencies on in-place legacy code. This appendix summarizes the pros and cons of moving existing legacy code to Java. It identifies a spectrum of approaches to accomplishing software transition and discusses the issues involved with each approach. It also covers approaches to translating C and C++ code to Java. This appendix assumes that the transition of C/C++ code to Java is being performed by a moderately large software organization. Some of the software porting issues become insignificant if only a few small programs are translated into Java.

Why Move to Java?

When deciding whether to move existing applications to Java, a tradeoff between the advantages and disadvantages of such a move must be considered. This section identifies many of the advantages of Java programs over C- and C++-based applications. The following section considers some disadvantages of using Java and roadblocks to any software transition effort.

Platform Independence

One of the most compelling reasons to move to Java is its platform independence. Java runs on most major hardware and software platforms, including Windows 95 and NT, the Macintosh, and several varieties of UNIX. Java applets are supported by all Java-compatible browsers. By moving existing software to Java, you are able to make it instantly compatible with these software platforms. Your programs become more portable. Any hardware and operating system dependencies are removed.

Although C and C++ are supported on all platforms that support Java, these languages are not supported in a platform-independent manner. C and C++ applications that are implemented on one operating system platform are usually severely intertwined with the native windowing system and OS-specific networking capabilities. Moving between OS platforms requires recompilation, as a minimum, and significant redesign, in most cases.

Object Orientation

Java is a true object-oriented language. It does not merely provide the capability to implement object-oriented principles—it enforces these principles. You can develop object-oriented programs in C++, but you are not required to do so—you can use C++ to write C programs as well. Java does not allow you to slip outside the object-oriented framework. You either adhere to Java's object-oriented development approach or you do not program in Java.

Security

Java is one of the first programming languages to consider security as part of its design. The Java language, compiler, interpreter, and runtime environment were each developed with security in mind. The compiler, interpreter, and Java-compatible browsers all contain several levels of security measures that are designed to reduce the risk of security compromise, loss of data and program integrity, and damage to system users. Considering the enormous security problems associated with executing potentially untrusted code in a secure manner and across multiple execution environments, Java's security measures are far ahead of even those developed to secure military systems. C and C++ do not have any intrinsic security capabilities. Can you download an arbitrary untrusted C or C++ program and execute it in a secure manner?

Reliability

Security and reliability go hand in hand. Security measures cannot be implemented with any degree of assurance without a reliable framework for program execution. Java provides multiple levels of reliability measures, beginning with the Java language itself. Many of the features of C and C++ that are detrimental to program reliability, such as pointers and automatic type conversion, are avoided in Java. The Java compiler provides several levels of additional checks to identify type mismatches and other inconsistencies. The Java runtime system duplicates many of the checks performed by the compiler and performs additional checks to verify that the executable bytecodes form a valid Java program.

Simplicity

The Java language was designed to be a simple language to learn, building on the syntax and many of the features of C++. However, in order to promote security, reliability, and simplicity, Java has left out those elements of C and C++ that contribute to errors and program complexity. In addition, Java provides automated garbage collection, freeing you from having to manage memory deallocation in your programs. The end result of Java's focus on simplicity is that it is easy to get up to speed writing Java programs for those who have programmed in C or C++. Java programs are also less complex than C and C++ programs due to the fact that many of the language elements that lead to program complexity have been removed.

Language Features

The Java language provides many language features that make it preferable to C or C++ for modern software development. On the top of this list is Java's intrinsic support for multithreading, which is lacking in both C and C++. Other features are its exception-handling capabilities, which were recently introduced into C++; its strict adherence to class and object-oriented software development; and its automated garbage-collection support. In addition to these features, Java enforces a common programming style by removing the capability to slip outside the class- and object-oriented programming paradigm to develop C-style function-oriented programs.

Standardization

Although C and C++ have been standardized by the American National Standards Institute (ANSI), many C and C++ compilers provide custom enhancements to the language, usually through additional preprocessor directives. Because these enhancements usually make their way into source code programs, a general lack of standardization results. Java does not yet suffer from any standardization problems because its syntax and semantics are controlled by a single organization.

The Java API

The predefined classes of the Java API provide a comprehensive platform-independent foundation for program development. These classes provide the capability to develop Windows and network programs that execute on a wide range of hosts. The Java I/O stream classes also provide a very useful set of filters for I/O processing. Whereas C and C++ may provide more extensive software libraries, none of these libraries provides as much platform-independent power as Java's API.

Transition to Distributed Computing

Sun has taken important steps to support fully distributed computing with its support of Remote Objects for Java. This product provides the capability to develop remote interfaces between Java objects and objects developed in other languages. The Java Interface Definition Language (IDL) can be used to support Common Object Request Broker Architecture (CORBA) integration.

Rapid Code Generation

Because Java is an interpreted language, it can be used to rapidly prototype applications that would require considerably more base software support in languages such as C or C++. The Java API also contributes to the capability to support rapid code generation. The classes of the Java API provide an integrated, easy-to-use repository for the development of application-specific software. Because the Java API provides high-level windows and networking support, custom application prototypes can be constructed more quickly using these classes as a foundation.

Ease of Documentation and Maintenance

Java software is essentially self-documenting when doc comments and the `javadoc` tool are used to generate software documentation. The excellent Java API documentation is an example of the superior documentation capabilities provided by Java. Because Java software is inherently better structured and documented than C or C++ software, it is generally easier to maintain. In addition, the package orientation of Java software affords considerable modularity in software design, development, documentation, and maintenance.

Reasons Against Moving to Java

Java provides many benefits that make it an attractive language to use to develop new applications and to which to port existing legacy code. The previous section discussed some of the advantages of porting existing code to Java. This section identifies some of the disadvantages of any C- or C++-to-Java migration effort.

Compatibility

Although Java is supported on many platforms, it is not supported on all of them. If your target hardware or software platform does not support Java, you are out of luck. Your alternatives are to switch to a different platform or wait for Java to be ported to your existing software platform.

Compatibility may also be a problem at a design level. Suppose that your target software platform does, in fact, support Java. If your legacy code is designed in such a manner that it is unstructured and incompatible with a class- and object-oriented model, the effort required to migrate the software may be prohibitive.

Performance

Java is interpreted, and although its execution is efficient, it might not meet the performance demands of those applications in which execution speed is of paramount importance. Examples of these types of applications include numerical "number crunching" programs, real-time control processes, language compilers, and modeling and simulation software. Just because your application fits into one of these categories does not necessarily rule out Java, however. For example, the Java compiler is written in Java and performs admirably for small programs. However, its performance is greatly enhanced when it is compiled into native machine code instructions. Java-to-C translators allow programs to be developed in Java and translated into C for native machine code compilation. The translation process generally improves the performance of Java programs.

Retraining

Although Java is simple, easy to learn, and based on C++, some training may be required to get programmers up and running writing Java code. This is especially true if the programmers have been using C++ in a nonstructured, non-object-oriented fashion. I never really appreciated the object-oriented programming features provided by C++ before I began programming in Java. Until I had adopted the Java program-development mindset, I was trying to apply my outdated and inefficient C++ programming techniques to Java software development. After I had made the mental transition to the Java object-oriented programming model, I became much more comfortable and efficient in writing Java programs.

Impact on Existing Operations

Moving legacy code to Java may result in adverse affects on company operations that are supported with legacy software. This is especially true when the legacy code is implemented in a poorly structured, convoluted manner that typically evolves from extensive software patches and upgrades. If existing system software is tightly coupled and fragile, a transition to Java (or any other language) may break the software application to the point where a complete software redevelopment is required.

Cost, Schedule, and Level of Effort

Any software transition effort is subject to cost and schedule constraints. Moving current legacy software to Java might not be cost-effective given the current software investment and its expected operational life. The software transition may also have a significant impact on system availability and previously scheduled activities. Transition from C or C++ to Java might also require a significant level of effort that would exceed the expected budget for the maintenance of the legacy code.

Transition Approaches and Issues

There are many ways to integrate Java into existing software applications. This section identifies some of these approaches and explores the issues involved in transitioning to a Java-based software environment.

Interfacing with Existing Legacy Code

One of the easiest ways to introduce Java to an operational environment is to use it to add functionality to existing legacy code. Java programs do not replace existing legacy software; they merely enhance it to support new applications. This approach involves minimal impact to existing software, but does introduce a potentially thorny maintenance issue with Java being added to the current list of languages that must be used to maintain the system.

Incremental Reimplementation of Legacy Code

An incremental approach to reimplementing legacy code in Java can be used to cut over to a Java-based software-development approach while minimizing the impact on existing legacy software. This approach assumes that the legacy software is developed in a modular fashion and can be replaced in an incremental manner. If this is the case, legacy software can be migrated to Java on a module-by-module basis with the legacy code ultimately replaced by new Java software.

Off-Boarding Access to Legacy Objects

If in-place legacy code can be upgraded using Java software that is implemented on separate hardware platforms, Java can be used to "off board" many of the functions performed by the legacy code. The use of off-board server software allows the investment in legacy code to be preserved while expanding the services provided by the system as a whole.

Full-Scale Redevelopment

In some cases, it is more cost-effective to keep legacy code in place while completely redeveloping system software from scratch. This is typically the case when the system is subject to large-scale reengineering or when it is so fragile that it breaks as the result of the simplest upgrades. Full-scale system redevelopment being necessary is actually an advantage to Java software development because the developed software is under no legacy compatibility constraints and can take full advantage of Java's capabilities.

Translation Approaches and Issues

Translation of existing C and C++ code into Java can be performed in several different ways, depending on the compatibility of the existing software with Java. This section describes some of the different approaches to software translation.

Automated Translation

Tools and utilities have been developed that allow Java source and bytecode to be translated into C to support native machine code compilation. Future Java-integrated software-development environments are planned where either Java or C++ code may be generated based on the configuration of the development software. These development tools will allow easy movement between C++ and Java. These tools require a common set of libraries that can be used by either Java or C++ programs. Automated translation between these two languages will be supported to some extent.

The degree to which C++ programs may be automatically translated into Java will depend on the planning and effort put into the code's design to develop it in a way that makes it more amenable to automated translation. Factors to be considered include the use of compatible libraries, the use of single inheritance, the use of object-oriented programming capabilities, and minimization of the use of incompatible language features.

Manual Translation

Manual translation of C and C++ to Java will probably be the most common approach to moving C and C++ legacy programs to Java. This approach requires you to use two editor windows—one for the legacy C++ code being translated and the other for the Java program being created. Some of the translation is accomplished by cutting and pasting C++ statements into the Java window, making the corrections necessary to adjust for language differences. Other parts of the translation require that new Java classes, interfaces, variables, and methods be developed to implement C++ functions and data structures that cannot be directly translated from C++ to Java. The effectiveness of the manual translation process will be determined by the degree to which the C++ legacy code meets the compatibility considerations identified at the end of the previous section.

Source-Level Redesign

In many cases, manual translation may be hampered by the fact that the C++ legacy code might be written in a style that renders it impossible to migrate using cut-and-paste–based translation methods. In these cases, a class- and object-oriented design of the legacy code needs to be extracted from the legacy code and used as the basis for the Java source code development. A two-level approach to software translation is followed. The legacy code is reverse-engineered to an object-oriented design, and the recovered design information is used to develop a Java software design which is, in turn, translated into Java source code. Code is not translated from one language to another. Instead, legacy code is translated into general design information that is used to drive the Java design and implementation.

I

Index

Symbols

A

B

C

D

E

F

G

H

I

J

K

L

M

N

O

P

Q

R

U

V

W

X

Y-Z

Teach Yourself Netscape 2 Web Publishing in a Week

— *Wes Tatters*

Teach Yourself Netscape 2 Web Publishing in a Week is the easiest way to learn how to produce attention-getting, well-designed Web pages using the features provided by Netscape Navigator. Intended for both the novice and the expert, this book provides a solid grounding in HTML and Web publishing principles, while providing special focus on the possibilities presented by the Netscape environment. Learn to design and create attention-grabbing Web pages for the Netscape environment while exploring new Netscape development features such as frames, plug-ins, Java applets, and JavaScript!

Price: $39.99 USA/ $56.95 CDN User Level: Beginner–Intermediate
ISBN: 1-57521-068-1 450 pages

Teach Yourself CGI Programming with Perl in a Week

— *Eric Herrmann*

This book is a step-by-step tutorial of how to create, use, and maintain Common Gateway Interfaces (CGIs). It describes effective ways of using CGI as an integral part of Web development. Adds interactivity and flexibility to the information that can be provided through your Web site. Includes Perl 4.0 and 5.0, CGI libraries, and other applications to create databases, dynamic interactivity, and other enticing page effects.

Price: $39.99 USA/$56.95 CDN User Level: Intermediate–Advanced
ISBN: 1-57521-009-6 500 pages

Teach Yourself Java in 21 Days

— *Laura Lemay and Charles Perkins*

The complete tutorial guide to the most exciting technology to hit the Internet in years—Java! A detailed guide to developing applications with the hot new Java language from Sun Microsystems, *Teach Yourself Java in 21 Days* shows readers how to program using Java and develop applications (applets) using the Java language. With coverage of Java implementation in Netscape Navigator and HotJava, along with the Java Developer's Kit, including the compiler and debugger for Java, *Teach Yourself Java* is a must-have!

Price: $39.99 USA/$56.95 CDN User Level: Intermediate–Advanced
ISBN: 1-57521-030-4 600 pages

Creating Web Applets with Java

— *David Gulbransen and Kenrick Rawlings*

Creating Web Applets with Java is the easiest way to learn how to integrate existing Java applets into your Web pages. This book is designed for the non-programmer who wants to use or customize preprogrammed Java applets with a minimal amount of trouble. It teaches the easiest way to incorporate the power of Java in a Web page, and covers the basics of Java applet programming. Find out how to use and customize preprogammed Java applets. Includes a CD-ROM full of useful applets.

Price: $39.99 USA/$56.95 CDN User Level: Casual–Accomplished
ISBN: 1-57521-070-3 350 pages

Teach Yourself Web Publishing with HTML 3.0 in a Week, Second Edition

— Laura Lemay

Ideal for those people who are interested in the Internet and the World Wide Web—the Internet's hottest topic! This updated and revised edition teaches readers how to use HTML (Hypertext Markup Language) version 3.0 to create Web pages that can be viewed by nearly 30 million users. Explores the process of creating and maintaining Web presentations, including setting up tools and converters for verifying and testing pages. The new edition highlights the new features of HTML, such as tables and Netscape and Microsoft Explorer extensions. Provides the latest information on working with images, sound files, and video, and teaches advanced HTML techniques and tricks in a clear, step-by-step manner with many practical examples of HTML pages.

Price: $29.99 USA/$42.95 CDN User Level: Beginner–Intermediate
ISBN: 1-57521-064-9 518 pages

Web Page Construction Kit (Software)

Create your own exciting World Wide Web pages with the software and expert guidance in this kit! Includes HTML Assistant Pro Lite, the acclaimed point-and-click Web page editor. Simply highlight text in HTML Assistant Pro Lite, and click the appropriate button to add headlines, graphics, special formatting, links, etc. No programming skills needed! Using your favorite Web browser, you can test your work quickly and easily without leaving the editor. A unique catalog feature allows you to keep track of interesting Web sites and easily add their HTML links to your pages. Assistant's user-defined toolkit also allows you to add new HTML formatting styles as they are defined. Includes the #1 best-selling Internet book, *Teach Yourself Web Publishing with HTML 3.0 in a Week, Second Edition,* and a library of professionally designed Web page templates, graphics, buttons, bullets, lines, and icons to rev up your new pages!

PC Computing magazine says, "If you're looking for the easiest route to Web publishing, HTML Assistant is your best choice."

Price: $39.95 USA/$55.95 CAN User Level: Beginner–Intermediate
ISBN: 1-57521-000-2 518 pages

HTML & CGI Unleashed

— John December and Marc Ginsburg

Targeted to professional developers who have a basic understanding of programming and need a detailed guide. Provides a complete, detailed reference to developing Web information systems. Covers the full range of languages—HTML, CGI, Perl C, editing and conversion programs, and more—and how to create commercial-grade Web applications. Perfect for the developer who will be designing, creating, and maintaining a Web presence for a company or large institution.

Price: $49.99 USA/$70.95 CDN User Level: Intermediate–Advanced
ISBN: 0-672-30745-6 830 pages

Web Site Construction Kit for Windows NT

— Christopher Brown and Scott Zimmerman

Web Site Construction Kit for Windows NT has everything you need to set up, develop, and maintain a Web site with Windows NT—including the server on the CD-ROM! It teaches the ins and outs of planning, installing, configuring, and administering a Windows NT–based Web site for an organization, and it includes detailed instructions on how to use the software on the CD-ROM to develop the Web site's content—HTML pages, CGI scripts, imagemaps, and so forth.

Price: $49.99 USA/$67.99 CDN User Level: All Levels
ISBN: 1-57521-047-9 430 pages

Book ISBN 1-57521-069-X

State Sales/Use Tax

In the following states, add sales/use tax: CO–3%; GA, LA, NY–4%; VA–4.5%; KS–4.9%; AZ, IA, IN, MA, MD, OH, SC, WI–5%; CT, FL, ME, MI, NC, NJ, PA, TN–6%; CA, IL, TX–6.25%; MN, WA–6.5%; DC–5.75%.

Please add local tax for: AZ, CA, FL, GA, MO, NY, OH, SC, TN, TX, WA, WI.

Order Information:

- Please allow 2–4 weeks for processing your order.
- Please attach the order form with your payment.
- No P.O. boxes and no C.O.D.s accepted.
- Order form good in the U.S. only.
- If you are tax-exempt, please include exemption certificate or letter with tax-exempt number.
- Resellers not eligible.
- Offer not valid with any other promotion.
- One copy per product, per order.
- Special offer expires 6/30/96.

Installing Your CD-ROM

The companion CD-ROM contains the Java Developer's Kit from Sun Microsystems, many useful third-party tools and utilities, plus the source code and Java samples from the book.

Windows 3.1 or NT Installation Instructions

1. Insert the CD-ROM into your CD-ROM drive.
2. From File Manager or Program Manager, choose Run from the File menu.
3. Type `<drive>CDSETUP`, where `<drive>` corresponds to the drive letter of your CD-ROM, and press Enter. For example, if your CD-ROM is drive D:, type `D:CDSETUP` and press Enter.
4. Follow the onscreen instructions in the installation program. Files will be installed to a directory named `\JAVADG`, unless you choose a different directory during installation.

`CDSETUP` creates a Windows Program Manager group called Java Dev Guide. This group contains icons for exploring the CD-ROM.

Windows 95 Installation Instructions

1. If Windows 95 is installed on your computer, and you have the AutoPlay feature enabled, the Guide to the CD-ROM program starts automatically whenever you insert the disc into your CD-ROM drive.

Macintosh Installation Instructions

1. Insert the CD-ROM into your CD-ROM drive.
2. When an icon for the CD appears on your desktop, open the disc by double-clicking on its icon.
3. Double-click on the icon named Guide to the CD-ROM and follow the directions that appear.

Technical Support from Macmillan

We can't help you with Windows or Macintosh problems or software from third parties, but we can assist you if a problem arises with the CD-ROM itself.

E-mail Support: Send e-mail to `support@mcp.com`.

CompuServe: Type `GO SAMS` to reach the Macmillan Computer Publishing forum. Leave us a message, addressed to `SYSOP`. If you want the message to be private, address it to `*SYSOP`.

Telephone: 317-581-3833

Fax: 317-581-4773

Mail: Macmillan Computer Publishing
Attention: Support Department
201 West 103rd Street
Indianapolis, IN 46290-1093

Here's how to reach us on the Internet:

World Wide Web (The Macmillan Information SuperLibrary): `http://www.mcp.com/samsnet`